# The Epistle to the Hebrews

**John Brown**

*Sovereign Grace Publishers, Inc.*
*P.O. Box 4998*
*Lafayette, IN 47903*

***The Epistle to the Hebrews***
***Paperback Edition***
Copyright © 2002
By Jay P. Green, Sr.
All Rights Reserved

ISBN: 1-58960-564-0

*Printed In the United States of America*
*By Lightning Source, Inc.*

# BIOGRAPHICAL INTRODUCTION

EARLY one morning in the year 1738 a shepherd boy with homespun clothes and bare feet, stood at the counter of Alexander McCulloch's bookshop in the University city of St. Andrews. The startled shopkeeper was yet more surprised when he heard the youth's request, it was for a Greek New Testament. "Boy," exclaimed the Professor of Greek who happened to be in the shop at that moment, "if you can read that book, you shall have it for nothing." Soon a rather thick leather volume was in the lad's hands and to the astonishment of all present he read a passage and won his prize. By the afternoon sixteen year old John Brown was back amongst his flock on the hills of Abernethy, having walked some forty-eight miles since the previous evening to obtain his treasure.

To see the far-flung consequences of that walk to St. Andrews we must pass on nearly seventy years to the 6th of February, 1806. On that day in the Secession Church at Biggar, with snow sweeping over the silent moorland and surrounding hills, another John Brown stands to be ordained into the ministry of the Christian Church. He was too young to remember his grandfather, being only three years old when John Brown of Abernethy had died in 1787, but the spirit and influence of that great man lived on in the grandson. For the shepherd boy of Abernethy had risen to become one of the greatest preachers and divines in Scotland and his thirty-six years ministry at Haddington had made the name of that East Lothian town known all over the English speaking world.[1] Though in his last twenty years John Brown of Haddington (as he is best described) became the Divinity Professor of his denomination—training students during the summer months together with his ministerial

[1] Cf. the fascinating biography, *John Brown of Haddington*, by Robert Mackenzie, 1918. He was perhaps best known for his *Self-Interpreting Bible*, which was so popular that twenty-six editions of it are to be found in the British Museum.

work—and though his learning was such that he mastered nearly a dozen languages, yet he remained to the last singularly devoted to one aim, the exposition and preaching of the Word of God. He preached, men said, as though he had read no other book.[1]

There is no doubt that it was partly due to the fact that John Brown, the author of this book, was the grandson of such a man that he became one of the greatest Scottish exegetes of the nineteenth century. Unlike his grandfather he started with no small advantages: his own father, John Brown of Whitburn (1754–1834), was a minister of no mean stature; his theological professor, Dr. George Lawson, was one of Scotland's saintliest expositors;[2] and his mother was a woman of uncommon piety and ability.[3] These factors, and others, all moulded his outlook. From his earliest days at Biggar he viewed commentating on the Scriptures as his highest privilege and duty for, said his biographer, "he did not at all share the loose and unscriptural opinion that the duties of the pastor were superior or even equal in importance to those of the public teacher of Christianity".[4]

The main facts of the author's long ministry of fifty-two years can be quickly told. From 1806 till 1822, he laboured quietly and studiously at Biggar, a small town twenty-eight miles south-west of Edinburgh on the old high-road to Moffat. During this period the year 1815 stands out not only because it marked his first appearance as an author,[5] but because from this

---

[1] "Brown of Haddington used to preach as if he had read no other book than the Bible."—R. M. M'Cheyne in an Ordination Sermon on 2 Tim. iv., 1, 2.

[2] The memory of Dr. Lawson, whose life was written by John Macfarlane in 1862, has been recently deservedly revived by the republication of his *Exposition of Ruth and Esther*, Sovereign Grace Publishers, 1960.

[3] Isabella Cranston met the eldest son of John Brown of Haddington when he was preaching in London just after completing his studies for the ministry. His father doubted if it was a suitable match and sent his other son, Ebenezer, to London to ascertain the position. Ebenezer returned with the astonishing report, "Father, if John does not marry her, I am going to marry her myself!" John did marry her and their eldest son, the third John Brown, was born on July 12, 1784.

[4] *Memoir of John Brown*, by John Cairns, 1860, p. 62. Such was the time and study which he devoted to the Scriptures in his early years that after his death Andrew Thomson declared, "I believe there was scarcely a text or a paragraph of the Bible on which he had not formed a deliberate and definite opinion."

[5] *Strictures on Mr. Yates Vindication of Unitarianism.*

date his ministry, always orthodox and serious, "was pervaded by a visibly increased earnestness and unction." The details of the spiritual conflict which led to this progress are not known, but it may well be they were connected with the death of his wife who died in the spring of the following year. "Prayer, meditation and temptation make a minister," said Luther, and in his days at Biggar John Brown found it to be so.

In 1822, at the age of thirty-eight, Brown was called to a wider sphere of usefulness in Edinburgh. For seven years he ministered in Rose Street Secession Church, then in 1829 he was translated to Broughton Place Church in the same city, where he remained until his death on October 13th, 1858. Throughout all the vicissitudes of his long years in Edinburgh—amidst the temptations of popularity, the struggles of controversy[1] and the responsibilities of leadership in his denomination—John Brown remained a spiritual Christian. He never forgot the passionate entreaty which old John Brown of Haddington when dying had addressed to his father, "Labour, labour for Christ while ye have strength." He was deeply interested in the prosperity of the cause of Christ in all denominations at home and abroad and his last illness was brightened by news of the 1858 revival in America. He was known for his attachment to vital religion and for his fear of worldliness in the Church.[2] Brown, said Spurgeon, "is a modern Puritan," and if that was so it was in no small measure due to the fact that those old spiritual writers were his constant companions. At the commencement of his ministry his father had charged him to be "more acquainted with evangelical and practical divinity, such as Ebenezer

[1] He was very much engaged in the Voluntary Controversy of 1835–43, respecting the separation of Church and State—and in the Atonement Controversy of 1840–45. In the latter controversy Dr. Brown held a more or less Amyraldian position on the extent of the atonement and the serious consequences of this lapse are shown in Dr. John MacLeod's *Scottish Theology*, pp. 243–4.

[2] The following solemn words are characteristic of the spirit of the Brown "dynasty": "A ministry destitute of vital religion is one of the most unnatural of all things and one of the deadliest curses which can light on a Christian body; and to the individual himself it is full of eternal hazard. An unregenerate man, after joining a Christian Church, is less likely to be converted than he was previously. If he became a student of divinity, the probabilities of final impenitence are prodigiously multiplied; and if he enter on the function of ministry, the hope of his being saved is faint indeed." *Hints to Students of Divinity*, p. 27.

Erskine's, Dr. Owen's, Trail's, etc." And he obeyed the charge for even on his death bed we find him still studying John Owen and exclaiming with his very last words that he felt, "*wonderfully well.*"

John Brown possessed his grandfather's gift in being at the same time a true scholar and an earnest preacher. His words brought both light and life and while he was probably most at home amongst students he nevertheless maintained a widely varied congregation of between 1,200 to 1,600 people at Broughton Place. Dr. Brown's most distinctive abilities were recognised by his denomination in 1834 when he was appointed to the chair of Exegetical Theology.[1] The conception of this chair was new to Scottish theological training and it was due to John Brown's own suggestion that this branch of study was introduced into the curriculum of the students who were training for the ministry of the Secession Church. The purpose was not only to teach principles of Biblical interpretation—they had long been taught in Scotland—but to *apply* these principles in the actual exposition of large portions of Scripture in the original languages. Dr. Brown was profoundly disturbed at the all too common custom of ministers preaching a truth which was nevertheless not *the* truth of the text upon which they based their sermon. "It is of radical importance to you," he would repeatedly declare to his students, "that your views be not only consistent *with*, but derived *from* a careful exegesis of the 'words which the Holy Ghost teacheth' . . it has been my sincere desire to bring out of the inspired words what is really in them, and to put nothing into them that is not really there; impressed with the conviction that imaginary exposition is one of the worst ways of adding to 'the words of the prophecy of this book,' and that he who thus adds to God's Word, 'deceiving and being deceived,' is in great danger of 'proving himself a liar'."[2] *Expositio non imposito*, was his curt definition of an interpreter's business and nothing developed an exegetical conscience in the Secession students so much as the example of their professor gripped with the tremendous responsibility of

---

[1] Since his grandfather's day the number of professors had been increased to four but as the training of students was still confined to the summer months, the professors were able to continue their pastorates.

[2] *Memoir of John Brown*, p. 369 and p. 293.

bringing out the mind of God as he expounded to them from the Prophets, the Gospels or the Epistles. "Here is an old man," exclaimed John Brown on his death bed to a fellow minister, "going away to give in the account of his stewardship." But though a new experience, this was the end which he had strived to keep in view in all his preaching and commentating.

The fundamental importance of accurate exegesis was very much neglected in Britain in the first half of the nineteenth century, and it was the opinion of no less an authority than Dr. William Cunningham, that the publication of Dr. Brown's first great commentary, *Expository Discourses on the First Epistle of Peter*, in 1848, "formed a marked era in the history of scriptural interpretation in this country. . . . Too many of those who hold the office of ministers of the Word," wrote Cunningham, "attempt something in the way of applying the Scriptures, without being well qualified to ascertain and to establish their true and correct meaning, and without labouring to found the application upon its only sufficient basis, viz. a careful and accurate exposition of their actual import. . . . This is the right and the only right mode of employing the Sacred Scriptures, and it is because we get so little of this either from the pulpit or the press, that we attach the highest value to Dr. Brown's expository works."[1]

Dr. Brown was already sixty-five when his first great commentary, mentioned above, appeared in 1848, but in the ten years that remained he produced a further eight expository volumes not including this present work on Hebrews which he more or less finished for the press[2] but which was not published until three years after his death. The explanation of the abundant

[1] *The British and Foreign Evangelical Review*, edited by William Cunningham, Vol. VI, 1857, p. 231–32. A review of Dr. Brown on *Hebrews* will be found in the same journal, Vol. XI, p. 710–11.

[2] Dr. David Smith who supervised the publication of Dr. Brown's work on *Hebrews* says that the author had prepared it for publication, having paragraphed it, drawn up the table of contents and marked on the margin various directions for the printer. There is one respect, however, in which the commentary might have been more complete had the author lived to publish it. During his last years John Brown preached several sermons on the Epistle to the Hebrews and it is possible he would have embodied some of the material from these in the commentary itself. Dr. Smith originally published this commentary on Hebrews in two volumes and appended the sermons to the second volume; in this edition in order to contain the complete commentary in one volume it has been necessary to omit the discourses.

literary output of the closing years of his ministry is that the commentaries he then published had been reaching their final form over a period of many years. He had, for example, expounded the Epistle to the Hebrews at Rose Street and at Broughton Place. With the exception of his exposition of Galatians, his commentary on Hebrews was written before any of his others and it was read several times to his divinity students being revised and enlarged in the process. Probably all Dr. Brown's commentaries went through the same process of composition, being expounded in somewhat differing forms to both his congregation and his students, and it is this fact which serves to explain the somewhat unusual combination to be found in his writings of the teaching of the professor's chair with the preaching of the pulpit. While this method has some defects it undoubtedly helped to preserve the devotional tone of the author's commentaries; he never concentrates merely on the intellectual side of the Scriptures, nor did he—as so many German commentators of the same period—treat exegesis as an end in itself, for though essential as true exegesis is, it was for him only an instrument "to bring the minds of his hearers or readers into *immediate contact* with the mind of the Spirit."

Dr. Brown, says his biographer, not only employed his entire powers in the study of the Scriptures, but resigned "his whole being to the empire of the Word of God." Without doubt, it is this spiritual quality of high devotion which has given to his commentaries much of their enduring value. "If I have written anything that will live after me," he declared, "it is because it has been linked on to the everlasting Word of God." This was a true prophecy. The explanation of the success of his life and the abiding worth of his works is all to be found in the text which he chose for his gravestone, "All flesh is grass. The Word of the Lord endureth for ever."

IAIN MURRAY

*February*, 1961.

# CONTENTS

|  | PAGE |
|---|---|
| BIOGRAPHICAL INTRODUCTION | iii |
| INTRODUCTION | 3 |

## PROLEGOMENA

| | |
|---|---|
| Section 1. Of the Author of the Epistle | 7 |
| 2. Of those to whom the Epistle was written | 8 |
| 3. Of the Original Language and Style of the Epistle | 9 |
| 4. Of the Date and Place of the Epistle | 9 |
| 5. Of the Canonicity of the Epistle | 10 |
| 6. Of the Subject and Division of the Epistle | 10 |
| 7. Of the Interpreters of the Epistle | 11 |
| Note: A | 12 |

## PART I—DOCTRINAL

### Chapter I.—X. 18

| | |
|---|---|
| Introductory Statement. The Two Revelations contrasted, i. 1–3 | 15 |

PAGE

### CHAPTER I

### THE SUPERIORITY OF JESUS CHRIST TO THE ANGELS, ESSENTIAL AND OFFICIAL    36

Section 1. The Proof, i. 4–14 . . . . . . . 36
    2. Practical Inference and Exhortation, ii. 1–4 . . 70
    3. An Objection met and answered, ii. 5–18 . . 84

Notes . . . . . . . . . 140

### CHAPTER II

### THE SUPERIORITY OF JESUS CHRIST TO MOSES    148

Introductory Address, iii. 1 . . . . . . 150

Section 1. The Fact stated, iii. 2–6 . . . . 158
    (1) The Resemblance . . . . . 158
    (2) The Superiority . . . . . . 161
    2. The Fact practically improved, iii. 7–iv. 13 . . 170

### CHAPTER III

### THE SUPERIORITY OF JESUS CHRIST TO THE AARONICAL PRIESTHOOD . . . . 222

Section 1. General Introductory Statement and Exhortation, iv. 14–16 . . . . . . . . 225
    2. The Nature, Design, and Functions of the Aaronical Priesthood, v. 1–3 . . . . . . 236

|  | PAGE |
|---|---|
| Section 3. Our Lord's High-priesthood proved by His Divine Appointment, v. 4–6 | 242 |
| 4. Our Lord's High-priesthood proved by His successful Discharge of the Functions of that Office, v. 7–10 | 248 |
| 5. The Superiority of our Lord's High-priesthood proved from His being called of God a High Priest after the Order of Melchisedec, v. 10–vii. 25 : | |
| (1) General Statement, v. 10 | 260 |
| (2) Cautionary Digression, v. 11–vi. 20 | 263 |
| (3) Particular Illustrations of the Argument for the Superiority of our Lord's Priesthood from Ps. cx. 3, vii. 1–25 : | |
| 1. The Order of Melchisedec superior to the Order of Aaron, vii. 1–10 | 322 |
| 2. The Prediction that a perpetual Priest was to arise after the Order of Melchisedec, a Proof of the Inferiority of the Priesthood to be superseded, and of the Superiority of the Priesthood that was to supersede it, vii. 11–19 | 335 |
| 3. The Superior Solemnity of the Institution of the Priesthood of our Lord a Proof of its Superiority, vii. 20–22 | 345 |
| 4. The Superior Permanence of our Lord's Priesthood proves its Superiority to the Levitical Priesthood, vii. 23–25 | 350 |
| 6. The Superiority of our Lord's High Priesthood proved from the Superiority of His Qualifications, vii. 26–viii. 5 | 352 |

PAGE

Section 7. The Superiority of our Lord's Priesthood to that of the Levitical Priesthood proved from the Superiority of the Covenant with which it was connected, viii. 6–13 . . . . . . 367

8. The Superiority of our Lord's Priesthood to the Levitical proved by a direct Comparison between them, ix. 1–x. 18 . . . . . . 375

 (1) General Comparison, ix. 1–12 . . . 376

  1. Facts with regard to the Levitical Priesthood, ix. 1–10 . . . . . . 376

  2. Contrasted Facts respecting our Lord's Priesthood, ix. 11, 12 . . . . 390

 (2) More Particular Comparison, ix. 13–x. 18 . 397

  1. The Efficacy of our Lord's Priesthood is of a higher kind than that of the Levitical Priesthood, ix. 13–24 . . . . 398

  2. The Efficacy of our Lord's Priesthood is more perfect in Degree than that of the Levitical Priesthood, ix. 25–x. 18 . . 426


PART II—PRACTICAL

Chapter x 19—xiii 25

Section 1. General Exhortation and Warning, x. 19–xii. 29 . 453

 2. Particular Exhortations, xiii. 1–14 . . . 671

Conclusion, xiii. 15–21 . . . . . . . 703

Postscript, xiii. 22–25 . . . . . . . 728

# INTRODUCTION

THE observation, though commonplace, is true and important, that principles, in themselves not only innocent but laudable, may, from their being excessive in degree or ill-timed in their display, be, to a great extent, mischievous in their consequences. Excess of patriotism, not unfrequently, has not merely brought destruction on the patriot's head, but plunged his country into deeper calamities than those from which he was attempting to save it; and some of the bloodiest persecutions of the Christian Church have originated in " a zeal of God, but not according to knowledge."

The remark has perhaps never been more strikingly verified than in the malignant influence which a veneration for the Mosaic institutions exercised over the minds of the great body of the Jewish nation in the primitive age of Christianity, and which it continues to exert over the minds of their deluded and unhappy posterity till the present day. That this principle was, in its own nature, highly praiseworthy, there can be no doubt. The institutions they venerated were of Divine origin. The Mosaic economy was the work of God. It was introduced with the most impressive solemnity, confirmed by the most signal miracles, and had been productive to the nation of the most important advantages. It was owing to this that, in a religious and moral point of view, the Jews were so much more happily situated than the Gentiles. It was owing to this "that to them were committed the oracles of God,—that to them pertained the adoption and the glory, and the covenants, and the giving of the law, and the service of God, and the promises;"[1] and this economy having now existed for a long course of ages, and outlived repeated revolutions of the civil institutions in the surrounding nations, in addition to its claims on their reverential attachment, from its high origin and advantageous results, it possessed, in no ordinary degree, that charm of venerable ancientness which has so powerful an influence over the human mind. In such circumstances, for the Jews not to have been fondly and religiously attached to the Mosaic institute, would have argued a destitution of everything that is amiable and respectable in individual or national character. Yet there can be no doubt that an excessive and unenlightened veneration for this economy hardened the great body of the Jews in their opposition to Christianity, and riveted the fetters of their unbelief and impenitence; and that even in the case of many of those who, borne down by the overpowering force of evidence, were constrained to admit the Messiahship of Jesus, it was the source of important misapprehension and dangerous corruption of the principles of their new birth.

No part of the system of Christianity was less palatable to the Jew, or furnished him with more plausible objections against receiving it, than its obvious tendency and its avowed purpose to abolish and supersede the Mosaic economy. This venerable institution, they were well aware, was Divine in its origin, and they believed with equal firmness, though on more questionable grounds, that it was destined to perpetual endurance. When Christianity, then, in no obscure language, declared Judaism to be radically an imperfect and introductory institution, a local and temporary economy, and proclaimed itself the universal and everlasting dispensation of religious truth and duty, fitted and intended for mankind of all countries and all ages, not merely were all their strongest prejudices roused into a state of most excited exasperation, but irrefragable evidence seemed presented to them of the falsehood and impiety of the new system.

[1] Rom. iii. 1, 2, ix. 4.

While their veneration for the Mosaic institute thus led the majority of the Jews to reject Christianity altogether, the same principle operated in a malignant manner on the minds of many of the minority who were induced to embrace that religion. It led into misapprehension of its general nature and design, and into dangerous mistakes respecting some of its most important doctrines. Instead of perceiving that under the new order of things there was neither Jew nor Gentile, but that, without reference to external distinction, all believers in Christ Jesus were now to live together in the closest bonds of spiritual attachment in holy society, they dreamed of the Gentiles being admitted to the participation of the privileges of the Jewish Church through means of the Messiah, and that its external economy was to remain unaltered to the end of the world.

The correction of this excessive and ignorant veneration of the Mosaic institution, by giving just views of its nature and design, is an object which the Apostle Paul in his writings frequently adverts to, and sometimes professedly prosecutes by a continuous series of illustrations and arguments; and the propriety and necessity of this will be apparent when we recollect that a very considerable proportion of the primitive converts, in almost every country, had been originally Jews, and, of consequence, laboured under Jewish prejudices. The fullest discussion of this interesting subject is, however, to be found, where it was to be expected, in that Epistle which is addressed exclusively to the Hebrew nation, and which is generally, on probable evidence, considered as the work of the great Apostle of the Gentiles. In this very remarkable composition it is shown, with a profusion of Jewish learning, an ingenuity and force of reasoning, and a fire of impassioned eloquence, which are indeed wonderful, that the Jewish institution was in many respects imperfect, and in its very nature emblematical and introductory,—that in Christ Jesus, and the economy which He had introduced, was to be found the completion of that dispensation of which the Mosaic institute was the introduction, the substance of which it was the figure,—that the new order of things possessed all the excellences, and was free from all the defects of the old, while it possessed a variety of excellences peculiar to itself, and that, of consequence, it was folly and crime to cleave to an institution which had already served its purpose, and reject the last and best institution of Divine truth and mercy to mankind.

Previously to our proceeding to examine more in detail the manner in which the great object of this Epistle is prosecuted, it will be useful, if not necessary, to make a few preliminary remarks respecting its writer—the persons to whom it was addressed—the language in which it was written—the period when it was written—the place whence it was written—its canonicity—the general outline of the argument which it unfolds—and its principal interpreters.

# PROLEGOMENA.

### § 1.—*Of the Author of the Epistle.*[1]

WITH regard to the first of these subjects, it is obvious that, though the Epistle is anonymous, there was no design on the part of the writer to conceal himself from those to whom he was writing. He speaks of himself as one on whom they had compassion in his bonds, requests an interest in their prayers, and intimates a hope of soon seeing them again.[2] There can be little doubt, that when they gave copies of the Epistle to other churches, they did not conceal the name of the writer; and if a tradition be found early received and generally prevailing, unless there be very strong internal evidence of its falsehood, the probability is that that tradition is true. Such a tradition we find prevailing towards the end of the second century, and since that period it has been generally received in the Christian Church. That tradition ascribes the Epistle to the Apostle Paul as its author. The only objection of importance to this opinion rises out of the dissimilarity of the language and style of the Epistle to those of the acknowledged writings of the Apostle Paul. This is an argument on which, however, but little dependence can be placed. Variety of subject is calculated to produce variety of style; and there is not a greater dissimilarity between the Epistle

---

[1] It has been questioned whether this book be an Epistle at all, or not rather a kind of homiletical discourse. This is a question of little interest. The ancients always termed it an Epistle, and the expression in ch. xiii. 22, διὰ βραχέων ἐπέστειλα ὑμῖν, seems to determine the question. It, however, partakes much more of the character of the rhetorical discourse than of the familiar epistle.

[2] Heb. x. 34, xiii. 18, 19.

to the Hebrews and the other Epistles of Paul, than there is between the Gospel, the Epistles, and the Apocalypse—all of them the admitted writings of the Apostle John. After considering with some care the evidence on both sides of this question, I am disposed to think that, though by no means absolutely certain, it is in a high degree probable, that this Epistle was written by the Apostle Paul.[1]

§ 2.—*Of those to whom the Epistle was written.*

As to the persons to whom the Epistle was addressed, it contains internal evidence that they were Jews who had been led to embrace the profession of Christianity. The greater part of its contents is applicable to persons in their circumstances, wherever they might have their residence; yet, as the letter obviously was addressed to a particular church, or collection of churches residing in the same country, the probability is, that it was primarily intended for the church in Jerusalem, or the churches of Judea.[2]

---

[1] FORSTER has an elaborate work defending the ordinary opinion, but the ablest defence of the Pauline origin of the Epistle is that of Moses Stuart, in his Preliminary Dissertation to his Commentary. An excellent summary of the arguments *pro* and *con* is to be found in the first chapter of Kuinœl's Prolegomena to his Commentary. The opinion of Origen, whom Stanley justly terms "the profoundest of all the ancient Fathers," as preserved by Eusebius (H. E. vi. 25), deserves to be quoted:—"The style of the Epistle to the Hebrews has not the rudeness of the language of the Apostle, who confessed himself to be rude in speech, *i. e.*, in diction. The Epistle is more purely Greek in its composition, as would be confessed by every one who is any judge of the difference of styles. On the other hand, that the thoughts of the Epistle are wonderful, and not inferior to the acknowledged works of the Apostle, would be agreed on by every one who has paid any attention to the reading of the Epistle. My own judgment then is, that the thoughts are the Apostle's, but the language and composition those of some one who noted down the Apostle's views (τὰ ἀποστολικά), and, as it were, commented as a scholiast on what had been said by his master. If then any church hold to this Epistle as Paul's, let it have the credit of so doing—for it was not without reason that the ancients left it as Paul's. But as to who *wrote* it, the truth is known to God."

[2] Braunius, Baumgarten, and Heinrichs consider it as written to the Christian Jews wherever dispersed. Storr supposes it written to the Christians of Jewish origin in the region of Galatia. Bengel, C. F. Schmid, and Cramer think it likely that it was written to the same persons as Peter's

## § 3.—*Of the Original Language and Style of the Epistle.*

Clement of Alexandria, Eusebius, and Jerome hold that this Epistle was originally written in Syro-Chaldaic, the vernacular language of Palestine, and that we have in the New Testament a translation. This opinion is supported by the ingenious Hallet. The opinion is a highly improbable one. The Epistle, as we have it, has none of the characters of a version from another language.

## § 4.—*Of the Date and Place of the Epistle.*

It is impossible accurately to fix the date of the Epistle; but it is plain that it was written before, and probably not long before, the final overthrow of the Jewish polity on the destruction of Jerusalem.[1]

The Epistle itself affords no means of saying with certainty whence it was written. The words ch. xiii. 24 by no means prove that it was written in Italy. They only prove that some who might be called οἱ ἀπὸ τῆς Ἰταλίας were with its author when he wrote it. The subscription of the Epistle is no authority.—Some have supposed it written from Rome, some from Corinth, some from Macedonia, but nothing in the shape of evidence can be adduced in favour of any of these opinions.

Epistles. Wetstein thinks it was probably written to the Christian Jews of Rome. Weber pleads for the Judæo-Christians at Corinth—Schmidt for those of Alexandria—Ludwig, following a conjecture of Jerome, for those of Spain,—Hasæus for the Nazarenes or Ebionites living in some remote town of Judea. The opinion we have denominated more probable, is that adopted generally by the Fathers, and by most of the learned among the moderns, particularly by Michælis, Bertholdt, Bleek, Kohler, and Schott. From the Epistle itself it is plain that it was addressed to a church or churches of not recent origin, ch. v. 12, x. 32; and that it or they constituted a large body, ch. xiii. 24. Stanley considers it as addressed to that portion of the Jewish nation who spoke the Hebrew tongue—the aristocracy of the race undefiled by any contamination of Grecian custom or language—to prepare them for the dreadful necessity of choosing once for all between those ancient institutions, in which, up to this time, the Apostles had not refused to join, and that eternal polity which could alone endure the convulsion which was "to shake not the earth only, but also heaven."

[1] Heb. viii. 4, ix. 6, xiii. 10.

## § 5.—*Of the Canonicity of the Epistle.*

With regard to the canonical authority of this Epistle, Clement of Rome, who wrote before the close of the first century, frequently refers to it, and appeals to it as Scripture. Justin Martyr, who flourished about the middle of the second century, quotes it; and about this time it seems to have had a place among the canonical writings both of the Eastern and Western churches. For obvious reasons, the Arians called in question its canonical authority. Some Protestant divines,—as well as Cajetan and Erasmus among the Roman Catholics,—have doubted its Pauline origin and canonical authority; and some of them have regarded it as belonging not to the first, but to the second or third class of canonical books. No sufficient reason has ever been assigned for questioning its canonicity.[1]

## § 6.—*Of the Subject and Division of the Epistle.*[2]

The Epistle divides itself into two parts—the first Doctrinal, and the second Practical—though the division is not so accurately observed as that there are no duties enjoined or urged in the first part, and no doctrines stated in the second. The first is by far the larger division, reaching from the beginning of the Epistle down to the 18th verse of the tenth chapter. The second commences with the 19th verse of the tenth chapter, and extends to the end of the Epistle. The superiority of Christianity to Judaism is the great doctrine which the Epistle teaches; and constancy in the faith and profession of that religion is the great duty which it enjoins. The superiority of Christianity is illustrated by showing that Jesus Christ, who is not only the Author, but the great Subject of that religion, is superior,—first

---

[1] Every careful student of it will be disposed to say with Origen,— "the thoughts of the Epistle are amazing, and not inferior to the acknowledged apostolic writings" (EUSEB. H. E., vi. 25),—or with the learned Cunæus (lib. iii., cap. iii., p. 317, Sam. 1674), "I do not know whether there is any New Testament book after John's Gospel in which there is more deep and profound theology."

[2] See Note A.

to the angels, through whose instrumentality the law of Moses was given; secondly, to Moses himself; and thirdly, to the Jewish high priest. These were the great objects of the admiration of the Jews; and the author of the Epistle shows that Jesus, the Angel and the Mediator of a Better Covenant, the Apostle and great High Priest of our profession, infinitely transcends them all. The comparison with angels begins at the 4th verse of the first chapter, and ends with the conclusion of the second chapter. The comparison with Moses begins with the third chapter, and ends at the 13th verse of the fourth chapter. The comparison with the Jewish high priest begins at the 14th verse of the fourth chapter, and ends with the 18th verse of the tenth chapter. The Practical part of the Epistle divides itself into two parts; the first, consisting of a general exhortation to constancy in the faith and profession of Christianity, begins at the 19th verse of the tenth chapter, and reaches to the close of the twelfth chapter; the second, consisting of a variety of particular exhortations, occupies the whole of the thirteenth chapter, with the exception of the last six verses, which form the conclusion of the Epistle. It is of importance to mark these great divisions of the Epistle. The keeping of them steadily in view, will be found to conduce materially to the more distinct and satisfactory apprehension of the meaning of the statements and the force of the argument contained in the Epistle.

§ 7.—*Of the Interpreters of the Epistle.*

The best of the ancient interpreters of this Epistle is Theophylact. His commentary is a compend of Chrysostom's more copious work, generally in Chrysostom's words. The best of the older continental interpreters are, Hyperius, Erasmus, Drusius, Grotius, Capellus—both James and Lewis, Limborch. Among the later, Carpzovius, Schmidius, Braunius, Nemethus, Ernesti, Abresch, Heinrichs, Böhme, Kuinœl, Ebrard, may be named. Of English commentators, the chief are Gouge, Owen, Lawson, Duncan, Peirce and Hallet, Sykes, M'Lean, Moses Stuart, Turner.

## NOTE A, p. 10.

The following eloquent outline of the Epistle by Stanley is well worth quoting:—" It is necessary once for all to place before our minds the feelings of the Hebrew Christians. Their national existence was, as I have said, on the eve of destruction; the star of their ancient glory was about to set in blood; their institutions had ' decayed and waxed old ' and were ' ready to vanish away ' (Heb. viii, 13); but still for this very reason there was the fond attachment which clings to what all the world beside has abandoned; there was the longing lingering look which a dying nation casts behind to its earlier life; there was the despair which cherished the more dearly the vestiges of it that still remained. The ' chariots of God, even twenty thousand of angels ' (as inferred from Heb. i. 3–13. See Ps. lxviii. 17; 2 Kings vi. 17), amidst which the Law had been delivered ' in the holy place of Sinai,' they might still believe to watch unseen around the walls of Jerusalem, as when they guarded the prophet of old at Dothan. The recollections of Moses and of Joshua (as inferred from Heb. iii. iv), the possession of the Law and of the promised rest, still seemed to them pledges of the Divine protection. The Temple still stood in all its magnificence on Mount Moriah; the priestly ministrations still continued day by day according to the exact letter of the Levitical law; the pontificate of Aaron, after the vicissitudes of fifteen hundred years,—after the disappearance of Judge, and King, and Prophet, through the splendour of the monarchy and the oppressions of the captivity,—still remained unshaken and unimpaired as when it was first ordained amongst the mountains of Horeb. What wonder if the better spirits of the nation should be fascinated by the spell, which rallied even the blood-thirsty ruffians of the final siege round the ruins of the burning sanctuary, which awakened a glow of patriotic enthusiasm in the breast even of the renegade Josephus while he described his descent (Josephus, Vita, c. 1. Comp. Contra Apionem, i. 7. ii. 21) from the house of Levi, which invested the high-priesthood (John xi. 51) even of Caiaphas with a character of Divine inspiration? What was there, they might well ask, what was there in the whole world beside, which could compensate to them for the loss of recollections so august, of institutions so sacred?

" It was to meet this need that the Epistle to the Hebrews was written. And now, if we compare its opening words with those of the Gospel of St John, it is the natural result of what has just been said, that—whereas in the latter we are carried beyond the limits of the visible world to that ' beginning in which the Word was with God and the Word was God,'—in the former we are brought down to the close of the long series of ages in which, after ' having in times past spoken unto the fathers by the prophets. God in these last days spoke to them by His Son.' If the Ephesians, Colossians, and Philippians, were taught to look to Him who was ' the First-born of every creature, the Head of the Church, the Lord of heaven and earth,' we find that the Hebrew Christians are especially reminded that there was One far above all their own ministering angels; One who was to be ' counted worthy of more glory ' than their great law-giver

Moses; One who was to guide them into a deeper rest, than even their great deliverer who, with the same significant name of 'Joshua' or 'Jesus,' had led them to their earlier rest in Canaan; that there was a true sense in which the glory not only of Aaron, but even of the mysterious patriarch king of Salem, was transferred to Him who was to be the whole human race 'a Priest for ever after the order of Melchisedec.'

" Every name, every feeling, every institution, which had existed under the older covenant was still to continue, but invested with a higher meaning,—a meaning, new indeed in itself, but yet fulfilling for the first time what had before been dimly shadowed forth; 'the first was taken away' only that the 'second might be established.' It was indeed no visible hierarchy of angelic forms, to which their thoughts were now directed, but He who was the same always, and 'whose years could never fail;' it was no earthly Sabbath to which He was to guide them, but the eternal 'rest which remains for the people of God;' no weapons of human warfare, like those which won the land of Canaan, but the 'word of God, quick and powerful, and sharper than any two-edged sword;' the Law was to be written not on tables of stone, but 'in their hearts and in their minds;' the Sacrifice was to be offered up in no earthly sanctuary; the Priest was to minister within the veil, 'not in the holy places made with hands, but in heaven itself, now to appear in the presence of God for us.' But still it was something to be told that the past and the future were not to be suddenly snapt in sunder,—something to feel that the new wine was not rudely to be forced on those whose natural feeling would still make them say that 'the old was better,'—something to be assured by apostolic teachers that the words, the thoughts, the associations with which they had been familiar would not perish in the approaching catastrophe, but would endure, as humanly speaking through the medium of this very Epistle they have endured, to become the stay and support of thousands in every age and country, to whom the difficulties, the sentiments, the very existence of the original Hebrew Christians would be utterly unknown and unintelligible. Yet, gradual as this preparation was, tenderly as they were accustomed by 'the milk of babes' to receive 'the strong meat which belongeth to them that are of full age,' it still remained to touch some faculty or feeling in their own hearts which should respond to this higher strain, which should raise them from 'the first principles of the doctrine of Christ to go on unto perfection,' which should prevent them when in sight of 'so great salvation' from sinking back into the wretched state of the apostate nation, 'rejected and nigh unto cursing, whose end was to be burned.' That feeling was 'Faith,' the same 'Faith' which had been so triumphantly brought forward by the great Apostle of the Gentiles in his conflict with Judaism, but which was now insisted upon not in vehement controversy, but in earnest exhortation; a faith not condemned like mere Jewish faith, as in the Epistle of St James,—not set in distinct opposition to the works of the Law, as in the Epistle to the Galatians,—but traced back through all its various stages from its most general manifestation by which in its earliest effort the Jewish mind had 'understood that the worlds were framed by the word of God,' down to its latest workings in the heroic struggles of the Maccabean age, 'destitute, afflicted, tormented.' With such a confidence (ὑπόστασις) in things hoped for, with such an evidence of things not seen,' they might well rise above the visions of outward dominion and array of legal ceremonies which hovered before the earth-bound senses of their countrymen; they might still have ' patient trust that in a little while He that shall come will come and will not tarry;' they might well be assured that although not like their fathers in the presence of ' the terrible sight of the mountain that might be touched and that burned with fire,' they were even amidst the impending ruin of their earthly home, brought within ' the city of the living God, the heavenly Jerusalem, to the innumerable company of angels, the general assembly and Church of the first-born which are written in heaven, and God the Judge of all, and the spirits of just men made perfect, and Jesus the Mediator of the new covenant.' "

# PART I.

## DOCTRINAL.

### INTRODUCTORY STATEMENT.

#### THE TWO REVELATIONS CONTRASTED.[1]

THE first three verses form the introduction to the Epistle, and distinctly enough state the great theme of the subsequent discussions—the superiority of Christianity to Judaism. There

---

[1] The bird's eye view of the contents of the Epistle by Valcknaer is sketched with a masterly pencil :—" It was written to half-Christians from among the Jews, people who were over-attached to Mosaic ceremonies. The author believed that he had been given the task of strengthening such Christians in the faith which they had received, and of weaning them away from the ceremonies and shadows of former days. To that end, he compares Christ with the angels, Moses, and Aaron (or the Levitical priesthood), and proves him to be far superior to them. He explains that, as shadows are scattered and vanish at sunrise, so likewise the shadows of former days passed away at the rising of Jesus, the Sun of righteousness. They had looked forward to Christ, and were to be abolished at his appearing. He explains that the priestly function had been transferred to Christ, who was far superior to Aaron and Moses. To that same end, he shows that the Law was wholly imperfect, for the fathers were justified, not by the Law, but by faith. Finally, this noble divine crowns the Epistle magnificently with practical injunctions adapted to the moulding of character and the good ordering of life." His remarks on the style of the Epistle are still better :—" The complexion of the writing is not such as could come from a translator. The style is entirely different from a translator's style. The Epistle to the Hebrews, though marked by Hebraisms, is terse, polished, elegant, thoroughly Greek, sublime and full of majesty. But the eloquence that must be sought in it is that to which Greek-speaking Jews aspired. Only an ignoramus would look for the eloquence of a Demosthenes or Isocrates in a Hellenistic Jew. The fact that Tollius, in his notes on Longinus' *On the Sublime*, speaks of the Epistle to the Hebrews as surpassing the sublimity of all Gentile writers, or certainly as equalling it, must be explained primarily as a reference to the nobility of the topics that are handled in it."

is something peculiarly sublime and impressive in these introductory verses.

Verses 1-3.—God, who at sundry times, and in divers manners, spake in time past unto the fathers by the prophets, hath in these last days spoken unto us by His Son, whom He hath appointed heir of all things, by whom also He made the worlds; who, being the brightness of His glory, and the express image of His person, and upholding all things by the word of His power, when He had by Himself purged our sins, sat down on the right hand of the Majesty on high.[1]

In these words the Divine origin both of the Jewish and of the Christian revelation is distinctly asserted; and so asserted, as that the superior importance of the latter is strikingly exhibited. The Divine origin of the Jewish revelation is clearly stated; 'God, spake[2] to the fathers,[3] by the prophets, at sundry times and in divers manners in time past." By "the fathers," we are plainly to understand the distant ancestors of those to whom he was writing—the Israelitish people, from the time of Moses to the time of Malachi. "God spake to them." Occasionally Jehovah spoke to the Israelitish people, or to individuals among them, by an audible voice, as when, from amid the clouds and darkness which covered Mount Sinai, the Ten Commandments were delivered in the hearing of all the people; but it is plain that the word "spake" is to be understood in a more general sense here, as equivalent to "revealed His will." It is by speaking chiefly that we communicate our thoughts to one another; and there-

---

[1] "The structure of this period has been justly noticed as remarkable for its beauty. The period is as perspicuous as it is long, and rich, and complicated: a fine succession of thoughts expressed in a form finished even to the minutest detail, gives it a claim to rank among the finest periods of the Greek authors."—EBRARD. The superscription usual in the apostolic Epistles is here wanting. It is impossible to give with certainty the true account of this peculiarity. The composition is like the First Epistle of John, which has the same characteristic,—partakes more of the nature of a treatise than an Epistle; and both might probably be accompanied by a short letter.

[2] "λαλεῖν is used in the sense of דִּבֶּר, to denote the revealing utterance of God.—Ch. ii. 2, ix. 19; Acts iii. 24; James v. 10; 2 Pet. i. 21."—EBRARD.

[3] In some codd. ἡμῶν is added to πατράσιν, but there can be little doubt it is the *gloss* of a transcriber. Paul commonly uses the word without the pronoun.—Rom. ix. 5, xi. 28, xv. 8.

fore a revelation of the Divine will, whatever be the particular mode of revelation, is termed God's speaking to men.[1]

When He revealed His will to the ancient Israelites it was by "the prophets."[2] The word *prophet* properly signifies one who speaks of things before they happen, who foretells future events. Its meaning here, however, and in other passages where it occurs in the New Testament, is to be sought for by inquiring into the signification of the word used in the Old Testament, as the term here employed is a translation. In its original signification it seems to have been applied to any person who stood in a peculiarly close relation to God. Thus, Abraham is termed a *prophet*.[3] And God is represented as saying, by His peculiar and miraculous care of the patriarchs, to those among whom they sojourned, "Touch not Mine anointed, and do My prophets no harm."[4] It came afterwards to be employed in the more restricted sense of an inspired person—a person supernaturally instructed in the will of God, and commissioned to make known that will to men, whether that will referred to future events or not.

Though the Divine origin of Christianity and the inspiration of the writings of the New Testament may be demonstrated without any reference to a preceding revelation, yet it is quite evident that in the New Testament the Divine origin of the Jewish religion, and the Divine inspiration of the Old Testament Scriptures, are uniformly supposed and often expressly assumed. Our Lord refers to the ancient Scriptures as of paramount authority. The Apostle Paul asserts that "all Scripture is given by inspiration of God," and the Apostle Peter—that "the prophecy came not in old time by the will of man, but holy men of God spake as they were moved by the Holy Ghost."

The Lord spake to the prophets, and by them to the fathers.[5]

---

[1] Luke v. 3, 4; Acts viii. 25.

[2] Crellius conjectures that ἀγγέλοις is the true reading, but it is a mere conjecture.

[3] Gen. xx. 7.   [4] Ps. cv. 15.

[5] The phrase, ἐν τοῖς προφήταις, has by some been interpreted as = in the writings of the prophets, as in Matt. v. 17; Luke xxiv. 27. That this is not its meaning is plain from the contrast— ἐν υἱῷ. 'Εν is here and in many other places = διά,—John i. 4. It is a translation of the Hebrew particle בְּ.

The following is the account which one of these inspired men gives of the nature and extent of his own inspiration: "The Spirit of the Lord spake by me and His word was in my tongue." The subject of inspiration is an interesting and difficult one. It is easy to ask many questions about it which no learning or ingenuity can answer. It is enough for us, however, on the authority of our Lord and His apostles, to know the fact that the Old Testament Scriptures, as well as the New, are inspired (*i.e.*, are an infallible statement of the will of God), and it is anything but reasonable or philosophical to deny or even to doubt of it merely on account of the difficulty which we may experience in reconciling certain appearances with this well established fact.[1]

These revelations, which God made to the ancient Israelites through the instrumentality of these inspired men, were given "at sundry times and in divers manners." By many learned interpreters these two phrases are considered as synonymous, and as intended together to describe the diversified manner of the Old Testament revelation. The passages commonly quoted for the purpose of supporting this interpretation prove merely that they may be used in this way, not that they uniformly and necessarily are so used. They admit of distinct senses, and while these senses are appropriate, as in the present case, why should they not be attributed to them? No man, especially an inspired man, is reasonably to be presumed to use words having a distinct meaning in an indefinite way. We are rather disposed to consider them as expressing different ideas. The word rendered "at sundry times" properly signifies, *in many portions, manifoldly*, implying the idea of different periods rather than expressing it. The Old Testament was not completed at once. It was not given forth as a whole. The will of God was gradually revealed, as the circumstances of the Church required. First were given the Five Books of Moses—then the Historical, Poetical, Didactic, and Prophetic books at irregular intervals, during a period of more than a thousand years. In adverting to this character of Old Testament revelations, it is not unlikely that it was the intention of

---

[1] On the subject of inspiration, the writers best worth consulting are Meyer, Doddridge, Parry, Dick, and Henderson, and there is an excellent article by Dr Vaughan in a late number of the *British Quarterly Review*. Rosenmüller runs into one extreme—Haldane and his followers into another.

the writer to suggest the idea that, valuable and divine as they were, they contained but an incomplete development of the divine will.

This occasional character of the Old Testament writings, when viewed in all its bearings, yields no inconsiderable corroborative evidence of their divine origin. It removes everything like the appearance of human art or contrivance, proves that, if harmony exists, it could not be the result of a preconcerted plan, and leads us to inquire for a reason—which can only be found on the admission of the infinite wisdom of their Author—why writings so plainly occasional in their origin, should, notwithstanding, so admirably serve the purpose of a universal and permanent rule of faith and manners.

The Old Testament revelation was not only given in different portions—which implies its being given at sundry times—but also "in divers manners." Some have supposed that the Apostle here refers to the various modes of revelation to the prophets.[1] Sometimes God made known His will to them by dreams, at other times by visions, at other times by voices, at other times by internal impulses, at other times by the ministry of angels. But the Apostle is not speaking of the variety of the modes of revelation, as made to the prophets, but as made by them to the fathers. The revelation was sometimes communicated by typical representations and emblematical actions, sometimes in a continued parable, at other times by separate figures, at other times—though comparatively rarely—in plain explicit language. The revelation has sometimes the form of a narrative, at other times that of a prediction, at other times that of an argumentative or hortatory discourse; sometimes it is given in prose, at other times in poetry.

Thus did God make a revelation of His will—in successive portions and in a variety of ways—to the Israelitish people *"in time past."* The word literally signifies long ago, and is pro-

---

[1] The force of the two words, πολυμερῶς and πολυτρόπως, is very well given by Kypke.—" Under the Old Testament, revelations were made at various times, through various persons, consisting in various laws and teachings, with varying degrees of clarity, under various shadows, types, and figures, by various means of revelation, through dreams, visions, etc." Dr HENDERSON, in his admirable work on Inspiration, considers πολυμερῶς as = in divers parts, and πολυτρόπως as referring to the various modes or forms of Old Testament revelation.

bably meant to convey the idea, not only of the venerable antiquity of the Old Testament revelation, but also the long period which had elapsed since that revelation was closed. It was nearly fifteen hundred years since the first portion of the inspired volume was written, and nearly four hundred since the last.

Having thus described the Jewish revelation, he goes on to give an account of the Christian, and he gives it in an antithetical form. The God who spake to the fathers, now speaks to us. The God who spake in old time, now speaks in these last days. The God who spake by His prophets, now speaks by His Son. There is nothing in the description of the Gospel revelation that answers to the two phrases—"*at sundry times* and *in divers manners;*" but the ideas which they naturally suggest to the mind are, the completeness of the Gospel revelation compared with the imperfection of the Jewish, and the simplicity and clearness of the Gospel revelation compared with the multiformity and obscurity of the Jewish. Thus, to use the language of a living author: "In that revelation of the divine will which the Bible contains, we have a series of communications, stretching through a course of many centuries, conveyed through individuals of different habits, tastes, education, and talents, and characterized by the greatest variety of form and style. Amid all this diversity, however, of outward circumstances, the great Author of the whole remained from the first to the last the same. By whomsoever the message was borne to men, whether by patriarchs or prophets, or by the Son of God Himself; at whatever period it was announced, whether in the early dawn of the world's history, or after 'the fulness of the time' had already come; and in whatever form it appeared, whether clothed in symbols, or conveyed in the language of direct communication; whether set forth by some silent, yet significant type, or proclaimed by the living voice of some gifted seer; whether uttered in brief and naked terms, or wrapt in the gorgeous mantle of impassioned poetry, it was throughout the same Divine Spirit who inspired the messenger and authorized the message. As in the natural world, the media through which the rays of the sun pass, and the degree of warmth and illumination experienced in consequence at the earth's surface, are different at different times—non habet officii Lucifer omnis idem—whilst it is, in every case and at all times, the same luminary to which we are indebted for whatever of light and heat our atmosphere may transmit to us: so in the spiritual world,—it hath pleased the Sovereign of the universe, that the radiance of divine truth, flowing, as it ever must, from the fountain of His own eternal mind, should descend in different degrees and with diversified hues, upon those to whom it was originally sent." [1]

Let us examine with somewhat more minuteness the description of the Christian revelation.

The same God who spake to the fathers, *hath spoken to us.* The pronoun *us* refers directly to the Jews of that age, to which class belonged both the writer and his readers; but the statement is equally true in reference to all, in every succeeding age, to whom the word of this salvation comes. God, in the completed revelation of His will, respecting the salvation of men through Christ Jesus, is still speaking to all who have an opportunity of reading the New Testament or of hearing the Gospel. The Christian revelation is to be traced to the same origin as the Jewish revelation. It is the same God that speaks to us, who spake to the fathers; and as that God is *one,* the two revelations must be harmonious. The Law cannot be against the Promise. The Jewish revelation cannot be inconsistent with the Christian; and that must be a misinterpretation of the former, which would lead men to refuse belief or obedience to the latter.

After a silence of nearly four hundred years, God, who had *anciently* revealed His will, now spake *in these last times;* or, according to a more approved reading, *in the end of these times.*[2] There is plainly here a reference to the Jewish mode of speaking with regard to the times of the law and the times of the Messiah. The Jews were accustomed to call the first the present age or world, the second the coming age or world,

---

[1] ALEXANDER's Connection of the Old and New Testaments, sect. ii., p. 67, 68.

[2] Ἐπ' ἐσχάτου τῶν ἡμερῶν, the literal version of בְּאַחֲרִית הַיָּמִים, is to be found in the LXX, Numb. xxiv. 14; Ezek. xxxviii. 16; Jer. xxiii. 20. We have the same Hebrew phrase rendered ἐπ' ἐσχάτων τῶν ἡμερῶν, Gen. xlix. 1; Deut. iv. 30; Isa. ii. 2. Τούτων is = the period referred to, or begun in *these* last days. Ἐπ' ἐ.τ.ἡ.τ. is contrasted with πάλαι, just as אַחֲרִית הַיָּמִים is with מִימֵי קֶדֶם, Isa. xxxvii. 26.

and they spoke of the age of the Messiah as the last or latter days. If we follow the reading, *in these last times*, the meaning seems to be, in that era spoken of by the prophets, under the appellation, *the last times*, as being the period of the *final* dispensation of divine mercy to mankind. If, with the best critics, we prefer the reading *in the end of these times*, then the meaning is, towards the conclusion of the Jewish dispensation. It seems equivalent to the expressions used by the Apostle, 1 Cor. x. 11,[1] "the ends of the world are come"—the conclusion of the Mosaic economy; Gal. iv. 4,[2] "the fulness, or the fulfilment of the time"—the accomplishment or termination of the period assigned for the duration of the Mosaic economy; Eph. i. 10,[3] "the dispensation of the fulness of the times"—the economy which was to be introduced when the times of the Mosaic economy were fulfilled; Heb. ix. 26,[4] "the end of the world," literally " of the ages"—the period of the termination of the Mosaic economy—the time when the present age or world was about to be changed into the coming age—the world to come.[5] The Christian revelation was begun to be made in the conclusion of the Jewish age. It was before the conclusion of that age that God spake to the Jews by His Son, who, according to our Lord's parabolical representation, was sent *last of all* to the husbandmen: "He sent forth His Son made under the law." His personal ministry, and for some time that of His Apostles, was confined to them; and though by His death the Mosaic economy was virtually abrogated, yet it was not in fact dissolved till forty years afterwards, in the destruction of the Temple by the Romans, and the consequent final cessation of its services.

The point, however, on which the writer wishes particularly to fix the attention of his readers, and on which he grounds chiefly the superiority of the Christian to the Jewish revelation, is that while anciently He spake to the Fathers *by the prophets*, He, in the end of these days, spake to them *by His Son*.[6] There

---

[1] Τέλη τῶν αἰώνων.  [2] Τὸ πλήρωμα τοῦ χρόνου.

[3] Οἰκονομία τοῦ πληρώματος τῶν καιρῶν.

[4] Συντέλεια τῶν αἰώνων.

[5] The Jews expected the Messiah so completely to change the state of things, as to make a new world. One of the rabbinical writers, on Gen. xlix. 1, says, "extremum tempus omnium doctorum consensu sunt dies Messiæ."

[6] Chrysostom's note is ἐν υἱῷ ἀντὶ τοῦ διὰ τοῦ υἱοῦ.

can be no doubt that the inspired writer here refers to Jesus Christ, but he refers to Him in a particular aspect, intimating that He was not only like the prophets, an inspired man, but a Divine person; not only like them, the messenger, but also the Son of God.[1] It has been very common among a certain class of interpreters to say, that the Son of God and the Messiah are synonymous terms; but the use of such language betrays great confusion of thought. The two designations belong to the same person, just in the same way as the designations, Prince of Wales, Eldest son of the monarch of Great Britain, Heir apparent of the British throne, usually belong to the same individual, but it would be absurd to say that these designations are synonymous. The prophets had intimated that the Messiah was to be the Son of God; and many of the Jews, who do not seem generally to have had clear notions of the import of that appellation, in using it, very probably employed it just as a name for the Messiah, though the notion of the Messiah generally entertained by the Jews of that age seems to have been a celestial being, superior to the angels—proceeding from God before all worlds—employed by Him in creating and governing the world—who was to come into the world, assume a human form, and effect the great deliverance promised by the prophets. Kuinœl, in his prolegomena to John, on the Λόγος, has given a succinct statement of the evidence on which these views are attributed to the Jews of the time of our Lord and His Apostles. The views of the Jews, however, do not materially affect the question as to the true meaning of the designation, or the manner in which it is employed by the inspired writers.

The principle on which such words as *son*—words borrowed from human relations to express divine relations—are to be interpreted, seems to me a very simple and obvious one, whatever difficulty there may be occasionally in its application. The word is to be understood as bearing its proper meaning as far as, and no farther than, we know from other sources, that it is not inapplicable to the object to which it is in a figurative sense applied. Let us apply this rule to the case before us. What are the ideas suggested by the word *son* in its proper application to mankind? They are, I apprehend, chiefly the following:—

[1] He very probably had our Lord's words in his mind; ὕστερον δὲ ἀπέστειλ πρὸς αὐτοὺς τὸν υἱὸν αὐτοῦ, Matt. xxi. 37.

Identity of nature, derivation of being, posteriority, inferiority, affection both on the part of the father and the son, and resemblance. Now, when in the Scriptures I find angels and saints represented as God's sons, I understand by it that they derive their being from Him, both as creatures and as holy creatures, that they are the objects of His kind regard, that He is the object of their dutiful regards, and that there is a resemblance between them and God; but I do not conclude that they are of the same nature, and for this reason, not that the word *son* does not naturally suggest the idea, but because I know, from the most certain sources of information, that angels and saints do not belong to the same order of being with divinity. When I find the same appellation given to Jesus Christ, and given to Him in a way quite peculiar, I consider it as signifying identity of nature with God, as well as that He is the object of the Divine kind regard, and that the Father is the object of His kind regard, and that He resembles the Father. And so I understand it for this reason, that this is the natural meaning of the word *son*; and I find from other passages of Scripture, that Jesus Christ is really possessed of this identity of nature with His Father: and I consider it as not signifying derivation of being, posteriority, or inferiority, for this reason, that though the word *son* naturally enough suggests these ideas, yet I know from other plain passages of Scripture, what is, indeed, implied in the leading idea of identity of nature, that Jesus is the eternal God—God over all, and, of course, neither posterior nor inferior to His Father. This appears to me the true mode of interpreting such phrases; and had it been generally adopted on this subject, it would have prevented, on the one hand, much rash speculation about the eternal generation of the Son, and the communication of the divine nature to Him by the Father; and on the other, the adoption of what appears to me the unscriptural dogma of a mere economical sonship, to which some good men have resorted, under the mistaken idea that sonship here necessarily implies posteriority and inferiority. The Son of God, then, though an appropriated appellation of the Messiah, is not a synonymous term with the Messiah, but intimates that He who wears it is a possessor of the Divine nature. He is so the Son of God as to be one with His Father. He is so the Son of God as to be equal with God.

When the Apostle, then, calls Jesus Christ the Son of God, and asserts that God had spoken to the Jews by Him, we consider him as asserting that, as He had formerly spoken by inspired men, He now had spoken by One who, as equal partaker of His own infinite nature, and all its excellences, was most intimately related to Him, and inconceivably dear to Him.

The claims of a revelation, delivered by a personage so exalted, are further developed by the inspired writer in his subsequent statements. The Son of God, by whom God had spoken in the end of these days, had "been appointed heir of all things."[1]

The word *heir*, properly speaking, signifies a person who, on the death of another, becomes possessed of his property. It is in this sense the word is used when Abraham, previously to the birth of Ishmael, says of Eleazar his steward, " One born in my house is my *heir;*" and in the parable, " This is the *heir*, come let us kill him, that the inheritance may be ours." It is not at all uncommon, however, to use the word as equivalent to *possessor* or proprietor, without reference to the manner in which the property is acquired. This is plainly its meaning here. The Father dieth not; nor does He divest Himself of His natural, necessary, and inalienable property in all things; but He hath given all things into the hand of His Son—He has constituted Him the proprietor of all things. The whole universe of creatures, material and spiritual, animate and inanimate, rational and irrational, is His property, to be managed according to His pleasure.

This proprietorship is the result of the appointment and gift of the Father. " God hath *appointed* Him *heir* of all things." As a divine person, Jesus Christ has an inalienable property in the universe which He has made. He is the *first-born*, or Lord and proprietor of all creation ; " for by Him were all things created that are in heaven and that are in earth, visible and invisible, whether they be thrones, or dominions, or principalities, or powers ; all things were created by Him and for Him : and He

---

[1] Κληρονόμος, properly heir, Luke xx. 14 ; Gal. iv. 1; secondarily, lord, possessor :—ἔθηκεν = κατέστησεν, ἐποίησε, v. 13 *inf.*; 1 Thes. v. 9 ; 1 Tim. 1. 12; Acts xiii. 47. THEOPHYLACT very well interprets the whole phrase—τοῦ κόσμου παντὸς ἐποίησε κύριον.

is before all things, and by Him all things consist."[1] But He who was "in the form of God," voluntarily "took on Him the form of a servant." The Only-begotten became a man, and in human flesh obeyed, and suffered, and died, for the honour of Divinity and the salvation of mankind. In this character, in which He had voluntarily divested Himself, not of His divine perfections or His supreme proprietorship and rule, for that was impossible, but of the visible display of them,—in this character, as the Mediator between God and man, the man Christ Jesus, He was, as the reward of His generous exertion, made proprietor of the universe, "and all power in heaven and earth was given Him, that He might give eternal life to as many as the Father had given Him."

Yet even the Mediatorial dignity, which was the result of appointment and gift, proves the *divinity of the Saviour*. Such property and dominion is infinitely too great for a creature to receive, and could be managed by no power and wisdom inferior to infinite. Indeed, in plain words, this appointment of the incarnate Son to be the heir of all things, seems just to be an ordination that that property in the universe which belongs to Deity should, in its exercise, appear to belong to Him "who was given for our offences, and raised again for our justification."

In this divine appointment there was a peculiar propriety, inasmuch as by the Son, God had in the beginning "made the worlds."[2] The Jewish Doctors were accustomed to divide the universe of created things into so many worlds:—the world of angels and spirits—the world of sun, moon, and stars—the world of our earth and sea. To make the worlds, is a phrase just equivalent to, to create the universe. The creation of the universe, then, is, in the plainest terms, ascribed to the Son of God,

---

[1] Col. i. 16, 17.

[2] Αἰών, like the Hebrew עֹלָם, properly denotes time, either past or future; and then comes to signify things formed and done in time—the world, Ecc. iii. 11; Matt. xiii. 39; Ps. lxvii. 7. The LXX and the New Testament writers generally use the word in the plural, as more suitable to such a prodigious and complicated system as the universe. The αἰῶνες is plainly the synonym of the τὰ πάντα in the preceding clause. Creation is ascribed to the Son at v. 10, and in many other passages of the New Testament, John i. 2, 3, 10; 1 Cor. viii. 6; Col. i. 16; Heb. xi. 3, so that there can be no reasonable doubt that αἰῶνας is = the universe.

our Saviour, Jesus Christ. Nor is it ascribed to Him in this passage alone. The Evangelist John states that "all things were made by Him, and that without Him was there nothing made that was made;"[1] and the Apostle Paul—that "by Him were all things created that are in heaven and that are in earth, visible and invisible, whether they be thrones, or dominions, or principalities, or powers; all things were created by Him."[2] The ascription of the creation of the universe to the Son is a most satisfactory proof of His proper divinity. To bring the universe into existence from nothing—to establish such perfect harmony as pervades all its parts, obviously requires a power and wisdom altogether infinite. The eternal power and Godhead of the Creator are so obviously deducible from His works, that the Apostle declares the heathen without excuse who do not worship the Creator as God. Are not they still more clearly without excuse who, reading in what they profess to consider as a well accredited divine revelation, that *the Son* created the world, yet refuse to honour Him as they honour the Father. Creative power was plainly regarded by the Jewish prophets as the appropriate and peculiar attribute of the Supreme God.[3] The argument, couched in these and in many other similar passages, would be utterly inconclusive if creation did not infer proper supreme divinity in the Creator.

It is not wonderful that those who deny the divinity of Jesus Christ, should have exerted themselves to the utmost to explain away the testimony contained in the text before us, to the fact, that He is the Creator of the universe. They have done this in a variety of ways. This very variety of ways is a strong presumption that no one of them is satisfactory.

Some tell us that there is no reference to creation, properly so called, and that the words should have been rendered, *by whom He constituted the ages*—i.e., by whom He arranged the various dispensations of religion,—or, that if rendered as they are, they are to be considered as referring to the new creation— that new order of things which He has introduced. The shortest and most satisfactory answer to this, is to appeal to the writer of this Epistle himself, as to the sense in which he uses the phrase.[4] The word *worlds* is never used of the new order

[1] John i. 3.
[2] Col. i. 16, 17.
[3] Isa. xxxvi. 16; Jer. ix. 10–16.
[4] Heb. xi. 3.

of things. The word *world* is once employed with this signification; but then the qualifying phrase, *to come*, is added.¹ Indeed, in this figurative sense, making the world, so far from being a distinguishing characteristic of the Son, might, with still greater propriety be ascribed to the apostles, whose ministry was more extensive and successful than that of their Master.

Others, admitting that the words do refer to proper creation, endeavour to exclude the force of the argument for the divinity of Christ in one or other of the two following ways. Some translate the phrase—" on whose account God made the world." But this would require either a change in the text, for which there is no authority, or a gross violation of one of the laws of the original language.²

Others maintain that God made the world by the Son, as an *instrument*, or as a created inferior agent. It is difficult to attach meaning to these words. Surely He who makes all things, " without whom nothing was made that was made," was not Himself a creature. Omnipotence and infinite intelligence—both of which are necessary in the Creator—cannot surely be delegated. There is, no doubt, an order in the operations of the divine Father and Son in nature as well as in grace. All things are of or from the Father, and by or through Christ Jesus; but this does not imply superiority in the one to the other. In Hos. i. 7, Jehovah promises to save His people by Jehovah; and in Gen. xix. 24, Jehovah is said to rain fire and brimstone out of heaven on Sodom and Gomorrha from Jehovah. No person who understands the meaning of the word Jehovah, will draw the inference, that the last Jehovah is inferior to the first.

When God is said to have created the world by his Son, we are taught that there is a distinction between the Father and the Son; and we are also taught that the Godhead, in the person of the Son, was in an especial manner concerned in the creation

¹ Heb. vi. 5.

² Δἰ ὅν instead of δἰ οὗ, would be requisite. The author of this Epistle never confounds the two phrases. They are obviously distinguished, ch. ii. 10, δἰ ὅν καὶ δἰ οὗ. The one expresses αἰτίαν, the end—the other ὄργανον, the means. The distinction is marked in Rev. iv. 11; Κύριε, ἔκτισας τὰ πάντα—i.e., πάντα ἐκτίσθησαν διὰ σοῦ, or διὰ τῆς δυνάμεώς σου, καὶ διὰ τὸ θέλημά σου εἰσὶ καὶ ἐκτίσθησαν. GRIESBACH (Opusc. Acad.) conjectures that δἰ οὗ is written by mistake for διότι; but it is mere conjecture.

of the universe. And what is there either impossible or improbable in this? And how does it in the slightest degree infringe on the argument for the divinity of the Son, from His being the Creator of the world?[1]

The dignity of the Author of the Gospel revelation is still further exhibited in the words which follow:—Ver. 3. "Who, being the brightness of His glory, and the express image of His person, and upholding all things by the word of His power, when He had by Himself purged our sins, sat down on the right hand of the Majesty on high."

When Jesus Christ is termed "the brightness of God's glory," the idea intended to be conveyed seems to be this, the true and proper representation of the infinite perfection of the Deity. "He is that to the Divine Father, which the solar light, falling on our world, is to the same light at the source of its emanation."[2] The glory of God is the supreme beauty of His perfections, His holy, wise, and benignant excellency—that moral goodness, without which omnipotence, eternity, and immensity, would be awful, but not lovely. This perfect glory, this complete divine majesty, resides in Christ, and shines forth from Him, so that He is the communicator of its knowledge and enjoyment to mankind.[3]

It is, to say the least, highly probable that in using this phraseology in speaking to Jews, the Apostle refers to that visible glory which was an emblem of the presence of God with His ancient people. This visible glory was seen by Moses in the bush,—it resided in the miraculous cloud which conducted Israel out of Egypt,—it appeared on Mount Sinai, at the giving of the law,—took possession of the tabernacle, where it sometimes appeared to all the people, but more ordinarily in the Holy of Holies within the vail, hovered over the mercy-seat between the cherubim. From the midst of this glory God spake to Moses; and towards this holy beauty all religious worship was directed

---

[1] Philo has a passage very similar to this. Λόγος ἐστὶν εἰκὼν Θεοῦ δι' οὗ σύμπας ὁ κόσμος ἐδημιουργεῖτο. De Monarch., Λόγ. β'.

[2] Pye Smith.

[3] The most satisfactory exegesis of the phrase, $d.\ \tau.\ \delta.$, seems to be that which considers the genitive τῆς δόξης as = the descriptive adj. ἔνδοξον—the glorious effulgence,—just as the God of mercy = the merciful God.

to Jehovah dwelling in it. This visible glory resided also in the first temple; and it is likely to it the Apostle refers in his enunciation of the peculiar privileges of Israel, when he says, "To them belonged the glory." Jesus Christ is the substance of which this natural glory was the shadow. In His person as God-man, in His saving work, and in the revelation He makes of both in His word, the excellences of the Divine character are more illustriously displayed than in any or in all the works of nature, or dispensations of providence. These are dim, indistinct intimations of His excellences; some of one, some of another; the incarnate Son is the bright manifestation of the whole of these excellences, the perfect harmony of which constitutes His glory.[1]

"The express image of His person."—The term *person* is not here used in the sense which it bears in systematic theology, as expressive of the distinctions which exist in the one Divinity—a sense which the words did not assume till about the beginning of the fourth century. The phrase seems more analogous to another theological term, the Person of Christ,—which means just Christ Himself. The person, or substance, or mode of subsistence of God, is just equivalent to God Himself;[2] and when Christ is called the express image of God's person, the idea is, the exact resemblance of His Father, as the figure engraved is a resemblance of the object it represents. It is the same truth which the Apostle states, when, in the Epistle to the Colossians, he terms Jesus Christ the image of the Invisible God. He is the manifestation of God—the manifested life or living one—God manifest in flesh.

As in the former case the Apostle seems to allude to the Shekinah, or visible glory, in which there was no similitude, but merely a supernatural radiance, so here he very probably alludes to that glorious vision of the likeness of a man in the

---

[1] Δόξα τοῦ Θεοῦ ἐστιν ἐν προσώπῳ Ἰησοῦ Χριστοῦ. 2 Cor. iv. 6. The second clause is exegetical. BASIL, in one of his homilies (Opp. ii. p. 102), very happily says, "What is the brightness, and what is the glory? The apostle himself explained this, by continuing: 'and the express image of his person.' 'Person' is the same as 'glory', 'express image' as 'brightness'," etc.

[2] This phrase is perhaps best interpreted on the principle just applied to that which precedes it. It seems = χαρακτὴρ ὑποστατικὸς, not a shadow or sketch, but a real complete representation,—to use the Apostle's own distinction,—not σκιά, but αὐτὴ ἡ εἰκών. Heb. viii. 5, x. 1.

midst of that glory, which Moses and the elders of Israel saw on Sinai, and which Isaiah and Ezekiel describe as having been seen by them in a prophetic ecstasy.[1] Of this glorious appearance, as of the former, the Incarnate Only-begotten is the substance. Among the many causes of the extreme attachment of the Jews to the Mosaic economy, this was no doubt one, that such splendid displays of the Divine majesty had been made in connection with it; but the Apostle points them to *the glory that excelleth*, and intimates to them, that humble as was the external appearance of Jesus of Nazareth, He was the true Shekinah, in whom dwelt the Godhead bodily—the real, substantial, adequate representation of the King eternal, immortal, and invisible, whom no eye hath seen, or can see. It is the same sentiment as that expressed by the Evangelist John, when he says, " The Word who was with God, and was God, became flesh, and dwelt among us; and we beheld His glory, the glory as of the only-begotten of the Father, full of grace and of truth."—" No man hath seen God at any time; the only-begotten who is in the bosom of the Father, He hath declared Him."—" For the Life," or the Living One, " was manifested, and we have seen Him, and bear witness, and show unto you that eternal life, as being one who was with the Father, and was manifested to us;" and by our Lord Himself when He says, " I and My Father are one,"—" Hitherto My Father worketh and I work,"—" Whatsoever things the Father doth, the same doth the Son also,"—" I am in the Father, and the Father in Me,"—" The Father, that dwelleth in Me, doth the works,"—" He that hath seen Me, hath seen the Father."

The Apostle proceeds in his description of the grandeur and majesty of Him by whom God now speaks to us, and declares that He " upholds all things by the word of His power." The term *uphold* seems to refer both to preservation and government.[2] " By

---

[1] Ex. xxiv. 10; Is. vi. 1-5; Ezek. i. 26-28.

[2] CHRYSOSTOM explains it as = governing, controlling the course of events. THEOD. says, for not only has he made all things, but he also guides and steers them. VALCKNAER'S note is good—Scholia, vol. ii. p. 272, "φέρω means bear, carry: what we carry, we support, sustain, or uphold. What I uphold, I rule, keep steady, guide, govern." The Latins use *vehere* in the same sense. SENECA, in his 31st Epist., says, "God is the greatest and most mighty One, and he carries along (*vehit*) all things."

Him the worlds were made"—their materials were called into being, and arranged in comely order, and by Him, too, they are prevented from running into confusion, or reverting into nothing. The whole universe hangs on His arm; His unsearchable wisdom and boundless power are manifested in governing and directing the complicated movements of animate and inanimate, rational and irrational beings, to the attainment of His own great and holy purposes; and He does this by the word of His power, or by His powerful word. All this is done without effort or difficulty. He speaks, and it is done; He commands, and it stands fast.[1]

The enemies of the doctrine of our Lord's divinity, would interpret the clause, as if the word of power were not the Son's word, but the Father's,—and as if the Apostle's statement were, that the Son sustains the world by the power of the Father. The power by which the world is sustained is the power of Divinity, which equally belongs to the Father and the Son; but it is quite plain to an unprejudiced reader, that the Apostle's object throughout the whole of this passage, is to excite in the minds of his readers exalted ideas of the dignity, and authority, and power of Christ; and that, had it not been thought necessary to serve a particular purpose, such a mode of interpretation would never have been thought of.[2]

This glorious person is introduced to our notice in the next clause, in very different, but to us sinful men, in a still more interesting aspect:—" When He had by Himself purged our sins, He sat down on the right hand of the Majesty on high."— The Apostle here discovers exquisite wisdom in the manner in which he introduces the great leading truth of Christianity, the death of Christ on a cross. This was the great stumbling-block. The Apostle could not conceal this without mutilating, without destroying, the system; but when he brings it forward he does so in connection with the great, benevolent, absolutely necessary purpose which it was intended to serve, and the glorious conse-

---

[1] ‛Ρῆμα = command, order. As men express their will by their command, so the Heb. expresses the exercise of the Divine will, which is all-powerful, by the phrase, דְּבַר יְהֹוָה. Ps. xxxiii. 6, cxlviii. 5; Gen. i. 3, 9; Heb. xi. 3; Apoc. iv. 11.

[2] BÖHME very justly remarks, that αὐτοῦ naturally refers not only to τῆς δυνάμεως, but to the whole phrase, ῥήματ, τ. δ.

quences with which it had been followed. He purged *our* sins,[1] or made a cleansing of our sins. The term cleansing is sometimes used to signify moral renovation, the destruction of sinful dispositions and habits; but here, and indeed throughout this Epistle, the word, and its cognate expressions, plainly refer to expiation.[2] To purge our sins, or to expiate our sins,—to make atonement for them,—is just to do what, in the estimation of infinite wisdom and righteousness, is necessary in order to our being delivered from the natural consequences of our sins, in a way consistent with the honour of the Divine perfections, and the stability and prosperity of the Divine moral administration,—to do what may make it just in God to justify the ungodly, and lay a foundation for fitting man for intercourse with God.

This the Son of God effected *by Himself*.[3] This phrase is explained in the subsequent part of the Epistle by such expressions as these:—" By His own blood,"[4]—" by means of death,"[5]—" by the sacrifice of Himself."[6] By taking the place of those whom He came to save—by doing what they were bound to do—by suffering what they deserved to suffer, He manifested the evil of sin, and the holiness and righteousness of the Divine law, and the Divine Lawgiver, in a far more striking manner than the everlasting punishment of a guilty world could have done, and thus laid a foundation for the honourable exercise of mercy towards the guilty and condemned children of men. This doctrine, understood and believed, wipes away for ever the offence of the cross, and makes the enlightened mind regard the scene of the Saviour's deepest humiliation as the scene, too, of the brightest display of His glory. The omnipotence—the infinite wisdom—the immaculate holiness—the inflexible righteousness—the inconceivable kindness of the Divinity, never shone forth with greater radiance in Him, who is " the brightness of the Divine

---

[1] Ἡμῶν is wanting in some of the best Codd. Mill, Bengel, Griesbach, and Morus, consider it as no part of the orig. text.

[2] Καθαρισμός properly describes physical cleansing; and as sin is considered as polluting the soul, making it an object of dislike to God, the removal of sin, both in its condemning and depraving influences, is represented by cleansing. Καθαρισμὸν ποιεῖσθαι seems just = ἱλάσκεσθαι τὰς ἁμαρτίας, ch. ii. 17.

[3] The genuineness of δι' αὐτοῦ is doubtful.

[4] Heb. ix. 12.    [5] Heb. ix. 14.    [6] Heb. ix. 26.

glory, the express image of God," than when He thus by Himself made expiation for the sins of His people. There is probably here a tacit contrast of Jesus Christ, Himself both priest and sacrifice, and the Aaronical high priests. They had for ages been attempting to purge sin, but in vain: He had at once, and completely, gained that great object. They endeavoured to gain this end by the blood of slain beasts; He fully gained it by the sacrifice of Himself. The efficacy of our Lord's sacrifice is to be traced to the dignity of His person. It was because He gave Himself, the *Son*, the *brightness of God's glory, the express image of His person*, that He succeeded in purging our sins. We have redemption through His blood, even the forgiveness of sin; for He is the image of the invisible God, the Lord of the whole creation.

Here we have in their germ the leading arguments for the superiority of Christianity to Judaism, from the greater excellence of the priesthood of its Author than that of the family of Aaron, which, with so much force and beauty, he brings out in the following part of the Epistle:—First, that He offered Himself; Secondly, that He was the Priest, and made expiation, not for a nation, but for the race; Thirdly, the completeness of His sacrifice, so that on its being offered He immediately leaves earth and goes to heaven; and Fourthly, His never-ending dignity and power, following and obtained by His expiatory sacrifice, "Having made expiation for sin by the sacrifice of Himself, He sat down on the right hand of the Majesty on high."[1]

The *Majesty* is a strong expression for the Supreme Being, who is here represented as seated on a glorious throne in the high places, *i.e.*, in the heaven of heavens; and Jesus, having finished the expiation of human guilt, is represented as sitting down on this throne, at the right hand of His Divine Father. It is very difficult to say how far these words are literal and how far they are figurative. I am not prepared either to assert or to deny, that in that local heaven, where the glorified humanity of Jesus Christ resides, there is a visible display of the Divine Majesty—analogous, but infinitely superior, to that which dwelt in the tabernacle and temple,—in the midst of which, or on the

---

[1] The complete phrase is ἐκάθισεν ἑαυτόν· μεγαλωσύνης ἐν ὑψηλοῖς = τῆς μεγαλωσύνης τῆς ὑψηλοτάτης.

right hand of which, the God-man who died on the cross, appears to angels and the spirits of just men made perfect, as the possessor and administrator of universal government; though, I confess, there is much that leads me to think this probable, and to apprehend that there may be less of pure figure in the descriptions of the upper world than we sometimes suppose. But whatever there may be in this, there is no doubt that the words intimate that, as the reward of His expiatory sufferings, Jesus Christ is elevated to the highest conceivable station of dignity and authority. His place is not a seat on the right hand of the throne merely, but a seat on the throne at the right hand of Him that sitteth on it. 'Jesus having overcome sat down with His Father on His throne.'[1] The throne of Jehovah is the throne of Jesus. It is the same throne, the throne of God and the Lamb. Is it not evident, then, that Jesus, in His official dignity, is infinitely superior to the angels? 'By the working of God's mighty power He hath raised Him from the dead, and set Him at His own right hand in the heavenly places, far above all principality, and power, and might, and dominion, and every name that is named, not only in this world, but also in that which is to come; and hath put all things under His feet.' 'God hath highly exalted Him, and given Him a name which is above every name: that at the name of Jesus every knee should bow, of things in heaven, and things on earth, and things under the earth; and that every tongue should confess that He is Lord, to the glory of God the Father.'[2] He is 'gone into heaven, and is on the right hand of God; angels, and authorities, and powers, being made subject to Him.'

This glory was conferred on the incarnate Son in consequence of His having purged our sins by Himself. It was on account of that suffering of death, in which He tasted death in the room of every one of His people, that "He was clothed with glory and honour." It was because He humbled Himself, that God thus highly exalted Him. It is not improbable that there is here, too, an allusion, by way of contrast, to the Jewish high priest. When he performed the most sacred part of his ministry on the great day of atonement, by entering alone into the Holy of Holies, and sprinkling the blood of the expiatory sacrifice on the mercy-seat, he stood in the attitude of a servant;

[1] Rev. iii. 21.      [2] Eph. i. 20, 22; Philip. ii. 9-11.

and when he had finished it, instead of sitting down on the mercy-seat between the cherubim, he was not allowed to sit down at all in the presence of the symbol of the Divine Majesty, but immediately retired. But the great High Priest of our profession, when He appeared in the presence of God,—having finished the work given Him to do,—presenting, as it were, the blood of His sacrifice,—instead of retiring, sat down as an abiding priest, there—and He sat down not only in the divine Presence, but on the divine throne—on the divine right hand, —to sway the sceptre of the universe, and to be head over all things, to His body, the Church.

# CHAPTER I.

### THE SUPERIORITY, ESSENTIAL AND OFFICIAL, OF JESUS CHRIST TO THE ANGELS.

#### § 1.—*Scriptural Proof of this.*

4. Being made so much better than the angels, as He hath by inheritance obtained a more excellent name than they. 5. For unto which of the angels said He at any time, Thou art My Son, this day have I begotten thee? And again, I will be to Him a Father, and He shall be to Me a Son? 6. And again, when He bringeth in the first-begotten into the world, He saith, And let all the angels of God worship Him. 7. And of the angels He saith, Who maketh His angels spirits, and His ministers a flame of fire. 8. But unto the Son He saith, Thy throne, O God, is for ever and ever; a sceptre of righteousness is the sceptre of Thy kingdom. 9. Thou hast loved righteousness, and hated iniquity; therefore God, even Thy God, hath anointed Thee with the oil of gladness above thy fellows. 10. And, Thou, Lord, in the beginning hast laid the foundation of the earth; and the heavens are the works of Thine hands: 11. They shall perish, but Thou remainest; and they all shall wax old as doth a garment; 12. And as a vesture shalt Thou fold them up, and they shall be changed: but Thou art the same, and Thy years shall not fail. 13. But to which of the angels said He at any time, Sit on my right hand, until I make Thine enemies Thy footstool? 14. Are they not all ministering spirits, sent forth to minister for them who shall be heirs of salvation?

THE Apostle proceeds to show the pre-eminent dignity of the Author of the Gospel revelation, by citations from the Old Testament Scriptures. The first thing to be done for their satisfactory interpretation, is to endeavour distinctly to apprehend what is the principle to establish which the Apostle brings forward these quotations; and this must be done by inquiring into the meaning of the fourth verse of the chapter: "Being made so much better than the angels, as He hath by inheritance obtained a more excellent name than they." We have here the first of many instances in the Epistle, of that characteristic of Paul's writings,—the announcement of a new theme, in the last clause of the immediately preceding sentence.

There is plainly a comparison or a contrast stated between the Author of Christianity and a certain class of beings denominated angels. The word, which signifies messengers, is most usually employed in Scripture to denote an order of unembodied spiritual beings, superior in intellectual and active faculty to mankind, who are employed by God as His messengers in the administration of the government of the universe. To them—in the estimation of the great body of interpreters, ancient and modern—there is a reference in the passage before us. It has appeared, however, to some, that the angels, or messengers, here alluded to, are not these unembodied spirits at all, but the prophets, or inspired men, mentioned in the first verse. There can be no doubt that the appellative denomination 'messengers,' may, with perfect propriety, be given to the Old Testament prophets;[1] and that to understand it in this way, would give a beautiful unity to the Introductory Statement. And if there had been no more said about angels, I should have been disposed to consider this as the right way of explaining the passage. But a lengthened discussion follows, which obviously is just the following up the assertion contained in these words,—and whatever be the meaning of the word angels in that discussion, must be its meaning in the passage before us. Now, there can scarcely be any reasonable doubt, that in the quotations both from the 97th and from the 104th Psalm, the re ference is to the angels, properly so called,—that 'ministering spirits sent forth to minister,' is a much more appropriate descrip-

---

[1] The word ἄγγελος is thus employed, Matt. xi. 10; Luke ix. 52; and πνεῦμα seems used in a similar way, 1 Cor. xii. 10; 1 John iv. 1. But while this is true, it is not less true, as ABRESCH remarks : " there is no place in the whole New Testament where the word 'angels', standing without qualification, signifies anything but heavenly intelligences."

tion of them than of the prophets,—and that the description of man, or the Messiah, 'being made a little lower than the angels,' will not at all apply to the prophets; and the declaration that He, *i.e.*, Christ Jesus, took not on Him the nature,—or rather, laid not hold, in order to deliver, on the angels, but on the seed of Abraham, is equally conclusive as to the reference being to the order of beings ordinarily called angels. We therefore proceed on this principle in the interpretation of the passage, that the comparison or contrast is between Jesus Christ and the angels, properly so called.

The introduction of this topic, in an illustration of the superiority of Christianity to Judaism, will not appear strange to any who reflect that angels were employed in some way or other in the giving of the law;[1] and that this was one of the circumstances in which Christianity must have appeared to a Jew to have a disadvantage in comparison with the system which it professed to supersede; and the manner in which it is introduced in the close of the sentence, will not appear unnatural to any one acquainted with the writings of the Apostle Paul, who very frequently introduces, in a sort of appended clause at the close of a sentence, the subject to the illustration of which the subsequent paragraph is devoted. Of the manner in which the angels were employed in the giving of the law, we have no particular account. But the fact seems plainly enough stated both in the Old Testament and the New. There is nothing said about them in the historical account of the giving of the law in the 19th chapter of Exodus; but in the 33d chapter of Deuteronomy, verse 2, we are told that 'Jehovah came from Sinai with ten thousand of His holy ones;' and in Psalm lxviii. 17, the chariots of God are said to be 'twenty thousand, even thousands of angels. The Lord is among them, as in Sinai, in the holy place.' Stephen, a man full of the Holy Ghost, declares that the Jews received the law 'by the disposition of angels;'[2] and Paul, in his Epistle to the Galatians, iii. 19, states, that the law was 'ordained by angels, in the hand of a mediator.' These angels are described as "excelling in strength," and as far raised in the scale of being above man; and, therefore, their employment in the giving of the law stamps a dignity and importance on that economy.

[1] Deut. xxxiii. 2; Psa. lxviii. 17; Gal. iii. 19; Heb. ii. 2; Acts vii. 53.
[2] Acts vii. 53.

The Christian revelation had not been introduced with the same public display of angelic ministration,—but it was not on this account to be considered as inferior to the Mosaic; for its Author, in sitting down as the appointed heir of all things on the right hand of the Majesty in the heavens, had been " made so much better than the angels, as He hath by inheritance obtained a more excellent name than they."

These words have been considered by many as just equivalent to a declaration, that the Author of the Christian revelation is superior to the angels, and that this is proved by His receiving a more honourable name than any conferred on them. We cannot help thinking they contain in them much more than this. They intimate that He is, by being set "on the right hand of the Majesty on high," raised to higher honours than any ever bestowed on angels. They intimate also,—whatever these words may mean, and we shall inquire into their meaning immediately,—that He has obtained by inheritance a more excellent name than the angels; and they intimate that there is something like a proportion between the greater height of dignity to which He is raised, and the greater excellence of the name that He has inherited. The last part of the verse is not a proof of the first. The first part of the verse asserts His official superiority to the angels; the second, His essential superiority to them; and the whole verse asserts that there is a proportion between these. For the distinctly bringing out of the Apostle's idea, it will be necessary to begin with the concluding clause of the verse. The author of the Christian revelation 'has received by inheritance a more excellent name than the angels.'[1] The word *name* is not unfrequently in Scripture used to signify high rank or reputation. Thus, the descendants of the unhappy intermar-

---

[1] Παρ' αὐτούς. A classic writer would have said διαφορώτερον αὐτῶν. It is a peculiarity of the Epistle to the Hebrews to use παρά in comparison with the accusative, ch. iii. 3, ix. 23, xi. 4, xii. 24. 'It is remarkable,' says VALCKNAER, 'that this mode of construction is not to be found in any of the Epistles of Paul which bear His name;' but this seems rashly said, for we seem to have an instance of it, Rom. i. 25, where μᾶλλον seems to be supplied; though Valcknaer might have questioned this, and interpreted παρά in a way not implying comparison. Besides, there is no word in the comparative degree in Rom. i. 25, which, in Paul's writings, is always followed by the genitive. Κληρονομεῖν is here=ἐπιτυγχάνειν, potiri, to possess, ch. vi. 12,—κληρονομῶ=ἐπιτυγχάνω, verse 15.

riages between the descendants of Cain and Seth—between the sons of God and the daughters of men,—are said to have been men of *name;* or, as our translators render it, very properly, "renown."[1] The conspirators against Moses, in the matter of Korah, are said to have been "men of *name*, princes of the assembly, famous in the congregation."[2] "I have made thee a *name*," says Jehovah to David, "like the name of the great men who are on the earth."[3] The Father is said to have given Christ "a *name* above every name."[4] It is not, however, in this way that the word is to be explained here. It is of Christ's *name*, in the sense of rank and dignity, that the Apostle speaks in the first clause,—His being "made much better than the angels;" and he illustrates this by comparing it, not surely with itself, but with something else. To understand it in this way here, would make the Apostle's assertion altogether nugatory, viz., who is as much superior to the angels, as the dignity to which He has attained is elevated above theirs. The term *name* here refers to some peculiar designation. The name of angels is not their dignity, but their designation *spirits;* and the name of Christ here, is not His official dignity, but His proper designation, *the Son of God.* Fully to understand the force of the expression, however, it is necessary to remark that, in the Hebrew language, by a reference to which much of the phraseology of the New Testament is to be explained, names are usually significant; and that, under the Old Testament, names were often given by God to describe the leading circumstances in the character or fortunes of individuals; and, hence, for a person to have a particular name given him, is often equal to his being what that name expresses. Thus, God declares His own *name* to Moses;[5] that is, He declares His character. When Isaiah says of the Messiah, "His name shall be called Wonderful, Counsellor, The mighty God, The everlasting Father, The Prince of Peace," he plainly means "He shall be Wonderful, Counsellor, The mighty God, The everlasting Father, The Prince of Peace." The meaning, then, of the Apostle in the passage before us, according to this principle of interpretation, is—the descriptive designation given to Christ Jesus, when contrasted with that given to angels,

---

[1] Gen. vi. 4.  
[2] Numb. xvi. 2.  
[3] 1 Chron. xvii. 8.  
[4] Philip. ii. 9; Eph. i. 21.  
[5] Exod. xxxiv. 5.

marks Him as belonging to a higher order of being. Their name is created spirits. His name is the only begotten Son of God.

This *name* he is said to have obtained by inheritance. I do not know if this phrase signifies any more than that He is possessed of such a name. The word often is used in this general sense. If there be any peculiarity of meaning, it intimates that the dignity expressed by the name, originates in His essential relation to the divine Father.

But the Author of the Christian revelation is not only essentially superior to the angels as possessing a name which, in the way in which it is given Him, necessarily implies divine perfection; He is also officially superior to the angels. In being set down as the proprietor and governor of all things " on the right hand of the Majesty on high," in consequence of His having purged our sins by Himself, He has "been made much better than the angels."[1] To be "made better than the angels," is to be raised to a higher state of dignity than the angels. When the only begotten of God "became flesh and dwelt among men," He was for a little while made lower than the angels; but when, having finished the work which the Father had given Him to do, "He sat down on the right hand of the Majesty on high," He was raised to a dignity far superior to that of the highest angel. However exalted is their station, they are all servants. He reigns along with God, having " all power in heaven and earth." His place is on the throne,—their place is before it.

And this superiority of official dignity is so great, that the superiority of essential dignity is employed as a kind of measure of it. He is made as " much better than the angels," as He possesses "a more excellent name than they." The distance between them and Him is immeasurable. He is not only exalted above them as far as heaven is above the earth, but as the name, 'the Son of God,' and that eternal independent divinity of nature which it expresses, is inconceivably above the name, 'creature of God,'

[1] Γενόμενος is here=factus. Some consider it as=ὤν, but the first interpretation is preferable; indeed it is contrasted with ὤν in ver. 3. Compare the fuller statements of the manner in which Jesus Christ obtained official superiority to the angels, Phil. ii. 9; Eph. i. 20. Παρά, in comparison, is=the Latin preposition *præ*. It is of the same force as ἢ quam, the Hebrew מ, and our *than*, Heb. ii. 7; Gen. xxxvii. 3, LXX; Heb. iii. 3.

and that limited dependent nature which it expresses; so the dignity of the Son, as Sovereign Lord of the universe, is inconceivably superior to any dignity which can attach itself to those who hold subordinate places in the system of divine government.

The Apostle proceeds now to prove from the Old Testament Scriptures, that the Messiah was to be a person both essentially and officially superior to the angels. He does not formally first prove the one and then the other; but everything that is said will be found to bear either on the one or other of these points. It is plain, that as he was reasoning not with unbelieving Jews, but with Jews acknowledging the Messiahship of Jesus, though in danger of apostatising, he, in this argument, takes for granted the Messiahship of Jesus, and that whatever is said of the Messiah in the Old Testament Scriptures, is true of Him.[1]

The first two quotations he makes, go to prove the essential superiority of Jesus Christ to the angels; or, that "He has received by inheritance a more excellent name than they."

The first proof which he brings forward, is a quotation from the second Psalm.—Ver. 5. "For to which of the angels said He at any time, Thou art My Son, this day have I begotten Thee?" The manner in which he brings forward his proof deserves notice. He puts it in the form of a question which admitted of but one answer: 'To none of them.' We have a similar use of the interrogative form, 1 Cor. ix. 7.

---

[1] By many of the German exegetical writers, the whole of this argument is considered as merely *ad hominem*. One of the more moderate of these rationalistic interpreters thus expresses himself :—" The excellence of the dignity of Jesus the Messiah is confirmed by several passages culled from the Old Testament, of which, however, many, indeed most, have nothing to do with the Messiah at all. But the Jewish doctors in the time of Christ, following the allegorical method of interpreting the sacred writings, used to take any glorious and great thing that was said of pious men and Israelite kings in the Old Testament books, as referring to the Messiah, and to explain it accordingly. Wisely, the New Testament writers held on to this method of interpretation, in order to secure a passage, so to speak, for the principles of the Christian religion into Jewish minds." If the writers of the New Testament did this, unconscious of thus misinterpreting the Old Testament writings, assuredly they might be honest men, but they could not be inspired men. If they did it consciously, what were they? The observations of ABRESCH on this subject are quite in point :—" If in passages of this sort, where the point made by an approved author is clearly and carefully stated and explained, there could be room for such a thing as accommodation, and

The second Psalm is certainly one of those Psalms which are written of Christ. The Messianic reference is very ably defended by Rosenmüller. Some interpreters consider it as having a primary reference to David or to Solomon; but there is no foundation for this opinion. There is much in the Psalm altogether inapplicable to either of these monarchs; and in the New Testament it is clearly stated to be a prophecy of the Messiah. The passage here quoted has, by many expositors, been considered as referring to Christ's being constituted Son of God. Those who hold the doctrine of the divine, and of course eternal, Sonship, consider the meaning of the words to be,— "Thou art My Son"—'From eternity Thou hast stood in that relation to Me.' Those who think that the only kind of Sonship which belongs to Jesus Christ is that which originates in His miraculous conception, refer it to His incarnation. Those who hold that Christ Jesus was constituted the Son of God when He was raised to the throne of the world as Mediator, consider it as meaning,—' By Thy resurrection and exaltation I have constituted Thee My Son, higher than the kings of the earth.'

We are not disposed to go entirely into any of these modes of interpretation. The two clauses, "Thou art My Son,"—"I have begotten Thee," seem to us, according to that parallelism which forms one of the most remarkable characteristics of Hebrew poetry, to be expressions of the same sentiment.[1] If

for imposing upon the passages quoted a different sense from that which they bear in their own contexts—then this finally disposes, I will not say of the apostles' inspiration (θεοπνευστία), but of their good faith ; and the verdict to be passed on them is that, instead of properly establishing what they allege, and claim to have ascertained, from these passages in support of their case, they have pulled the wool over their readers' eyes. I know what our latter-day reformers, who follow Richard Simon and John le Clerc, usually say of the method of argument employed by Christ and the apostles, and by Paul in particular—that it was *ad hominem* (κατ' ἄνθρωπον). But I should very much like to be told what force and authority, in that case, all their arguments have for us Christians. Or was the doctrine of the gospel meant for Jews alone, so that it was sufficient to display its truth and certainty just by means of arguments that would appeal to Jews? The man who could believe this would believe anything !"—*Paraph. Ep. ad Heb.* p. 198. The whole subject of accommodation is treated in a very masterly and satisfactory manner in ALEXANDER'S work on the Connection and Harmony of the Old and New Testaments, p. 188–202.

[1] Vide Jer. ii. 27.

there be any difference in the meaning of the two clauses, the second defines the first, and intimates that the relation is, strictly speaking, a natural relation.[1]

The principal difficulty lies in the word *to-day*. Those interpreters—though some of them of great name, such as Athanasius and Augustine, and lately Munburgh and Weber—are certainly in a mistake, who say that this phrase, by itself, is ever in Scripture used to signify eternity; though we have no hesitation in saying, that that which lies at the foundation of the divine Sonship of Christ, is not to be viewed as a *past act*, but as an *essential property* of the Divinity; so that at any period—if I may use the expression—in the past eternity, or in time, or in the coming eternity, the language in the text might, with propriety be used. But to make the Apostle his own interpreter, he says, in reference to this very phrase in another case, that when God uses it, " He limiteth a certain day."[2] And what that time is, we find little difficulty in ascertaining; for the Apostle, in his discourses to the Jews in the synagogue of Antioch, thus applies the oracle to the incarnation of Christ.[3] But as, I apprehend, few truths are more plainly stated in the New Testament than that our Saviour was the Son of God, in the highest sense in which this analogical expression is employed in reference to Him, before His incarnation, from the unbeginning ages of eternity, the words must be understood, not of the constitution, but of the declaration of His Sonship. The words are equivalent to, 'I proclaim Thee My Son—My begotten Son.' The Apostle has as it were paraphrased them, when, recording their fulfilment, he says that Jesus Christ was powerfully proved[4] and declared to be the Son of God according to the Spirit of holiness—in divine nature—in opposition to what He was according to the

---

[1] It was with great satisfaction that I found the learned and acute Hengstenberg taking this view of the clause. "Thou art My Father," says he, "and Thou hast begotten Me, are used as synonymous; but this can be the case only when the literal sense of the word *Son* is retained, and not when it is used in a mere moral sense. The parallelism then requires that the words, 'Thou art My Son,' should be taken literally."—*Introd. to Messianic Psalms.*

[2] Heb. iv. 7.

[3] Acts xiii. 32-34. The ἀναστήσας in the 33d verse seems plainly used in contrast to the ἀνέστησεν ἐκ νεκρῶν of the 34th; the first referring to the incarnation, the second to the resurrection.

[4] ὁρισθείς, Rom. i. 4.

flesh, the Son of David. It was for declaring that He was the Son of God—so the Son of God as to be equal with God—that the Jews put Him to death; and God, by raising Him from the dead, crowned Him as His Son, and made it demonstrably manifest that His claims were well founded. This is in accordance with a principle which, though not peculiar to the Hebrew language, is often exemplified in it—that things are often represented as done when they are declared to be done; *e.g.*, Isa. vi. 10; Jer. i. 10.

The Apostle's argument, in which you will at once see the prophetic oracle and its fulfilment, is thus a most conclusive one. The Messiah, who is Jesus, possesses a more excellent name than the angels, for God had solemnly declared Him and proved Him to be His begotten Son—His Son according to the Spirit of holiness—a name never conferred on any of the angels.

The second quotation brought from the Old Testament in support of the declaration, that the Messiah possessed " a more excellent name" than the angels, is taken from 2 Sam. vii. 14, or 1 Chron. xvii. 13. The only principle, as it appears to me, on which the conclusiveness of the Apostle's reasoning from this passage can be distinctly made out, is that the prediction from which it is quoted is a direct prophecy of the Messiah. Very similar language is used in reference to Solomon, 1 Chron. xxii. 10, xxviii. 6. But there is much, very much, in the prediction here quoted which will not apply to Solomon.[1] The words, considered as a prediction of the Messiah, may either signify, that He should be the Son of God in a sense peculiar to Himself; or that God would make it evident that He was the Messiah's Father—that it should be clearly manifested that the Messiah was his Son. Both passages prove that He possesses a name never given to any of the angels, and far more excellent than any name that belongs to them.

The truth is, that the more closely the divine oracle here quoted, which was revealed, not to David, but to Nathan, is scrutinized, the clearer will the evidence appear that it has a

---

[1] ἐγὼ ἔσομαι αὐτῷ εἰς πατέρα, καὶ αὐτὸς ἔσται μοι εἰς υἱόν. The construction is Hebrew. The Greek idiom would require ἐ. ἔ. π. α—κ. α. ἔ. μ. υ. It is more than merely, 'I and He shall stand in the relation of Father and Son,' it is, 'I will treat Him as My Son—He shall conduct Himself to Me as His Father,' implying, however, the relation.

direct reference to the Messiah. It is quite a different prophecy from that referred to by David as made to himself. It refers to a son to be *raised up* after David had gone to be with his fathers, whereas Solomon was not only born but crowned before David's death; and the person to be raised up, whosoever he is, was to be settled 'in God's house and kingdom,' and His throne was to be 'established for evermore,'—words certainly not applicable, in their full extent, to Solomon, and very different from the words employed in the prophecy that unquestionably refers to him. It is, moreover, an unconditional prophecy, which is not the case with that made in reference to Solomon. Indeed, had it not been for what we conceive a mistranslation of the words which immediately follow, I apprehend they never would have been explained in any way but that which the Apostle's argument requires. "If he commit iniquity," certainly cannot refer to the Messiah; but the words may be fairly rendered, 'Whosoever shall commit iniquity,'—and its true meaning is best illustrated from what is plainly a commentary on it, Ps. lxxxix. 30–33 : "If his children forsake My law, and walk not in My judgments; if they break My statutes, and keep not My commandments; then will I visit their transgression with the rod, and their iniquity with stripes. Nevertheless My loving-kindness will I not utterly take from him, nor suffer My faithfulness to fail."

The third quotation, to the consideration of which we are now about to proceed, seems to refer primarily to His official superiority, though this, when rightly understood, necessarily supposes His essential superiority. The substance of the argument is this:—The Messiah, as the supreme Administrator of the government of the universe, is the appointed object of religious homage for the angels; and, therefore, He has, on being invested with this office, been made much better than they. Let us examine a little more attentively the quotation, and the use which the Apostle makes of it. Ver. 6.—" And again, when He bringeth in the first-begotten into the world, He saith, And let all the angels of God worship Him."

The quotation here made is from Ps. xcvii. 7, which, in the Greek version of the Old Testament then used, is thus rendered: "Worship Him, all ye His angels." The words here quoted are to be found in our copies of the LXX., in Deut.

xxxii. 43, in a clause inserted between the first and second clauses. As, however, these words are not in the Hebrew text, nor in any of the other ancient versions, except the Italic, there is no evidence that they were written by Moses, and they are, in all probability, an interpolation by some Christians at an early age, more zealous than either wise or honest. The only difference between the passage as quoted here, and as it stands in the Hebrew text, is, that it is put in the indirect instead of the direct form, and the word *gods* is translated, or rather explained, " angels,"— an explanation of the translator which is here sanctioned by the inspired writer, and which is obviously the only intelligible meaning which can be given to the word in the connection in which it stands, as it were an absurdity to suppose that the heathen divinities, many of whom were mere ideal beings, should be called on to worship Jehovah the King.[1] The word *again* is by some connected with the expression, *bringeth in*, as if the meaning was, 'When He—that is, God, bringeth in again, or the second time, the first-begotten into the world.' The words will bear this, but there is no reference to a first bringing Him in; and we consider our translators as having given the true meaning, when they use the word "again" merely as the mark of an additional confirmation of the truth the Apostle is establishing—the superiority of Jesus Christ to the angels.[2]

By the *first-begotten*, we are plainly to understand Jesus Christ. Some suppose it equivalent to *His Son;* but it deserves notice that, though Jesus Christ is repeatedly termed the only-begotten of God, and the first-born of Mary, He is never represented as the first-begotten of God. The phrase, wherever it occurs, is the first-begotten, or the first-born, and seems plainly used in the secondary sense, as descriptive of dignity and dominion. Thus, when Christ is termed "the first-begotten of every creature," the meaning is, 'the Lord of the whole creation;' when He is termed "the first-born from the dead," the meaning

---

[1] The Hebrew אֱלֹהִים sometimes denotes angels. Gen. xxxv. 7; Ps. viii. 5, lxxxii. 1, lxxxvi. 8.

[2] "Ὅταν δὲ πάλιν is, by *metathesis* or transposition, put for πάλιν δ' ὅταν. Examples of similar trajection you find in Rom. i. 20, v. 6; 1 Cor. i. 2; Acts xii. 27; 1 Cor. iv. 18; 2 Cor. vii. 6; 1 Thes. i. 8. Πάλιν = 'on another occasion,' as John i. 35, viii. 12, 21; Acts xvi. 32. The π. here is parallel with π ver. 5.

seems to be, 'the risen again Lord;' and when He is termed, "the first-born among many brethren," the meaning is 'the Head of the family of God.' "The first-begotten"[1] is apparently quite synonymous with the "appointed heir of all things."

The greatest difficulty in the passage lies in the phrase, "*bringing in* the first-begotten into the world."[2] Some consider this as referring to the presenting the only-begotten Son to the angels, immediately after their creation, as the object of their worship; others refer it to the incarnation; others refer it to the resurrection. The most satisfactory way of settling this question, is to refer to the place from which the quotation is here made. It is plain that the subject of the 97th Psalm must be the "bringing in of the only begotten into the world," whatever the meaning of that phrase may be. Now, when we turn to the 97th Psalm, we find that it is a poetical celebration of the reign of Jehovah. It is plain that the reign there celebrated is neither the natural dominion of Deity over the universe, nor His particular sovereignty over the Jews, but that order of things which is so frequently in the New Testament called "the kingdom of God"—"the kingdom of Christ"—"the kingdom of heaven." The Psalm is a beautiful description of "Messiah the Prince," who is the Lord of hosts, taking possession, in the exercise of divine power, of the kingdom assigned Him; and it is while He is thus engaged that the divine mandate comes forth, "Worship Him, all ye His angels."[3] The phrase, "*bringeth him into* the world," seems borrowed from the language used in reference to the putting Israel in possession of the promised land—an event analogous to, and probably emblematical of, Messiah the Prince being put in possession of the heritage of the nations. The following passages from the Old Testa-

---

[1] Τὸν,—as Valcknaer, with characteristic acuteness, notices,—giving emphasis to the word.

[2] "Mark," says the accomplished scholar just referred to,— "Mark the stylistic refinement (which some in the past have overlooked) whereby the phrase 'bringeth in' is used instead of 'describes', or 'foretells', the 'bringing in', or the 'fact that he is to be brought in'," You have instances of the same peculiarity of expression, ch. vii. 16, 18, x. 9.

[3] Calvin takes this view of the passage:—"If you go through the whole Psalm, you will see the kingdom of Christ, and that only ; . . . the subject-matter of the Psalm is, so to speak, just an official letters patent, whereby Christ is sent to take possession of his kingdom."

ment seem to me to cast light on the phrase before us :—" Thou shalt bring them in, and plant them in the mountain of Thine inheritance, in the place, O Lord, which Thou hast made for Thee to dwell in; in the sanctuary, O Lord, which Thy hands have established."—" To drive out nations from before thee—to bring thee in to give thee their land."—" Their children also multipliedst Thou as the stars of heaven, and broughtest them into the land concerning which Thou hadst promised to their fathers, that they should go in to possess it."[1] The Apostle himself seems to explain the phrase in the beginning of the next chapter, when he says, " He hath not put in subjection the world to come,"[2]—that is, the world during the age succeeding the Law, or the age of the Messiah. The " bringing into the world," and the " putting the world under subjection," are equivalent phrases.[3] The meaning of the passage plainly is,—' While God is establishing the kingdom of His Son in the world,—while He is putting all things under His feet, —while, by the exercise of divine power, all opposing powers and authorities are in process of being subjected to Him, whom He has appointed heir of all things, the first-born or ruler of the whole creation, and who " must reign till all His enemies are made His footstool,"—it is the revealed will of God the Father to the angels,[4] that they honour the Son as they honour Himself.'

It is His clearly manifested and well-understood will, that "every knee" in heaven as well as on earth " should bow" to Him, and " every tongue" in heaven as well as on earth acknowledge His supreme lordship and dominion. And we know that the mandate is cheerfully obeyed. Whatever diversity of opinion there may be among men as to worshipping Christ Jesus, there is

---

[1] Exod. xv. 17; Deut. iv. 38; Nehem. ix. 23.   [2] Heb. ii. 5.

[3] We thus see a peculiar propriety in using the appellation, πρωτότοκος, rather than any other title of the Messiah—a term which designates Him as Prince and Proprietor. Ps. lxxxix. 27; Rom. viii. 29; Col. i. 15, 18; Rev. i. 5.

[4] Λέγει.—Who says? Some supply γραφή; but the proper supplement is Θεός—He who " bringeth the first begotten into the world." The objection some have raised from the expression being, not 'My angels,' but " the angels of God," could spring only from a very careless consideration of the manner in which in the inspired writings the Supreme Being is often represented as speaking: Ps. l. 14; Exod. xx. 7.

obviously but one mind and one heart in heaven. "I beheld," says John the divine, when a window was as it were opened to him into heaven, and all the glories of the celestial state burst on his astonished and delighted view, "and, lo, in the midst of the throne and of the four beasts, and in the midst of the elders, stood a Lamb as it had been slain, having seven horns and seven eyes, which are the seven Spirits of God sent forth into all the earth. And He came and took the book out of the right hand of Him that sat upon the throne. And when He had taken the book, the four beasts and four and twenty elders fell down before the Lamb, having every one of them harps, and golden vials full of odours, which are the prayers of saints. And they sung a new song, saying, Thou art worthy to take the book, and to open the seals thereof: for Thou wast slain, and hast redeemed us to God by Thy blood, out of every kindred, and tongue, and people, and nation; and hast made us unto our God kings and priests: and we shall reign on the earth. And I beheld, and I heard the voice of many angels round about the throne, and the beasts, and the elders: and the number of them was ten thousand times ten thousand, and thousands of thousands; saying with a loud voice, Worthy is the Lamb that was slain, to receive power, and riches, and wisdom, and strength, and honour, and glory, and blessing. And every creature which is in heaven, and on the earth, and under the earth, and such as are in the sea, and all that are in them, heard I saying, Blessing, and honour, and glory, and power, be unto Him that sitteth upon the throne, and unto the Lamb, for ever and ever."[1] In the Apocalypse, which is just an anticipated history of Jehovah's "bringing in the only begotten into the world," it is interesting to observe how ready the chorus of angels are to break in, on every new triumph of Messiah their Prince, in songs of congratulation and triumph. When the King who sits at the right hand of Jehovah "strikes through kings in the day of His wrath, judges among the heathen, fills the places with dead bodies, wounds the heads over many countries,"[2] the angel of the waters lifts up his voice, and says, "Thou art righteous, O Lord, which art, and wast, and shalt be, because Thou hast judged thus: for they have shed the blood of saints and prophets, and Thou hast given them blood to drink; for

[1] Rev. v. 6–13.   [2] Ps. cx. 5, 6.

they are worthy." And another angel out of the altar—one of the spirits of the slaughtered martyrs—responds, " Even so, Lord God Almighty, true and righteous are Thy judgments."[1] As the final destruction of His most obstinate enemy approaches, a voice from heaven is heard, saying, " Reward her even as she rewarded you, and double unto her double, according to her works: in the cup which she hath filled, fill to her double. How much she hath glorified herself, and lived deliciously, so much torment and sorrow give her : for she saith in her heart, I sit a queen, and am no widow, and shall see no sorrow. Therefore shall her plagues come in one day, death, and mourning, and famine; and she shall be utterly burned with fire : for strong is the Lord God who judgeth her."[2] And when that wicked one is completely destroyed by " the breath of His mouth and the brightness of His coming," "a great voice of much people is heard in heaven, saying, Alleluia; Salvation, and glory, and honour, and power, unto the Lord our God: for true and righteous are His judgments; for He hath judged the great whore, which did corrupt the earth with her fornication, and hath avenged the blood of His servants at her hand. And again they said, Alleluia. And her smoke rose up for ever and ever. And the four and twenty elders, and the four beasts, fell down and worshipped God that sat on the throne, saying, Amen ; Alleluia. And a voice came out of the throne, saying, Praise our God, all ye His servants, and ye that fear Him, both small aad great. And I heard as it were the voice of a great multitude, and as the voice of many waters, and as the voice of mighty thunderings, saying, Alleluia : for the Lord God omnipotent reigneth."[3] And when the seventh angel sounds, there are " great voices in heaven, saying, The kingdoms of this world are become the kingdoms of our Lord, and of His Christ ; and He shall reign for ever and ever."[4] And when the end is come,—when He has " brought back the kingdom to the Father,"—when He has " put down all rule, and authority, and power,"—when all things shall have been made new, O how loud and how sweet shall be the anthem of praise " to Him who hath overcome !"—" Salvation to our God, and the Lamb, for ever and ever."—" Now is come salvation, and strength,

[1] Rev. xvi. 5–7.  
[2] Rev. xviii. 6–8.  
[3] Rev. xix. 1–6.  
[4] Rev. xi. 15.

and the kingdom of our God."[1]—" Alleluia: for the Lord God omnipotent reigneth."

Need we now ask, Has He not indeed been made much higher than the angels? Has He not been "made as much better than the angels, as He has obtained by inheritance a more excellent name than they"?

In illustrating the superiority of Jesus Christ, the Apostle's statements hitherto have all had a direct reference to *Him*. In the quotation he next makes, the reference is directly to the *angels*. He has shown us what *He* is; he now shows us what *they* are. He has shown His superiority; now he shows their inferiority. Ver. 7.—" And of[2] the angels He saith, Who maketh His angels spirits, and His ministers a flame of fire."

This is a quotation from Psalm civ. 4.[3] Considerable difference prevails among interpreters as to the meaning of these words as they occur in the Old Testament scripture, and as to the manner in which the sacred writer here derives an argument from them for the inferiority of the angels to Jesus Christ. The words, as they stand in the original Hebrew, admit of different renderings, according as you make the words, "angels" and "messengers," the subject or the predicate of the proposition, or as you translate, "who maketh," of employment or treatment, or of creation properly so called. They may be rendered, 'Who maketh the winds His angels or messengers, and the lightning His servants;' or, 'Who employeth His angels as the winds, and His ministers as the lightning;' or, 'Who creates His angels spirits, and His ministers a flame of fire.'

Supposing the first of these the right rendering, an argument for the inferiority of the angels to the Son might be thus deduced. ' "Angel" is by no means so high and dignified a name as may be supposed. It denotes nothing more than a subordinate agent; and it is given even to material things, such as the winds and the lightning. While the name " Son of God" is

---

[1] Rev. xii. 10.

[2] Πρός is here = περί—' *de*, of, concerning.' This is in conformity to the Hebrew usage of corresponding particles. אֶל is used for עַל, Gen. xx. 2; 2 Kings xix. 32; Ps. lxix. 27. Λέγει is either impersonal, = λέγεται, or has for its subject ἡ γραφή; comp. ver. 6.

[3] Cited apparently *memoriter* from the LXX. The only difference is, the Apostle says, πυρὸς φλόγα, instead of πῦρ φλέγον.

peculiar to Him who possesses it, the name " angels" is common to the spiritual beings who possess it, and to winds and lightning.' But whatever there may be in this argument, it is obviously not the Apostle's; for though the Hebrew words will admit of being thus rendered, the Apostle's translation of them will not; and we must hold that his interpretation is the only true one.[1]

Supposing the second mode of rendering the words the just one, 'Who maketh—*i. e.*, who employeth—His angels as the winds, and His ministers like the lightning,' the argument for the inferiority of the angels to the Son might be thus expressed: 'The angels, however exalted, are merely instruments of the divine agency, like the winds and the lightning. The place they occupy is, therefore, far inferior to His, "who doth according to His will in the army of heaven, and among the inhabitants of the earth," to whom "all power in heaven and earth" belongs.' The principal objection to this mode of interpretation is, that, admitting it, there is no statement of the essential inferiority of the angels, corresponding to the statement of the essential superiority of the Son. We find a statement of their official inferiority—" they are ministering spirits" (ver. 14)—answering to the statement of His official superiority—" He has been made much better than the angels;" and it is certainly but natural to expect a statement as to their essential inferiority, corresponding to the declaration that He has obtained " by inheritance a more excellent name than they." And if, without using any violence on the words, either as they occur in the Psalm or in the passage before us, we can find in them such a statement, —still more if the connection and design of the quotation in the Psalm where it occurs seem naturally to lead to such a view, there can be very little doubt that this is the true way of interpreting it.

I am, on these grounds, disposed to prefer the third mode of rendering the words, both in the Psalm and in the passage before us. " Who maketh"—*i. e.*, 'who createth'—" His angels

---

[1] His words, πρὸς μὲν τοὺς ἀγγέλους, clearly show that he considered the angels as the subject of the proposition. What sort of an argument would this be? An inspired writer states that God uses the winds as His messengers; therefore the Son of God has a higher office than the unembodied spirits called angels. Paul, even though uninspired, could never have been guilty of a paralogism like this.

spirits," or 'winds,' "and his ministers a flame of fire." The word rendered "maketh," is used in reference to creation in Gen. i. 31. The Psalm is a hymn of praise to Jehovah, as the Creator, and Preserver, and Governor of the universe. It begins with the celebration of His glories as the Creator. The creation of the heavens is the subject of the 2d and 3d verses; the creation of the earth, of the 5th and some succeeding verses. What so natural as to consider the 4th, the intermediate verse, as a description of the creation of the inhabitants of the heavenly world?[1] The verse, literally rendered, would run thus, connecting it with all the clauses of the Psalm, and with the introduction: " Bless Jehovah—creating His angels spirits," or winds, " and His ministers a flame of fire." These words, " creating His angels spirits," may either mean, 'creating them spiritual beings, not material beings,' or 'creating them winds'—*i. e.*, like the winds, invisible, rapid in their movements, and capable of producing great effects. The last mode of interpretation seems pointed out by the parallelism—" and His ministers"—or ' servants,' who are plainly the same as His angels—" a flame of fire," *i. e.*, like the lightning. The statement here made about the angels seems to be this: 'They are created beings, who in their qualities bear a resemblance to the winds and the lightning.'

The argument to be deduced from this statement for the inferiority of the angels is direct and powerful:—He is the Son; they are the creatures of God. *Only begotten* is the description of His mode of existence; *made* is the description of theirs. *All* their powers are communicated powers; and however high they may stand in the scale of creation, it is in that scale they stand, which places them infinitely below Him, who is so the Son of God as to be " God over all, blessed for ever."

The fifth quotation, to which our attention is now more particularly to be directed, is taken from Psalm xlv. 6, 7, a passage referring primarily to our Lord's official superiority, though, like most other passages of the same kind, necessarily implying His essential superiority. Let us examine it with all the attention in our power. Ver. 8. "But unto the Son he saith, Thy throne, O God, is for ever and ever; a sceptre of righteousness is the

---

[1] The Jews held that the angels were created on the second day. PIRKE R. Eliezer, c. iv.

sceptre of Thy kingdom. 9. Thou hast loved righteousness, and hated iniquity; therefore God, even Thy God, hath anointed Thee with the oil of gladness above Thy fellows."

The 45th Psalm, from which the quotation is made, is considered by many interpreters as a marriage song on the nuptials of Solomon with an Egyptian princess,—having, however, a mystical reference to the relation between Christ and the Church. We apprehend, however, that this opinion, which is inconsistent with that both of Jewish and Christian antiquity, is not only without evidence, but opposed to evidence. There is much to prove that the sovereign here celebrated is not Solomon—is not, indeed, any mere mortal monarch, but is Messiah our Prince. The hero of this divine poem is a warrior, who girds His sword on His thigh, rides in pursuit of His flying foes, thins their ranks by His sharp arrows, and reigns at last over His conquered enemies.[1] Solomon was no warrior, but enjoyed a long reign of forty years of uninterrupted peace. The prince here celebrated has a numerous progeny. We do not know that Solomon had any other son than Rehoboam. No earthly prince could with propriety be addressed as God; and to no *mortal* could belong a perpetual dominion. Every particular in the description, interpreted according to the ordinary principles on which Old Testament prophecy is explained, is applicable to the Messiah. Though we had no direct assertion that this is one of the Psalms in which "it is written" of Christ, yet on these grounds we should have been warranted to have come to this conclusion. But with all who admit the divine inspiration of the writer of this Epistle, the words before us are of themselves sufficient to settle the question as to the subject and reference of the passage quoted. "Unto[2] the Son he"—*i.e.*, the psalmist or prophet—"saith,"— or, 'the Scripture saith;' or, understanding it impersonally, 'it is said,'—"Thy throne, O God,[3] is for ever and ever."

A throne is the seat on which a king sits when he administers judgment, or performs other royal functions, and is naturally employed as a figurative expression for royal power and authority. A tottering throne is expressive of insecure dominion; the subversion of the throne is an emblem of a revolution; a

---
[1] Henley.      [2] Πρός. δὲ=ἀλλά.
[3] ὁ Θεός for ὁ Θεέ. AQUILA thus renders the passage. Similar constructions are to be found, Matt. xi. 26, xx. 30; Mark v. 41; Luke viii. 54.

stable throne expresses well-established authority; and an everlasting throne, a perpetual kingdom. When it is said of the Son that "His throne is for ever and ever," the meaning is, that He is invested with supreme dominion, and this dominion shall never be taken from Him.

The argument for the Son's official superiority to the angels from this passage, is direct and conclusive. *He* has a throne; *they* have a station before it. He is the ruler; they are but subjects. And His rule is not temporary, but perpetual: He reigns, and He shall reign for ever and ever.[1]

There is also a strong additional argument for the *essential* superiority of Jesus Christ to the angels contained in the appellation here given Him: "Thy throne, *O God*, is for ever and ever." This is a proof that "He has received a more excellent name than they." Angels are called "gods," just as they are called "sons of God;" but to none of them was either the one or the other of these appellations given in the way in which they are given to Jesus Christ. To none of the angels was it ever said, 'Thou art the Son of God;' to none of them was it ever said, ' O God, Thy throne is for ever and ever.'

It may be said, that He who is here addressed as God, is represented as having Himself *a God*: "God, even Thy God;" or, "O God, Thy God." But to the person who holds the plain scriptural doctrine, that the incarnate Son, as Mediator, is subordinate to His Father, who in the economy of grace sustains the majesty of the Godhead, there is nothing unaccountable in this. He who was God, equal with the Father, was, in His assumed character of the Mediator and Saviour, placed by the Father—who was His God, as the man Christ Jesus—on a throne elevated far above every earthly throne, secured from all fluctuation, and destined to endure for ever.

Those who deny our Lord's divinity have been greatly per-

---

[1] It may appear to some that this declaration is scarcely consistent with the Apostle's statement in 1 Cor. xv. 24-28. Some suppose that "for ever and ever" means merely to the end of the present order of things. Other passages, however, seem to teach plainly the strictly everlasting duration of the mediatorial reign of Christ. It is termed "the everlasting kingdom of our Lord and Saviour." The passage in 1 Cor. xv. 24-28 admits of an interpretation which not only is consistent with, but strongly supports, the doctrine of the perpetuity of our Lord's mediatorial dominion.—*Vide* STORR, i. 272, etc.

plexed by this passage, and have attempted to get rid of the argument by rendering the words, 'God is Thy throne for ever and ever.' But this is not only contrary to the usage of the language,[1] but it would utterly destroy the force of the Apostle's argument. If the words, 'God is Thy throne,' mean anything, they mean, 'God is the support of Thy throne'—a declaration which is true of every throne.[2] It also completely destroys that parallelism which is one of the characteristic beauties of Hebrew poetry. It is kept up when it is said, 'Thy dominion is perpetual, Thy administration is righteous;' but it is utterly lost when it is said, 'God is the support of Thy dominion, and Thy administration is righteous.'

"A sceptre of righteousness is the sceptre of Thy kingdom." The sceptre has from the earliest ages been one of the badges of royalty. It was originally nothing but a straight slender rod, studded sometimes, for ornament, with nails of gold. It was an emblem of the integrity of the monarch in administering justice. The expression, "a sceptre of righteousness," is literally 'a sceptre of straightness;' *i.e.*, according to a Hebrew idiom, a straight sceptre. A crooked sceptre was an emblem of an unjust government; a straight sceptre, of a righteous government. The meaning of the poetical description, in plain terms, is—'The administration of Thy kingdom is strictly and invariably just.'

The Apostle's argument here is founded on the word *sceptre*—an emblem of royal power. The Son is the King; the highest dignity belonging to the angels is, that they hold the first rank among His subjects. It is a mistake to suppose, that when a quotation is made for the sake of argument from the Old Testament by a New Testament writer, every part of the quotation is intended to be argued from. In many cases, a considerable part of the quotation may be made merely for the sake of connection. This is plainly the case also in the passage before us: "Thou hast loved righteousness, and hated iniquity; therefore God, even Thy God, hath anointed Thee with the oil

---

[1] *Vide* STUART and MIDDLETON.

[2] MICHAELIS very justly terms this exegesis "a forced explanation;" and adds, "Who ever called, or would call, the upholder of a throne, a throne? What instance of such unprecedented usage could be adduced from any Hebrew source, to confirm this explanation?"

of gladness above Thy fellows." It is on the last clause here only that the Apostle builds his argument. The first clause is quoted merely for the sake of connection.

These words, "Thou hast loved righteousness, and hated iniquity," have by many been considered as an expansion of the sentiment in the preceding verse : " A sceptre of righteousness is the sceptre of Thy kingdom." But if we look attentively at the passage, we will clearly see that they are a description of the character and conduct of the Messiah previously to His being constituted Supreme Ruler; for it is stated as the reason why ' God, even His God, has anointed Him with the oil of gladness above His fellows,' that He ' loved righteousness, and hated iniquity.' These words are very descriptive of the whole of the character and conduct of our Lord Jesus, who " knew no sin"— who "always did the things which pleased the Father"—who was equally free from hereditary and personal guilt, from original and acquired depravity—whose character combined every species of moral excellence in its highest degree, and whose life was an uniform tenor of unspotted holiness—whose conformity to the divine will was perfect in its principle, perfect in its extent, and perfect in its duration. But there is, I doubt not, a peculiar reference to the manifestation of His love of righteousness and His hatred of iniquity in voluntarily submitting to do and suffer all that was necessary to the vindication of the divine righteousness, and the display of the divine mercy in the salvation of a lost world. To this there is plainly a reference in that remarkable prediction in the 40th Psalm, ver. 8. This is the interpretation given of it by the Apostle in the 10th chapter of this Epistle, vers. 5–10. In consequence of, and as the reward for, this extraordinary manifestation of love of righteousness and hatred of iniquity, by which His fitness for the administration of righteous government was illustriously manifested, "God, even His God, anointed Him with the oil of gladness above His fellows." The words might with equal propriety be rendered, ' O God, Thy God hath anointed Thee with the oil of gladness[1] above Thy fellows.'[2]

The unction of Christ here plainly refers to His investiture

[1] In the phrase, " oil of gladness," there is a reference to the refreshing, enlivening influence of certain medicated odoriferous unguents.

[2] Above His μετόχους, kings—" King of kings," " Lord of lords."

with royalty. One "anointed with oil," as appears from David's lamentation over Saul,[1] is just a synonym for a king. To be "anointed with oil," is just to be made a king; and to be anointed with the "oil of gladness," is to be invested with such a regal office as is well fitted to communicate satisfaction and happiness. It is plain, that to seek here a reference to what the Apostle calls "Christ's anointing with the Holy Ghost," is to seek what is not to be found. The reference is not to divine destination or divine preparation for the work of a Mediator generally, but divine investiture with supreme dominion. This view of the matter clears of all difficulty the phrase, "above Thy fellows," which has greatly perplexed interpreters; some referring it to angels, and others to saints, and others to all anointed persons—prophets, priests, or kings. It is plain that it is to be interpreted so as to correspond with the train of thought in the passage. The Apostle and Psalmist are both speaking of Jesus the Messiah as a prince, and their sentiment is, 'God, even Thy God, hath raised Thee to a kingdom far more replete with enjoyment than that ever conferred on any other ruler. He has given Thee a kingdom which, for extent and duration, and multitude and magnitude of blessings, as far exceeds any kingdom ever bestowed on man or angel as the heaven is above the earth.'

It particularly deserves notice, that the elevation of the Messiah to His supreme and perpetual throne is represented as the reward of His meritorious display of 'love of righteousness, and hatred of iniquity.' It strikingly corresponds with the declaration of the Apostle: "But made Himself of no reputation, and took upon Him the form of a servant, and was made in the likeness of men; and being found in fashion as a man, He humbled Himself, and became obedient unto death, even the death of the cross. Wherefore God also hath highly exalted Him, and given Him a name which is above every name."[2]

The bearing of the last clause on the Apostle's argument is direct and powerful: 'He is made much better than the angels, for God has raised Him to royal honours far superior to those conferred on any prince, whether angelic or human.'

The sixth quotation is from Ps. cii. 24–27, and bears on the essential superiority of the Son to the angels.

[1] 2 Sam. i. 21.      [2] Philip. ii. 7–9.

Ver. 10. "And, Thou, Lord, in the beginning hast laid the foundation of the earth; and the heavens are the works of Thine hands: 11. They shall perish, but Thou remainest; and they all shall wax old as doth a garment; 12. And as a vesture shalt Thou fold them up, and they shall be changed: but Thou art the same, and Thy years shall not fail."

The quotation is made from the Septuagint. The first thing to be inquired into here, is the connection of this passage with what precedes it. The most natural method is to connect it with what immediately goes before, and to consider it as another quotation in support of the supremacy of the Son to the angels. "To[1] the Son," or in reference to the Son, "he says, Thy throne, O God, is for ever and ever;" and also he says to or of the Son, "Thou, Lord, in the beginning," etc.

It has been proposed to connect it with the 7th verse, considering the 8th and 9th verses as a parenthesis. But there is none of the ordinary signs of a parenthesis here; and without giving a very unusual meaning to the word *heavens*, and adopting altogether a very unnatural mode of interpretation, it is impossible to find anything said directly of the angels in this quotation.

The passage is obviously brought forward to illustrate directly, not the inferiority of the angels to the Son, but the superiority of the Son to the angels. Admitting this, it has been alleged by those interpreters who deny the proper divinity of Jesus Christ, that the quotation is not to be considered as an address to the Messiah, but to God the Father, and that its bearing on the argument of the Apostle is merely this : 'The perpetuity of the Messiah's throne is secured by the eternity and immutability of God.' But unless the Messiah is Himself God, it would be difficult to make out the conclusiveness of this argument; and at any rate, if the quotation from the 45th Psalm be an address to the Messiah, it is impossible to give a good reason why this quotation, wearing the same form of direct address, and introduced in the same way, should be interpreted on a different principle. Indeed, but for the strong sanction which the words, understood in their natural sense, give to the doctrine of our Lord's proper divinity, we may safely say, another sense would never have been accorded to them.

[1] Πρός, ver. 8.

## THE SUPERIORITY OF CHRIST TO ANGELS. 61

It may then be laid down as a principle, that the author of the Epistle quotes this passage as an address to the Son; and his honesty as a good man, and his inspiration as an Apostle, secure us from the hazard of being misled by him. He could not misapprehend the meaning and reference of the Psalmist; and he could not wilfully impose on us, by giving a meaning to the Psalmist's words that he knew did not belong to them. Even, then, although we might find some difficulties in seeing distinctly that the words, as they stand in the 102d Psalm, are an address to the Son or Messiah, if we admit the divine authority of the Epistle, we must attribute these difficulties to any cause rather than misapprehension or misinterpretation on the part of the inspired writer.[1]

On examining the passage, however, where it occurs in the 102d Psalm, I apprehend we will find it one of those which, though we would not readily have applied them to the Messiah unless an inspired writer had done so, now that they are applied, we can not only on his authority implicitly believe, but can distinctly enough see, are applicable. The 102d Psalm was written probably during the Babylonian captivity or the Syro-Macedonian persecutions. It contains in it a plaintive description of the depressed and languishing state of the Church of God, and a prophecy of its revival and extension among the Gentiles. The prediction plainly refers to the kingdom of the Messiah. No occurrence in the history of the Jews previously to the coming of Christ affords anything like an adequate fulfilment of it. "Thou shalt arise, and have mercy upon Zion: for the time to favour her, yea, the set time, is come. For Thy servants take pleasure in her stones, and favour the dust thereof. So the heathen shall fear the name of the Lord, and all the kings of the earth Thy glory. When the Lord shall build up Zion, He shall appear in His glory. He will regard the prayer of the destitute, and not despise their prayer. This shall be written for the generation to come: and the people which shall be created shall praise the Lord. For He hath looked down from the height of His sanctuary; from heaven did the Lord behold the earth; to hear the groaning of the prisoner; to loose those that are appointed to death."[2] After contemplating the glories of Messiah's reign, the delight

[1] See Note A.     [2] Ps. cii. 13-20.

of the inspired poet is checked by the reflection of his own mortality, and the thought that he would never see those glorious events which the spirit of prophecy enabled him to foresee afar off. To relieve his mind from this distressing feeling, he seeks refuge in the contemplation of the unchangeableness of the great Preserver, and Deliverer, and Protector of His Church, and the certainty that He would fulfil His promises to the latest posterity of His faithful people. And who was this Preserver, and Protector, and Deliverer, but Messiah the Prince, Jehovah the Saviour? Even although the original reference to the Messiah in the Psalm could not be so satisfactorily made out as it is, the argument to a Christian is quite a conclusive one. Language plainly applicable only.to a divine person is by an inspired author referred to Jesus Christ: therefore He is divine; and because He is divine, infinitely superior to the angels.

Let us now look at the passage itself somewhat more particularly. The person addressed is termed *Lord*. The word "Lord" is not in the Hebrew text in the verse quoted; but the person addressed is repeatedly, in the course of the Psalm, called *Jehovah*: vers. 1, 12, 15, 16, 19,—an appellation descriptive of the eternal and independent existence of the Divinity. The phrase, *in the beginning*, plainly refers to the first words of Genesis, "In the beginning God created the heaven and the earth." To "lay the foundation of the earth," is just a figurative term for creation. It very often occurs in Scripture: Ps. xxiv. 2, lxxxix. 11, civ. 5; Job xxxviii. 4; Isa. xlviii. 13; Zech. xii. 1. "The heavens being the work of Christ's hands," is an expression of similar import, and signifies 'the creation of the heavens.' Thus Ps. viii. 4, 6; "the heavens the work of Thy hands," is just equivalent to "the sun and the moon which Thou hast ordained." "The heavens and the earth" are a common scriptural expression for all things. This is evident from such passages as Gen. i. 1; Neh. ix. 6; Ps. cxxxiv. 3. These words, then, distinctly ascribe the creation of all things to the Son. To attempt to explain the creation here mentioned of a moral creation, and to try to convince men that "the earth" means the Jewish dispensation, and "the heavens" the Christian, or that "the foundation of the earth" means human rulers, and "the heavens" *angelic* princes, only shows to what absurd extremes men will run to support a favourite hypothesis.

## THE SUPERIORITY OF CHRIST TO ANGELS. 63

The doctrine here taught is plainly the same doctrine which is taught by John in his Gospel, ch. i. 3, " All things were made by Him; and without Him was not any thing made that was made;" and by Paul in his Epistle to the Colossians, ch. i. 16, " For by Him were all things created that are in heaven, and that are in earth, visible and invisible, whether they be thrones, or dominions, or principalities, or powers; all things were created by Him, and for Him."

But in the passage quoted by the Apostle, the Son is represented not only as the Creator of all things, but as the Author of all the changes through which they are to pass. " They"—*i.e.*, the heavens and the earth—" shall perish, but Thou remainest; and they all shall wax old as doth a garment, and as a vesture Thou shalt fold them up, and they shall be changed." We have no reason to think there is such a thing as annihilation in God's world; but these words certainly do intimate that the present system of things is to undergo a great change. This world is to perish, just as the old world perished, though by different means. " For this they willingly are ignorant of, that by the word of God the heavens were of old, and the earth standing out of the water and in the water: whereby the world that then was, being overflowed with water, perished: But the heavens and the earth which are now, by the same word are kept in store, reserved unto fire against the day of judgment and perdition of ungodly men.—But the day of the Lord will come as a thief in the night; in the which the heavens shall pass away with a great noise, and the elements shall melt with fervent heat, the earth also, and the works that are therein, shall be burnt up."[1] Of these changes the Son is to be the author: " Thou shalt fold them up;" or, as it is in the Hebrew text, " Thou shalt change them." How this is to be done we do not know, but we know who is to do it. He who creates the world alone destroys it. The perfect ease with which these mighty changes are to be effected is beautifully pointed out—" Thou shalt fold them up," as a put-off garment.

But amid all the changes which take place among the works He has made, He remains unchanged, unchangeable. " He is the same, and His years do not fail." In His nature there is

[1] 2 Pet. iii. 5–7, 10.

no change; in His duration, no circle to run—no space to be measured—no time to be reckoned—all is eternity, infinite and onward. Such is the plain meaning of this quotation. Its bearing on the Apostle's object is direct, and obvious. The Son has received the appellation " Jehovah," *i.e.*, the eternal, independent Being; and in doing so, He possesses " a more excellent name" than any of the angels. He " was in the beginning," when neither man, nor angel, nor creature of any kind existed—when there was nothing but God in the universe—when God was all. He created all things—while they are the works of His hands. As He established, so He shall change, the present order of things, which all the angels of heaven cannot do; and while they are mutable beings, He "remains"—"the same, yesterday, to-day, and for ever."

The seventh quotation, to which our attention is now to be directed, is taken from Ps. cx. 1, and bears directly on our Lord's official superiority to the angels. Ver. 13.—" But to which of the angels said He at any time, Sit on My right hand, until I make Thine enemies Thy footstool?"

There are none of the Psalms concerning which we may more confidently assert that in them "it is written" of Christ, than that from which the quotation in the passage before us is made. All the ancient Jewish interpreters explain it of the Messiah. Even on the principles of the typical system, it is impossible to refer it to any mere human prince; and in the New Testament it is no fewer than eight times quoted and reasoned from, in a way which makes it evident that our Lord and His Apostles considered it as having a direct and sole reference to Him.[1]

To a person acquainted with the style of the prophetic writings, the first verse of the 110th Psalm—"The Lord," or Jehovah, "said to my Lord, Sit Thou at My right hand, until I make Thine enemies Thy footstool"—will appear a prediction that, at the period to which the oracle refers, Messiah should be placed at the right hand of God, and continue there while all His enemies were being made His footstool. To perceive the force of the Apostle's argument from this passage in support of the official superiority of Jesus Christ to the angels,—of His being " made

[1] Rosenmüller's and Jahn's proof of the Messianic reference of this Psalm are very masterly.

much better than they," it will be necessary to inquire into the meaning of the phrase, 'sitting at the right hand of God.'

In inquiring into the meaning of a prediction clothed in figurative language, like that before us, it is of primary importance that we have a distinct apprehension of the imagery presented to the mind of the prophet. What then was before the mind's eye of the inspired poet when he said, " The Lord said unto my Lord, Sit Thou at My right hand, until I make Thine enemies Thy footstool?" It is the very ingenious conjecture of a most learned interpreter,[1] that the imagery of this sacred ode is borrowed from the most sacred part of the Jewish sanctuary, the Holy of Holies. There, amid the thick darkness, resided the emblem of the divine presence,—there was the throne of Jehovah, the God of Israel, between the cherubim; and the ark of the covenant was as it were His footstool. The heaven-opened eye of the prophet penetrates the veil, and his heaven-opened ear hears the voice of Jehovah inviting Messiah the Prince to sit down with Him on His throne, while from the sanctuary the lightnings of divine power are sent forth to overwhelm with discomfiture His obstinate foes. Under these emblems, he apprehends, is exhibited the vast superiority of dignity which belongs to the Messiah, when compared either with the Jewish kings, who were not allowed to enter into the Holy of Holies at all, or with the Jewish high-priests, who, though allowed to enter once a year with the blood of atonement, were not allowed to remain, and, even while there, ministered standing. This view of the imagery receives something like support from the 11th and 12th verses of the tenth chapter of this Epistle : " Every priest *standeth* daily ministering, and offering oftentimes the same sacrifices, which can never take away sins : but this man, after He had offered one sacrifice for sins, for ever *sat down* on the right hand of God."

We apprehend, however, that the images present to the prophet's mind are not those of Jehovah in the Holy of Holies as the object of the worship of His people, but Jehovah in heaven as the great Sovereign of the universe. There is nothing in the Psalm that naturally leads the mind to the temple, while the whole of it answers to such a representation as was made to Daniel, and is so strikingly described in the seventh chapter of

[1] Michaelis.

his prophecies: "I beheld, and the Ancient of days did sit, whose garment was white as snow, and the hair of His head like the pure wool: His throne was like the fiery flame, and His wheels as burning fire. A fiery stream issued and came forth from before Him: thousand thousands ministered unto Him, and ten thousand times ten thousand stood before Him." "I saw, and, behold, one like the Son of man came with the clouds of heaven, and came to the Ancient of days, and they brought Him near before Him. And there was given Him dominion, and glory, and a kingdom, that all people, nations, and languages, should serve Him: His dominion is an everlasting dominion, which shall not pass away, and His kingdom that which shall not be destroyed."

The glories of the presence-chamber of the celestial palace of the Great King, the Lord of hosts, burst on the prophet's view; Messiah the Prince, in the form of a man, draws near to the "throne high and lifted up;" while from the inaccessible light in which He dwells who sits thereon, there comes forth a voice of complacent invitation, "Sit Thou at My right hand, till I have made Thine enemies Thy footstool." Such seems to be the imagery of the prophetic oracle. Let us now inquire into its significancy.

How much there may be of literal accomplishment of this sublime prediction, it is impossible for us to tell. No sound thinker can doubt that there may be in that local heaven, where the glorified God-man Christ Jesus is, some visible representation of the presence of the Divine Majesty, infinitely transcending our highest conceptions of grandeur and beauty, in the midst of which He dwells; while there are many passages of Scripture which may incline a devout believer to the opinion that there is. But whatever there may be in this, it is evident that the words are intended to convey to our minds the idea of the greatest conceivable dignity of station as conferred on the Messiah.

A king seated on his throne issues forth his orders, administers justice, and displays the splendour and majesty of his office. To sit near the king at any time, is the emblem of being on terms of familiarity and friendship with him, for all but his peculiar favourites *stand* in his presence; but to sit near him when on the throne, is an emblem of rank, and dignity, and power in the kingdom. A seat on the right hand and a seat on the left of the king are just other words for the two most dignified stations in the kingdom. Thus, when Salome asked of our Lord, that her sons should sit, one on His right, and one on His left hand, the meaning is, that they should be His prime ministers. But there are obviously two different ways of sitting at the right hand of the king. There is sitting on an inferior seat at the right hand of the throne, and there is a sitting on the throne at the right hand of the king. The last of these stations is a much more honourable one than the former. It denotes not only honour, but royal honour. It indicates that he who sits there reigns along with the king. That the phrase is to be understood in this last sense, when used in reference to our Lord, is obvious; for the Apostle Paul, arguing from this very passage, says, " He must *reign* till He hath put all His enemies under His feet;"[1] and our Lord Himself says, " I have overcome, and am set down with My Father on His throne."

The declaration, then, that the Messiah sits on the throne of God, at the right hand of His divine Father, is just equivalent to a declaration that He is the Ruler of the universe. The following passages of Scripture are the best illustration of this amazing sentiment, ' The God-man Christ Jesus is the Ruler of the universe :'—" For the Father judgeth no man, but hath committed all judgment unto the Son : that all men should honour the Son, even as they honour the Father. He that honoureth not the Son, honoureth not the Father which hath sent Him." " And Jesus came and spake unto them, saying, All power is given unto Me in heaven and in earth." " Which He wrought in Christ, when He raised Him from the dead, and set Him at His own right hand in the heavenly places, far above all principality, and power, and might, and dominion, and every name that is named, not only in this world, but also in that which is to come." " Who is the image of the invisible God, the first-born of every creature : for by Him were all things created that are in heaven, and that are in earth, visible and invisible, whether they be thrones, or dominions, or principalities, or powers; all things were created by Him, and for Him ; and He is before all things, and by Him all things consist." " Who is

---

[1] 1 Cor. xv. 25.

gone into heaven, and is on the right hand of God; angels, and authorities, and powers, being made subject unto Him."[1]

The ultimate design of this government is the glory of God in the final salvation and happiness of those whom He has given to Him; and in order to gain this, all things are subjected to His control that can directly or indirectly affect their interests. It is thus in the character of the Saviour, "the Mediator between God and man," that He possesses this high dignity, and exercises this unlimited authority.

This dignified place Jesus Christ is to occupy until God, even His God, "make His enemies His footstool." By the enemies of Jesus Christ, we are to understand whoever and whatever opposes the great purposes of His wise and benignant government: Satan and all his legions—obstinately unbelieving and impenitent men—all institutions, civil or ecclesiastical, which are inconsistent with, and opposed to, that reign of truth, and purity, and order, and happiness, which it is His purpose to establish.

For these enemies to become the "footstool" of Messiah, is plainly equivalent to their being completely subjected to His dominion—entirely deprived of all power to oppose His purposes. Some interpreters have supposed that there is here an allusion to a custom, of which we have traces in Scripture, of conquerors putting their feet on the necks of their vanquished foes. But the figure is not here that of a warrior on the field of battle triumphing over his foes, but a prince secure on his throne,— his enemies being so far from being able to disturb him, or overturn his throne, that they are as it were his footstool—so completely subjected to him, as that he can employ them, in any way he pleases, however degrading to them, which may be subservient to his dignity or comfort.

The expression, "I will make Thine enemies Thy footstool," intimates that the power by which the enemies of the Messiah are put down, is the power of God. As mediatorial King, as well as mediatorial Priest, He is subservient to His Father, the representative of essential Divinity. He is subject to Him who is "putting all things under Him."

The phrase, "*until* I make Thine enemies Thy footstool,"

[1] John v. 22, 23; Matt. xxviii. 18; Eph. i. 20, 21; Col. i. 15–17; 1 Pet. iii. 22.

does not by any means intimate, that when all things are put under Him—that when all His enemies are made His footstool—He shall reign with His Father no longer. That the word does not necessarily imply this, is plain from the two following passages in the Book of Daniel, ch. i. 21, x. 1. It intimates that our Lord's mediatorial dominion will continue "*till* all His enemies are made His footstool;" but it does not intimate that it is *then* to terminate.

He who would wish to have vivid impressions of the nature, and extent, and energy, and final results of the Messiah's mediatorial sovereignty, would do well to read with care the Book of the Apocalypse, in which we see Him directing all the events of Providence, and prosperously carrying forward, amid all the revolutions of empires, the great ends of His high and holy government.

The bearing of this quotation on the Apostle's argument is so direct and obvious as scarcely to require to be pointed out. 'Jesus is made very much higher than the angels. His place is on the throne—theirs is before it; He is the King—they are servants, and His servants.' Nay, more than this, they are the servants of those for whom He lived and died, suffered and reigns, to save and bless. For "are they not all ministering spirits, sent forth to minister to them who shall be heirs of salvation?"

This text wears an interrogative form; but it is just equivalent to a strong affirmation. 'It is certain no angel sits on the throne of God; it is certain that they are all *ministering* spirits, sent forth to minister to them who are the heirs of salvation.' A minister is a servant—a person who occupies an inferior place, who acts a subordinate part, subject to the authority and regulated by the will of another. The angels are "*ministering* spirits;" they are not *governing* spirits. *Service*, not *dominion*, is their province. Some have supposed the idea intended to be conveyed by " ministering spirits," to be just the same as that suggested by the phrase, " ministering to the heirs of salvation." They consider the latter of these phrases as merely the expansion and interpretation of the former. We rather think that in the first phrase there is an expression of their being God's ministers or servants; in the second, that He *sends forth*, commissions, these servants of His, to minister to them who shall be heirs of salvation. They are His servants, and He uses their instrumentality for promoting the happiness of His peculiar people. There is a double contrast. The Son is the co-ruler—they are servants; the Son sits—they are sent forth.

"Salvation" is a word which is expressive of deliverance in general from danger and suffering; and its meaning in any particular case must be learned from attending to the particular dangers and miseries of the individuals who are represented as saved. In the place before us, and generally in the New Testament, it refers to that deliverance from guilt, and depravity, and misery, and that corresponding state of enjoyment of the divine favour, conformity to the divine image, and everlasting happiness, which has been obtained for mankind through the mediation of Jesus Christ, and in which men obtain a personal interest through the faith of the truth.

To be "an heir of salvation," or to inherit salvation, is to be *saved*. At the same time, I am disposed to think that there are two very important collateral ideas suggested by the phrase, "*heirs* of salvation," as applied to Christians, which would not have been suggested by the simpler phrase, 'saved.' It seems to me to mark at once the gratuitousness of the salvation, and the secure tenure by which they hold it. The salvation is freely bestowed and securely possessed.

The angels are employed by God—" sent forth" by Him—to minister to the saved, to promote their improvement and add to their enjoyment, till they obtain the full possession of their inheritance, " even the salvation that is in Christ, with eternal glory."[1]

## § 2.—*Practical Inference and Exhortation.*

CHAP. ii. 1-4.—Therefore we ought to give the more earnest heed to the things which we have heard, lest at any time we should let them slip. For if the word spoken by angels was stedfast, and every transgression and disobedience received a just recompense of reward; how shall we escape, if we neglect so great salvation; which at the first began to be spoken by the Lord, and was confirmed unto us by them that heard Him; God also bearing them witness, both with signs and wonders, and with divers miracles, and gifts of the Holy Ghost, according to His own will?

The paragraph is plainly parenthetical. It is introduced in the midst of the discussion of the superiority of Jesus Christ to

[1] See Note B.

the angels, which is resumed at the 5th verse. It is obviously an inference from what has been already stated. *Therefore* is equivalent to, 'Since Jesus Christ is as much better than the angels, as He hath received by inheritance a more excellent name than they—since He is both essentially and officially inconceivably superior to these heavenly messengers, His message has paramount claims on our attention, belief, and obedience.' "We ought to give the more earnest heed to the things which we have heard."

" The things which we have heard" is plainly an elliptical expression for the things we have heard of Him who is the Son, equivalent to 'the things spoken by the Lord'—the principles of the Christian religion—the profession of our faith. ' Now,' says the Apostle, ' we ought to give earnest heed to those things,[1]— we ought to give the more earnest heed.'[2] He uses the pronoun of the first person, per κοίνωσιν, rather than of the second—*we* instead of *ye*—to show those to whom he was writing that the obligation he pressed on them was felt and acknowledged by himself.

To "give heed," is to apply the mind to a particular subject, to attend to it, to consider it. It is here opposed to "neglecting the great salvation." No person can read the Scriptures without observing the stress that is laid on *consideration*, and the criminality and hazards which are represented as connected with inconsideration. Nor is this at all wonderful, when we reflect that the Gospel is a moral remedy for our moral disease. It is by being believed that it becomes efficacious. It cannot be believed unless it is understood; it cannot be understood unless it is attended to. Truth must be kept before the mind in order to its producing its appropriate effect; and how can it be kept before the mind, but by our giving heed to it?

On subjects of this kind it is not enough to rest on general precepts. Many persons are so unaccustomed to mental discipline, that when called on to take heed to—to consider a

---

[1] Προσέχειν. The expression is elliptical; the full phrase is προσέχειν τὸν νοῦν, Xen. Mem. iv. 7, 2, and is opposed to παρακούειν.

[2] Περισσοτέρως has been connected with προσέχειν. In that case the sense is, 'We ought to attend more closely than we have hitherto done.' From the collocation of the words, it would seem better to connect it with δεῖ: ' We are more bound to attend, than if these things had not been so.'

subject, they do not know very well how to set about it. It is therefore of importance to be somewhat more particular in our directions—to show men how they are to " take heed to the things which are spoken."

The revelation made by Jesus Christ consists of doctrines and precepts. In order to take heed to one of the doctrines of Christ,—for example, the doctrine of the atonement,—the first thing is to endeavour to obtain distinct ideas of this doctrine, as stated by Christ—to apprehend clearly the meaning of the declarations in the Christian revelation on this subject. We cannot properly give heed to anything, till we have distinctly ascertained what it is. This is the radical part of the duty of consideration; and if we go wrong here, we are giving heed, not to the things which we have heard of Christ, but, it may be, to the things we have heard of men only, or to the unauthorized suggestions of our own mind. Distinct apprehensions of the meaning of Christian truth, are plainly, then, of primary importance.

Having ascertained the meaning of a doctrine, we should "take heed" to its evidence, satisfying ourselves as to the divine origin of the statement which contains it. This is obviously necessary, as its claim on our faith depends on this, and as it is only as believed that the doctrine will be effectual for the purposes it is intended to serve.

Having ascertained the meaning and evidence of a doctrine, we ought to " give heed" to its importance—view it in its various relations to the perfections of the divine character, the principles of the divine government, the constitution and circumstances, the duties and interests, of mankind.

And then as to the duties enjoined in the Christian revelation—to " give heed" to them, is first to attend to the terms in which the injunction is given, that we may clearly understand what is required of us, and then to attend to the motives which urge us to comply with the requisition, especially those which rise out of the character of God, and our relation to Him, as in Christ reconciling the world to Himself. Such is the duty recommended by the Apostle, and such the manner in which we ought to discharge it.

But we ought not only to give heed to the things which we have heard of the Lord, but we ought to " give the more earnest heed." The qualifying words, "more earnest," convey one of two ideas closely connected,—that Jesus Christ has a stronger claim on our attention than any angel or divine messenger; or, that the consideration of the essential and official glories of Jesus Christ, which are altogether unrivalled, should lead us to give a greater degree of attention to the statements He makes, than we would have been disposed to yield in other circumstances. The general idea is, that the personal and mediatorial excellences of Christ suggest strong additional motives to a diligent study of the revelation He has made. 'We ought; it is reasonable and right, seeing He is so much better than the angels, that we give the closest attention our minds are capable of to a revelation coming from so high a source, and through so dignified a medium.'

The Apostle adds, "lest at any time we let them slip." The meaning of these English words is plain enough—' lest at any time we forget them, so as not to be influenced by them, or lest at any time we be induced to give them up—to apostatize.' The original term is a figurative one, and the figure is a different one from that expressed in the translation. The figure in the translation is that of a person letting go his hold of something; the figure in the original is borrowed from water. The words may be rendered, either, ' lest we should run out, like a leaky vessel,'—or, ' lest we flow by, as a vessel borne by the violence of the stream or tide past the harbour into which it was the purpose of the mariner to steer her.' The use of the language admits of either mode of interpretation.

In the first case, the meaning is substantially the same as in our translation. 'If we do not take heed to the things which we have heard, they will gradually, as it were, vanish out of our minds, as water out of a leaky vessel, and their purpose will be entirely lost, so far as refers to us.'[1]

In the second case, the meaning is equivalent to, ' lest we come short of the rest of God—a promise in reference to entering into which has been given us—by a turning back unto perdition.' I am disposed to prefer this mode of interpretation, both because it gives greater energy to the Apostle's exhortation, and because this is the idea which he immediately proceeds to ex-

---

[1] In support of this view, the Sept. Vers. of Prov. iii. 21 is appealed to. Υἱέ, μὴ παραῤῥυῇς, τήρησον δὲ ἐμὴν βουλὴν καὶ ἔννοιαν.

pand and illustrate,—the fearful consequences of not taking heed to the things which have been spoken of the Lord.[1]

There is something very instructive in this figurative representation. The Christian is embarked in his little vessel on the stream of life, and he is bound to the New Jerusalem. The winds of temptation, the tides of corrupt custom, and the powerful under-current of depraved inclination, all present such obstacles in the way of his reaching the desired haven, that he is in great apparent hazard of being carried past the celestial city, and of making shipwreck on the shores of the land of Destruction. He is in reality quite safe—he safely depends on the power and faithfulness of his Lord and King, whose will all the elements obey; but that power and faithfulness are manifested according to fixed laws, and this is one of them, that the Christian mariner constantly attend—"give earnest heed," to the instructions he has received. Christians are "kept by the mighty power of God," but it is "through faith." They are "saved by the Gospel which is preached to them;" but they must "keep it in memory." They "shall never fall;" but it is in "doing these things." They shall be made "partakers of Christ," but they must "hold fast the beginning of their confidence stedfast unto the end." If any man who seemed to others, or seemed to himself, a believer, do not "give heed to the things which are spoken,"—if the truth, in its meaning, its evidence, and its importance, is not kept before his mind, he will most assuredly come short of the celestial blessedness; he will be floated past the harbour of rest, and destruction in its most fearful form will ultimately overtake him.

The idea of the absolute certainty and the inconceivable severity of the punishment of the neglecter of the Christian revelation, who does not "give earnest heed," arising out of the dignity of the person who is the Author of that revelation, is very strikingly brought out in the following verses, by contrasting the Christian revelation with the Old Testament, and especially the Mosaic revelation. Ver. 2. "For if the word spoken by angels was stedfast, and every transgression and dis-

---

[1] In the other mode of interpretation, if not tautological, the words are spiritless,—'We must remember, lest we forget.' This does not accord with the nervous, pointed style of the Epistle. Besides, παραρρυῶμεν does not seem opposed to προσέχειν, but is intended to express the consequence τοῦ μὴ προσέχειν.

obedience received a just recompense of reward; 3. How shall we escape, if we neglect so great salvation; which at the first began to be spoken by the Lord, and was confirmed unto us by them that heard Him; 4. God also bearing them witness, both with signs and wonders, and with divers miracles, and gifts of the Holy Ghost, according to His own will?"

By "the word spoken by angels," some understand whatever revelation God made through the medium of angels under the former economy. Others suppose that there is a peculiar reference to the Mosaic law, which was "ordained by angels," as Paul phrases it, or as Stephen expresses it, given "by the disposition of angels." This last mode of interpretation corresponds best with the context, and the whole design of the Epistle. In this case, there is a beautiful contrast between the *word*—"the letter that killeth," the ministration of condemnation and death—and the *salvation*, the revelation of mercy, the ministration of justification and life, and between the signs and wonders by which both these divine dispensations were confirmed.

The only difficulty seems to arise out of the express declaration made by the sacred historian, that Jehovah spake all the words of the law. But the difficulty is more apparent than real. What lies at the foundation of the Apostle's whole argument is, *God* spake both the law and the Gospel. Both the one and the other are of divine origin. It is not the origin, but the *medium* of the two revelations, which he contrasts. 'He made known His will by the ministry of angels in the giving of the law; He makes known His will by the ministry of His Son in the revelation of mercy.'

It seems probable from these words that the audible voice in which the revelation from Mount Sinai was made, was produced by angelic agency. In using the word *angels*, the sacred writer obviously refers to its meaning, *messengers;* and the force of the contrast is, ' If the word spoken by *messengers* was stedfast, how much more the word spoken by the Lord of these messengers?' That "word," or revelation, "spoken"—made known —"by" the instrumentality of "angels was *stedfast*." It was confirmed and ratified—the divine dispensations were regulated according to it. "*And*[1] every transgression and disobedience re-

[1] καί is here exegetical: This is the meaning of the law being *stedfast*. It was not a dead letter—it was "quick and powerful."

ceived a just recompense of reward." The two words here are nearly synonymous. "Transgression" points out the violation of the law under the figure of stepping over the bounds prescribed by the law—our doing what it forbids; "disobedience" expresses that violation of the law which consists in a refusal to listen to its requisitions, so as to obey them. Every violation of that law "received a just recompense of reward,"—was punished according to its demerit. The sanction of the law ran thus: "The soul that sinneth, it shall die." "Cursed is every one who continueth not in all things written in the book of the law, to do them." All sins were not indeed actually punished with death under the law, but the offering of expiatory sacrifice went on the principle that they deserved death.

Some very good interpreters suppose that there is a reference here only to those more flagrant violations of the Mosaic law for which there was no expiatory sacrifice; but we rather think the inspired writer's idea is, 'Under the law, transgressions received an adequate punishment: the same general principle holds under all dispensations; and adequate punishment of the neglecters of the Gospel must be severer punishment than adequate punishment of the violators of the law.'

Let us now turn our attention to the other elements of the Apostle's argument. "The great salvation spoken by the Lord was confirmed by those who heard Him; and testified to by God by divers signs, and wonders, and gifts of the Holy Ghost, according to His will."[1]

"Salvation" signifies deliverance from danger and suffering generally; and is usually in the New Testament employed as a general name for that deliverance from the dangers and

---

[1] This verse, obviously, should not have been disjoined from what precedes it. It is a very just remark of VALCKNAER—"It is a somewhat perverse practice to cut up the New Testament epistles, Paul's especially, into the tiny fragments which we call verses. For the latter are too often regarded as so many separate aphorisms, having no connection with what goes before or what comes after them. This epistle, or address, to the Hebrews has in several places been wrongly divided up in this way. A case in point is ch. iii. 15–19, which should stand at the beginning of the following chapter. This practice was not known to any Christian till the time when so-called Concordances began to be compiled, so that every single line of the text could be precisely identified. It was then that our holy books were cut up into verses by the hurried labours (sandwiched between his travels) of Robert Stephanus."

miseries which rise out of a state of guilt and depravity, which has been effected through the mediation of Jesus Christ for all who believe. In the passage before us, the word has usually been explained by the best interpreters as a designation of the Gospel revelation. The grounds on which they go in thus interpreting the term are the following:—There is an antithesis between the "word spoken by angels" and the "salvation spoken by the Lord." You may contrast the deliverance by Moses with the deliverance by Christ, and the revelation by angels with the revelation by Christ; but there is no proper contrast between a word, or revelation, and a deliverance. This salvation is said to be "spoken," "confirmed," "testified to,"—all which modes of expression seem better to agree with the idea of a statement about salvation, than with that of salvation or deliverance itself. Besides, they remark that it is not uncommon to give to a statement or document the name of its subject. Thus the piece of paper or parchment containing an authenticated statement of the king's having pardoned a criminal, is termed *his pardon*. And they further remark, that there is a peculiar propriety in giving the name "salvation" to the Gospel, not merely because it is substantially an account of the deliverance through Christ—a statement of what it consists in, how it was effected, and how the individual sinner may be interested in its blessing,—but also as it is the grand means which the Holy Spirit employs for putting men in possession of these blessings. It is through means of the Gospel, understood and believed, that men are justified, and sanctified, and comforted —that they are saved from ignorance and delusion, and guilt, and depravity, and misery—that they are made wise, and good, and happy.

These statements are replete with important truth; but they do not convince me that *salvation* is here a designation of the Gospel. In some passages of the New Testament there can be no doubt that the term "salvation" signifies the Saviour.[1] But I have not discovered one where it certainly signifies the Gospel. The appellation, "great"—"so great," is obviously one more applicable to the Christian salvation than to the Gospel revelation. I have no doubt that the Apostle here uses the word "salvation" in its ordinary signification; and if we look

[1] Acts xiii. 47.

carefully at the passage, we will find the antithesis sufficiently preserved, and a perfect propriety in the use of the terms, "confirmed," and "testified to." It is the "salvation" as spoken of, or revealed by, the Lord,—*i.e.*, in other words, the revelation of the salvation, which he contrasts with "the word spoken by angels;" and it is this revelation which was "confirmed by them who heard" the Lord, and "testified to" by such a variety of divine wonders. The peculiar phraseology of this passage is greatly illustrated by a passage in the Epistle to Titus: "For the grace of God that bringeth salvation hath appeared to all men."[1] "The grace of God" has here usually been interpreted of the Gospel. But it has its ordinary signification—' the free favour of God,—which free favour extending salvation to men of every kindred and character, has been manifested;' and this manifestation of the free favour of God, which is the Gospel, "teaches men."[2]

The salvation here, then, is the deliverance of man through the mediation of Jesus Christ. This salvation is spoken of by the Apostle as unspeakably great: not merely a great salvation, nor even *the* great salvation, but "so great salvation"—an expression peculiarly fitted to express his high estimate of its importance. And who that knows anything about that deliverance can wonder at the Apostle using such language?

What are the evils from which it saves us? The displeasure of God, with all its fearful consequences in time and eternity; and "who knows the power of His anger?" We must measure the extent of infinite power, we must fathom the depths of infinite wisdom, before we can resolve the fearful question. We can only say, "According to Thy fear, so is Thy wrath." The most frightful conception comes infinitely short of the more dreadful reality. A depravity of nature ever increasing, and

---

[1] Titus ii. 11.

[2] Michaelis takes this view of the subject: "$\Sigma\omega\tau\eta\rho\iota\alpha$ does not mean the gospel itself (that would be a very harsh and unusual mode of speech), but that which the gospel teaches and preaches. The Hebrews were neglecting this by abandoning and deserting the gospel. But the words in which Paul depicts the heinousness of this sin of leaving Christ's camp are extremely powerful. What an enormity it is to despise (1) not inflexible rules, as the laws of Moses were, but the offer to us of *salvation*, (2) and that not a trifling, but a *great* salvation, (3) and one that had been preached, not by angels, but by *the Lord himself*, (4) and had been confirmed by so many *miracles* from God!"

miseries varied according to our varied capacities of suffering —limited in their intensity only by our powers of endurance, which an Almighty enemy can enlarge indefinitely, and protracted throughout the whole eternity of our being,—these are the evils from which this salvation delivers.

And what are the blessings to which it raises? A full, a free, an everlasting remission of all our sins—the enjoyment of the paternal favour of the infinitely powerful, and wise, and benignant Jehovah—the transformation of our moral natures—a tranquil conscience—a good hope while here, and in due time perfect purity and perfect happiness for ever, in the eternal enjoyment of God.

And how were these evils averted from us?—how were these blessings obtained for us? By the incarnation, obedience, suffering, and death of the only-begotten of God, as a sin-offering in our room. And how are we individually interested in this salvation? Through the operation of the Holy Spirit, in which He manifests a power not inferior to that by which the Saviour was raised from the dead, or the world was created. Surely such a deliverance well merits the appellation, a "great salvation."

This salvation "began to be spoken by the Lord,"[1]—*i.e.*, 'it was first plainly revealed by the Lord.' We know that this salvation was the leading subject of all former revelations; but these were comparatively obscure and indistinct. "Of which salvation the prophets have inquired and searched diligently, who prophesied of the grace that should come unto you: searching what, or what manner of time, the Spirit of Christ which was in them did signify, when it testified beforehand the sufferings of Christ, and the glory that should follow. Unto whom it was revealed, that not unto themselves, but unto us, they did minister the things which are now reported unto you by them that have preached the Gospel unto you with the Holy Ghost sent down from heaven; which things the angels desire to look into."[2] Do I need to recall to your mind the words of our Lord Jesus respecting this " so great salvation?" I trust you remember, and will never forget them: —" As Moses lifted up the serpent in the wilderness, even

---

[1] ἀρχὴν λαβοῦσα λαλεῖσθαι is = ἐν ἀρχῇ λαληθεῖσα.
[2] 1 Pet. i. 10–12.

so must the Son of man be lifted up; that whosoever believeth in Him should not perish, but have eternal life. For God so loved the world, that He gave His only begotten Son, that whosoever believeth in Him should not perish, but have everlasting life. For God sent not His Son into the world to condemn the world; but that the world through Him might be saved." "I am the living bread which came down from heaven. If any man eat of this bread, he shall live for ever: and the bread that I will give is My flesh, which I will give for the life of the world. The Jews therefore strove among themselves, saying, How can this man give us His flesh to eat? Then Jesus said unto them, Verily, verily, I say unto you, Except ye eat the flesh of the Son of man, and drink His blood, ye have no life in you. Whoso eateth My flesh, and drinketh My blood, hath eternal life; and I will raise him up at the last day. For My flesh is meat indeed, and My blood is drink indeed." "If any man thirst, let him come unto Me and drink."[1]

The appellation here given to Jesus Christ, "the Lord," is emphatic. It is contrasted with the messengers, "the angels." 'The Mosaic revelation was spoken by messengers; but the revelation of the great salvation is made by *the Lord*,'—the Lord of angels and of men—'the Lord of all—King of kings, and Lord of lords.'

What the Lord spoke concerning this great salvation, "was confirmed," says the inspired writer, "to us by them who heard Him." Some interpreters conceive that in the use of the pronoun of the first person here, they have evidence that Paul was not the author of the Epistle, as he obtained his knowledge of the Christian salvation, as he states to the Galatians, not from men, but by the revelation of Jesus Christ. I do not think there is much in this. He is speaking of himself in common with those to whom he was writing, few or none of whom probably had heard the Gospel from the lips of the Lord Himself; and though Paul did not obtain his knowledge of the Gospel from the other Apostles, he might justly say, it was confirmed to him by those who heard the Saviour.

The idea intended to be conveyed by these words is, 'Though we did not hear the Lord speak of the great salvation, we

---

[1] John iii. 14–17; vi. 51–55; vii. 37.

know both that He did speak about it, and what He said about it, from ear-witnesses;[1] we have the most satisfactory evidence—the attestation of credible witnesses in abundance—that these things were spoken by the Lord.' The number of these witnesses was more than sufficient to confirm any truth. They were all united in their testimony. They were plain, undesigning men, incapable of forming and executing any deep-laid complicated plan. Their veracity and integrity were unimpeachable. They had no worldly interest to serve by their testimony, but quite the reverse. They exposed themselves to, and many of them endured, sufferings, and even death, rather than conceal or clog their testimony. No shadow of counter evidence was ever brought forward by their opponents; though it is plain that they would eagerly have invalidated their testimony, had it been in their power.

Nor is this all. We have not only their testimony, we have the testimony of God to the truth of their declaration; for "God also hath borne witness, both by signs and wonders, and by divers miracles, and gifts of the Holy Ghost, according to His own will." There is here obviously a reference to the miracles performed by the Apostles and the other primitive teachers of Christianity. The Acts of the Apostles are the best illustration of this passage.[2]

It is not very easy to point out the precise meaning of the different terms here employed. It has been supposed, with much probability, that "signs and wonders" refer to such miraculous operations as were common to the Law and the Gospel. These are the terms usually employed in the Old Testament respecting the Mosaic miracles. They are the terms used by Stephen when referring to these miracles, Acts vii. 36. They likely refer here to the more terrific and awful displays of the divine power—such as the supernatural earthquake and

---

[1] The testimony referred to is that of those who heard Him, whom Luke i. 2, calls αὐτόπται καὶ ὑπηρέται τοῦ λόγου. Their testimony *confirmed* the fact that the Lord spoke, and that He spoke these things respecting the " great salvation," and confirmed it εἰς ἡμᾶς, *i.e.*, ἡμῖν. Some explain this as = 'in our minds.' Ernesti, Abresch, and Heinrichs seem in the right when they consider the phrase as a pregnant expression = ἦλθεν εἰς ἡμᾶς βεβαία. 'The Gospel was brought to us in such a form as that we could not doubt of its divine origin.'

[2] Acts xiv. 3.

darkness, similar to the wonders of Sinai, and the sudden death of Ananias and Sapphira, and the blindness of Elymas, similar to the fate of Korah, Dathan, and Abiram.

On the other hand, "divers miracles" serve to point out that species of miraculous operation which was peculiar to, and characteristic of, the Christian revelation. This is the word commonly employed for beneficent miracles.[1] The words seem equivalent to, 'God attesting not only by prodigious and fearful manifestations of His power, as in the case of the Law, but by various salutary miracles.'

"Gifts[2] of the Holy Ghost" refer plainly to the miraculous gifts of the Holy Spirit, referred to by the Apostle in 1 Cor. xii.[3] The words, "according to His own will," refer to God, not to the Holy Spirit—'God bearing witness according to His own will;' and may, in conformity with the usage of the language of Scripture, be interpreted either, 'according to His benignity, His good pleasure,' or, 'according to His sovereign will.' It does not matter much which of these modes of interpretation is adopted.[4]

These, then, are the Apostle's premises : 'There was a revelation made by angels. There has been a revelation made by the Lord respecting an inestimably important subject; and we have the fullest evidence that such a revelation has been made. The first revelation was ratified, and every transgression and disobedience received an adequate and appropriate punishment.' His conclusion is: 'It is still more evident that the second revelation must surely stand stedfast also, and that he who neglects or despises it must receive adequate and appropriate punishment; and if he does so, his punishment must be far

---

[1] Mark vi. 5 ; Acts viii. 6, 7, 13.

[2] μερισμοῖς—the gifts of the Spirit as *distributed* among Christians : 1 Cor. xii. 11.

[3] By these various methods God συνεπιμαρτυρεῖ. This is one of the ἅπαξ λεγόμενα. They go beyond who seek to translate both the prepositions, 'bearing witness over and above, and along with;' they fall short who translate the word just as if it were simply μαρτυρεῖ. 'God confirming their testimony,' seems the idea : God being co-witness, as Stuart has it.

[4] Probability, however, is given to the interpretation which refers αὐτοῦ to π. ἁ., instead of to Θ., by 1 Cor. xii. 11,—a passage which, supposing it to have been written before the Epistle to the Hebrews, which is probable, we can scarcely help thinking was in the writer's mind.

severer than that of the neglecter or despiser of the first revelation.' That conclusion is not formally drawn, but it is expressed with far more emphasis in that most striking interrogation, "How shall we escape if we neglect so great salvation?"

The language is elliptical. The full expression is, 'How, if we neglect so great salvation, shall we escape a just recompense of reward?' and it is plain that the question is equivalent to a very strong negative: 'It is impossible that we should escape.'

'To neglect the great salvation spoken to us,' is materially the same thing as 'not to take heed to the things heard of the Lord.' It is to remain inattentive, ignorant, and unbelieving. It seems here to refer particularly to persons who have made a profession of Christianity making shipwreck of faith, silently abandoning or openly renouncing their profession.

It is impossible for such persons to "escape." That it is so must be plain; for the "great salvation" is the only salvation, and taking heed to what the Lord has spoken is the only way in which we can enjoy it. To neglect the great salvation is a peculiarly aggravated sin, and therefore, under the administration of a just and holy God, must expose to peculiarly severe punishment. The declarations of Scripture on the impossibility of the neglecters of the great salvation escaping, are most explicit. "The Lord Jesus shall be revealed from heaven in flaming fire, taking vengeance on them that know not God, and that obey not the Gospel of our Lord Jesus Christ: who shall be punished with everlasting destruction from the presence of the Lord, and from the glory of His power." "He that despised Moses' law died without mercy under two or three witnesses: Of how much sorer punishment, suppose ye, shall he be thought worthy, who hath trodden under foot the Son of God, and hath counted the blood of the covenant, wherewith he was sanctified, an unholy thing, and hath done despite unto the Spirit of grace? For we know Him that hath said, Vengeance belongeth unto Me, I will recompense, saith the Lord. And again, The Lord shall judge His people. It is a fearful thing to fall into the hands of the living God."[1]

[1] 2 Thess. i. 8, 9 ; Heb. x. 28-31.

## § 3.—*An Objection met and answered.*

CHAP. ii. 5-18.—For unto the angels hath He not put in subjection the world to come, whereof we speak. But one in a certain place testified, saying, What is man, that Thou art mindful of him? or the son of man, that Thou visitest him? Thou madest him a little lower than the angels; Thou crownedst him with glory and honour, and didst set him over the works of Thy hands: Thou hast put all things in subjection under his feet. For in that He put all in subjection under him, He left nothing that is not put under him. But now we see not yet all things put under him: but we see Jesus, who was made a little lower than the angels for the suffering of death, crowned with glory and honour; that He by the grace of God should taste death for every man. For it became Him, for whom are all things, and by whom are all things, in bringing many sons unto glory, to make the Captain of their salvation perfect through sufferings. For both He that sanctifieth and they who are sanctified are all of one: for which cause He is not ashamed to call them brethren, saying, I will declare Thy name unto My brethren; in the midst of the Church will I sing praise unto Thee. And again, I will put My trust in Him. And again, Behold I and the children which God hath given Me. Forasmuch then as the children are partakers of flesh and blood, He also Himself likewise took part of the same; that through death He might destroy him that had the power of death, that is, the devil; and deliver them who through fear of death were all their lifetime subject to bondage. For verily He took not on Him the nature of angels; but He took on Him the seed of Abraham. Wherefore in all things it behoved Him to be made like unto His brethren, that He might be a merciful and faithful high priest in things pertaining to God, to make reconciliation for the sins of the people. For in that He Himself hath suffered, being tempted, He is able to succour them that are tempted.

This paragraph is certainly one of the most difficult of interpretation in the whole inspired volume. A considerable portion of that difficulty originates in the uncertainty as to the precise object which the Apostle had in view in writing it. Nothing is of greater importance to the right understanding of an author's particular statements, arguments, and illustrations, than a clear apprehension of the general object he has in view. Without this, the most accurate statements may seem incorrect, the most apposite illustrations irrelevant, and the most cogent arguments inconclusive.

Our first attention, then, must be directed to this question, —What is the design of the Apostle in the paragraph which we have quoted, and which we must now attempt to explain? There are two views which may be taken of this subject, neither of which is without plausibility, and neither of which is completely free of difficulty. The paragraph may be considered, either as the prosecution of the argument for the superiority of Jesus Christ to the angels—interrupted by that beautiful and impressive practical inference which formed the subject of the last section—and as containing evidence that the Son has indeed been " made much better than the angels;" or, it may be considered as an answer to an objection, which might not unnaturally rise in the mind of the reader, to this doctrine of the superiority of Jesus Christ to the angels, from the consideration of His being a man—a mortal man—" a man of sorrows and acquainted with grief "—a man who actually died, and died in circumstances of peculiar agony and ignominy.

In the first case, the Apostle must be considered as asserting, in corroboration of his statement that Jesus Christ is " made much better than the angels," that *the world to come,*—whatever may be the meaning of that term,—is not subjected to them, but to Him: in which case the quotation from the 8th Psalm must be viewed as brought forward in proof of this; and the argument in the 8th and 9th verses, as intended to show that that quotation cannot with propriety be applied to any but to Him. This plan of interpretation, though recommended by its apparent simplicity, appears to me to labour under insurmountable difficulties. The Apostle is reasoning with the Jews on their own principles. The outline of his whole argument is this: ' You acknowledge Jesus to be the Messiah: all, then, that the prophets say of the Messiah must be true of Him. The prophets represent the Messiah as superior to angels ; therefore Jesus is superior to the angels.' Now, we have no reason to think the Jews understood the 8th Psalm as a direct prediction of the Messiah; and if they did not, the argument could have no force to them. Indeed, no person, on reading the 8th Psalm carefully, could easily persuade himself that it is such a direct prediction ; a plain proof of which is to be found in the very various methods in which Christian interpreters have endeavoured to show how this Psalm refers to the Messiah, after the Apostle has in this passage distinctly enough asserted that it has some kind of a reference to Him. Were the Messiah the direct subject of the Psalm, He would not have been indefinitely styled *man,* but *the man,* or *this man.* There is plainly a contrast stated between the subject of the Psalm and Jesus Christ in the 8th and 9th verses: "We see not yet all things put under *him*; but we see *Jesus*." The argument which this mode of interpretation puts into the Apostle's mouth is obviously a sophism, in which that is taken for granted which is at the same time proposed to be proved. The argument, as they state it, is this: 'Jesus is superior to the angels, as the world to come is subjected to Him, and not to them; and the proof of this is to be found in the 8th Psalm, where all things are said to be put under the feet of man and the son of man. And the proof that this refers to Jesus is to be found in the fact, that what is here said is not true of any other man, but is true of Him; for He is crowned with glory and honour.' I cannot believe that so acute a person as the author of this Epistle, putting his inspiration out of the question altogether, could have imposed on himself by such an argument; and I can still less believe that he, knowing it to be an inconclusive argument, would have employed it to impose on others. Besides, this plan of interpretation guides us only a certain length in the explication of the passage, down to the middle of the 9th verse, where, though there is no intimation of any such thing in the construction of the passage, a new train of thought must be considered as commencing. Indeed, this alone, I apprehend, would be fatal to this plan of exposition, as there can scarcely be a doubt that, from the 5th verse down to the close of the chapter, there is but one subject of discussion, whatever that may be.

In the second method of interpretation, this paragraph is considered, not as the continuation of the proof that Jesus Christ is "made as much better than the angels, as He hath obtained by inheritance a more excellent name than they," but as an illustration of the perfect harmony, and indeed close connection, of this fact with the apparently incongruous fact of His being a man, a mortal man, a man who died, and who died in circumstances of peculiar agony and ignominy. The train of thought, according to this scheme of interpretation, is the following: 'That Jesus Christ, a man, 'a suffering man, should be placed at the head of the divine administration in the new economy, is not wonderful; for God has subjected that economy, not to angels, but to men. The design of that economy is to raise men to the highest place among the creatures of God; and this design is accomplished by His becoming a man, and submitting to suffering and death, and thus obtaining both for Himself and His people that state of transcendent dignity and honour which an ancient prophet predicted would be possessed by men in the world to come.' That this mode of interpretation is free of difficulties, I am by no means prepared to say, but it does not appear to me encumbered with either so many or so great difficulties as the other system already adverted to; and it has this great advantage, that it gives connection and unity to the whole paragraph. We will, however, be better able to judge both of its advantages and disadvantages after attempting to apply it to the various parts of the paragraph as they lie before us.[1]

Ver. 5. "For unto the angels hath He not put in subjection the world to come, whereof we speak." It is not very easy to fix the connection of these words, indicated by the particle

---

[1] The following sentences are quoted from EBRARD:—"That not merely the Son as the eternal only begotten of the Father, or the first-born ($\pi\rho\omega\tau\acute{o}\tau o\kappa o\varsigma$) of every creature, is higher than the angels, but that *man also as such* is called (of course in Christ) to a much more immediate union with God than belongs to angels, and that therefore man, as regards his proper destination, is higher than the angels,—is a statement which at first sight will appear surprising, as we are generally wont to regard the angels as *superior* beings. And, indeed, it is not without reason that we do so. For, according to the statements of the Holy Scripture, the angels are endowed with higher and less limited gifts and powers; and although as creatures they cannot be conceived of as unlimited by space, and consequently as incorporeal, still they have an unspeakably freer and less circumscribed relation to space and to matter than men have in their present state. They clothe themselves with visible matter and put off this garment again; they transfer themselves to wheresoever they please; they are not bound to a body of clay; and as they are without sexual distinction (Matt. xxii. 30), there exists among them neither any development of the individual from childhood through the various steps of age, nor of the race, through successive generations. The entire species has come from the creative hand of God *complete* in all its individuals, complete as the diamond which sparkles with perpetual and unchanging lustre.—How now shall we reconcile it with this, that our author should place above the angels poor weak *man*, hemmed in by space and a gross body, developing himself upon the basis of animal sexuality? Just in the same way as we can reconcile it with the weakness and meanness of the rose-bush, that there is in it, notwithstanding, a more excellent life than in the diamond. The enamel of the rose, when it has reached its bloom, is something far superior to the glitter of the diamond. So also will man, when he reaches the bloom of his *glorified* life, unspeak-

translated "for."[1] Some would connect them with the words immediately preceding, after this manner,—'It appears, then, that our religion has been confirmed by the most splendid manifestations of the divine approbation, though not by such angelic ministration as the Mosaic economy; which, indeed, would not have been appropriate, as God has not subjected the new economy, as He did the old, to the rule of angels.' Others, as Kuinœl, connect them thus: 'How can we escape, if we neglect this great salvation, which the Lord, far superior to the angels, has taught? for not to the angels, but to the Lord, has God subjected the world to come.' Others would connect them with the last verse of the first chapter, considering the first four verses of this chapter as parenthetical: 'Are not the angels all ministering spirits, sent forth to minister to them who shall be heirs of salvation? For God has not, under the new economy, appointed them to rule, but to serve. Their place is a subordinate place. *Man* occupies the first place under this order of things.' I am rather disposed to consider the last as the preferable mode of stating the connection.

"The world to come" is a Jewish phrase for the state of things

ably excel the angels in glory. Man's superiority lies just in his *capability of development*. When the diamond is once disturbed by the ray of a burning reflector it is irrecoverably gone; so are the angels, once fallen, for ever lost, according to the doctrine of Scripture. The rose can with difficulty be hurt, and even from its root it will still send forth new life; so was man rendered capable even by sin (the possibility of which, though not its actual entrance, was necessary in consequence of his freedom) of entering into full spiritual life-fellowship with God, through the help of the Saviour entering into him, nay, capable of receiving the person of the redeeming Son of God as a member into his race. Hence also it is the planet-system that has been assigned to man as the habitation and the theatre of that absolute revelation of God in Christ,—the planet-system, in which the antithesis between the fixed-star-like, or angel-like, independent *sun* and the animal-like dependent *moon* finds its genuine human reconcilement in the *planets*, and most completely in the *earth*; while the angels, as the 'hosts of heaven,' have their dwelling-place in the fixed stars, where there is no opposition between illuminating and illuminated bodies, where planets do not revolve round suns, but fixed stars around fixed stars."

[1] Γάρ. The importance of rightly apprehending the meaning of the particles can scarcely be over-estimated. As VALCKNAER remarks, "They are, so to speak, the nerves and sinews which are essential to the making up of the body of a language." Macknight's loose interpretation of the particles is one of the worst features of his exegesis.

under the Messiah: it seems nearly equivalent to, " the kingdom of heaven"—" the kingdom of God"—" the kingdom of Christ." All these are terms of very extensive meaning, embracing the whole divine administration in its bearing on the salvation of man. The Apostle fixes its meaning by adding, " of which we speak," or, 'concerning which we are discoursing.' Now, it is plain that the whole of the Apostle's discussions throughout the Epistle refer to the new order of things introduced by Jesus Christ. Some, by " the world to come," understand the new heavens and earth wherein righteousness is to dwell; others understand by it the celestial state. I apprehend it includes both, but it is not confined to either; it is, generally, the order of things introduced by the Messiah.[1]

"Now," says the Apostle, " He"—*i. e.* plainly God—" hath not put this world to come, this order of things, in subjection to the angels." I think many good interpreters have been led much out of their way, by supposing that there is here meant a very striking contrast between the world that had been—the order of things before Christ, and the world to come—the order of things under Christ. 'The former was,' say they, 'subjected to the angels, the latter is not;' and they have endeavoured, though I do not think by any means very satisfactorily, to show that under the Old Testament dispensation everything almost was done by angels, while under the New Testament they occupy a much humbler place. The words of the Apostle do not by any means necessarily imply that the Mosaic economy was subjected to angels; they only assert that the present—the Christian— is not.

But what are we to understand by this " world to come" not being subjected to angels? I apprehend the meaning is, they do not hold the first place in it. They are not the most important beings in this "world"—this order of things. They are not " the heirs of salvation;" they are but " the ministers to the heirs of

---

[1] ἡ οἰκονομία τῆς καινῆς διαθήκης. There is great probability in the suggestion of ABRESCH, a most accurately learned and acutely critical interpreter, that there is an allusion to the land of Canaan as enjoyed by the Israelites, which is called οἰκουμένη, Luke ii. 1; Acts xi. 28; and the peaceful enjoyment of which was a type of the New Testament state. We find the same allusion in the *Captain of salvation* leading the children of God into glory, plainly referring to Joshua leading Israel into the promised land.

salvation." In the restorative dispensation they hold but a subordinate place, they act but a subordinate part. The Lord of that world—the Chief of that order of things—should belong to the class of paramount importance in it.

But who are that class? To whom hath God subjected "the world to come?" Who occupy the principal station in it? To that question might be answered in plain words, Men—human beings. They are the "heirs of salvation." They hold the first place in the kingdom of the Messiah—in "the world to come." But the Apostle chooses rather to let his readers draw the inference from what an Old Testament writer says, than to make the statement directly himself. 'God hath not assigned to angels the first place in the world to come. Ver. 6. "But one in a certain place testified, saying, What is man, that Thou art mindful of him? or the son of man, that Thou visitest him? 7. Thou madest him a little lower than the angels; Thou crownedst him with glory and honour, and didst set him over the works of Thy hands: 8. Thou hast put all things in subjection under his feet."'

There is something peculiar in the manner in which this quotation is made. Neither the writer nor the book is mentioned. Both, however, were well known both to the writer and to those to whom he wrote; and perhaps this peculiar mode of quotation is employed to suggest the idea, that we ought to be so familiar with our Bibles as to be able to find out a quotation, though the particular place which it is taken from should not be specified.[1] We know that the certain person referred to is David, and the certain place the 8th Psalm. The words, which form the 5th, 6th, and 7th verses of the Psalm, are accurately

[1] This mode of quoting the ancient Scriptures is common in Philo: μαρτυρεῖ δέ που τῷ λόγῳ ὁ ἱερώτατος χρησμός. . . . Εἶπε γάρ τις. Lib. 3, leg. Alleg. p. 85 A, p. 4 E, CARPZOV. SCHOETGEN, in his Horæ Heb., shows that the Jewish writers were accustomed to the same formula of reference. ŒCUMENIUS states the reason of so indefinite a mode of citation: ὡς εἰδότας τὰς γραφὰς διαλεγόμενος, οὐ τίθησι τῶν λεγόντων τὰ ὀνόματα. THEODORET says, to the same effect, οὐ λέγει τὸ ὄνομα τοῦ εἰπόντος, ἅτε πρὸς ἐπιστήμονας τῶν γραφῶν διαλεγόμενος. We find a similar indefiniteness of reference in ch. iv. 4. The place of the citation is not specified, because it is taken for granted that it is well known; as, to use EBRARD'S illustration, "a writer or speaker of our time might refer to Luther's famous dictum—'One has said, Here I stand, I can do nothing else.'"

## AN OBJECTION MET AND ANSWERED. 91

quoted from the Septuagint Version, which justly gives the meaning of the Hebrew original.

From the manner in which the Apostle quotes this passage, it is plain he means to represent it as an account of the state of things in what he terms "the world to come;" and he brings it forward for the purpose of showing to whom that world is subjected, or who occupy the most distinguished place in it,—that they are not angels, but men. I have already stated to you that this is one of the passages from the Old Testament quoted and applied in the New Testament, in a way which it never could have entered into our minds to have done; yet I apprehend it is also one of those passages about which, as to their fitness for answering the purpose for which they are applied, we may obtain complete satisfaction.

On first reading the Psalm, we are apt to consider it as a humble, grateful acknowledgment of the goodness of God to man in assigning to him so high a place in the scale of created being. But if we examine it somewhat more closely, we will find considerable difficulty in explaining it on this principle. It certainly does not accurately describe the state of mankind generally in their fallen state; and it is equally plain that it cannot refer to Adam, for the word used to denote man is a word expressive of his state as fallen;[1] and his state of dignity is represented as succeeding a state of humiliation, for the word *made lower*[2] does not signify to be created originally in a lower condition, but it signifies to be brought down from a higher situation to a lower. The Psalm's being expressed, not in the Future, but in the Past time, will not be felt as an objection to its being considered as a prediction, this being quite common in the prophetic style. The most of the predictions, for example, in the 53d chapter of Isaiah are expressed in the Past time.

Let us now look a little more attentively at the Psalm, and particularly at the portion of it quoted here, in the light in which the words of the Apostle constrain us to view it, as a prophetic description of the place which man was to hold in "the world to come," under the order of things to be introduced by the Messiah. The sacred ode opens with an expression of de-

[1] אֱנוֹשׁ.

[2] חָסֵר, ἐλαττόω. 2 Sam. iii. 1: The house of Saul ἠσθένει, LXX.; ἠλαττοῦτο, Sym. The Syriac Version translates ἠλαττωμένον, *depressum.*

vout admiration of the infinite excellence and glories of Jehovah. The second verse is considerably obscure. The general idea seems to be—'By the most feeble means Thou accomplishest the most glorious purposes, and in this displayest Thy wisdom, to the confusion of Thine enemies.' It is alluded to by our Lord; and the songs of the children in the temple, hailing Him as the King of Zion, the Son of David, come in the name of the Lord to save men, are represented by Him as a verification of it, though this seems rather an accommodation than an explication of the ancient oracle, as appears from the mode of citing or referring to it, Matt. xxi. 16. It is one of those general predictions which had their fulfilment in innumerable particular events. The success of the preaching of the Gospel by the Apostles—and, indeed, its success in every instance when it is preached by men—may be considered as accomplishments of this prophecy. Or, perhaps, it may be considered as the argument of the ode in a condensed form:—'Man, human nature, degraded and expelled, is yet to be raised to a state of dignity and dominion by God, which shall illustriously display His glory, and cover with confusion His enemies, who in the degradation of the creature sought the dishonour of the Creator.'

The Psalmist then, after contemplating the magnitude and glory of God's works in the visible heavens, exclaims, "What is man, that Thou art mindful of him? or the son of man, that Thou visitest him?" These words admit of a twofold interpretation. They are either equivalent to, 'How dignified is man! God is mindful of him, God visits him;' or, 'How insignificant a being is man, that God should be mindful of him, that God should visit him!' The train of thought is either, 'The sun, moon, and stars are very glorious beings, but man is a still more dignified being—remembered, visited, blessed by his God;' or, 'What is man amid the magnificence of the creation, that God should bestow on him such favours?' It might not be easy to say which of these two modes of interpretation was to be preferred, were it not that we find the same words employed by the Psalmist in another place, where there can be no doubt as to their meaning; and it is not likely that the same words would be employed with two different, indeed opposite, significations. The passage I allude to is Ps. cxliv. 3 and 4. We therefore consider these words as expressive of this idea: 'It is amazing that, amid the number and magnificence of the divine works, man—human nature, degraded human nature—should be so honoured.'

"Thou madest"—or rather, " Thou hast made—him lower than the angels." These words are ordinarily understood as equivalent to, 'Thou didst create him in a state lower than the angels;' but this is, as we have seen, not the meaning either of the original word, or of the Greek word by which it is rendered. They signify, 'to bring down.' We cannot doubt that man, even in his best estate, was in some respects inferior to the angels; but in some points he was on a level with them. One of these was immortality; and it deserves consideration, that this is the very point referred to when it is said of the raised saints, the children of the resurrection, "They die not, being equal to the angels." We cannot help, then, thinking that "Thou madest him lower than the angels" is a part of the description, not of man's exaltation, but of his humiliation, and that it is noticed to exalt our ideas of the kindness of God to man. "Thou didst make him" mortal, and thus didst reduce him " below the angels" in a point in which he once was on a level with them.

The word *a little*, both in the Hebrew and Greek, is applied both to degree (2 Kings x. 18; Prov. x. 20, xv. 16; Heb. xiii. 22) and to time (Ps. xxxvii. 10; Hos. viii. 10; Luke xxii. 58). *A little* may either be a little space, or a short while. It is in the last of these senses I would understand it here. It is the sense which best suits the phrase as applied to Jesus Christ; and it were strange if it were used in two different senses in a continuous argument. We find the word employed in this way, Acts v. 34; 1 Pet. v. 10. 'Thou didst reduce him to a state of mortality and suffering, but that state is not to be perpetual,—in comparison of the eternity before him, it is but a little while.'

"Thou hast crowned him with glory and honour," etc. These words scarcely need particular explication. Their general meaning is obvious. 'Thou hast bestowed on man such honours as Thou hast bestowed on none of Thy creatures; Thou hast set him at the head of the created universe.'[1] The words have

---

[1] Many codd. of the highest character omit the words καὶ κατέστησας αὐτὸν ἐπὶ τὰ ἔργα τῶν χειρῶν σου. Mill and Wetstein consider them as spurious; Knapp and Vater put them within crotchets; and Griesbach,

certainly an allusion to the address of God to Adam after his creation, Gen. i. 28; but they are more comprehensive, and intimate the amazing and delightful truth, that man, debased man, is to be raised to an elevation far superior to that from which he has fallen.[1]

The greatness of that elevation, as expressed in these words, we would scarcely have dared to have conjectured, had not the Apostle distinctly stated it to us in his explanatory note, in the second clause of the 8th verse. Ver. 8. "For[2] in that He hath put all things under him, He hath left nothing that is not put under him."

From this passage it appears, that with the single exception of Him who is to put all things under him, *i.e.*, God, all things are to be put under man. In *the world to come*, the new order of things, even angels are subordinate to man. Man is next to God in that world. The meaning of the passage, then, viewed as a prediction of "the world to come," or the kingdom of God, is this,—'Man, though for a season reduced below the level of angels, is yet destined to occupy the highest place among the creatures of God.'

I know of only two objections that can with any show of reason be made against this interpretation, which the words plainly warrant, and which the reasoning of the Apostle seems absolutely to require. It may be said, 'This is a meaning which could not be present to the mind of the Psalmist when he wrote the Psalm.' And we readily admit this. We have no reason to think the Psalmist saw so far into the mystery of redemption as this would necessarily imply. But what then? Is not this just an exemplification of the statement of the Apostle Peter? "Of which salvation the prophets have inquired and searched diligently, who prophesied of the grace that should

---

Matthæi, and Schott, exclude them from the text. Πάντα ὑπέταξας, κ.τ.λ., is a mode of expression borrowed from the Oriental custom of putting the feet on the necks of the vanquished.

[1] It is a strange dream of the learned Œderus, "The sheep, oxen, beasts of the earth, fowls of the air, fish of the sea," are figurative descriptions of different classes of men to be subjected to the saints when they take the kingdom. Well may it be said, What absurdity is there which has not had the support of a learned man?

[2] The particle γάρ, perhaps compounded of γὶ and ἄρα, is not here a *causal*, but an *illative* particle. It is = ἄρα, igitur.

come unto you: searching what, or what manner of time, the Spirit of Christ which was in them did signify, when it testified beforehand the sufferings of Christ, and the glory that should follow. Unto whom it was revealed, that not unto themselves, but unto us, they did minister the things which are now reported unto you by them that have preached the Gospel unto you with the Holy Ghost sent down from heaven; which things the angels desire to look into."[1] It is quite possible, and highly probable, that the prophet knew that this was a prediction that man, who for a period was to be lower than the angels, was ultimately to be exalted to a state of the highest honour and dignity. Now, this is still the meaning, though we, from the fuller revelation respecting the Christian salvation, can see more of the particulars that are included in the general statement. It is no argument against an interpretation of a prophecy, that the prophet himself could not possibly understand it so; though, I apprehend, it would be a strong presumption against the interpretation, if it could be made out that the prophet must have understood by it something irreconcilable with the interpretation we put on it. But there is nothing of this kind in the passage before us.

The only other plausible objection to this mode of interpretation is, that it is not accordant with facts; for all men are not ultimately thus to be honoured and exalted. But the text does not say, 'all men;' it says, *man*. Had a prediction been uttered five hundred years ago that the Guelph family should have all Britain subjected to them, would not that prediction have been fulfilled in the elevation of George I. to the throne of Great Britain, and in so many of his descendants being the first class in these kingdoms, though many of that family never had rule or honour there? We speak of the salvation of *man*, though all men are not saved; and the prophecy is fulfilled in the exaltation of the redeemed from among men, and their reigning with their Lord and Prince in human nature for ever and ever.

> "Lord, what is man? Extremes how wide
> In his mysterious nature join!
> The flesh to worms and dust allied;
> The soul immortal and divine,—

[1] 1 Pet. i. 10–12.

"Divine at first—a holy flame,
  Kindled by the Almighty's breath;
Till, stain'd by sin, it soon became
  The seat of darkness, strife, and death.

"But Jesus—O amazing grace!—
  Assumed our nature as His own,
Obey'd and suffer'd in our place,
  Then took it with Him to His throne.

"Now what is man, when grace reveals
  The virtue of a Saviour's blood?
Again a life divine he feels,
  Despises earth, and walks with God.

"And what in yonder realms above
  Is ransom'd man ordain'd to be?
With honour, holiness, and love,
  No seraph more adorned than he.

"Nearest the throne, and first in song,
  Man shall his hallelujahs raise;
While wondering angels round him throng,
  And swell the chorus of his praise."

In that part of the Apostle's statement which now comes under review, he proceeds to show how the sufferings and consequent glory of Jesus Christ were the begun fulfilment, and how they will lead to the complete accomplishment, of that ancient oracle in which such glorious things had been said of man. Ver. 8. "But now we see not yet all things put under him: 9. But we see Jesus, who was made a little lower than the angels for the suffering of death, crowned with glory and honour; that He by the grace of God should taste death for every man."—By those interpreters who consider the first part of this paragraph as a continuation of the Apostle's proof of the superiority of Jesus Christ to the angels,—who view the passage quoted from the 8th Psalm as a direct prophecy of the Messiah, brought forward for the purpose of establishing the superiority of Jesus Christ to the angels by showing that "the world to come" is subjected to Him, and not to them, and who regard the words which immediately follow the quotation as intended to intimate that so unlimited a subjection of all creatures as is predicted in the Psalm could refer only to the Messiah,—the words, "Now we see not yet all things put under him," are considered as intended to convey this sentiment: 'We do not, indeed, yet see this prediction fully accomplished, but we see its begun accomplishment. All things are, indeed, already put under Him, inasmuch as He already is invested with full authority over them; but all things are not yet put under Him, inasmuch as there are many things which are not actually, fully, and finally subdued to Him. But notwithstanding this, in His being crowned with glory and honour, we have the commencement and the sure earnest of His ultimately subduing all things to Himself.'

I have stated at some length the reasons which prevent me from adopting this mode of interpretation, and which lead me to consider the quotation from the 8th Psalm as referring not directly to the Messiah, but to man. Of course I consider these words as referring to man,—" We see not yet all things put under man."[1]

The following appears to me the track of the Apostle's thoughts :—' In the world to come, in the new order of things, men, not angels, are to occupy the first place. An ancient oracle, which refers to the world to come, clearly proves this. The place to be occupied by man in that world is not only a high place, but it is the first place among creatures. The words of the oracle are unlimited. With the exception of Him who puts all things under man, everything is to be subjected to him. This oracle must be fulfilled. It obviously has not yet been fulfilled. In the exaltation of Christ, after and in consequence of His humiliation, we have the begun fulfilment of the prediction, and what, according to the wise and righteous counsels of Heaven, were the necessary, and will be the effectual, means of the complete accomplishment of it in reference to the whole body of the redeemed from among men.'

The stage at which we are arrived in our illustrations of this closely connected train of thought is,—The ancient oracle respecting all things being subjected to man in " the world to come" is not yet accomplished. " We see not yet," says the inspired writer—and after the lapse of nearly eighteen centuries, we may still say—" We see not yet all things put under *man*." Man may, in a limited sense, be said to be the lord of the lower

---

[1] There is no contrast between ὁρῶμεν and βλέπομεν, as if the first referred to physical, and the other to intellectual vision. Both are equivalent : ' We *know* that all things are not yet,' etc. ; ' but we also *know* that Jesus,' etc.

world; but it is plain his authority is but little acknowledged or regarded. The great material powers of nature are completely beyond his control. He "cannot lift up his voice to the clouds, that abundance of water may cover him." He "cannot send out the lightnings, that they may go; neither will they say to him, Here we are."[1] The great body of the brutal tribes are beyond his control, and not unfrequently with success employ their force against him. The uncivilised part of mankind are, instead of lords of the world, fugitives and vagabonds on the face of the earth; and even with regard to those who are in the highest state of civilisation, how far are they from having all things put under them!

Even those who through faith in Christ Jesus have been brought within that mystic enclosure where the curse which rests on our world has lost its withering influence—even the heirs of salvation, to whom alone the prediction refers—have not yet had all things put under them. Though rightful inheritors of the world, they are not in visible possession of their inheritance. We know, indeed, that "all things are working together for their good,"—that "all things belong to them, whether Paul, or Apollos, or Cephas, or the world, or life, or death, or things present, or things to come;" but, generally speaking, the faithful followers of Jesus Christ, instead of having all things put under their feet, have been considered as the "filth of the earth, and the offscouring of all things."

The words, "we see not yet all things put under man's feet," plainly intimate, especially when taken in connection with the words of the prophecy, that a period is coming when all things shall be put under his feet. Of this no person can entertain a doubt who believes the "sure word of prophecy." "The saints shall take the kingdom, and possess the kingdom for ever and ever." "The kingdom, and dominion, and the greatness of the kingdom under the whole heaven, shall be given to the people of the saints of the Most High, whose kingdom is an everlasting kingdom, and all dominions shall serve and obey him." "He that overcometh, and keepeth My works unto the end, to him will I give power over the nations." "He that overcometh shall inherit all things."[2] Those prophetic oracles which belong to the same class as the 8th Psalm must in due

[1] Job xxxviii. 35.     [2] Dan. vii. 18, 27; Rev. ii. 26, xxi. 7.

time, during the continuance of " the world to come," to which they refer, have their accomplishment. But it is plain, as the inspired writer says,—it is plain that they are not yet accomplished.

But though we see not their full accomplishment, we see their begun fulfilment. Though the body is yet in a state of humiliation, the Head is exalted. " We see not all things yet put under man: but we *see* Jesus, who was made a little lower than the angels for the suffering of death, crowned with glory and honour; that He by the grace of God should taste death for every man." It scarcely requires remark, that the word *see* here is used, not in reference to bodily vision, but to mental perception. It is equivalent to, ' We know, we are sure, that Jesus is exalted to the throne of the universe, crowned with glory and honour.'

There is some difficulty in ascertaining the precise manner in which the clauses of this verse hang on one another. It is plain that the primary idea of the verse is, ' We see Jesus crowned with glory and honour—we do not see man in general, we do not see even redeemed man, raised to that dignity to which we know he is destined in the world to come; but we do see Jesus raised to that dignity. The oracle is fulfilled with respect to the man Christ Jesus.' The phrase, " for the suffering of death," may either be viewed as connected with the phrase, " made lower than the angels," or " crowned with glory and honour." In the first case, it expresses the design of His being made lower than the angels: ' He was made lower than the angels for the suffering of death—that He might suffer death—He became mortal that He might die.' In the second case, it expresses the cause of His exaltation: ' He was crowned with glory and honour, because of, in consequence of, His suffering death.' It is not easy to say which of these is the true way of connecting the phrase. A single circumstance turns the balance, in our minds, in favour of the last mode of explication. According to the first mode, the clauses, " for the suffering of death," and " that He might taste death for every man," are expressive of the very same idea; whereas in the second, they convey a distinct and an important idea,—one well fitted to answer the Apostle's object, too—the wiping away the reproach of the cross. It must be evident to most readers, that the last clause of the verse does not hang by that which immediately precedes it. Jesus was not " crowned with glory and honour that by the grace of God He should taste death for every man;" on the contrary, " He tasted death for every man, that He might be crowned with glory and honour."[1] It obviously depends on the first clause, " made a little lower than the angels;" and it does so either singly, or as an explication of the phrase, " for the suffering of death." We apprehend the sense of the passage will be more distinctly perceived by a slight transposition; thus,—" We see Jesus, who was made a little lower than the angels that by the grace of God He might taste death for every man, for the suffering of death crowned with glory and honour;" or thus,—" We see Jesus crowned with glory and honour for the suffering of death—Jesus, who was made a little lower than the angels that He might taste death for every man."[2]

" Jesus was made a little lower than the angels." I have already stated the reasons which induce me to think that " a little" here, as well as in the 8th Psalm, to which there is a plain allusion, refers not to degree, but to time: 'Jesus was made for a little while lower than the angels;'—and also the reasons which induce me to consider the phrase, " lower than the angels," as intended to convey the idea of mortality and subjection to suffering. The statement of the inspired writer then is, 'Jesus for a season became a mortal,

---

[1] Ebrard's remarks are ingenious, but not satisfactory, by which, connecting it with " crowned," he endeavours to bring out this sense : " Jesus must be exalted, in order that His death may be $ὑπὲρ \ παντός$, for the benefit of all. So long as He was only the crucified man Jesus, so long indeed His death was an objective vicarious death of atonement for guilt not His own, but it yielded no fruit. Not till the Incarnate One was exalted and glorified, and crowned King in heaven, did it become possible for Him to send the Holy Spirit, and thus to effect, on the part of man, the appropriation of the salvation which had been objectively wrought out."—Pp. 86, 87.

[2] We have similar examples of this $συγχυσις$, as rhetoricians term it; as Ps. xlv. 5, LXX., $τὰ \ βέλη \ σου \ ἠκονημένα· \ λαοὶ \ ὑποκάτω \ σου \ πεσοῦνται \ ἐν \ καρδίᾳ \ τῶν \ ἐχθρῶν \ τοῦ \ βασιλέως$. The obscurity here is removed by reading the middle clause as a parenthesis. Phil. i. 21, $ἐμοὶ \ τὸ \ ζῆν \ Χριστός, \ καὶ \ ἀποθανεῖν \ κέρδος$. The right way of resolving this seems to be, $Χριστὸς \ ἐμοὶ \ κέρδος \ ἐστί, \ καὶ \ εἰς \ τὸ \ ζῆν, \ καὶ \ εἰς \ τὸ \ ἀποθανεῖν$.

Stuart considers $ὅπως$ as = cum, postquam, and refers to Acts iii. 19 ; but this passage does not seem to support his exegesis. See Note C.

suffering man.' This is a statement with which our ears are very familiar; but if our minds but distinctly apprehended its meaning and its evidence, it would fill us with adoring wonder and gratitude. Jesus—He who " has obtained by inheritance a more excellent name than the angels," even the name of the "only-begotten" of God—"the brightness of His Father's glory, and the express image of His person"—the Creator and Upholder of the universe—He has become a man—a frail, suffering, mortal man. "The Word has become flesh"—the Son of God has " put on the likeness of sinful flesh." The wonder grows on us as we proceed. Jesus for a season became a mortal, suffering man, " that by the grace of God He might taste death for every man." He became capable of suffering that He might suffer; He became mortal that He might die.

To *taste death*, is a Hebrew idiomatical expression for ' to die,' Matt. xvi. 28; John viii. 52.[1] Some have supposed that there is a peculiar emphasis in the word, and that it is intended to denote at once the reality of our Lord's death, and His short continuance in the state of the dead. 'He did taste of death; but He only as it were tasted of it.' I think it very doubtful if any such thought was in the inspired writer's mind, or that he meant to express any other idea than merely that of death.[2] Jesus became for a season a mortal, that He might die—die for every man. Universal terms are used in reference to it, but they have been variously explained.

The extent—the design, reference, and effects—of the death of Christ has been a fruitful subject of controversy in the Christian Church: some holding that He so died for all, that all shall be saved by Him; others holding that He died for all, inasmuch as His sufferings and death removed the obstacles, arising out of the divine moral character and government, in the way of the

---

[1] The classic Greeks have a similar use of the word; *e.g.*, Hercules, in Sophocles' Trachiniæ v. 1101, says, Ἄλλων τε μόχθων μυρίων ἐγευσάμην. "I have performed, or experienced, a thousand other labours."

[2] *Gustare* in Latin is used in this way, as = primis labris, or leviter attingere, but not γεύεσθαι in Greek. Γεύεσθαι μαθημάτων is severam navare literarum studiis operam; γεύεσθαι φιλοσοφίας, philosophiæ se dedere. Some very learned and ingenious men have supported this "arguta exegesis;" but Calvin, with his never-failing good sense, remarks, not without something of a sarcastic smile, "I doubt whether the apostle meant to say anything so subtle."

pardon and salvation of sinners generally; and others holding that He died for all " whom the Father has given Him," and in no sense for any other. I do not think the present a proper opportunity for entering on a full discussion of this subject;—indeed, as Moses Stuart says, it is a question rather for the theologian than for the commentator to discuss;—but only observe, that the passage before us, when rightly interpreted, furnishes no support to either of the first two of the theories mentioned. The universality here specified is plainly a limited universality. The word in the original is not 'every man,' 'every human being;' it is "every one,"—a word that naturally leads you on to ask, 'Every one of whom?' And when you look into the context you find a particular class of persons mentioned,—"the heirs of salvation"—the "many sons" of God—the "sanctified" ones—the "brethren" of Christ—the "children" of Christ, "whom God had given Him."[1] It was for "every one" of these, that Jesus, when He became mortal, laid down His life. He died *for* them; *i.e.*, He died on their account, He died in their room. He died, not on account of His own sins, but on account of theirs. "He was wounded for their transgressions, He was bruised for their iniquities;" He died for their sins. He "suffered for them, the just for the unjust;" He "gave Himself a ransom for them." When we think that those for whom He died are " an innumerable com-

---

[1] Peirce's note deserves to be quoted for its candour:—" I own I have not the least doubt of the truth of that doctrine, that Christ died for all mankind, for the proof of which this text has commonly been alleged. I am satisfied that Christ ' gave Himself a ransom for all,' 1 Tim. ii. 6; that ' He is the propitiation for the sins of the whole world,' 1 John ii. 2; and that God showed His ' love to the world,' that is, to all mankind, in giving His only begotten Son to die for them, John iii. 16. But still, as He died for the whole world, He did it to save them only in a way of believing, ' that whosoever believeth in Him should not perish, but have everlasting life.' And therefore, as believers only shall share in the final advantages of His death, He may very properly, and consistently with the foresaid extent of His death, be said to die for them. And hence, what brings the matter nearer to my purpose, He is spoken of as showing a peculiar regard to His Church in His death. Eph. v. 25, ' Christ loved the Church, and gave Himself for it.' And, to say the truth, it appears most natural to me, from the context and scope of this writer, to understand every man in this place under such a limitation. Nor will it be easy for a man to avoid seeing this, who attentively considers what follows in our author's discourse."

pany, out of every kindred, and people, and tongue," and when we reflect on the number, and variety, and duration of the blessings which He has secured for every one of these, we cannot help perceiving, that if the dignity of His person stamped an infinite value on His sacrifice, the efficacy of that sacrifice reflects back a glorious light on the dignity of His person.

When Jesus, in His mortal nature, died in the room of all His people, He did so " by the grace of God."[1] It is impossible to trace the appointment of this mysterious sacrifice to any principle in the divine mind but free, sovereign mercy. " God so loved the world, that He gave His only begotten Son, that whosoever believeth in Him should not perish, but have everlasting life." " God commendeth His love toward us, in that, while we were yet sinners, Christ died for us." " Herein is love, not that we loved God, but that He loved us, and sent His Son to be the propitiation for our sins." The expression seems a pregnant one: ' That He might taste death for every one of the heirs of salvation, and by that death secure that they, as well as He, according to the ancient oracle, should be crowned with glory and honour.'

The statement of the design of Christ's sufferings and death was in itself calculated to do more than reconcile the minds of the Hebrews to what to every Jew must at first be a stumblingblock; but, still further to gain his end, he turns their attention not merely to the design of His sufferings and death, but to their consequences. ' We see Him who became for a season mortal that He might die in the room of His people—we see Him crowned with glory and honour, and crowned with glory and honour for the suffering of death.' Jesus is crowned with glory and honour. I have had occasion so fully to illustrate the subject of the mediatorial glory of Jesus Christ already, that nothing more is necessary here than to turn your attention to

[1] There is a very remarkable various reading here, which deserves some notice. Some MSS. read χωρὶς Θεοῦ. Bengel prefers this to the textus receptus, on the principle that it is easier to see how χάριτι should be substituted for χωρὶς than the reverse. The direct evidence, both external and internal, is however decidedly in favour of the text. rec. The probability is, that originally it was merely a note to the words in the middle clause of the 8th verse, suggested by 1 Cor. xv. 27, and that some subsequent transcriber, mistaking it for a correction of χάριτι Θεοῦ, transferred it into the text.

one or two of the passages in which that glory is described: Eph. i. 20-23; 1 Pet. iii. 22.

This "glory and honour" not only followed, but was the result, as the meritorious reward, of His sufferings and death. He is "crowned with glory and honour for the suffering of death." The expression, "suffering of death," seems emphatic. 'He not only died, but He suffered death,—death was to Him a scene of fearful endurance. On account of His unspeakable sufferings when He died in the room of every one of His people, God has bestowed on Him the highest honours.' This connection between our Lord's sufferings and His glory is strongly marked, both in the predictions of the prophets and the statements of the apostles: Isa. liii. 10-12; Phil. ii. 8, 9. You see, then, how the Apostle advances towards the gaining of his object, in putting down the prejudices against Christianity originating in the sufferings and death of its Author. A prediction of Old Testament Scripture secures that man shall, in "the world to come," or the Messianic economy, be at the head of the created universe. That prediction is not yet accomplished. The exaltation of the man Christ Jesus is the commencement of that fulfilment. His sufferings and death were necessary to His exaltation as the man Christ Jesus; and the two events, closely connected together, shall, in fulfilment of the wise and righteous plan of Him by whom are all things, and for whom are all things, ultimately lead to the whole of the human redeemed family of God being brought to glory.

To the gaining of this end—when the natural condition of the objects of the divine sovereign favour, and when the situation and character of God as the Ruler of the world, are taken into consideration—the sufferings of the Saviour were absolutely necessary as a propitiatory sacrifice; while they at the same time produced a capacity and disposition in the Saviour to sympathize with the saved amid the afflictions to which they are exposed, which, in the nature of things, would otherwise have been impossible. Such appears to me the substance of the statements and reasonings contained in this very interesting paragraph. The verse which follows is clearly connected with that which immediately precedes it. Jesus Christ, "by the grace of God, tasted death for every one" of His people—died in their room—died for their salvation, and on this ground has been "crowned with glory and honour;" and this mode of obtaining salvation for them is in every way worthy of God as the Moral Governor of the world. By our Lord's sufferings and death, not only has He obtained for Himself "glory and honour," but He has become an all-accomplished Saviour, so that all the chosen children of God shall be assuredly brought by Him to glory; and in this arrangement there is a glorious display of the character of the Divine Being, as "Him for whom and by whom are all things," whose glory is the end, and whose will is the law, of the universe.

Let us examine this interesting passage somewhat more particularly. Ver. 10. "For it became Him, for whom are all things, and by whom are all things, in bringing many sons unto glory, to make the Captain of their salvation perfect through sufferings."

The first thing to which our attention is naturally called, on looking at this verse, is the appellation here given to the Supreme Being.[1] He is styled, He, "for whom are all things, and by whom are all things."[2] The expression, *all things*, is one as comprehensive as language can furnish. It includes all beings and all events. All beings and all events are *for* God; *i.e.*, the ultimate reason why the one exist and the other occur, is the manifestation of the glories of His character. All beings and all events are *by* God; *i.e.*, the one exist, and the other occur, in consequence of His will—they all originate in His appointment and in His agency. His glory is the end, His will is the law, of the universe.

There is a beautiful appropriateness in the descriptive appellations given to God in the inspired writings. They have almost uniformly a peculiar reference to the statement in the course of which they occur. When the Apostle prays that the Roman Christians may be "likeminded one towards another," he addresses the prayer to "the God of all patience and consolation;" when he speaks of spiritual illumination, he describes God as "Him who commanded the light to shine out of darkness." We see the same appropriateness in the appellation

---

[1] There can be no doubt that αὐτῷ here refers not to Jesus Christ, but to God. The person spoken of is ὁ τελειώσας, and is distinguished from the ἀρχηγὸς τῆς σωτηρίας, who is represented as τετελειωμένος.

[2] A similar description of God is to be found, Rom. xi. 36.

here given to the Divinity, as will appear more distinctly when we come to show how the dispensation here referred to had a congruity with the character of God as "Him, for whom are all things, and by whom are all things."

This glorious Being, in the exercise of His high sovereignty, had formed a purpose of mercy with respect to a large portion of the human race, all of whom had by sin forfeited every claim on His kind regard, and rendered themselves the fit objects of His judicial displeasure and moral disapprobation. It was His determination to "bring many sons to glory." He "predestinated them to the adoption of children," having "chosen them before the foundation of the world." Though in any past age of the Church they have formed a very small minority of mankind, yet, considered collectively, they are "a multitude which no man can number, out of every kindred, and people, and tongue, and nation."

The whole of this chosen family are to be brought "to glory" —are to be raised to a state of the greatest dignity and honour to which creatures can be raised. The word "glory"[1] is used obviously in reference to the quotation from the eighth Psalm, and suggests the idea, that it is in the case of these *sons*, these "heirs of salvation," that the ancient oracle respecting the future dignity of man in "the world to come" is to be realized. I cannot help thinking that the language is here borrowed from the history of God's ancient people. Israel was God's son— His first-born; and He delivered him from Egypt, and brought him into Canaan, where He gave him the heritage of the Gentiles. In like manner God leads His spiritual children from that state of inferiority to the angels, as mortal, suffering beings, onward to the heavenly Canaan, where they are to become inheritors of all things.

In executing this purpose of mercy, He constitutes His own Son in human nature "the Captain of their salvation." The word translated "Captain" occurs in reference to our Lord in three other passages of Scripture. One of these is in the 12th chapter of this Epistle, ver. 2, where He is termed "the *Author* of our faith." The other two are in the Acts of the Apostles: chap. iii. 15, where He is termed "the *Prince* of life;" and chap. v. 31, where He is termed "a *Prince* and a Saviour."

[1] This is plainly = σωτηρία.

The idea intended to be conveyed is, plainly, that He is the Author of their salvation[1]—the person who procures salvation for them. The passage is precisely parallel to chap. v. 8, 9, where the Apostle, after remarking that Jesus Christ, "though a Son, learned obedience by the things which He suffered," adds, "and being made perfect, He became the Author," or source, "of eternal salvation to all who obey Him." As God constituted Moses, and afterwards Joshua, the deliverer of Israel, so He constituted His incarnate Son the Saviour of His people, in all the extent of that word, both as implying that He procures salvation for them, and conducts them safely into the enjoyment of the salvation He has procured for them.[2]

It is a beautiful remark of Dr Owen, that, in employing this peculiar phrase, "the Holy Ghost intimates that the way whereby God will bring His sons to glory is full of difficulties, perplexities, and oppositions, as that of the Israelites into Canaan also was; so that they have need of a Captain, Leader, and Guide, to carry them through it. But all is rendered safe and secure to them through the power, grace, and faithfulness of their Leader. They only perish in the wilderness and die in their sins, who, either out of love to the pleasures of this world, or being tempted by the hardships of the warfare to which He calls them, refuse to go up under His command."

To secure that the "many sons" shall be brought "to glory" under this "Captain of their salvation," God saw meet to "make Him perfect through suffering." Interpreters are by no means agreed as to the signification of the word rendered by our translators, *make perfect*. It is plain that, in the sense which the English term most naturally suggests, it is not applicable to Jesus Christ. The character of Jesus Christ was perfect; He did not stand in need, as good men do, of a course of discipline to cure them of their faults, and to improve their virtues. It is indeed said, that "He learned obedience by the things which He suffered;" but the meaning of that expression is not that He learned to obey, but that He learned by experience what obedience is. To avoid this difficulty, some have represented the word as signifying 'to consecrate, to set apart to.' There can be little doubt that the word is employed in this way,[3] as

---

[1] Αἴτιος, ὁ τὴν σωτηρίαν τεκών, as Chrysostom explains it.
[2] See Note D.   [3] Lev. xxi. 10, viii. 28, 33.

the consecration of a priest was an intimation that he was fully possessed of the qualifications the law required in those who filled that office, and in that sense perfected, accomplished for the discharge of its functions. Others consider it as signifying 'to glorify, to bring to glory, to crown with glory and honour, to render perfectly happy and glorious.' I am rather disposed to understand the word as equivalent to 'to accomplish—completely to fit or qualify for the discharge of His office as the Captain of salvation.' This is a common use of the term: Heb. vii. 19, ix. 9, x. 1, 14.

To perform the office of a Saviour of lost men, three things were necessary—merit, power, and sympathy. It pleased the Father that the incarnate Son should, as the Saviour of men, obtain all these by suffering.[1] The Saviour of men must deserve so well of the Moral Governor of the world, as that He, in consistency with the perfections of His character and the principles of His government, may on the Saviour's account reverse the sentence of condemnation passed on those in whose behalf He has interposed, and bestow on them blessings to which on their own account they have no claim. The Saviour of men must be possessed of "all power in heaven and earth"—He must have the command of those divine influences which are necessary to make ignorant, foolish, depraved, miserable men, wise, and good, and happy; He must, too, have the control of all events which, directly or indirectly, bear upon their interests. And, still further, the Saviour of men must, to fit Him for the discharge of His office, be able to enter into the feelings of those whom He is to deliver.

All these accomplishments are necessary to His being a perfect Saviour; and all these accomplishments were obtained by our Lord Jesus "through suffering." It was the patient, cheerful endurance of those penal evils which the law of God had denounced against sinners by the incarnate only begotten of God, that "magnified the divine law and made it honourable," and made it not merely consistent with, but gloriously illustrative of, the righteousness as well as the mercy of God, to pardon and save the guiltiest of the guilty believing in Jesus. The

---

[1] Διὰ παθημάτων has the same reference as πάθημα τοῦ θανάτου; but the plural is used to denote that the sufferings which terminated in death were numerous and varied.

power and authority bestowed on Jesus Christ as Mediator are uniformly represented as the meritorious reward of His voluntary obedience unto the death. "Yet it pleased the Lord to bruise Him; He hath put Him to grief: when Thou shalt make His soul an offering for sin, He shall see His seed, He shall prolong His days, and the pleasure of the Lord shall prosper in His hand. He shall see of the travail of His soul, and shall be satisfied: by His knowledge shall My righteous servant justify many; for He shall bear their iniquities. Therefore will I divide Him a portion with the great, and He shall divide the spoil with the strong; because He hath poured out His soul unto death: and He was numbered with the transgressors; and He bare the sin of many, and made intercession for the transgressors."—"And being found in fashion as a man, He humbled Himself, and became obedient unto death, even the death of the cross. Wherefore God also hath highly exalted Him, and given Him a name which is above every name."[1] The power and disposition to sympathize with His people were obtained, and indeed could be obtained, in no other way but by suffering. If our High Priest can be "touched with the feeling of our infirmities," it is because "He was in all things tempted like as we are, yet without sin." Without suffering, sin could not have been expiated; without the expiation of sin, the Saviour could not have obtained all power to give eternal life to men; and, from the very nature of the case, without suffering He would have been very imperfectly capable of sympathizing with the sufferers. But by suffering He expiated sin; by suffering He obtained for Himself the control both of that inward influence and that physical power which are necessary to the salvation of His people, and He also acquired that experimental acquaintance with trial which peculiarly fits Him to succour them who are tried.

We are now in some measure prepared for inquiring into the meaning of the Apostle's declaration when he says, "It became Him, for whom are all things, and by whom are all things, in bringing many sons to glory, to make the Captain of their salvation perfect through suffering."[2] The phrase, "it became

[1] Isa. liii. 10–12; Phil. ii. 8, 9.
[2] "Επρεπε denotes what is becoming, and in a moral point of view, taking into consideration the character of the individual, necessary—what

Him," etc., is equivalent to—'It was congruous to His place and character as the Supreme Governor of the universe, whose will is the law and whose glory is the end of all things, in saving men through His Son, to save them not without His suffering, but by His sufferings.' It is the doctrine of many divines of very high name, that the salvation of a lost world through the expiatory sufferings of His incarnate Son is to be resolved entirely into the divine sovereignty—that the fact is plainly revealed, that the salvation of men was accomplished in this way—that we ought to believe the fact, and acquiesce in this appointment—that God has not in any degree made known to us the reasons of this appointment, nor explained to us in what manner the death of His Son has been efficacious in procuring our salvation.

It is my earnest desire to avoid anything like an intrusion into things which God has not revealed, but it is equally my earnest desire to avoid that "voluntary humility" which keeps a man ignorant of what has been revealed. The salvation of a lost world, indeed, originates in the sovereignty of God. It was for Him, in the exercise of this high attribute, to determine whether all, or some, or none of the fallen family of mankind should be saved; but on the supposition that some are to be saved, the method of their salvation must be of such a kind as will illustrate those perfections of the divine character, and vindicate those rights of the divine government, which the sin of man had dishonoured and violated. Without subjecting ourselves to the charge of presumptuously pronouncing judgment on a question placed beyond the reach of our faculties, we may assert, that it would not have become "Him, for whom are all things, and by whom are all things," to have saved men without displaying His displeasure at sin in a way equally strong as would have been done by executing on the sinner the penalty of the law, to which he had exposed himself.[1] If "all things"

honour and consistency require. It is equivalent in meaning with ἀναγκαῖον, ch. viii. 3 ; ὀφείλει, in the 17th verse of this chapter, = δεῖ, Matt. iii. 15 ; Acts iii. 21 ; Eph. v. 3 ; Heb. vii. 26 ; Ecclus. xxxiii. 28. Compare with this passage Luke xxiv. 26.

[1] Πρέπει here, like ὤφειλεν in ver. 17, and δεῖ, Luke xxiv. 26, denotes not a fatalistic necessity, but what, in the circumstances of the case, could not take place in any other way under the government of God, infinitely wise, just, and good.

are "for" God—if "all things" are "by" Him—if His will be the law, if His glory be the end, of all things,—sin, which is the violation of His will, and which, of course, naturally leads to His dishonour, cannot be tolerated permanently in His world. It "becomes Him, for whom are all things, and by whom are all things," to make it evident, that whatever disturbs the order of His government is an evil thing; and the direct and obvious way of doing this is to punish the sinner. But if God, in His sovereign kindness, determine to save the sinner, it must be in such a way as that the honour of the divine character and law are at least equally supported as they would have been by the punishment of the sinner.

Nothing can be plainer than that the will of God, who is infinitely wise, should be the law of the universe; and that the glory of God, who is infinitely excellent, should be the end of the universe—the happiness of all intelligent creatures depending on the glories of the divine character being displayed by Him and apprehended by them. Not merely, then, the regard which the all-perfect Being must have for Himself, but His regard to the good order and happiness of His intelligent creation, require, that if a sinner—a violator of that order, a doer of that which, if it were becoming universal, would put an end to everything like happiness in the creation—is to be saved, it must be in a way consistent with all the rights of God as the Moral Governor of the world, and all the interests of His intelligent creatures; and therefore it is, that in saving men through His Son, "it became *Him*" to accomplish Him as a Saviour by sufferings. This was a way in which all the perfections of His nature were gloriously and harmoniously displayed, and the seemingly incompatible characters conjoined, of the just God and the Saviour.

The question has sometimes been put—'Could not God have saved man in some other way, in consistency with, and in illustration of, His holiness and justice?' I feel much disposed to use the three Jewish children's words to Nebuchadnezzar in reference to the question: "We are not careful to answer thee in this matter." But if obliged to speak, I would say, 'If a less costly sacrifice would have served the purpose, would not God have spared His Son? and if a less costly sacrifice could not have served the purpose, where could, even among the resources of Omnipotence, a more costly, or an equally costly one, have been found?' The words, fairly interpreted, teach us, not that the incarnation and sufferings of Jesus Christ, the Son of God, were abstractly necessary, but that, on the supposition of the salvation of man being determined, they were necessary—necessary not because appointed merely, but rather appointed because necessary and sufficient for their purpose. He *must* become "a propitiation in His blood," if the just God is to become " the justifier of the ungodly."

The design of the inspired writer in that part of the paragraph which yet remains to be considered, seems to be, to show that the incarnation of the Son of God in order to His being the Saviour of men was necessary, both as the fulfilment of Old Testament prophecy, and as in the nature of things absolutely requisite to His accomplishing their salvation. The first of these ideas is illustrated in the 11th, 12th, and 13th verses; the second in verses 14–18. The proposition which the Apostle means to establish is this : ' The incarnation of the Son of God, in order to His being the Saviour of men, ought not to offend any one, for the ancient prophets predicted it, and it was absolutely necessary to His effecting the salvation of mankind.' Let us inquire a little more particularly into the manner in which he illustrates and proves the two different parts of this proposition.

Ver. 11. "For both He that sanctifieth and they who are sanctified are all of one : for which cause He is not ashamed to call them brethren, 12. Saying, I will declare Thy name unto My brethren; in the midst of the church will I sing praise unto Thee. 13. And again, I will put My trust in Him. And again, Behold I and the children which God hath given Me." The object of the Apostle in these and the following verses seems to be, to show that to gain the great ends of His mission— to " bring many sons to glory"—to place degraded human nature at the head of the creation, it was necessary that He should be a man—a suffering, dying man. The words now before us seem to me to express this general idea: ' That the Saviour and the saved must belong to the same class, and, of course, that the Son of God, if He is to be the Saviour of man, must Himself be a man, is obvious from the language of Old Testament prophecy.'

No person can doubt that by "the Sanctifier" we are to understand Jesus Christ, and by "the sanctified" His saved people. The Sanctifier is obviously the same person as "the Captain of salvation;" and the sanctified ones, the "many children" whom He is conducting to glory. But what is the import of the related appellations here given to Christ and His people—"The Sanctifier and the sanctified?" The word usually rendered 'sanctify' signifies 'to set apart to a particular purpose.' Thus the Medes are represented as God's sanctified ones, because destined by Him to overthrow the Babylonian empire.[1] The Israelites are represented in many passages as holy or sanctified to the Lord—separated from the rest of the nations, and devoted to important purposes in the great scheme of divine government; and in 2 Tim. ii. 21, the Christian minister who carefully abstains from everything unbecoming his character is represented "a vessel sanctified unto honour," *i.e.*, set apart to an honourable purpose.

To apprehend the precise import of the word in any particular passage of Scripture, it is necessary to attend to the nature of the person or thing said to be sanctified, and the nature, too, of the purpose to which they are sanctified or set apart. To the sanctification of inanimate things, such as the tabernacle and temple, and their furniture, or of irrational animals, as the victims offered in sacrifice, certain divinely instituted rites were necessary, as indications that they were by the divine appointment set apart for religious purposes. To sanctify a Jew for the external service of Jehovah as the God and King of his nation, his having submitted to circumcision, and if he had contracted political guilt or ceremonial defilement, his having gone through certain propitiatory and lustratory ritual services, were necessary. The sanctification here referred to is of a higher character, corresponding to the spiritual nature of the order of things to which it belongs. "Ye are," says the Apostle Peter in reference to Christians, "a holy," or sanctified, "nation,"—ye are devoted to God to serve an important purpose —"a holy priesthood, to offer up spiritual sacrifices."[2] Christians are separated from the world lying under the wicked one, and devoted to the service and enjoyment of God in all the faculties of their nature, and during the whole eternity of their being.

[1] Isa. xiii. 3.  [2] 1 Pet. ii. 5, 9.

It should not be difficult, then, to determine what is implied in their sanctification, or, in other words, what Jesus Christ does when He sanctifies them—what that is in consequence of which He receives the appellation of the "Sanctifier," and they of the "sanctified." They are naturally guilty; *i.e.*, they have, by the violation of the divine law, placed their happiness in opposition to the honour of the divine character and the principles of the divine government. While in that state, they are as it were separated from the innocent part of God's intelligent creation to destruction. In order to their being separated to the enjoyment and service of God, the first thing that is necessary is expiation or atonement. Something must be done to make their salvation consistent with, and illustrative of, the perfections of a holy and just God. This is done by the obedience to the death of our Lord Jesus Christ. This opens a way for the communication of those divine influences which are necessary to give to the sinner the moral capacity of spiritually and acceptably serving God; for those who are to be brought "to glory" are not only guilty, but depraved. They are so indisposed as to be morally incapable of serving God. Now, by the shedding forth on them of these divine influences (the barriers raised by guilt in the way of communicating which having been removed by His atonement), He inclines and enables them to devote themselves to God "as living sacrifices;" and thus His giving Himself for them as a sacrifice and offering ends in their being brought to God, "a peculiar people, redeemed from all iniquity, zealous of good works." You see then what is meant by sanctification in the case of Christians—you see how Jesus Christ receives the appellation, "the Sanctifier," and His people that of the "sanctified" ones. By shedding His blood for them, He made it consistent with the honour of God to take them to be His peculiar people; and by the influence of His Spirit, He fits them for the privileges and duties of this high calling, for the enjoyment and for the service of their God and Father.[1]

[1] Ἁγιάζειν thus does not here denote sanctification—the moral change produced by faith in the atonement, as distinguished from the relative change in justification, and just as little this relative change as distinguished from the moral change. It includes both, and, as Ebrard says, denotes the total change in reference to God, which takes place in the members of the New Covenant—expiation, justification, sanctification, glorification,—all that makes them separated ones, a peculiar people, a sacred nation.

## AN OBJECTION MET AND ANSWERED. 115

'Now,' says the inspired writer, 'Jesus Christ, the Sanctifier, and His people, the sanctified ones, are all *of one.*' The language is plainly elliptical. The ellipsis[1] has been variously supplied by interpreters. Some consider the statement as equivalent to—'they are all the descendants of one person, they are all of one father;'[2] and some suppose the father referred to, to be God; others, to be Adam; others, to be Abraham. It is no doubt true that in all these respects "He who sanctifies and they who are sanctified are all of one." Jesus is the Son of God, and all His people are the sons of God—"heirs of God, and joint heirs with Christ Jesus." He is His Father and their Father, His God and their God. It is plain, however, to every person who reads the passage, that it refers to the common human nature possessed by the Sanctifier and the sanctified, and, of course, that the reference is not to the common spiritual relation in which they stand to their heavenly Father. It is equally true that Jesus is the Son of Adam, and so are all who are saved by Him; but as the name of our first parent does not occur at all in the context, I do not think it natural to supply the ellipsis by it. It is also true that Jesus Christ was not only literally a son of Abraham, but He was the "Seed" by way of eminence, "in which all the nations of the earth were to be blessed;" and all His people are Abraham's seed too, according to the promise.[3] But it seems plain that what the Apostle is doing here, is to account for the incarnation of the Son of God. It was not to his purpose to state—'The people He came to save were the spiritual seed of Abraham, therefore He must be the spiritual seed of Abraham too;' but it was directly to his purpose to remark—'The people He came to save were men, therefore He must be a man;' and we find this is just the argument which he states and illustrates in the succeeding verses. I am disposed to

---

[1] ἐξ ἑνὸς πάντες, scil. εἰσί.　　　　[2] ἐξ ἑνὸς πατρός.

[3] This interpretation, at first sight, appears peculiarly plausible. In the first quotation, establishing that the ὁ ἁ. and the οἱ ἁ. are ἐξ ἑνός, the words cited are followed by—" Ye the seed of Jacob, glorify Him; and fear Him, all ye the seed of Israel." The next quotation seems to refer to that faith or trust in God which is the *basis* of the filial character of good men, and by which "the first born among many brethren" was pre-eminently distinguished; and then this satisfactorily accounts for the use of σπέρμα Ἀβραάμ in the 16th verse. But, notwithstanding all this, we cannot agree with Peirce and Michaelis in this exegesis.

go along with those interpreters who would supply the ellipsis thus: 'Both He that sanctifieth and they who are sanctified are all of one family or race.'[1] Both the Sanctifier and the sanctified are men; and to both of them does the ancient oracle above quoted, respecting the dignified place intended for man in "the world to come," belong.

The evidence derived from the Old Testament Scriptures, on which this assertion rests, is introduced by the inspired writer remarking, "For which cause He is not ashamed to call them brethren." The general sentiment plainly is—'This community of nature is the reason why, in the Old Testament Scriptures, the Messiah is represented as the brother of those whom He comes to deliver.' But there is something peculiarly beautiful and touching in the way in which the sentiment is expressed: "He is not ashamed to call them brethren." These words plainly intimate that it was an act of condescension to call them brethren. If Jesus had not been possessed of a nature superior to the human, this language could never have been applied to Him. For one who was no more than a man to refuse to acknowledge the bond of brotherhood which binds him to the rest, would have been intolerable haughtiness and pride; for him so readily to admit it, could be no proof of humility.[2]

---

[1] Γένους, or σπέρματος, or αἵματος. Perhaps the expression ἐξ ἑνός may be intended to express generally the conformity of the Sanctifier and the sanctified, in *condition* as well as in character—κατὰ πάντα ὁμοιωθῆναι τοῖς ἀδελφοῖς. This would enable us to see the appropriateness of the quotations from Isa. viii. In this case, the general idea of conformity is resolved into its two parts in the succeeding context—conformity of nature, ver. 14 —conformity of condition, vers. 17, 18. There seems, as Peirce has ingeniously remarked, more intended by the use of the word πάντες, which, according to the ordinary mode of interpretation, is not necessary to bring out the meaning. He conceives "that πάντες is added with a special regard to οἱ ἁγιαζόμενοι: that these being of two sorts, Jews and Gentiles, and the former objecting and cavilling against the favour showed to the latter, our author here, the more strongly to assert their right, uses this term; but yet in a manner that would give as little offence as possible to the Jews to whom he was writing. It is worth while to compare with this Rom. iv. 11-16, Gal. iii. 26-29, both on account of the argument and the emphasis laid on πάντες." Paul never forgets that he was the Apostle of the Gentiles.

[2] Photius on Œcumenius well says—" By saying ' he is not ashamed ', he showed the difference (sc., between him and us). For he is not man's brother by nature, though he is truly man, but by love, since he is also

But it is a subject of wonder to angels and men that the Sanctifier, who "is the brightness of the Father's glory, and the express image of His person," the Creator and Lord of the universe, should not be ashamed, even when He became incarnate, to call the sanctified ones His "brethren." He might well be expected to be ashamed to recognise them as so closely related to Him. When we think of Him only as a perfectly pure and holy man, His condescension is evident. Those whom He sanctifies, when He finds them, are sunk in guilt and depravity, and at best, while here below, they are full of imperfections and faults: yet He does not say, "Stand by, I am holier than thou;" but He calls them "brethren." When we reflect on the miseries they had involved themselves in, we have a further proof of His condescension. The prosperous are not fond of owning close relationship to the unhappy. He readily owned His relationship to us, though He knew the doing so would cost Him dear. By claiming us, poor debtors to divine justice, as His "brethren," He, "though rich, was made poor." He well knew that the throne of the universe was destined for Him as the incarnate Son of God; and yet, in the prospect of all this aggrandisement, aye, and in the possession of it, He calls the meanest of His redeemed people 'Brother.' But nothing places His condescension in so strong a point of light as the consideration of His divinity. That He, who is the only begotten of God—" God over all, blessed for ever," should acknowledge so close a relationship to guilty, depraved, self-ruined man, is a mystery of kindness which will never be fathomed. We can do nothing but exclaim with the Apostle, "O the depth!"

The inspired writer now proceeds to quote a variety of passages from the Old Testament in proof of his assertion, that both the sanctified and the Sanctifier are of one common nature. The proof is, He speaks of them as brethren in a way which shows that He is possessed of the same nature with them.

The first passage quoted is from Psalm xxii. 22: "I will declare Thy name unto My brethren; in the midst of the church will I sing praise unto Thee." There can be no reasonable doubt that the whole of the 22d Psalm is spoken in

truly God." And well does Abresch, after quoting this passage, add: "Very true indeed. For make Jesus to be mere man, and then what force will the statement have, that he is not ashamed of *man*, that he honours *men* by calling them brethren?"

the person of the Messiah. Many passages in it are applied to Him in the New Testament, and will apply to none but Him. Comp. vers. 1, 7, 8, 16, 18, with Matt. xxvii. 46, 43, 35, 39, 40; John xx. 25. These words are plainly descriptive of what the Messiah was to do after His sufferings. The passage refers, I apprehend, to His making known the true character of God, by His Gospel accompanied by the effectual working of His Spirit, to all His brethren, to all whom the Father has given Him,— "preaching peace to them who are afar off, and to them who are nigh;" thus bringing together into one church, or assembly, the whole of "the children of God scattered abroad;" and, as the High Priest of the redeemed family, leading the worship of them all,—offering up their sacrifice of praise and thanksgiving with acceptance to His Father and their Father, to His God and their God.

It is a subject of dispute among interpreters, whence the second of the inspired writer's proofs that "the Sanctifier and the sanctified are all of one," namely, "I will put my trust in Him," is taken. Some have supposed that it is taken from Isa. viii. 17, where words very similar are to be found, words which immediately precede the following quotation. Had it not been for the words *and again* intervening, we should have been disposed to go into this view; but these words seem naturally to suggest the idea that the two quotations are taken from different places.[1] We agree with those who consider these words as quoted from the 18th Psalm, ver. 2. The 18th Psalm is one of those which speak of "the sufferings of Christ, and of the glory which should follow." Quotations from it in the New Testament are represented as spoken by the Messiah, and there is much in it which is utterly inapplicable to David. It appears to be the Messiah's song of praise to God for raising Him from the dead, making

---

[1] It is a strange hallucination of the learned Schoetgen, *Hor. Heb. et Tal.* vol. i. 933, that the passage referred to is the first clause of Isa. xlii. 1, which he renders, 'Behold My servant, I rest Myself in—sustain Myself on—Him,' and grounds the argument on what follows, vers. 2 and 3; the tender sympathy shown by the Messiah to those whom He comes to deliver, proving that He regards them as brethren, and is partaker of a common nature. Nothing can be more far-fetched than this. The student of exegesis will find abundant evidence that it is not only of philosophers that Cicero's pungent saying holds true : "Nothing is too absurd for some philosopher to have said." De Nat. Deor.

Him victorious over all His enemies, exalting Him to universal power and dominion, and giving Him a people from among the Gentiles. But it may be said, How do these words prove that "the Sanctifier and the sanctified are all of one?" The most satisfactory answer that I can give to this question is the following :—'The Son of God in His original state was not in circumstances in which He could exercise *trust*. The language intimates that the person who uses it needs to rely on God, and is therefore possessed of a created and dependent nature. Trust in God is the natural sentiment of a sanctified human spirit; and in uttering it, the Messiah shows that He and His people are all of one.'[1]

The third quotation is taken from Isa. viii. 18: "Behold I and the children which God hath given Me." That the passage referred to is a prediction of Christ is plain, from the way in which it is quoted not only here, but in other parts of the New Testament. Paul applies the 14th and 15th verses to Christ in Rom. ix. 33; and Peter, in 1 Ep. ii. 7. Our Lord obviously alludes to it, Matt. xxi. 44; and Simeon, under the inspiration of the Holy Spirit, Luke ii. 34. Some suppose that it refers typically to Isaiah and his children, and ultimately to Christ and His people. I rather think it a direct prophecy of the Messiah. The person here spoken of is called Immanuel, ch. vii. 14,—a name that is explained and applied to the Virgin's Son, Matt. i. 23. And what other person can be intended by that name in Isa. viii. 8? Surely neither the prophet nor any of his sons could be called Immanuel. Nor was the land of Judea their property. Verses 14 and 15, as we have already seen, are applied to Christ in different places of the New Testament, and to none but our Lord are the words applicable. "And He shall be for a sanctuary" to believers; "but for a stone of stumbling, and for a rock of offence, to both the houses of Israel," for their unbelief. These things do not apply to Isaiah or any of his sons, but were exactly verified in the

---

[1] Abresch's note deserves quotation :—"Would you ask what the apostle is proving from these words? The same thing that he proved from the proof-text that went before : that is, Christ's likeness to his brethren, i.e. to men. For trust in God in Holy Scripture is predicated of man alone, and that when he is poor and burdened with many troubles and sorrows. Hence Christ's true manhood and distressful condition can be expressed by this phrase."

different effects of the Gospel upon the Jews when "the elect obtained, and the rest were blinded."[1] The words, "Bind up the testimony,"—whether they mean, as some think, that the Mosaic economy was to cease among Christ's disciples, as having attained its end, or, as we are more inclined to maintain, that the true sense of the law and testimony was to be bound up and sealed from the understanding of the body of the Jewish people, and deposited among His disciples,—must in either case be viewed as the words of the Messiah, among whose disciples alone the prediction was fulfilled. If this be admitted, the words quoted by the inspired writer must also be viewed as spoken by the Messiah. He calls those whom He had formerly denominated disciples, *children*, *i. e.*, children of God—children given to Him by God,—entrusted to His care by God, to redeem, to preserve, and to conduct to glory. Our Lord often speaks of His people as given to Him by His and their Father: John vi. 37, 39, xvii. 2, 6, 24. He also denominates them children, John xiii. 33, xxi. 5. Being the children of God, they are His brethren. It is added in the prophecy—" They are for signs and for wonders in Israel from the Lord of hosts, which dwelleth in Mount Zion." The best commentary on these words is to be found in Luke ii. 34, " And Simeon blessed them, and said unto Mary His mother, Behold, this child is set for the fall and rising again of many in Israel; and for a sign which shall be spoken against;" and in 1 Cor. iv. 9, "For I think that God hath set forth us the Apostles last, as it were appointed to death: for we are made a spectacle unto the world, and to angels, and to men."[2]

Such is the Apostle's proof that, according to the ancient prophecies, the Messiah who comes to redeem men was Himself to be a man. The Sanctifier and the sanctified were to be all of one nature.[3]

The statement contained in the words which follow is substantially the following:—' The Son of God assumed human

---

[1] Rom. xi. 7.

[2] Peirce's long note, or rather dissertation, on this paragraph well deserves perusal.

[3] Ebrard, with great ingenuity, yet we think fruitlessly, endeavours to prove that the Apostle's object in these words is to show from the Old Testament Scripture that the Messiah was to raise His people to the dignity of being, like Himself, children of God—thus leading them to glory. The discussion deserves to be read and considered.

## AN OBJECTION MET AND ANSWERED.

nature—a nature capable of suffering and death; He became a man, that He might die, and by dying destroy the power of the great enemy of man, and deliver His people from his dominion.' "Forasmuch then as the children are partakers of flesh and blood, He also Himself likewise took part of the same; that through death He might destroy him that had the power of death, that is, the devil; and deliver them who through fear of death were all their lifetime subject to bondage."

The connection between this verse and the preceding context may be thus stated :—' Since " it became Him, for whom are all things, and by whom are all things, in bringing many sons unto glory, to make the Captain of their salvation perfect through suffering ;" and since, according to Old Testament prophecies, the Sanctifier and the sanctified, the Saviour and the saved, must be of the same race; and since the saved are human beings,—the Son of God, the appointed Saviour, assumed a nature capable of suffering and death—even the nature of man, whom He came to save, that in that nature He might die, and by dying accomplish the great purpose of His appointment, the destruction of the power of Satan, and the deliverance of His chosen people. In other words; since the honour of God as the Moral Governor of the world, whose will is the law, and whose glory is the end of the universe, rendered it impossible that the deliverer of guilty man could be an accomplished Saviour—could obtain that merit, that power and authority, and that sympathy, which were necessary to effect man's salvation—without submitting to suffering, to suffering even to the death; since, as appears from ancient oracles, the Saviour and the saved must have a common nature, and since in this case the saved are men,—the Son of God became a man that He might suffer and die, and by suffering and dying accomplish the deliverance of His people from the power of their enemy, and bring first Himself, and then them, to that glory to which His Father and their Father, His God and their God, had destined them.' Let us now proceed to examine somewhat more minutely the different parts of this most interesting statement.[1]

---

[1] According to Ebrard, the connection is, ' As the Son, the Captain of salvation, leads to glory His chosen people by making them, like Himself, sons of God, children of the resurrection, so, in order to this, it was necessary that He should come down to be a son of man, in order to His making

"The children are partakers of flesh and blood." "Flesh and blood" is a common expression for mankind, or human nature. "Flesh and blood hath not revealed this unto thee," said our Lord to Peter; *i.e.*, 'No man gave you this information.' "I consulted not with flesh and blood," says Paul; *i.e.*, 'I asked no man's advice; I followed not the impulses of my nature as a man.' To be a "partaker of flesh and blood," is just to be a man. "The children" were men. "The children" here are plainly "the heirs of salvation"—the sons of God to be brought "to glory"—the "brethren" of the Messiah. They receive this name here plainly from the circumstance of their being denominated "children" in the last of the quotations brought forward by the Apostle to prove that, according to the Old Testament predictions, "the Sanctifier and the sanctified are all of one."[1] The children of God, delivered by Him into the hands of His Son to be saved and brought "to glory," are "partakers of flesh and blood;" *i.e.*, they have a common nature, and that common nature is the human; or, they are a portion of the human race.

Now, as the Sanctifier and the sanctified must, according to the ancient oracle, be possessed of a common nature, and as they were men, He became a man also—He took part of the same flesh and blood. The qualifying phrase *likewise*[2] seems intended to suggest the idea, that He not only assumed the nature, but also the condition, of those whom He came to save. He took human nature, not in its primitive glory, but in the degraded state in which they wore it. He was indeed *without sin;* but He appeared in "the likeness of sinful flesh." He assumed human nature with all those physical infirmities which in others are the effect of sin.

men sons of God. The Son of God must become man to do the great work of the Messiah.'

[1] Τὰ παιδία is = 'these children.' The course of reasoning is, ' It was necessary that the Messiah should be a man, a suffering man. The Sanctifier and the sanctified must be ἐξ ἑνός. So they are; they are in the Old Testament Scriptures represented as " brethren," and as Father and children. Now these children were men—men exposed to suffering, and so must He be; and this is the true account of the incarnation and suffering of one so exalted as *the Son of God.*'

[2] Παραπλησίως, according to Chrysostom, is = οὐ φαντασίᾳ, οὐδὲ εἰκόνι ἀλλ' ἀληθείᾳ. It indicates, as Theophylact says, that He *really* became a man, οὐ κατὰ φαντασίαν καὶ δόκησιν.

The language of the inspired writer seems obviously intended to suggest the idea of the pre-existence of the Deliverer of men before He became a man. He does not say, what he might have said, 'Inasmuch as the children were partakers of flesh and blood, He also was a partaker of flesh and blood.' He intentionally changes the expression, so as to convey the important truth, that He was possessor of another nature than the human. 'He was a man; but He was—he existed, before He was a man. He became man; He voluntarily assumed human nature into personal union with that divine nature of which from eternity He was the possessor.'

This is a truth which, from its being familiar to us from our infancy, fails of producing that sentiment of wonder which it is so well calculated to excite; and from the weakness of our faith, if not our utter want of faith, fails of calling forth that adoring gratitude which, wherever it is really believed, it must awaken in the mind. "Great," great indeed, "is the mystery of godliness,"—unfathomable are the depths of wisdom, and power, and righteousness, and kindness which it opens to the astonished and delighted mind of the believer,—"God was manifest in flesh."

The design of the Saviour in assuming the nature of the saved—a nature capable of suffering and death—was, that He might be capable of suffering and dying,—that He actually might suffer and die, and thus accomplish what, in consistency with the perfections of the divine moral character, and the principles of the divine moral government, could not be otherwise accomplished—the destruction of the power of the great enemy of His people, and their complete and everlasting deliverance from his dominion. He "took part of flesh and blood, that through death He might destroy him that had the power of death, that is, the devil; and deliver those who through fear of death were all their lifetime subject to bondage."

The ends of our Lord's incarnation, both proximate and ultimate, are here brought before the mind. The first is plainly implied; the second is expressly stated. The proximate end of our Lord's incarnation was, that He might be capable of that suffering and death without which He could not have been the accomplished Saviour of men. The ultimate end of our Lord's incarnation was, that by thus suffering and dying He might be perfected, fully accomplished as a Saviour, that He might deliver man by vanquishing his great enemy. The Son of God, previously to His incarnation, had power enough, and wisdom enough, and benignity enough, to effect the salvation of men. But from the very perfection of His divine nature, He could not suffer and die. As a divine person, He is " the King eternal and immortal." Had He never been anything but the great God, He could not have been our Saviour. Had he never been anything but God, He no doubt could have annihilated or punished in ten thousand ways " him that had the power of death," but He could not have " destroyed him" by dying; and this was the only way in which his destruction could have been our salvation. The Saviour of man must expiate man's guilt; and this could be done only by suffering and death. The Saviour of man must be a high priest—He must offer a propitiatory sacrifice; and when the only begotten Son assumes that character, He must have somewhat to offer, He must be placed in circumstances in which He can obey and suffer. To His executing the will of His Father " in bringing the many sons to glory," suffering and death are necessary; and therefore He gladly took on Him *the body* which had been " prepared" for Him, that in it, infinitely dignified by its union with the divine nature, He might have a suitable and an available sacrifice to lay on the altar of divine justice, as the expiation of the sins of His people. How do wonders—wonders of divine wisdom and divine grace—thicken on us while contemplating the economy of salvation through the sufferings and death of the only begotten of God!

While the proximate end of our Lord's incarnation is plainly suggested by the words under consideration—His being rendered capable of suffering and death—the ultimate end forms their principal subject: "that through death He might destroy him that had the power of death; and deliver them who through fear of death were all their lifetime subject to bondage." The ultimate end of our Lord's incarnation is one—the salvation of His people in a way not merely consistent with, but gloriously illustrative of, the perfections of the divine character, and the principles of the divine government. But it is here presented to us under a twofold aspect: in reference to the great enemy from whom they are delivered, and in reference to them who are emancipated from his yoke. Viewed in reference to him, it is destruction; viewed in reference to them, it is deliverance. Let us contemplate it for a little in these two aspects.

He "took part" of "flesh and blood"—or, in other words, He assumed a human nature capable of suffering and death— "that through death He might destroy him that had the power of death, that is, the devil." He does not say, 'that He might destroy death,' though he might have said it; for the last enemy *shall* be destroyed—destroyed by Him, destroyed by Him as the result of His death. But Jesus, as Ebrard well observes, has not freed us from death absolutely and in every respect. It remains, but its sting, its power is removed. The death of Christians is, as the Heidelberg Catechism says, "not a payment for sin, but an entrance into life." We are not left in any doubt as to the being to whom the awfully significant appellation is here given—"Him that had the power of death." It is "the devil,"—the chief of those unseen and powerful beings who kept not their first estate, but left their original habitation, and who are constantly endeavouring to uphold and extend that empire of evil which they have established in the universe of God.[1] But though there can be no doubt as to the reference of the expression, there is some difficulty in fixing its precise meaning. What are we to understand by the devil having the power of death?[2] Some interpreters of considerable name have endeavoured to explain this, as well as the appellation given to the saved in the next verse—"those who were all their lifetime subject to bondage from fear of death,"—from the opinions entertained by the Talmudists respecting death, and the power of the devil in reference to it. They teach that the devil, whom they call "the angel of death,"[3] is continually urging God to allow him to put men to death; that death in all its forms is the work of the devil; that when a man is ready to die, the devil, as the

---

[1] It is pleasant to hear from a late German exegete, that even in his country the time is happily gone by for representing the devil as but a personification of the evil principle.

[2] A learned man says $ἔχων$ is = having for his object to obtain, seeking by all means to secure. Michaelis well says, "I can only say in reply that I am completely ignorant of this meaning of the word $ἔχω$." How many ingenious but unlearned interpretations in common currency might be put down by these few weighty words!

[3] Asmothe and Samael.

angel of death, appears to him with a sword steeped in poison in his hand, and that it is this poison which occasions dissolution; and that he carries them down along with him into the abyss, where they are tormented by him, till they obtain deliverance through the prayers of their friends. These statements, no doubt, represent the devil as "having the power of death," and those who believe them must, no doubt, be "in bondage through fear of death;" but we have no reason to think that these absurd opinions are of so ancient a date as the primitive age. They are among the strong delusions to which the unbelieving Jews have been given up, as the punishment of their impenitence and unbelief. And, at any rate, though they had been then prevalent, it is impossible that an inspired writer could have given his sanction to them: if he had alluded to them at all, it would have been to have exposed their absurdity and falsehood.

The *power of death* has by some been considered as a phrase of the same kind as *the sorrows of death.* "The sorrows of death" are deadly or deathlike sorrows; and in the same way they suppose that "the power of death" is deadly, destructive power, just in the same way as "the Spirit of life" is the living or life-giving Spirit,—"the water of life," life-giving water, etc. In this way of interpreting, the appellation is just equivalent to, 'Him who is possessed of destructive power—him who is mighty to destroy.' This makes good sense, and is agreeable, as we have seen, to the usage of New Testament language, but it does not suit the context. The mention of death in the preceding clause of this verse, and the "fear of death" in the next verse, naturally lead us to expect that the word is used in its ordinary sense.

To "have the power of death" is an expression that naturally suggests the idea of having influence, or authority, or active power in reference to men's dying. We know most certainly that our lives are not at the disposal of the devil. Miserable as the world is, in this case it would be far more miserable. Our times are wholly in God's hand. It is because He bids us live that we live, and it is because He bids us die that we die. That fallen angels have been employed for the infliction of evils of various kinds, some of them terminating in death, we cannot doubt, if we believe the Bible in the plain meaning of the statements; but that they have any power or authority generally in reference to life and death, is in the highest degree improbable.

The idea which I am disposed to consider as intended to be conveyed by the words is this: that he is the author, the introducer, of death among mankind,—death in the case of all mankind being, as the Apostle shows at length in the concluding part of the fifth chapter of the Romans, the penal effect of the first sin of the first man. It is a just remark of an apocryphal writer, that God created man to be immortal, and made him to be an image of His own eternity; nevertheless, through envy of the devil came death into the world. And on infinitely higher authority we know that "by one man," under the influence of the devil, "came death into the world, and death by sin; and so death passed upon all men." We apprehend that the idea of the Apostle is the same as that of his Master when he calls the devil "a murderer"—"a murderer from the beginning." All the death that is in the world may be in this way considered as the work of the devil.

I cannot help suspecting, however, that there is something more implied in the words. "The strength of death" and "the sting of death" seem nearly parallel expressions. Now we know that "the sting of death is sin," or guilt. When the devil, therefore, is said to "have the power of death," I apprehend that it is intimated, that it is through his malignity that death has that penal character which belongs to it, and which chiefly makes it terrible. It is easy to suppose that some change similar to death might be necessary to man's rising to a higher place in the scale of being. Such a death—and, by the mercy of our God, through the death of Christ the death of Christians has become such—is a powerless thing to injure. The sting is not there. But in consequence of the malignant craft of the devil introducing guilt, death is powerful, giving over the body to what, if Christ had not died, would have been hopeless dissolution, and giving over the soul to what, if Christ had not died, would have been hopeless, endless misery.

Now the inspired writer states that the design of the Son of God in becoming man was, "that He might destroy him that has the power of death." To "destroy" the devil, I need scarcely remark, does not mean to annihilate him. He shall exist for ever, to bear the punishment which he deserves. The word rendered *destroy* properly signifies, 'to make void, to render inefficient.'[1] To "destroy him that has the power of death" is to strip him of his power. It is said by the Apostle John, that "for this purpose was the Son of God manifested, to destroy the works of the devil;" *i.e.*, ignorance, error, depravity, and misery. In the passage before us, the destruction is restricted to the peculiar aspect in which the devil is viewed. To destroy him, is so to destroy him as having "the power of death," —to render him, in this point of light, powerless in reference to the children; *i.e.*, to make death cease to be a penal evil. Death, even in the case of the saint, is an expression of the displeasure of God against sin; but it is not—as but for the death of Christ it must have been—the hopeless dissolution of his body; it is not the inlet to eternal misery to his soul. Death to them for whom Christ died consigns, indeed, the body to the grave; but it is in the sure and "certain hope of a glorious resurrection," and it introduces the freed spirit into all the glories of the celestial paradise.

This rendering the devil, as "him who had the power of death," inefficient and powerless with regard to the children of God, was brought about by the death of the incarnate Son of God. It is "through death that He destroyed him that had the power of death." Our Lord's obedience to the death was the expiation of the sins of His people. He endured in their room what, in the estimation of infinite wisdom and righteousness, was abundantly sufficient to make the remission of their guilt not merely consistent with, but gloriously illustrative of, the divine faithfulness and justice, as well as of the divine mercy and grace; so that from death as the work of the devil—from death as the destroyer either of body or soul—they are completely delivered. The devil is entirely baffled and disappointed in reference to *them*; and what he had created as an entrance to hell, is, by means the most extraordinary, converted into the "gate of heaven."

The other view of the ultimate object of our Lord's incarnation refers directly to the saved. It is deliverance. He "took part" of human nature that He might die, and by dying "deliver them who all their lifetime were subject to bondage through fear of death." A slight change in the translation—warranted, perhaps required, by the original text—will make this verse some-

[1] Καταργεῖν = ποιεῖν ἀεργον. Rom. iii. 3–31, vi. 6; 2 Tim. i. 10.

what more perspicuous: "And deliver them from bondage who all their lifetime were subject to fear of death."[1]

The first question here is, Who are the persons thus described? Some have considered the inspired writer as referring to the Jews; others, as referring to all mankind. There is nothing to limit the description to the Jews,—the words are descriptive of what is true with regard to all mankind; but the context plainly requires us to refer them to the only class of persons the Apostle is speaking about throughout the whole paragraph—"the heirs of salvation," the "brethren" of Christ, "the sons of God." They are represented as "subject to fear of death." These words are very ordinarily considered as meaning, 'constantly haunted by distressing fears of death.' This is the case with some individuals, but it is not generally the case with mankind. The greater part of men pass through life without being very much incommoded by the "fear of death." The words do not imply this; they literally signify, 'liable to the fear of death.' All men by nature, and "the heirs of salvation" among the rest, are doomed to death as a penal evil. The awful truth on this subject may be brought before their mind in its meaning and evidence; and if it is, they must be agitated with fear. In these circumstances they feel the sharpness of "the sting of death." They see before them nothing but death—ever-during death, and destruction—total, everlasting destruction. Had it not been for the salvation of Christ, all men would have been, *during their whole life*,[2] liable to be attacked by such fears of death. They are also represented as in *bondage*: they are in a state of slavery to "him who has the power of death."

Now, the design of Christ in assuming human nature is said to be, to deliver from "bondage" those who all their lifetime were liable to the "fear of death," and to do this by dying. Many have supposed that the Apostle refers to the death of Christ here as connected with His resurrection. We rather think that he refers to it in the light in which it is uniformly considered in this Epistle, as an expiation for sin. By enduring,

---

[1] ἔνοχος may be construed with the Genitive, but it usually governs the Dative, and ἀπό governs the Genitive. In thus construing the words, I follow the learned De Rhoer (ad Porphyr. pp. 289, 343), Abresch, and Teller.

[2] Διὰ παντὸς τοῦ ζῆν. The Infinitive in the room of the noun = διὰ πάσης τῆς ζωῆς.

in the room of His people, death as a curse, He has converted death into a blessing to them. They need no longer be afraid of it. They may look forward to it with tranquillity, and even desire. They may say, "O death, where is thy sting? O grave, where is thy victory? The sting of death is sin; and the strength of sin is the law. But thanks be to God, which giveth us the victory through our Lord Jesus Christ."

The subject is continued in the following context. Ver. 16. "For verily He took not on Him the nature of angels; but He took on Him the seed of Abraham."[1]

The meaning of these words, as they stand in our English version, is sufficiently obvious: 'The Son of God assumed into connection with His divine nature, not the nature of angels, but the nature of man; and He did so by becoming a descendant of Abraham.' This is an important truth, but it does not appear to me to be the truth intended by the inspired writer. A careful reader will notice that our translators have inserted a very important word—*the nature*—in the first clause of the verse, to bring out the sense; which, indeed, would have required to be repeated in the second clause—' but He took on Him *the nature* of the seed of Abraham,' as the expression ' seed of Abraham' never in Scripture means anything but the descendants, either natural or spiritual, of that patriarch; and, in strict accuracy, perhaps the words *on Him* should have been marked as a supplement also.

The words as they stand in the original are: "For verily He took not angels, but He took the seed of Abraham." The word rendered "took" never, either in sacred or profane writers, is used to signify, ' to assume, or to put on;' the ordinary and primary signification is, 'to lay hold of.' The sense given in our version, though conveying an important truth, does not well suit the context. The words seem a reason assigned for the statement made in the 14th and 15th verses. The leading statement there is, "Inasmuch as the children are partakers of flesh and blood, He also took part of the same." Now, surely the Apostle would never assign as the reason of this, "For verily He took

---

[1] Δήπου is a particle of asseveration—*certainly*. The Nominative to ἐπιλαμβάνεται is not expressed. Schulzius strangely supposes that θάνατος or διάβολος is to be supplied. There can be no reasonable doubt the Nominative is, ὁ ἀρχ. τ. σ., ὁ ἁγιάζων: He who took part of flesh and blood.

not on Him the nature of angels, but that of man;"—that were just to say, 'He became incarnate, for He became incarnate.' It is not in this way that the author of the Epistle to the Hebrews reasons, though his translators and interpreters have sometimes made him appear to reason so inconclusively.[1]

The real connection is: 'He assumed *human* nature, not *angelic* nature; for He is the Saviour not of angels, but of men.' The word properly signifies 'to lay hold of, to lay the hand on a person or thing.'[2] I may lay hold of a person for different and even opposite purposes. I may lay hold of him to punish him. I may lay hold of him to help him or deliver him. The word in itself merely denotes 'to lay hold of,'—the purpose must be gathered from the context. There is no difficulty in the passage before us. Salvation, deliverance, is the subject spoken of, and the word is to be understood in reference to that subject. "He laid not hold on angels"—*i. e.*, to save them—"but He laid hold on the seed of Abraham," to save them. Understood in this way, there is a close and important connection between these words and the preceding statement. He became a partaker of "flesh and blood," for His object was to save not angels but men. It deserves notice, also, that the word is not in the past, but in the present time: 'He lays not hold on angels, but He lays hold.' The assumption of human nature is a past event, but the salvation of His people is the constant employment of the Saviour.

Having thus fixed the signification and connection of the words, let us briefly attend to the sentiment they convey. "He" —that is, the Son of God—" lays not hold on angels," to save them: He is not the Saviour of angels. The declaration is

---

[1] FROMMANN (Opusc. p. 274) very justly remarks, "If this interpretation stands, Paul must be said to have repeated one and the selfsame thought three times; for this would be the thread of his utterance: 'Forasmuch as the children are partakers of flesh and blood, he also himself likewise took part of the same: for he took not the nature of angels, but of the seed of Abraham. Wherefore it behoved him in all things to be made like to his brethren.' What would this mean, but— 'Christ became a partaker of true human nature: for he became a partaker, not of the nature of angels, but of human nature. Wherefore it behoved him to become a partaker of human nature.' Who, now, would think such stuff tolerable in the utterance, I will not say of a divine writer, but of a mere human writer? 'Christ is the deliverer, not of angels, but of men.'"

[2] Heb. viii. 9.

quite general, and we have no right to limit it. It is true of angels universally, that "He lays not hold on them," to save them. He is not the Saviour of the angels who kept their first estate. We have reason to believe that their happiness is greatly increased by the mediatorial economy. Jesus Christ is not only their Creator and Lord, as God : He is also their Lord and Benefactor, as Mediator ; but He is not their Saviour. They have no guilt to be expiated—no depravity to be destroyed —no misery to be removed. They cannot be saved, for they have not been lost. He is not the Saviour of the angels who left their original habitation. They are guilty, and depraved, and miserable. They need salvation ; but there is nothing in Scripture which would lead us to suppose that a Saviour is provided for them. No. They have been cast into hell; and they are kept in chains, under darkness, to the judgment of the great day. For them is prepared, not salvation, but eternal punishment. The Author of salvation " lays not hold" on them.

But He does lay hold on "the seed of Abraham." "The seed of Abraham" signifies the descendants of Abraham. Sometimes the word is used in reference to the natural descendants of Abraham, sometimes in reference to his spiritual descendants. The Apostle speaks of a seed which is of the law, and a seed which is of faith. It is in the last sense that Abraham is "the father of many nations"—"the father of us all," as the Apostle says. And we are told that he was justified previously to his circumcision, "that he might be the father of all them that believe, though they be not circumcised ; that righteousness might be imputed unto them also." "Therefore it is of faith, that it might be by grace; to the end the promise might be sure to all the seed : not to that only which is of the law, but to that also which is of the faith of Abraham, who is the father of us all (as it is written, I have made thee a father of many nations), before Him whom he believed, even God, who quickeneth the dead, and calleth those things which be not as though they were."[1] "If ye be Christ's," says the same Apostle in the Epistle to the Galatians, "then are ye Abraham's seed." It scarcely admits of a doubt that in the passage before us it is used in the signification of the spiritual seed. It is just equivalent to "the heirs

[1] Rom. iv. 11, 16, 17.

of salvation," "the family of God,"—the Messiah's "brethren," for every one of whom He "tasted death." He does lay hold on every one of the elect family of God, all of whom are "partakers of flesh and blood."

There is something very striking in the language. They are lost—in themselves, hopelessly lost; they are rushing forward to destruction; they are falling into hell. But He stretches forth the arm of omnipotent grace; He "apprehends" them, to use a parallel expression of the Apostle in reference to himself; and, having laid hold of them, He will never, never quit His grasp. "I lay down My life for the sheep." " I give unto them eternal life; and they shall never perish, neither shall any pluck them out of My hand."

What an overwhelming subject of contemplation is this! He is not the Saviour of angels, but of the elect family of man. We are lost in astonishment when we allow our minds to rest on the number and dignity of those whom He does not lay hold of, and the comparative as well as real vileness of those of whom He does take hold. A sentiment of this kind has engaged some good, but in this case not wise men, in an inquiry why the Son of God saves men rather than angels. On this subject Scripture is silent, and so should we be. There is no doubt that there are good reasons for this as for every other part of the divine determinations and dispensations; and it is not improbable that in some future stage of our being these reasons will be made known to us. But, in the meantime, I can go no further than, " Even so, Father, for so it hath seemed good in Thy sight." I dare not " intrude into things which I have not seen," lest I should prove that I am " vainly puffed up by a fleshly mind." But I will say with an apostle, " Behold the goodness and severity of God: on them that fell, severity" —most righteous severity ; " but to them who are saved, goodness"—most unmerited goodness.[1]

The direct and principal point in discussion hitherto has been the propriety of the Divine Saviour's being conformed as to nature with the saved, in order to the accomplishment of their salvation. In the concluding verses the inspired writer adverts more immediately to the important ends served by His being conformed to them not only in nature, but in condition—*in*

[1] See Note E.

*all things,* as he phrases it. Ver. 17. "Wherefore[1] in all things it behoved Him to be made like unto His brethren, that He might be a merciful and faithful high priest in things pertaining to God, to make reconciliation for the sins of the people. 18. For in that He Himself hath suffered, being tempted, He is able to succour them that are tempted."

The connective particle *wherefore* may either be considered as looking backward or forward. If it look backward, its force is, 'Since He is the Saviour not of angels but of men, it behoved Him to be made like unto His brethren.' If it look forward, its force is, 'For this reason it behoved Him to be made like unto His brethren, that He might be a merciful and faithful high priest in things pertaining to God, to make reconciliation for the sins of the people.' It does not matter much which reference is given to the word, though I am disposed to prefer the latter.

The Apostle's assertion is, that it "behoved" the Divine Saviour " to be made like unto His brethren *in all things.*" The expression, "in all things," though in itself universal, is plainly to be limited. It is to be limited, plainly, to the whole of those things necessary to the end in view. And even with regard to these the conformity is not necessarily a complete and perfect conformity. It plainly was not necessary that He should be conformed to His brethren in personal guilt or depravity. This, so far from conducing to the gaining of the object in view, would have completely obstructed it. The conformity referred to includes a conformity of nature. They were men; and it was necessary that He should be a man, possessed of a body capable of suffering death, and a soul endowed with all the faculties and affections of human nature. But the conformity was not complete. His human nature was formed in a miraculous manner, and did not subsist by itself, but in union with the divine. These particular differences were as necessary as the general conformity in nature was to the great end of His being a successful Saviour. He was conformed to His people not only in nature, but in condition. They are in a suffering condition; and He, when on earth, was in a suffering condition—exposed to the same kind of sufferings as those to which they were exposed; though these sufferings produced very

---

[1] ὅθεν as an illative nowhere occurs in the Epistles bearing Paul's name, though it does in one of his recorded speeches, Acts xxvi. 19.

different effects on His innocent and all-perfect mind from what they do on the minds of guilty, depraved men.

This conformity both of nature and condition was becoming and necessary. "It behoved Him." On the supposition of His being divinely appointed to save men as a high priest, this conformity was absolutely necessary. He could not have made "reconciliation for the sins of His people"—He could not in the same degree have executed the duties of a Saviour—had He not been "in *all* things made like unto His brethren."

The language here, as well as in the preceding context, seems intentionally so fashioned as to convey the idea that our Saviour was not originally conformed to His brethren: "It behoved Him to be *made* like" to them.

The great object to the gaining of which this conformity of Christ to His brethren is necessary, is His being " a faithful and merciful high priest," " to make reconciliation for the sins of His people."[1] The object is twofold: that as a high priest He might "make reconciliation for the sins of the people;" and that, in the discharge of His duties as high priest, He might show Himself at once " faithful and merciful." We have already seen that His conformity to His brethren implied two things—participation of their nature, and fellowship with them in their state of suffering. The first of these was necessary to His being a high priest, and " making reconciliation for the sins of the people;" the second was necessary to His being " a merciful and faithful high priest," in the way and degree in which His people stood in need of mercy and faithfulness.

To be a "high priest in things pertaining to God," is just to manage the religious interests of those for whose benefit the person invested with the priestly office performs its functions;[2] and the grand primary duty of the High Priest of guilty men is to make expiation of their guilt, or, as the Apostle here expresses

---

[1] By the λαός are plainly to be understood those who are called, ver. 16, σπέρμα 'Αβραάμ, the peculiar people of God under the new economy: ch. xiii. 12, iv. 9; Acts xv. 14; Tit. ii. 14. Εἰς τὸ ἱλάσκεσθαι τὰς ἁμαρτίας —the full expression is, ἱλ. τὸν Θεὸν κατὰ τ. ἁ. τ. λ.—Vide Grot. de Satisfactione, quoted by Wolfius.

[2] To look after τὰ πρὸς τὸν Θεόν—the full phrase, κατὰ τὰ πράγματα τὰ πρὸς τὸν Θεόν—our affairs Godward. Xenophon well discriminates the object of the priestly and the kingly office: Ἱερεῖ μὲν τὰ πρὸς τοὺς θεούς, στρατηγῷ δὲ τὰ πρὸς τοὺς ἀνθρώπους.—XEN. Rep. Laced. 13, *fin*.

it, "to make reconciliation for the sins of the people,"—to do and suffer what was necessary to render the pardon of sin consistent with, and illustrative of, the divine justice as well as mercy. To do this, it was absolutely necessary that the Divine Saviour should become man—should become "like unto His brethren" by participating of their nature. Every high priest for men must be "taken from among men." Expiation is not a work for angels, nor even for God, merely as God. The duty which He had to perform as the Great High Priest, who was to "give Himself a sacrifice, the Just One in the room of the unjust," made it necessary that He should be conformed to His brethren by assuming their nature.

And as He could not have been a high priest at all, as He could not have made reconciliation, without being conformed to His brethren as to nature, so He could not, in the degree and manner in which they required mercy and fidelity, have been "a merciful and faithful high priest," if He had not been conformed to His brethren in His condition. It is finely observed by Dr Owen, "that in a perfectly holy human nature He should exactly discharge the will of God, was all that was required in order to His being a high priest. But this was not all that the estate and condition of the brethren required. Their sorrows, tenderness, weakness, miseries, disconsolations were such, that if there be not a cotempering of His sublime holiness and absolute perfection in fulfilling all righteousness, with some qualifications inclining Him to condescension, pity, and compassion, and tender sense of their condition, whatever might be the issue of their safety in the life to come, their comforts in this life would be in continual hazard."

To be "a merciful[1] high priest," is to be a tender-hearted, compassionate manager of all our religious interests—to be ever ready, under the influence of a tender sympathy, to support, and comfort, and deliver. To be "a faithful[2] high priest," does not, I apprehend, mean, as some interpret it, a true, a legitimate high priest; nor, as others, a high priest who is generally faithful to God and man both in the discharge of his duties; but a high

---

[1] For illustration of ἐλεήμων, see Matt. v. 7, and Ps. cxlv. 8.

[2] For illustration of πιστός, see 1 Tim. i. 15; 1 Cor. iv. 2; Heb. iii. 2. Πιστός may either signify *fidelis*, who is faithful to his trust, or *fidus*, who deserves to be trusted. Either sense suits very well.

priest who is trustworthy, exact, constant, and careful in attending to his people amid all their varied temptations and sufferings.

To be such " a merciful and faithful high priest," it behoved the Divine Saviour not only to be conformed in nature, but in condition, to the brethren. There is a kind and degree of compassion and fidelity in giving comfort and relief which nothing but fellowship in suffering can teach. Suppose two friends, equally benevolent in their temper, equally attached to you; the one, a person who had never suffered under the afflictions to which you are exposed; the other, one who had experienced the same, or at least a very similar course of trials: would there not be a tenderness, and a suitableness, and a minuteness of appropriate attentions and consolations experienced from the latter, which, in the very nature of things, it is impossible that the former, however kindly disposed, should yield? Who is not struck with astonishment and delight at observing in the plan of salvation such an intimate knowledge of all the peculiarities of our nature, and such a benevolent use made of this intimate knowledge, in securing for man not only the great substantial blessings of salvation, but their being conferred on him in the way best fitted to soothe and comfort him amid the remaining evils of the present state?

This idea of the capacity of the Saviour to sympathize with and relieve His people under their trials, in consequence of His having Himself been tried, is very beautifully amplified in the verse with which this division of the Epistle closes. 18. " For in that He Himself hath suffered, being tempted, He is able to succour them that are tempted."

The connection of this verse with what goes before is abundantly plain. 'It was a wise arrangement to make Him "like unto His brethren," in order to His being " a merciful and faithful high priest;" "for in that He Himself hath suffered, being tempted, He is able to succour them that are tempted."' The words, "in that He hath suffered, being tempted," may either be considered as equivalent to, 'because He hath suffered, being tempted,'[1] or, 'in whatever suffering He has sustained, being tempted,'[2] He is able to succour those who are tempted

---

[1] Considering ἐν ᾧ adverbial, as equivalent to *quoniam*: Rom. viii. 3; 1 Pet. i. 6.

[2] As Rom. ii. 1; Acts v. 8, vi. 17, i. 2.

in the same way. I prefer the latter way of interpretation. The Apostle seems to have in view what he said in the preceding verse: "It behoved Him to be made in ALL things like His brethren, that He might be a merciful and faithful high priest in things pertaining to God, to make reconciliation for the sins of the people." And why in ALL things? Because in whatever trials He was conformed to them, in these He would be peculiarly fitted and disposed to comfort and help them.

Our Saviour is here said to have "suffered, being tempted." The word "tempt," in the modern usage of the English language, is nearly restricted to the sense of enticement to sin; but in the Bible generally, it is just equivalent to trial. "He suffered, being tempted," is therefore equivalent to, 'He suffered, being tried.'[1] He was exposed to every variety of suffering to which innocent human nature could be exposed. He speaks of His whole life as one scene of trial: "Ye have continued with Me in My temptation"—during My trial.[2] Poverty, reproach, hunger, thirst, weariness, pain even to agony, unkind treatment from relations and friends, temptation in the strict sense of the term, especially from the great enemy of God and man, and the loss of the delights arising from sensible communion with His Father,—these are some of the things in which "He suffered, being tried."

Now in all these things, wherein "He suffered, being tried, He is able to succour those who are tried." "Those who are tried" is just another description of that class of persons to whom the whole discussion refers,—"the heirs of salvation"—"the children of God"—the "brethren" of Christ and "the seed of Abraham"—the people for whose sins atonement is made. "The heirs of salvation," while in the present state, are exposed to a variety of trials—trials as men, trials as Christians. But their Saviour is able to "succour" them—to give them the help which they need under them. He is *able* to do this. The word "able" is expressive both of physical and moral ability. He both can and will; He is able and disposed. The word able is often used in this way in reference to God and Christ: Rom. iv. 21, xi. 23, xiv. 4, xv. 14, xvi. 25; 2 Tim. i. 12.[3]

---

[1] It may either be $\pi\acute{\epsilon}\pi ov\theta\epsilon v\ \pi\epsilon\iota\rho\alpha\sigma\theta\epsilon\acute{\iota}\varsigma$ or $\pi\epsilon\pi ov\theta\grave{\omega}\varsigma\ \grave{\epsilon}\pi\epsilon\iota\rho\acute{\alpha}\sigma\theta\eta$.

[2] Luke xxii. 28.

[3] Carpzov well remarks: "the 'can' and the 'will' must be linked

He is able to succour those who are tried *in that wherein He has suffered, being tried.* And there is, as we have already remarked, no suffering which innocent human nature can endure that our Saviour was a stranger to.

How admirably is the plan of the Christian salvation suited to the circumstances of men! And how rich and abundant the consolation which this particular part of it is calculated to administer to the afflicted Christian! He not only knows that "the High Priest of his profession" has "made reconciliation" for his sin, and will one day call him up to heaven to sit with Him on His throne,—he not only knows that all his afflictions are measured out to him by infinite wisdom and infinite love,—he knows also that his compassionate Saviour enters into all his feelings; exercises towards him a most tender, and wise, and watchful care; and will not withhold from him that measure and degree of consolation under, and deliverance from his trials, which He sees best fitted for promoting his spiritual improvement and everlasting salvation. Oh! could Christians by a living faith but realize all this, would they not "glory in tribulation," and count it all joy when they are brought into manifold trials! Who does not sympathize with Mr Stuart in his devout interjectional note? and who does not feel such a note a refreshment in reading an exegetical work?—" Wonderful condescension of divine love! Here is the great mystery of godliness: 'God made manifest in the flesh.' And while Jesus sits on the throne of the universe as Lord over all, the Christian is reminded that he does this in his nature, as his brother. In the person of Jesus, man is exalted above angels: yea, he himself is to attain a rank superior to theirs; for, while Jesus passed them by, He laid down His life for us, in order to exalt us above them. Deeper and deeper still becomes the mystery. The debt of gratitude appears boundless when viewed in this light; and the baseness of ingratitude and disobedience as boundless too. What can we do less than lie down in the dust, overwhelmed with a sense of our guilt, and exclaim with the prophet, 'Who is like unto Thee,—a God forgiving iniquity, and passing by the offences of Thine heritage?'"

together, for τὸ δύνασθαι. means both." Rom. xv. 14 : δυνάμενοι ἀλλήλους νουθετεῖν.—Chrysostom understood the phrase well. He explains it, "he will stretch out his hand with great readiness, he will feel for us."

## NOTE A, p. 61.

"The supposition that the author of the Epistle to the Hebrews by mistake, *i.e.*, from complete ignorance of the context from which he took the passage, considered those words as an address directed to *Christ*, is too awkward to find any acceptance with us. The author of the Epistle to the Hebrews can scarcely be conceived of as so senseless, that, without any occasion, he should use words which apply to God as if they applied to the incarnate Son of God. So coarse a mistake would certainly not have escaped detection; for it is not to be forgotten that his *readers* were also in a certain sense his *opponents*, and would scarcely have allowed themselves to be drawn away from their deep-rooted prejudice in favour of the Old Covenant and the Old Testament Israel, by *bad* and *untenable* arguments. That supposition is all the more improbable when it is considered, that the author has evidently not quoted all these passages from memory, but carefully copied them from the LXX., so that he could not possibly be ignorant of their original context. In general, however, it is a very superficial and shallow view that would lead us all at once to consider the use of Old Testament passages in the New Testament as parallel with the exegetico-dogmatic method of argumentation pursued by the Rabbins. The Apostles and apostolical men have, indeed, exhibited in their epistles such a freedom from the spirit of Jewish tradition, such an originality and youthful vigour of new life, such a fineness and depth of psychological and historical intuition; and the whole system of Christianity in its freshness and originality stands in such contrast to the old, insipid, anti-Messianic Judaism, and appears so thoroughly a new structure from the foundation resting on the depths of Old Testament revelation, and not a mere enlargement of the pharisaico-rabbinical pseudo-Judaism; that it were indeed wonderful, if the same apostolical men had in their interpretation of Old Testament passages held themselves dependent on the Jewish exegesis and hermeneutical method. In reality, however, the apostolical exegesis of the Old Testament stands in directest opposition to the Jewish-rabbinical, so that one can scarcely imagine a more complete and diametrical difference. In the rabbinical interpretation it is always *single words*—studiously *separated* from the context—from which inferences, arbitrary of course, are drawn. The Rabbins affirm, for example, that when a man lies three days in the grave, his entrails are torn from his body and cast in the face of the dead; *for it is written* in Mal. ii. 3, 'I will also cast the filth of your festivals in your face.' (Sepher joreh chattaim, num. 66.) Nay, the later Rabbinism, as a direct result of this arbitrary procedure, went the length of drawing inferences even from single letters. They taught, for example, the transmigration of the soul, and that the souls of men ever continue to live in men; thus the life of Cain passed into Jethro, his spirit into Korah, his soul into the Egyptians (Ex. ii. 12 ss.), for it is written, Gen. iv. 24, יקם קין, and ׳, ק, and ם, are the first letters of Jethro, Korah, and מצרים. (Jalkut rubeni, num. 9.) The genuine pharisaical principle which forms the basis of all this is, *that the letter as such* is what is most significant. The New

Testament writers, on the contrary—as we have seen in reference to Heb. i. 6-9, and as we shall see more and more as we proceed with the Epistle—drew all their arguments from *the spirit* of the passages *considered in their connection*. Nothing at all is inferred from the mere letter of the passages quoted. In Ps. xlv. there is not a syllable about *angels*. When the author, notwithstanding, has adduced that passage as a proof that the Messiah is superior to the angels, he has, as we have seen, necessarily reckoned on a *rational consideration of the passage on the part of his readers*, and a *reflective logical comparison* of the passage with that in Ps. civ. 4, and the force of the argument proceeds only from such a judicious interpretation and attentive examination of the ideas and references objectively contained in both passages.

"The procedure which he uniformly follows is not that of collecting passages in which the *words* 'Son' and 'angel' occur, and arbitrarily interpreting them—thus the Rabbins would have done—but of adducing the weightiest passages in which the Messianic salvation is prophesied of (substantially, although not at all under the name 'Messianic'), and from these developing the *idea of this salvation*. Thus in vers. 7-12, the simple and fundamental idea which he wants to show is, that while the angels are employed by God as *ministering in temporary appearances of nature*, the Messianic salvation, on the contrary, is ever represented as the lifting up of the man, the theocratical king, immediately to *God*; as the immediate saving act of God Himself; *i.e.*, in one word, as an immediate relation of God to men without the intervention of mediation by angels. He finds this *idea* of the Messianic salvation in those expressions of the Psalms, but not dry outward statements respecting the *person* of Christ."—EBRARD'S *Commentary*, Engl. Transl.

NOTE B, p. 70.

In a sermon on Heb. i. 14, preached by the author in October 1854, the following statements occur, on the continued ministry of the angels under the present dispensation, and the ends answered by that divine arrangement. After mentioning various instances of angelic ministrations to the saints, recorded in Scripture, the author proceeds :—

As we have no reason to think that the kind interposition of angels in behalf of the people of God was one of the peculiar characteristics of the patriarchal and Mosaic dispensations, so we have no reason to think that, under the new economy, it was intended to be confined to its commencement. Though, in accordance with its spiritual character, their interposition is not so obvious, we have no reason to think it less extensive or real. In that revelation of Jesus Christ which God gave to John the divine, and which was sent and signified to him by His angel, is a prophetic narrative of the fates of the church and of the world ; and nothing is more remarkable in it than the prominence given to the fact, that angels are leading agents in the terrible revolutions by which the enemies of truth and righteousness are to be punished, and the kingdoms of this world to become the kingdom of our Lord and His Christ. The promises already quoted from the Book of Psalms[1] have nothing in them which would lead us to restrict their reference to any age of the Church; and our text is of itself quite sufficient to warrant the assertion, that *all* those who shall be heirs of salvation are the objects of continual angelic guardianship. As they watch over them through life, we have reason to believe that in the last trial they take a deep interest, and conduct the parted spirit into the regions of eternal rest. What else can mean the declaration of our Lord in the parable, that "the soul of Lazarus, when he died, was carried by angels into Abraham's bosom?" It has been beautifully said, "To our natural feelings, a deathbed scene is in a high degree revolting and afflicting. We behold a helpless human being, emaciated by disease, panting for breath, and convulsed with pain; his countenance pale, his lips quivering, and his brow bedewed with a cold sweat; and with his expiring groans are mingled the lamentations of his disconsolate friends. But were not the spiritual world hidden by a veil, we should see the glorious inhabitants of heaven surrounding his bed, and sympathizing with the sufferer—for even the Lord of angels has a fellow-feeling of the infirmities of His people—yet rejoicing at his unmurmuring patience and stedfast hope; and when the struggle was over, bearing his spirit away to their own abode, where there is no more death, neither sorrow, nor crying, nor any more pain."[2]

"And at the second coming of the Lord, the angels shall appear as "ministering spirits, sent forth to minister to them who are heirs of salvation." At the great harvest, the angels are to be the reapers; and as they shall pluck up the tares, and throw them into the fire, so shall they gather the wheat into the garner. The Lord, "the Son of Man," the Son of God, "will send His angels, with a great sound of a trumpet, and they shall gather together His elect"—those who shall be heirs of salvation—"from the four winds, from one end of heaven to another." Such is a summary of the statements made in Scripture concerning the ministry of angels.

Let us now, for a little, turn our attention to the question which naturally arises, What are some of the ends which are answered, and which, we have reason to think, were meant to be answered, by the divine arrangement which we have been considering? Why does God choose to bestow benefits on the objects of His special favour, the heirs of salvation, through the instrumentality of angels, rather than directly, without instrumentality, or through some other instrumentality? It were enough, though in reply to that question we could only say, "Even so, Father, for so it hath seemed good in Thy sight." We are never to forget, however, that while God acts sovereignly, He does not act capriciously. There are always the best reasons for what He does; and though in every case we are but imperfectly acquainted with them—though in many cases we are entirely ignorant of them,—yet in many cases they are discoverable; and when they are so, it is not only lawful, but dutiful, devoutly to inquire into them. In the present case, the reasons of the divine appointment are, within certain limits, abundantly apparent. I shall merely enumerate a few of them. This arrangement brings in a striking manner before the mind the magnitude and order of the divine government,—what our great

[1] Ps. xxxiv. 7; xci. 10-12.     [2] Dr Dick.

poet calls "the throne and equipage of God's almightiness." It exercises the holy principles of obedience and benevolence in the angels themselves, and leads them into a deeper acquaintance with the manifestation of the divine character in the wonderful economy of human redemption, learning from the development of that plan to the Church, to which they minister, "the manifold wisdom of God." It is a delightful proof of the tender care which God cherishes towards His people, and is in this way well fitted to support and comfort them. It establishes a happy intercourse between the different parts of God's holy, happy family, and lays up materials for their permanent enjoyment when they are united into one holy society in their Father's house of many mansions above. But what particularly deserves our attention, from its bearing on the Apostle's object in the whole of the discussion which occupies this section of the Epistle, this divine appointment sheds a peculiar lustre over the character and work of our Lord Jesus Christ. The angels are not only made subject to Him as their Lord—called on to worship Him as their God—but they are employed in watching over the safety, and promoting the happiness of His people, amid the trials, and imperfections, and sorrows of this mortal life—many of them being "not wise men after the flesh, or mighty, or noble, but foolish and weak" in the world's estimation—poor, despised sufferers. What an honour to our Lord, for the highest class of intelligent beings to reckon themselves, then, honoured, not only in directly ministering to His honour, but in ministering to the lowest necessities of these poor, despised ones, because they belong to Him! Their joyful engagement in such services, to such persons, for such a reason, is the finest of all illustrations of the force of their anthem, as they mean it, "Worthy is the Lamb to receive glory and honour."—ED.

## NOTE C, p. 100.

It is due to the author to state that he appears to have somewhat modified his views of the construction and meaning of Heb. ii. 9; as will be seen by the following extract from a sermon preached by him in Sept. 1854. After illustrating four important truths contained in the text—1st, That Jesus originally existed in a state of superiority to the angels; 2d, that He was made lower than the angels; 3d, that when thus made lower than the angels He suffered death; and 4th, that He has for His suffering of death been crowned with glory and honour;—the author proceeds to remark:—

"Thus *in* Him did the ancient oracle in the 8th Psalm find its accomplishment. But the direct subject of that oracle is not *Jesus*, but *man*—lost and redeemed man; and *by* him the oracle, in this its direct and principal reference, is in due time to be completely fulfilled. The Captain of salvation, Himself "made perfect through suffering," will lead every one of the "many sons" to fellowship with Him in the "glory and honour" with which He has been crowned.

"This is the last great truth intimated by the text, in these words, "that by the grace of God He might taste death for every man"—literally, 'for every one;' *i. e.*, for all the sons He is bringing to glory—all the children whom He is to present to the Father—all who are to be "heirs of salvation." The concluding clause of the verse is the only part of it, the interpretation of which involves any difficulty. It seems strange to say that Jesus Christ should be crowned with glory and honour "that He might taste death for every one" of the heirs of salvation. Some have endeavoured to remove this difficulty by transposing the clauses of the verse thus: 'We see Jesus, who for a season was made lower than the angels, that He might taste death for every man, crowned with glory and honour on account of the suffering of death.' This is important truth, clearly stated; but not only does the construction of the language forbid the use of such a liberty of transposition, but in this case there is no reference to what is obviously the Apostle's object, to show how the making of Jesus "lower than the angels," and "for the suffering of death" "crowning Him with glory and honour" secures the fulfilment of the oracle, that men, made lower than the angels in consequence of sin, are yet in the world to come to be raised to a higher state than that of the angels. Others would give a different meaning to the particle rendered *that*, in order that. Some would render it 'after that,' others 'so that;' but neither of these plans seems satisfactory. I think the meaning is, 'that Jesus Christ, made lower than the angels, after having suffered, and on account of having suffered death, was crowned with glory and honour, that His tasting death—which is just His dying—might be, and might appear to be, so *for*—i. e., for the benefit of—every one of the heirs of salvation, as that they all might, according to the ancient oracle, no longer inferior to the angels, be crowned with glory and honour also;' as it is expressed in the following verse, He, as the Captain of salvation, was "made perfect through suffering" that He might lead them, "the many sons," to glory. They could not have been raised from their state of inferiority to angels had He not become inferior to angels; they could not have been delivered from death had He not died; they could not have been raised to glory had He not been raised to glory. And, on the other hand, His becoming inferior to angels, suffering death, and being crowned with glory, absolutely secures their being raised from their inferiority to the angels, by His incarnation, death, and exaltation on the ground of His meritorious death. The cause which produced mortality, and other more dreadful proofs of the divine displeasure against man,—in other words, guilt is removed by the all-efficacious atoning death of the incarnate Son of God, by which "He put away sin;" and the glory and honour thus obtained for Himself, implying "all power in heaven and on earth," secure that those whom He so loved as to descend to their level so far as that was possible, and die the death they deserved and were doomed to die, should be made, so far as their nature admits, participants of His glory and honour—a glory and honour far superior to any that belongs, or ever can belong, to angels. God, as the reward of the Son's "glorifying Him on the earth" by "finishing the work given Him to do," which was the "offering of His body once for all," glorifies Him by giving Him all "power over all flesh," "all power in heaven and earth," "that He may give eternal life," and crown with glory and honour "all those whom He has given Him."

"In raising man, who had been justly, on account of sin, made lower than the angels—subjected to death in all the extent of meaning belonging to that awful word—to a height of dignity and happiness so exalted, by such means—the bringing down the only begotten Son to man's level, that He might be capacitated to make atonement for him, and the raising Him as incarnate to the throne of the universe, that He might have at once the authority and power necessary to save man—in these dispensations what a display is given of the grace of God—His free, sovereign benignity! Well might the Apostle say that it was " by the grace of God" that He " tasted death for every one of His saved ones." Whether you look upward to God, or downward to man—whether you look at the misery averted, or the happiness secured—whether you look at the number, and variety, and value of the benefits, or at the wonderful means by which they are obtained, and through which they are bestowed—you equally are led to the conclusion that the whole economy is " according to the riches of divine grace." The blessings were unmerited, unsolicited, by guilty depraved man, and can be traced to no principle in the divine nature but self-moved love. "Herein is love, that God gave His Son to be the propitiation for our sins." " God has commended His love to us, in that, while we were yet sinners, Christ died for us." " Behold what manner of love the Father hath bestowed on us, that"—in order that—"we should be called the sons of God!" "Behold what manner of love He hath bestowed on us" in making us sons, "heirs of God, joint heirs with Christ Jesus"—heirs of the world, "inheritors of all things!"—ED.

NOTE D, p. 107.

I have sometimes thought that ἡ σωτηρία may here be used as a denomination of the saved, as ἡ μετοικεσία, the captivity, is a name for the captives: " He led captivity captive." The meaning of the phrase in this case is peculiarly appropriate—The Leader of the redeemed. He conducts them all to glory by a path similar to that by which He Himself entered into glory.

Ἀγαγόντα is by some connected with αὐτῷ, by others with ἀρχηγόν; referring in the one case to God, in the other to Christ. The grammatical objection to the first mode of interpretation might be got over; for ἀνακόλουθα of this kind are not unfrequent in Paul's writings: Rom. ii. 8, viii. 3; 2 Cor. xii. 17; Col. iii. 16; Eph. iv. 2; 2 Cor. ix. 10; Acts xv. 22; and such anomalous constructions are to be found in the best classic writers, as has been shown, for instance, by Hoogeveen ad Viger. Idiotism. pp. 264, 267, 271. But, setting this objection aside, there seem strong reasons for preferring the second interpretation. These are very well stated by EBRARD: —" With respect to the construction of the tenth verse, it is self-evident, a, that ἔπρεπε γὰρ αὐτῷ is the governing clause; b, that the relative clause δι' ὃν depends on αὐτῷ; c, that the subject to ἔπρεπε is formed through the infinitive τελειῶσαι; and d, that τὸν ἀρχηγόν depends on τελειῶσαι as its object. The only doubtful point is, whether the accusative ἀγαγόντα, with what belongs to it, is *accusative of the subject* to τελειῶσαι (consequently, together with τελειῶσαι, forms an acc. c. inf.), or, whether ἀγαγόντα is in *apposition* to the *accusative of the object* ἀρχηγόν. In the latter case, the word in apposition would be placed before its principal word, in order that the latter may receive all the greater emphasis (just as in ver. 9, the attribute ἠλαττωμένον was placed first, and Ἰησοῦν followed for the sake of the emphasis). That the αὐτὸς δι' ὅν, as subject of the verb τελειῶσαι, is different from the ἀρχηγός as the object of this τελειῶσαι, as also, that the ἀρχηγός is Christ, is self-evident; the αὐτὸς δι' ὅν is, therefore, God the Father. If now, following the former construction, we render the words thus (with Olshausen): 'It became Him, for whom and through whom are all things, in bringing many to glory, to make the Leader of their salvation perfect through suffering,' then God the Father is here the one to whom the action expressed by the ἄγειν belongs, and this whole clause, πολλοὺς υἱοὺς εἰς δόξαν ἀγαγόντα, receives the place of a mere *accessary* limitation, to some extent a conditional limitation. If God (thus we might explain the idea)—if God would bring many sons to glory, then must He make Him whom He has chosen as their Captain perfect *through suffering*. The emphasis rests here on the words διὰ παθημάτων. That the *suffering was necessary*, is the kernel of the thought; all the rest serves only for preparation.—If again, following the other construction, we render the passage thus: 'For it became Him, for whom and through whom are all things, to make the *Captain* of their salvation perfect through suffering, as one who should bring *many* sons to glory,' then the emphasis here rests evidently on πολλοὺς υἱοὺς ἀγαγόντα and ἀρχηγόν. It is, however, precisely one of the peculiarities of our author's style to place such principal clauses, as it were, in the *periphery* of his sentences, and this of itself would suffice to give the preference to this second construction. In addition to this, there is the beautiful parallelism resulting from this construction between the Ἰησοῦν placed after, and the ἀρχηγόν, in like manner, placed after. Moreover, the two ideas are thus placed antithetically to each other: at present, *Jesus* alone is exalted; but He is exalted as a *leader of others*. The train of thought, then, absolutely requires that the emphasis in ver. 10 should rest upon this—that through Jesus *the rest of mankind also* attain to glory, consequently, on the *end* and *result* of the suffering of Jesus—but not on the means, the suffering itself. And how strong the emphasis which the author lays upon that *result* he shows by giving a twofold expression to the idea, that through Jesus many attain to glory, first, in the words πολλοὺς υἱοὺς ἀγαγόντα, and then in the word ἀρχηγός. We are not, therefore, at liberty to sink the clause, πολλοὺς υἱοὺς ἀγαγόντα, into a mere accessary limitation, which, according to the former construction, would be unavoidable, but must necessarily give the preference to the second construction. Ver. 10 is connected with ver. 9 as an explanation of it; there, as we saw, all the stress lay on ὑπὲρ παντός; in ver. 10, too, it must therefore be shown how *others also* attain to glory through Jesus. And the same idea is followed out also in ver. 11. It is shown in ver. 11 how the glory of *Christ* is participated in by *man*, but not why it was necessary that Christ should *suffer* in order to procure this glory. We render the passage accordingly: 'It became Him, for whom and through whom all things subsist, to make perfect through suffering the *Captain* of their salvation, as one who should bring *many sons* unto glory.' The idea that Christ could not be a first fruits of others without suffering, finds its explanation in the passages, John xiv. 2, 3, xvi. 7. Πρέπειν, as also ὀφείλειν, ver. 17, seems to denote not a fatalistic necessity, but a necessity lying in the nature of the thing, and, therefore, in God's own wise, world-governing will. That the Father is here designated by δι' οὗ τὰ πάντα, which is usually a term of designation for the Son (Rom. xi. 36 ; 1 Cor. viii. 6 ; ἐξ οὗ is generally said of the Father), is explained partly by the paronomasia with δι' ὅν, partly by this,— that the Father is here regarded not as the Creator, but as the Governor of the world, through, and under, whose guidance the work of salvation is accomplished."—*Comm.* pp. 87–89.

### Note E, p. 133.

"But why a philanthropy rather than a philangely? Why a redemption for men and not for devils? Here men give their conjectures. Man, say some, sinned by seduction, but devils by self-motion. In the fall of men, say others, all the human nature fell ; but in the fall of the angels all the angelical nature fell not. Others allege that the sin of angels was more damnable than man's, because their nature was more sublime than his. Others yet affirm that men are capable of repentance, but devils not, because whatever they once choose, they do *immobiliter velle* : the devil sinneth from the beginning. 'Tis not said he sinned, but he sin*neth* ; because from his first apostasy he sinneth on incessantly. But, alas, who can limit the Holy One? Might not His boundless mercy have saved the self-tempted devils? What if His devouring justice had broke out against devil-seduced men, nay, against all the race of men? Who should accuse Him for the nations which perish, which He made, and sin hath marred? Wisd. xii. 12. Could not the blood of God have washed out the blackest spots of fallen angels? Was not the Almighty Spirit of grace able to melt a devil into repentance? Had we poor worms been to dispute with the devil about the body of Christ, as Michael did with him about the body of Moses, O how easily would he have reasoned us out of our Redeemer! What! (would he have said) shall the tender bowels of God be let down to you on earth, and restrained to us in heaven? Will the all-wise God repair His clay images in the dunghill of this lower world, and neglect His fairer pictures once hung up in His own palace of glory? May not the Son of God be a Redeemer at an easier rate without stepping a foot from His Father's house, and will He travel down so far as an incarnation? How much better were it for Him to spot Himself with an assumed cherub than to take flesh into His glorious person? But the great God hath neither given angels a day to plead for a Redeemer, nor man a license to pry into His ark. Wonder then, O man, at this astonishing difference made by the Divine Will alone. Angels must be damned, and men may be saved ; golden vessels are irreparably broken, and earthen pots are set together again ; inmates of glory drop to hell, and dust and ashes fly up to heaven. When I consider Thy heavens, and the stars glistening there, Lord, what is man, that Thou mindest him? Ps. viii. 4. But when I consider the heaven of heavens, and Thy angels dropping thence into utter darkness, Lord, what is man, that Thou savest him? 'Misericordia Domini plena terra est ; quare non dictum est " plenum est cœlum?"

quia sunt spirituales nequitiæ in cœlestibus, sed non illæ ad commune jus indulgentiæ Dei, remissionemque peccatorum pertinent,' as holy Ambrose expresses it. Even so, gracious Father, because so it seemeth good in Thy sight."—POLHILL's *Divine Will*, pp. 174-177.

## CHAPTER II.

### THE SUPERIORITY OF JESUS CHRIST TO MOSES.

#### INTRODUCTORY.

IN that illustrious assemblage of great and good men with whom the Old Testament Scriptures make us acquainted, there is none who has higher claims on our attentive consideration than Moses, the legislator of Israel. Whether we attend to his intellectual endowments or moral excellences—to the gifts he received from nature, or to the acquirements made by his own exertions—to his personal virtues, or to his public services—to the important revolutions accomplished through his instrumentality during his life, or to the invaluable legacy which he left behind him in his writings,—it will be difficult to find, in the records either of profane or sacred history, an individual whose character is so well fitted at once to excite attachment and command veneration, and whose story is so replete at once with interest and instruction. From his earliest years he was marked out by the peculiar care of Providence as a person destined to act no common part on the theatre of the world. Exposed, in common with his infant brethren, to imminent danger from the barbarous policy of a jealous tyrant, he was for three months protected by maternal tenderness; and when at last the cruel necessity of circumstances deprived him of this natural guardianship, he was, by a series of remarkable events, in which even a sceptic must be constrained to acknowledge the hand of God, placed in circumstances of security and comfort, under the immediate care of the daughter of that king who had doomed him to an untimely death. Under her patronage—probably with the name, certainly with the advantages, of her son—Moses spent his childhood and youth. These precious seasons were not, however, wasted by him in the trifling employments and luxurious pleasures with which a court abounds, but were busily devoted to the acquisition of those branches of knowledge for which Egypt at the time was pre-eminently distinguished. But neither the splendours of the Egyptian court, nor the charms of Egyptian learning, could extinguish in the bosom of Moses the fire of patriotism, make him forgetful that he was an Israelite, or insensible to the multiplied and severe oppression under which his enslaved nation groaned. An incident occurred soon after his arriving at maturity, which strikingly displayed that love of liberty and of his country, and that hatred of oppression and oppressors, which afterwards shone forth so brightly in the character and conduct of the deliverer of Israel. As the qualifications which render a man truly great are not all to be acquired in the busy haunts of men, this incident was rendered by Divine Providence the means of removing him from the dangerous pleasures and ensnaring studies of the Egyptian metropolis, and procuring for him the advantages of seclusion and meditation. He fled into the land of Midian, and spent a considerable term of years in the humble labours of pastoral life. We have no detailed account of the manner in which Moses spent these years of retirement; but it is reasonable to suppose that they were spent in reflection on his former acquirements, in adding to his stock of useful information, and in the cultivation of communion with God in the duties of life and in the exercises of a sublime and affectionate devotion. But the uncommon powers and acquirements of Moses were not always to remain thus unemployed. When the instrument was fully prepared, it was devoted to its appropriate work. While engaged in the duties of his employment as a shepherd, the God of his fathers appeared to him, and invested him with that most dignified of all characters, the emancipator of the enslaved. Armed with the delegated power of miraculous operation, he accomplished the great work of the deliverance of his countrymen. Having first overcome their prejudices, and then baffled at once the policy and power of their oppressors, he led them forth towards the land which God had promised to their ancestors. By him, under the inspiration of God, was given that system of religious and political institutions, so remarkable in themselves, and so superior to anything which mere human wisdom has ever devised, by which the Israelites continued for a long course of ages so favourably distinguished from the rest of mankind; and for forty years, during their wanderings in the deserts of Arabia, to which they were doomed on account of their unbelief and rebellion, he managed their affairs with consummate wisdom. It was not at all wonderful that such a man should establish for himself a paramount place in the reverential esteem of all succeeding generations of his countrymen; and that, whoever might be the second, Moses would be the first name in the splendid roll of Israelitish worthies.

Ver. 1. "Wherefore, holy brethren, partakers of the heavenly calling, consider the Apostle and High Priest of our profession, Christ Jesus."—These words form the commencement of the second great section of the doctrinal part of the Epistle, or, perhaps, rather are the transition from the first to the second. The subject of the section already considered is the superiority of Jesus Christ to the angels. The subject of the section on the consideration of which we are about to enter, is the superiority of Jesus Christ to Moses.

The particle *wherefore*, with which the section opens, may be considered as either retrospective or prospective in its reference. In the first case it is equivalent to: 'Since Jesus Christ is so incomparably superior to the angels both in nature and in office, and since His incarnation and sufferings are so closely connected both with His exaltation and our salvation, we ought most seriously to fix our minds on Him in those characters in which the Gospel exhibits Him.' In the second case it is equivalent to: 'For this reason we ought to contemplate with reverence and affection Christ Jesus, that while He strikingly resembles, He infinitely excels, Moses, the legislator of Israel.' It does not matter much which of these two views of the connection of the passage is adopted.

There are two points to which our attention must be successively directed: (1) The appellations here given by the inspired writer to the Hebrew Christians; and (2) the exhortation which he addresses to them. The appellations are, "Holy brethren," "partakers of the heavenly calling;" and the exhortation is, "Consider Christ Jesus, the Apostle and High Priest of our profession."

The first appellation which he gives to the Hebrew Christians is, "Holy brethren." All mankind may be considered as one family, and may be addressed as *brethren*. "God hath made of one blood all the nations of men who dwell on the face of the earth." "Have we not one Father? hath not one God created us?" I am not aware, however, that the word is ever employed in the Scriptures in this most extensive sense. The appellation is sometimes used to convey the idea that the persons addressed belong to the same nation,—as when Peter, addressing the Jews, Acts ii. 29, says, "Brethren, let me freely speak unto you;" and as when Paul says, "I have continual sorrow of heart for my brethren," which he immediately explains by adding, "my kinsmen according to the flesh," Rom. ix. 3. See also Acts xxii. 5, xxviii. 21. It is most frequently used by the Apostle to denote that spiritual relation in which true Christians stand to one another as children of the same heavenly Father, members of the same holy family. We are all the children of God "through faith in Christ Jesus," and therefore we are all brethren: Acts vi. 3; 1 Cor. v. 11; Col. i. 2; 1 Thess. v. 25. It is sometimes—though not, I apprehend, often—used to denote ministers in contradistinction to private Christians; as in Phil. iv. 21: "The brethren which are with me salute you. All the saints salute you." There can be little doubt that in the case before us the appellation is given to the whole body of the Hebrew Christians, and that it is intended to express the idea, not of their being the brethren of the writer, according to the flesh, but of their belonging to that spiritual brotherhood to which he also belonged. I am disposed to think, however, that the primary idea in the term, as used here, is not so much the mutual relation between them and the writer, and between each other, as their common relation to Christ—HIM who is "the first-born among many brethren." The use of the appellation was probably suggested by what the Apostle said at the 11th verse of the preceding chapter: "HE is not ashamed to call them *brethren*, saying, I will declare Thy name unto My brethren." This is a view of the state of true Christians peculiarly replete both with instruction and consolation. They are mutually brethren; but what lies at the foundation of this mutual relation is, their common relation to their great Elder Brother. How high the honour, how rich the privilege, how numerous, how weighty the obligations, that are connected with this relation!

The Apostle addresses the Hebrew Christians not only as brethren of Christ, but as "*holy* brethren." The epithet, as well as the appellation, seems to have been suggested by the previous train of thought: "Both the Sanctifier and the sanctified"—both He who makes holy and they who are made holy—"are all of one." The appellation "holy" signifies separated from a common to a sacred purpose—devoted, dedicated to God. It intimates their being set apart by God for Himself—separated from "the world lying under the wicked one"—dedicated to God by "the sprinkling of the blood of Jesus, and the washing of regeneration." I can scarcely doubt that, in using this epithet, the writer of this Epistle had a reference to the appellations given to the Jewish nation, in the same way as the Apostle Peter, when addressing the same class of persons, says, "But ye are a chosen generation, a royal priesthood, *a holy nation*, a peculiar people."[1] What an interesting and delightful view is thus presented to our minds of genuine Christians scattered over all the earth—belonging to almost every kindred, and people, and tongue, and nation—distinguished from one another in an almost infinite variety of ways, as to talent, temper, education, rank, and circumstances, yet bound together by an invisible band, even the faith of the truth, to one great object of their confidence, and love, and obedience, Christ Jesus—forming one great brotherhood, devoted to the honour and service of His Father and their Father, His God and their God! Do we belong to this holy brotherhood? The question is an important one; and, as affording one of the shortest and most certain methods of resolving it, I beg your attention to an interesting incident in the Gospel history: "While He yet talked to the people, behold, His mother and His brethren stood without, desiring to speak with Him. Then one said unto Him, Behold, Thy mother and Thy brethren stand without, desiring to speak with Thee. But He answered and said unto him that told Him, Who is My mother? and who are My brethren? And He stretched forth His hand toward His disciples, and said, Behold My mother and My brethren! For whosoever shall do the will of My Father which is in heaven, the same is My brother, and sister, and mother."[2]

But the inspired writer addresses those to whom he is writing not only as "holy brethren," but as "partakers of the heavenly calling." The word 'call' has two meanings: to name or designate, and to invite. It is used in the first sense when it is

[1] 1 Pet. ii. 9.  [2] Matt. xii. 46-50.

said, "He shall be *called* Jesus, because He shall save His people from their sins;" and in the second, when the king is said to send out his servants to *call* men to the marriage feast of his son. The word "calling" in the passage before us admits of two different interpretations, corresponding to the different meanings of the word from which it is derived. "The heavenly calling" may be understood as just equivalent to 'the heavenly appellation,' and be considered as descriptive of the title, "holy brethren,"—'sacred brethren, partakers of so high and holy a name.' This makes good sense, but the ordinary usage of Scripture language leads us to prefer the other interpretation. There are few appellations more frequently given to Christians than *the called*; and their *calling* is very often spoken of in the apostolical epistles. *The called* are just those who have been invited and induced to accept of the invitation to participate in the blessings of the Christian salvation; and their *calling* is, properly speaking, *their invitation*.

As the word 'faith' often signifies, not the act of believing, but the truth believed; as the word 'promise' often signifies, not the promise made, but the promise fulfilled, or the blessing promised; so the word 'calling' seems not unfrequently to signify not so much the invitation, as the blessings to the enjoyment of which we are invited. Thus 1 Cor. i. 26–30; Eph. i. 18; 2 Pet. i. 10, 11. The "calling" here then, I apprehend, is just the blessings to which Christians are invited in the Gospel, and which, on accepting the invitation, they are made secure of. The Apostle gives us a very interesting view of these when he says in 1 Cor. i. 9, God had "called them to the fellowship of His Son," *i.e.*, as he explains it elsewhere, to be "heirs of God, and joint heirs with Christ Jesus,"—"to the obtaining the glory of our Lord Jesus Christ:" 2 Thess. ii. 14.

This *calling*, or these blessings to which they are called, are denominated "heavenly;" for they are not earthly, but heavenly and divine in their origin and nature, and are enjoyed in all their perfection only in heaven.[1]

The "holy brethren" are represented as "*partakers* of the heavenly calling." The idea is plainly that of common participation in those blessings which are termed "the heavenly

---

[1] At ch. ix. 15 believers are termed οἱ κεκλημένοι τῆς αἰωνίου κληρονομίας, and their calling is termed ἡ ἄνω κλῆσις, Phil. iii. 14.

calling;" but it is not improbable that this peculiar mode of expression was adopted to suggest the idea that this calling was by no means peculiar to them. The privileges of their new calling were not, like those of their former calling, peculiar to the descendants of Abraham, but were enjoyed by the believing Hebrews in common with believers " out of every kindred, and people, and tongue, and nation." And here, as in the former case, let us pause and ask ourselves, Does this appellation belong to us? Are we " partakers of the heavenly calling?" The invitation has been addressed to us, but has it been accepted? The call has come to us in word, but has it come " in power," and with the accompanying energy of the Holy Spirit? It should not be difficult to determine this question when we consider what the call is: " Wherefore, come out from among them, and be ye separate, saith the Lord, and touch not the unclean thing; and I will receive you."[1] Such are the appellations which the Apostle gives to the Hebrew Christians.

Let us now attend to the exhortation which he addresses to them: " Consider the Apostle and High Priest of our profession, Christ Jesus."

For the right understanding of this exhortation, we must first inquire into the meaning of the phrase, "our profession;" then into the signification of the titles here given to our Lord, "the Apostle and High Priest of our profession;" and then we shall be prepared to discern the import of the exhortation, "*Consider* the Apostle and High Priest of our profession."

By some very learned interpreters, the word translated *profession* is understood as equivalent to *covenant* or *dispensation*. 'Moses was the apostle of the former covenant, or dispensation, or economy; Aaron was the high priest of that economy: Jesus Christ is both the Apostle and High Priest of the New Covenant.' This is truth; but whatever may be the classical use of the word, it does not seem ever used in the New Testament as equivalent to 'covenant' or 'dispensation;' and the New Covenant is often called God's covenant, but never the covenant of Christians. The word signifies acknowledgment or confession. Our acknowledgment or confession may signify that which we acknowledge and confess—our belief on religious subjects, our faith, our religion. This would suit one of the appellations very well—'The

[1] 2 Cor. vi. 17.

## THE SUPERIORITY OF CHRIST TO MOSES.   155

Apostle of our religion,' *i.e.*, the person employed by God to make known to us the truth we believe and profess; but it would not equally suit the other appellation—'the High Priest of our faith.'

The simplest and most satisfactory way of explaining the phrases, seems to me to consider them as expressions of similar construction with "the God of my praise," *i.e.*, 'the God whom I praise.' "The Apostle and High Priest of our profession"—acknowledgment or confession—is the person whom we profess, acknowledge, or confess, to be an Apostle and High Priest to us; just as we call a minister whom a congregation have chosen to be their pastor, 'the pastor of their choice.' "The Apostle and High Priest of our profession," then, is He whom we acknowledge as Apostle and High Priest.[1]

Let us now attend to the meaning of the titles here given to Christ Jesus. He is "the Apostle" whom we acknowledge. The meaning of the word 'Apostle' is, one sent forth by another[2] to execute some affair of importance, and is nearly equivalent to legate or ambassador. It is in ordinary language nearly restricted to those twelve persons sent forth by our Lord to lay the foundations of His kingdom, with the addition of Matthias and Paul. It is seldom, even in the original language of the New Testament, applied to any others; though Epaphroditus is styled the Apostle of the Philippians, and the brethren chosen to take charge of the pecuniary contributions of the Gentile churches for the poor saints at Jerusalem are termed the Apostles of the churches. It is nowhere else in Scripture applied to our Lord, though in the New Testament the word from which the title is borrowed is very often used in reference to Him. He is called by way of eminence, "He whom God hath sent."[3] When He is called the *Apostle*, or *the Sent One*, He is plainly marked out as the person whom God had promised to the fathers to send to the Church as the great Revealer of His will—the "Prophet like unto Moses," whom He was to "raise up," and whom they were to "hear" and to obey. 'The Apostle we acknowledge,' is, then, equivalent to 'the great Pro-

---

[1] Chrysostom thus explains it: ἀπόστολον ἡμῶν καὶ ἀρχιερέα ὁμολογούμενον, and is followed by Tho. Aquinas, Luther, Calovius, Storr, etc.

[2] = ὁ ἀπεσταλμένος.

[3] John iii. 34, v. 36, 38, vi. 29, x. 36, ὃν ὁ πατὴρ ἡγίασε καὶ ἀπέστειλεν εἰς τὸν κόσμον.

phet whom we acknowledge as the supreme authority in matters of religion.'[1] The language of their acknowledgment is—'This is God's beloved Son, we will hear Him. To whom can we go but to Him? He has the words of eternal life. One is our teacher, even Christ.'

But He is represented not only as the Apostle whom we acknowledge, but as the "High Priest" whom we acknowledge. A high priest is described as one "taken from among men, ordained for men in things pertaining to God, to offer both gifts and sacrifices for sins." The great duty of a high priest was to bring men into the favourable presence of God—so to manage their religious interests as that they might be reckoned and treated by God as His people.

Now Jesus is the High Priest of the Christian's profession or acknowledgment. He has done and suffered all that is necessary to obtain for His people the pardon of their sin, free access to God as their God and Father, and the enjoyment of all those blessings which spring from His favour and fellowship. To Him, and to Him alone, they look for these blessings. They do not acknowledge the Jewish high priests; they do not acknowledge the Pagan high priests; they do not look for these blessings either from man or angel, but only from Jesus Christ. The language of their acknowledgment in reference to Him as their High Priest is, "In Him we have redemption through His blood, the forgiveness of sins, according to the riches of His grace." "Through Him we have access by one Spirit unto the Father."

It now only remains that we inquire into the import of the exhortation, "Consider the Apostle and High Priest of our profession, Christ Jesus." The phraseology is peculiar. The usual order of the names, Jesus Christ, is reversed. Michaelis is probably right in thinking this was intended to bring out this thought: 'Consider the Apostle and High Priest whom we acknowledge—the Messiah, Jesus.' Some have supposed that the exhortation here is just equivalent to that in the beginning of the second chapter. To "consider the Apostle of our profession," and to

---

[1] Another probable interpretation of the term is that which considers it as the translation of the Heb. שׁלִיחַ—the curator of the synagogue, who was over the house of God. The first, however, is the preferable one. God said to Moses—Exod. iii. 10, 12, 14, 15—שְׁלַחְתִּיךָ, I have sent thee, I have made thee My Apostle.

"give heed to the things spoken by Him," if not the same, are very closely allied; but to "consider the High Priest of our profession," is obviously a different thing from "taking heed to the things spoken by Him," though it is only by taking heed to the things spoken by Him that we can consider Him as our High Priest, as He alone, by His Spirit, has revealed the truth respecting His priestly office and functions. To "consider" our Lord as "the Apostle and High Priest of our profession," is just to make the truth revealed to us in His word respecting Him, as the Great Prophet and the only High Priest whom we acknowledge, the subject of deep habitual thought, that we may understand it and believe it, and be led into a corresponding course of affection and conduct in reference to Him.[1]

This is a duty of radical importance to Christians. It is because we think so little, and to so little purpose, on Christ, that we know so little about Him, that we love Him so little, trust in Him so little, so often neglect our duty, are so much influenced by "things seen and temporal," and so little by "things unseen and eternal." If the Apostle could but get the Hebrew Christians to "*consider* the Apostle and High Priest of their profession," his object of keeping them steady in their attachment to Him was gained. It is because men do not know Christ that they do not love Him; it is because they know Him so imperfectly that they love Him so imperfectly. The truth about Him as the Great Prophet and the Great High Priest well deserves consideration—it is "the manifold wisdom of God." It requires it; it cannot be understood by a careless, occasional glance. Angels feel that even their faculties are overmatched with this subject. They are but "desiring to look into" it, as they do not yet fully understand it. It is only by "considering" the truth about Jesus Christ as "the Apostle and High Priest of our profession" that we can personally enjoy the benefits of His teaching as a Prophet, and of His expiation and intercession as a High Priest. We cannot be too deeply impressed with a conviction of this, that all spiritual blessings come to us through the faith of the truth respecting the Apostle and High Priest of our profession. Truth must be understood in order to its being believed, and it must be considered in order to its being understood. The con-

---

[1] Chrysostom explains it very well, κατανοήσατε—τουτέστι, Γνῶτε, τίς ἐστιν ὁ Ἀρχιερεὺς, καὶ ποταπός.

sideration of Jesus Christ is not only necessary to the production of faith, but to its continued existence, and to its gradual improvement. An inconsiderate man is never likely to succeed in life. An inconsiderate Christian is necessarily a very unsteady and a very uncomfortable one. The grand radical duty of the Christian is "looking to Jesus;" and the sum and substance of the message which the ministers of Christ have to deliver is, 'Behold Him, behold Him.'

We all acknowledge Jesus Christ as "the Apostle and High Priest." Let us treat Him accordingly. Believe nothing but on His authority. On His authority believe everything that He reveals. In religion acknowledge no other ultimate authority but His. Expect pardon and salvation in no other way but through His atonement and intercession; and confidently expect them through this medium. You equally do Him dishonour when you trust to anything but His sacrifice, and when you refuse to trust implicitly and unsuspectingly to that sacrifice. In the New Economy, Jesus Christ is "all in all"—*Prophet, Priest, King*, Saviour, Lord. Let us then seek all from Him; let us receive all that He is appointed to bestow—knowledge, pardon, sanctification, eternal life; and let us cheerfully ascribe to Him all the glory.

The second great division of this Epistle is occupied with showing that great as Moses, the giver of the Law, confessedly was, Jesus Christ, the Author of the Gospel, was still greater than he.

### § 1.—*The Fact stated.*

CHAP. iii. 2–6.—Who was faithful to Him that appointed Him, as also Moses was faithful in all His house. For this man was counted worthy of more glory than Moses, inasmuch as He who hath builded the house hath more honour than the house. For every house is builded by some man; but He that built all things is God. And Moses verily was faithful in all His house, as a servant, for a testimony of those things which were to be spoken after; but Christ as a Son over His own house; whose house are we, if we hold fast the confidence and the rejoicing of the hope firm unto the end.

The resemblance between Jesus Christ and Moses is pointed out in the second verse: the superiority of Jesus Christ to Moses is illustrated in the 3d, 4th, and 5th verses.

### (1.) *The Resemblance.*

Let us now turn our attention, first, to the resemblance

## THE FACT STATED.    159

which the Apostle states as subsisting between Jesus Christ and Moses.—Ver. 2. "Who was faithful to Him that appointed Him, as also Moses was faithful in all His house."[1]

The key to the whole paragraph is to be found in the meaning of the figurative term "house," which so often occurs in it. By supposing that the word "*house*" here is equivalent to *edifice*, the whole passage is involved in inextricable perplexity. "*House*" here does not signify a building, but a family or household. This mode of using the word is an exemplification of a common figure of speech, by which the name of what contains is given to what is contained. A man's family usually resides in his house, and hence is called his house. This use of the word is common in the Bible. "The house of Israel," "the house of Aaron," "the house of David," are very common expressions for the children, the descendants, the families of Israel, Aaron, and David. We have the same mode of speech in our own language: 'The house of Stuart,' 'the house of Hanover.' Keeping this remark in view, the verse we have now read will be found, short as it is, to contain in it the following statements: —Moses was appointed by God over the whole of His family: Moses was faithful in discharging the trust committed to him. Jesus is appointed by God over the whole of His family: Jesus is faithful in the discharge of the trust committed to Him.

Moses was divinely appointed over the whole family of God, —*i.e.*, plainly, over the whole Israelitish family of God. The reference here is not to the superintendence of the services of the tabernacle, which, so far as we recollect, never receives the name of the *house* of God, as the temple very often does, and which was subjected to the immediate control of Aaron, the high priest. The house, as Chrysostom very justly remarks, is not the temple,[2] but the people[3] of God. Moses was divinely appointed over the Israelites as the peculiar people or family of God. He was constituted at once their instructor and governor under Jehovah. He made known to them the laws, both religious and civil, which God revealed to him; and, under the direction of the Spirit of judgment, while he lived he administered these laws among them. He was placed at the head of that economy.

And in the discharge of the duties connected with so important a trust, Moses acted faithfully—he was faithful in

[1] οἴκῳ αὐτοῦ.    [2] ὁ ναός.    [3] ὁ λαός.

reference to the whole family. The Apostle here plainly alludes to the testimony given by God to His servant Moses on occasion of the sedition of Miriam and Aaron: Num. xii. 7, 8. The words are obviously intended to convey the idea, 'Moses is entrusted by Me with the highest authority in My family, and he is faithful in the discharge of the duties connected with this trust.' He kept back no part of the divine revelation with which he was entrusted; he made no additions to that revelation. In everything he said and did, as the prophet and chief human magistrate of Israel, he conformed himself exactly to the instructions he received from God: Exod. xl. 16.

We see here the wisdom of the inspired Apostle. He begins his illustration of the superiority of Jesus to Moses by making as strong a statement respecting the dignity of Moses' situation, and the excellence of his conduct in that situation, as the most bigoted Jewish zealot could desire. He thus conciliates the Hebrews by showing that he had no wish to deny Moses the honours that belonged to him, that he was no blasphemer either of him or of his law, and that, in his estimation, the honour of Moses and the honour of Christ were by no means incompatible.

Like Moses, Jesus Christ is appointed[1] over the whole family of God,—*i. e.*, plainly, over the spiritual family of God, of which the Jewish family was a type. Jesus Christ is appointed over the spiritual Church of God under the New Economy, as Moses was over the external Church under the Old Economy. He is their Great Apostle; He is their Lord and Sovereign. They must believe and profess as religious truth nothing but what He has taught; they must observe as religious institutions nothing but what He has appointed. He " is head over all things to His body the Church." The will of God on this subject is clearly revealed. "From the most excellent glory a voice came forth, This is My beloved Son, hear ye Him." He is the "Prophet like unto Moses," raised up from among the Israelites, whom all men are bound to listen to, believe, and obey, under the most awful sanctions.

And as, like Moses, Jesus Christ was appointed, or made, over the whole family of God, so, like Moses, He was faithful to the trust reposed in Him. He sought not His own glory, but the

---

[1] ποιεῖν is not unfrequently used as = to constitute, to appoint: 1 Sam. xii. 6, comp. with ver. 8; Mark iii. 14; Acts ii. 36.

glory of Him who sent Him. He declared plainly that He came not in His own name, but in the name of His Father. He turned not His message to His own advantage and honour, but prosecuted uniformly the great end of Him who appointed Him. He uniformly declared that His words were not so much *His*, as His Father's who sent Him. He kept back none of the revelation with which He was entrusted. "The words," said He, "which Thou hast given Me, I have given them." And rather than conceal or retract any part of the message He was entrusted with, He laid down His life. To *teach* and to *die* were the two great commissions given to Jesus by His Father, and He was faithful to both: John x. 18, xii. 49. Thus was Jesus "faithful" in reference to the whole family of God over which He is appointed, as Moses was "faithful" in reference to the whole family of God over which he was appointed.

### (2.) *The Superiority.*

Thus far the Apostle has stated the similarity between Jesus Christ and Moses. Now he proceeds to assert His superiority. Ver. 3. "For this man was counted worthy of more glory than Moses, inasmuch as He who hath builded the house hath more honour than the house."

*For*, here, is just equivalent to 'further' or 'moreover.' It is plain that the statement in the 3d verse is not a reason for the statement made in the 2d verse.[1] It is an additional reason for complying with the exhortation in verse 1, "Consider the Apostle and High Priest of our profession, Christ Jesus." If Jesus Christ has been faithful in reference to the whole family of God over which He has been appointed, as Moses was faithful in reference to the whole family of God over which he was appointed, then surely He must be worthy of equal honour. But He is not only worthy of equal honour, but of far superior honour.[2] He "is counted worthy of more honour than Moses, inasmuch as He that buildeth the house hath more honour than the house."[3]

---

[1] Or γὰρ may look back to κατανοήσατε, ver. 1, though this is not very natural or easy.

[2] πλείονος is explained by Chrysostom as = μείζονος.

[3] In the beginning of the verse the reader is left to supply κατὰ τόσον, to correspond with the καθ' ὅσον that follows. It is more usual in Greek, in such a case, to use the Dative, τόσῳ and ὅσῳ.

The phrase, 'to build' the house, is equivalent to, be the founder of the family. This kind of phraseology is by no means uncommon. It is said, Exod. i. 21, that God "made houses" to those humane women who refused to second the barbarous policy of Pharaoh in destroying the infants of the Israelites; *i.e.*, He established their families, giving a numerous and flourishing offspring. In Ruth iv. 11, Rachel and Leah are said to have built the house of Israel. And Nathan says to David, 2 Sam. vii. 11, "Also the Lord telleth thee that He will make thee a house;" and what the meaning of that phrase is, we learn from what immediately follows, ver. 12.

The latter part of the verse admits of being interpreted in two ways: 'The founder of the family is worthy of more honour than the family;'[1] or, ' the Founder of the family is entitled to the greater'—in the sense of greatest—' honour of the family.' The meaning in both cases is materially the same, though the last is probably the writer's idea. The founder of the family is entitled to the highest honour in the family. Jesus Christ, who is the Founder of the family of God, is entitled to the highest honour in that family; and if so, He is worthy of more honour than Moses, who was not the founder of the family, but a member of the family raised to an official superiority over the other members of the family. Moses was not the founder of the Israelitish family of God. They were God's people previously to his being raised up. He was placed over a family already in existence. Jesus Christ is the Founder of that family over which He is placed. He finds them not God's

---

[1] As if it had been said, παρὰ τὸν οἶκον. In the second case it is an instance of the use of the Genitive *Hebraico more*, of which we have many cases in the New Testament, signifying some relation or connection;—thus ὁ ἀμνὸς τοῦ Θεοῦ, the lamb destined for sacrifice to God, John i. 29; τὴν δωρεὰν τοῦ Θεοῦ, the benefit destined by God for you, John iv. 10; ζῆλος Θεοῦ, zeal about God or religion, Rom. x. 2; αἱ ἐπαγγελίαι τῶν πατέρων, promises made to the fathers, Rom. xv. 8; πίστις τοῦ υἱοῦ τοῦ Θεοῦ and Χριστοῦ, faith of the truth respecting Christ, Gal. ii. 20; Phil. iii. 9; τὴν παραθήκην μου, the deposit committed to me, 2 Tim. i. 12; δικαιοσύνη Θεοῦ, the righteousness approved or commanded by God, James i. 20. In the same way τιμὴν οἴκου may be = τιμὴν ἐν οἴκῳ, the greatest honour in the family. The use of the comparative degree for the superlative is not uncommon in the Greek language: μείζων is used for μέγιστος, Matt. xviii. 1, 4, xxiii. 11; 1 Cor. xiii. 13. Our translators, in Luke vii. 42, 43, render πλεῖον 'most.'

people, and He makes them God's people. This family are "God's workmanship, created in," or by, "Christ Jesus to good works." The new as well as the old creation is the work of God by Christ Jesus. Whatever honour may be due to Moses, who occupies a very distinguished place in the family, it is plain that that honour must be inferior to His who is the Founder of the family. The force of the argument seems just to be this: 'Moses did not make men children of God. Jesus Christ does. Therefore Jesus Christ deserves to be more highly honoured than Moses.' It has been supposed that the Apostle had in his mind the remarkable promise regarding the Messiah, "He shall build the temple of the Lord, and He shall bear the glory."[1]

The Apostle brings forward another argument in support of the superiority of Christ to Moses. Viewing the Church as the family of God, he states that Jesus Christ is the Son over the whole family, whereas Moses was but a servant in the family. But before proceeding to the statement of this argument, he remarks, as it were by the way—ver. 4, "For every house is builded by some one; but He who built all things is God."

This is a passage which has extremely perplexed interpreters.[2] Taking the words by themselves, it is not difficult to make a good, an important, sense out of them. The argument for the existence of Deity from the works of nature could scarcely be more shortly and strikingly stated. But it is plain that that has nothing to do with the Apostle's subject of discourse. It might also be considered as embodying a satisfactory proof of our Lord's divinity; but this also seems inconsistent with the train of thought. Were the verse entirely omitted, we would feel no hiatus; but there is no ground to consider it as otherwise than genuine, and therefore we must endeavour to interpret as best we may.

There can be no doubt, I think, that the word "house" here retains the meaning it had in the preceding context. "Every house is built by some one,"—*i.e.*, 'every family has its founder,' —"but He who built all things is God." The expression, "all things," does not seem to me to refer to the universe, but to all the things which the Apostle is speaking of—the family over

---

[1] Zech. vi. 13. The words of the LXX. are οἰκοδομήσει τὸν οἶκον Κυρίου.

[2] Exegetes tie themselves in grievous knots trying to connect this verse with what went before; several give up, and leave it out altogether. —CARPZOVIUS.

which Moses was placed, and the family over which Christ is placed.[1] 'The great Founder of all these things—both of the Jewish and Christian families—is God.'

These words have by some very good interpreters been referred to our Lord; thus, 'Jesus Christ, the Founder of all these things—the Author of both churches, both families—is God, and therefore infinitely superior to Moses.' Though this is a truth, I cannot think it the truth here taught. The most natural meaning of the words seems to me to be this: 'Jesus Christ, when contrasted with Moses, is the Founder of the family over which He presides, which Moses was not; yet, viewing the matter in a somewhat more extended way, *God* may be considered as the Founder of both families. Yet, even in this view of it, Moses is far inferior to Jesus Christ. For Moses is only a servant in the family of God: Jesus Christ is God's Son, having a natural property in the family, and a natural superiority over it.' The general meaning of this verse, in connection with that which follows it, seems to be: 'God is the Author of both orders of things; but the place which Moses and Christ occupy in the two orders of things is very different indeed.' Wherein the difference consists, is stated in the words which follow.[2]

---

[1] It is equivalent to πάντα ταῦτα, as Grotius observes. In this way we have τὰ πάντα in 2 Cor. v. 17, and, it may be, in Eph. i. 10, iii. 9.

[2] "It smells too much of scholastic subtlety."-Abresch. On reconsidering this *locus vexatus*, though still disposed to adhere to the interpretation just given, I think it right to state Abresch's opinion, which, as usual with him, is supported with great learning and ingenuity. He considers the direct reference to be to God the Father; but he conceives that there is what he calls a " tectum et obliquum" reference to Jesus Christ. Throughout the whole passage God is considered as the Head of the family—the Proprietor of the families over which Moses and Christ were respectively placed. Whatever, however, God does in reference to the salvation of man, He does through the intervention of, with a reference to, Jesus Christ: Eph. ii. 10, iii. 9; Heb. i. 10, ii. 15, iv. 15, 16; 2 Cor. v. 18, 19; Col. i. 20. And this is not only true as to the Christian economy properly so called, but also as to the Mosaic economy, which was an introductory, preparatory, subsidiary economy. That the Son was the Author of both economies, the Founder of both families, seems plainly the doctrine of Scripture: Acts vii. 38; Isa. lxiii. 9. Comp. 1 Cor. x. 4, 9. In all that He did in either case, He is represented as the Father's agent—His "Αγγελος—the מַלְאַךְ בְּרִית of Malachi —the Angel who was with the Church in the wilderness. All things in both economies were ἐκ τοῦ Θεοῦ, διὰ 'Ιησοῦ Χριστοῦ. Abresch, on these

## THE FACT STATED.

Ver. 5. "And[1] Moses verily was faithful in all his house, as a servant, for a testimony of those things which were to be spoken after; 6. But Christ as a Son over His own house." Moses was entrusted with the management of the whole family, and was faithful to that trust, in the character of a servant. In a divine dispensation—in a family of which God is the Founder—Moses occupied an important place, and faithfully discharged the duties of that place. But what was that place? It was the place of a servant—a highly honoured servant, but still nothing more than a servant. He had no property in the family—no natural authority over the family; the family was not his, but God's. The Apostle obviously refers to the passage already quoted, Num. xii. 7, 8, "Moses, *My servant*."[2]

Moses was God's servant in the family over which he was placed, "for a testimony of those things which were to be spoken after." These words have often been considered—they obviously were by our translators—as stating that the great design of Moses, as a minister in the Israelitish family, was, in the economy he introduced, to give a testimony respecting another economy, in due time to be revealed. The righteousness of God now manifested was witnessed in the law. "The law which came by Moses was a shadow of good things to come." There can be no doubt as to the truth and importance of this sentiment; but it does not appear to me to be expressed here.[3]

---

grounds, thinks the full expression of the Apostle's thought is: ὁ δὲ τὰ πάντα κατασκευάσας Θεός ἐστι, διὰ Ἰησοῦ Χριστοῦ. All that is said here is true; but has the Apostle *said* it? I rather think not. Ebrard has thrown light on the passage by considering it as thrown in to reconcile vers. 2, 3. In ver. 2, Jesus is represented as *appointed* by God; in ver. 3, as building or arranging the οἶκος. These representations seem not very harmonious. Ver. 4 contains the principle of conciliation. 'Every οἶκος has a founder; but above all such God stands as the great Founder of all; so that Christ, though a Founder of His family, was yet in a situation to exercise faithfulness towards One still superior to Him.' In this way it is a link attached both to vers. 2, 3, and ver. 5.

[1] Καὶ is here '*porro*, moreover.'

[2] Θεράπων is a more honourable appellation than δοῦλος or οἰκέτης. The correlate of δοῦλος is δεσπότης; of θεράπων, πατήρ, κύριος, or βασιλεύς. The δ. does all by constraint, and in fear; the θ. acts with freedom and affection. Δοῦλος is opposed to ἐλεύθερος; θεράπων to τὰ τέκνα, or to ὁ υἱός.

[3] With Abresch, "I would say this is over-ingenious, for nothing at all is found in the context to suggest it."

The Apostle's idea seems to be that Moses was a servant, and his ministry consisted in testifying or revealing those things which it was the will of God should be spoken to His people.

The place which Christ occupies is a very different and a far higher one. "But Christ as a Son over[1] His own house." The language is plainly elliptical: 'but Christ is faithful as a Son over His own house.' It is in the character of "the first-born among many brethren," the natural Ruler of the family, that Christ presides over the family of God. It is not necessary for me to enter at large into an illustration of the dignity which belongs to Jesus Christ as the Son of God, and which raises Him not only above Moses, but above angels—above all creatures. A son, especially the first-born, is not only superior to a servant, from his near relation to the father of the family, but also as being heir and lord of all. This is the peculiar dignity and prerogative of Jesus Christ: "The Father loveth the Son, and hath given all things into His hand." "For the Father judgeth no man, but hath committed all judgment unto the Son."[2]

Our translators seem to have considered the words as intimating another idea,—'the property He had in the family as the first-born—a Son over His own house.' The Church is Christ's property, being purchased with His own blood; but it is so in consequence of the Father's appointment. And as the pronoun *His*, in vers. 2, 5, without doubt refers to God the Father, I do not see any reason for supposing that the reference is different in the verse before us. The comparison is between Moses, a faithful servant *in* God's house, and Christ, a faithful Son *over* it.[3]

---

[1] ἐπί is here plainly contrasted with ἐν:—'The servant *in*,' 'the Son *over*.' In ἐπὶ τὸν οἶκον there is a reference to the Heb. עַל־הַבַּיִת, Isa. xxii. 15: Shebna, the treasurer, was the superintendent of the palace, the royal family.

[2] John iii. 35, v. 22.

[3] The editions of the G. T. vary. Some—the Plantin and Geneva editions, Erasmus and Wechelius—give αὑτοῦ, referring to Christ. Stephens' and the Complutensian editions of the elder, and Bengel's, Wetstein's, Griesbach's of the modern impressions, give αὐτοῦ, referring to God. A strong objection to the first way of reading the word is, that it brings into the ἀπόδοσις an important idea not in the πρότασις, so that the two members of the sentence do not well correspond. It is plain the 6th verse should not have been separated from the 5th: they form parts of one sentence.

The Apostle, in the concluding words of this verse, shows what he means by that house or family over which Christ as a Son presides. Ver. 6. "Whose house are we, if we hold fast the confidence and the rejoicing of the hope firm unto the end;"[1] *i.e.,* 'We are the family of God over which Jesus Christ presides as a Son, if we hold fast the confidence and the rejoicing of the hope firm unto the end.'[2]

The pronoun *we*, in the apostolical epistles, is used with a considerable variety of reference. It always signifies the writer along with some other individuals who have something in common with him. It is sometimes 'we apostles,' sometimes 'we Christian ministers,' sometimes 'we Jews,' sometimes 'we Christians,' sometimes 'we sinners,' sometimes 'we men.' The particular reference may generally, without difficulty, be discovered from the context. Here it is plainly, 'We believing Jews, not as Jews, but as believers,' belong to the family of God over which Jesus Christ presides as a Son.

This figurative view of the state of believers in Christ Jesus as the family of God, under the management of His Son, suggests many very important truths in reference to the relation in which they stand—to God, to Jesus Christ, and to one another—to the privileges which they enjoy, and to the duties which are incumbent on them. The idea which the words of the Apostle seem intended to bring before the mind, is the honour and happiness of the situation of the believing Hebrews as members of this family of God. God is their Father; the incarnate Son is their Elder Brother; angels are their ministers; the heavenly Canaan is their inheritance. They are "heirs of God, and joint heirs with Christ Jesus." This is the truth in reference to all genuine believers, of every country, and in every age; but it is the truth only in reference to genuine believers; and the only permanently satisfactory evidence of the genuineness of their faith, is their continuing to manifest by their conduct that they are under the influence of this faith. Accordingly, the Apostle adds, We are the family of God, "*if we hold fast the confidence and the rejoicing of the hope firm unto the end.*"

[1] It is a question whether ὅς οἶκος or οὗ οἶκος is the genuine reading. Much may be, and much has been, said on both sides. The meaning is not materially affected, however the controversy be decided.

[2] Words, as Abresch says, ἐμφατικώτατα.

These words are not intended to suggest the sentiment, that persons may belong to the family of God under the government of His Son—in other words, may be the children of God through faith in Christ Jesus—and yet not " hold fast the confidence and rejoicing of the hope stedfast unto the end ;" for this is plainly inconsistent with many plain declarations of Scripture. While their inheritance is " reserved for them in heaven," they are " kept to it by the mighty power of God through faith." But it is intended to teach us this important truth, that none but those who " hold firm to the end the confidence and rejoicing of their hope," really belong to the family of God which is entrusted to the care of His Son Jesus Christ.

*The hope* here spoken of is what by way of eminence may be called the Christian hope—the expectation of everlasting happiness through Christ Jesus. This is the hope which has been brought to us in " the word of the truth of the Gospel," and which is awakened in every heart into which the faith of the Gospel enters.

But what are we to understand by the " confidence of this hope," and " the rejoicing of this hope?" The primary and ordinary meaning of the word rendered " confidence," is freedom and boldness of speech, as expressive of full conviction and the absence of fear—opposed to silence and hesitation, as expressive of doubt and timidity. The force of the word is illustrated by the following passages in which it occurs :—John vii. 26, xviii. 20 ; Acts iv. 13 ; 2 Cor. iii. 12, vii. 4 ; Phil. i. 20 ; 1 Tim. iii. 13. Open, unhesitating, fearless profession of the Christian hope, seems to be the Apostle's idea. The Apostle Peter exhorts Christians to be " always ready to give an answer to every one who asketh them a reason of the hope that is in them."[1]

This constant readiness to state and defend those truths and their evidences on which rests our hope, is what is here termed "the confidence of the hope," the free and fearless profession of the hope. This was indeed dangerous in the primitive times, and the Hebrew Christians were exposed to very strong temptations to desist from it ; but it is absolutely necessary to the continuance and progress of the Gospel in the world, and it is very plainly enjoined by our Lord, Matt. x. 32, 33.

Of the free and fearless profession of the truth, we have

[1] 1 Pet. iii. 15.

a very striking specimen in the manner in which the three Israelitish young men witnessed a good confession before the Babylonian king. They beheld an absolute monarch the form of whose visage was changed with fury, and a flaming furnace of fire, into which they were to be instantly cast if they would not let go their profession. They ask not a moment's space for deliberation. They make an unhesitating, fearless profession of their faith and hope.[1] Such, too, was the profession made by Stephen, when, amid his exasperated persecutors, with the instruments of his death in their hands, he said, " I see the heavens opened, and the Son of man standing on the right hand of God." Such was the profession made by Basil, when the Emperor Julian would have given him time to consult whether he would renounce Christianity : " Do what you intend, for I will be the same to-morrow that I am to-day." This, then, is the meaning of the phrase, " confidence of the hope,"—free, fearless profession of the truth on which rests our hope.

The other phrase, " the rejoicing of the hope," is of kindred meaning. The word translated " rejoicing" is the same as that which is usually rendered ' glorying,' or ' boasting.' Thus we glory in the hope of the divine approbation. " The rejoicing of the hope," or ' the gloriation in the hope,' is the contemning all things which would come in competition with it. What is meant by " the rejoicing of hope" will be best understood by the following specimens :—" For I reckon, that the sufferings of this present time are not worthy to be compared with the glory which shall be revealed in us." " For which cause we faint not; but though our outward man perish, yet the inward man is renewed day by day. For our light affliction, which is but for a moment, worketh for us a far more exceeding and eternal weight of glory; while we look not at the things which are seen, but at the things which are not seen : for the things which are seen are temporal; but the things which are not seen are eternal."[2] On believing the truth, the Hebrew Christians had made an open profession of their hope by submitting to bap-

---

[1] Dan. iii. 16–18.

[2] Rom. viii. 18 ; 2 Cor. iv. 16–18. It has been suggested by a very acute scholar (Abresch), that $\pi\alpha\dot{\rho}\dot{\rho}\eta\sigma\iota\alpha$ and $\varkappa\alpha\dot{\upsilon}\chi\eta\mu\alpha$ are used as = adjectives; the whole phrase being thus = the heart-nerving, mouth-opening, triumph-giving hope.

tism, and had then felt that eternal life, which was the object of their hope, made every object of human desire which could be put into competition with it grow dim or disappear.

To "hold fast the confidence and rejoicing of the hope," then, "to the end,"[1] is to maintain till the close of life that open, fearless profession of the Gospel, and that heart-satisfying estimate of the value of that eternal life which that Gospel reveals, which naturally grow out of the firm faith of "the truth as it is in Jesus."[2] Such is the character of the members of the family of God, and such the way in which they are to enjoy the comfort arising from an assurance that they are the members of this family.

But it may be said, Are we to remain in a state of uncertainty and doubt as to our belonging to the family till the end of life? This does not by any means result from the Apostle's statement. In "the confidence and rejoicing of the hope,"—in the faith of the truth producing its appropriate effects, in an honest profession of the truth both in words and in actions, and in satisfying the heart with the salvation it reveals as a portion,—the Christian has most satisfactory evidence of his belonging to the family; but he can continue in possession of it only in the degree in which he continues to "hold fast" this confidence and rejoicing of hope.

### § 2.—*The Fact Practically Improved.*

From these statements respecting Jesus Christ, as far superior to Moses as the head of a divine family, and respecting the Hebrews as professed members of this family, the Apostle takes occasion to warn them against apostasy, and to point out the awful consequences which would result from disobedience and rebellion against Him whom God had appointed as a Son over His family.

CHAP. iii. 7-iv. 13. Wherefore (as the Holy Ghost saith, To-day, if ye will hear His voice, harden not your hearts, as in the provocation, in the

---

[1] Μέχρι τέλους, to the end of life; ch. vi. 11; John xiii. 1; 1 Cor. i. 8.
[2] Βεβαίαν. From καύχημα we should have expected βέβαιον; from π. κ. κ. we should have expected βεβαία. But both in Greek and Latin we find the same construction—an adjective equally connected with two nouns put in the gender of the former.

day of temptation in the wilderness; when your fathers tempted Me, proved Me, and saw My works forty years. Wherefore I was grieved with that generation, and said, They do alway err in their heart; and they have not known My ways. So I sware in My wrath, They shall not enter into My rest.) Take heed, brethren, lest there be in any of you an evil heart of unbelief, in departing from the living God. But exhort one another daily, while it is called To-day; lest any of you be hardened through the deceitfulness of sin. For we are made partakers of Christ, if we hold the beginning of our confidence stedfast unto the end; while it is said, To-day, if ye will hear His voice, harden not your hearts, as in the provocation. For some, when they had heard, did provoke: howbeit not all that came out of Egypt by Moses. But with whom was He grieved forty years? was it not with them that had sinned, whose carcases fell in the wilderness? And to whom sware He that they should not enter into His rest, but to them that believed not? So we see that they could not enter in because of unbelief.

Let us therefore fear, lest, a promise being left us of entering into His rest, any of you should seem to come short of it. For unto us was the Gospel preached, as well as unto them: but the word preached did not profit them, not being mixed with faith in them that heard it. For we which have believed do enter into rest; as He said, As I have sworn in My wrath, if they shall enter into My rest: although the works were finished from the foundation of the world. For he spake in a certain place of the seventh day on this wise, And God did rest the seventh day from all His works. And in this place again, If they shall enter into My rest. Seeing therefore it remaineth that some must enter therein, and they to whom it was first preached entered not in because of unbelief: (Again, He limiteth a certain day, saying in David, To-day, after so long a time; as it is said, To-day, if ye will hear His voice, harden not your hearts. For if Jesus had given them rest, then would He not afterward have spoken of another day. There remaineth therefore a rest to the people of God. For He that is entered into His rest, He also hath ceased from His own works, as God did from His.) Let us labour therefore to enter into that rest, lest any man fall after the same example of unbelief. For the word of God is quick, and powerful, and sharper than any two-edged sword, piercing even to the dividing asunder of soul and spirit, and of the joints and marrow, and is a discerner of the thoughts and intents of the heart. Neither is there any creature that is not manifest in His sight: but all things are naked and opened unto the eyes of Him with whom we have to do.

There is some difficulty in determining the right method of construing the first of these paragraphs. Some interpreters connect the particle " wherefore" with the quotation from the 95th Psalm, including the words " as the Holy Ghost saith" in a parenthesis, and consider the Apostle as adopting the words of the Psalmist as his own, and directly addressing them to his readers. Others connect the particle " wherefore" with the

12th verse, and include the whole quotation in a parenthesis. They do not consider the Apostle as addressing these words directly to the Hebrews, but as quoting a passage of Old Testament Scripture which had an important bearing on the subject of consideration, and from which he afterwards proceeds to reason. It is not a question of vital importance as to the right interpretation of the passage. It does not matter much which side we take in it; but the latter mode of construing it seems to us preferable.

Let us first, then, examine the quotation which the inspired writer makes from the Book of Psalms.[1] The Psalm quoted is the 95th,—a Psalm which does not contain in it any of those very decisive marks of the time and circumstances in which it was composed which many of the other Psalms do, but which, on highly probable grounds, has been considered as composed in the Maccabæan times. This opinion is in no way inconsistent with the inspired writer's saying in the next chapter, "Again He limiteth a certain time, saying *in David;*" the whole Book of Psalms going under the name of David, though it is certain he was not the writer of all these sacred odes.

The words of this Psalm are represented as the words of the Holy Ghost. It was true of all the psalmists of Israel as well as of the royal psalmist that "The Spirit of the Lord spake by them, and His word was in their tongue." "All Scripture is given by inspiration of God;" and the "holy men of old, who spake as they were moved by the Spirit of God," spoke not in words which man's wisdom taught, but in words taught them by the Holy Spirit.

The passage is generally an exhortation to the Jewish people to listen to, and believe, and obey the voice of God, promising to lead them into His rest; and warning them of the fearful consequences which would flow from their disregarding this exhortation, by pointing out to them the dreadful results of their fathers' disbelieving and disobeying the voice of God when He invited them to enter into the rest of Canaan.

---

[1] The form of quotation, καθὼς λέγει τὸ Πνεῦμα τὸ ἅγιον, does not occur often. We have it ch. x. 15, and Acts i. 16, xxviii. 25. It has a peculiar propriety here, as the quotation is a prophetic oracle in the strict sense of the phrase; and as, Isa. lxiii. 10, *the Holy Spirit* is particularly mentioned as *vexed* by the conduct here referred to.

"To-day" is equivalent to, 'This is the day in which God is inviting you to enter into His rest, as He invited your fathers long ago to enter into the rest of Canaan. The reign of Heaven is approaching; Messiah is at hand.'

"If ye will hear His voice." These words are obviously elliptical; and, consistently with the Hebrew idiom, the ellipsis may be filled up in either of the two following ways:—' If ye hear His voice, ye shall enter into His rest;' or, ' Oh, if ye would but hear His voice!' This is a common form of expressing a wish in the Hebrew idiom. "If thou hadst known, in this thy day, the things which belong to thy peace!"

"Harden not your hearts." The heart is in Scripture just equivalent to the mind, viewed as endowed both with intelligence and affection. To "harden the heart," is to be inattentive, unbelieving, impenitent, disobedient.

The prophet calls on his countrymen not to be inattentive, unbelieving, impenitent, and disobedient, as their ancestors were "in the provocation, in the day of temptation in the wilderness." This is a reference to what happened at a place which received names from the undutiful conduct of Israel towards Jehovah —"Meribah," the striving or provocation; and "Massah," the trial or temptation: Exod. xvii. 2, 7. These are particularly referred to, because it was then that the scene of provocation and temptation commenced, which continued down to the period that the awful sentence was pronounced on them, that they should not enter into God's rest.

The history of the Israelites is a history of continued provocation. In the wilderness of Sin they murmured for the want of bread, and God gave them manna. At Rephidim they murmured for want of water, and questioned whether Jehovah was with them; and He gave them water from the rock. In the wilderness of Sinai, soon after receiving the law, they made and worshipped a golden image. At Taberah they murmured for want of flesh; and the quails were sent, followed by a dreadful plague. At Kadesh-barnea they refused to go up and take possession of the land of promise, which brought down on them the awful sentence referred to in the Psalm; and after that sentence was pronounced, they presumptuously attempted to do what they had formerly refused to do. All these things took place in little more than two years after they left Egypt.

Thirty-seven years after this, we find them at Kadesh again, murmuring for want of water and other things. Soon after this, they complained of the want of bread, though they had manna in abundance, and were punished by the plague of fiery flying serpents. And at Shittim, their last station, they provoked the Lord by mingling in the impure idolatry of the Moabites. So strikingly true is Moses' declaration: "Remember, and forget not, how thou provokedst the Lord thy God to wrath in the wilderness: from the day that thou didst depart out of the land of Egypt, until ye came unto this place, ye have been rebellious against the Lord." "Ye have been rebellious against the Lord from the day that I knew you."[1]

They " tempted Him, and proved Him, and saw His works forty years." To "tempt" God and to "prove" Him, are nearly, if not altogether, synonymous expressions. They refer to men as it were making experiments, whether He be indeed the powerful, holy, just, and faithful God He has declared Himself to be. Instead of believing His declarations, and acting accordingly, they seemed, as it were, bent to discover, though at the hazard of their own destruction, whether He really was able or meant to execute either His promises or threatenings.

That part of the quotation contained in the 10th verse slightly differs both from the Hebrew text and the Greek version in common use when the Apostle wrote. In them it reads, " Forty years long was I grieved with that generation." The Apostle refers the " forty years" to their seeing God's works; the Hebrew text and the Septuagint, to the time during which they grieved God. It comes, however, materially to the same thing; for they both saw His works and grieved Him during these forty years.[2]

The word translated "grieved," properly signifies 'grievously

---

[1] Deut. ix. 7, 24.

[2] It is curious to know that the ancient Jews believed that " the days of the Messiah were to be forty years." Thus Tanchuma, F. 79, 4, " How long do the days of Messiah last ? R. Akiba said, 40 years, as the Israelites were 40 years in the desert." It is remarkable, that in forty years after the ascension, the whole Jewish nation were cut off equally as they who fell in the wilderness.

Καί, the rendering of the Heb. גַּם, may be rendered *and, also*; or it may be rendered *although*. ' They tempted and grieved Me for forty years, though all that time they saw the manifestations I made of My power and

## THE FACT PRACTICALLY IMPROVED. 175

offended.' Jehovah was displeased with that generation; *i.e.*, their conduct was the object of His moral disapprobation; and the ends of His wise and holy government required that this should be manifested by its becoming the object of His judicial punishment. His determination, and the reasons of it, are shortly, but most emphatically, stated in the close of the 10th and in the 11th verse.

These words, " they do alway err in their heart," are not to be found in Num. xiv.; but the inspired Psalmist expresses the sense of what Jehovah said on that occasion. " They do alway err in their heart." They are radically and habitually evil. "They have not known My ways."[1] God's " ways" may mean either His dispensations or His precepts. The Israelites did not rightly understand the former, and they obstinately refused to acquire a practical knowledge—the only truly valuable species of knowledge—of the latter. The reference is probably to God's mode of dealing: Rom. xi. 33; Deut. iv. 32, viii. 2, xxix. 2–4.

Such a people deserved severe punishment, and they received it. " So I sware in My wrath, They shall not enter into My rest."[2] The original words both in the Hebrew text and here are, " If they shall enter into My rest." This elliptical mode of expressing oaths is common in the Old Testament: Deut. i. 35; 1 Sam. iii. 14; Ps. lxxxix. 35; Isa. lxii. 8. This awful oath is recorded in the 14th chapter of Numbers: " But as truly as I live, all the earth shall be filled with the glory of the Lord. Because all those men which have seen My glory, and My

wisdom on their behalf.' Arthur Johnston, in his poetical version, gives a turn something like this to the words:
" Illius hic quamvis lassatus murmure signa
Roboris invicti non dubitata dedi."
Καί is not unfrequently used for καίπερ, εἰ, etc. John xvii. 25, καὶ ὁ κόσμος, "although the world," etc. Comp. Neh. vi. 1; Ps. cxxix. 2.

[1] δὲ is here either = καί, which is the word in the LXX., or to γάρ, which is often the force of the Heb. ן: Ps. vii. 10; Hos. xii. 2.

[2] In explaining such terms as ὀργή in reference to God, great caution is necessary. There is hazard both in overstating and understating their import. To attribute internal commotion to the divine mind, which always is an element in what we call ὀργή in man, and still more, to attribute malignant feeling to Him who is love, is utterly wrong. But, on the other hand, to say that ὀργή is to be understood merely *synecdochicè*, as the rhetoricians say—that it describes merely punishment—is certainly not right. I entirely agree with the following cautiously expressed sentiment of a learned interpreter and judicious divine :—" In Basil's words (*Opera*,

miracles which I did in Egypt, and in the wilderness, have tempted Me now these ten times, and have not hearkened to My voice; surely they shall not see the land which I sware unto their fathers, neither shall any of them that provoked Me see it: but My servant Caleb, because he had another spirit with him, and hath followed Me fully, him will I bring into the land whereunto he went; and his seed shall possess it. (Now the Amalekites and the Canaanites dwelt in the valley.) To-morrow turn you, and get you into the wilderness, by the way of the Red sea. And the Lord spake unto Moses and unto Aaron, saying, How long shall I bear with this evil congregation, which murmur against Me? I have heard the murmurings of the children of Israel, which they murmur against Me. Say unto them, As truly as I live, saith the Lord, as ye have spoken in Mine ears, so will I do to you: Your carcases shall fall in this wilderness; and all that were numbered of you, according to your whole number, from twenty years old and upward, which have murmured against Me."[1] The words of the oath seem here borrowed from the account in Deut. i. 35. There are many threatenings of God which have a tacit condition implied in them; but when God interposes His oath, the sentence is irreversible.

The curse was not causeless, and it did come. We have an account of its actual fulfilment, Num. xxvi. 64, 65. The "rest" from which they were excluded was the land of Canaan. Their lives were spent in wandering. It is termed "God's rest," as there He was to finish His work of bringing Israel into the land

---

l. 511) : 'it is impious to allow either (anger, or fury) to be predicated of God in a proper sense. The words are metaphorical : for God has no passions, nor is his actual substance subject to them.' So that no excitement or turmoil of mind, or desire to wreak vengeance or do hurt, can be conceived of in that which is by far the most exalted and perfect nature that there is. But yet I would believe that, by reason of the holiness and righteousness of his mind, he is touched by human ungodliness with a real and keen feeling, which by accommodation to the lowliness of our understanding, and because there is some analogy between the two things, is called *wrath* or *hatred*; and it impels and moves him with the full consent of his will to punish."—ABRESCH. The ideas intended to be expressed are moral disapprobation and judicial displeasure. Sin is opposed to the divine character, and inconsistent, if unpunished, with the ends of His government. Lactantius, the Christian Cicero as he has been called, has some excellent observations on this subject in his book, *De ira Dei*.

[1] Num. xiv. 21–29.

promised to their fathers, and fix the symbol of His presence in the midst of them,—dwelling in that land in which His people were to rest from their wanderings, and to dwell in safety under His protection. It is *His* rest, as of His preparing, Deut. xii. 9. It is *His* rest—rest like His, rest along with Him. We are by no means warranted to conclude that all who died in the wilderness came short of everlasting happiness. It is to be feared many of them, most of them, did; but the curse denounced on them went only to their exclusion from the earthly Canaan.

Such is the passage of Old Testament Scripture to which the Apostle refers in his exhortation to the believing Hebrews, and from which he proceeds to reason in the subsequent context. ' Wherefore, seeing Jesus Christ, who presides over the family of God of which you profess to be members, is so far superior to Moses, who presided over the family of God in a former age,—calling to mind what an inspired writer has said of the fearful judgments which overtook those of the family under Moses who were unbelieving and disobedient, ver. 12, " take heed, brethren, lest there be in any of you an evil heart of unbelief, in departing from the living God." The evils to which unbelief and impenitence exposed the Israelites were dreadful; but the evils to which they will expose you will be just as much more dreadful, as the New Economy exceeds the Old in dignity, as Jesus Christ is superior to Moses.'

The Apostle cautions the Hebrew Christians against an " evil heart of unbelief." A " heart of unbelief" is just an idiomatical expression for an ' unbelieving heart;'[1] and for a person to have in him an unbelieving heart, is just to doubt or disbelieve. When the Apostle, then, says, " Take heed lest there be in any of you a heart of unbelief," his exhortation is just equivalent to, ' Beware lest any of you doubt or disbelieve those statements which have been made to you by Him who is so far superior both to Moses and the angels.'

The unbelieving heart is styled an *evil* heart. The word " evil" sometimes signifies 'wicked, diseased,' and sometimes ' mischievous or destructive.' In all its senses it is very applicable to unbelief. To doubt or disbelieve the revelation which God has made to us by His Son, which is a plain and well-accredited revelation, is wicked. It originates in immoral principles—in

[1] Καρδία ἀπιστίας = καρδία ἄπιστος.

the love of sin—or in thoughtlessness, which in such a case must be highly criminal—or in pride, whether the pride of wealth and station, or of intellect, or of self-righteousness. To doubt or disbelieve the revelation which God has made to us by His Son, is most pernicious and ruinous. Faith naturally leads to holiness and happiness, to purity and peace; and unbelief as naturally produces guilt, depravity, and ruin. It is probably the last of these ideas—that of mischievousness—that the Apostle meant to convey by the epithet 'wicked,' as he immediately proceeds to show how unbelief excludes him who indulges it from the rest of God, into which only those who believe can enter.

The words which follow—" in departing from the living God"—point out the native tendency of an evil, unbelieving heart. The whole exhortation may be thus stated: 'Take heed lest any of you have in you an evil, unbelieving heart, leading you to depart—or manifesting itself in a departure—from the living God. Beware of departing from the living God, under the influence of a wicked, unbelieving heart.'

To "depart from the living God" is just an expression for apostasy from Christianity,—in the case of those whom the Apostle was addressing, the renouncing the profession of the faith of Christ and returning to Judaism. Those who did so, no doubt, flattered themselves that they were not departing from, but returning to God; but the Apostle presses on them this truth, that they could not abandon Christ without abandoning God. There is but one God,—He is "the God and Father of our Lord Jesus Christ,"—He is " God in Christ reconciling the world to Himself;" and, of course, he who renounces Christ abandons God.

The appellation *living God* is emphatic. Some have supposed it just equivalent to the *true* God;[1] as if the Apostle had said, 'In apostatizing from Christianity to Judaism, you as really depart from the living God as if you were becoming the worshippers of idols.' I am rather disposed to think that the expression "living" is intended to convey the idea of power. 'Dead' is often equivalent to powerless; 'living,' to powerful. This is remarkably the case in two passages in this Epistle: "The word of God is quick (*living*) and powerful, sharper than a two-edged sword, piercing even to the dividing of the soul

---

[1] Jehovah is the living God as opposed to idols wanting life: Jos. iii. 10; Acts xiv. 15; 1 Thess. i. 9.

and spirit." "It is a fearful thing to fall into the hands of the *living* God." It is quite safe to depart from *dead* gods. No spiritual advantage can be obtained by adhering to them; no danger is incurred in abandoning them; they cannot punish the apostate. But it is otherwise with him who apostatizes from the *living* God. He departs from Him "with whom is the fountain of life," and who alone can make him happy; he departs from Him who *can* execute all the threatenings which He has denounced against those who forsake Him.

There is need of constant watchfulness on the part of the professors of Christianity, lest under the influence of unbelief they "depart from the living God." "Take heed," says the Apostle. There is nothing, I am persuaded, in regard to which professors of Christianity fall into more dangerous practical mistakes than this. They suspect everything sooner than the soundness and firmness of their belief. There are many who are supposing themselves believers who have no true faith at all,—and so it would be proved were the hour of trial, which is perhaps nearer than they are aware, to arrive; and almost all who have faith suppose they have it in greater measure than they really have it. There is no prayer that a Christian needs more frequently to present than, "Lord, increase my faith;" "deliver me from an evil heart of unbelief." All apostasy from God, whether partial or total, originates in unbelief. To have his faith increased—to have more extended, and accurate, and impressive views of "the truth as it is in Jesus"—ought to be the object of the Christian's most earnest desire and unremitting exertion. Just in the degree in which we obtain deliverance from the "evil heart of unbelief" are we enabled to cleave to the Lord with full purpose of heart, to follow Him fully, and, in opposition to all the temptations to abandon His cause, to "walk in all His commandments and ordinances blameless."

To prevent so fearful and disastrous a result as apostasy from the living God, the Apostle calls on them to strengthen each other's faith by mutual exhortation, and thus oppose those malignant and deceitful influences which had a tendency to harden them in impenitence and unbelief. Ver. 13. "But exhort one another daily, while it is called To-day; lest any of you be hardened through the deceitfulness of sin."

For the explanation of this verse, it will be necessary to turn our attention first to the evil into which the Hebrew Christians were in danger of falling—the being "hardened through the deceitfulness of sin;" and then to the means which he recommends to be employed for preventing this evil—the "exhorting one another daily, while it is called To-day."

To be hardened is to become insensible to the claims of Jesus Christ, so that they do not make their appropriate impression on the mind, in producing attention, faith, and obedience. He is hardened who is careless, unbelieving, impenitent, and disobedient.

Into this state the professors of Christianity among the Jews were in danger of falling "through the deceitfulness of sin"— that is, through sin's deceiving them. By "sin" I apprehend we are to understand anything inconsistent with the law of Christ, whom professing believers acknowledge as their Lord and Master; for example, the neglecting to assemble themselves together for the observance of the ordinances of Christianity, to which the Apostle particularly refers in a subsequent part of the Epistle.

But how is such a sin as this calculated to deceive them, and by deceiving to "harden" them—to make them careless, unbelieving, and disobedient, so as that they depart from Christ, and, in departing from Him, depart also from "the living God?" It is natural for man to wish to stand well with himself. Self-condemnation is one of the most intolerable of all feelings. When a man has, from whatever motive, done something that is inconsistent with the law of Christ, he naturally sets himself to extenuate, to excuse, and, if possible, to defend his conduct. There is perhaps an attempt made to convince the mind that there is really no violation of the law of Christ; that the ordinary way of interpreting that law is unduly strict; or that, if there was a violation, it was in his circumstances scarcely avoidable, and, if not justifiable altogether, yet deserving of but very slight blame. In this state of mind, doubts of the reasonableness of the law he has transgressed, and of the authority to which it lays claim, present themselves to the mind, and, instead of being immediately dismissed, meet with a welcome reception. These naturally lead to a repetition of the act of violation of the law of Christ, or to other violations of the law of Christ; and just as the backslider proceeds in his downward course, the process of thought above described is apt to become more and more habitual to him, till at last he becomes completely hardened against the claims which the word of Christ has on his attention, faith, and obedience, and finally " makes shipwreck of faith and a good conscience."

Unbelief thus naturally leads to disobedience, and disobedience as naturally hardens in unbelief. It is equally true that the great obstacle in the way of a man's believing the Gospel, and the most powerful incentive to apostasy from the Gospel, is the love of sin. The truth can be kept only in a good and honest heart; it can be held only in a pure conscience. Apostates from the truth often flatter themselves that they have yielded to the force of argument; but the just statement of the fact is that given by the prophet—" a deceived heart has turned them aside;" or by the Apostle—they have been " hardened by the deceitfulness of sin."

The means which the Apostle prescribes for preventing this evil is quite appropriate to its nature. " Exhort one another," says he, " daily, while it is called To-day." The food of faith is truth and its evidence. All that *man* can do to produce faith, and maintain faith, is just to place these before the mind. It is the duty of every Christian, knowing that there is in him " an evil heart of unbelief," often to turn his own mind to a serious consideration of the truth and its evidence, as contained in the Volume of Inspiration; and it is his duty, too, knowing that in every fellow-Christian there is also " an evil heart of unbelief," and especially if he perceive this evil heart manifesting itself in anything like a tendency to apostasy, to bring before his mind the truth and its evidence, that he may continue " stedfast and unmoveable," rooted, and grounded, and stablished in the faith wherein he has been taught. This is, I apprehend, the mutual exhortation to which the Apostle refers.

It deserves notice that the word rendered *exhort* is the same word which is often translated ' comfort;' and it is very probably used to suggest the idea, that nothing is better fitted to prevent apostasy than bringing before the mind the truth as to the " exceeding great and precious promises," made to those who " hold fast the confidence and rejoicing of the hope firm to the end." It is the *good news*—the consolatory message of a **free** and full salvation through Christ Jesus—it is this, believed, which binds the heart to the Saviour and to His law. It is quite right to imitate the Apostle in placing before the mind of the backslider the awful results of apostasy; but such statements *alone* will produce but little effect. The voice of a reconciled God behind him, proclaiming, " Return to Me, thou backsliding child, for I have redeemed thee," when heard, will do more to prevent apostasy, and induce him to turn his feet to God's testimonies, than all the terrors of the tenfold damnation which awaits the apostate, though presented to the mind in the most striking and alarming form.

The duty of public exhortation forms an important part of the duty of Christian pastors; but it is plain from the passage before us that it is the duty of all Christians, as they have opportunity, privately to exhort and admonish one another,[1] lest they " be hardened by the deceitfulness of sin." It is too much the practice of professors of Christianity in our times, when they perceive in one of their brethren a tendency, as they think, to " depart from the living God," to speak of it to every person rather than to the one to whom alone in the first instance it ought to be spoken of—to lament over it in the presence of others, instead of endeavouring to remove the evil by friendly exhortation to the individual himself, and earnest prayer to God to render the use of the means prescribed by Himself effectual for the purpose for which He has appointed it.

This mutual exhortation the Apostle enjoins to be engaged in " daily, while it is called To-day."[2] They were to exhort one another *daily*, *i.e.*, frequently, and without delay. Whenever we observe in brethren what appears to us an indication of departure from the path of Christian truth and duty, we are to use the means prescribed by the inspired writer for bringing them back. Every step they take in the downward path makes their recovery more difficult; and yet a little while, and they will be removed beyond the reach of our exertions. If any of us have a friend whom we think in danger of that greatest of all evils, the loss

---

[1] ἑαυτούς = ἀλλήλους, as in ch. x. 24; 1 Cor. vi. 7; 1 Pet. iv. 8-10; 1 Thess. v. 13. That the word is not to be understood, as the Vulgate has understood it, as a command to the Hebrews to press the truth each of them on his own mind, is plain from the words that follow: they are not ἵνα μὴ σκληρυνθῆτε, but ἵνα μὴ σκληρυνθῇ τις ἐξ ὑμῶν.

[2] καλεῖται = κηρύσσεται—while the proclamation continues to be made, " To-day, etc." There is a *paronomasia* in παρακαλεῖτε and καλεῖται.

of the soul, let us be speedy, diligent, earnest, whether by instruction, admonition, or prayer. Ah! how soon may he be in that world where warning is too late! "What thy hand findeth to do" in this way, "do it with thy might; for there is no work, nor device, nor wisdom, nor knowledge in the grave, whither thou goest." This idea seems intended to be suggested by the additional clause, "while it is called To-day;" *i.e.*, 'while the voice of God still invites men to enter into His rest.' As God's fellow-workers, we should "beseech them not to receive the grace of God in vain." "For He saith, I have heard thee in a time accepted, and in the day of salvation have I succoured thee. Behold, now is the accepted time: behold, now is the day of salvation." "The deceitfulness of sin" and the precariousness of time are considerations which greatly strengthen each other. As time wastes, the sinner hardens: not only is the season passing away, but the work is becoming more difficult.

It is plain that the duty here enjoined on the Hebrew Christians is, from the nature of the case, obligatory on Christians in all countries and in all ages. So long as there are "evil hearts of unbelief" in professors of Christianity—so long as they are exposed to the fascinating influences of an evil world, and the endlessly varied devices of the crafty "old serpent,"—so long will they need to be "exhorted daily, lest they be hardened by the deceitfulness of sin."

To the right discharge of this duty, much Christian wisdom and affection are necessary; but when rightly performed, I am persuaded it very seldom fails of producing a happy effect. Surely, when we consider the interests at stake, we ought not to be so backward, as I am afraid we generally are, to the discharge of this duty. What a power of motive is contained in these words of the Apostle James: "Brethren, if any of you do err from the faith, and one convert him; let him know, that he who converteth a sinner from the error of his way shall save a soul from death, and shall hide a multitude of sins."

The importance of taking heed lest there was in any of them an evil heart of unbelief, and of their exhorting one another daily, is placed in a strong point of light by the declaration made by the Apostle in the 14th verse. "For we are made partakers of Christ, if we hold the beginning of our confidence stedfast unto the end."

The striking analogy between these words and those in the 6th verse, which have been already explained, must be obvious to all,—"Whose house are we, if we hold fast the confidence and the rejoicing of the hope firm unto the end." Some interpreters have considered the words, "we are made partakers of Christ," as equivalent to, 'we shall be made partakers of Christ' —understanding by that, we shall be made participants of all the blessings of the Christian salvation—'if we hold the beginning of our confidence stedfast to the end.' But the words will not admit this mode of exposition. The words, literally translated, are, "We have been made partakers of Christ;" and the following clause, "if we hold the beginning of our confidence stedfast unto the end," does not express the means of attaining the fellowship of Christ as something future, but the evidence of our having already attained that fellowship.

To be a "partaker of Christ," is a phrase which nowhere else occurs in Scripture; but we have parallel expressions—such as, to "put on Christ," to "be in Christ," to "be members of His body, of His flesh, and of His bones." It is a very unduly attenuated sense to affix to the words, 'to be partakers of the doctrine of Christ,' or even 'to be partakers of His benefits.' It is the result of the first, the cause of the second. To be a "partaker of Christ," is to be so closely related to Him as that God treats us not as *we* deserve, but as *He* deserves to be treated—so intimately connected with Him, as that, " by His Spirit dwelling in us," we are made partakers of His views and feelings, His mind and will. This is to be a "partaker of Christ"—this is to be a true Christian. He is so joined to the Lord as to be one spirit with Him. Whoever professes to be a Christian, professes to be thus a "partaker of Christ;" but many make a false profession. All do so who do not "hold fast the beginning of the Christian confidence stedfast unto the end."

The word translated "confidence" is not the same as that rendered by the same term in the 6th verse. There, "the confidence of the hope" means, as I endeavoured to show, the free and fearless profession of the Christian hope both in word and in deed. "Confidence" here means, *firm persuasion*. It is the same word which the Apostle makes use of in his definition, or rather description, of faith in the 11th chapter: "Faith is the substance of things hoped for"—the persuasion of things hoped for. The Christian confidence or persuasion is just the faith of the Gospel—the knowing and being sure that "God so loved the world that He gave His only begotten Son, that whosoever believeth in Him might not perish, but have everlasting life"—the persuasion that "Christ Jesus came into the world to save sinners, even the chief"—that "His blood cleanseth from all sin," and that "He is able to save to the uttermost all that come unto God by Him."

"The beginning," or commencement, "of our confidence," is, I apprehend, just our first, or our original, confidence or persuasion.[1] It is by the faith of the truth which I have just stated that a man becomes a Christian; and it is by perseverance in that faith alone that he can obtain satisfactory evidence that he is a Christian. It is not the person who is "carried about with every wind of doctrine," but it is the person who is "rooted, and grounded, and stablished" in the faith of the truth, that manifests that he is a "partaker of Christ." Continued faith in the truth, manifesting itself in those fruits of peace, and joy, and holiness which it uniformly produces just in the degree in which it exists, is the only permanently satisfactory evidence that we are united to Christ Jesus, and interested in the blessings of His salvation. When the Hebrews first received the Gospel as good news of a full and free salvation to sinners, their faith and hope manifested itself in lively devotion, brotherly love, patience under suffering for Christ; and it was only by their holding fast this, their original faith and hope, that they could continue to enjoy the satisfaction of knowing that they were "partakers of Christ Jesus."

The words quoted in the 15th verse have already been explained. The only thing that requires to be remarked on, is the connection in which they stand, and the purpose for which they are introduced. A sentence seems begun here which is never completed. Some very learned interpreters have connected it with the beginning of the fourth chapter, considering the last four verses of this chapter as included in a parenthesis.[2] It ap-

---

[1] Ἀρχὴν τῆς ὑποστάσεως is a Hebraistic expression = ὑ. ἣν εἴχετε ἐν ἀρχῃ, which is = τὴν πρώτην ὑπόστασιν; or, as Paul has it in 1 Tim. v. 12, ἡ πρώτη πίστις.

[2] The occurrence of the particle οὖν in iv. 1, among other things, forbids the adoption of this connection.

pears to us more natural to consider it as connected with the 13th verse—the 14th being parenthetical—and as an expansion of the idea suggested by the words, "while it is called To-day;" thus, 'Exhort one another, inasmuch as it is said, To-day,' etc., —'Exhort one another, from its being said,' etc.[1] 'As one of the means of preserving each other from apostasy, frequently bring before each other's minds the dreadful consequences which resulted from unbelief in the case of your ancestors.'

It is easy to perceive how well the topic of mutual exhortation was chosen. The example is taken from their *ancestors*, for whom the Jews had a special reverence. The evil to be guarded against is the same in both cases—*unbelief*. The circumstances of their ancestors were similar to their own—both placed under a new economy. The consequences of unbelief in their case would be the same as in the case of their ancestors— exclusion from God's rest; while their guilt would be much more aggravated than that of their fathers, from the superior dignity of the Head of their dispensation, and their punishment much more severe—exclusion from a happiness of which peaceful residence in the Holy Land was but an imperfect figure. We cannot help in this perceiving the "wisdom given to the Apostle," as Peter expresses it.

In the verses which follow, he points out to them those circumstances in the history which were peculiarly fitted to impress their minds with the criminality and danger of apostasy from the faith of Christ. Vers. 16–18. "For some, when they had heard, did provoke: howbeit not all that came out of Egypt by Moses. But with whom was He grieved forty years? was it not with them that had sinned, whose carcases fell in the wilderness? And to whom sware He that they should not enter into His rest, but to them that believed not?" Let us proceed to examine the passage somewhat more particularly. Ver. 16. "For some, when they had heard, did provoke: howbeit not all that came out of Egypt by Moses."

These words, as they stand in our version, express this sentiment,—'that they who offended God so highly in the wilderness as to induce Him to exclude them by a solemn oath from any part in the rest of Canaan, were but a part of those who came out of Egypt under the care of Moses;' and did we know no

[1] *Vide* Peirce.

more of the matter than what is stated in these words, we would naturally conclude that they formed but a small part. From the history itself, we know that the whole of the male adult Israelites who left Egypt under Moses—with the exception, probably, of some of the Levites, and certainly of Caleb and Joshua—were involved both in the sin and punishment to which the Psalm refers. It is not very easy to see the bearing which the words have on the Apostle's object. There does not seem coherence in the exhortation, 'Be not rebellious, as your fathers were in that provocation, where some, but not all, rebelled.' It seems strange to use the word *some* as descriptive of many thousands—the great majority, and to suppose that the words " not *all*" refer merely to a small minority—Caleb and Joshua, and a few Levites.

These considerations have led many of the most learned and judicious interpreters to prefer another mode of rendering the words, which they will bear, and which brings out a sense more agreeable to the facts of the history, and more obviously bearing on the Apostle's great object, which plainly is, from the history of their ancestors to impress on the minds of the Hebrew Christians the criminality and danger of unbelief and apostasy. They[1] consider the 16th verse, as well as the 17th and 18th, as consisting of two interrogations. 'For who were they who, when they had heard, did provoke? Were they not all they who came out of Egypt by Moses?' These questions, like those in the succeeding verses, are just equivalent to a strong assertion. It is as if the Apostle had said, 'There is one fact in the history which peculiarly deserves your attention. All who came out of Egypt by Moses, after having heard, provoked.' The only objection to this version is, that it seems not exactly to express the fact; for there were exceptions, as we have already noticed. It is, however, quite common in the Scriptures, as well as in other writings, to use universal terms when the exceptions are comparatively few: Mark i. 5; John iii. 26; Phil. ii. 21; Acts iii. 18, x. 43; and we do find such universal terms used in the very history referred to, and from which it seems probable that the inspired writer borrowed them: Num. xiv. 1,

---

[1] They alter the accent in τινες from the last to the first syllable, making it signify *quinam* instead of *quidam*,—interrogative instead of demonstrative.

2, 10, 22, 23, 29, 35, 36. The sentiment in this verse, then, is, 'Almost all—the great body—of those who came out of Egypt by—through the instrumentality of—Moses, after having heard, did provoke Jehovah.'[1] This mode of interpretation has the great recommendation that it gives symmetry to the paragraph—the word rendered *some* occurring in the two following verses as an interrogative; and it rids us of the difficulty of giving a reason for its being stated that only some, and not all that came out of Egypt with Moses, heard and provoked. It is to be recollected that the accents and divisions of the sacred text were the work, not of the inspired writers, but of transcribers, who had no claim to infallibility, as their frequent blunders sufficiently show, and that the Greek language had no point of interrogation.

The words, "when," or "after, they had heard," have by many been supposed to refer to the Israelites hearing the divine communications made to them by Moses, and especially hearing the voice of God in awful solemnity pronounce, from amid the darkness which covered Mount Sinai, the law of the ten commandments. But I apprehend they directly refer to their having heard the command of God to go up and take possession of the land of Canaan, and the promise that God would enable them to do so. They did not "mix faith" with the annunciation made to them. On hearing, instead of believing the promise and obeying the command, they provoked God by calling in question His kind intentions, and obstinately refusing to do what He had commanded them. The following passage from Deuteronomy is a striking commentary on the statement in the text: "And when we departed from Horeb, we went through all that great and terrible wilderness, which ye saw by the way of the mountain of the Amorites, as the Lord our God commanded us; and we came to Kadesh-barnea. And I said unto you, Ye are come unto the mountain of the Amorites, which the Lord our God doth give unto us. Behold, the Lord thy God hath set the land before thee: go up and possess it, as the Lord God of thy fathers hath said unto thee; fear not, neither be discouraged. And ye came near unto me every one of you, and

---

[1] ἀλλά, both by itself—especially in the beginning of a sentence, as Rom. vi. 5; 2 Cor. vii. 11; Phil. i. 18—and joined to οὐ, οὐκ, or οὐχ, has the power of giving force to a clause, and answers to the Latin *omnino, sane, utique*.

said, We will send men before us, and they shall search us out the land, and bring us word again by what way we must go up, and into what cities we shall come. And the saying pleased me well; and I took twelve men of you, one of a tribe: And they turned, and went up into the mountain, and came unto the valley of Eshcol, and searched it out. And they took of the fruit of the land in their hands, and brought it down unto us, and brought us word again, and said, It is a good land which the Lord our God doth give us. Notwithstanding ye would not go up, but rebelled against the commandment of the Lord your God: and ye murmured in your tents, and said, Because the Lord hated us, He hath brought us forth out of the land of Egypt, to deliver us into the hand of the Amorites, to destroy us. Whither shall we go up? our brethren have discouraged our heart, saying, The people is greater and taller than we; the cities are great, and walled up to heaven: and, moreover, we have seen the sons of the Anakims there. Then I said unto you, Dread not, neither be afraid of them. The Lord your God, which goeth before you, He shall fight for you, according to all that He did for you in Egypt before your eyes; and in the wilderness, where thou hast seen how that the Lord thy God bare thee, as a man doth bear his son, in all the way that ye went, until ye came into this place. Yet in this thing ye did not believe the Lord your God, who went in the way before you, to search you out a place to pitch your tents in, in fire by night, to show you by what way ye should go, and in a cloud by day."[1]

This statement—'Almost all who came out of Egypt with Moses, after having heard the promise and command of God, provoked Him, by refusing to believe the promise and obey the command'—was well fitted to excite a salutary fear in the minds of the Hebrew Christians. It cautioned them against resting in privileges, and thinking themselves safe merely because they had by profession forsaken Judaism, and had heard the promises and commands of God made known by Jesus Christ and His apostles. All who left Egypt did not enter Canaan. All who by profession leave the world lying in wickedness do not, of course, enter into the heavenly rest. Men may hear the Gospel, and yet not believe it. The grace of God may come to them,

[1] Deut. i. 19-33.

and yet come to them in vain. But this is not all. The great majority—almost all who came out of Egypt with Moses, almost all who heard the promise and command of God—were unbelieving and disobedient. Was not this a most striking demonstration of the strength of the natural tendency to unbelief and disobedience in the human heart? and was it not reasonable and right that the Hebrews should take heed lest there was in any of them "an evil heart of unbelief," when it was so plain that there was such a heart in the great majority of their ancestors? Every new proof of the tendency of human nature to unbelief and disobedience should make us the more "jealous over ourselves with a godly jealousy."

The Apostle proceeds to turn the attention of the Hebrew Christians more particularly to the punishment, and to the cause of the punishment, of the majority of their ancestors.— Ver. 17. "But (and) with whom was He grieved forty years? was it not with them that had sinned, whose carcases fell in the wilderness? 18. And to whom sware He that they should not enter into His rest, but to them that believed not?"

These questions are equivalent to an assertion. 'On account of the unbelief and disobedience of the ancient Israelites, God was grievously offended with them, and manifested His displeasure by excluding them by an oath from Canaan, and dooming them to die in the wilderness.' "He was grieved," or rather offended, "with them for forty years." For the long period of forty years, by keeping them in the wilderness, and by a variety of severe judicial inflictions, He showed His displeasure at them. It is probably to this that Moses refers in the 90th Psalm, when he says, "For we are consumed by Thine anger, and by Thy wrath are we troubled. Thou hast set our iniquities before Thee, our secret sins in the light of Thy countenance. For all our days are passed away in Thy wrath; we spend our years as a tale that is told."[1]

Their "carcases fell in the wilderness." The word translated "carcases," properly signifies limbs, or members of the body. The awful sentence, "Your carcases shall fall in the wilderness," is equivalent to, 'Your limbs shall bestrew the desert,'[2]—your bones shall whiten amid its sands.' It was executed not merely by such awful judicial inflictions as took place

---

[1] Ps. xc. 7–9.    [2] κατεστρώθησαν is the Apostle's word, 1 Cor. x. 5.

in consequence of the rebellion of Korah, Dathan, and Abiram, the plague of the fiery serpents, and the joining in the impure rites of the Moabitish idolatry—but also by retaining the people in the wilderness till the whole of that unbelieving and disobedient generation, who did not perish in these judgments, were in the ordinary course of things brought to their graves.

These circumstances in the history of the ancient Hebrews were well fitted to excite in the minds of those to whom the Apostle wrote, a holy fear of unbelief and disobedience. Jehovah is "the same yesterday, to-day, and for ever." If unbelief and disobedience offended Him in them, they will offend Him in us also. If unbelief and disobedience to the will of God as "spoken by Moses" brought down on our fathers such judgments, what may we expect if we are unbelieving and disobedient when He makes known His will to us "by His Son?" Death in the wilderness, exclusion from Canaan, will be found but very feeble figures of the evils in which unbelief and disobedience to Him will involve us.

But what the Apostle wishes chiefly to impress on the minds of his readers is, that unbelief lay at the foundation of all their sins and all their judgments. Ver. 19. "So we see that they could not enter in because of unbelief;" *i.e.*, 'It is plain, from the history of the Israelites, that it was their unbelief that prevented their obtaining possession of Canaan.' The Apostle seems to have had in his mind the words of Jehovah, "How long will this people provoke Me? and how long will it be ere they believe Me?"[1]

Some interpreters would understand the expression, "they *could* not," as equivalent to 'they would not.' The word is not unfrequently used in this way. Joseph's brethren "*could* not"— *i.e.*, they would not—"speak peaceably to him."[2] "I cannot," says the man in the parable,—"I cannot rise and give it thee;" where the meaning plainly is, 'I am not disposed to rise and give it thee.'[3] This is true, but it does not seem to be the truth here taught. That seems plainly to be, 'Unbelief was the cause why they were excluded from the rest of God.' Unbelief was by no means the only sin of which that wicked generation were guilty. They had made and worshipped a golden calf; they had

[1] Num. xiv. 11.     [2] Gen. xxxvii. 4.
[3] Luke xi. 8. John viii. 43; Mark vi. 5.

often rebelled and murmured. But, notwithstanding all their sins, if they had—even down to the period when God sware in His wrath they should not enter into His rest—believed the divine promise, and shown that they believed it by acting accordingly, they would have obtained possession of the promised land. They *could not*, continuing unbelieving, enter in; for their unbelief prevented their doing what was absolutely necessary to their entering in; and, continuing unbelieving, it would not have been becoming in God, and therefore it was impossible, that He should bring them in. This is distinctly stated in reference to the worship of the golden calf, Exod. xxxii. 34. Unbelief was the source of all their other sins; and it was in consequence of obstinate perseverance in unbelief that the irreversible sentence of exclusion was pronounced. They attempted afterwards to enter, but they found it was too late: Num. xiv. 45. Previously to the oath of God, their unbelief prevented them from entering by inducing them to refuse to go up at the command of God; and afterwards, their unbelief, as the procuring cause of the divine sentence of exclusion, made all attempts on their part fruitless.

The conclusion to which the Apostle wished the Hebrew Christians to come from the consideration of this fact in reference to their ancestors is this, 'If unbelief was so mischievous in the case of our fathers, it cannot be less so—it must be more so—in ours; if unbelief shut them out of Canaan, have we not reason to think unbelief will shut us out of heaven?' It deserves notice that, under the Gospel, it is unbelief that by way of eminence excludes men from the celestial blessedness. There is no sin so great but it may be pardoned, if the sinner believe. There is no sinner so guilty but he may be saved through the faith of the truth. Unbelief prevents salvation, both as it keeps us away from the Saviour, and because, as direct opposition to the favourite purpose of God in the New Economy, it draws down the severest influences of His righteous indignation.

It may be proper, before concluding our remarks on this chapter, to correct a mistake into which some good men have fallen with regard to the nature of that unbelief which led to the exclusion of the Israelites from Canaan, and which has led, we are disposed to think, to important and dangerous misapprehension respecting the nature of that unbelief by which a man is excluded from the celestial rest. The promise of bringing the Israelites into Canaan has been considered by some as an absolute, unconditional promise made to that generation; and the faith required of them, as a belief on the part of every individual that *he* would infallibly enter into the possession of the land; and that the unbelief for which the Israelites were punished, was the disbelief of the promise viewed in this light. And as there is plainly an analogy between the promise revealed to the Israelites and the promise revealed in the Gospel, they have argued that there is an absolute promise of salvation made to every hearer of the Gospel, and that the faith required of him is a belief that he himself shall be saved and enter into the possession of the heavenly rest.

Let us look at the promise made in reference to Israel entering into the promised land : " I will bring you in unto the land, concerning the which I did swear to give it to Abraham, to Isaac, and to Jacob; and I will give it you for an heritage : I am the Lord."[1] This is a promise which refers to Israel as a people, and which does not by any means necessarily infer that all, or even that any, of that generation were to enter in. No express condition is mentioned in this promise—not even the believing it. Yet, so far as that generation was concerned, this, as the event proved, was plainly implied; for, if it had been an absolute, unconditional promise to that generation, it must have been performed, otherwise He who cannot lie would have failed in accomplishing His own word. There can be no doubt that the fulfilment of the promise to them was suspended on their believing it, and acting accordingly. Had they believed that Jehovah was indeed both able and determined to bring His people Israel into the land of Canaan, and, under the influence of this faith, gone up at His command to take possession, the promise would have been performed to them. This was the tenor of the covenant made with them. "Now therefore, if ye will obey My voice indeed, and keep My covenant, then ye shall be a peculiar treasure unto Me above all people: for all the earth is Mine. And ye shall be unto Me a kingdom of priests, and an holy nation. These are the words which thou shalt speak unto the children of Israel. And Moses came, and called for the elders of the people, and laid before their faces all these

[1] Exod. vi. 8.

words which the Lord commanded him. And all the people answered together, and said, All that the Lord hath spoken we will do. And Moses returned the words of the people unto the Lord. And the Lord said unto Moses, Lo, I come unto thee in a thick cloud, that the people may hear when I speak with thee, and believe thee for ever. And Moses told the words of the people unto the Lord." Again, "Behold, I send an Angel before thee, to keep thee in the way, and to bring thee into the place which I have prepared. Beware of Him, and obey His voice, provoke Him not; for He will not pardon your transgressions: for My name is in Him. But if thou shalt indeed obey His voice, and do all that I speak; then I will be an enemy unto thine enemies, and an adversary unto thine adversaries. For Mine Angel shall go before thee, and bring thee in unto the Amorites, and the Hittites, and the Perizzites, and the Canaanites, the Hivites, and the Jebusites; and I will cut them off. Thou shalt not bow down to their gods, nor serve them, nor do after their works; but thou shalt utterly overthrow them, and quite break down their images."[1] Their unbelief and disobedience are constantly stated as the reasons why they did not enter in. "Because all those men which have seen My glory, and My miracles which I did in Egypt, and in the wilderness, have tempted Me now these ten times, and have not hearkened to My voice." "For the children of Israel walked forty years in the wilderness, till all the people that were men of war, which came out of Egypt, were consumed, because they obeyed not the voice of the Lord: unto whom the Lord sware that He would not show them the land which the Lord sware unto their fathers that He would give us, a land that floweth with milk and honey."[2] And the Apostle says, "They could not enter in because of unbelief." God promised to bring Israel into the land of Canaan; but He did not promise to bring them in whether they believed and obeyed or not. No promise was broken to these men, for no absolute promise was made to them. But their unbelief did not make the promise of God of none effect. It was accomplished to the next generation. "And the Lord gave unto Israel all the land which He sware to give unto their fathers; and they possessed it, and dwelt therein."[3]

[1] Exod. xix. 5–9, xxiii. 20–24.   [2] Num. xiv. 22; Josh. v. 6.
[3] Josh. xxi. 43.

Joshua appeals to the Israelites themselves for the completeness of the fulfilment of the promise. "And, behold, this day I am going the way of all the earth: and ye know in all your hearts, and in all your souls, that not one thing hath failed of all the good things which the Lord your God spake concerning you; all are come to pass unto you, and not one thing hath failed thereof."[1] That generation believed the promise that God would give Canaan to Israel, and, under the influence of this fact, went forward under the conduct of Joshua, and obtained possession of the land for themselves.

The Gospel promise of eternal life, like the promise of Canaan, is a promise which will assuredly be accomplished. It is sure to all "the seed." They were "chosen in Christ before the foundation of the world." Eternal life was promised in reference to them before the times of the ages, and confirmed by the oath of God. They have been redeemed to God by "the blood of the Lamb," and are all called in due time according to His purpose. Their inheritance is "laid up in heaven" for them, and "they are kept for it by the mighty power of God, through faith unto salvation." And they shall all at last "inherit the kingdom prepared for them from the foundation of the world."

But the Gospel revelation does not testify directly to any one that Christ so died for him in particular, that it is certain that *he* shall be saved through His death: neither does it absolutely promise salvation to all men; for in this case all must be saved,—or God must be a liar. But it testifies that "God is in Christ, reconciling the world to Himself, not imputing to men their trespasses—seeing He ever liveth to make intercession for them;" and it promises that "whosoever believeth in Christ shall not perish, but have everlasting life." It proclaims: "He that believeth shall be saved—he that believeth not shall be damned." It is as believers of the truth that we are secured of eternal life; and it is by holding fast this faith of the truth, and showing that we do so, that we can alone enjoy the comfort of this security. "The purpose of God according to election must stand," and all His chosen will assuredly be saved; but they cannot know their election—they cannot enjoy any absolute assurance of their salvation—independent of their continuance in the faith, love, and obedience of the Gospel. "And besides this, giving all dili-

[1] Josh. xxiii. 14.

gence, add to your faith, virtue; and to virtue, knowledge; and to knowledge, temperance; and to temperance, patience; and to patience, godliness; and to godliness, brotherly-kindness; and to brotherly-kindness, charity. For if these things be in you, and abound, they make you that ye shall neither be barren nor unfruitful in the knowledge of our Lord Jesus Christ. But he that lacketh these things is blind, and cannot see afar off, and hath forgotten that he was purged from his old sins. Wherefore the rather, brethren, give diligence to make your calling and election sure; for if ye do these things, ye shall never fall: for so an entrance shall be ministered unto you abundantly into the everlasting kingdom of our Lord and Saviour Jesus Christ. Wherefore I will not be negligent to put you always in remembrance of these things, though ye know them, and be established in the present truth."[1] And to the Christian, in every stage of his progress, it is of importance to remember, that he who turns back, turns "back to perdition;" and that it is he only who believes straight onward—that continues in the faith of the truth—that shall obtain "the salvation of the soul."

The exhortation which follows, as is plain from the connective particle *therefore*, rises out of the statements made in the preceding chapter. These statements are the following:—Jesus Christ is placed over the family of God under the New Economy, as Moses was placed over the family of God under the Old. Jesus Christ is faithful in the discharge of the duties rising out of this high trust, as Moses also was. In these points Jesus Christ is entitled to the same attention, reverence, faith, and obedience from all who are under His care, as Moses was from all placed under his care. But this is a great under-statement of the truth. He has much higher claims on our attention, and reverence, and faith, and obedience than Moses; for He is the Founder of the family over which He is placed, which was not the case with Moses; and He is a Son over the family of His Father, instead of being, like Moses, merely a servant in the family of his Master. The Israelites who obstinately disbelieved and disregarded the promise and command of God in reference to entering into the rest of Canaan, given by Moses, provoked the divine displeasure, and by an oath were excluded from that rest, and doomed to die in the wilderness.

[1] 2 Pet. i. 5–12.

From these statements, the Apostle—knowing that all these things happened to them for ensamples, and were written for the admonition of those on whom the ends of the Mosaic age had come—draws the conclusion, that inattention, unbelief, and disobedience to the command of God given by Jesus Christ, would be attended with consequences more dreadful than inattention, unbelief, and disobedience to His command given by Moses, in proportion to the superior dignity of Christ to Moses; and that, if in the one case they led to exclusion from the rest of Canaan, in reference to which a promise and command had been given by Moses, they would, in the other, lead to exclusion from that better rest, in reference to which a promise and command had been given by Jesus Christ; and on these principles he founds the exhortation contained in the first verse of the fourth chapter. —Ver. 1. "Let us therefore fear, lest, a promise being left us of entering into His rest, any of you should seem to come short of it." The paragraph on the consideration of which we are now entering requires most careful attention; for, as Tholuck justly remarks, "few commentators have succeeded in clearly tracing out the connection of the ideas." The cause, however, is not to be found in the passage, but, as Ebrard says, "in the commentators bringing too much of their own ideas with them, and wanting the self-denial simply to surrender themselves to the words of the writer."

These words admit of two different interpretations, according to the meaning attached to the clause, " a promise," or " the promise, being left." The word *us*, you will observe, is a supplement. These words may either be considered—as it is plain our translators considered them—as the statement of a fact: ' A promise of entering into God's rest was not peculiar to the Israelites —a promise of this kind is revealed to us as well as to them ;' or they may be viewed as expressing the way in which the evil cautioned against is likely to be incurred : ' Let us fear, lest, the promise being left or abandoned, any of us should come short— lest, by abandoning, or losing hold of, or giving up the promise, any of us should come short of the rest to which it refers.' The original text will bear either interpretation, and both bring out an important and appropriate truth. In the first case the sense is, ' Since a promise of entering into God's rest has been made known to us as well as to the Israelites, let us fear, lest we, like the unbelievers among them, come short of that rest.' In the other case the sense is, ' Let us fear, lest, by leaving or rejecting the promise, we fall short of the rest of God.'

But we apprehend that the mode of interpretation followed by our translators is the preferable one.[1] It is plain that the foundation of the Apostle's exhortation is, ' A promise of entering into God's rest has been exhibited to us Christians, as well as to the Israelites;' and the following verses are employed in proving this.

"A promise is left to us of entering into the rest of God." These words are equivalent to,—' In the words of the Psalm which I have quoted,—To-day, if ye will hear My voice, harden not your hearts,—there is an implied promise of entering into God's rest, which is addressed to us under the Christian economy.' For that the closing words of the 95th Psalm refer, and refer solely, to the Messianic times, the argument of the inspired writer in the following part of the chapter forbids us to doubt. 'The Israelites had a promise of entering into God's rest in Canaan : we have a promise of entering into God's rest, of which the rest of Canaan was only a figure; and this promise is implied in the quotation from the Book of Psalms which I have just made.'

These words bring before the mind a very instructive view of the Gospel revelation. It is "a promise of entering into God's *rest.*" The "rest" of God has, very generally, by commentators, been considered as descriptive of the celestial blessedness. I think that a juster view of the meaning of the phrase is taken by those who consider it as a general name for that happiness, whether enjoyed on earth or in heaven, on the possession of which men enter when they believe the Gospel; and it is termed "God's rest," both because it is substantially the same kind of happiness which God enjoys, and because it is at once prepared and bestowed by Him. The Gospel, viewed in the aspect in which it is here held up to us, may be considered as including a discovery of this rest of God, an account of the way in which we are to enter into it, an invitation to enter, and a promise to all who accept the invitation that they shall assuredly be brought in and put in possession of all its blessings.

---

[1] Had the other been the Apostle's idea, he would probably have said, μήποτε καταλείπων ἐπαγγελίαν—δοκῇ τις.

Since such "a promise of entering into God's rest has been left" to Christians, the Apostle exhorts them to "fear, lest any of them should seem to come short of it."[1] The expression *come short* may refer either to the promise or the rest promised. To come short in reference to the promise, is to remain in unbelief. There is a promise given: a personal interest in that promise can be obtained only by believing. It is the believer only who embraces the promise; the unbeliever "comes short." The promise is as it were no promise to him. In this case the meaning of the exhortation is, 'Let us fear, lest, a promise being left us, any of us should, by continuing in unbelief, not lay hold on that promise.' Though this makes good enough sense, yet I apprehend the expression *come short* naturally refers, not directly to the promise, but to the thing promised—the rest of God. The allusion is plainly to the people of Israel who, under the influence of unbelief, "came short of"—never reached—the promised rest of Canaan, but died in the wilderness. To "come short" of the rest of God, is to fail of obtaining that state of holy happiness both on earth and in heaven which is in the Gospel promised to believers.

There is a peculiarity in the phraseology which deserves notice. The Apostle does not say, 'Lest any of you come short of this rest of God;' but, "Lest any of you *seem* to come short of it." We take notice of this chiefly to correct a mistake into which some have fallen in reference to it. They consider it as intended to intimate this sentiment: 'You cannot, indeed, fall short of the rest of God, but you may *seem* to fall short of it.' This is certainly to destroy the force of the caution. The unbelieving Israelites not only seemed to fall short, but actually fell short of Canaan; and professors of Christianity who believe not, not merely in appearance, but in reality, exclude themselves from the enjoyment of that holy happiness which in the text before us is called the "rest" of God. The truth is, that the word rendered *seem* is generally held to be often used, both in the New Testament and in profane writers, as an expletive. "That which he seemeth to have," and "that which he hath," are synonymous expressions as used by Luke, ch. viii. 18, xix. 26. In Luke xxii. 24, "which of them should be accounted the

[1] The meaning of ὑστερεῖν may be learned from Luke xxii. 35; Rom. iii. 23; 1 Cor. i. 7; Heb. xii. 15; Eccles. xi. 12, xiii. 6.

greatest," is just equivalent to, 'which of them should be the greatest.' In 1 Cor. xi. 16, "If any man seem to be contentious," is equivalent to, 'if any man be contentious.' If the word have any distinct meaning, it is probably intended to suggest this idea, 'That men may, like the Israelites, appear to be on the fair way to the promised rest of God, and yet never actually reach it.'[1] Since, then, a promise is left us in reference to entrance into the rest of God,—since men, to whom this promise is left, may, like the Israelites, seem to be on the way to this rest, and yet through unbelief never enter into its enjoyment,[2]—"Let us," says the Apostle, "*fear*."

The expression *let us fear* is just synonymous with "let us take heed," "let us be cautious," "let us be watchful."[3] These words are not to be understood as an exhortation to believers to be fearful in reference to their ultimate salvation. To all believers it is distinctly promised that "they shall never perish, but have everlasting life." To all believers the words of our Lord to His disciples may be considered as addressed: "Fear not, little flock; it is your Father's good pleasure to give you the kingdom." "I give unto My sheep eternal life, and they shall never perish, neither shall any pluck them out of my hand. My Father, who gave them Me, is greater than all; and

---

[1] Schmid translates δοκῇ by *audeat*, 'lest any one *dare* to come short of it.' He considers it as opposed to Φοβηθῶμεν: *non audet qui timet*. This is a good sense, but I scarcely think it is consistent with the usus loquendi. Schmid appeals to Matt. iii. 9, as a similar passage.

[2] ὑστερηκέναι admits of a somewhat different interpretation. The proper meaning of ὑστερεῖν is, 'to come on the following day—to come too late.' It has been supposed there is a reference to τὸ σήμερον: 'lest the day pass away without your entering into the rest of God—lest, as the prophet Jeremiah says, "the harvest should pass, and the summer end, while ye are not saved;" or as our Lord has it, "lest the good man of the house should rise up and shut to the door ere ye have entered."' This affords a good and impressive sense, but the ordinary way in which ὑστερεῖν is used in the New Testament and LXX. seems to require us to prefer the common mode of exegesis. Ebrard gives a somewhat different turn to the words δοκῇ and ὑστερηκέναι: "Let us take heed, therefore, lest, while a promise of entering into God's rest remains to be fulfilled, any one of you should nevertheless imagine that he has come too late namely, that he lives in a time when all such promises have been long ago fulfilled." This is ingenious, but not satisfactory.

[3] βλέπωμεν, ch. iii. 12; ἐπισκοπῶμεν, ch. xii. 15; or σπουδάσωμεν, ver. 11 *infra*.

none can pluck them out of My Father's hand." It never can be the duty of a believer to doubt the fulfilment of the promises which God has made to believers; and the more firmly he believes them, the more active will he be in the discharge of every duty,—"the joy of the Lord will be his strength." This in them is a fruit of unbelief, and obviously cannot be right.[1]

But believers ought to fear and guard against the "evil heart of unbelief;" knowing that he who is completely under its influence cannot at all "enter into God's rest"—must be a stranger, both in time and through eternity, to that holy happiness in reference to which "a promise has been left us;" and knowing also, that just in proportion to the degree in which we are influenced by it, we "come short" of the enjoyment of that rest into which men enter by believing, and into which, from the very nature of the case, it is impossible for them to enter in any other way. It is only in the way of believing that the rest of God can be enjoyed on earth. It is only by continuing in "the faith of the truth" till the end that we can enter on its full enjoyment in heaven. Whatever, then, has a tendency to shake our faith in the testimony of God—whatever has a tendency to draw away our minds from that saving truth which is the source at once of our comfort and our holiness—ought to be an object of cautious fear to every Christian.

"Many have adopted a scheme of doctrine which tends to set believers free from every kind of fear, as being inconsistent with faith, which, they think, is a person's believing that he will be saved at all events; and especially if he has been once enlightened, and has received the word with joy, it is supposed that he can never fall away; so that, whatever symptoms of

---

[1] Turner proposes to render the words, "lest, by some possibility, some of you should after all forget this promised rest. The Apostle's exhortation is not, Fear that you shall come short of the promised rest; but, *Fear*, fear God—fear sin—that you may not come short of it. *Hope* that you shall, but, at the same time, *fear* that you may not." Calvin says well— " Here fear is commended to us, not to destroy the certainty of faith, but to instil such great carefulness that we may never lapse into complacent torpor." " It is ever," as a late American commentator remarks, " the teaching of the Scriptures, that while we exercise an implicit and triumphing confidence in the fidelity of God, we should exercise a jealous watch over the treachery of our own hearts. These ideas are here also by implication. The promise abides; it is we who may seem to come short."

apostasy may appear, he is to consider them only as the infirmities and failings of God's children, but has no cause to fear lest he finally come short, which, in their estimation, is the great sin of unbelief. But the author of this Epistle had no idea that a cautious fear of coming short by unbelief was itself unbelief. On the contrary, it was to guard them against unbelief, and its dreadful consequences, that he inculcates this fear upon them. Faith, in general, is the belief of God's word, and respects His threatenings as well as His promises; and so gives credit to the motives of fear as well as of hope, both of which are necessary to believers while in this world.

"Both believers and unbelievers have their fears; but they arise from different sources, and have quite opposite effects. The fear of unbelievers and the unbelieving fears of believers arise from unworthy thoughts of God—a distrust of His power, faithfulness, and goodness—a prevailing love of 'the present evil world' and its enjoyments, which makes them more afraid of worldly losses and sufferings for righteousness' sake than of forfeiting the divine favour. Such fears not only indispose the mind for obedience, but lead directly to sin. But that godly fear, which is peculiar to believers, which arises from a just view, reverence, and esteem of the divine character—a supreme desire of His favour as their chief happiness,—is a fear lest they should offend Him, and incur His just displeasure,—such a fear of Him as outweighs all the allurements of sin on the one hand, and all the terrors of suffering for righteousness' sake on the other. This is that fear which Christ inculcates on His disciples, Luke xii. 4, 5. This is to sanctify the Lord our God in our hearts, and to make Him our fear and our dread.

"Happy is the man that thus feareth always. This godly fear, instead of dejecting or abasing the mind, inspires a noble courage and freedom. Fearing our God, we know no other fear. It preserves from slothful security, checks self-confidence and high-mindedness, and makes us cautious and vigilant in reference to everything which may endanger the safety of the soul."[1] May we all have grace to serve our God with this reverence and godly fear.

The paragraph which follows, verses 2-11, contains in it an illustration and proof of the fact on which the exhortation

[1] M'Lean.

contained in the 1st verse of this chapter proceeds—that a promise of entering into God's rest is left, or remains, for those who are under the New Testament dispensation, and that that promise is embodied in the quotation which has been made from the 95th Psalm, "To-day, if ye will hear His voice, harden not your hearts." The words, "A promise has been left us of entering into God's rest," may be considered as the theme, and these verses are the illustration of it.

'A promise,' says the Apostle, 'has been left us of entering into the rest of God.' Ver. 2. "For unto us was the gospel preached, as well as unto them."

The meaning and design of these words have been very much obscured by the use of the technical word "gospel," which, though originally signifying 'good news' in general, has come by long use to be appropriated as the name of the best news which ever reached our world—the revelation of mercy to guilty man through the mediation of the only begotten of God. It is not the design of the Apostle in these words to state that "the Gospel," in the ordinary sense of that word, was preached to the Hebrews as well as to their ancestors. The meaning which his words naturally convey, and which his argument plainly requires, is, *For unto us has a joyful annunciation been made, as well as to them.* 'They were invited to enter into the rest of Canaan: we are invited to enter into that rest of holy happiness which Christ has obtained for His people, both on earth and in heaven.' The joyful annunciation made to them was: "Ye are come unto the mountain of the Amorites, which the Lord our God doth give unto us. Behold, the Lord thy God hath set the land before thee: go up and possess it, as the Lord God of thy fathers hath said unto thee; fear not, neither be discouraged."[1] The joyful annunciation made to us is: "Come unto Me, all ye that labour and are heavy laden, and I will give you rest." "To-day, if ye will hear His voice."

"But the word preached did not profit them." "*The word preached*," or the word of the report made to the Israelites, is plainly the joyful annunciation just referred to.[2] This "did not profit them;" it was of no use to them—they were none the better for it. They did not obtain the blessing in reference

---

[1] Deut. i. 20, 21.

[2] ὁ λόγος τῆς ἀκοῆς,—a Heb. for ὁ ἀκουσθεὶς λόγος.

to which a promise was given them: they did not enter into Canaan—they died in the wilderness.

The cause why they were not the better for the joyful annunciation which was made to them is stated in the next clause. "The word of the report was not mixed with," or by, "faith in them which heard it."[1] It is by believing a principle that it becomes influential, as it is by digesting food that it becomes nutritive. Food not mingled with the mass of vital fluids, in consequence of the process of digestion, does not serve its purpose. Truth, unless believed, mingled with the springs of moral action, cannot serve its purpose either. When the Israelites heard the joyful annunciation, they would not go up; for they did not believe the Lord their God. If they had believed the divine declaration, Deut. i. 30, that "the Lord their God would go before them and fight for them," the joyful annunciation would have "profited" them. They would have gone up, and they would have entered in and obtained possession. But because they did not believe, they would not go up, and "rebelled against the commandment of the Lord;" and instead of being "profited" by the joyful annunciation, it became the occasion of more heinous guilt and more aggravated punishment. The following sentiment, though not expressed, is obviously intended to be suggested by this statement:—'And the joyful annunciation made to us will not profit us unless it be mingled with faith in us when we hear it. The mere hearing the Gospel will do us no good. It must be believed in order to its serving the purpose of leading us into the enjoyment of God's rest.'

Ver. 3. "For," continues the Apostle, "we who have believed do enter into rest." The Apostle here speaks of believers of all ages as a body, to which he and those to whom he was writing belonged, and says, 'It is we who believe, and we alone, who under any dispensation can enter into the rest of God.'[2]

---

[1] It is doubtful whether $\sigma \upsilon \gamma \kappa \varepsilon \kappa \rho \alpha \mu \acute{\varepsilon} \nu o \varsigma$ or —$o \upsilon \varsigma$ be the true rendering. Mill., Wet., Griesb., Matthæi, prefer the latter. The meaning in the latter case is, 'because they were not mixed by faith with those who heard,'—i. e., listened, believed, obeyed, such as Caleb and Joshua. The general meaning is the same: 'The good news did them no good, because it was not believed by them.'

[2] οἱ πιστεύσαντες is here used emphatically as opposed to οἱ ἀπειθήσαντες. It is = persevering believers. The word is used in the same way, John vi.

## THE FACT PRACTICALLY IMPROVED. 205

They who heard and disbelieved the invitation to enter into Canaan, did not enter into that rest: they that hear and disbelieve the invitation to enter into the Gospel rest, shall not enter into that rest. And the reason is, it is only they who believe that enter into rest. In neither of these cases was this an arbitrary arrangement. In the nature of things, in neither of the cases could the unbeliever enter into God's rest,—faith being the appropriate means for the end of entering; and in both cases, too, *unbelief*, as rebellion against God, deserved to be punished by exclusion from God's rest.

As a corroboration of his statement, that it is *believers*, and *believers only*, who enter into God's rest, the Apostle quotes a part of the 95th Psalm, already more than once referred to: "As He," *i.e.*, God, "said, As I have sworn in My wrath, if they shall enter into My rest;" *i.e.*, according to the Hebrew idiomatical, elliptical mode of expressing an oath, '*they* shall not enter into My rest.'

To see the bearing of this quotation on the Apostle's argument, it is only necessary to ask, 'And who were *they* who were thus awfully excluded from the rest of God?' "To whom sware He that they should not enter into His rest, but to them who believed not?" The unbelievers are excluded. It is the believers alone who can enter.[1] Thus far the meaning and design of the Apostle are clearly manifest.

The passage that follows wears a peculiarly disjointed appearance, and has occasioned great perplexity to interpreters.[2] I apprehend the last clause of the 3d verse should be disconnected from the words immediately preceding, and should be connected with those which immediately follow it. Along with the 4th and 5th verses, it appears to me a kind of explanatory note

---

64, ii. 11, xi. 15; 1 John v. 13. Πίστις, in a similar way, occurs Eph. i. 15; Col. i. 4; 2 Thess. i. 4; Heb. x. 39, xiii. 7. Words must be considered as to be interpreted emphatically when the ordinary interpretation yields either no sense, or no appropriate sense, or a very tame and frigid sense.

[1] As Calvin happily says, "The argument is from opposites. Only unbelief excludes; where there is faith, the entry lies open." Some would supply before καθώς: ἧς ὑστερήσουσιν οἱ ἀπειθήσαντες.

[2] "The punctuation and, here at any rate, Robert Stephanus' inept division of the verses in what comes after quite impede the sense."—CARPZOVIUS. "The clipped brevity of expression here has given rise to obscurity."—ABRESCH.

on the expression, "*the rest of God.*" "A promise is left us of entering into *His rest.*" The "rest" of God, in its primary use in the Old Testament Scriptures, is descriptive of that state of cessation from the exercise of creating energy, and of satisfaction in what He had created, into which God is represented as entering on the completion of His six days' work, when in the beginning "He formed the heavens and the earth, and all their hosts." In this sense the phrase was plainly not applicable to the subject which the Apostle is discussing; but in these words he shows that the phrase, the *rest of God*, is not in the Scriptures so appropriated to the rest of God after the creation as not to be applicable, and indeed applied, to other subjects. Vers. 4, 5. "Although the works were finished from the foundation of the world (for He spake in a certain place of the seventh day on this wise, 'And God did rest the seventh day from all His works'), yet in this place again, 'If they shall enter into My rest.'"[1] In this way the three apparently disjointed members are formed into one sentence; and that one sentence expresses a sentiment calculated to throw light on the language which the Apostle is employing.

*God's rest* is an expression originally used in reference to the divine rest after the creation; but in using it in reference to that holy happiness into which Christians enter by believing, the Apostle does not use an undue freedom with the language of inspiration, for it is plain from this passage in the 95th Psalm that the phrase is applied to other things besides that, to express which it was primarily used. It would have been a happy thing for the Christian Church if human interpreters had discovered an equal carefulness with that shown here by the Apostle, of not attaching to inspired phrases sentiments different from those which they were intended to convey.

---

[1] Καίτοι may signify, indeed—nempe, nimirum, et quidem. Καί in the beginning of the 5th verse may be rendered, *yet, nevertheless:* Matt. vi. 26, x. 29, xii. 5; John i. 10, vi. 70, vii. 19, ix. 30, xvii. 25; Gal. iv. 14; 1 John ii. 4; Rev. iii. 1; LXX. 2 Sam. iii. 8; Mal. ii. 14. Moses Stuart's mode of connecting καίτοι, etc.—thus, My rest, *i.e.*, rest from the works which were finished—is utterly unsatisfactory; for neither of the rests referred to in the 95th Psalm is the rest of the Sabbath. Kuinoel's plan, borrowed from Abresch, of supplying εἴρηκε—And this He said, though, etc.—is much preferable, and brings out the same sense as our rendering.

The 6th verse is plainly an unfinished sentence: "Seeing therefore it remaineth that some must enter therein, and they to whom it was first preached entered not in because of unbelief." When in reading any author we meet with an unfinished sentence, we conclude that what interrupts the sense is what is termed a parenthesis—something thrown in which may be useful for the complete elucidation of the subject; and we expect that by and by we shall meet with the close of the period. Now, I apprehend this is just what occurs in the passage before us. All that is introduced from the close of the 6th verse to the close of the 10th is parenthetical, and in the 11th verse you have the conclusion of the sentence commenced in the 6th: "Let us labour therefore to enter into that rest, lest any man fall after the same example of unbelief."

As the design of the parenthesis seems plainly to establish the principle on which this exhortation proceeds,—viz., that *there is a rest of God remaining for us* under the Gospel dispensation, into which we may enter,—it will be conducive to our more distinct apprehension of the meaning and force of the Apostle's discussion, if we endeavour first to explain the parenthesis, and then proceed to illustrate the exhortation grounded on the principle established in it.

Ver. 7. "Again, He limiteth a certain day, saying in David, To-day, after so long a time; as it is said, To-day, if ye will hear His voice, harden not your hearts." The Apostle had already shown from the words in the 95th Psalm, "I sware in My wrath that they should not enter into My rest"—words plainly referring to the enjoyment of Canaan,—that the phrase, *rest of God*, is not exclusively descriptive of the rest of God after the creation. He now goes on to show from another part of the same Psalm, that there is *a rest of God* different not only from the rest of the creation, but from the rest of Canaan. "Again, He"—*i.e.*, the Holy Spirit—"limiteth a certain day"—fixes on a particular period during which men may enter into the rest of God,— "saying in David"—*i.e.*, in the Book of Psalms, which goes by David's name—"*To-day*, after so long a time." The phrase, *after so long a time*, has by many been supposed to refer to the period between Israel's entry into the possession of Canaan and the time when the writer of the Psalm lived. I confess that, viewing the 95th, as well as the 96th, and 97th, and 98th Psalms, as a direct prediction of the Messiah,[1] I am disposed to consider the *long time* as descriptive of the period elapsing between the conquest of Canaan and the commencement of the Christian dispensation; as if the Apostle had said, 'We find the Holy Spirit in the Psalms fixing on a period which was not to commence for a very long time, which He terms To-day; and during which He plainly supposes that men may enter into the rest of God, when He says, "To-day, if ye will hear His voice, harden not your hearts."'

Now, this prophetic Psalm makes it quite plain that there is a divine rest into which men are invited to enter different from, and long subsequent to, the rest of Canaan. Ver. 8. "For if Jesus had given them rest, then would He not afterwards have spoken of another day." *Jesus* here, as in Acts vii. 45, is the Greek form of the name of Joshua, the conqueror of Canaan; and in both cases the Hebrew word should have been retained.[2] If there had been no other rest of God but the rest of Canaan into which Joshua conducted the Israelites, then there would not have been any mention made of a period called a day, long posterior to the era of entering Canaan, during which men are invited to enter into the rest of God. But since mention is made of such a period, and as nothing that can be called *a divine rest* has been entered into by men since Israel entered into Canaan, it is plain that we must come to the Apostle's conclusion, ver. 9. "There remaineth therefore a rest for the people of God."

These words, interpreted, as so many other passages of Scripture are, without reference to their connection, are usually explained of the celestial blessedness, and considered as intimating, that whatever may be the afflictions, and troubles, and labours of the saint here below, there remains for him rest above. This is truth, but it is not the truth here taught. The rest here is that state of holy happiness which Christians enjoy on earth as well as in heaven, and into which they enter by the "belief of the truth." There is a rest far better than the rest of Israel in

---

[1] Kimchi, who speaks the belief of the ancient Jews, says, that "all the Psalms from the 93d to the 101st relate to the Messiah."

[2] Indeed, wherever Old Testament characters are introduced in the New Testament they should have their Hebrew, not their Grecised names: Elijah, not Elias; Elisha, not Eliseus, etc. Joshua did give them rest—or rather, God gave them rest by Joshua,—as it is said, Josh. xxi. 44, καὶ κατέπαυσεν αὐτοῖς (vel αὐτοὺς) Κύριος κυκλόθεν.

Canaan, which remains—after the rest of Canaan has passed away—for the peculiar people of God, the spiritual Israel under the New Economy;[1] and into this we are invited in the Gospel to enter by believing.

The word *rest*[2] in this passage is not the same as that employed in the preceding context: it is a word equivalent to the *rest of God*, a *sabbatism*—a sacred rest; and the Apostle states the reason why he gives it this appellation in the 10th verse. "For he that is entered into his rest, he also hath ceased from his own works, as God did from His." These words have by some interpreters of great name (Dr Owen and Dr Wardlaw) been referred to Christ. But, though it is true that Christ has entered into rest, and has ceased from the work of expiation as God has ceased from the work of creation, yet, as Christ is not mentioned in the immediate context, as He is never anywhere by way of eminence called, 'He who hath entered into rest,' and as this statement, however important in itself, has no bearing on the Apostle's object, this mode of interpretation cannot be acquiesced in.[3] "He that is entered into his rest" is a description of the same persons as "*the people of God*." Those who consider the rest of God as exclusively descriptive of heaven, consider the words as expressing this idea: 'They who have entered on the enjoyment of the celestial inheritance are completely at rest, as God was after the creation; they rest from their labours; and their rest resembles God's.' The words, viewed in this light, no doubt express a truth; but it is difficult to see how that truth is connected with the Apostle's design, which seems to be, to show how the rest which, as appears from the 95th Psalm, yet "remains for the people of God," and into which they enter by believing, deserves to be called a sacred rest—a sabbatism—the rest of God. By "him that is entered into rest," I understand the man who by believing is introduced into that state of holy happiness which is begun on earth and perfected in heaven.

[1] Ὁ οἶκος τοῦ Θεοῦ, ch. iii. 6, over which Christ ὡς ὁ Υἱὸς presides.

[2] σαββατισμός.

[3] Michaelis considers the words as a general proposition forming part of an argument: No man can be said to have entered into God's rest who is not completely delivered from toil and sorrow; the people of God are not in this condition; therefore there is yet a rest remaining, into which they are to enter. This is more ingenious than satisfactory, like many of the interpretations of this very learned and very acute critic.

This state of rest is called a sabbatism,[1] or sacred rest—the rest of God; and it deserves the name, for he who has entered into it has fellowship with God—rests along with God.

Some have supposed that in the words, "*hath ceased*," or rested, "*from his works, even as God did from His*," there is a reference to the believer ceasing for ever from the vain attempts in which he previously engaged to make himself happy, and resting in the enjoyment of that happiness which through believing he possesses as the gift of God through Jesus Christ his Lord. He does not go about to establish his own method of justification, but he submits to God's method of justification. He does not say, "Who will show me any good?" but, "This is the rest, and this is the refreshing."

We are disposed to think the primary idea is that already hinted at: 'He who has entered into his rest has fellowship with God—rests along with God; and therefore the rest well deserves to be called a sabbatism—a sacred rest. He who believes the truth enters on the enjoyment of a happiness which is of the same nature, and springs from the same sources, as the happiness of God. Jehovah rests and rejoices in the manifestation made of His all-perfect character in the person and work of Jesus Christ; and he who believes enters into this rest, and participates of this joy.'[2] Such, we apprehend, is the Apostle's illustration of the principle—a promise of entering into God's rest has been left us, or a divine rest remains for us.

We are now prepared for attending to the exhortation founded on this principle, and on the fact, so frequently stated, as to those who had been invited formerly to enter into a divine rest coming short of it through unbelief. That exhortation is

---

[1] Eusebius, in his Commentary on Ps. xci. according to the LXX.—Ps. xcii. in our Bibles—gives the following beautiful description of σαββατισμός: Τὸ τέλειον σάββατον καὶ τὴν τελείαν καὶ τρισμακαρίαν κατάπαυσιν ἐν τῇ τοῦ Θεοῦ βασιλείᾳ—ἔνθα ἀπέδρα ὀδύνη, καὶ λύπη, καὶ στεναγμός· ἔνθα τῆς θνητῆς καὶ φθαρτῆς ζωῆς ἀπαλλαγέντες, καὶ ἀργίαν ἀργήσαντες τὴν θεοφιλῆ καὶ μακαρίαν, τῶν τε σωματικῶν πράξεων καὶ τῆς δουλείας τῆς σαρκὸς ἐλευθερωθέντες, σὺν αὐτῷ τῷ Θεῷ, καὶ παρ' αὐτῷ γενόμενοι, σαββατίσομεν καὶ ἀναπαυσόμεθα.

[2] Dr Owen's theory of interpretation—of the three rests: the paradisiacal Sabbath-rest, the Jewish rest in Canaan, and the Christian Sabbath-rest—is ingenious, but unsatisfactory. It is wonderful to see so *sound-minded* a theologian and interpreter as Dr Wardlaw adopting it in his useful, but unequal, and in some points unsatisfactory, work on the Sabbath.

contained in the 6th and 11th verses : " Seeing therefore it remaineth that some must enter therein, and they to whom it was first preached entered not in because of unbelief—Let us therefore labour to enter into that rest, lest any man fall after the same example of unbelief."

The Apostle's exhortation rests on two principles—the first expressed in these words : " It remaineth that some must enter into the rest of God ;" the second in these words: " They to whom it was first preached did not enter in because of unbelief." To an English reader the first of these phrases seems equivalent to, ' It is evident that some must enter into the rest of God—there is a necessity that some should enter into it.' I do not apprehend that the original words express this idea.[1] There is nothing certainly in the Apostle's reasoning that brings out this conclusion, and it is not at all necessary to the object he has in view. The principle the Apostle is illustrating in the whole of the parenthetical passage is this—*a divine rest remains for us;* and this is the principle on which he builds his exhortation. The verb "remaineth" is not used impersonally, as our translators seem to have supposed—the nominative to it is " a rest"—a divine rest; and the word *must* ought to have been marked as a supplement.[2] The Apostle's statement is—' Since, then, a divine rest remains, that some may enter into it—since we have a rest of God set before us to enter into.' This is the first principle on which the exhortation proceeds.

The second principle is—"*Seeing they to whom it was first preached entered not in because of unbelief.*" More literally, ' They to whom on a former occasion a joyful annunciation was made, entered not in because of unbelief ;' *i.e.,* ' Seeing your ancestors, who on a former occasion were invited to enter into a divine rest in Canaan, failed of attaining it through unbelief.' The exhortation consists of two parts—an injunction and a caution, corresponding to the two principles on which it is founded. ' Seeing a divine rest remains, to be entered into, let us labour to enter into it;' and, ' Seeing the great body of those who on a former

---

[1] Carpzov endeavours to show that ἀπολείπεται is used to mark the progress of an argument—as *sequitur, efficitur,* ' *it follows,*'—but he fails.

[2] Abresch supposes ἐπαγγελία to be the word that should be supplied, from verse 1. It does not matter : only the whole phrase must be supplied —ἐπαγ. εἰσελθεῖν εἰς τὴν κατάπαυσιν Θεοῦ.

occasion were invited to enter into a divine rest, did not enter because of unbelief, let us therefore labour lest we *fall*[1] after the same example of unbelief—lest we, through unbelief like theirs, should, like them, come short of the promised rest.' The word "labour" is equivalent to 'eagerly and perseveringly seek.' The manner in which the Hebrew Christians were to "labour to enter into rest," was by believing the truth, and continuing "stedfast and unmoveable" in the faith of the truth, and in the natural results of the faith of the truth.

A better illustration of this labouring cannot be given than in the Apostle's account of his own experience: "But what things were gain to me, those I counted loss for Christ. Yea doubtless, and I count all things but loss for the excellency of the knowledge of Christ Jesus my Lord: for whom I have suffered the loss of all things, and do count them but dung, that I may win Christ, and be found in Him, not having mine own righteousness, which is of the law, but that which is through the faith of Christ, the righteousness which is of God by faith: that I may know Him, and the power of His resurrection, and the fellowship of His sufferings, being made conformable unto His death; if by any means I might attain unto the resurrection of the dead. Not as though I had already attained, either were already perfect; but I follow after, if that I may apprehend that for which also I am apprehended of Christ Jesus. Brethren, I count not myself to have apprehended: but this one thing I do, forgetting those things which are behind, and reaching forth unto those things which are before, I press toward the mark, for the prize of the high calling of God in Christ Jesus."[2] And the Apostle Peter's exhortation: "And besides this, giving all diligence, add to your

---

[1] πέση—often used, like the Heb. נָפַל, to signify 'to become miserable, to perish;' Prov. xi. 28, xxiv. 16; Rom. xi. 11; Ecclus. ii. 8. The word is probably used in preference to any other, because the doom of the Israelitish unbelievers was *falling* in the wilderness, and so coming short of Canaan. Πέση, as Calvin well remarks, "is taken for 'perish', or, to speak more clearly, not for the sin, but for the punishment."

"'Απειθείας is dependent on ὑποδείγματι. The separation of the Genitive from its governing word by an interposing word or phrase, is by no means unusual in the New Testament: Phil. ii. 10; 1 Tim. iii. 6; Heb. viii. 5."—SAMPSON.

[2] Phil. iii. 7-14.

faith, virtue; and to virtue, knowledge; and to knowledge, temperance; and to temperance, patience; and to patience, godliness; and to godliness, brotherly-kindness; and to brotherly-kindness, charity. For if these things be in you, and abound, they make you that ye shall neither be barren nor unfruitful in the knowledge of our Lord Jesus Christ. But he that lacketh these things is blind, and cannot see afar off, and hath forgotten that he was purged from his old sins. Wherefore the rather, brethren, give diligence to make your calling and election sure; for if ye do these things, ye shall never fall: for so an entrance shall be ministered unto you abundantly into the everlasting kingdom of our Lord and Saviour Jesus Christ. Wherefore I will not be negligent to put you always in remembrance of these things, though ye know them, and be established in the present truth."[1] The fearful consequence of unbelief in the case of the Israelites ought to be felt as a motive to stedfastness in the faith, and to a diligent use of the means for obtaining stedfastness in the faith. They through unbelief came short of Canaan; and all unbelievers, whatever privileges they may enjoy, whatever professions they may make, must come short of *the rest of God*, into which men can only enter by believing.

The words which follow are a further enforcement of the exhortation contained in the 6th and 11th verses. 'Seeing a rest remaineth that some may enter into it, and seeing they who were formerly invited to enter into God's rest did not enter because of unbelief; let us labour to enter into that rest, lest any man fall after the same example of unbelief.' Ver. 12. "*For the word of God is quick, and powerful, and sharper than any two-edged sword, piercing even to the dividing asunder of soul and spirit, and of the joints and marrow, and is a discerner of the thoughts and intents of the heart. Neither is there any creature that is not manifest in His sight: but all things are naked and opened unto the eyes of Him with whom we have to do.*" The appropriateness and force of the motives presented in these words will become distinctly apparent when their meaning is clearly apprehended.

*The word of God* has, by many of the ancient, and some of the modern interpreters, been explained here as a title of Jesus Christ, the Messiah, in His pre-existent state;[2] as it is without doubt employed by the Apostle John, in his Gospel, in his

---

[1] 2 Pet. i. 5–12.     [2] Ὁ λόγος Θεοῦ ὑποστατικός.

First Epistle, and in the Book of Revelation. The use of the expression, "Word of God," as an appellation of Jesus Christ, seems, however, peculiar to that inspired writer; and though much of what is here said of the word of God might with truth be said of Jesus Christ, other expressions cannot without extreme violence be applied to Him, and neither the words themselves nor the context require us to give so uncommon a meaning to the expression; on the contrary, both seem naturally to lead us to understand the phrase in its ordinary signification, of the revelation of the divine will.[1] At the same time, it seems plain that it is not to the Scriptures generally that the inspired writer refers, but to that "word of God" of which he has been speaking, which excludes the unbeliever from the divine rest, and denounces on him the divine vengeance. In the inspired oracle on which he grounds his exhortation—"To-day, if ye will hear My voice, harden not your hearts"—there is implied not only a promise, that if they hear God's voice they shall enter into His rest, but also a *threatening*, that if they do not hear His voice, but harden their hearts, they shall not enter into His rest.

Now, *this* "word of God is quick and powerful." It is scarcely necessary to remark that the word *quick* is not here used in the sense in which it is almost exclusively now employed—of 'rapid, or speedy,'—but in the way in which it is used in the phrase, "the *quick* and the dead." It is equivalent to *living*. "The word of God is living." The general proposition, "the word of God is living," taken by itself, might, in consistency with the analogy of Scripture language, mean—'The word of God is as it were instinct with a living spirit, which it communicates to men.' "My words, they are spirit, and they are life."[2] It is a quickening word; but from the connection here it is plain that the meaning is—'The word of God in reference to the punishment of unbelievers is not dead but living.' It is not a meteor flash, but the real thunderbolt of heaven; no pointless dart, but "a sharp two-edged sword;" it is not inoperative, but powerfully efficient. We say of a law that is never executed, that it is "a dead letter." The phrase "word," as referring to a threatening, occurs Isa. ix. 8 : "The Lord sent a word to Jacob, and it hath lighted on Israel." "The word of God" is just God Himself declaring His will and purpose. A

---

[1] Ὁ λόγος Θεοῦ προφορικός.   [2] John vi. 63.

threatening may be a dead, inefficient word, either because he who uttered it never meant to execute it, or because he has changed his mind, or because he has not the means of carrying it into execution. The declaration, that the unbeliever shall not enter into the rest of God, is the annunciation of the unalterable determination of Him who is infinitely powerful and infinitely faithful. The vital energy of the divine denunciation is strikingly illustrated by its being compared to one of the most destructive of weapons. It "is sharper than a two-edged sword." We have the same image—a sword which has two mouths, two foresides and no back, cutting both ways, peculiarly trenchant—Isa. xlix. 2; Rev. i. 16, ii. 12, 16, xix. 15, 21.[1] He who is exposed to it is in a situation far more hazardous than he into whose vitals a sharp two-edged sword seems just about to be plunged.

This figurative description is amplified in the words which follow:—"It pierces to the dividing asunder of the soul and spirit, and of the joints and marrow." The meaning of these words is not, 'piercing not only the skin and flesh, but penetrating to the very inmost core of the individual—to that point where there is a division of the soul and spirit, and of the joints and marrow;' for there is no such point. The meaning is, 'piercing so as to divide the soul from the spirit, and the joints from the marrow.'[2]

These words, "the word of God pierces even to the dividing asunder of soul and spirit," have often been used as descriptive of the power of the word of God, when accompanied by divine influence, to produce conviction; to unfold to the sinner in the light of truth the falsehood and wickedness of his inmost thoughts and desires; and to lodge in his mind a conviction that these are the objects of the divine knowledge and disapprobation, and that therefore "for all these things he must be brought into judgment." This is truth, and important truth; it is truth, too, which the words, taken by themselves, are not ill fitted to convey; but, viewed in their connection, I think there can be no

---

[1] ὑπέρ is often by Greek writers used in comparison as = πλεῖον or μᾶλλον. In the New Testament it occurs only here and Luke xvi. 8.

[2] Some have explained ψυχή of corrupt, and πνεῦμα of regenerated, human nature. Others, certainly with greater probability, understand ψυχή of the principle of animal life and action, and πνεῦμα of the principle of rational life and action—a distinction which undoubtedly was made by the ancients.

doubt that it is not the truth taught in this clause. The phrase is expressive of the *destructive* energy of the divine threatening. The *soul*, as distinguished from the *spirit*, was among the ancients the denomination of the principle of animal life; and the *spirit*, as distinguished from the *soul*, was the principle of rational life. These in the living man are closely connected, and death is the necessary consequence of their being divided. To "divide the soul from the spirit" is just another expression for, 'to produce death.'

That this is its meaning seems plain not only from the general scope of the passage, but from the expression that immediately follows, and which appears intended to be a further description of the destructive energy of "the word of God." It pierces so as to " divide asunder the joints and marrow." "The joints," or limbs of which the bones are the frame and support, " and marrow," are most intimately connected. They cannot be divided without the exertion of great force, without occasioning intense pain to the individual, and without indeed producing death.[1]

When, then, " the word of God" is represented as " sharper than a two-edged sword, piercing so as to divide the soul from the spirit, and the joints from the marrow," the idea intended to be conveyed is—'The threatening of God against unbelievers is a threatening which will assuredly be executed; and when executed, an intensity of suffering, a completeness and extent of destruction and misery, will be the result; of which the torturing and deathful energy of a two-edged sword, wielded by the most powerful arm, affords only a very distant and imperfect figurative representation.'

It can scarcely be doubted that the fearful consequences of the divine threatening against the unbelieving Israelites were present to the Apostle's mind. That " word of God"[2] was not dead and inefficient, but "quick and powerful." The whole of that generation, under the influence of that denunciation, died in the wilderness. In consequence of it the carcases of some hundreds of thousands of Israelites strewed the desert;—most of them dying a natural death, though that was probably hastened by the hardships to which they were exposed, but not a few of

---

[1] We have similar phrases in Jer. iv. 10, LXX., "Ἥψατο ἡ μάχαιρα ἕως τῆς ψυχῆς; and in Luke ii. 35, καὶ σοῦ δὲ αὐτῆς τὴν ψυχὴν διελεύσεται ῥομφαία.
[2] Num. xiv. 28.

them perishing under the immediate stroke of divine vengeance, by miraculous inflictions.[1]

The threatening denounced against unbelievers under the New Testament Economy will certainly not be less "living and powerful." The evils it subjects to are far more dreadful. It excludes not from Canaan, but from heaven; it dooms not only to the grave, but to hell. And its execution will not be less certain. The curse is not causeless, and it must come. Its execution is secured by the word and oath of Jehovah. "He has lifted up His hand to heaven, and sworn by Himself, who lives for ever and ever," that He will "whet His glittering sword," that "His hand will lay hold on judgment," that He "will render vengeance to His enemies, and recompense them that hate Him."

We should consider him as a madman who, in the expectation that that "word of God" which gives to fire its consuming quality, was to lose its power in his case, should leap into a burning fiery furnace; and certainly he who, though he may be counted wise in his generation, continues in unbelief, and yet hopes to escape the punishment denounced against the unbeliever, is labouring under a still more deplorable species of insanity. The first appointment rises entirely out of the will of God. He who gave fire its consuming energy can deprive it of that energy if He pleases. But the second rises out of the nature of God; and unless God cease to be God, the obstinate unbeliever must perish. No length of time can deprive this word of denunciation of its destructive energy. Some of the Israelites who incurred the curse in the wilderness, and who were allowed to live almost forty years afterwards, might be beginning to think it had lost its force, and would not be executed in reference to them. But they were disappointed. Every one of that generation died in the wilderness. No intermediate season of impunity, however protracted, secures the unbeliever from the execution of the curse. It is still living; and by and by, if he

[1] What a picture do the words of Michaelis, who had a good deal of the poet in his composition, bring before the mind! "Siste tibi imaginem illam veterum Israelitarum, quorum cum sexcenta essent millia, post quadraginta annos non nisi bini minax Dei verbum fugerunt. Fac observentur animo tuo illæ in deserto factæ strages, quæ sæpe unico die xx millia absumpserunt: acutius omni gladio ancipiti fateberis divinum verbum."

flee not for "refuge to the hope set before us in the Gospel," it will prove itself powerful, and he will find that it is indeed "a fearful thing to fall into the hand of the *living* God." This consideration of the awful nature and certain execution of the denunciation against unbelievers was admirably fitted to serve the purpose for which the Apostle here employs it, as a motive to the Hebrew professors of Christianity to "labour" to enter into the rest of God, lest any should fall after the example of their unbelieving and disobedient forefathers.

But besides the awful energy of the threatening, there is another of its distinguishing characters which was well fitted to make a salutary impression on the minds of the Hebrew Christians in their present circumstances; and that is the spiritual reference of the divine command and threatening. This threatening refers not only to external acts of apostasy, but to movements of the mind and heart tending to them. This word is a "*discerner* of the thoughts and intents of the heart." The word translated *discerner* has been interpreted as equivalent to 'a judge, a condemner, a punisher.' The meaning plainly is—'This word of threatening takes cognizance of, refers, not only to external actions, but to thoughts and feelings, to opinions and desires. Its destructive energy will be exerted not only against the open apostate, but against the secret unbeliever—the backslider in heart from the faith and love of the truth as it is in Jesus.' It is the unbeliever who is excluded from the rest of God, and it is the evil heart of unbelief against which especially the Apostle guards the Hebrew Christians. The passage on which he grounds the whole of his exhortation has an express reference to the state of the mind and heart. Both the promise and the threatening which it implies—and, as we have seen, it implies both—have a reference to the thoughts and feelings. "To-day, if ye will hear His voice, harden not your hearts."

It can never be too strongly stated—it can scarcely be too frequently repeated—that the religion of Christ is pre-eminently a spiritual religion; that to have the mind and heart, the thoughts and the affections, subjected to the divine authority, conformed to the divine will, forms its essence; and when these are wanting, it does not exist, however ingeniously the man may speculate, however fluently he may talk, however plausible may be his profession, and however regular his performance of the external offices of Christian devotion. "Keep thy heart with all diligence," is an injunction which ought to be constantly before the mind of all who are called by the name of Christ. "As a man thinketh in his heart, so is he." The word of God, whether of promise or of threatening, refers to principles as well as to actions, and to actions only so far as they are the result and expression of principles. If our minds and hearts are not in accordance with God's word, we sin; and we may rest assured that "our sin," though not manifesting itself strongly in outward acts, "will," as Moses says, "find us out."[1] However orthodox, then, may be our professed creed, however regular our external conduct, if our views of truth are not conformed to the mind of Christ, if our tempers and dispositions are not regulated by the statements of His word and subjected to the influence of His Spirit, though we may be called by His name, though we may be students and preachers of His word, we "are none of His." We are in reality unbelievers; and the threatening of God, that the unbeliever shall not enter into His rest, is as really pointed against us as against the professed infidel or the open apostate, and will as certainly be executed in reference to us as in reference to them.

This truth is always seasonable, but it is peculiarly so at present, in our country, where a profession of a pure Christianity is all but universal, and where, under the influence of early education and general example, multitudes assume the garb of discipleship, and attend to the external ordinances of the Gospel, who in "the thoughts and intents of the heart" are utter strangers to the influence of an enlightened faith of "the truth as it is in Jesus."

A human threatening directed against a peculiar state of mind and heart, except so far as these are manifested in conduct, would be nugatory. Man has not the means of directly discovering the state of the thoughts and feelings, the sentiments and desires; but it is otherwise with Him of whose threatening the Apostle is speaking, for—"Neither is there any creature which is not manifest in His sight."[2]

---

[1] Num. xxxii. 23.

[2] Michaelis's note is very ingenious. He considers it as likely that κτίσις is here used in the way in which the Heb. יֵצֶר is: יֵצֶר לֵב with Moses is the thought of the heart. No thought is invisible to Him.

The word "creature" here is plainly used as in Rom. viii. 39,—not as restricted to 'created things' strictly speaking, but as equivalent to 'thing,' including thoughts, feelings, actions, as well as the beings who think, feel, and act. "There is nothing that is not manifest in *His* sight." The word *His* either refers to God, mentioned in the preceding verse, or to "Him with whom we have to do," mentioned in the close of this verse. I think it most probable that the last is its true reference; and that by "Him with whom we have to do"—with whom our business is,[1] or "Him of whom we are discoursing,"[2] or "Him to whom we must give an account,"[3]—for the expression will admit of all these renderings,—we are to understand Jesus Christ, of whom the Apostle is discoursing—" with whom," as the family of God, "we have to do," and "to whom we must all give an account."[4]

It does not matter much in which of these three ways we interpret the phrase—in all of them it is strikingly applicable to our Lord; but we apprehend our translators have been very happy in the selection they have made. It is with Christ that "we have to do." It is not with Moses "we have to do," or with the angels, or with the Aaronical high priests: it is with Christ "we have to do." He is the "*one* Mediator between God and man;" for it is not directly with God as essential Divinity "we have to do." All our religious business, if I may use the expression, must be transacted immediately with Christ.

If this is the truth, what are we to say of the religion of many who call themselves Christians, but in whose religion there is little or no reference to Christ—who think, and feel, and act in religion, as if it were not with Christ that they "had to do?" They have no habitual sense of the necessity of *His* mediation— no habitual trust in *His* atonement—no habitual reliance on *His* Spirit—no habitual submission of mind and heart to *His* authority. In the New Economy Christ is "all in all;" and he does not act like one who is under that economy, who does not habitually treat Christ as "Him with whom we have to do,"—on whose sacrifice we must depend, to whose laws we are subject,

---

[1] Judg. xviii. 7, 28.      [2] = περὶ οὗ λαλοῦμεν, ch. ii. 5.
[3] Luke xvi. 2; Rom. xiv. 12; 1 Pet. iv. 5; Heb. xiii. 17.
[4] Theophylact expounds it thus:—ᾧ μέλλομεν δοῦναι τοὺς λόγους καὶ τὰς εὐθύνας τῶν πεπραγμένων.

by whose Spirit we must be guided, before whose judgment-seat we must stand.

Now all things are "manifest in *His* sight." Omniscience, —in particular, the knowledge of "the thoughts and intents of the heart,"—is repeatedly in Scripture ascribed to our Lord. " He needs not that any should testify of man, for He knows what is in man." " He searches the reins and the hearts."[1] It is utterly impossible to impose on Him. He knows " the thoughts and intents of the heart ;" and therefore He is furnished with the means of executing His threatenings against those who, in " the thoughts and intents of the heart," are unbelievers or apostates.

The intimate knowledge of our Lord is strikingly described in the second clause of the verse : " All things are naked and opened unto the eyes of Him." Many learned interpreters suppose that there is here a reference to the manner in which the priests inspected the victims intended for sacrifice. After being killed, they were hung up by the neck, the skin was stripped off them, the bowels taken out, and the back-bone cleft; so that the internal part of the animal was completely laid open, and the priest had an opportunity of seeing any blemish which might unfit it for being offered as a sacrifice. Others suppose the reference to be to a person's head drawn back, so as completely to expose the countenance. Chrysostom supposes the reference to be to sacrificial victims lying on their backs, that the haruspex might have an opportunity of contemplating the entrails.[2]

Whatever be the reference, the meaning of the passage is plain : ' He is acquainted with the inmost thoughts and feelings—He knows the forming design, and the rising desire.' There is no possibility of imposing on Him by false professions or plausible appearances. He requires of us conformity of mind and heart to Him ; and if we do not yield it, He is perfectly aware of this, and can and will deal with us, not according to what we appear to be, but according to what we really are, and what He knows us to be. It is not only a truth that " we all must appear," or rather be made manifest, " before the judg-

---

[1] Rev. ii. 23.
[2] ——————— pecudumque reclusis
Pectoribus inhians spirantia consulit exta.
—VIRG. *Æn.* iv. 63, 64.

ment-seat of Christ,"[1] but already all our thoughts are manifest before Him, and He knows us much more intimately than we do ourselves.

## CHAPTER III.

### THE SUPERIORITY OF JESUS CHRIST TO THE AARONICAL PRIESTHOOD.

No part of the Mosaic economy had taken a stronger hold of the imaginations and affections of the Jews than the *Aaronical High-priesthood*, and that system of ritual worship over which its occupants presided. The gorgeous apparel, the solemn investiture, the mysterious sacredness of the high priest —the grandeur of the temple in which he ministered—and the imposing splendour of the religious rites which he performed— all these operated like a charm in riveting the attachment of the Jews to the now over-dated economy, and in exciting powerful prejudices against that simple, spiritual, unostentatious system by which it had been superseded. In opposition to these prejudices, the Apostle shows that the Christian economy is deficient in nothing excellent to be found in the Mosaic; on the contrary, that it has a more dignified High Priest, a more magnificent temple, a more sacred altar, a more efficacious sacrifice; and that, to the spiritually enlightened mind, all the temporary splendours of the Mosaic typical ceremonial wax dim and disappear, amid the overwhelming glories of the permanent realities of the Christian institution.[2]

This most interesting topic forms the subject of the third great section of the Epistle to the Hebrews. The great object of this Epistle is to establish the Hebrew Christians in the faith

---

[1] 2 Cor. v. 10.

[2] Some have strangely supposed that such discussions were only of a topical and temporary interest, suited to the Jewish Christians in the primitive times, but of little use to us. This is a very mistaken view of the subject. "The Christian religion," to use the language of Abresch, "rests on the Jewish. It is unquestionably of the highest importance for us to hold fast, as we should, what long ago was symbolically expressed

and profession of their new religion, in opposition to the strong temptations to which they were exposed to relapse into Judaism. The most appropriate means of gaining this end, was the demonstration of the superiority of Christianity to Judaism. Such a demonstration, therefore, forms the great subject of the doctrinal part of the Epistle; and it is conducted in a way peculiarly fitted to gain its object. It takes the form of an illustration and proof of the superiority of Jesus Christ—the Author and subject, the sum and substance, of Christianity—to the three great objects of Jewish veneration: the angels, by whose ministry the law was given; Moses, their great legislator; and the Aaronical priesthood, by whom the most sacred functions under that economy were performed. We have already considered the Apostle's illustration and proof of the superiority of Jesus Christ to the angels and to Moses: we are now about to enter on the illustration and proof of His superiority to the Aaronical high-priesthood.

We have here a very striking instance of the want of judgment often manifested in the division of the New Testament into chapters. No division takes place at the 14th verse of the 4th chapter, where the Apostle obviously enters on a new topic, and a division is made after the 16th verse; while it is plain that there is a continued description of the subject introduced at the 14th. This third section is by much the longest of the three into which the doctrinal part of the Epistle is divided. It reaches from the 14th verse of the 4th chapter down to the 18th verse of the 10th chapter. And as it is the longest, so is it the most important section.

The two former sections are occupied with what, though intimately connected with, is yet to a certain extent extrinsic to, the merits of the two systems—the comparative dignity and excellence of the agents employed in their revelation and establishment. In this section the comparative value of the two

and prefigured concerning the Messiah and his saving work. For by it the certainty, and importance, and indeed the nature and character, of saving doctrine is made the more plain—yes, and is actually confirmed and established. For is there not in the typical sacrificial system a most powerful argument for the vicarious death of Jesus? And, without doubt, the propitiation of Christ is one of those things which are certain, true, and unchangeable throughout eternal ages, for it determines the pattern of saving faith."

systems, viewed in reference to the attainment of the great objects of a religion—the expiation of guilt, the transformation of character, the attainment of the divine favour and eternal happiness—comes to be considered, and the infinite superiority of Christianity is most triumphantly established.

Nothing is of greater importance to the right understanding of an author's particular statements, illustrations, and arguments, than a clear apprehension of the general object he has in view. Without this, the most accurate statements may seem incorrect, the most apposite illustrations irrelevant, and the most cogent arguments inconclusive. The design of the whole section, on the illustration of which we are entering, is plainly to establish the superiority of Jesus Christ, the High Priest whom Christians acknowledge, to the Aaronical high priests, whom the Jews acknowledged. The Apostle begins with asserting the facts, which he afterwards at length proves and illustrates, that in Christ Jesus, the Son of God, we have a High Priest—a great High Priest—a High Priest who has "passed into the heavens" —a High Priest who can be "touched with the feeling of our infirmities." He then gives a short description of the Levitical priesthood, with whom it is his design to compare and contrast Christ Jesus. He describes a Levitical high priest as a man divinely selected and ordained to manage the religious interests of his fellow-men, by offering in their stead, and for their benefit, "gifts and sacrifices for sin;" and qualified to sympathize with those in whose place he stood, and for whose behalf he acted, from the circumstance of his being himself, like them, a man surrounded with infirmity. The inspired writer then applies this description to the purpose he had in view, the establishment of the reality and excellence of the high-priesthood of our Lord Jesus. He shows (1.) that Jesus Christ has been legitimately invested with the office of a High Priest; and (2.) that He has proved Himself a qualified High Priest, by actually performing with success the functions of that office; and in doing this, he not only directly proves that Jesus Christ is really a High Priest, but he indirectly brings forward much evidence, of which he avails himself in his subsequent discussions, of the superiority of His priesthood to that of Aaron and his sons.

## § 1. *General Introductory Statement and Exhortation.*

CHAP. iv. 14-16. Seeing then that we have a great High Priest, that is passed into the heavens, Jesus the Son of God, let us hold fast our profession. For we have not an high priest which cannot be touched with the feeling of our infirmities; but was in all points tempted like as we are, yet without sin. Let us therefore come boldly unto the throne of grace, that we may obtain mercy, and find grace to help in time of need.

These verses may be considered as containing a brief announcement of the subject, to the illustration of which the whole of the third section of the Epistle is devoted. Ver. 14. " Seeing then that we have a great High Priest that is passed into the heavens, Jesus the Son of God, let us hold fast our profession."

These words are not a deduction from what goes before, as may appear from the particle *then;* for what immediately precedes is an illustration of the superiority of Jesus to Moses as the Superintendent of the family of God under the New Economy, and in no previous part of the Epistle is there any extended illustration of the priesthood of Christ. This subject has merely been cursorily adverted to in three passages: in chap. i. 3, where He is said to have " purged," or expiated, " our sins by Himself;" in chap. ii. 17, where His incarnation is said to be necessary in order to His being " a merciful and faithful High Priest;" and in chap. iii. 1, where He is termed " the High Priest of our profession," or the High Priest whom we acknowledge. The particle *then* is merely connective, denoting transition to another, but connected subject. It probably does look back to the 1st verse of the 3d chapter, where the Apostle calls on his readers to contemplate Jesus Christ as " the Apostle and High Priest of their profession," *i.e.*, the Apostle and High Priest whom they acknowledged. He had already exhibited Him to them as the Apostle whom they acknowledged, and shown how the truth about Him in this character was calculated to operate as a motive to perseverance; and he now proceeds to exhibit Him to them as the High Priest whom they acknowledged, and to show that the truth about Him in this character suggested not less powerful inducements to continue rooted and built up in Him, and stablished in the faith they had been taught.

" We have a High Priest;" *i.e.*, ' We Christians have a High

Priest.' The unbelieving Jews would be apt to say to their Christian brethren, 'Your new religion is deficient in the very first requisite of a religion—you have no high priest. How are your sins to be pardoned, when you have none to offer expiatory oblations for you? How are your wants to be supplied, when you have none to make intercession for you to God?' The answer to this cavil is to be found in the Apostle's words, "We have a High Priest."

The high priest among the Jews was the principal religious minister of their economy, the inferior priests being merely his deputies, as it were, and executing such parts of his office as personally it was impossible for him to overtake. The high-priesthood intimated that God was offended with men, and would not have direct favourable intercourse with them; that He was disposed to be reconciled to them; and that the medium through which He was disposed to confer saving blessings on them, was that of vicarious sacrifice and intercession.

When the Apostle says that "we have a High Priest," he means, 'We Christians have One to interpose with God in our behalf; we have One who has offered up an availing expiatory sacrifice in our room—who has done what renders it consistent with, and illustrative of, the divine moral character to pardon and save us; and One too who makes intercession for us, securing us in the enjoyment of everything that is necessary to our final and complete salvation.'

But the Apostle affirms not merely that we have a High Priest, but that "we have a *great* High Priest." By some interpreters the whole phrase, rendered by our translators "*great* High Priest," has been considered as just equivalent to High Priest,—the word they thus translate[1] being sometimes applied to the heads of the twenty-four orders of priests. These are the "chief priests" so often spoken of in the New Testament. "We have a great Chief Priest," *i.e.*, a High Priest who was the first of the chief priests. We apprehend, however, as the word in the singular is never in the New Testament applied to any one but the high priest, that the epithet *great* here is meant to convey a superadded idea, and is equivalent to *distinguished* or *illustrious*. 'We have not only a High Priest; but our High Priest infinitely transcends, both as to personal and official dig-

---

[1] ἀρχιερεύς.

nity, all who ever bore that name. He Himself belongs to a higher order of being than the Aaronical high priests; and His priesthood is of a far more dignified character than theirs.'

The words used in reference to His superiority to the angels may be justly applied to His superiority to the Jewish priests. 'He has, as a Priest, been made so much better than Aaron and his sons, as He has received by inheritance a more excellent name than they. He has been made better than Aaron and his sons, for He is entered into the heavens; and He has received by inheritance a more excellent name than they, for He is Jesus the Son of God.'

He is "passed into the heavens." These words literally rendered are, "He has passed through the heavens." This seems a plain reference to the Jewish high priest entering into the Holy of Holies on the great day of atonement. Having offered sacrifices of expiation, he entered first into the holy place, and then through the second vail into the holiest of all, to sprinkle the blood of atonement, and to burn incense before Jehovah, who dwelt between the cherubim.[1] In allusion to this most sacred of all the functions exercised by the Jewish high priest, Jesus, our High Priest, is represented as having "passed through the heavens," *i.e.*, the visible heavens, which as a vail conceal from mortal view the glories of "the heaven of heavens." The meaning plainly is, 'He has passed through the visible heavens into that glorious place where the Divine Being gives the most remarkable displays of His presence and excellences.'[2]

The object of the inspired writer in making the remark seems threefold. First, to account for our having no high priest on earth. It is as if he had said, 'To be sure we have no high priest on earth; but the reason is, having finished His work on earth, He has passed through the heavens into the immediate presence of God.' The second object seems to be, to mark the superiority of Jesus to the Aaronical high priest. The Aaronical high priest having offered sacrifice, entered through the first vail into the sanctuary, and then through the second vail into

---

[1] Lev. xvi.
[2] Ernesti somewhat rashly, not as he is wont, terms this "a stupid comment;" and Abresch says, "An explanation displaying more of ingenuity than of learning and truth." It is the plain meaning of the words, and is supported by Owen, Bengel, Peirce, and Kuinoel.

the most holy place, into the presence of the symbol of Divinity; but our great High Priest has passed through the visible heavens into the heaven of heavens—the place of the real, not the symbolical presence of God; or, as the inspired writer himself expresses it: "For Christ is not entered into the holy places made with hands, which are the figures of the true; but into heaven itself, now to appear in the presence of God for us."[1] The third object seems to be, to suggest the efficacy of His sacrifice, and the prevalence of His intercession. Had not His sacrifice been acceptable to God, He would not have passed through the heavens; and if His sacrifice has been acceptable, and has been proved to be so by His passing through the heavens, then there can be no reason to fear that His continued interference in our behalf shall be unsuccessful.

But not only is our High Priest *great, illustrious,* inasmuch as " He has passed through the heavens," but inasmuch also as He is "*the Son of God.*" We have already had occasion at considerable length to illustrate the import of this appellation, as descriptive of identity of nature and equality of perfection with the Divine Father. We have for our High Priest not a son of Aaron, but "*the* Son of God"—not a mere man, but "God manifest in flesh."

Such, then, is the Apostle's statement. 'We Christians, though we have no such religious minister as the Jewish high priest, are not without a high priest. We have a High Priest— one who, having purged our sins, ever lives to make intercession for us,—an illustrious High Priest, who is not on earth, just because He has finished His work on earth, and ascended through the skies into heaven; whereby He is raised to an infinite superiority above the Jewish high priest, who only passed through the symbolical heavens into the symbolical presence of God, whereas He has passed through the real heavens into the real presence of God—a clear evidence that His sacrifice has been acceptable, and that His intercession will prove effectual.'

The exhortation grounded on this statement is, "Let us hold fast our profession."[2] When illustrating the 1st verse of the 3d

---

[1] Heb. ix. 24.

[2] Κρατῶμεν is = βεβαίως κατάσχωμεν, chap. iii. 6, 14, and κατέχωμεν τὴν ὁμολογίαν ἀκλινῆ, chap. x. 23.

chapter, I had occasion to explain the word translated *profession*. It is equivalent to ' acknowledgment'—that which we have acknowledged. It may either be considered as referring generally to the acknowledgment made by a man when he became a Christian, or particularly to the acknowledgment made in reference to Christ as our High Priest. In the first case it is equivalent to, ' Let us hold fast the whole doctrine of Christ, which we have acknowledged to be true.' In the second case it is equivalent to, ' Let us hold fast the acknowledgment we have made of Jesus Christ as our High Priest.' It does not matter much which of these two views we take of it.

To " hold fast our profession," or acknowledgment, is to abide by it—to persevere in it. In whatever view we understand the word " profession," the statement made by the Apostle contains in it abundant reason why we should hold it fast. It were madness to abandon a religion which so abundantly provides for our eternal interests; and if we give up acknowledging " Jesus the Son of God," who " has passed through the heavens," for our High Priest, where can we find a substitute? Where shall we find one who can expiate our sins? Where shall we find one who in our behalf is either able or willing to appear before the throne of God? Whatever may be the difficulties, or dangers, or sufferings in which stedfastness in the faith of Christ may involve us, it is our duty and our interest to be stedfast and immoveable.

There was much in the peculiar circumstances of the Hebrews to make such an exhortation necessary, and to give it peculiar force. Paul had been in chains in Jerusalem—James slain by the sword—very possibly the Christians debarred from mingling in the sacred assemblies of the Jews. How precious in these circumstances the truths—We have a better temple, a better High Priest, a better sacrifice than these! No, we will not be tempted to purchase the continuance of the latter by the abandonment of the former. We will cleave to our High Priest at all hazards, though we should be obliged to go to Him " without the gate, bearing His reproach." And what a powerful confirmation of their constancy is to be found in the statement which immediately follows!

In the verse following we have a further statement of the excellences of Jesus Christ as a High Priest, and of course an additional reason for our continuing steady in the acknowledgment of Him under that character. Ver. 15. "For we have not an high priest which cannot be touched with the feeling of our infirmities; but was in all points tempted like as we are, yet without sin."

The connection between this verse and that which precedes it has been variously stated. It is the opinion of a very learned and generally judicious expositor,[1] that the whole passage, from the beginning of this verse to the end of the 3d verse of the 6th chapter, is a digression; and that the exhortation, "Let us hold fast our profession," immediately connects with the 4th verse of the 6th chapter. This does not appear to me at all probable.

By some the statement in the 15th verse is considered as intended to obviate an objection likely to rise in the mind from what is stated in the 14th verse: 'But if Jesus Christ be both essentially and officially so inconceivably exalted, He is removed at such a distance from us that He cannot be expected to take any very deep interest in us, or in our concerns.' The Apostle answers: 'Highly exalted as He is above us, He is both capable and disposed to take an interest in us, and in all our concerns; for though a divine person originally, and though now made higher than the heavens, He is a partaker of our nature, and when on earth submitted to all the various kinds of trials to which we are exposed.'

The most natural mode of stating the connection seems to be this: The Apostle has been exhorting them to "hold fast their profession," on the ground of their having "a High Priest"—"a great High Priest"—"a High Priest passed through the heavens"—"a High Priest who is the Son of God;" and he here suggests further reasons for their holding fast their profession, rising out of their High Priest's capacity and disposition to sympathize with them amid all the sufferings to which attachment to His cause might expose them, and which, when connected with His having "passed into the heavens," and being "the Son of God," secure that He will in every case of difficulty and danger successfully interpose in their behalf with the reconciled Divinity, and obtain for them those divine aids which were at once necessary and sufficient to enable them to "hold fast the confidence and the rejoicing of the hope stedfast to the end."

[1] Ernesti.

"We have not a high priest who cannot be touched with the feeling of our infirmities." The word rendered "infirmity" is employed in various senses in the New Testament. Here it seems obviously used as equivalent to 'afflictions,' and probably has a direct reference to afflictions undergone in consequence of a profession of the Christian faith, and in their nature tending to shake the resolution to remain stedfast in that profession. It seems used in the same way as it is by the Apostle in the 2d Epistle to the Corinthians, xii. 5, 10. "Our infirmities" there are our afflictions, especially such as arise from our being Christians.

To be "touched with the feeling of our infirmities," or in one word to sympathize with us, is to feel that kind of interest in us under them which can only be felt by a person who has experienced the same or similar afflictions, and which naturally excites a desire to relieve us. It is pity; but it is something more than pity: it is the pity which a man of kind affections feels towards those who are suffering what he himself has suffered. 'Now,' says the Apostle, 'we have not a high priest who cannot sympathize with us in the trials to which we are exposed. The belonging to a different order of being—the being possessed of an inconceivably more elevated station—might be supposed to incapacitate or indispose our great High Priest, passed into the heavens, Jesus the Son of God, for sympathizing with His people in their afflictions. But no. "We have not an high priest which cannot be touched with the feeling of our infirmities; but was in all points tempted like as we are, yet without sin."' This double negation is equivalent to a very strong assertion: 'We have a Priest who can be touched with the feeling of our infirmities. He has at once the natural and moral capacity of sympathy.[1] He is both able and disposed to sympathize.'

The Son of God, had He never become incarnate, might have pitied, but He could not have sympathized with His people. To render Him capable of sympathy, it was necessary that He should become *man* that He might be susceptible of suffering, and that He should actually be a sufferer that He might be susceptible of sympathy. It is to this the Apostle refers when he says, "It behoved Him to be in all things"—in nature and in

[1] δυνάμενον is used emphatically, as at chap. ii. 18.

condition—"made like unto His brethren, that He might be a faithful and merciful High Priest."

But He has not only a natural, but also a moral capacity—not only the power, but the disposition. Words strictly expressive of power often are intended to convey the idea of disposition: Rom. iv. 21, xi. 23, xiv. 4, xvi. 25; 2 Tim. i. 12. The truth is, He not only can be touched, but cannot but be touched. The assertion is not, It is possible that He may sympathize; but, It is impossible that He should not.[1]

"But was in all points tempted like as we are, yet without sin"—literally, "having been tempted in all points," etc.[2] The sentiment is the same as that expressed in the 2d chapter, at the 18th verse: "For in that He Himself hath suffered, being tempted, He is able to succour them that are tempted." Our High Priest was "tempted," *i.e.*, tried. He was exposed to affliction, and to affliction as a trial. He met with much affliction, the native tendency of which was to try the steadiness of His regard to the will of His Father. A very large proportion of our Lord's sufferings were of a kind which were brought on Him by the performance of His duty, and which might have been avoided by His following a different course.

He was "tempted," or tried, "*in all points*,"—literally, "in reference to all things." He was exposed to *trials* suited to all the various principles of human nature,—poverty, reproach, pain, desertion of friends: every variety of suffering was familiar to "the man of sorrows."

The force of the phrase, *like as we are*—literally, 'according to likeness'[3]—is not very easily determined. It may signify—what our translators obviously understood by it—'In every way in which we are tried He has been tried;' or it may signify, 'He was tried in reference to all things, conformably to the similitude of His nature and circumstances to ours.' That conformity was extensive, but it was not complete. He was "made in the likeness of sinful flesh," but not sinful flesh. He was tried in all things so far as His conformity to us admitted. To all trials, except those which rose out of per-

---

[1] It is not improbable that there is here an implied contrast between Jesus Christ and the superseded Jewish high priests, many of whom were haughty and overbearing.

[2] δέ is used as = ἀλλά.       [3] καθ ὁμοιότητα.

sonal guilt and depravity, He was exposed. We are disposed to prefer the first mode of explication—*being assimilated to us in all manner of trials;* though the words seem to admit of either.

" *Yet without sin.*" These words may be considered as conveying this idea: 'Our High Priest sustained all His trials. Though He was tempted in all things, He sinned in nothing,—He continued stedfast and unmoveable.' Or it may be considered as just stating the fact, that Jesus Christ, our High Priest, is *without sin.* All the trials and afflictions we are exposed to are the consequences of sin. It was not so with our great High Priest. He was "holy, harmless, undefiled, and separate from sinners." And here, as we will by and by see, is a most important distinction between Him and the Aaronical high priests. They, being sinners, were obliged to offer expiatory sacrifices equally for themselves as for the people; but He, though exposed to trial by human weaknesses and afflictions, needed to offer no sacrifice for Himself,—being absolutely innocent, and indeed perfect,—but had the expiation of the guilt of others as the sole object of His offering.

From the consideration of all these truths in reference to Jesus Christ as our High Priest, the Apostle exhorts the believing Hebrews in all their trials to apply to God as the reconciled Divinity, in the assurance of obtaining from Him every aid their circumstances might require. Ver. 16. " Let us therefore come boldly to the throne of grace, that we may obtain mercy, and find grace to help in time of need."

The language here is obviously borrowed from the most sacred religious observances of the Ancient Economy. In the expression, "the throne of grace," there is undoubtedly an allusion to the mercy-seat in the Holy of Holies, over which the Shekinah, the emblem of the divine presence, hovered; and which might therefore with sufficient propriety be represented as the throne of Jehovah, who " dwelt between the cherubim." The question of greatest importance to us is, What under the New Economy answers to the mercy-seat? What is "the throne of grace" to which the believing Hebrews are exhorted to "come boldly?" Some consider the mercy-seat as emblematical of our Lord Jesus Christ, grounding their opinion chiefly on Rom. iii. 25, where God is represented as " setting forth His

Son a propitiation"[1]—or, as they would render it, a propitiatory or mercy-seat—"in His blood." We apprehend, however, that the true meaning of the word propitiation in that passage is, 'propitiatory victim;'[2] and it plainly better suits the entire connected system of emblems to consider the whole of the mystic furniture of the Holy of Holies—the Shekinah hovering above the mercy-seat, sprinkled with blood—as a figurative representation of the Divinity propitiated by sacrifice. It is common in our own language, as well as in that in which the Scriptures were originally written, to speak of a monarch under the names of things which are characteristic of his royal dignity. We speak of the prerogatives of the *crown*, and of addressing the *throne*, when we mean the prerogatives of him who wears the crown, and addressing him who sits on the throne. In like manner, "the throne of grace" is a figurative expression for God as seated on a throne of grace,—"the God of peace," the propitiated Divinity,—" God in Christ reconciling the world to Himself, not imputing to men their trespasses, since He hath made Him to be sin for us who knew no sin, that we might be made the righteousness of God in Him." For, as the Apostle expresses it in the Epistle to the Ephesians, iii. 12, it is in or "by Christ that we have boldness and access with confidence by the faith of Him."

To this propitiated Divinity the inspired writer exhorts the believing Hebrews to *come* or draw near. It is plain that the phrase is figurative. To draw near to the propitiated Divinity, as seated on His "throne of grace," is, in the firm faith of the truth respecting His reconciled character, and in the exercise of those religious affections which this truth believed naturally excites, to render Him religious homage,—to present the desires of our heart before Him. When we thus worship the reconciled Divinity, we are to do it *boldly*: not with that trembling apprehension with which the Israelites, who were ignorant of what might be the event, approached, not to, but towards the mercy-seat, while their high priest entered for them within the vail,—but with a confidence arising from the certain knowledge that our High Priest has " passed into the heavens" with the "blood that cleanseth from all sin," and that "He is able to save to the uttermost, seeing He ever liveth to make interces-

---

[1] ἱλαστήριον.   [2] Not ἱλαστήριον ἐπίθεμα, but ἱλαστήριον θῦμα.

sion." "Boldness" is here not opposed to godly fear, but to slavish dread.

The object of "coming boldly to the throne of grace" is, "that we may obtain mercy, and find grace to help in the time of need." The words "mercy" and "grace" seem here nearly synonymous; as are also the phrases, to "obtain mercy" and "find grace." Both the words properly signify the principle of benignity in the divine mind,—in the first case, in its exercise to us as miserable; in the second, as undeserving,—but they are here, and in many other places, by a common figure of speech, used to denote the manifestations of that principle. To "obtain mercy," to "find grace," is just to receive manifestations of the divine favour,—proofs that God is our reconciled Father and Friend ; and these proofs are given by affording, in answer to our prayer, such assistance as is needful for us in the day of trial, to enable us to " hold fast our profession"—to persevere in the faith, and profession, and obedience of the truth;—*literally*, "that we may obtain mercy, and find grace for seasonable help."[1] The reference is not here to forgiveness of sins, though it is our duty to come to "the throne of grace" for that purpose, but to those aids which are requisite amid the trials of life, to enable us to "hold fast our profession."

This exhortation is grounded on the statements made respecting Jesus Christ as our High Priest. This is intimated to us by the word "*therefore*." 'Since we have a High Priest—one to interpose with God in our behalf—one to expiate our sins and to make intercession for us; since our High Priest is an illustrious personage, who has entered into the immediate presence of God, thus proving the acceptance of His sacrifice and the prevalence of His intercession; since He is indeed the only begotten of God, the divinity of whose nature gives infinite virtue to His sacrifice, and secures uniform success to His interpositions; and since, though so inconceivably great and glorious, He is notwithstanding, from His having assumed our nature and submitted to our condition, at once capable of and disposed to sympathize with us in all our trials, having Himself, so far as the absolute purity of His nature admitted, been exposed to the same trials,—let us persevere in the acknowledg-

[1] εὔκαιρον βοήθειαν.

ment we have made, and instead of falling before the temptations to abandon Christ and His cause, let us, in the exercise of an enlightened and affectionate devotion, seek from God, the propitiated Divinity, in the exercise of His pity for our weakness and misery, and of His grace towards us who are utterly undeserving, those aids of His good Spirit which are at once absolutely necessary and abundantly sufficient to enable us to "hold fast the beginning of our confidence stedfast to the end," amid all the trials to which we are exposed.' The exhortation was peculiarly appropriate to the Hebrew Christians in their circumstances. It is suited, however, to Christians of all countries and all ages. The grand leading outlines of state, character, and education of true Christians are independent of the circumstances of time and place. The two great duties of the Christian are, the believing study of the truth respecting Jesus Christ, and the cultivation of a habitual affectionate intercourse with God as the God of peace, under the influence of the faith of "the truth as it is in Jesus."

These three concluding verses of the fourth chapter, with which the third section of the Epistle commences, contain in them a kind of epitome of the principles which are more fully stated and illustrated in the sequel. After their general annunciation, the Apostle enters on this more extended statement and illustration. In the course of the section he makes it evident, that whatever was essential to the office of a high priest was to be found in Christ Jesus,—that whatever imperfections belonged to the Aaronical high-priesthood were not to be found in Him, —and that a variety of excellences were to be found in Him of which none of the Aaronical priests were possessed.

### § 2. *The Nature, Design, and Functions of the Levitical High-Priesthood.*

As the foundation of such a series of illustrations, Paul in the following passage gives a brief but comprehensive account of the Levitical high priest, with whom he is about to compare at length Jesus Christ, the High Priest of our profession. Vers. 1-3. "For every high priest, taken from among men, is ordained for men in things pertaining to God, that he may offer both gifts and sacrifices for sin: who can have compassion on the ignorant, and on them that are out of the way; for that he himself also is compassed with infirmity. And by reason hereof he ought, as for the people, so also for himself, to offer for sins." This is the general description of a Levitical high priest. Let us examine somewhat more minutely its several parts.

"*For*" is here obviously to be understood as neither stating a reason for, nor drawing an inference from what goes before: it is neither *causal* nor *illative;* but is merely a particle of connection, equivalent to 'Now.'

The phrase, *every high priest*, though in itself unlimited, is plainly to be understood of every high priest of the order of which the Apostle is speaking—the Aaronical or Levitical high-priesthood.

"It will tend, we apprehend, to diffuse light over some of the succeeding discussions, to make a few preliminary remarks respecting the priestly office in general, and the manner in which it became fixed in the family of Aaron. By the priesthood, we understand a particular class of men divinely appointed to manage the concerns of their brethren with the Divinity— by means of vicarious atonement and intercession; to avert His displeasure, propitiate His favour, and secure friendly intercourse with Him,—in the acceptance of services *from* them, and the communication of blessings *to* them. This is the Apostle's account of the matter: 'Every high priest, taken from among men, is ordained for men in things pertaining to God, that he may offer both gifts and sacrifices for sin.'

"Immediately after the fall, an intimation was made to man of the determination of God to redeem him; and the manner in which this was to be accomplished, was shadowed forth by the significant rite of sacrifice—a rite which at once exemplified the death to which men were doomed for transgression, and represented the death to be undergone by the Redeemer of mankind for their salvation. Whether, during the earlier ages of the world, every man was allowed to offer up sacrifices for himself, or whether this office was from the beginning appropriated to a particular body, and, in this case, what was the body of men entrusted with this honourable function, are questions, the full resolution of which would involve us in a long discussion, which, though neither uninteresting nor unimportant, would not well answer our present design.

"There seems, however, to be reason to suppose, that for some time every father of a family was the prophet, priest, and king of his own household; and that afterwards the priesthood formed an important part of that birthright which belonged to the first-born. In the Book of Exodus we read of 'the priests who came near the Lord,' and of 'young men of the children of Israel, who offered burnt-offerings, and sacrificed peace-offerings to the Lord,' at a period prior to the choice of the tribe of Levi, or the consecration of Aaron and his family; and it deserves notice, that the Chaldaic paraphrasts, and some of the more ancient versions, interpret 'these priests and young men' of the first-born among the Israelites."[1]

At the commencement of the Mosaic dispensation, the priesthood was appropriated to Aaron and his family. The dignity of the priesthood centred in Aaron—he being constituted high priest, his sons, during his life, his assistants and substitutes, and the high-priesthood made hereditary in his family. It is of Aaron, then, and his descendants that the Apostle gives a description in the paragraph under consideration.

The expression, "taken from among men,"[2] may be considered either as defining the particular kind of high priests, of all of whom he is about to give a description, or as the first part of that description. Viewed in the first light, in which our translators seem to have considered it, it is equivalent to, 'every mere human priest—every priest who is nothing more than a man;'—tacitly suggesting, what he elsewhere distinctly states, the superiority of our High Priest in this respect: "the law making *men* priests who have infirmity, but the word of the oath constituting the Son a priest, consecrated for evermore." Viewed in the second light, the words must be rendered, 'being taken from among men, is ordained,' or, 'is taken from among men and ordained;' and they teach us that the

---

[1] *Vide* Sermon on the Priesthood of Christ—Discourses Suited to the Administration of the Lord's Supper, pp. 144, 145, 3d Ed.

[2] Λαμβανόμενος may be considered as a Latinism—a Latin idiom expressed in Greek, instances of which, as Grotius has shown, are not rare in the writings of Luke. A Greek writer would scarcely have used λαμβάνεσθαι of the election to the priesthood. But *capi* was the very word employed in the Roman sacerdotal law for such a purpose. "Eximie," says Aulus Gellius, i. 12, "virgines vestales, sed Flamines quoque Diales, item Pontifices et Augures, CAPI dicebantur."

## THE LEVITICAL HIGH-PRIESTHOOD. 239

Levitical priests were partakers of human nature in common with the rest of mankind—that they had no natural superiority over their brethren, but that they were taken or selected by God "from among men" to serve an important purpose. It does not matter much in which way the phrase is understood, though I am disposed to prefer the latter mode of interpretation.

The purpose for which the high priest was taken from among his fellow-men is described in the words which follow. Being "taken from among men," he was "ordained for men in things pertaining to God, that he might offer both gifts and sacrifices for sin." He was *ordained, i.e.*, divinely appointed, *for men.* The particle *for* sometimes signifies in the room of: John x. 11; Philemon 13. At other times, and more usually, it signifies in behalf of, for the benefit of: 1 Tim. ii. 1. Here we are disposed to think it is to be understood in the first sense, which includes the second. He was appointed to be the substitute of his fellow-men, to do for them what was necessary to be done, but which the emblematical nature of the Jewish economy required should be done by another standing in their place. The principle lying at the foundation of our Saviour's priesthood, of which the Levitical priesthood was emblematical, is this: God is displeased with man on account of sin, and cannot have direct favourable intercourse with him. There must be a mediator—one to deal for man with God. He was appointed in the room and for the benefit of his fellow-men "in things pertaining to God."[1] He was ordained to manage their religious interests, to do for them what must be done with God—to expiate their sins, and to secure the acceptance of their religious services.

The meaning of the phrase, "in things pertaining to God," is explained in the clause that follows—"that he may offer both gifts and sacrifices for sin." By some interpreters, "gifts and sacrifices" are understood as two names for the same thing.[2]

---

[1] τὰ πρὸς τὸν Θεόν, religious duties and interests—man's business with God.

[2] In defence of this exegesis, Ebrard's note deserves to be quoted. "Δῶρα is not the more general, and θυσίαι the more special term, for ὑπὲρ ἁμαρτιῶν refers to προσφέρῃ, and therefore both to δ. and θ. These two terms are (just like τέρατα and σημεῖα) only two designations of one and the same thing, regarded from different points of view. Sacrifices are called δῶρα because the person for whom the atonement is to be made gives

There can be no doubt that sacrifices for sin were viewed as given to God by the offerer as the price of pardon; and when our Lord's sacrifice is spoken of, He is said to have "given Himself for us a sacrifice and offering." Yet at the same time it seems more natural, and it is agreeable to the fact, to understand "gifts" of religious oblations generally, or particularly of eucharistic offerings, and "sacrifices for sin" of propitiatory oblations. Such was the design of the Levitical priesthood. Now for their qualifications. Every high priest is one "who can have compassion on the ignorant, and on them who are out of the way."

The persons in whose room and for whose benefit he officiates are not innocent beings; in this case his services would not have been needed. They are persons who have sinned—persons who are *ignorant and out of the way*. These words do not describe merely those who, through want of information, have fallen into some neglect of duty, or the commission of some fault. In the Bible all sin is represented as the result of ignorance, but of blameable ignorance. It is of sinners the Psalmist says, "They know not, neither do they understand. They walk on in darkness." "The Lord looked down from heaven upon the children of men, to see if there were any that did understand, and seek God. They are all gone aside, they are all together become filthy; there is none that doeth good, no, not one. Have all the workers of iniquity no knowledge? who eat up My people as they eat bread, and call not upon the Lord."[1] Every sin shows a want of the knowledge of the truth, as well as want of true wisdom. Every sinner is a fool. "Those who are out of the way" is a figurative expression for the sinner. The law of God marks out a particular path in which men should walk; and when a person breaks that law, either by neglect or by actual violation, he goes "out of the way." I do not think that these words are descriptive of two different classes of sinners. The ignorant

them to the priest for God; they are called θυσίαι because they must be slain to have an atoning efficacy. The person whose guilt is to be atoned for must take the victim *from his own property*, that it may appear a representative of himself; and then the victim must suffer the death which its owner had deserved."

[1] Ps. xiv. 2–4.

and the erring are the same class; and it includes here the whole people of Israel, in whose room the high priest was appointed, and for whose benefit he officiated, with the exception of those presumptuous and obstinate sinners for whom no sacrifice was to be offered.

Now, as it was with these persons that the high priest had to do—as it was their interests he had to manage with God, it was necessary that he should be a person who "*could* have—who was capable of having—compassion on them."[1] The word translated "have compassion," is rendered in the margin, *reasonably bear with*. A person could not be expected to do the duties of a high priest aright if he could not enter into the feelings of those whom he represented. If their faults excited no sentiment in his mind but disapprobation—if they moved him to no feeling but anger, he would not be fit to interpose in their behalf with God—he would not be inclined to do for them what was necessary for the expiation of their guilt, and the acceptance of their services. But the Jewish high priest was one who was capable of pitying and bearing with the ignorant and the erring; "for he himself also was compassed with infirmity."[2]

"Infirmity," here, plainly is significant of sinful weakness, and probably also of the disagreeable effects resulting from it. The Jewish high priest was himself a sinner. He had personal experience of temptation, and the tendency of man to yield to temptation—of sin, and of the consequences of sin; so that he had the natural capacity, and ought to have had the moral capacity, of pitying his fellow-sinners. Of this truth, of which the Apostle makes use afterwards in illustrating the superiority of Jesus Christ to the Levitical high priests, we have a striking proof in the undeniable fact, that they were appointed

---

[1] μετριοπαθεῖν δυν. = δυν. συμπαθῆσαι.

[2] περίκειται ἀσθένειαν. The allusion is to the body as a garment—the body the seat of frailty, and the occasion and instrument of sin. In Greek a bride is said to be νυμφικὴν ἐσθῆτα περικειμένη, clothed with bridal attire. The Stoical philosophers, as well as the Apostle, considered the body as a cumbrous garment, to be laid aside at death; SENECA, Ep. xcii.; 2 Cor. v. 4. The words of the Roman poet in reference to this figure are very beautiful:—

"Quod si immortalis nostra foret mens
Non jam se moriens dissolvi conquereretur,
Sed magis ire foras, vestemque relinquere ut anguis,
Gauderet, praelonga senex aut cornua cervus."—LUCRET. iii. 611-614.

to offer sacrifices for "their own sins, as well as for the sins of the people,"—a plain proof that they needed pardon as well as those in whose room they stood. And it deserves particular notice, that the high priest was required first to offer sacrifice for himself that he might be purified and accepted in offering for the people,—an intimation that, in order to available interposition with God, the person who interposes must be considered as himself an object of His favourable regards. Lev. iv. 3, ix. 7, xvi. 6, 24. Such is the Apostle's description of the Levitical high priest. From what has been said it is plain that there is no human ministry under the New Economy which corresponds to the priesthood or high-priesthood under the law. There is an essential difference between the Christian ministry and the Levitical priesthood. Christians do not need a human priesthood. We *have* a great High Priest, who requires no coadjutors. His character and work are perfect.

### § 3. *Our Lord's High-Priesthood proved by his Divine Appointment.*

In the paragraph which follows, the Apostle proceeds to show that if this be the true description of a Levitical high priest, in Christ Jesus, the High Priest whom we acknowledge, we have *a High Priest—a great High Priest.* The first point to which the Apostle turns our attention is the divine constitution of our Lord's priesthood. A Levitical high priest was a man selected and ordained according to divine appointment to his office. Our High Priest is the Son of God, ordained by a divine oath to His office.

Vers. 4-6. "And no man taketh this honour unto himself, but he that is called of God, as was Aaron. So also Christ glorified not Himself to be made an high priest; but He that said unto Him, Thou art My Son, to-day have I begotten Thee. As He saith also in another place, Thou art a Priest for ever, after the order of Melchisedec."

By many, perhaps most interpreters, the 4th verse is considered as the conclusion of the Apostle's account of the Levitical priesthood. We are rather disposed to consider it as the commencement of his application of the description contained in the three preceding verses, to the object he has in view—the illustration of the reality and excellence of the priesthood of our Lord. The ordinary mode of interpretation represents the Apostle as proceeding in an inverted order in applying what he had said about the Levitical priesthood to the priesthood of our Lord, whereas the mode we are disposed to follow preserves the natural order. He shows, first, that He has been legitimately invested with the high-priesthood; and secondly, that He has successfully discharged the functions of the high-priesthood. The first of these topics is discussed in the 4th, 5th, and 6th verses; and the second in the 7th, 8th, and 9th verses; and in illustrating these two topics, he makes it evident that His high-priesthood is superior to the Levitical high-priesthood—that He is not only a High Priest, but a great High Priest. Let us turn our attention to his proof that our Lord is legitimately invested with the high-priesthood, and to the illustration of the superiority of our Lord's high-priesthood, involved in that proof.

"No man taketh this honour to himself, but he that is called of God, as was Aaron." *This honour*[1] is plainly descriptive of the high-priesthood. To be employed in managing the religious interests of his fellow-men, to be allowed a peculiarly intimate intercourse with the Divinity, was perhaps the highest honour which could be conferred on a mortal; and the gorgeous apparel and the elevated station of the Jewish high priest were external indications of the intrinsic dignity of the office. "No man," says the Apostle, "takes this" honourable "office to himself." These words are not to be understood as intimating that none had ever assumed to themselves the honour of priests and high priests among the Jews except those who were legally entitled to it. Their history, particularly in the latter ages of the republic, furnishes us with a number of instances of persons occupying the high-priesthood who had no title but what force or fraud could give them; and it is not at all unlikely that these words were intended by the Apostle to glance at this disgraceful fact. The words are equivalent to—'No man can lawfully

---

[1] τιμή is used of any office of dignity. Herodian, vii. 3, 8, speaks of ὑπατείας τιμή, the office of consulship. Xenoph. Mem. iii. 1, 1, speaking of the office of warlike leader, uses the expression, τῆς τιμῆς ταύτης τυγχάνειν, and ii. 6, 24, mentions τῶν πολιτικῶν τιμῶν κοινωνούς. The Romans used the word *honor* in the same way: Juv. xi. 87, has "dictatoris honore functus."

assume this honourable office unless he is divinely called, as was Aaron.[1] No man is a legitimate high priest unless he is divinely called to that office.'

When it is said that no man can be a legitimate priest except he be "called of God, as was Aaron," the meaning is not that his call must be exactly of the same kind as Aaron's; for in that case there never would have been a legitimate high priest except Aaron. The meaning is, 'No man can be a legitimate high priest without a divine call.' Aaron had a divine call, Exod. xxviii; and so had his sons, as the high-priesthood was by a divine appointment fixed in his family. Not only were Aaron and his sons "called of God" to the office of the high-priesthood, but all others, even of the tribe of Levi, were debarred from interfering or sharing with them its peculiar functions and honours. Korah, Dathan, and Abiram, with two hundred and fifty of their associates, were miraculously destroyed for presumptuously attempting to intrude into it; and fourteen thousand seven hundred of the children of Israel were cut off for murmuring at this manifestation of the divine displeasure. The exclusive right of Aaron and his family to the high-priesthood was also clearly proved by his rod being caused to blossom miraculously: Num. xvi. xvii. And when Uzziah attempted to perform one of the peculiar functions of the priesthood by burning incense, he was not merely severely rebuked, but permanently punished for his presumption: 2 Chron. xxvi. 16–21.

The principle on which the necessity of a divine call to the legitimate exercise of the priesthood rests is an obvious one. It depends entirely on the will of God whether He will accept the services and pardon the sins of men; and supposing that it is His will to do so, it belongs to Him to appoint everything in reference to the manner in which this is to be accomplished. God is under no obligation to accept of every one, or of any one who, of his own accord, or by the choice of his fellow-men, takes it upon him to offer sacrifices or gifts for himself or for others; and no man in these circumstances can have reason to expect that God will accept of his offerings, unless He has given him a commission to offer them, and a promise that He will be appeased by them. This, then, from the very nature of the case, was necessary to the legitimate discharge of the functions of a high priest.

---

[1] The word λαμβάνειν seems used in the same way, John iii. 27.

Now this requisite is to be found in "the High Priest of our profession," and is to be found in such a way as to prove not only that He is really a High Priest, but that He is a High Priest infinitely superior to the Levitical high priests. "So Christ also glorified not Himself to be called a high priest; but He that said unto Him, Thou art My Son, to-day have I begotten Thee."

These words are plainly elliptical. When the ellipsis is supplied they run thus: 'Christ glorified not Himself to be called a high priest; but He who said to Him, Thou art My Son, to-day have I begotten Thee, He glorified Him to be called a high priest.'[1] The words, "Christ glorified not Himself to be called a high priest," are just equivalent to—'Christ took not this honour unto Himself.' Jesus Christ did not intrude Himself into the office of a priest. In taking to Himself the name, performing the functions, claiming the honours of the high-priesthood, He was guilty of no presumption. "He was called of God, as was Aaron." He who said to Him, Thou art My Son, this day have I begotten Thee, He glorified Him to be called a high priest. He to whom the right belonged, invested Him with the honours of the high-priesthood. Some interpreters have sought in this quotation from the 2d Psalm evidence of our Lord's investiture with the high-priesthood;[2] some going on the very untenable principle, that 'Son of God,' and 'Messiah the Anointed One,' are terms of equivalent meaning; and others supposing that the Apostle's argument is founded on a part of the paragraph, the beginning only of which he quotes—"*Ask of Me,*"—intercession being a part of the official duty of the high priest. It does not appear to be possible to deduce a good argument for our Lord's call to the priesthood from these words; and there is no evidence that the Apostle introduces them for this purpose. They are an assertion, the evidence of which is contained in the succeeding verse. It is just equivalent to—
'Christ did not ultroneously assume the office of a high priest; but that God who acknowledges Him as His Son in a sense

---

[1] How admirably do the Apostle's words harmonize with our Lord's own! ἐὰν ἐγὼ δοξάζω ἐμαυτόν, ἡ δόξα μου οὐδέν ἐστιν· ἔστιν ὁ πατήρ μου ὁ δοξάζων με. John viii. 54.

[2] Some suppose that in the reference, ἐγὼ γεγέννηκά σε, is to be found the principle,—*whatever* the Messiah is, God has made Him.

which raises Him far above all creatures,—that God has constituted Him a high priest.'[1]  If it be asked why the Apostle uses the periphrasis, "He that said unto Him, etc.," rather than God, the answer is ready. He wishes to keep before the mind of his readers the fact of the divine nature of Jesus Christ, which sheds a peculiar and altogether unparalleled glory over all His mediatorial characters and functions.

There is something very striking in the language, 'God *glorified* His Son by investing Him with the high-priesthood.' The high-priesthood of our Lord, viewed in reference to the opportunities it afforded Him of manifesting the glories of His own character, in the vindication of the honour of the divine law and government, and in the everlasting salvation of innumerable millions—and in reference to the honours with which the discharge of its functions was ultimately to crown Him, may well be described as a glory conferred on Him.

The evidence that God, who acknowledges the Messiah as His Son, has also invested Him with priestly honours, is brought forward in the 6th verse: "As He saith also in another place, Thou art a Priest for ever, after the order of Melchisedec." These words are a quotation from the 110th Psalm, which was generally admitted by the Jews to refer to the Messiah, and indeed does not admit of being referred to any other person.[2] The Apostle's argument is most satisfactory. He is addressing persons who admitted that Jesus Christ was the Messiah. 'Now,' says he, 'in Christ Jesus we have a High Priest, a great High Priest; for ancient oracles which refer to the Messiah speak of Him both as the Son of God and as an High Priest.' There is much, very much, in these words themselves, and in the manner in which they are introduced, calculated to reflect light on the peculiar glories of the high-priesthood of Christ Jesus. This forms the subject of after-discussion by the Apostle; but the object for which they are introduced here is plainly to prove

---

[1] Camerarius, with his usual sagacity, says, "συλληπτικῶς hæc dicuntur μετ' ἐλλείψεως, ὁ X. οὐκ ἐδόξασεν ἑαυτὸν τοῦ γενηθῆναι ἀρχιερέα, ἀλλ' ὁ λαλήσας, Θ., ἐδόξασεν αὐτόν."

[2] Michaelis' note on this Psalm, in his Latin translation of Peirce, is admirable. The notes in that work are generally excellent. It is painful to think that that truly great man did not grow more sober-minded and more devout, as his treasures of erudition, great even when but a youth, accumulated so as to be unmanageable.

that Jesus Christ, if he was, as the Hebrew Christians admitted, really the Messiah, was also really a High Priest, " called of God, as was Aaron,"—separated by a divine appointment to hold the character and perform the functions of the priesthood.

The passage which I have attempted to explain has often been quoted, as if it contained a condemnation of those who, without being regularly called, assume the functions of the Christian ministry. It plainly has no reference to this subject; but it does place in a strong point of light the hazardous situation of those men who assume to themselves the name of priests, and pretend to offer up a sacrifice for the sins of the living and the dead. They act a part just as much more guilty than that of Korah, Dathan, and Abiram, as Christ is superior to Aaron; and if mercy prevent not, the depth of their perdition will correspond with the heinousness of their presumptuous iniquity.

But those religious office-bearers, in whatever church, who pretend to discharge sacerdotal functions, are not the only class who invade the honours of our New Testament High Priest. Whoever attempts to substitute anything in the room of His atoning sacrifice and prevalent intercession, incurs the divine indignation; and if he persists, will draw down upon himself " swift destruction." Had any Israelite attempted to substitute repentance and reformation in the room of the appointed sacrifice, or presented the sacrifice himself instead of employing the sons of Aaron, far from obtaining the remission of his sin, he would have involved himself in deeper guilt. And the sinner, under this last dispensation of the divine mercy, who, instead of submitting to the righteousness of God, goes about to establish his own righteousness, instead of obtaining pardon, commits a new and most aggravated transgression. He usurps the place of our great New Testament High Priest; and if he perseveres, " there remains for him no more sacrifice for sin, but a certain fearful looking for of judgment, which shall devour the adversaries."

§ 4. *Our Lord's High-Priesthood proved by His successful discharge of the Functions of that Office.*

As the theme of vers. 4-6 is, 'Jesus Christ has been divinely appointed to the priestly office,' so the theme of vers. 7-9 is, 'Jesus Christ has successfully executed the priestly office.' Let us examine this very interesting passage somewhat more minutely.

Vers. 7-10. " Who in the days of His flesh, when He had offered up prayers and supplications, with strong crying and tears, unto Him that was able to save Him from death, and was heard in that He feared: Though He were a Son, yet learned He obedience by the things which He suffered; and being made perfect, He became the Author of eternal salvation unto all them that obey Him; called of God an High Priest, after the order of Melchisedec."

These four verses form one long and complicated sentence. To the right interpretation of a complicated sentence the first step is to see its right construction. A distinct apprehension of what is the main body of the sentence, if I may use the expression, and what are the members attached to it—what, to vary the figure, is the trunk, and what are the branches which grow out of it—will often go far to make a sentence perspicuous that at first view appears exceedingly perplexed. The leading idea becomes in this way distinctly marked, and the subsidiary ones are seen in their relation to their principal.

To a person who looks at the passage as it stands in the original, there scarcely can be a doubt that the body of the sentence, expressing the great leading idea that Jesus Christ has successfully performed the functions of the high-priesthood, is to be found in these words,—" Who learned obedience by the things which He suffered, and is become the Author of eternal salvation to all who obey Him." The other clauses are all of them expressive of subsidiary ideas, defining, qualifying, or in some way or other relating to the primary one. The body of the sentence divides itself into two parts:—1. " He"—*i.e.*, plainly, Christ in the character of a priest—" learned obedience by the things which He suffered." 2. " He," in the same character, " has become the Author of eternal salvation to all that obey Him." The clauses, " in the days of His flesh," and " though He were a Son," qualify the general declaration, " He learned obedience by the things which He suffered;" and the clauses, " when He had offered up"—or having offered up—" prayers and supplications, with strong crying and tears, unto Him that was able to save Him from death," and " when He was heard"—or having been heard—" in that He feared," contain in them illustrations both of the nature and extent of those sufferings by which Christ learned obedience ; while the clause, " being made perfect," qualifies the second part of the sentence, connecting it with the first, and showing how His " learning obedience by the things which He suffered " led to His being " the Author of eternal salvation to all who obey Him." Such seems to me the true mode of resolving this somewhat complicated sentence.

" He"—*i.e.*, Jesus Christ as a priest—" learned obedience by the things which He suffered."[1] When it is said of a person, that ' he learned obedience by the things which he suffered,' the idea naturally suggested is that of a person previously rebellious and disinclined to obedience, but disciplined into it by sufferings to which he is exposed in consequence of disobedience. But it is quite plain that it were blasphemy to use the words with this sense in reference to our Lord. Had the only begotten of God been unwilling to obey and suffer, who could have compelled Him? His obedience was a most willing obedience. Had it been otherwise than voluntary, it could not have served its purpose. Constrained obedience could not have " magnified and made honourable" the divine law. The language of our Lord's conduct was, " Lo, I come ! to do Thy will I take delight ; yea, Thy law is in My heart."

Not more satisfactory is the mode of interpretation which makes the words mean that He learned how painful a thing obedience is. It is our depravity, our pride, our desire of independence, which makes obedience a painful thing. These principles did not exist in the mind of our Lord. What in itself was very disagreeable, became to Him desirable just because God had enjoined or appointed it. This sweetened to

---

[1] ἔμαθεν, ἔπαθεν,—paronomasia. It is not unlikely that the ancient Greek dictum was in the author's mind, παθήματα, μαθήματα—nocumenta, documenta. In Herodotus, lib. i. 207, Crœsus is represented as saying, γεγονέναι μαθήματα τὰ παθήματα, that he had become wiser by his misfortunes.

Him the bitterest cup, and lightened the heaviest load. So far from obedience being difficult to Him, merely as obedience, it was His " meat," " drink," etc. His meat and drink was to do the will of His Father, and to finish His work.

To " learn obedience," is, I apprehend, to become experimentally acquainted with obedience. When it is said of our Lord, that " He knew no sin," the meaning is, He was experimentally unacquainted with it—He never sinned : in like manner, when it is said, " He learned obedience," the meaning is, He became experimentally acquainted with obedience—He obeyed. The obedience here referred to is plainly obedience in the character of a high priest—the doing all that God, who had appointed Him, required in order to gain the end of His office,—the expiation of guilt, and the salvation of man. The commandment which, as the great High Priest, He received of His Father was, that He should lay down His life for His people, in whose place He stood, and for whose benefit He acted ; " and He became obedient unto death, even the death of the cross." The will of God which as High Priest He was to do, was the sanctification of His people by the offering of His body " once for all."[1] And thus we perceive the propriety of the phraseology here adopted, " He learned obedience by the things which He suffered," or from His sufferings. In the sufferings to which He was exposed, He experimentally learned what the obedience was which was due by Him, as the appointed High Priest of His people, to the righteous Majesty of Heaven ; and from these sufferings, however severe, He did not draw back. To use the language of the ancient prophet, " He was not rebellious, neither did He turn away back. He gave His back to the smiters, and His cheeks to those who plucked off the hair : He hid not His face from shame and spitting."[2] He by His sufferings became experimentally acquainted with the full extent of the demands of the divine law on Him as our High Priest, and completely answered them. The law of the Levitical high priest was, that he should offer gifts and sacrifices for the sins of Israel. The law of our great High Priest was, that He should " offer Himself for us a sacrifice and an offering ;" and He learned, He became experimentally acquainted with, obedience to this law by His sufferings.

[1] Heb. x. 9, 10.       [2] Isa. l. 5, 6.

It was " in the days of His flesh" that Jesus Christ, as our High Priest, thus "learned obedience by the things that He suffered." The word " flesh," and the phrase, " flesh and blood," are often expressive simply of human nature. " All flesh" is all men. "The Word was made flesh;" *i.e.*, the Word became incarnate. " Inasmuch as the children were partakers of flesh and blood"—*i.e.*, of human nature—" He also took part of the same." They are sometimes used as signifying human nature with the superadded idea of that frailty and liability to suffering and death by which it is distinguished in its present state: as in Ps. lxxviii. 39, " He remembered that they were flesh"—poor, frail, dying creatures—" a wind that passeth away, and returneth not again:" and in 1 Cor. xv. 50, " Flesh and blood"—*i.e.*, human nature in its present frail, mortal state—" cannot inherit the kingdom of God; neither doth corruption inherit incorruption." In the former sense, " the days of our Lord's flesh" commenced with His incarnation, and will continue for ever; in the latter sense, they commenced with His incarnation, and terminated at His resurrection. There can be no doubt that it is in the latter sense the phrase is here to be understood. " The days of His flesh" are plainly contrasted with His present condition, as having been " made perfect," and " become the Author of eternal salvation to all who obey Him." During the whole of His humbled state, from His cradle to His tomb, from Bethlehem to Calvary, " He learned obedience by the things He suffered." The whole of His humbled life was one great act of obedience to the will of God—one great sacrifice of expiation.

And He thus, during "the days of His flesh, learned obedience by the things which He suffered, *though He were a Son.*"[1] In the preceding context the inspired writer had stated that He whom God had constituted our High Priest is the same glorious person whom He acknowledges as His Son, in a sense in which that appellation cannot be given to the highest of the angels; and he brings this fact before the mind here to impress us with the conviction that the dignity of our High Priest did not prevent Him from performing all the functions of His office, whatever degradation and suffering they might involve, and thus to fill us with admiration of His condescension and love. Our

---

[1] καίπερ ὢν Υἱός. The true rendering seems to be, ' though He was the Son'—the glorious person described, ch. i. 1, etc.

great High Priest, "in the days of His flesh," "though a Son" —or "though Son" in a sense quite peculiar to Himself—yet "learned obedience" by His sufferings. "Though in the form of God," He did not refuse to take on Him "the form of a servant." Though "Lord of all," He did not refuse to "become obedient to death, even the death of the cross." Though "the brightness of the Father's glory, and the express image of His person," "He purged our sins by Himself." This is one of the numerous passages which show plainly that *Son of God* and Messiah are not synonyms—that "Son of God" is an essential and not an official appellation. Suppose that "Son of God" is just equivalent to Messiah, or divinely appointed Saviour,—and there is no force in the Apostle's remark. In that case he would have said, not 'Although He were,' but, 'Because He was a Son, He learned obedience by the things which He suffered.' But considering "Son of God" as an appellation denoting essential relation to His Divine Father—identity of nature, equality of perfection,—then there is inconceivable energy in the remark, 'Though He was the Fellow of the Almighty Father, He yet learned obedience by the things which He suffered; He yielded all, and suffered all, that was required to the full accomplishment of His duties as our High Priest.'[1]

We have an account of the exercise of the Saviour's mind while thus "learning obedience by the things which He suffered" during "the days of His flesh." "He offered up prayers and supplications, with strong crying and tears, to Him who was able to save Him from death, and was heard in that He feared." From the manner in which the words are rendered in our version, it is natural to conclude that the offering up of these "prayers and supplications" preceded our Lord's "learning obedience by the things which He suffered:"—"When He had offered," "and when He was heard," etc.: but this does not seem to be the meaning of the inspired writer. It seems to intimate to us that the "learning obedience" and the offering up of the "prayers and supplications" were contemporaneous. The word rendered "prayers" properly signifies deprecations, or prayers against evil, viewed as impending; such as, "Lead me not into temptation." The word ren-

---

[1] It is strange that Stuart, who is an advocate for the economical Sonship, takes no, or at any rate a very cursory, notice in his commentary, of the import of καίπερ ὢν Υἱός.

dered "supplications" signifies prayers for assistance under, or deliverance from, evil already experienced ; such as, " Father, let this cup pass from Me." Our Lord, while " learning obedience by the things which He suffered," offered up prayers of both kinds, and offered them up " with strong crying and tears "— indicating at once the intensity of His sufferings and the ardour of His devotional sentiments.

These " prayers and supplications" were addressed to " Him who was able to save Him from death," *i.e.*, to GOD His Father, under the character of " Him who was ABLE;" *i. e.*, as we have repeatedly seen, who had both the capacity and disposition, the power and the will, to save Him from death.[1] To " save from death" does not here mean, to deliver from the necessity of dying. Death under the curse was the ultimate term of that obedience which He was experimentally learning by suffering. It was necessary to the gaining of the great object for which He became a High Priest—it was necessary to the completion of the sacrifice—that He should " become obedient even to the death." No doubt God, who is omnipotent, abstractly speaking, could have prevented Jesus Christ from dying ; but He could not do so in consistency with the economy of human salvation. To " save from death" means, to deliver from death after having died. God manifested Himself as " Him who was able to save Him from death," when, as " the God of peace"—the pacified Divinity—" He brought again from the dead our Lord Jesus, that great Shepherd of the sheep, by the blood of the everlasting covenant."

It has been common to consider the Apostle, in these words, as referring entirely to the "prayers and supplications" offered up by our Lord in the immediate prospect of, and in the midst of, His last sufferings. I do not see any good reason for this restriction. "The days of His flesh" include more than the hour of agony in Gethsemane, and the hours of torture on the cross : they must include the entire period of His humiliation. The pressure of human guilt habitually weighed down His mind, and He was by way of eminence a man of prayer as well as " a man of sorrows." We read in one instance that, after dismissing

[1] It is worthy of notice that our Lord's express words in one of these prayers are, Ἀββᾶ, ὁ πατήρ, πάντα δυνατά σοι· παρένεγκε τὸ ποτήριον ἀπ' ἐμοῦ τοῦτο. Mark xiv. 35, 36.

the multitude and His disciples, He retired not to repose, but to prayer, Matt. xiv. 23, 25; on another occasion, that, rising up at a very early hour, He went out to a solitary place to pray, Mark i. 35; that on a third occasion He went up to a mountain to pray, and in that exercise spent the whole night, Luke vi. 12 ; and we are told that, after the observance of the Passover, He retired to the Mount of Olives, as He was wont, Luke xxii. 39. "He cried," according to the ancient oracle, "in the day-time; and in the night-season, there was no silence to Him."

But although I do not think there is an exclusive reference to what took place in the immediate prospect of His death, yet at the same time, as His prayers then are more circumstantially recorded than on any other occasion, they are, as a specimen of His devotional exercises, strikingly illustrative of the general declaration of the Apostle. "Now is My soul troubled; and what shall I say? Father, save Me from this hour: but for this cause came I unto this hour. Father, glorify Thy name. Then came there a voice from heaven, saying, I have both glorified it, and will glorify it again." "Then cometh Jesus with them unto a place called Gethsemane, and saith unto the disciples, Sit ye here, while I go and pray yonder.—And He went a little farther, and fell on His face, and prayed, saying, O My Father, if it be possible, let this cup pass from Me: nevertheless not as I will, but as Thou wilt.—He went away again the second time, and prayed, saying, O My Father, if this cup may not pass away from Me, except I drink it, Thy will be done." "And, being in an agony, He prayed more earnestly: and His sweat was as it were great drops of blood falling down to the ground." "But as for Me, My prayer is unto Thee, O Lord, in an acceptable time: O God, in the multitude of Thy mercy hear Me, in the truth of Thy salvation. Deliver Me out of the mire, and let Me not sink: let Me be delivered from them that hate Me, and out of the deep waters. Let not the water-flood overflow Me, neither let the deep swallow Me up, and let not the pit shut her mouth upon Me. Hear Me, O Lord; for Thy lovingkindness is good: turn unto Me according to the multitude of Thy tender mercies. And hide not Thy face from Thy servant; for I am in trouble: hear Me speedily. Draw nigh unto My soul, and redeem it: deliver Me, because of Mine enemies." "I will bless the Lord, who hath given Me counsel; My reins also instruct Me in the night-seasons. I have set the Lord always before Me: because He is at My right hand; I shall not be moved. Therefore My heart is glad, and My glory rejoiceth; My flesh also shall rest in hope: for Thou wilt not leave My soul in hell; neither wilt Thou suffer Thine Holy One to see corruption. Thou wilt show Me the path of life: in Thy presence is fulness of joy; at Thy right hand there are pleasures for evermore."[1] Such were the " prayers and supplications" which He " offered up to Him who was able to save Him from death." These words most strikingly intimate the intensity of our Lord's sufferings as the victim of human guilt. If the question be asked, Whence arose this remarkable intensity of suffering? the answer is ready. These sufferings were penal and vicarious. " The Lord laid on Him the iniquity of us all," and " therefore it pleased the Lord to bruise Him." " Exaction was made, and He became answerable." " His soul was being made a sacrifice for sin." They well intimate also the temper in which He sustained these sufferings,—viewing them as coming from God, submitting to them as sent by Him, looking up to Him for support under them and deliverance from them.

Nor did He look in vain. " He was heard in that He feared." —" He was *heard*." All His supplications were ultimately answered. The sum of all He asked was support under, and ultimate deliverance from them. And both were granted Him. Even the prayer, " Let this cup pass from Me,"—which many, supposing it to refer to *death*, have represented as rising unheeded and unheard,—received an answer. *This cup* seems to refer to that intense mental agony which He then felt, and which threatened to dissolve the connection between soul and body. That cup passed from Him, inasmuch as " an angel was sent to strengthen Him,"—and He regained composure to act with propriety before His judges, and to suffer what He had yet to endure before He reached the cross. The whole history of our Lord's humbled life may be given in the words of the Psalmist: " This poor man cried, and the Lord heard him, and saved him from all his troubles." His prayers for support and deliverance from particular evils were heard, even " in the days of His flesh;" and all His prayers fully answered when God brought Him from

[1] John xii. 27, 28; Matt. xxvi. 36, 39, 42; Luke xxii. 44; Ps. lxix. 13–18, xvi. 7–11.

the dust of death, and "crowned Him with glory and honour." Then the "Man of Sorrows," according to the ancient prophetic oracle, exclaimed, "Thou hast heard Me."[1]

"He was heard *in that He feared.*" The last clause, *in that He feared*, has occasioned much trouble to expositors. Some have rendered it, 'He was heard on account of His pious reverence to God.' This is a truth, but I do not think either the original words or the connection will allow us to consider it as the truth taught here.[2] Some, considering the expression *heard* as equivalent to 'deliver,'[3] would render it, 'and was delivered from that which He feared,' *i.e.*, from all the evils to which He was exposed, and which were to Him as a human being, who from his very constitution dislikes suffering, objects of fear and aversion. Others, with our translators, consider the words as meaning, 'and was heard in reference to what He feared.' This appears to me, upon the whole, the simplest and best way of explaining the phrase.[4] He obtained the answer of His prayers and supplications in reference to those events which were the object of fear to Him,—fear here being put for the object of fear.

All suffering is, from the very constitution of a human being, the object of aversion and fear; and our Saviour had all the innocent feelings of humanity. A good man once said, "I am not afraid of death, but I am afraid of dying." Our Saviour was not afraid of sinking under His sufferings, however severe, because God had promised to support Him under them; but these sufferings were in themselves objects of aversion, dislike, and terror; and God, in answer to His prayers, not only supported Him under them, but ultimately completely delivered Him from them.

This, then, is the first part of the Apostle's statement as to Jesus Christ, "the High Priest of our profession," having successfully discharged the functions of His office: 'In the days of His humbled state, He became experimentally acquainted, by the sufferings He endured, with the obedience required by His office; and, while acquiring this painful but necessary experi-

---

[1] Ps. xxii. 23, 24.

[2] In this case the inspired writer would have said: $\delta\iota\grave{\alpha}$ $\tau\grave{\eta}\nu$ $\epsilon\grave{\upsilon}\lambda\acute{\alpha}\beta\epsilon\iota\alpha\nu$.

[3] *Vide* Job xxxv. 12 LXX.; Ps. cxviii. 5, xxii. 22.

[4] $\mathring{\alpha}\pi\acute{o}$, like the Heb. ב, is used like $\pi\epsilon\rho\acute{\iota}$ = *quod attinet ad*, in reference to: Acts xvii. 2.

mental knowledge, the intensity of His sufferings and the holiness of His character were manifested in His habitual, earnest supplications—which supplications were heard and answered.' The second part of the statement is :

'Having thus been made perfect through such intense, obediential, pious suffering—having thus obtained all the merit, all the power and authority, all the sympathy, which are necessary to the discharge of the high functions of Saviour,—" He is become the Author of eternal salvation to all who obey Him."'

This is the second statement which the Apostle makes in illustration of the principle, that our Lord has proved Himself qualified for the office to which He has been divinely appointed by a successful discharge of its functions. The subsidiary clause, *being made perfect*, connects this second statement with the first; showing how our Lord's "learning obedience by the things which He suffered in the days of His flesh"—His humbled state —led to His being now, in His exalted state, "the Author of salvation to all who obey Him."

I had occasion, at considerable length, when explaining the 10th verse of the second chapter of this Epistle—"It became Him, for whom are all things, and by whom are all things, in bringing many sons unto glory, to make the Captain of their salvation perfect through sufferings,"—to illustrate the meaning of the phrase, *to be made perfect*, as applied to our Lord. I endeavoured to show that it refers to official qualification, and that the meaning of that sublime statement is, 'Our Lord's attainment of all the qualifications of a completely accomplished Saviour—merit, legitimate power, and sympathy, by means of suffering—is a divine appointment which admirably harmonizes with the character of God as the Moral Governor of the world, whose glory is the end, and whose will is the law, of the universe.' Here the phrase occurs with precisely the same meaning. "Being made perfect" is just equivalent to—'having thus obtained every necessary qualification for actually saving man; having, by becoming experimentally acquainted with obedience by sufferings—sufferings inconceivably severe, and endured in a spirit of the most enlightened and affectionate devotion—so "magnified and made honourable" the divine law as to make it safe, and wise, and just in the supreme Moral Governor to pardon sin and save the sinner, from regard to this "obedience to the death;" having obtained, as the reward of this obedience, "power over all flesh"—"all power in heaven and in earth"—"to give eternal life to as many as the Father has given Him;" and having also by this obedience and these sufferings become capable both physically and morally—having obtained both the power and the disposition—to sympathise with those whom He is appointed to save, in all their anxieties, and fears, and afflictions.' Being thus by His obediential sufferings completely qualified as a Saviour, "He has become the Author of eternal salvation to all who obey Him."

To be "the Author of salvation," is, in the fullest extent of the word, to be the Saviour.[1] "Being" thus "made perfect"—having thus obtained all necessary merit, power, and sympathy—He is at once the procurer and the bestower of salvation. He has done everything that is necessary to make the salvation of His people consistent with, and illustrative of, the perfections of the divine character and the principles of the divine government; and He actually does save His people from guilt, depravity, and misery—He actually makes them really holy and happy here, and will certainly make them perfectly holy and happy hereafter.

The epithet *eternal* is here emphatic. The Jewish high priest, when he had performed his functions in behalf of his countrymen in the due order,—when, accomplished for his work, his hands filled with the blood of the finished sacrifice and with the sacred incense, he entered into " the holy place made with hands,"—obtained for them *a salvation*, a deliverance from the evils to which their sins would have exposed them according to the principles of that peculiar economy under which they were placed. But that deliverance, as it was inferior in nature to the deliverance accomplished by our High Priest, so it was temporary in its duration. The Jewish atonement could not remove moral guilt, and therefore could not secure permanent salvation. But Jesus Christ is become the Author of an eternal deliverance, a complete and ever-enduring salvation from evil, in all its forms and all its decrees. " The gift of God through Jesus Christ is eternal life."

Of this eternal salvation He is the Author *to all who obey Him*. Obedience necessarily presupposes a revelation of the will of the person to be obeyed. I cannot obey Christ unless I

---

[1] "Non *doctor* tantum, sed *dator*, imo *causa*, *effector* salutis, in quo ratio insit, cur æternum servemur."

know what is the will of Christ. It not merely presupposes a revelation of the will of Christ, but also a belief of that revelation. Without faith there can, in the very nature of the thing, be no acceptable obedience; and where the revelation of the will of Christ is really understood and believed, obedience to that will is the natural and uniform consequence. He obeys Christ, then, who, crediting God's testimony concerning His Son, submits to be saved by Him in the way of His appointment; and, trusting to Him as the only "Author of eternal salvation," acknowledges Him as his Lord and Master, and pays a conscientious regard to "all things whatsoever He has commanded him."

To "all" persons of this description, and to persons of this description alone, will Jesus Christ ultimately be "the Author of eternal salvation." *All*, whether Jew or Gentile, "who obey Him" shall be saved by Him. *None* who do not obey Him shall be saved by Him. There is, there can be, no salvation through Christ to men living and dying in unbelief, impenitence, and disobedience.

Those persons miserably misunderstand and abuse this passage who consider it as forbidding the greatest sinner, believing the truth, immediately to hope for eternal salvation through Christ, and as making our sincere but imperfect obedience to the will of Christ the ground of our expectation of eternal life through Him. It merely characterizes the persons who are saved by Christ Jesus, and teaches us that it is only in *obeying* Him, in believing the truth about Him, and in living under its influence, that we can enjoy that eternal salvation which He died to procure, and is exalted to bestow.

The three verses (4-6) which formed the subject of the immediately preceding exposition are devoted to the statement of the argument for the priesthood of Christ from His being legitimately invested with that office:—No man can lawfully bear the character of a high priest, unless he has been divinely called;—now, on the supposition that Jesus is the Messiah, there can be no doubt entertained of His priestly character; for Jehovah, who in one ancient oracle acknowledges the Messiah as His Son, in another declares, with the solemnity of an oath, that He is "a priest for ever, after the order of Melchisedec." This is most satisfactory evidence of the *reality* of our Lord's high-priesthood; but in the manner in which it is brought forward, much illustration is also afforded of its *excellence*. There is proof not merely that in Christ Jesus we have a High Priest, but a *great* High Priest; inasmuch as our High Priest, previously to His investiture with that character, was not a mere man, but the Son of God; inasmuch as He is a Priest of a higher order than that of Aaron—even that of Melchisedec; inasmuch as He is invested, not with a temporary, but with a perpetual priesthood; and inasmuch as His investiture was signalized by the peculiar solemnity of a divine oath.

The Apostle, accordingly, now proceeds to speak of the superiority of Christ's high-priesthood, as implied in the order, after which He is called.

§ 5. *The Superiority of our Lord's High-Priesthood proved from His being "called of God a High Priest, after the order of Melchisedec."*

(1.) *General Statement.*

Jesus Christ, our High Priest, having "learned obedience by the things He has suffered," and being thus perfectly accomplished, is become "the Author of eternal salvation to all who obey Him;" and of this we have evidence in the 110th Psalm, which proves that He had been divinely invested with the priestly office. Ver. 10. "Called of God a High Priest, after the order of Melchisedec."[1]

These words were formerly quoted to prove that Jesus, being the Messiah, is really a Priest: the argument then rested on these words—"The Lord said to Messiah, Thou art a Priest." Here they are plainly introduced as containing evidence of His being such a Priest as the inspired writer had represented Him —a perfected Priest, a Priest the Author of eternal salvation; and the argument now rests on His being pronounced "a Priest after the order of Melchisedec."

The word rendered *called*, here, is not the same as that employed in the 4th verse. *Called of God* in the 4th verse means, appointed by God; *called of God* here signifies, addressed by God under this appellation.

---

[1] These words seem introduced abruptly, but they are closely connected with what goes before: "He is the Author of *eternal* salvation ;" and, "for God has pronounced Him an *everlasting priest*," which is = "able to save εἰς τὸ παντελές."

The question of principal importance here is, What is meant by "a Priest after the order of Melchisedec?" To answer this question, it is necessary to reply to the previous one, Who was Melchisedec? We know no more of him than what is contained in a fragment of ancient history in the 14th chapter of Genesis: "And Melchizedek king of Salem brought forth bread and wine: and he was the priest of the Most High God. And he blessed him, and said, Blessed be Abram of the Most High God, possessor of heaven and earth: and blessed be the Most High God, which hath delivered thine enemies into thy hand. And he gave him tithes of all."[1] Some interpreters have supposed that Melchisedec was but another name for *Shem* the son of Noah; while others have strangely held that he was the Son of God. All that the sacred history informs us respecting him is, that he was "the king of Salem," and "the priest of the Most High God."

"A Priest after the order of Melchisedec" has been by many supposed just equivalent to—'a priest like Melchisedec, after the similitude of Melchisedec.' We rather think there is more implied in the phrase than this. Melchisedec was a priest under the primitive or patriarchal dispensation, which was not limited like the Jewish economy, but of a universal character. He was a priest, not of the law, but of the promise. He offered up sacrifices, not for men as members of a particular family, but as partakers of human nature; not as descendants of Abraham, but descendants of Adam. The first religious dispensation was of the most liberal kind; and the Apostle Paul plainly teaches us, that the Christian dispensation is but the full expansion or development of the original economy. The restrictive economy of the law, to which the Aaronical priesthood belonged, "was added because of transgressions," till the Seed should come in reference to whom the promise was made. Melchisedec belonged to an order of priests not fettered by the Mosaic ordinances—an order of priests who were attached to an economy in which there was "neither Jew nor Gentile."

I am the more disposed to take this view of the subject, from noticing that the Apostle Paul in the Epistle to the Galatians[2] calls what we render "Jerusalem above,"—but which, contrasted

[1] Gen. xiv. 18–20.
[2] Gal. iv. 26. See Exposition of the Epistle to the Galatians.

as it is with "Jerusalem that now is," ought probably to have been translated, as the words admit, "the ancient Jerusalem,"—"the mother of us all." Salem, of which Melchisedec was king, was probably the same city afterwards called Jerusalem. We know that Salem was one of the names of that city: Ps. lxxvi. 2. I think it probable that the name Zedek also was anciently given to Jerusalem. I find the king of Jerusalem in Joshua called Adonizedek, or the lord of Zedek; just as the king of Bezek is called Adonibezek, or the lord of Bezek. Melchisedec may be rendered 'king of Zedek,' as well as 'king of righteousness,' which the word Zedek signifies. And it is not improbable that the prophet Isaiah refers to these circumstances, Isa. i. 21–26.[1] Jerusalem, under Melchisedec, was a seat of the primitive religion; and ancient Jerusalem might then, with equal propriety, in the allegory be made the emblem of the spiritual Church under the promise, as Jerusalem which then was is made the emblem of the external Church under the law. I am far from bringing forward these statements as undoubtedly certain, but they appear to me probable; and they certainly afford a more distinct, palpable meaning to the phrase, *a priest after the order of Melchisedec,* than can be given on any other hypothesis. When it is said of Christ that He is "a priest after the order of Melchisedec," according to this view the statement is equivalent to—'He belongs to a more ancient and honourable order of priests than that of Aaron; His priesthood has a reference not to a particular nation, but to the race of man, without reference to such distinction as Jew or Gentile.'[2]

It would not be right in us to enter further here into an account of Melchisedec and his priesthood, nor to proceed to show how Christ's belonging to this order proves the superior grandeur of His priesthood to that of the order of Aaron, as the Apostle defers the prosecution of this subject till the commencement of the 7th chapter. The passage seems quoted to serve this purpose among others—to meet the objection which was so likely to rise in the mind of a Jew, 'How can Jesus be a High Priest? He is no descendant of Aaron; He is not even of the

---

[1] *Vide* Vitringa.

[2] Perhaps "the order of Melchisedec" may mean that order of priesthood which has royalty connected with it. Jesus is, like Melchisedec, a "priest on His throne."

tribe of Levi.' 'Doubtless,' as if the Apostle had said, 'He is not; but what then? He belongs to a higher order of priesthood: solemnly addressed by His Father as a High Priest after the order of Melchisedec.'

### (2.) *Cautionary Digression.*

On quoting this passage, that train of thought, so admirably fitted for showing the superiority of Jesus Christ to the Levitical high priests, which he follows out in the 7th chapter, seems to have opened on the Apostle's mind; but he is checked by the fear that, owing to their deficiency in habits of attention, and in distinct knowledge of Christian truth, he would find it difficult, if not impossible, to make his readers apprehend the force of his arguments and the appositeness of his illustrations; and therefore he goes into a digression, in which he reproves them for their ignorance and slothfulness, with the intention of stirring them up to a more diligent attention to what he had to bring forward on this interesting subject. Ver. 11. "*Of whom*," or of which—*i.e.*, of Melchisedec, or of his priesthood—"we have many things to say, and hard to be uttered," or rather, of difficult explanation, "seeing ye are dull of hearing."

The connecting phrase may be rendered, either 'concerning whom,' *i.e.*, Melchisedec; or, 'concerning which,' *i.e.*, the priesthood of Christ "according to the order of Melchisedec." It matters not in which of these ways it be rendered. Of Melchisedec the Apostle had "many things to say." He perceived that this ancient oracle might be turned to great account in a variety of ways in illustrating the pre-eminent glory of Christ's high-priesthood; but he, as it were, hesitates as to entering on the subject, for it was "hard to be uttered," or rather, it was of difficult explanation.[1]

A subject may be difficult of explanation from a variety of causes. It may be so in consequence of the nature of the subject. The eternity of God—His unbeginning, unsuccessive existence—and the existence of unity and plurality in His nature, are difficult of explanation from this cause. It may be so from the limited extent of the revelation. The way of salvation through the Messiah was difficult of explanation in this way,

---

[1] λόγος δυσερμήνευτος.

till "the mystery which was kept secret from former ages was made manifest." It may be so from the ignorance or unskilfulness of him who attempts to explain it. An ignorant man would find the motions of the heavenly bodies difficult of explanation. It may be so from the want of the necessary information, or the want of the necessary capacity, on the part of the persons to whom the explanation is to be made. It is impossible to explain the principles of the higher astronomy to a man ignorant of mathematics: it is impossible to explain anything that requires close connected thought to a person whose mind has never been at all disciplined to thinking.

It is not difficult to determine in what sense the doctrine of the resemblance of our Lord's high-priesthood to that of Melchisedec is here represented as "hard of explanation." The statement, that Jesus Christ, the incarnate Son of God, is a high priest "after the order of Melchisedec," is a plain proposition, easily enough understood in itself, and very distinctly stated in the Old Testament Scriptures; and there is nothing peculiarly difficult in the subject itself. The Apostle was fully enlightened in this particular department of Christian doctrine, as in all other, and was completely qualified for stating the truth on this subject in the way best fitted for the edification of the Church. The difficulty of interpretation here referred to arose entirely out of the state of the minds of the persons to whom the explanation was to be given. They were deficient both in the habit of attention and in the degree of information which were requisite to the ready and distinct apprehension of the truth on this subject, when stated to them. The truth about Christ's being "a Priest after the order of Melchisedec," and the evidence it involves of the dignity and excellence of His priesthood, were difficult of explanation to the Hebrew Christians, because "*they were*," or rather, had become, "*dull of hearing.*"

I need scarcely say, that to be slow or "dull of hearing" is not here descriptive of that defect in the external organ of hearing which is termed deafness, but is expressive of a mental deficiency which bears some analogy to it. It is common in all languages thus to describe mental habits in terms properly expressive of the exercise of the external senses. Thus we call a man of distinct perceptions clear-sighted; a man of uncommon sagacity and acuteness, far-sighted; a man of confused and limited thought, short- or dim-sighted. To be "dull of hearing" is descriptive of that state of mind in which statements may be made without producing any adequate corresponding impression —without being attended to—without being understood—without being felt. In one word, it is descriptive of mental listlessness. To a person in this state it is very difficult to explain anything; for nothing, however simple in itself, can be understood if it is not attended to.

Such was the state of mind in which many of the Hebrew Christians were; and, what made it the more melancholy, they had once discovered a better state of mind. The words, "ye are dull of hearing," properly signify, 'ye are become dull of hearing;' and that this is their meaning, is plain from the language of the following verse: "Ye have need that one teach you again which be the first principles of the oracles of God;" ye "are become such as have need of milk, and not of strong meat." When the Gospel was first preached to them, it aroused their attention—it exercised their thoughts; but now with many of them it had become a common thing. They flattered themselves that they knew all about it. It had become to them like a sound to which the ear has long been accustomed,—the person is not conscious of it—pays no attention to it.

I am afraid this is a very common habit among hearers of the Gospel in the present age. They have been accustomed to hear the Gospel from their infancy; they fancy they know and understand it perfectly; and under this impression, if they continue to read the Scriptures or hear the Gospel, it is almost entirely without anything that can be called intellectual effort. They indolently assent to what their teacher states, but they do so in a way which makes it plain they do not understand it— they are not interested in it.

The necessary consequence of the prevalence of this habit is strikingly described by the Apostle in the following verse. Ver. 12. "For when for the time ye ought to be teachers, ye have need that one teach you *again* which be the first principles of the oracles of God; and are become such as have need of milk, and not of strong meat."

The habit of spiritual dulness of hearing not only prevents progress, but it absolutely produces retrogression. The man not only does not improve, but he "loses the things which had been already wrought in him." Instead of the obscure becoming clear, the clear becomes obscure. As the Apostle Peter (2 Ep. i. 9) says, they become "blind, and cannot see afar off,"[1] either backward, or forward, or upward. The Hebrews had been for a long time favoured with the Gospel. To them it was first published, and of them were the first Christian churches formed. They had, some of them, heard Christ Himself preach the Gospel: they had enjoyed the ministry of the Apostles. Their previous knowledge of the Old Testament revelation afforded them great facilities for obtaining accurate and extended views of Christian truth.

I do not know but the expression, *for the time*,[2] may refer, not only to the length of the period they had enjoyed these privileges, but also to the peculiar character of that period. It was a time of a very remarkable character: on earth, distress of nations, with perplexity,—wars, "rumours of wars,"—"men's hearts failing them for fear," and for looking for the things which were coming upon the earth. It was a season peculiarly fitted for raising to serious thought, and for inducing those who had embraced the Gospel to give themselves up to a devout study of its principles, and a diligent practice of its duties.

Looking altogether at their privileges, the Apostle states that they ought to have been "teachers of others." Had they availed themselves of the advantages they possessed, they might have been capable of instructing others in Christianity; and, acting on the principle that we are to "do good to all as we have opportunity," they ought to have been engaged in communicating this most precious benefit to their ignorant brethren. But instead of this, "they had need that some one teach them what were the first principles of the oracles of God."

The *oracles of God* is a phrase here plainly descriptive of the same thing as *the doctrine of Christ*. It refers to the inspired Scriptures, of which Christ is at once the great Author and Subject. The word *oracle*, in the singular, signifies the place where God revealed His will in a supernatural way to the high priest, when he consulted Him by the Urim and Thummim:

---

[1] τυφλός ἐστι, μυωπάζων.

[2] διὰ τὸν χρόνον has been explained '*after* so long a time,' Matt. xxvi. 61; Mark xiv. 58, ii. 1; Acts xxiv. 17; Gal. ii. 1. The true meaning is, '*on account of* the time.'

1 Kings vi. 19; Ps. xxviii. 2. In the plural, it signifies the revelations supernaturally made, whether in that or in any other way, and recorded in the Holy Scriptures: Acts vii. 38; Rom. iii. 2.

*The first principles* of these oracles—literally, ''the elements of the beginning of the oracles of God'—are what may be called the rudiments of Christianity,—such principles, without the knowledge and belief of which a man cannot be a Christian. The word translated "principles" is descriptive of elementary rudiments.[1] The alphabet, for example, contains the principles of reading. The principles referred to by the Apostle bear the same relation to a full knowledge of Christian truth as the alphabet does to a complete acquaintance with the art of reading. He refers plainly to such principles as the spirituality of the religion of Christ, the guilt and depravity of man, pardon through the atonement, sanctification by the Spirit; or, to use his own selection, "repentance from dead works," "faith towards God," "the resurrection of the dead," "eternal judgment." So listless had they become, that their apprehension even of such truths as these had become dim, and their faith wavering. They needed as it were to be sent back to the first form in the school of Christ, like children who once had made some progress towards learning to read, but who, through thoughtlessness, have almost forgot their alphabet.

To explain to such persons some of the higher principles of Christianity—to make them acquainted not merely with the facts, but with the connections and dependences of these facts—to unfold to them the philosophy of Christianity, if I may use the expression—to point out to them its harmony and grandeur as one great connected system,—is nearly as impracticable as to instruct in the abstrusest principles of abstract science those who have never studied its elements.

The Apostle further describes the state of inaptitude for receiving instruction on the higher principles of Christianity, into which the Christian Hebrews had brought themselves by their indolence, by comparing them to children who require milk for their food, and contrasting them with full-grown men who can digest a more substantial kind of nourishment. This he does in the close of ver. 12, and the two following verses: "Ye are

---

[1] $\sigma\tau o\iota\chi\epsilon\tilde{\iota}\alpha\ \tau\tilde{\eta}\varsigma\ \dot{\alpha}\rho\chi\tilde{\eta}\varsigma = \tau\dot{\alpha}\ \pi\rho\tilde{\omega}\tau\alpha\ \sigma\tau o\iota\chi\epsilon\tilde{\iota}\alpha$,—what Horace and Quintilian term *prima elementa*. HOR. Sat. i. 1, v. 26. QUINT. Inst. i. 1.

become such as have need of milk, and not of strong meat. 13. For every one that useth milk is unskilful in the word of righteousness; for he is a babe. 14. But strong meat belongeth to them that are of full age, even those who by reason of use have their senses exercised to discern both good and evil."

It seems common in all languages to compare instruction to nourishment.[1] Truth is to the mind what food is to the body; and as the body, in different states, requires different kinds of nourishment, so the mind, according to its capacities and attainments, requires different modes of instruction. This is the principle which lies at the foundation of the figurative illustration contained in these words.

Milk, as the appropriate food of babes and sickly persons, is a fit emblem of elementary instruction, suited to imbecile minds and limited acquirements. "Milk" here means the same thing as "first principles of the oracles of God"—the principles of Christ. "Strong meat," the food of fully grown and healthy men, is a fit emblem of a higher kind of instruction, suited to persons of well-informed and well-disciplined minds. Milk and meat are used in the same sense as in the passage before us, when the Apostle says to the Corinthian believers, "And I, brethren, could not speak unto you as spiritual, but as unto carnal, even as unto babes in Christ. I have fed you with milk, and not with meat: for hitherto ye were not able to bear it, neither yet now are ye able."[2] In another place, milk is used to signify Christian truth generally, as the appropriate food of the new-born soul: "Wherefore, laying aside all malice, and all guile, and hypocrisies, and envies, and all evil-speakings, as new-born babes, desire the sincere milk of the word, that ye may grow thereby."[3]

---

[1] Philo, de Decal. p. 745, calls the divine laws τροφὰς διανοίας.—Ψωμιεῖ αὐτὸν (σοφία) ἄρτον συνέσεως, καὶ ὕδωρ σοφίας ποτίσει αὐτόν, Ecclus. xv. 3.— Οἱ ἐσθίοντές με (σοφίαν) ἔτι πεινάσουσι, καὶ οἱ πίνοντές με ἔτι διψήσουσι: Prov. x. 11; Ez. ii. 8; John iv. 10, vii. 38; 1 Pet. ii. 2; Rev. x. 8. A passage of Cicero is remarkable, from the similarity of the sentiment to that contained in the words before us : " As a child cannot cope with solid strong meat, by reason of the tenderness of its stomach, but is fed with soft liquid milk until its strength is established and it can take something stronger, so he who cannot yet receive divine witness should be offered the witness of men, i.e. of philosophers and historians, so that he may ideally be refuted by the very authors whom he claims as his."—Cic. de fin. v. 4, 6.

[2] 1 Cor. iii. 1, 2.     [3] 1 Pet. ii. 1, 2.

When the Apostle says, "Ye have need of milk, and not of strong meat," he does not mean to deny that it was a matter of great importance that they should be instructed in the higher principles of Christianity, but merely to state that an elementary course of instruction better suited their present state of spiritual imbecility. Every Christian has need both of milk and strong meat, in order to his "coming to the measure of the stature of a perfect man;" but some have more need of the one, and others more need of the other.

It deserves especial notice, that the Apostle does not say, "Ye have need;" but, "Ye are become such as have need." They were once in more favourable circumstances for spiritual instruction. They had, by their indolent neglect of the proper nourishment of the mind, spoiled their spiritual appetite and power of digestion, bringing themselves back as it were to a state of second childhood. They had forgotten what they had learned,—they had lost in a good measure the habits they had acquired.

The words which follow in the 13th and 14th verses seem to me to be just as it were two explanatory notes—the one referring to the phrase, "milk," and the other to "strong meat." "For" is plainly merely connective. It is just as if he had said, 'By a person who uses or who stands in need of milk, I mean a person who is unskilful in the word of righteousness; for such a one is indeed spiritually a child.' 'He that uses milk,' does not describe the person who relishes the elementary principles of Christianity, but the person who can relish and digest nothing else. A healthy man may be fond of milk, but he will require something besides. It were a sign, in ordinary circumstances, of something wrong about his constitution if he could relish and digest nothing else. He who uses milk, is just equivalent to—he who lives on milk, who confines his attention to elements, and seems incapable of comprehending anything but elements.[1]

That person is one unskilful in *the word of righteousness*. In interpreting Scripture, it is of much importance to distinguish

---

[1] The Jewish Rabbins were in the habit of calling their catechumens Tinokoth, 'sucking children.' Philo, speaking of the same class of persons as the Apostle, says, ἀχρί τίνος ἡμεῖς οἱ γέροντες ἔτι παιδές ἐσμεν; τὰ μὲν σώματα χρόνου μήκει πολιοί, τὰς δὲ ψυχὰς ὑπ' ἀναισθησίας κομιδῇ νήπιοι,— "How long shall we old men yet be children? In body, hoary through age; but in mind, for unskilfulness, still infants."

between the *meaning* of a word or phrase and its *reference*. For example, the appellations "Messiah," "Son of God," "Saviour of the world," "Brightness of the Father's glory," have all the same reference, but they have by no means all the same meaning. In the same way, in the passage before us, "the oracles of God," "the doctrine of Christ," and "the word of righteousness," have all the same reference—they all refer to the revealed will of God about man's salvation through Christ Jesus,—but they have all of them different meanings. They hold up the same thing, each of them in a different aspect; they communicate, each of them different information on the same subject.

In many cases, the reference is plain where the meaning is obscure; and sometimes the reverse holds. In the first chapter of John, for example, the meaning of the appellation, *the Word*, is somewhat obscure, but its reference is quite plain. Whatever that term means, it is an appellation of Jesus Christ. In such cases the general meaning of a passage may be understood satisfactorily, while the particular import of a word or phrase is doubtful, or even altogether unknown.

In the case before us, the reference of the phrase, "the word of righteousness," is perfectly evident, but its precise meaning is somewhat obscure. To the question, 'What does the phrase refer to?' we can answer readily, 'To the revelation of the divine will respecting man's salvation through Christ;' but it is not quite so easy to reply to the question, 'Why is this revelation termed "the word of righteousness?" What truth about this revelation is intended to be conveyed to our minds by this appellation?'

Had I met with the phrase in the Epistle to the Romans or to the Galatians, I should have scarcely hesitated to have said, that as the word "righteousness" in both these Epistles is used with an almost uniform reference to justification, the meaning of the phrase was, 'the word or doctrine of justification'—that it is an expression of the same kind as "the word of faith" in the 10th chapter of the Romans, ver. 8; and that the divine revelation receives this appellation, because "the righteousness of God"—the divine method of justification—is manifested in the Gospel, and "witnessed by the law and the prophets:" the great subject of divine revelation is the divine method of justifying sinners.

At the same time, as the doctrine of justification is not directly discussed in this Epistle, and as I am not aware that the term occurs anywhere in its course in the sense just noticed, I am rather inclined to think that the phrase, "word of righteousness," is a description of the Gospel, to be interpreted on the same principle as that nearly synonymous appellation, "the word of truth, the Gospel of our salvation"—*i.e.*, 'the true word' by a Hebraism. In Hebrew, truth and righteousness are words often employed as synonymous. "The word of righteousness" is then here, we apprehend, equivalent to—'the righteous, the true word.' The epithet is intended to express the excellence of the Gospel revelation as the very "truth most sure."[1]

He, then, who cannot be made to attend to anything but elementary principles, is a person unskilled in this true and righteous word; he is unpractised in its study, and therefore very imperfectly acquainted with its meaning,—*for he is a babe.* To be a babe, is sometimes expressive of simplicity—freedom from guile, teachableness; as when our Lord says, "Except ye become as little children, ye can in nowise enter into the kingdom of God;" and when the Apostle Peter says, "As new-born babes, desire the sincere milk of the word, that ye may grow thereby;" and the Apostle Paul, "In malice be ye children." Here, plainly, it is equivalent to—'weak and ignorant.'

The 14th verse contains the Apostle's explication of what he means by "strong meat," and those who are capable of using it. "Strong meat," as opposed to "milk," is the proper food of men as opposed to children. The phrase translated, "them that are of full age," is, literally, *the perfect.*[2] I notice this, because without noticing it the connection with what follows cannot be so distinctly perceived—"let us go on to perfection." "The perfect" is plainly the mature—the man in age and in strength. "Strong meat" is the appropriate food of *men.*

The adage is true literally and figuratively. "Strong meat" is descriptive of those illustrations and arguments which refer to the connections and dependences of the various parts of the grand scheme of restoration, such as those that follow respecting the superiority of our Lord's high-priesthood to that of the family of Aaron. To enter into such discussions requires an extent of information, and a discipline of mind, which can be ob-

---

[1] It seems a phrase of the same kind as ὅπλα δικαιοσύνης, καρποὶ δικαιοσύνης, ἥλιος δικαιοσύνης.

[2] τελείων.

tained only by a diligent study of divine truth, and which mark maturity of spiritual understanding.

The spiritually mature man, who is fit for "strong meat," is the man "who by reason of use has his senses exercised to discern between good and evil." A child is easily imposed on as to food. Its nurse may easily induce it to swallow even palatable poison. But a man, "by reason of use," has learned so to employ his senses as to distinguish between what is deleterious and what is nourishing. The spiritually mature man is a person who, by the use of his faculties, under the influence of the Divine Spirit, in the study of divine truth, can examine doctrines, make a distinction between the things that differ, "refuse the evil and choose the good;" and from this habit thus acquired he is qualified for entering, with pleasure and advantage to himself, on the study of every part of the Christian economy.[1]

A careless reader of the Epistle to the Hebrews, as it stands in our version, would be very apt to conclude that one of the leading divisions of the Epistle commences here: that the former part of the Epistle has been devoted to "the first principles" of Christianity, and that the Apostle is now proceeding to the more recondite and complicated doctrines of that religion. No conclusion could be more wide of the truth. These words do not commence a new section. They occur in the midst of a digression, into which the inspired writer was naturally led when entering on the discussion of this principle—'Jesus Christ is superior to the Aaronical high-priesthood.'

In proving the reality of the priesthood of Jesus Christ, he quotes a passage from the 110th Psalm—a Psalm admitted by the Hebrews to be prophetic of the Messiah—in which Jehovah is represented as addressing the Messiah in these words, sanctioned by the solemnity of a divine oath: "Thou art a Priest for ever, after the order of Melchisedec." The heaven-enlightened mind of the inspired writer clearly perceived that this passage not merely proved that Jesus Christ was a High Priest, but a great High Priest; that it afforded evidence not merely of the reality, but of the pre-eminence of His high-priesthood.

But he is checked in his course; he is prevented from immediately following the impulse of his mind, to enter on this wide

---

[1] Διάκρισιν καλοῦ καὶ κακοῦ is borrowed from the Hebrew יָדַע טוֹב וָרָע —Gen. ii. 17; Deut. i. 39; Isa. vii. 15, 16; Jonah iv. 11.

and fair field of argument and illustration which opened before him, by the recollection that many of those to whom he was writing were, from their very limited knowledge, and from their habits of inattention, but ill qualified for accompanying him. 'I have many things,' says he, ' to say of Melchisedec and his priesthood, illustrative of the pre-eminent glories of the High Priest of our profession; but I feel it difficult to bring them before your minds in a way which would secure your attending to them and understanding them, for ye have become very inapt to receive spiritual instruction. Though enjoying advantages which, if rightly improved, would have fitted you to instruct others in Christianity, you have lost in a great measure the knowledge you once possessed, and stand in need of being yourselves instructed a second time in the very elementary principles of our divine religion.' He illustrates this statement by comparing them to " babes," who are capable of digesting nothing but " milk," as contrasted with men of " mature age," who require for their nourishment " strong meat;"—and he explains the force of this figurative illustration by remarking, that by the spiritual "babe," who can digest nothing but " milk," he means the person who is but imperfectly acquainted with " the word of righteousness," and unfurnished with those habits of mind which are necessary for a thorough knowledge of it; while by the men of " mature age," who are capable of, and indeed require, a more nutritious diet, he understands those who have extensive and accurate views of divine truth, and who, from these extensive and accurate views, and from the habits of mind naturally formed in acquiring them, are able to make a distinction between what is true and false, good and evil.

The words with which the 6th chapter commences immediately follow.

Ver. 1. "Therefore, leaving the principles of the doctrine of Christ, let us go on unto perfection; not laying again the foundation of repentance from dead works, and of faith toward God, 2. Of the doctrine of baptisms, and of laying on of hands, and of resurrection of the dead, and of eternal judgment. 3. And this will we do, if God permit."

The first point which requires our attention, is the *connection* of this short paragraph, or, in other words, the force of the particle *therefore*. It has been common to consider the word as having a retrospective reference, and as intimating that this is an inference from what has been stated. But the premises stated seem to demand a different conclusion. It seems strange arguing, ' Ye have need of milk ; therefore I will not give it you. You are not capable of digesting strong food; therefore I will present you with it. You have need of some one to teach you again the first principles of the oracles of God,; therefore let us leave these first principles. You require elementary instruction; therefore let us plunge at once into the depths of the Christian mysteries.' This certainly is not the connection. Apart from the influence of inspiration altogether, it is plain that the writer of the Epistle to the Hebrews was utterly incapable of arguing thus.

This difficulty has been perceived by interpreters ; and they have adopted different methods for removing it. Some would connect this verse immediately with the 11th in the preceding chapter, thus :—' I have many things to say of Melchisedec which are difficult of explanation ; therefore let us, leaving the elements, proceed to the exposition of these things.' Others would connect it with the 14th verse, thus :—' Since solid food befits grown-up men, I will feed you with this nourishing diet.' Others would connect it with ver. 12 :—' Since ye ought, for the period ye have been under Christian instruction, to be teachers of others, it is time that, instead of milk, ye should have strong meat : setting aside that mode of instruction which we employ for the novice, we will adopt a style of teaching more befitting the adept.' None of these modes of stating the connection appears satisfactory.

I am inclined to think that the true way of getting rid of the difficulty, is to consider the word "therefore" as having, not a retrospective, but a prospective reference. The reason for the Apostle's " leaving the principles of the doctrine of Christ, and going on to perfection," is to be found, I apprehend, not in the preceding, but in the following context. The improbability, the moral impossibility, of reclaiming those of the Hebrews who, after having once been enlightened, had sunk into such a state of spiritual apathy as that described in the preceding verses, is the reason why the Apostle, instead of wasting time on them, proceeds to unfold the higher principles of Christianity to those of them who were disposed and capable of entering with advantage on their study. This view of the matter not only removes the difficulty above adverted to, but also gives a satisfactory account of the introduction of the awfully impressive paragraph that follows, and of the force of the particle *for*, by which it is prefaced. That the word *therefore* is used sometimes with a reference to what follows, is plain from the commencement of the second chapter of the Epistle to the Romans: " Therefore thou art inexcusable, O man, whosoever thou art that judgest ;" *i.e.*, not for the reason just mentioned—for no reason has been mentioned—but for the reason just about to be mentioned.

The next question that must be answered—and it, too, is of a preliminary kind—is, What is the reference of the plural pronoun *we*? The Apostle obviously uses the figure of speech which grammarians call Communicatio.[1] But whether does he identify himself with the Hebrews, and urge them in the most persuasive manner to do their duty; or does he identify the Hebrews with himself, and in the least assuming form intimate the design which he was about to prosecute? I apprehend that the latter is the true view of the expression. To "lay the foundation," is more properly descriptive of what is done by the teacher than the learner, as the Apostle plainly enough intimates, 1 Cor. iii. 10, 11. Besides, it would be difficult to show how the 3d verse could apply to the Hebrews, " And this we will do, if God permit."

The words, then, appear to be an intimation of the Apostle's determination, not to enter into a statement of first principles for the use of those who had once known them, but had now forgotten them, and become careless of them,—a statement which, in their circumstances, was likely to serve little purpose; but to proceed forward to the unfolding of those illustrations of the pre-eminence of Christ's priesthood, implied in the ancient oracle already quoted, which belonged to the higher principles of the Christian faith.

*The principles of the doctrine of Christ* have been considered by some learned and ingenious interpreters as descriptive of the *typical facts and institutions of the Jewish economy*. These they consider as " the first principles of the oracles of God"—the " milk" for " babes." This mode of interpretation is not at all satisfactory. The literal meaning of the phrase, " the principles of the doctrine of Christ," is *the word*, or *dis-*

---

[1] Κοίνωσις, or κοινοποιΐα.

*course, of the beginning of Christ;* i.e., the elementary principles of Christianity. This is certainly not a natural description of the typical events and institutions of the Old Economy. These are never represented as the *foundation* of Christianity. An account of these, certainly, was not the " milk" with which he fed the Corinthian believers; and the specimen which he gives us of what he accounts " first principles of the doctrine of Christ," in the 2d verse, is not taken from among these typical events and institutions.

" The first principles of the oracles of God," and " the principles of the doctrine of Christ," are just the elementary principles of Christianity.[1] The Apostle then intimates his intention to " leave" these[2] on the present occasion; not to enter on a statement of them to those to whom they had often been stated—and stated, as regarded many of them, to little purpose, —but " to go on to perfection."

The word " perfection" here refers to the phrase, men " of full age," in the preceding verse,—literally, ' perfect men.' *Perfection* here describes that higher species of spiritual instruction which formed the appropriate nourishment of spiritual men of full stature and mature age.

The Apostle further explains his purpose by adding, " not laying again the foundation." " The word of the beginning of Christ," or " the principles of the doctrine of Christ," are the foundation,—those principles, the knowledge and belief of which are absolutely necessary in order to a man's being a Christian. Some interpreters consider " the foundation" as something totally distinct from all the principles afterwards enumerated—something on which they all rest. But it is difficult to attach a distinct idea to " the foundation of the resurrection of the dead"—" the foundation of eternal judgment." It seems far more natural to consider the six particulars which are enumerated as specimens of these " first principles," which form, as it were, " the foundation" of Christianity, and into the statement of which it was the purpose of the Apostle not at present to enter.

The first of these fundamental principles mentioned by the

---

[1] Τὸν τῆς ἀρχῆς τοῦ Χριστοῦ λόγον = τὸν πρῶτον λόγον τοῦ Χ.—*i.e.,* περὶ τοῦ Χ., ' the elementary instruction respecting Christ.'

[2] ἀφιέναι, ' to pass over in silence.'

Apostle, is " repentance from dead works ;" *i.e.*, plainly, ' the doctrine of repentance from dead works.' He did not intend to enter on a statement of this doctrine. *Repentance*, in the New Testament, usually signifies a change of mind; and one of the primary doctrines of Christianity is, that a change—a complete change of mind, is necessary in order to a man's being a Christian. " Except a man be born again," said our Lord, " he cannot enter into the kingdom of God." " If any man be in Christ, he is a new creature." The sum of the preaching of Jesus, and of both His forerunner and His Apostles, was, " Repent"—change your minds—" and believe the Gospel." This change of mind is sometimes described as a change of mind towards God—" repentance towards God ;" *i.e.*, a change of mind leading the man, who was formerly far from God, and going farther and farther from Him, in the direction Godwards; and here it is described as a change of mind " from dead works."

The phrase, *dead works*, is a somewhat peculiar one. Some have interpreted it as equivalent to ' useless, unprofitable works,' referring to the Levitical services. They consider it as analogous to such phrases as—" without works, faith is *dead*," *i.e.*, useless ; " without law, sin is *dead*," *i.e.*, powerless. Into this mode of interpretation we might have been disposed to go, had it not been that the phrase occurs in another passage in this Epistle, where its meaning is clearly fixed to be something different from this : ch. ix. 14. " Dead works" there can signify nothing else but sins—guilty actions. If any extrinsic evidence were necessary to confirm this assertion, the parallel passage, ch. x. 22, furnishes it. " An evil conscience," is plainly a guilty conscience. Sins are called *dead works*, either because they produce death or misery, or because they are the works of men who in a spiritual sense are dead. The phrase seems the translation of a Hebraism for the *works of death*, ' works worthy of death ;' just as ' a man of death,' 1 Kings ii. 26, is ' a man worthy of death.' " Repentance from dead works," or a change of mind from sinful actions, is a change of mind leading men to abandon sinful actions. This, then, is the first of " the principles of the doctrine of Christ" that the Apostle specifies ;—the doctrine of the necessity of such a change of mind as will lead a man to turn from every wicked way. That the doctrine of repentance is a first principle of Christianity, is plain from such passages as these: "From that time Jesus began to preach, and to say, Repent: for the kingdom of heaven is at hand." "The time is fulfilled, and the kingdom of God is at hand: repent ye, and believe the Gospel." "Then Peter said unto them, Repent, and be baptized every one of you in the name of Jesus Christ for the remission of sins, and ye shall receive the gift of the Holy Ghost." "And the times of this ignorance God winked at; but now commandeth all men everywhere to repent."[1]

The second principle of the doctrine of Christ is "faith toward God."[2] The "faith" here mentioned has been variously explained; some considering it as descriptive of the belief that there is a God, or the belief that there is but one God, or the belief of the providence of God. The circumstance of its being mentioned as one of "the principles of the doctrine of Christ" should have prevented such very limited views of the subject. It is the faith of the truth about God, as that is stated in the revelation of mercy—the belief that He is "the God and the Father of our Lord Jesus Christ;" that "He so loved the world, as to give His only begotten Son" for it; that He is "in Christ reconciling the world to Himself, not imputing their trespasses unto them." It is a "first principle of the doctrine of Christ," that this faith in God is indispensably necessary to salvation. When we take this view of the subject, we cease to wonder, as some have done, that in this enumeration we do not find 'faith in Christ;' for "faith toward God," as revealed in the Gospel, and faith in Christ, are substantially the same thing. That this is an element of Christianity, is plain from the following passages: "And Jesus answering, saith unto them, Have faith in God." "Let not your heart be troubled: ye believe in God, believe also in Me." "But without faith it is impossible to please Him: for he that cometh to God must believe that He is, and that He is a rewarder of them that diligently seek Him."[3]

---

[1] Matt. iv. 17; Mark i. 15; Acts ii. 38, xvii. 30.

[2] There is no peculiar force in ἐπί. The forms of πίστις or πιστεύειν ἐπὶ Χριστὸν and Θεόν, εἰς Χριστὸν and Θεόν, ἐν Χριστῷ and Θεῷ, and even πίστις Χριστοῦ, and πιστεύειν, without a preposition, are indiscriminately employed.

[3] Mark xi. 22; John xiv. 1; Heb. xi. 6.

The next two "principles of the doctrine of Christ"—the doctrine of baptisms, and the laying on of hands"—have given occasion to a great deal of critical discussion. It is a very ingenious conjecture, that these words are not intended to express two new principles, but that they are merely explanatory of what goes before. Previously to a man's being acknowledged a Christian by baptism and the imposition of hands, he was instructed in the necessity of repentance and faith; and this instruction, it has been supposed, is here termed "the doctrine of baptisms, and the laying on of hands"—the doctrine which a man must have learned before he could be baptized, or have the hands of the Apostles laid on him. Had the phrase been 'the doctrine of baptism,' not "of baptisms," and had the whole clause occurred either at the beginning or at the end of the enumeration, and not, as it does, in the midst of it, I would have been strongly inclined to consider this as the true mode of interpretation; but, as it stands, I cannot doubt that these are intended by the Apostle as two other specimens of what he means by "principles of the doctrine of Christ;" and, therefore, all that remains for us is, to inquire into what is meant by "the doctrine of baptisms," and the doctrine of "the laying on of hands."

Those who interpret these principles of the typical events and institutions of the former economy, refer "the baptisms" to the various ceremonial washings, and "the laying on of hands" to the rite of transferring the guilt of the sinner to the victim by the imposition of the hands of the high priest on its head. Indeed, it seems to have been this phrase more than anything else which led them into that particular view of the passage. We have already stated the reasons why we cannot go into this mode of interpretation.

"The doctrine of baptisms" has by many been considered as just equivalent to—'the doctrine about Christian baptism;' and they endeavour to get over the difficulty arising out of the plural form of the word by saying, that there is a reference to the double baptism of water and of the Spirit, or to the trine immersion which in the ancient Church took place at baptism; or, that the baptism of a number of persons may properly be termed "baptisms;" or, that it is an instance of what sometimes occurs, a plural noun used to express what is in reality but *one*. All this seems to me very unsatisfactory.

"The doctrine of baptisms," which with the Hebrews was a "principle of the doctrine of Christ," was a statement of the nature and design of Christian baptism, as distinguished from the baptism of John and the ceremonial washings or baptisms under the law. Before any man was acknowledged a Christian by baptism, he was instructed in the meaning of baptism, and, if a Hebrew, in the difference between this baptism and the baptisms under the former economy.

In like manner, as the primitive Christians, after baptism, had the hands of an Apostle—frequently at least—laid on them, as an emblem of their receiving the Holy Spirit;[1] so, previously to their submitting to this rite, as in Christianity everything is "a reasonable service," they were instructed in its meaning. Some refer this to the imposition of hands in the ordination of office-bearers; but it is not likely that instruction on this subject formed a part of the rudiments of primitive Christianity.

The next fundamental principle of Christianity mentioned by the Apostle, is the "resurrection of the dead." This is a most important article of the Christian faith,—so important, that the denial of it as it were unchristianizes a man. This principle is very clearly stated by our Lord: "Marvel not at this: for the hour is coming, in the which all that are in the graves shall hear His voice, and shall come forth; they that have done good, unto the resurrection of life; and they that have done evil, unto the resurrection of damnation."[2] It formed a leading doctrine with the Apostles: "And I have hope toward God, which they themselves also allow, that there shall be a resurrection of the dead, both of the just and unjust."[3]

The last fundamental article mentioned, is the "eternal judgment." Those who seek these principles among typical events and institutions refer this to the ancient judgments inflicted on Pharaoh the Egyptian, and on the rebellious Israelites in the wilderness. It plainly refers to the general, final judgment, which Jesus Christ is appointed to pronounce and execute on all mankind: John v. 22, 27; Acts xvii. 31; 2 Cor. v. 10. This judgment is called the "eternal judgment," because its results are final: Matt. xxv. 46.

Such are some of the principles of Christianity, on the illustration of which the Apostle is not about to enter—principles

[1] Acts ii. 38, xix. 6.     [2] John v. 28, 29.     [3] Acts xxiv. 15.

which a man must know and believe in order to his being a Christian—principles which, if he have once known and seemed to believe, and afterwards silently "let slip," or openly abandon, there is very little probability, to say the least, of his ever being renewed to repentance.

Ver. 3. "And this will we do, if God permit." These words admit of a twofold interpretation :—"This we will do;" *i.e.*, 'we will not insist on these fundamental principles, but proceed to something more recondite :' "if God permit;" *i.e.*, 'depending on the assistance of God.' Or, 'Though we are to leave the principles, etc., just now, yet on another occasion I will readily enter on these subjects, on which many of you need as much instruction as if ye had never received any'—"I will do this, if God permit;" *i.e.*, 'if God spare my life, and give me an opportunity, and if your apostasy, of which I am fearful, does not unhappily make it unnecessary. I shall be glad to give you such explications; but I am afraid, in reference to some of you, they may come too late.' In either way we have a good sense, agreeable both to the use of the language and the context. I am, upon the whole, disposed to prefer the former mode of interpretation.[1]

There is a plain reference in the paragraph that follows to some of the peculiarities of the state of things which characterized the primitive age of Christianity, which forbids us to conclude that the statement it contains is in all its parts applicable to those who live after that state of things has passed away; while, at the same time, that statement, like all similar ones in the New Testament, goes upon general principles, which have a universal and perpetual application. The legitimate way of ascertaining these principles, and thus discovering "what these things are to us," is by, in the first instance, endeavouring distinctly to apprehend the meaning of the statement in reference to those to whom it was primarily applicable in all its particular details.

This passage is one which it is impossible to read without feeling that it has strong claims on our attentive consideration; and this conviction will be strengthened in no ordinary degree if we advert to the history of its interpretation. As it is certainly one of those passages in Paul's writings which are

---

[1] The words are just = 'Jam agite igitur, Deo auxiliante.' He never forgets ἡ ἱκανότης ἡμῶν ἐκ τοῦ Θεοῦ : 2 Cor. iii. 5.

somewhat "hard to be understood," so, perhaps, none of this class of passages has been more "wrested" by "the unlearned and unstable."

At a very early period of the Church, a misapprehension of the meaning of this, and a parallel passage in the tenth chapter of this Epistle, gave origin to the formation of a sect, the leading peculiarity of which was the peremptory and final exclusion from church communion of all who after baptism had fallen into open sin, especially the sin of outward compliance with idolatrous worship in time of persecution, whatever signs of penitence they might discover.

On the other hand, a similar misapprehension on the part of the Roman Church as to the meaning of these passages, led them for a considerable period to refuse to this Epistle a place among the canonical books, as teaching doctrine inconsistent with that taught in the indisputably inspired writings of the Apostles.

In later ages, it has been considered by those who deny the doctrine of the perseverance of the saints as one of the strongholds of their system; and I am afraid that the defenders of that important doctrine, in their extreme eagerness to wrest the weapon out of the hands of their adversaries, have in this, as in many similar cases, been more intent on confuting them, than on giving a fair and satisfactory view of the meaning of the inspired writer.

Misapprehension of this passage has also, I believe, in many cases occasioned extreme distress of mind to two classes of persons,—to nominal professors, who, after falling into gross sin, have been awakened to serious reflection; and to real Christians, on their falling under the power of mental disease, sinking into a state of spiritual languor, or being betrayed into such open transgressions of the divine law as David and Peter were guilty of: and this has thrown all but insurmountable obstacles in the way of both "fleeing for refuge, to lay hold on the hope set before them in the Gospel." All this makes it the more necessary that we should carefully inquire into the meaning of the passage. When rightly understood, it will be found to give no countenance to any of the false conclusions which have been drawn from it, but to be, like every other part of inspired Scripture, "profitable for doctrine, for reproof, for correction, and for instruction in righteousness,"—well fitted to produce caution, no way calculated to induce despair. Let us then proceed to examine this interesting passage somewhat more particularly.

Vers. 4–6. "For it is impossible for those who were once enlightened, and have tasted of the heavenly gift, and were made partakers of the Holy Ghost, and have tasted the good word of God, and the powers of the world to come, if they shall fall away, to renew them again unto repentance; seeing they crucify to themselves the Son of God afresh, and put Him to an open shame."

The connection of this passage, intimated by the particle "for," was illustrated, when pointing out the force of the word *therefore* in the beginning of the first verse. We considered that particle as equivalent to—' for the reason I am just about to assign;' and the words before us contain that reason,—thus: 'Instead of again laying the foundation—instead of again teaching those who have already been taught, but have forgotten what they learned—" what be the first principles of the oracles of God," I will proceed to some of the higher branches of Christian instruction; for there is little or no probability of any good result from such an attempt to re-teach those who have willingly unlearned all that has been taught them. They seem in the direct road to open apostasy; and that is a state from which I have no hope that anything I could say would reclaim them. "For it is impossible for those who were once enlightened, and have tasted of the heavenly gift, and were made partakers of the Holy Ghost, and have tasted the good word of God, and the powers of the world to come, if they shall fall away, to renew them again unto repentance; seeing they crucify to themselves the Son of God afresh, and put Him to an open shame."'[1]

A slight transposition, which the English idiom seems to demand, will make the sentence run more smoothly, and will even make it more easily understood by a mere English reader: "For it is impossible to renew again to repentance those who

---

[1] Abresch, who considers the third verse as = 'I will enter on a statement of these elements at some future period, if God permit,' states the connection thus: "If God gives an opportunity; but if general apostasy take place, such an opportunity may never be given, for," etc.

were once enlightened, and have tasted of the heavenly gift, and were made partakers of the Holy Ghost, and have tasted the good word of God, and the powers of the world to come, if they shall fall away." There are three topics brought before us for consideration : First, a description of a particular class of persons; second, a statement with regard to them; and third, a reason assigned for that statement.

The first thing to be done here is, to inquire into the meaning of the Apostle's description of the persons of whom he is here speaking. They are persons "who have been enlightened, who have tasted of the heavenly gift, who have been made partakers of the Holy Ghost, who have tasted the good word of God, and the powers of the world to come." They are persons who have enjoyed great privileges, and made considerable attainments in religion ; and they are persons who, notwithstanding this, have apostatized—"fallen away."

They had "been enlightened." It is common with some of the Fathers to call baptism illumination, and the baptized the illuminated; but there is no reason to think these modes of expression so ancient as the apostolic age. To be "enlightened," according to the ordinary meaning of this figurative expression in the New Testament, is to be instructed.[1] A person is enlightened on any subject on which he possesses information. An unenlightened man is an ignorant man; an enlightened man is a well-informed man. The phrase here plainly refers to Christianity; and to be enlightened as to Christianity is to be acquainted with its principles: 2 Cor. iv. 6. In the parallel passage, chap. x. 26, they who are here said to be enlightened, are described as having "received the knowledge of the truth." And the Apostle Peter, when describing the same class of persons, speaks of them as having "the knowledge of the Lord and Saviour Jesus Christ," and as having "known the way of righteousness" (a phrase, by the way, well fitted to illustrate the phrase, "word of righteousness," and to support the view we gave of it).[2] The persons here described, then, are persons who had been, from an acquaintance with the principles of Christianity, induced to prefer it to heathenism or to Judaism.

The second statement made in reference to them is, that

[1] Eph. i. 18, iii. 9.      [2] 2 Pet. ii. 20, 21.

they had "tasted of the heavenly gift." By "the heavenly gift," some interpreters understand Jesus Christ; others, the Holy Spirit; others, the forgiveness of sins by faith; others, the Lord's Supper. I apprehend " the heavenly gift" is equivalent to 'this heavenly gift;' and that this clause, according to the Hebrew usage, repeats—placing in a new aspect however—the idea expressed in the preceding one.[1] "The gift of God" is, I apprehend, the Gospel, or the revelation of mercy through Jesus Christ. The making this revelation is a striking manifestation of the divine sovereign benignity. This "gift" well deserves the appellation *heavenly*. The Gospel revelation is not a "cunningly devised fable," it is not a curiously constructed theory, it is not a humanly composed history—it is a divine revelation: it is, as the Apostle expresses it, "the Gospel of God."[2]

To "taste this heavenly gift," is to have experience of it. This is plainly the general idea, as appears from the following passages where the figurative term is employed:—" She perceiveth that her merchandise is good: her candle goeth not out by night." " O taste and see that the Lord is good: blessed is the man that trusteth in Him." " If so be ye have tasted that the Lord is gracious."[3] To "taste" the Gospel revelation, is to know, not merely from report but from personal experience, what the Gospel is—to understand in some measure its meaning, and in some measure, too, to enjoy those pleasurable sensations of mind which the Gospel, when understood, naturally produces. I think it likely that it was the figurative description of instruction in the preceding context, under the emblem of food, that led the inspired writer to employ the word *taste* here, and in a subsequent clause.

The following remark of Dr Owen is ingenious, and the sentiment it conveys is just and important; whether the words of the Apostle were intended to suggest the idea conveyed in it, may admit of a doubt:—"Tasting does not include eating, much less digesting and turning into nourishment what is so tasted; for its nature being only thereby discerned, it may be refused, yea, though we like its relish and savour, on some other consideration. The persons here described, then, are persons who have to a certain degree understood and relished the revelation of

---

[1] The use of the particle τὶ is favourable to this view.
[2] Rom. i. 1. [3] Prov. xxxi. 18; Ps. xxxiv. 8; 1 Pet. ii. 3.

mercy: like the stony-ground hearers, they have received the word with a transient joy."[1]

The third statement made in reference to these persons is, that they had been "made partakers of the Holy Ghost." "The Holy Ghost" is the proper name of that divine person who, along with the Father and the Son, exists in the unity of the Godhead. By an easy figure of speech, the term is often employed to signify His gifts, influences, or operation. This is its meaning in such phrases as, to be "baptized with the Holy Ghost," to be "full of the Holy Ghost." To "partake of the Holy Ghost," is to be a sharer of His gifts or influences. It is highly probable that the inspired writer refers principally to the miraculous gifts and operations of the Holy Spirit by which the primitive dispensation of Christianity was characterized. These gifts were by no means confined to those who were "transformed by the renewing of their minds." Under the former economy, we find Balaam and Saul endowed with miraculous prophetic gifts. We have no reason to doubt that Judas Iscariot, as well as the other Apostles, had the power of working miracles. The words of our Lord,—"Many will say to Me in that day, Lord, Lord, have we not prophesied in Thy name? and in Thy name cast out devils? and in Thy name done many wonderful works? And then will I profess unto them, I never knew you: depart from Me, ye that work iniquity;" and of the Apostle, "Though I speak with the tongues of men and of angels, and have not charity, I am become as sounding brass, or a tinkling cymbal. And though I have the gift of prophecy, and understand all mysteries, and all knowledge; and though I have all faith, so that I could remove mountains, and have not charity, I am nothing,"[2]—seem to intimate that the possession of these by unrenewed men was not very uncommon in that age; at any rate, they plainly show that their possession and an unregenerate state were by no means incompatible.

While, I apprehend, the reference is chiefly to miraculous gifts and operations, I dare not limit the meaning of the word so far as to exclude all reference to influences and gifts not of

---

[1] This view of the meaning of γινέσθαι, as if it were = 'to taste *labris extremis*—to have a glimpse of,' is not warranted by the Scripture use of the term. Indeed it occurs in this sense but rarely even in the classics.

[2] Matt. vii. 22, 23; 1 Cor. xiii. 1, 2.

an extraordinary and miraculous kind. I am strongly disposed, from a number of passages of Scripture, to believe that men who are never converted are yet the subjects of a divine influence, and that it is their resisting this influence which constitutes one of the greatest of their sins. The persons here described, then, were persons who not only enjoyed what has been termed the common influences of the Holy Spirit, but His miraculous gifts —who not only witnessed the effects of these gifts in others, but were partakers of them themselves.

The fourth statement made in reference to these persons is, that they had " tasted the good word of God." By the *good word of God* many interpreters understand the Gospel. There can be no doubt that the Gospel well deserves that name ; but if we explain it in this way, the two clauses, " who have tasted the heavenly gift," and "who have tasted the good word of God," would be precisely synonymous, which is not at all likely. I would understand by *the good word of God*, the promise of God respecting the Messiah, the sum and substance of all. It deserves notice that this promise is by way of eminence termed by Jeremiah "that good word."[1] To " taste," then, " this good word of God," is to experience that God has been faithful to His promise—to enjoy, so far as an unconverted man can enjoy, the blessings and advantages which flow from that promise being fulfilled. To " taste the good word of God," seems just to enjoy the advantages of the new dispensation.

This interpretation is greatly supported by the clause which follows, and which is very closely connected[2] with that which we have just been explaining—" and the powers of the world to come." " The world to come" sometimes in the New Testament refers to the future state: Eph. i. 21; Luke xviii. 30. In this Epistle, however, I apprehend it is used, according to the Jewish idiom, as a description of the age of the Messiah—the New Economy. The name " Everlasting Father," given to the Messiah by the prophet Isaiah, is translated by the LXX. " the Father of the coming age," or " of the world to come ;" and it was common among them to speak of " the present age," or

---

[1] Jer. xxxiii. 14. In Josh. xxiii. 15, הַדָּבָר הַטּוֹב, the promise, is contrasted with הַדָּבָר הָרָע, the threatening.

[2] It is connected by the particle τέ.

"the present world"—*i.e.*, the state of things under the law, and "the future age," or "the world to come"—*i.e.*, the state of things under the Messiah. We endeavoured to show that this is the meaning of the parallel phrase in chap. ii. 5.

But what are we to understand by "*the powers* of the world to come?" Many very excellent interpreters understand by "the powers of the world to come," the external miraculous gifts of the Holy Spirit which belonged to that economy. The word is no doubt used with this signification.[1] According to this mode of interpretation, to "taste the powers of the world to come," is equivalent to—'to possess the power of working miracles.' Now, though the words by themselves will admit of this interpretation—though, perhaps, viewed by themselves, it is their most natural meaning,—yet there are two things which induce me to prefer another mode of interpretation. In this way it is just a repetition of the statement, "and were made partakers of the Holy Ghost;" and from the way in which this clause is connected with that which immediately precedes it, we are led to expect that the phrase, "tasting the powers of the world to come," should be an amplification and explication of the phrase, "tasting the good word of God."

By "the powers" of the new dispensation, I would understand all those circumstances peculiar to the new dispensation which are calculated to have power over the mind and heart of man. Everything that is striking and convincing in its evidence,—everything in its statements, as to the character of God, the person and work of Christ, the solemnities of the judgment-seat, the joys and miseries of eternity, which is calculated to persuade or alarm,—everything, in a word, which, in that economy, is fitted to exercise influence over men,—all this is included in the phrase, "the powers of the world to come." The ancient economy was comparatively weak as well as unprofitable, but the new economy is powerful. It has everything that can enlighten, and convince, and persuade, and alarm, and delight. It has the means of touching every spring of action—of stirring the human mind in its deepest recesses. To "taste" these powers, is just to be subjected to their influence—to be placed in circumstances in which the wondrous spectacles of God "not

---

[1] Matt. vii. 22, 23, δυνάμεις, rendered "wonderful works;" 1 Cor. xii. 10, ἐνεργήματα δυνάμεων, the *operations of powers.*

sparing His Son, but delivering Him up" for sinners—"the only begotten" in human flesh bleeding, groaning, dying—the world dissolving—the judgment set—the ineffable glories of heaven—the smoke of the torment of the finally condemned ascending up for ever and ever, are brought before our minds.[1]

Those persons who have thus been enlightened, etc., are represented as having " fallen away :" *If they fall away.* This is scarcely a fair translation; and there is some reason to fear that it was preferred to a juster one for the purpose of affording the means of repelling the objection to the doctrine of the perseverance of the saints, which has been founded on this passage; at any rate, it has been used in this way. It has been said that the Apostle does not assert that such persons did or could " fall away;" but that, if they did—a supposition which, however, could never become realized—then the consequence would be, they could not be " renewed again unto repentance." The words, rendered literally, are, " and have fallen away," or, " yet have fallen away."[2] The Apostle obviously intimates that such persons might, and that such persons did, " fall away." By " falling away," we are plainly to understand what is commonly called apostasy. This does not consist in an occasional falling into actual sin, however gross and aggravated; nor in the renunciation of some of the principles of Christianity, even though these should be of considerable importance; but in an open, total, determined renunciation of all the constituent principles of Christianity, and a return to a false religion, such as that of unbelieving Jews or heathens, or to determined infidelity and open ungodliness. This is, I apprehend, to " fall away"—to sin wilfully after men have received the knowledge of the truth.

The Apostle's statement, then, is this, that in the primitive age there were men who at one time were possessed of a knowledge of Gospel truth, and had a certain kind and degree of enjoyment from that knowledge—who were partakers of the common influences and miraculous gifts of the Holy Ghost—

[1] Carpzov seems to think this last clause a recapitulation of what goes before, and that—1. φωτισμός; 2. γεῦμα τῆς δωρεᾶς τῆς ἐπουρανίου; 3. Πνεῦμα ἅγιον; 4. καλὸν Θεοῦ ῥῆμα are themselves the powers referred to; and considers the force of the particle τε, in the phrase δυνάμεις τε, as = all which form the power and excellence of the New Economy.

[2] παραπίπτειν here is obviously = ἀποστῆναι, chap. iii. 12; παραρρυῆναι, chap. ii. 1; and ἑκουσίως ἁμαρτάνειν, chap. x. 26.

who enjoyed the advantages of the fulfilled promise as to the Messiah, and had their minds subjected to the influences of the new dispensation,—who yet, after all, "made shipwreck of faith and of a good conscience," and openly and totally abandoned the profession of Christianity. This was the primitive apostate.

This miserable class of men is not extinct, though they have lost some of the peculiar characters of their predecessors of the primitive age. The age of miracles has passed away, and, along with it, everything that grew out of that peculiarity of the primitive times; but still it is a truth, substantiated by but too abundant evidence, that men who have made very considerable attainments in the knowledge of Christianity—who seemed to have, who really had, considerable enjoyment in their religion—who were striven with by the Holy Spirit—who enjoyed in high perfection the advantages of the New Economy, and who had its powers brought to bear on them with considerable energy—have from a variety of causes renounced Christianity altogether, neglecting its ordinances, openly denying its divine origin, and living in habitual ungodliness.

Such is the class of men described by the Apostle, and such the corresponding class in our own times to whom what the Apostle here says is equally applicable. The persons here referred to are not mere nominal professors—*they* have nothing to fall away from but an empty name; neither are they backsliding Christians. They are men who have really had their minds and affections to a very considerable degree exercised about, and interested in Christianity; but who, never having been "renewed in the spirit of their mind," when exposed to temptation of a peculiar kind, make complete "shipwreck of faith and of a good conscience."

Respecting these most criminal and miserable men the Apostle declares, that "it is impossible to renew them again unto repentance; seeing they crucify to themselves the Son of God afresh, and put Him to an open shame."

There are here two questions which must successively engage our attention. What is meant by "renewing these men again to repentance?" and what by its being "*impossible* to renew these men again to repentance?" Some interpreters have connected the word *again* with "fall away"—'if they again fall away;' others have supposed it redundant, but without assigning any reason. But we have no doubt that it is intended to qualify the phrase, " to renew them to repentance." It is opposed to " once," ver. 4.[1] It naturally intimates that the persons had been *once* " renewed to repentance."

The word translated " repentance," means just a change of mind. To be " renewed to repentance," is for a man to be so far renewed as to have changed his mind—to have a new mind on some subject. To be " renewed," is a figurative expression to denote a change, a great change, and a change to the better. To be " renewed" so as to change a person's mind, is expressive of an important and an advantageous alteration of opinion, and character, and circumstances. And such an alteration the persons referred to had undergone at a former period. They were once in a state of ignorance respecting the doctrines and evidences of Christianity; and they had been " enlightened." They had once known nothing of the excellence and beauty of Christian truth; and they had been " made to taste that heavenly gift." They once had not known so much as that there was a Holy Ghost; and they had not only felt His common influence, but been the subjects of His miraculous operation. They once misunderstood the promise respecting the Messiah, and were unaware of its fulfilment, and, of course, were strangers to that energetic influence which the New Testament revelation puts forth; and they had been made to see that " that good word" was fulfilled, and had been made partakers of the external privileges and been subjected to the peculiar energies of the new order of things. Their views, and feelings, and circumstances were materially changed. How great the difference between an ignorant, bigoted Jew, and the person described in the preceding passage! He had become, as it were, a different man. A great change of mind had taken place. He had not, indeed, become, in the sense of the Apostle, " a new creature." His mind had not been so changed as unfeignedly to believe " the truth as it is in Jesus;" but still a great, and, so far as it went, a favourable, change had taken place.

Now, to " renew to repentance" such a person, who had " fallen away," or apostatized, is not, I apprehend, to bring him into what, in the technical language of theology, is called a

---

[1] Πάλιν has a reference to ἅπαξ.

regenerate state—for in this state there is no reason to believe he ever was; but it is just to bring him back to the state in which he once was,—as Storr says, "to produce another amendment"—to give him those views of Christian doctrine, and their evidence, which he once possessed. "To "renew" such a man "again to repentance," is so to change his mind as that he shall again, instead of counting Jesus Christ an impostor, acknowledge Him as the Messiah; and instead of considering Christianity as "a cunningly devised fable," or rather a hellish delusion, again regard it as a revelation of the will of God.

Let us now proceed to inquire what the inspired writer means when he says, "It is *impossible* to renew" such persons "to repentance."[1] Many good interpreters consider the word *impossible* as used here, not in a strict, but in a popular sense, as equivalent to—'very difficult,' or 'very improbable.' I am not aware, however, that the word ever occurs in this sense in Scripture. Certainly the passage usually brought to prove it is not at all in point: "With men this is *impossible*; but with God all things are possible;"[2]—the word "impossible," obviously, there having its ordinary strict meaning.

When anything is said to be impossible, the natural question is, Impossible to whom? for it is plain that what may be possible to one being, may be impossible to another being. If I were called to attempt to lift a stone of a ton weight, I would naturally say, 'No, I will not attempt it, for it is impossible,'—meaning, not that it is impossible that the stone should be lifted, but that it is impossible that I should lift it.

The impossibility in the case before us may either be considered as existing in reference to God, or in reference to man. If the restoration of these apostates to the state in which they once were be an impossibility in reference to God, it must be so either because it is inconsistent with His nature and perfections, or with His decree and purpose. In the first sense, "it is impossible for God to lie," or to "clear the guilty" without satisfaction. In the second sense, it was impossible that Saul and his posterity should continue on the throne of Israel. That the restoration of an apostate to his former state is an impossibility

---

[1] Some would supply the word ἑαυτούς,—' It is impossible for them to renew themselves.' This is obviously unsatisfactory.

[2] Matt. xix. 26.

in either of these points of view, is more than we are warranted to assert.

If we carefully examine the passage, I apprehend we will come to the conclusion, that the impossibility is considered as existing not in reference to God, but in reference to man,—that the Apostle's assertion is, that it is impossible, by any renewed course of elementary instruction, to bring back such apostates to the acknowledgment of the truth. He had stated that many of the Hebrews had unlearned all that they had learned, and "had need of some one to teach them again the first principles of the oracles of God." Yet he declares his determination not to enter anew on a course of elementary instruction, but to go on to some of the higher branches of Christian knowledge; for this cause, that there was no reason to expect that such restatements would be of any use in reclaiming those who, after being instructed in the doctrines and evidences of Christianity, had apostatized; while, on the other hand, there was every reason to hope that illustrations of the higher branches of Christian truth would be of the greatest use to those who "held fast" the "first principles," in establishing them in the faith and profession, in the comforts and obedience of the Gospel;—just as a farmer, after making a fair trial of a piece of ground, and finding that, though everything has been done for it in the most favourable circumstances, it still continues barren, desists, saying, "It is impossible to make anything of that field," and turns his attention to rendering still more fertile those fields which have already given evidence of their capability of improvement. 'It is not possible, by a renewed statement of Christian principles and their evidence, to bring back *these* apostates. Nothing can be stated but what has been already stated, which they seemed to understand, which they professed to believe, but which they now openly and contemptuously reject. No evidence, stronger than that which has been brought before their minds, and which they once seemed to feel the force of, can be presented to them. The meaning and evidence of Christian truth have been before their minds in as favourable circumstances as can be conceived.' The Apostle's assertion, then, appears to me to be just this— 'Statement and argument would be entirely lost on such persons, and therefore we do not enter on them.'

We must now attend for a little to the reason assigned by

the inspired writer, for the impossibility by anything he could do of bringing back these apostates. "It is impossible—seeing they have crucified to themselves the Son of God afresh, and put Him to an open shame."[1] These words have generally been considered as intended to place in a strong point of light the heinousness and aggravation of the crime of these apostates, and thus to account for what the words have been thought to teach—its unpardonableness. They no doubt do express strongly the heinous and aggravated nature of their sin; but the object of the Apostle in stating them seems plainly to be, to illustrate the hopelessness of attempting to reclaim them. They openly proclaimed Jesus Christ to be an impostor. They thus identified themselves with His crucifiers. The language of their conduct, and in many cases of their lips, probably was,—'Our fathers did right in bringing Him to the cross, as an impious deceiver.' It is doubtful if the idea of *re*-crucifixion be necessarily implied in the word.[2] They crucified Him *to themselves;*[3] i.e., *they involve themselves in the guilt of His crucifixion*—they entertain and avow sentiments which, were He on earth, and in their power, would induce them to crucify Him. "And they put Him to an open shame." They exposed Him to infamy—made a public example of Him. They did more to dishonour Jesus Christ than His murderers did. *They* never professed to acknowledge His divine mission; but these apostates had made such a profession—they had made a kind of trial of Christianity, and, after trial, rejected it. To refer to the parallel passage in the 10th chapter, "they trampled under foot the Son of God,

---

[1] It is remarkable that this clause is passed over without exposition in all the editions of Owen's Commentary. It is explained in his work on Apostasy, which was published before the part of the Commentary which treats of the 6th chapter. The passage seems to have been omitted by a printer's mistake. It should be inserted in future editions.

[2] If it be, the phrase is = 'they repeat the insult offered to Jesus Christ when He was crucified—they pronounce Him an impostor.'

[3] Ἑαυτοῖς. Michaelis explains it, *quantum in ipsis est*—'as far as is in their power;' Schott, *secum animo suo*—'in their intention;' Böhme, *quod ipsos attinet*—'so far as they are concerned.' Others consider it as = ἱκουσίως, Heb. x. 26,; Storr—'against themselves, to their own hurt.' Stuart considers it as pleonastic, as לְךָ in the Heb. phrase, לֶךְ־לְךָ, 'go for thyself,' *i.e.*, 'go;' לוֹ in the phrase, נָס לוֹ, 'he has fled for himself,' *i.e.*, 'he has fled;' or, as we say, '*as for him*, he has done the work.'

and they accounted the blood of the covenant, wherewith *He* was sanctified, an unholy thing,"—declaring Jesus Christ an impostor, and His blood but that of a criminal, who richly merited the ignominious death to which He was doomed.

Now to what purpose address statements and arguments to such men? This certainly would have been directly to contravene our Lord's command, "Cast not pearls before swine." Over such persons the Apostle might well lament and weep; but he must have clearly seen, and strongly felt, that to attempt, by statement or argument, to bring such persons back to their former profession, was utterly hopeless, and, indeed, to waste that time which might be better devoted to calling those who remained yet in ignorance, and in building up those who held fast the faith of Christ.

If we have succeeded in bringing out the true meaning of this somewhat difficult passage, it must be evident that it says nothing which would warrant a Christian church to refuse to admit into its communion a person who, though he has been guilty even of open apostasy from the faith of Christ, makes a credible profession of his repentance. The person here described is the open, determined apostate; and the statement is, It is impossible, by mere statement of the truth and its evidence, to reclaim him, and it is needless to try it. Nor does it throw any obstacles in the way of an apostate, supposing him to be convinced of his error and guilt, applying to God through Jesus Christ for pardon. This is just what he should do; and if he do it, he is sure of salvation. "The blood of Jesus Christ cleanseth us from *all* sin;" and "He is able to save to the uttermost *all* that come to God by Him;" and "him that cometh to Him, He will in no wise cast out." If no apostate ever was saved (though we durst not say so), the reason is, he continued in his apostasy, and therefore perished—not, he perished though he sought, but sought in vain, salvation through Christ.[1] Still less is the passage calculated, when rightly understood, to produce those fears which, ill understood, it often has occasioned in the minds of sincere, but weak-minded Christians, who not only have misapprehended the meaning of this text, but the true

[1] The passage respecting Esau in a subsequent part of the Epistle ch. xii. 17, is very generally misinterpreted. "Repentance" there refers to *a change of mind on the part of Isaac.*

state of their own minds. They are afraid that they have sinned wilfully after they have received the knowledge of the truth, and therefore think there can be no mercy for them. If they would but reflect that the sin described here, and in the 10th chapter, is a total and voluntary renunciation of Christ and His cause, and a joining with His enemies, their apprehension would be effectually relieved. The passage is also utterly unfit for a purpose to which it has often been applied, to invalidate the doctrine of the perseverance of the saints. Nothing is said of the persons here described but what is said of the stony-ground hearers, Luke viii. 13,—of those who may be destitute of Christian love, 1 Cor. xiii. 1-3,—of such as Christ will at last disown, as "workers of iniquity," Matt. vii. 22, 23.

The doctrine of the perseverance of the saints is a doctrine clearly taught in Scripture. Instead of "drawing back to perdition," they "believe straight onward to the salvation of the soul,"[1]—"they endure to the end."[2] If they were "chosen in Christ before the foundation of the world,"[3]—if they were given by the Father to the Saviour to be redeemed and "brought to glory,"[4]—if He has promised to "give unto them eternal life," and that "they shall never perish, nor any pluck them out of His or His Father's hand,"[5]—if they are "kept by the mighty power of God unto salvation,"[6]—surely it is as certain as anything of the kind can be, that they shall never finally "fall away."

But though the perseverance of the saints is certain, let us never forget that it is the perseverance of *saints* that is *thus* certain. Many who seem to others to be saints, who seem to themselves to be saints, do "fall away." And let us recollect that the perseverance of the saints referred to, is their perseverance not only in a safe state, but in a holy course of disposition and conduct; and no saint behaving like a sinner can legitimately enjoy the comfort which the doctrine of perseverance is fitted and intended to communicate to every saint, acting like a saint, "in a patient continuance in well-doing, seeking for glory, honour, and immortality." Let us take the Apostle Paul's caution, "Let him who thinketh he standeth take heed lest he fall;" and the Apostle Peter's advice, "Give all diligence to add to your faith, virtue; and to virtue, knowledge; and to know-

---

[1] Heb. x. 39.   [2] Matt. xxiv. 13.   [3] Eph. i. 4.
[4] Heb. ii. 10, 13.   [5] John x. 15, 17, 28, 29.   [6] 1 Pet. i. 4, 5.

ledge, temperance; and to temperance, patience; and to patience, godliness; and to godliness, brotherly-kindness; and to brotherly-kindness, charity. For if these things be in you, and abound, they make you that ye shall neither be barren nor unfruitful in the knowledge of our Lord Jesus Christ. But he that lacketh these things is blind, and cannot see afar off, and hath forgotten that he was purged from his old sins. Wherefore the rather, brethren, give diligence to make your calling and election sure; for if ye do these things, ye shall never fall: for so an entrance shall be ministered unto you abundantly into the everlasting kingdom of our Lord and Saviour Jesus Christ."[1]

The verses which follow seem to me to contain an account, couched in figurative language, of the Apostle's reasons for going forward to a statement of some of the higher and more recondite principles of Christianity, and for not engaging in a restatement of its elements. The Hebrews had been long blessed with the means of Christian instruction. Some of them had improved these well and wisely; they did not need a restatement of the elements; the instruction they had received had produced fruit; and they were ready for further and higher instruction, which, by God's blessing, would make them still more fruitful. Others of them had not improved these means of instruction; they had forgotten what they had once learned; they "had need of some one to teach them again what be the first principles of the oracles of God." They were on the brink of apostasy,—that state in which statements of Christian truth and evidence can serve no good purpose. They were quite unfit for *going on to perfection;* and, at the same time, while they needed elementary instruction, there was little reason to think it would do them any good; they had long enjoyed it, and yet remained ignorant—had become stupid. There was much encouragement for the Apostle to go forward in the instruction of the first class in the higher branches of Christian knowledge; there was no encouragement for him to restate to the second class what had often been stated to them without effect. The first class plainly were enjoying the blessing of God, which gives spiritual fruitfulness; the other seemed, from their perseverance in unbelief and ignorance amid all the means of knowledge and faith, doomed to spiritual barrenness and utter destruction. Such is, I apprehend, the con-

[1] 2 Pet. i. 5–11.

nection and general import of this passage. Let us proceed to examine it with more minuteness.

Ver. 7. "For the earth,[1] which drinketh in[2] the rain that cometh oft upon it, and bringeth forth herbs meet for them by whom it is dressed, receiveth blessing from God: 8. But that which beareth thorns and briars is rejected, and is nigh unto cursing; whose end is to be burned."

The two classes among the Hebrews are figuratively described as two fields, subjected to the same culture, but producing very different crops,—the one, a crop of good grain; the other, a crop of briars and thorns;—the one showing that it is blessed by God with fruitfulness, the other giving reason to fear that it is cursed by Him with barrenness. The emblem is a field often rained on, and drinking in the rain. This is a very significant emblem of a person who has long enjoyed the means of Christianity, and who has made such a use of these means as to obtain a knowledge of that religion sufficient to induce him to make a profession of it.

"Rain" is used in Scripture as the emblem, both of divine doctrine and of divine influence. It is used in the first way in Isa. lv. 10, "For as the rain cometh down, and the snow from heaven, and returneth not thither, but watereth the earth, and maketh it bring forth and bud, that it may give seed to the sower, and bread to the eater, so shall My word be;"—and in the last way, in Isa. xliv. 3, "For I will pour water upon him that is thirsty, and floods upon the dry ground: I will pour My Spirit upon thy seed, and My blessing upon thine offspring." "The ground which drinketh in the rain which often cometh on it," is descriptive of those who have long enjoyed the means of instruction, and who have often experienced the common influences of the Holy Spirit,—persons who "have been enlightened, and tasted the heavenly gift"—"the good word, and the powers of the world to come."

The Apostle supposes two of these fields or pieces of ground. Both are alike as to the means of fruitfulness here mentioned, but there is a contrast between the effect which these means produce.

---

[1] Γῆ is here = *ager*—'soil, ground:' Matt. xiii. 5; James v. 7.

[2] It seems common in all languages to express the earth's receiving the rain by the figure of drinking. Anacreon commences one of his odes—ἡ γῆ μέλαινα πίνει; and Virgil concludes his third eclogue with, "Sat prata biberunt."

The one field "brings forth[1] herbs meet for them by whom it is dressed." The phrase, "meet for them *by* whom it is dressed," is better rendered in the margin, " meet for them *for* whom it is dressed."[2] The reference is not to the cultivators, but to the proprietors of the soil. The word translated *meet*, as opposed to *rejected*, in the second clause, is equivalent to 'acceptable, well-pleasing.' The whole phrase, then, " herbs meet for them for whom it is dressed," is equivalent to—'herbs well-pleasing to the proprietors.'

The meaning of the figurative expression is not obscure. One class of those persons who have long enjoyed the means of Christianity make a wise improvement of them, and cultivate that kind of temper and that kind of conduct which are the objects of the approbation of Him whose they are. They are the persons who are "transformed by the renewing of the mind," and who "prove the good, and acceptable, and perfect will of God;" or, to use a figure similar to that employed in the passage before us, who, having received the word in a good and honest heart, keep it, and "bring forth fruit with patience,"— *i.e.*, 'perseveringly continue to bring forth fruit.'

This field, which thus, when watered from heaven, yields produce acceptable to its proprietor, *receiveth blessing from God*. These words do not, I apprehend, signify, that as a kind of reward for its fertility, the productive field receives a divine blessing. The words are equivalent to—'is blessed of God.' That field shows by its fertility that it is blessed of God, for it is the divine blessing that makes fields fertile. That field shows that it is the object of the kind regard of God.

The meaning of this part of the figurative representation is not far to seek. The person who, enjoying the means of Christianity, improves them, and under them becomes distinguished by that character and conduct which they are calculated to

---

[1] τίκτουσα. Lucretius employs the same figure:—
  " Humorum guttas Mater cum Terra recepit,
  Fœta parit nitidas fruges."—*Lib. II.* v. 992.

[2] Δι' οὕς is explained by many, like our translators, of the cultivators— 'by whom.' Διά, as Abresch remarks, when used with the accusative, never means *per*, by; δι' οὗ and δι' ὅν are always distinguished,—the first denotes *per quem*—the second, *propter quem*: ch. i. 2, ii. 10. The Church is represented as a vineyard, the property of God, cultivated by Christian teachers, 1 Cor. iii. 9; Matt. xxi. 33, xx. 1.

produce, and which is the object of the divine approbation—that person receives "blessing of God,"—he is blessed of God—he is the object of the kind regards of the Divine Being; and his spiritual fruitfulness is the evidence of it. If he wills and does, it is "of God's good pleasure." "It is God who works in him all the good pleasure of His goodness, and the work of faith with power." And as the past fertility of a field not only proves that God has blessed it, but gives reason to hope that He will continue to bless it, and encourages those who cultivate it to persevere in their labours, from the expectation that these labours will not be in vain; so the Christian improvement of individuals under the means of grace not only proves that they have been "blessed of God," but that they are permanently the objects of His kind regards; and therefore the Christian minister is greatly encouraged to use every means for their further Christian improvement, knowing that "this labour" in reference to them "shall not be in vain in the Lord."

The sentiment conveyed by these words, when expressed in plain language, is just this: 'Those persons who, under the means of grace, are gradually forming to that character which is the object of God's approbation, are plainly themselves the objects of the divine peculiar favour—the subjects of the divine peculiar blessing; and therefore there is the greatest encouragement to use the appropriate means for their further improvement. The divine blessing which rests on them will make the means effectual.'

But there is another field besides this which the Lord has blessed.[1] There is a field which, though it "drinketh in the rain that often comes on it," yet "brings forth nothing but briars and thorns." This field, like the fruitful one, enjoys frequent showers of fertilizing rain, and, like it too, "drinketh in the rain that comes often on it." The persons referred to have the same means of improvement as their neighbours. They have the Scriptures, and divine ordinances, and the common influences of the Holy Spirit. And this is not all. "The ground *drinketh in* the rain which cometh on it." The persons here described are not those who continue utterly ignorant and

---

[1] In the beginning of the 8th verse the words must be repeated, γῆ ἡ πιοῦσα τὸν ἐπ' αὐτῆς πολλάκις ἐρχόμενον ὑετόν, and the idea must be carried with us that this field also, like the other, γεωργεῖται.

openly infidel: the emblem of such persons is the rock, into which the rain cannot at all find its way. They seem to attend in some measure to instruction—to understand to a certain degree the truth, and they make a profession of believing it.

But notwithstanding the rain's falling and being "drunk in" by this field, it "produces"[1] nothing but "briars and thorns." The persons referred to are those who, with the means of Christianity, are so far improved, as that they are not grossly ignorant—are not avowedly unbelieving, yet continue worldly and wicked in their character and conduct. Uselessness and noxiousness are their leading characteristics. They bring forth not "the fruits of the Spirit," but "the fruits of the flesh."

This ground, fruitful only in briars and thorns, "is rejected." The word *rejected* properly signifies, 'disapproved of after trial.'[2] It is here opposed to the word in the former branch of the figure—*meet*, which signifies, 'acceptable, well-pleasing.' The persons of whom this field—productive only of a noxious, or at best an useless crop—is emblematical, are disapproved of God.

But this is not all. This field "is nigh unto cursing; whose end is to be burned." The field which produces nothing but briars and thorns "is nigh to"—*i.e.*, is in great danger of—"a curse; the end of which curse is burning;"—*i.e.*, 'it is in great danger of being doomed to have all its worthless productions consumed by fire' (for there is plainly no allusion to burning as a means of ameliorating the soil), 'and of having this doom executed.' The meaning of this with regard to the persons referred

---

[1] ἐκφέρουσα. Grotius supposes that this word is used rather than τίκτουσα, to express the idea of throwing out as an abortion; but this is *interpretatio nimium arguta*. Ἐκφέρειν is applied to the earth's most salutary productions: Strabo, lib. v., quoted by Elsner.

[2] ἀδόκιμος, 'disapproved.' The words δοκιμάζειν, δοκίμιον, δοκιμή, δόκιμος, ἀδόκιμος, properly refer to those who prove metals. The verb δοκιμάζειν signifies, to inspect coins, and distinguish the genuine from the spurious or adulterated. Δοκίμιον denotes that by which the proof is made —the fining-pot, the furnace, the touchstone: Prov. xxvii. 21. Δοκιμή is the proof or trial itself. Δόκιμον is that which is tried and approved, as χρυσίον δόκιμον, 2 Chron. ix. 17. The word δοκιμάζειν naturally, in a figurative sense, comes to signify, to judge a person or thing to be what they ought to be, to approve of one, 1 Thess. ii. 4; and the word ἀδόκιμος, properly applied to base or adulterated coin—ἀργύριον ἀδόκιμον, Isa. i. 22,— as naturally is employed to signify a person or thing of no value, and known to be of no value, from proof taken.—KUINOEL.

to is easily discovered. The caution of the inspired writer deserves notice. Of the productive ground he says, its productions are acceptable to, and it enjoys the blessing of, its owner. Of the unproductive he only says, "it is nigh unto cursing;" he does not say positively, it is cursed. Those persons who enjoy the means of spiritual fruitfulness and yet continue unfruitful, are *nigh unto cursing*. We dare not say they are entirely given up of God; we cannot say the curse of permanent barrenness has gone out against them. But this we will say, they are "nigh to cursing;" and the longer they continue unproductive, they are the nearer to it. They are barren fig-trees, "cumbering the ground." The command, "cut them down," may not yet have gone forth; but, continuing barren, it cannot be long before it do go forth.

"And the end is to be burned."[1] The "unprofitable servant" is "cast into outer darkness." Persons persisting in neglecting and misimproving the means of salvation must perish for ever. And as the continued barrenness of a field discourages the husbandman, and induces him to give over labouring to improve so thankless a soil, so long-continued unfruitfulness under the means of spiritual fertility disheartens the labourer in God's vineyard, and warrants him to bestow his principal attention where the blessing of God seems to accompany his exertions.

Such seems to be the meaning of this passage; and though it has, no doubt, a primary reference to the Hebrews in the circumstances in which they were placed, it is full of most important instruction and warning to persons enjoying a dispensation of Christian truth, and making a profession of the Christian religion.

[1] Some suppose $\mathring{\eta}_{\varsigma}$ to refer to $\varkappa\alpha\tau\acute{\alpha}\rho\alpha$, and this connection has been adopted in the text. Τέλος, 'the end—the *upshot* of which curse is *burning*, complete ruin.'

It is not the field apart from the crop, it is the field with the crop, that is spoken of; and the burning is opposed to reaping and storing. Virgil, Georg. i. 84, says :—

"Sæpe etiam steriles incendere profuit agros,
Atque levem stipulam crepitantibus urere flammis."

This was done to improve the field; but in Scripture, the burning up a field of useless herbage is uniformly the image of destruction: Nah. i. 10; Mal. iv. 1; Matt. iii. 12, xiii. 30.

These are our circumstances. We have been often rained on. Oh! how numerous—how valuable have been our privileges! From our infancy we have had the Bible to read, and the Gospel to hear; and most of us have read the Bible, and heard the Gospel. The labours of pious parents and pious ministers have been expended on us; "the powers of the world to come" have been brought to bear on us; plain statements of the meaning and evidence of divine truth have been often laid before our minds, and pressed on our attention; and the Spirit of God has not been wanting in striving with us, though we have often rebelled and grieved Him. We too have, many of us, "drunk in the rain." We know something about Christianity; we generally profess to believe it; we observe its ordinances.

But what fruits have we produced? Have we produced "the fruits of righteousness, which are by Christ Jesus, to the glory and praise of God?" Are we producing "the fruits of the Spirit?"[1] If we are, then all praise to Him who made us fruitful! To make a man holy in heart and conduct is the work of God—is the most striking proof God can give of His favour to the individual. None of us are so fruitful as we ought to be; but if we are really producing fruits "meet" for Him who is our great proprietor, it is an evidence that His blessing rests on us, and an encouragement to our abounding more and more in these fruits. "For He who has begun the good work will perform it till the day of Jesus Christ." Such persons, I trust, there are among us. May God increase their number, and, in their growing fruitfulness, make it more and more apparent to themselves and others that they are indeed "a field that the Lord hath blessed."

But have we not reason to fear that a very large proportion of professed Christians among us belong to the class of which the unfruitful field is the emblem? Have we not reason to fear, many of us, that with all the means of spiritual fruitfulness enjoyed by us, we have hitherto yielded no better produce than briars and thorns? Of how many professors of Christianity is not this the best you can say: 'They are not notoriously wicked people!' Where are their "works of faith?" Where are their "labours of love?" Their most intimate friends know nothing of these. Where is their love of God? Where is their deadness to

[1] Gal. v. 22-24.

the world? Where is their zeal for Christ's honour? Where is their " love of the brethren ?" Where is their sympathy with the spiritual and temporal miseries of their fellow-men? Let them be honest, and they will confess that they are nearly, if not altogether, strangers to these sentiments—that these are far indeed from being the animating and regulating principles of their conduct.

Let such persons be induced seriously to reflect on their most hazardous situation. They are already the objects of the divine disapprobation. God does not, He cannot, approve of your character and conduct. His language to you is : " What hast thou to do to declare My statutes, and to take My covenant in thy mouth ?" And you are " nigh to cursing." You need only to be exposed to temptations sufficiently strong, to plunge into the gulf of apostasy. Oh ! what tremendous disclosures would a season of persecution make among us! How many would " make shipwreck of faith and of a good conscience !" You are becoming every day more and more " hardened by the deceitfulness of sin." Every sermon you hear, every awakening dispensation of Providence you meet with, if they produce not their appropriate effect, operate in fixing you down more securely under the chain of unbelief. God only knows how soon the curse, the condemning sentence, may go forth ; and when it does go forth, all is over for ever as to happiness or hope, for its " end is burning"—destruction, " everlasting destruction, from the presence of the Lord, and the glory of His power." And oh ! must not this destruction be doubly dreadful to those who enjoyed the means, who indulged the hopes, of the Christian salvation ! " Let the sinners in Zion be afraid : let fearfulness surprise the hypocrites. Who can dwell with the devouring fire ? Who can dwell with everlasting burnings ?"

It may be that some conscience-struck, Gospel-hardened sinners may be disposed to say, ' What is to be done in our fearfully alarming circumstances ? What must we do to be saved ?' My answer is, Be in reality what you have so long professed to be. You have professed faith in Christ. " Believe in the Lord Jesus Christ, and ye shall be saved." Ye have professed repentance towards God. " Repent, and be converted, every one of you." " Let the wicked forsake his way, and the unrighteous man his thoughts ; and let him turn to the Lord, and He will have mercy on him; and to our God, for He will abundantly pardon." Embrace "the truth as it is in Jesus," and yield yourselves up to its influence. Bless God that He has not yet "commanded the heavens that they rain no rain" on you. The Gospel, in all its fulness and freedom, is not only written in the Scriptures, but proclaimed from many a pulpit in our land. The communication of divine influence is not restrained. God "waits to be gracious"—gracious even to you. His language to you is, "Hearken to Me, ye stout-hearted, and far from righteousness: behold, I bring near My righteousness to you." But a continuance in your present state must ultimately bring down divine vengeance. "If ye set at nought these counsels; if ye will none of these reproofs, He also will laugh at your calamity; He will mock when your fear cometh; when your fear cometh as desolation, and your destruction cometh as a whirlwind; when distress and anguish cometh upon you: Then shall they call upon Him, but He will not answer; they shall seek Him early, but they shall not find Him: for that they hated knowledge, and did not choose the fear of the Lord: they would none of His counsel; they despised all His reproof: therefore shall they eat of the fruit of their own way, and be filled with their own devices."[1]

It may be proper to observe, before closing our remarks on these two verses, that by some very learned interpreters they have been considered as a prophecy respecting the Jewish people. That portion of them who, improving the means of instruction with which they were favoured, continued to bring forth the fruits of faith and obedience, would, in the approaching calamities, be preserved and protected, and be distinctly marked as the objects of the peculiar favour and care of God; while, on the other hand, those who either continued in unbelief or fell into apostasy, would be involved in the execution of that curse or wrathful sentence which overhung their nation, and the end of which was to be the burning of their temple and city—"wrath coming on them to the uttermost." Even in this point of view the verses are full of warning and instruction; but I cannot help thinking that the view which has been given above, as better agreeing with the connection, exhibits the meaning of the inspired writer.

[1] Prov. i. 25–31.

Lest the Hebrews should be discouraged—as if the Apostle thought them all apostates, or, at any rate, trembling on the very verge of apostasy,—he, in the words which follow, in the most affectionate and winning manner assures them of his affection, and of his comfortable hope of the genuineness of their Christian profession. Ver. 9. "But, beloved, we are persuaded better things of you, and things that accompany salvation, though we thus speak. 10. For God is not unrighteous, to forget your work and labour of love, which ye have showed toward His name, in that ye have ministered to the saints, and do minister. 11. And (or rather *but*) we desire that every one of you do show the same diligence, to the full assurance of hope unto the end: 12. That ye be not slothful, but followers of them who through faith and patience inherit the promises."

The general meaning of this paragraph, all the parts of which are closely connected together, plainly is: 'The reason why I have made these awful statements about apostates, is not that I consider you whom I am addressing as apostates; for your conduct proves that this is not your character, and the promise of God secures that their doom shall not be yours; but that you may be stirred up to persevering steadiness in the faith, and hope, and obedience of the truth, by a constant continuance in which alone you can, like those who have gone before you, obtain, in all their perfection, the promised blessings of the Christian salvation.' The reason why the Apostle had stated so particularly the aggravated guilt and all but hopeless condition of apostates, was not that he considered the Hebrew Christians whom he was addressing as in a state of apostasy. No, he "was persuaded[1] better things of them"—"things accompanying salvation."

Some refer these "*better things*," and "things accompanying"[2]—*i.e.*, necessarily connected with—"salvation," to those truly holy dispositions by which genuine Christians are characterized, as opposed to those external privileges and those

---

[1] πέπεισμαι is not = 'I am certain,' but 'I entertain a strong hope.' The passage is very similar to one in the Epistle to the Galatians, ch. v. 10. The Apostle was quite sensible of the νωθρότης of the Hebrews, and of the ἄνοια of the Galatians; yet he had good hopes respecting both.

[2] ἔχεσθαι = *attingere, contingere, cohærere.* Ἐχόμενον τοῦ θυσιαστηρίου, Lev. vi. 10, is, 'near the altar.' Buildings are said to be ἐχόμενα that stand in the same row, and are joined together—contiguous.

spiritual gifts of which persons who ultimately apostatize may be possessed. Others refer them to that perseverance in a state of grace and that state of final and complete salvation which is secured to genuine Christians, as opposed to that state of all but unreclaimableness into which apostates fall, and that utter destruction which, if they are not reclaimed, must be their portion for ever. I think the words, which are general, are intended to include both.[1] These apostates were, no doubt, once possessed of high privileges and valuable gifts; but if the Hebrews were what the Apostle charitably hoped them to be, they were in possession of " better things,"—they were in possession of " sanctification of the Spirit, through the belief of the truth"—they were in possession of that "*love*" which is " the fruit of the Spirit," and which, in the 13th chapter of 1st Corinthians, the Apostle shows so far surpasses all the extraordinary gifts of the Holy Ghost. And these " better things" were " things accompanying salvation." All the privileges enjoyed by the apostate might be disjoined from salvation; but between that temper of mind to which they had been formed by the Holy Spirit, " through the faith of the truth," and final salvation, there is an inseparable connection. These things are indeed *salvation* begun—" the *earnest* of the inheritance."

And as the Apostle trusted that the Hebrews were in possession of " better things, even things which accompany salvation," in that truly sanctified character by which they were distinguished from the apostates, so he hoped for them a far happier destiny. He did not anticipate their " falling away," so as that it would be "impossible to renew them again to repentance." His expectation was, that they would "continue rooted and grounded in love," " established in the faith wherein they had been taught ;" and, instead of " turning back " again " towards perdition," that they would persevere in believing till the complete " salvation of the soul." Instead of foreboding for them " everlasting destruction from the presence of the Lord, and from the glory of His power," He anticipated " an abundant entrance into the everlasting kingdom of our Lord and Saviour Jesus Christ."

The grounds of his hopes respecting the character and prospects of the Hebrew Christians are stated in the following

---

[1] The expression, ἐχόμενα σωτηρίας, is used in contrast to κατάρας ἐγγύς. The apostate is κ. ἐ.—those who persevere are ἰ. σ.

verse: "For God is not unrighteous, to forget your work and labour of love, which ye have showed toward His name, in that ye have ministered to the saints, and do minister."

Their "work and labour of love, which they had showed toward the name of God, in having ministered, and in continuing to minister, to the saints," led him to hope that they were in possession of something better than the privileges and gifts which may be enjoyed by those who may yet finally apostatize. The "work and labour of love" is equivalent to—'the laborious, the toilsome work of kindness.' "The work of love" is either the work which love prompts, or the work which manifests love.

The love which prompted these exertions, and was manifested in them, was love *toward the name of God*.[1] The "name" of God, is just God Himself as revealed to us. The "name" of God here plainly refers to God as made known in the Christian revelation, as "the God and Father of our Lord Jesus Christ," and the God and Father of all who believe in Him—"God in Christ reconciling the world to Himself"—"the God of peace, who has brought again our Lord Jesus from the dead," and who in Him is "blessing us with all heavenly and spiritual blessings." The faith of the truth about the name of God, or His revealed character, produces love; and this love is manifested by a laborious work. This work consisted in "ministering to the saints."

To "minister to the saints," is to serve them by supplying their wants and relieving their distresses. It is a term of very considerable latitude of signification. It may include the giving of advice, comfort, and encouragement; but it seems primarily and principally to refer to the relief of bodily wants—the succouring of them in poverty and persecution. The Hebrews were at first very remarkable for this ministry of love: Acts ii. 45, iv. 34. The Apostle mentions with much gratitude their attention to himself: Heb. x. 34. It is likely that he refers to their ministry to him when a prisoner at Cæsarea, previously to his being sent to Rome.

---

[1] ἥς is placed for ἥν, which the construction requires. It is an extremely common Atticism. The case of the relative pronoun is attracted to the preceding noun, not governed by the following verb. We have instances of this idiom, Mark vii. 13; Acts i. 1.

May the force of εἰς τὸ ὄνομα αὐτοῦ not be 'with reference to His name;' i.e., from a regard to His authority?

This, then, was the evidence on which the Apostle rested in hoping that the Hebrews were in possession of something better than all the privileges and gifts of the apostate,—their laborious and persevering exertions to relieve the wants and mitigate the sufferings of their Christian brethren, rising from love towards the name of God. "Faith working by love" is the grand characteristic of the new creature. Love to God, manifesting itself in "love to the brethren," is the leading feature in the truly Christian character. "He that loveth is born of God." This is better than all supernatural gifts: 1 Cor. xiii. 1–4. The Apostle obviously judged of the Hebrews in the same way in which he judged of the Thessalonians: 1 Thess. i. 4. Such was the ground on which the Apostle thought well of the character of the Hebrews as Christians.

The ground on which he cherished a joyful hope that they would not "fall away" and perish, but persevere and be saved, is stated in these words: "God is not unjust, to forget your work and labour of love." The word "unjust" here is equivalent to 'unfaithful.' 2 Thess. i. 6 is a parallel passage. The whole phrase is equivalent to—'God is faithful, and will remember your work and labour of love.' This may either be considered as referring to preserving it for the present, or rewarding it at last. He it is that "hath wrought in you both to will and to do of His good pleasure;" and He has promised to take care of His own work: 1 Cor. i. 8, 9; Phil. i. 3, 5, 6; 1 Thess. v. 23, 24; 2 Thess. iii. 3. The faithfulness of God secures that the true believer shall continue, under the influence of his faith, to be distinguished by those "works of love" which are among the most satisfactory evidences of his being a child of God. I apprehend, however, that the direct and principal reference is to the gracious reward at last of this "laborious work of love." The faithfulness of God secures the gracious reward of all who, from a regard to God's "name," "minister to the saints;" and therefore the Apostle has a comfortable hope in reference to the final salvation of the Hebrews. The account of the transactions of the last day, as given in the 25th chapter of Matthew, is well fitted to illustrate the Apostle's declaration. "Then shall the King say unto them on His right hand, Come, ye blessed of My Father, inherit the kingdom prepared for you from the foundation of the world: for I was an hungered, and ye gave Me meat: I was thirsty, and ye gave Me drink: I was a stranger, and ye took Me in: naked, and ye clothed Me: I was sick, and ye visited Me: I was in prison, and ye came unto Me. Then shall the righteous answer Him, saying, Lord, when saw we Thee an hungered, and fed Thee? or thirsty, and gave Thee drink? When saw we Thee a stranger, and took Thee in? or naked, and clothed Thee? Or when saw we Thee sick, or in prison, and came unto Thee? And the King shall answer and say unto them, Verily I say unto you, Inasmuch as ye have done it unto one of the least of these My brethren, ye have done it unto Me. Then shall He say also unto them on the left hand, Depart from Me, ye cursed, into everlasting fire, prepared for the devil and his angels: for I was an hungered, and ye gave Me no meat: I was thirsty, and ye gave Me no drink: I was a stranger, and ye took Me not in: naked, and ye clothed Me not: sick, and in prison, and ye visited Me not. Then shall they also answer him, saying, Lord, when saw we Thee an hungered, or athirst, or a stranger, or naked, or sick, or in prison, and did not minister unto Thee? Then shall He answer them, saying, Verily I say unto you, Inasmuch as ye did it not to one of the least of these, ye did it not to Me."[1]

The substance of what the Apostle has said in these two verses is: 'The cause of my making these statements about apostates is not that I think you apostates; I entertain a very different opinion both in reference to your character and destiny. I hope you are genuine Christians; and I anticipate your perseverance in grace, and in due time your complete salvation. And these are my grounds for entertaining such an opinion: You are distinguished by a persevering, laborious service of kindness to Christians from a regard to God; and if this is your real character, I know that the faithfulness of God secures both your perseverance in the faith and obedience of the truth, and your ultimate and complete salvation.'

But it may be said still, 'Why make these statements to us? You have told us what was not your object in making them, but what was your object?' To this inquiry we have a satisfactory answer in the 11th and 12th verses. "And"—or rather *but*[2]—" we desire that every one of you do show the same diligence,

---

[1] Matt. xxv. 34–45.     [2] δέ.

to the full assurance of hope unto the end: that ye be not slothful, but followers of them who through faith and patience inherit the promises." The force of the particle *but* seems to be this: 'My design in making these remarks is not to suggest that I think *you* apostates, but this is the reason of my making such statements—my desire that every one of you should show the same diligence, to the full assurance of hope unto the end.'

It was the Apostle's wish that they should have "the full assurance of hope." Faith is the belief of what God reveals respecting the way of salvation; hope is the expectation of obtaining that salvation. "The assurance of faith" is a full persuasion of the truth of what God reveals; "the assurance of hope" is a full expectation of obtaining what God has promised. It was the Apostle's desire that the Hebrews should have "the full assurance of hope." So far from wishing to cloud their minds with fears of their own apostasy and ultimate ruin, he wished that the continual sunshine of an assured hope of eternal happiness should rest on them; but in order to the possession of this, he was persuaded that they must continue to show the same diligence by which they had formerly been distinguished. *To the end* seems to be connected with the phrase, "the same diligence." The Apostle's desire was, that they should use diligently every means fitted to produce "the full assurance of hope," and persevere in doing so. The means calculated for this purpose are just the faith of the Gospel, and living under the influence of the faith of the Gospel. Our faith and our hope will just be in proportion to each other, and our holiness will be in proportion to both.

The Apostle wished a "full assurance of hope" to the believing Christians, for the promotion not only of their comfort, but of their holiness: "that, having the full assurance of hope, ye be not *slothful*." The word "slothful" is the same that, in the 11th verse of the preceding chapter, is rendered *dull of hearing*. The hope of eternal life animates the mind, and makes us willing to do and suffer all that is necessary to the gaining the object of our hope. It gives strength both for labour and suffering. "But followers of them who through faith and patience[1] inherit the promises." Some have strangely supposed that by

---

[1] Διὰ πίστεως καὶ μακροθυμίας may be by hendiadys put for διὰ πίστεως μακροθυμούσης, as Calvin remarks.

"them who through faith and patience inherit the promises," we are to understand Gentile believers, who "through faith and patience" are become inheritors in this world of the promises made to Abraham and his seed; as if the Apostle had said, 'Imitate the steadiness of your Gentile brethren.' I think there can be no reasonable doubt the reference is to their believing forefathers, who, by continuing stedfast in faith amid all the trials to which they were exposed, were now "inheriting the promises"—*i.e.*, the promised blessings—in heaven.

It may be thought that the statement here is inconsistent with what the Apostle says, ch. xi. 13 : " These all died in faith, not having received the promises, but having seen them afar off, and were persuaded of them, and embraced them, and confessed that they were strangers and pilgrims on the earth." But the incompatibility is merely apparent. The Apostle had no idea of the sleep of the soul. He believed that when he became "absent from the body," he would "be present with the Lord;" and he believed that the holy patriarchs had a conscious existence and an enjoyment of blessedness after their death; for, long after that, God, who "is not the God of the dead, but of the living," declared Himself to be their God. Their death did not hinder their "inheriting the promises" in due time. Till then, the spirits of these good men enjoyed a state of blessed rest in heaven, while they waited for the accomplishment of the promise respecting Christ's first coming, and the good things to be brought in by Him. But when these things came to be fulfilled, they "inherited the promises" which they died in the faith of, and which must have been a great accession to their blessedness; so that when the Apostle wrote this, they were "inheriting the promises" in a more perfect manner than they could have enjoyed them on earth, being now "present with the Lord." There are promises which remain yet to be fulfilled, but in due time they shall inherit these also. These refer to the second coming of Christ, to the redemption of their bodies from the grave, their being openly approved in the judgment, and the complete felicity of their whole persons in the possession of the heavenly kingdom.

The only point that remains to be noticed, is the influence which the Apostle's statements respecting apostates was likely to have in securing the accomplishment of this desire. The fearful state of the apostate was well fitted to place in a strong light the evil of unbelief, which leads to apostasy, and to stir up the Hebrews to "take heed lest there should be in any of them an evil heart of unbelief"—to guard against the first movements of the mind and heart away from Christ, and diligently to use every method for the establishing of their faith and hope, and joy and holiness.

The train of thought in the paragraph which follows seems to be—'I have made these statements to you respecting the character and doom of apostates, that ye may be induced to use strenuously every fit method for attaining a confident and undoubting expectation of the blessings of the Christian salvation; that you may not be languid and inactive, but may imitate your pious ancestors, who through a persevering faith have entered on the enjoyment of the promised blessings. To make my meaning still more obvious, I will illustrate my general assertion by a particular example. Abraham, having obtained from God a promise, sanctioned by an oath, firmly believed it, and continued firmly to believe it; and, through his persevering faith, finally entered into the possession of the blessing promised. You have also received promises, sanctioned also by an oath. It becomes you to cherish, like Abraham, an undoubting and a persevering faith; and in this way you also shall become inheritors of the promises.' Let us proceed to examine the verses somewhat more minutely.

Ver. 13. "For[1] when God made promise to Abraham, because He could swear by no greater, He sware by Himself, 14. Saying, Surely blessing I will bless thee, and multiplying I will multiply thee. 15. And so, after he had patiently endured, he obtained the promise." The facts asserted by the Apostle in these three verses are the following:—God made a promise to Abraham; He confirmed that promise by an oath. Abraham believed the promise, and persevered in believing it; and, through his persevering faith, obtained the promised blessing.

God made a number of promises to Abraham, some of them referring to temporal, and others of them to spiritual blessings —some of them relating to himself personally, and others relating to his posterity, either natural or spiritual. Which is the

[1] Γὰρ introduces an illustration and proof—'The persons I refer to did through faith and patience inherit the promises; for,' etc.

particular promise referred to here, it is not difficult to discover. It was a promise confirmed by an oath; and the only promise with which this description agrees is that which was given to Abraham after he had proved his devotedness to God, by laying his son Isaac, in obedience to His command, on the altar. We find a narrative of the incidents referred to here in Gen. xxii. 16–18: "By Myself have I sworn, saith the Lord; for because thou hast done this thing, and hast not withheld thy son, thine only son: that in blessing I will bless thee, and in multiplying I will multiply thy seed as the stars of the heaven, and as the sand which is upon the sea-shore; and thy seed shall possess the gate of his enemies: and in thy seed shall all the nations of the earth be blessed; because thou hast obeyed My voice." The quotation is not made exactly according to either the Hebrew text or to the version of the LXX., then in ordinary use, but the sense is accurately given. "I will multiply thee," and "I will multiply thy seed," are plainly synonymous expressions, as the only way in which a man can be multiplied is in his posterity. It has been generally supposed by interpreters, that though the Apostle only quotes a part, he refers to the whole promise; and much labour has been devoted to the making of it evident that this promise, especially the concluding part of it, implies in it a promise of the Messiah, and of all the blessings which through His instrumentality should be bestowed on mankind. I have no doubt of the justness of such a representation; but it does not appear to me that the Apostle, in quoting the promise here, meant to fix the attention of his readers on the contents of the promise, or to reason from its import, but merely to state the facts: A divine declaration, confirmed by an oath, was made to Abraham, warranting his expectation of future blessings It was the design of God to give Abraham the most satisfactory evidence that the blessings promised should be bestowed, and therefore He not only made a declaration, but confirmed that declaration by an oath; and, as there was no being in the universe superior to Himself to whom He could appeal, or to whom He would be answerable for the performance of His oath, "He sware by Himself," appealing to His own being and perfections, and pledging them, as it were, for the truth and performance of His promise, so that He could as soon cease to be as break it. The declaration was not in reality made more certain by the addition of an oath, but so solemn a form of asseveration was calculated to give a deeper impression of its certainty.

Now, Abraham, having received a promise thus confirmed, believed the declaration it contained, expected the blessings it referred to, and "patiently endured," or rather, steadily persevered in believing and expecting, amid all the trials to which he was exposed; and then at last "obtained the promise," *i.e.*, plainly, the promised blessing. He obtained the partial fulfilment of the promise—"Surely blessing I will bless thee"—even in this world. He obtained the much more extended fulfilment of it at death, when he entered on the rest and joy of paradise, obtaining the heavenly country of which Canaan was but a type. He has, since that period, had the promise still more fully accomplished, in the multiplication of his natural posterity, and still more in the coming of the Messiah, and in the multiplication of his spiritual offspring.

This, then, is a specimen of the examples held up to the imitation of the Hebrews: 'Here is *one* who through persevering faith became an inheritor of the promised blessings.' The application of this, as at once a pattern and motive to the Hebrews in their circumstances, is contained in the concluding part of the chapter.

Before entering on it, however, the Apostle premises a remark explicatory of the nature and design of oaths in general, and of the divine oath in particular. Ver. 16. "For men verily swear by the greater: and an oath for confirmation is to them an end of all strife." These words convey this general idea: 'An oath by God—an appeal to Him, is the highest kind of assurance which can be given by one man to another of the truth of his declarations and the sincerity of his intentions.' This passage has been often quoted in the controversy with respect to the lawfulness of oaths, as a proof on the affirmative side of that question. It does not seem to me to have much bearing on the subject, being merely the statement of a fact; though, at the same time, if swearing were in all cases unlawful, it is in the highest degree probable that such a statement as that before us would not have been made without a caution, that the practice, though general, was not right, and that though God may swear, men *must* not. That those who interpret the words of our Lord and the Apostle

James on this subject—Matt. v. 34; James v. 12—as an absolute prohibition of oaths, are mistaken, appears to me quite evident from the following considerations: that oaths were used by the pious patriarchs before the law; that God expressly appointed the use of swearing in judgment, where necessary; that this appointment rests on general and permanent grounds; that, under the New Testament, our Lord swore by answering to the adjuration of the high priest; and the Apostle Paul repeatedly interposes the solemnity of an oath in his declarations. The prohibitions of our Lord and His Apostle refer to irreverent and profane swearing in common conversation, which prevailed very extensively among the Jews, and which prevails but too extensively among ourselves. These observations are merely by the way.

Having thus remarked that an oath is the highest kind of evidence which can be given of the truth of a declaration and the sincerity of a promise, the Apostle goes on to show that God has dealt with the Hebrews as with Abraham—He had given them this highest ground of faith and confidence; and leaves it with them to draw the conclusion, that they should continue, like him, to persevere, till, like him, they obtained the promised blessing. Vers. 17-20. "Wherein God, willing more abundantly to show unto the heirs of promise the immutability of His counsel, confirmed it by an oath; that by two immutable things, in which it was impossible for God to lie, we might have a strong consolation, who have fled for refuge to lay hold upon the hope set before us: which hope we have as an anchor of the soul, both sure and stedfast, and which entereth into that within the vail; whither the Forerunner is for us entered, even Jesus, made an High Priest for ever, after the order of Melchisedec."

The word translated *wherein* may, and we apprehend ought to be rendered, 'for this reason, or therefore.'[1] Because an oath is the highest species of evidence, "therefore God, willing more abundantly to show unto the heirs of promise the immutability of His counsel, confirmed it by an oath; that by two immutable things, in which it was impossible for God to lie, we might have a strong consolation, who have fled for refuge to lay hold upon the hope set before us."

---

[1] ἐν ᾧ = בַּאֲשֶׁר, Gen. xxxix. 9, xviii. 28; Jonah i. 14; Rom. ii. 1; just as ἐν τούτῳ is *propterea*, Luke x. 20; John xvi. 30; Heb. xi. 2.

The first question here is—What is it which God has confirmed by an oath to the heirs of promise? Most interpreters suppose that the reference is to the promise made to Abraham. I am disposed to think that the reference is to the declaration in the 110th Psalm—" Thou art a priest for ever, after the order of Melchisedec"—which introduced this discussion, and to the consideration of which, as an illustration of the pre-eminent excellence of the priesthood of Christ, the Apostle is just about to proceed. To this conclusion I am led by attending to the context and the train of thought. Every one must see that there is a close connection stated, as existing between this divine oath and the abundant consolation and firm hope which it is calculated to produce, and the constitution of Jesus Christ "a High Priest after the order of Melchisedec," mentioned in the last verse. The introduction of these concluding words seems to me inexplicable, on the supposition that the Apostle here refers to the promise made to Abraham; whereas they are just what we should expect, supposing the reference to be to the oath mentioned in the 110th Psalm. We see, too, why the hope is represented as " entering into that within the vail," where the true Melchisedec, the everlasting Priest, is, and resting on Him there, as having entered in the name of His people. The high importance of the constitution of Christ's high-priesthood by an *oath* is afterwards more particularly illustrated in the 20th, 21st, and 28th verses of the next chapter; and we know it is according to the Apostle's usual method to notice cursorily what he intends by and by more fully to discuss. It is obvious that the fact, that Jesus Christ is " a Priest for ever, after the order of Melchisedec," lies at the foundation of human hope. He is a Priest, a Priest in the immediate presence of God, a Priest on a throne,— a King as well as a Priest, a King and a Priest for ever. That fact implies in it, both that "His blood cleanseth from all sin," and that "He ever liveth to make intercession," and therefore "is able to save to the uttermost those who come to God by Him,"—both that " He has purged our sins by Himself," and that He has "sat down on the right hand of God." Let us proceed, then, to the interpretation of the passage, on the supposition that it is this truth which the Apostle represents as confirmed by the solemnity of a divine oath.

" God was willing "—was graciously disposed—" to show to

the heirs of promise,"—*i.e.*, to "those who should inherit salvation," to those on whom it was His determination to bestow eternal happiness, Abraham's spiritual seed, "the heirs of the promises," for to Abraham and his seed were the promises made,— "the immutability of His counsel."[1] He was disposed to give them the most satisfactory evidence that He would never change His purpose of mercy towards them. " He confirmed *it* " (observe that *it* is a supplement)—literally, interposed—" with an oath." He not only said, but He swore, that the Messiah should be " a Priest for ever, after the order of Melchisedec ;" and He did so for this purpose, " that by two immutable things, in which it was impossible for God to lie, we might have a strong consolation, who have fled for refuge to lay hold on the hope set before us." The two immutable things have commonly been said to be the promise and the oath of God. I cannot doubt they are the two oaths: the oath to Abraham—the word of the oath before the law, and the word of the oath since the law in the 110th Psalm. This is the opinion of Storr and Stuart.

The first thing here that requires consideration, is the description of the persons for whose "strong consolation" this remarkable confirmation of a declaration by an oath on the part of God was intended: " *We ;*" *i.e.*, plainly, 'such of you as, along with me, have fled for refuge to lay hold on the hope set before us.' "The hope" here has by some interpreters been explained of Jesus Christ, on whom the Christian's hope rests, and "who is," as the Apostle elsewhere says, "our hope;" and by most interpreters, of that everlasting life which he who believes the Gospel hopes for. That "the hope" is not Christ personally, seems plain from its being distinguished from Him in the close of the verse. 'Our hope enters into the holy of holies, where Jesus is.' That " the hope" is not here the object of hope, the heavenly blessedness, is also plain: that may be said to be laid up in heaven, as in Col. i. 5, but cannot be said to enter into heaven. This shows that they are wrong who consider the figure as drawn from the Grecian games : thus 'We who are running to lay hold on the thing hoped for, which is held up to us.' Nor do our translators, who obviously had the

---

[1] The adjective neuter is elegantly employed for the substantive. Similar instances: τὸ γνωστόν, Rom. i. 19 ; τὸ χρηστόν, ii. 4 ; τὸ ἀδύνατον, viii. 3.

manslayer fleeing from the avenger of blood to the city of refuge before their minds (Num. xxxv. 11, 12), seem to have been more fortunate in discovering the origin of the tropical phraseology. I rather apprehend that "the hope set before us" is just the expectation which the Gospel testimony warrants us to entertain. The persons described are persons who have been made to see that all expectations of final happiness, except that which the Gospel warrants, are unfounded—hopes that will make ashamed; and, chased out of these "refuges of lies," they have, by the faith of the truth, "laid hold of," obtained possession of, "the hope of eternal life." The meaning of the expression may, perhaps, be thus illustrated. I have a friend in very hazardous circumstances. A medical man states that he thinks he may recover: he holds out a hope—he sets it before me. If I believe that he is a man of skill, I will credit his statement, and in this way lay hold of the hope. The Gospel makes statements which, if believed, necessarily produce "the hope of eternal life;" and this hope becomes ours, is laid hold of, in believing. Now the declaration of God, confirmed by an oath, that Jesus Christ is "a Priest for ever, after the order of Melchisedec," is intended to give these persons "strong consolation." If "the blood of Jesus Christ cleanseth from all sin"—if "He is able to save to the uttermost," then, though everything else bid them despair, this bids them hope.

And these declarations are absolutely true—they have the sanction of the oath of God. These two declarations—the promise to Abraham, and the declaration in the 110th Psalm—are "two unchangeable things, in which it is impossible for God to lie." He cannot falsify either His word or His oath. This impossibility argues no want of power in God, but, on the contrary, the highest perfection of it. It is a deficiency of power or of goodness in men which makes them violate their promises or oaths. They either cannot make good what they sincerely promise, or they propose some advantage to themselves by falsehood. But this can never be the case with God, who is possessed of infinite power, goodness, and faithfulness; so that there is an utter impossibility, arising from His perfections, that His promise should fail. The tendency of a declaration, which implies in it a ground of expectation of happiness, to produce *consolation*, depends on the abundance of the evidence. The distinctly pledged word and oath of God confirm the declaration, and, of course, go to increase the *consolation* of those who believe it. The salvation of those who come to God through Christ is thus as certain as the destruction of those who, by continuing in unbelief, will not come to God by Him. Both are secured by the oath of God. The words admit of a somewhat different construction and rendering: "So that by two immutable things, concerning which it is impossible that God should lie, we who have sought a refuge might have strong persuasion to hold fast the hope that is set before us; which hope we cleave to as an anchor of the soul."[1] This mode of exegesis we are inclined to prefer. The repeated oaths of God respecting the Messiah, as He " in whom all nations were to be blessed," and " the Priest for ever, after the order of Melchisedec," offer strong persuasive motives to those who, feeling their danger, are seeking refuge somewhere, "to lay hold of," and to hold fast, "the hope set before us." If this hope fail, the pillared firmament is rottenness, and earth's base built on stubble.

The Apostle, having mentioned the hope of the Christian, gives a very interesting description of it: "Which hope we have as an anchor of the soul, both sure and stedfast, and entering into that which is within the vail." The words "sure and stedfast," and "entering within the vail," refer, we think, directly to the hope of the Christian, and are not to be considered as qualities of the *anchor*, to which it is figuratively compared.[2] This " hope of eternal life" through the priesthood of Jesus Christ is "sure and stedfast,"—*i.e.*, it cannot be disappointed; and it " enters into that which is within the vail"—it has a reference to heavenly blessings—its object is " the salvation that is in Christ with eternal glory," the " being with Him where He is," and the sharing of His glory. This is the Christian's hope. " It doth not yet appear what we shall be: but we

---

[1] Stuart. In this case κρατῆσαι hangs by ἵ. ἱ. π., and not by οἱ καταφυγόντες.

[2] The image of an anchor flying upward, and fixing itself in the adytum of the heavenly temple, exceeds the license of Oriental figure. This were indeed " delphinum silvis appingere, fluctibus aprum." There seems a tendency to mix metaphors when anchors are the leading image. The correct Virgil, Æn. vi. 3, 4, has—

" ———— tum dente tenaci
Anchora *fundabat* naves."

know that, when He shall appear, we shall be like Him, seeing Him as He is." The leading idea seems to be—'This hope rests on Christ. He is in heaven—the perfected High Priest, "the Author of eternal salvation to all that obey Him." Hope, conducted by faith, passes through these heavens into the heaven of heavens—"enters within the vail," and confidently trusts in *Him* who is there as our "Forerunner," who has entered on our account, for our advantage, as our representative.'

It "enters within the vail, whither the Forerunner has for us entered."[1] The finest illustration of these words is to be found in our Lord's farewell discourse to His disciples: "In My Father's house are many mansions: if it were not so, I would have told you. I go to prepare a place for you. And if I go and prepare a place for you, I will come again, and receive you unto Myself; that where I am, there ye may be also."

This "entrance" of Jesus, "the Forerunner, within the vail," as His introduction to the possession of celestial glory in His mediatorial character, is the great subject of the ancient oracle to which the Apostle is referring. "The Lord said unto my Lord, Sit Thou at My right hand, till I make Thine enemies Thy footstool." "The Lord hath sworn, and will not repent, Thou art a Priest for ever, after the order of Melchisedec." Thus, naturally, is the Apostle brought back, after his long digression, to this oracle, from which he intends to show at large the pre-eminence of our Lord's priesthood; and the illustration of the meaning and import of this oracle will make it more and more evident how its confirmation with an oath is fitted to give "the heirs of promise" abundant consolation.

"Now, this *hope*," says the Apostle, "is as an *anchor* of the soul;" *i.e.*, it is fitted to preserve the mind firm in the profession and obedience of the truth. He who has laid hold of, and who keeps hold of this hope, will not be "tossed to and fro with every wind of doctrine;" but he will "be rooted and grounded in love," "stablished in the faith as he has been taught," "abounding therein with thanksgiving." He will be, according to the Apostle's wish, "a follower of those who through faith and patience are become inheritors of the promise;" like Abraham, having "patiently endured, he will obtain the promise;" he will patiently "continue in well-doing;" and,

[1] $\pi\rho\delta\rho\rho\mu\rho\varsigma$, as to signification, seems = $\dot{\alpha}\pi\alpha\rho\chi\dot{\eta}$, 1 Cor. xv. 20, 23.

through this patient continuance in well-doing, he will "obtain glory, honour, and immortality."[1]

Of what high importance is the hope of the Gospel, both to the Christian's comfort and holiness! This hope rests on the faith of the Gospel. This faith springs from the knowledge of the meaning and evidence of divine truth. These are to be found in the Bible. The influence of the Divine Spirit is necessary to enable us to find them there. That influence is promised to all who ask it. "Search the Scriptures." "Seek ye out of the book of the Lord, and read." "Ask, and ye shall receive; seek, and ye shall find; knock, and it shall be opened to you."

(3.) *Particular Illustrations of the Argument for the Superiority of our Lord's Priesthood, grounded on Ps. cx. 3.*

1. *The Order of Melchisedec superior to the Order of Aaron.*

Having finished this digression, the Apostle resumes his great theme, the priesthood of Christ; and, having shown its reality, he now proceeds to demonstrate its excellence—its excellence not so much absolutely, as in comparison with the Levitical priesthood. His first illustration is drawn from the ancient oracle in the 110th Psalm. Jesus Christ is superior as a Priest to the Levitical priests; for He is constituted by a divine oath " a Priest for ever, after the order of Melchisedec." This is the theme of the whole of the 7th chapter, on the illustration of which we are now about to enter.

The first thing to be done in an argument of this kind is, to show that Melchisedec, to whom our Lord is compared, was a priest superior to Aaron, and his order of priesthood superior to the Aaronical order; and this is what the Apostle does in the first ten verses of the chapter. The first three verses consist of a statement of facts; and the following seven, of reasoning from these facts to the superiority of Melchisedec to Aaron, and of his order of priesthood to the Levitical order.

The first three verses form one sentence. Vers. 1-3. "For this Melchisedec, king of Salem, priest of the Most High God,

---

[1] Theodoret's note deserves to be cited. Ηὔξησε τὸ θάρσος τῇ τοῦ προδρόμου προσηγορίᾳ· εἰ γὰρ πρόδρομος ἡμῶν ἐστι, καὶ ὑπὲρ ἡμῶν ἀνελήλυθεν, ἀνάγκη καὶ ἡμᾶς ἀκολουθῆσαι, καὶ τῆς ἀνόδου τυχεῖν.

who met Abraham returning from the slaughter of the kings, and blessed him; to whom also Abraham gave a tenth part of all; first being, by interpretation, King of righteousness, and after that also King of Salem, which is, King of peace: without father, without mother, without descent, having neither beginning of days, nor end of life; but, made like unto the Son of God, abideth a priest continually."

The connection of this passage has been variously stated. Some would connect it with the 10th verse of the 5th chapter, and consider the paragraph as assigning the reason why the Messiah is termed " a Priest after the order of Melchisedec:" He is so, because Melchisedec " abideth a priest continually." But as this is obviously only one of the reasons why Christ is called " a Priest after the order of Melchisedec," and as the Apostle does not confine himself to the illustration of this one reason, but treats generally of the superiority of Melchisedec as a priest to Aaron and his sons, I apprehend that the particle *for* is here equivalent to *now*,—that it marks the Apostle's transition to another department of his argument, or his resumption of a topic which had been suspended. From the ancient oracle he had already proved the reality, now he proceeds to prove the pre-eminence, of our Lord's priesthood.

Before entering on the explication of the different parts of this account of Melchisedec, it will be proper to say a few words on a question which it is strange should ever have been agitated: To what order of beings did Melchisedec belong? One class of early heretics held that Melchisedec was the Holy Ghost; another, that he was a divine virtue, superior in power to Christ, after whose likeness Christ was formed by God; a third class held an opinion which has still some supporters, that he was the Son of God in human form; a fourth class were of opinion that he was an angel.

The only one of these opinions that deserves more than merely to be noticed, is the third, and that chiefly because it continues still to be held by some interpreters. To us it appears very plain, that Melchisedec and the Son of God are two different persons. Melchisedec is said to have been " made like unto the Son of God;" and the Son of God is said to have been " made a High Priest after the order of Melchisedec." It is scarcely possible to conceive two persons more clearly distinguished. Besides, to the exercise of the priesthood on the part of the Son of God, the possession of human nature was absolutely necessary, according to the Apostle; and further, to argue from the superiority of the priesthood of Melchisedec to Aaron and his sons to the superiority of the priesthood of Christ, supposing Melchisedec and Christ the same person, is obviously a paralogism.

Among those who consider Melchisedec as a man, there has been considerable variety of opinion as to who he was. Some have supposed that he was Enoch; others, Shem; others, Ham; others, Job. These are mere conjectures; and, indeed, all of them highly improbable, if not demonstrably false conjectures. The most probable opinion is, that he was one of the descendants of Japhet, who possessed the supreme authority over a small tribe in Canaan, of which Salem was the chief town,[1] among whom the true primitive religion was still preserved, and who was invested with the priestly as well as the regal office. The notion which some learned men have entertained, that he was endowed with immortality, and that, after having officiated for a time on earth both as a king and a priest, he was translated alive to heaven, has no foundation but a mistaken interpretation of the 8th verse.

We proceed now to the explication of the Apostle's account of this singular person.

He was " king of Salem." The most probable opinion as to the capital of Melchisedec is, that it was Jerusalem, of which it appears from Ps. lxxvi. that Salem was one of the names. On this supposition, there appears, as already remarked, a peculiar propriety in terming "*Jerusalem above*,"[2] or rather, ancient Jerusalem, as opposed to " Jerusalem *that now is*," " the mother of us all."[3]

But he was not only a king, but a priest in Salem. He was "priest of the Most High God."[4] The Hebrew word,[4] of which the Greek word here translated *priest* is the version, sometimes signifies *prince;* but the addition of " of the Most High God," and his blessing Abraham and receiving tithes from him—both priestly functions—make it plain that the title is to be under-

---

[1] Χαναναίων δυνάστης, as Josephus calls him, Ant. i. 10, 2.

[2] Ἡ ἄνω Ἱερουσαλήμ. Ἄνω is used in reference to time as well as place.

[3] Gal. iv. 25, 26. See p. 262.    [4] כֹּהֵן.

stood in its ordinary and peculiar meaning. He is called "Priest of the Most High God,"[1] to distinguish him from the priests of false deities, and probably also to intimate that he was the priest of a religion in which God was not made known as the God of a particular people, but in which He was viewed in His common relation to all mankind. Melchisédec's priesthood belonged to the primitive catholic dispensation of religion, not to that temporary and topical economy which "was added because of transgressions."

Melchisedec is further described as having " met Abraham returning from the slaughter of the kings." The passage of ancient history referred to is to be found, Gen xiv. 18, 19. A coalition of four kings had made a successful attack on the kings of Sodom and Gomorrah and their allies. According to the marauding practice of that age, they carried off the property of those whom they had conquered, along with many of its owners. Among the rest, they took captive Lot and his family. Abraham, on being informed of this, pursued them at the head of his numerous household, and succeeded in rescuing the captives and recovering the property. It was on his return from this expedition that the interview with Melchisedec took place. Whether any intercourse had previously taken place between these two venerable men, or whether they afterwards continued to have occasional intercourse, we cannot tell; though the probability seems to be, that Melchisedec was not a stranger to Abraham when he came forth to meet him, and that, in an age when the worshippers of the true God were comparatively few, two such men as Abraham and Melchisedec did not live in the same district of country without forming a close intimacy.

All that we know certainly is, that on this occasion *he blessed Abraham;* i.e., he solemnly invoked God's blessing on him, or rather, solemnly declared that he was blessed of God, and an object of *His* peculiar favour and care. This was a part of the priest's office, as we learn from Deut. xxi. 5, where Aaron's appointment to the priesthood is described as a separation " to bless the people in the name of the Lord."

---

[1] It deserves to be noticed, that in a fragment of Sanconiathon, preserved in Eusebius' Præparatio Evangelica, we learn that the name under which the Phœnicians worshipped the true God was Elion, 'Ελιοῦν· which is just the Hebrew word עליון, here rendered ὕψιστος.

But not only did Melchisedec perform the function of a priest in reference to Abraham, but Abraham also acknowledged him as a priest, by giving him " a tenth part of all ;" *i.e.*, plainly, not of all his property, but of the spoils which he had taken from the kings whom he had overcome in battle.

From this it appears, that the institution of tithes as the means of the support of the priests, though introduced into the Mosaic economy, belonged, like sacrifice, to a more ancient order of things. No argument, however, for the divine right of any class of Christian teachers to tithes can be legitimately drawn from the institution, either before or under the law. It supports the general principle, that ministers of religion should be maintained by those to whose spiritual interests they devote their time and their talents, but it does no more. The fact which the Apostle wishes to establish is obviously this: ' Abraham acknowledged Melchisedec as a priest.'

He then takes notice by the way, that both Melchisedec's appellations were significant ones; and I have no doubt that he did so with the intention that the Hebrews should notice that these appellations were very applicable to Him of whom Melchisedec was so illustrious a figure. "First being, by interpretation, *King of righteousness*,"—*i.e.*, ' his first appellation, Melchisedec, means King of righteousness, or a righteous king ;' " and then afterwards," *i.e.*, his second appellation, " King of Salem,"[1] means " King of peace." We know that names were often given, both to men and places, significant of some remarkable quality possessed by them, or some important event relating to them. It is not unlikely that to his remarkable justice Melchisedec owed his name, and that his capital was called Salem from the peace and happiness which his subjects enjoyed under his government.

Hitherto all has been plain enough. The statement contained in the 3d verse, however, sounds somewhat paradoxical. " Without father, without mother, without descent," or genealogy, " having neither beginning of days, nor end of life ; but, made like unto the Son of God, abideth a priest continually."

This is the statement which has led into so many strange opinions respecting Melchisedec. If he was, as we believe him

---

[1] מֶלֶךְ שָׁלֵם.

to have been, merely a man, these words cannot be understood in their most obvious meaning. It has been supposed that all that the Apostle means, is to assert that there is no account in the sacred writings of his parentage, or birth, or death. This is true: but it is difficult to see how the statement of such a fact bears at all on the Apostle's object; and if he had been about to state it, we should have expected him to have used plainer words.

The key to the true meaning of the passage is to be found in the peculiar view the Apostle is here taking of Melchisedec. He is speaking of him as a priest; and as a priest he is said to have had no father, or mother, or genealogy. The last statement is explanatory of the two former. The genealogy of the Levitical priests was very carefully preserved. It was absolutely necessary that a priest should have for his father a lineal descendant of Aaron, and for his mother a person qualified to be a priest's wife; and that this should be certified by a genealogical register. Accordingly, we learn that they who could not clearly prove their priesthood at the return from the captivity, were not allowed to officiate till God should give counsel in the matter by Urim and Thummim: Ezra ii. 62, 63; Neh. vii. 63, 64, 65. Melchisedec belonged to an order of priesthood where natural descent was not at all regarded—an order of things free from those artificial restrictions which formed a leading feature of the legal economy; and in this way he was a fit figure of our great New Testament High Priest, who did not belong to the family of Aaron or the tribe of Levi.

"Having neither beginning of days, nor end of life," is a phrase to be explained on the same principle. If Melchisedec was a man, there is no doubt that he began and ceased to live; but as a priest he did not belong to that order who had a fixed period for commencing, and a fixed period for concluding, their priestly existence. The Levitical priests were allowed at the age of twenty-five years to minister to their officiating brethren; at thirty they entered on the services peculiar to the priesthood; and at fifty there was an end of their priestly services. This was the beginning of their days and the end of their life as priests. But Melchisedec belonged, as I said before, to a less artificial order of things. When he was called to be a priest, we do not know; but it was not according to any statute law that the exercise of his functions as a priest commenced; and his priesthood seems to have been commensurate with his life.

In these respects he was "made like unto the Son of God."[1] It has been said that the want of all record in reference to Melchisedec's father, and mother, and genealogy—in reference to his birth and his death—were intended to fit him to be an emblem of Jesus Christ, who as God has no mother, and as man no father—"whose goings forth have been of old, from everlasting," and who is "the same yesterday, to-day, and for ever." But this is obviously not merely very unsatisfactory in itself, but it is utterly foreign to the Apostle's object. The meaning obviously is, 'In these respects Melchisedec resembles the Son of God; for He too did not belong to that order of priesthood whose descent from Aaron was a necessary qualification, and whose entering on and cessation from the priestly functions were regulated by express appointment.' The appellation, "Son of God," rather than the name Jesus Christ, is used, as it was under that appellation that He is introduced in the beginning of the Epistle, ch. i. 1.

There is little difficulty now in the concluding words: Melchisedec "abideth a priest continually." Some interpreters would insert the word *who*, and consider the phrase as applying, not to Melchisedec, but to Christ; but this is an unwarrantable freedom with the sacred text. The meaning is, 'Melchisedec continued a priest during the whole of his life. He did not, like the Levitical priests, at an appointed period cease to minister; while he continued to live he continued to minister.'[2]

In the paragraph which follows, these facts are reasoned from. They are employed to establish the superiority of Melchisedec as a priest to Aaron and his sons. The form of the Apostle's reasoning is very different from that which the same arguments would assume in the hands of a modern theologian; but a careful examination of it will convince us not only of the justness of the conclusion, but of the ingenuity and satisfactoriness of the means by which he arrives at it.

Ver. 4. "Now consider how great this man was, unto whom even the patriarch Abraham gave the tenth of the spoils." You

---

[1] Ἀφωμοιωμένος does not mean "made like to," but "likened to."
[2] A Roman dictator for life was called "Dictator perpetuus."

will notice *was* is a supplement. Perhaps the force of the argument would have been more clearly expressed had the supplement been, 'must have been:' 'Consider how great this man must have been, to whom even the patriarch Abraham gave the tenth of the spoils.'

The Apostle's argument consists of the following parts:—Abraham acknowledged the religious superiority of Melchisedec. Abraham, in a religious point of view, was a highly dignified character. He whom Abraham acknowledged as his religious superior must have been a more dignified character still. Abraham's giving tithes to Melchisedec after having received his priestly blessing, was a plain acknowledgment on the part of Abraham that he considered and honoured him as the " Priest of the Most High God."

Tokens of respect are either personal or official. The value of a personal token of respect depends on the wisdom and the worth of the person who yields it. The value of official tokens of respect depends on the dignity of the station of the person who yields it. It is plain that it is to an official token of respect that the Apostle here refers; and to ascertain its value, we must have a correct idea of the official rank of the person who offered it.

Now Abraham was a person of very high dignity. He was the founder of the Israelitish nation; he was the father of that people whom God chose to be the depositaries of His revealed will—the means of preserving true religion among mankind—and the means, too, of the development of the great economy of divine mercy. To him the promises of the peculiar privileges to be bestowed on his posterity were given. He was as it were, not the fountain indeed, but the reservoir from which they flowed out to his posterity. Every religious privilege they enjoyed, they enjoyed because they were his posterity. In his person there was concentrated all the sacred dignity which belonged to the peculiar people of God. Whatever was venerable and holy about the Israelites, or the system under which they were placed, was essentially to be found in their patriarch.

It obviously follows from these two facts—that Abraham was a person of high sacred dignity, and that he acknowledged the religious superiority of Melchisedec—that Melchisedec must have been a person invested with a very extraordinary degree of sacred dignity, and that the order of priesthood of which he was the representative must have been the highest order of priesthood. No person among the descendants of Abraham equalled their great progenitor in sacred dignity. All the sacred offices under the legal economy were but expansions as it were, or divisions of honour, which centred in the person of the patriarch. In the person of Abraham the whole legal economy did homage to another, a more spiritual economy, in the person of Melchisedec. It was a higher honour than if Moses and Aaron had paid tithes to Melchisedec. It was equivalent to David and Solomon, and all the illustrious prophets, and priests, and kings of Israel, doing homage to him in his priestly character. Were the Sovereign of Great Britain, who is the fountain of all civil honour in this country, to do homage to any individual, it would be a clear acknowledgment that that individual possessed a dignity superior to any British dignity. In like manner, Abraham's doing homage to Melchisedec is a plain proof that, in his sacred character, Melchisedec was superior to any of the religious officers under the legal economy.

This idea is brought more distinctly out in the two following verses:—Ver. 5. " And verily they that are of the sons of Levi, who receive the office of the priesthood, have a commandment to take tithes of the people according to the law, that is, of their brethren, though they come out of the loins of Abraham: 6. But he, whose descent is not counted from them, received tithes of Abraham, and blessed him that had the promises."

The substance of the Apostle's argument in these verses is this : ' It is a high honour which the Aaronical priesthood enjoy, in being acknowledged as possessed of a sacred dignity by their brethren, who equally with themselves are descended from Abraham; but it was a far higher honour which Melchisedec enjoyed, in having his sacred dignity acknowledged by Abraham himself.'

"The sons," or descendants, "of Levi, who received the priesthood," are plainly the lineal descendants of Aaron, to whom among the sons of Levi the priestly honours were restricted. They "had a commandment to take tithes." According to an express, positive law of Heaven, of which you have an account in the 18th chapter of Numbers, their maintenance was provided for. The Levites generally received the tithes, and the priests were supported by the tithe of these tithes. The paying tithes was an acknowledgment of the spiritual superiority of those to whom they were paid; and the value of that acknowledgment depended on the sacred dignity of those who yielded it. The Aaronical priesthood were not supported by a tax exacted from idolaters, but from the sacred nation. The Levites, their ministers, were supported by tithes paid by the great body of the Israelites; the priests, by tithes paid by this doubly sacred order of men, the Levites.

On these principles, how much more honourable was Melchisedec than Aaron or any of his sons! "He, whose descent is not counted from them, received tithes of Abraham, and blessed him that had the promises."

" He whose descent is not reckoned from them," or ' he who as to descent is not among them,' is plainly just a circumlocution for Melchisedec. He was "*without descent*," we are told in a former verse; *i.e.*, his priesthood was of a kind in which there was no reference to parentage. His name is not in the genealogy of the Levitical priests—he did not belong to their order. ' Melchisedec, a priest of another order than that of Aaron, received tithes of Abraham.'

I rather think there is an intended contrast between the phrases used in reference to the Levitical priesthood and Melchisedec, as to the acknowledgment of dignity implied in receiving tithes. They "have a commandment to take tithes of their brethren." If they receive them, it is not so much as a voluntary expression of homage to their spiritual dignity as in obedience to an express, positive law. But "he received tithes." Abraham freely gave them to him. It was a voluntary expression of his recognising him as the "priest of the Most High God;" and in this way corresponded to that spiritual, liberal, unrestricted economy to which Melchisedec's priesthood belonged, and under the most perfect earthly form of which we live.

And as Melchisedec " received tithes from Abraham," so he also officially pronounced a benediction on him. He "blessed him who had the promises." The benediction is recorded in Gen. xiv. 18. The Aaronical priesthood blessed their brethren. It was their duty solemnly to invoke the favour of God on the people of the Lord. But Melchisedec pronounced a solemn benediction on "him who received the promises;" *i.e.*, who was the head of the holy family—the founder of the holy nation—to whom God made the promises, of which all the privileges and honours conferred on his posterity were the fulfilment.

The Apostle adds, the more distinctly to bring out his argument, ver. 7. " And, without all contradiction, the less is blessed of the better." These words are plainly to be understood with limitations. It does not follow that, because a priest under the law blessed the king, he was in a civil capacity the king's superior, any more than that a Christian minister instructing or even reproving a man of high civil rank, who is a member of the church of which he is pastor, is civilly his superior. The Apostle's argument is, 'The person who accepts of priestly benediction from an individual acknowledges his spiritual superiority;' just as the highest authority in the land, if he were becoming a member of a voluntary Christian society, would acknowledge that its pastor was "over him in the Lord." Abraham's paying tithes and receiving a priestly blessing from Melchisedec, was a clear acknowledgment of Melchisedec's superiority in a religious point of view. It was a proof that Melchisedec was a priest of a higher order than that order, all whose dignities were centred in Abraham's person, who did homage to Melchisedec.

Hitherto the Apostle has argued for the superiority of Melchisedec's priesthood to that of the family of Aaron, solely from the facts of Melchisedec receiving tithes from, and pronouncing a benediction on Abraham. Now he proceeds to state an argument from the fact stated in the 3d verse, which, as I endeavoured to show is, that Melchisedec's priesthood was not of a kind restricted to a particular family, or exercised only for a restricted period. Ver. 8. " And here men that die receive tithes; but there he receiveth them, of whom it is witnessed that he liveth."

"Here" plainly is equivalent to—' under the Mosaic economy;' and "there," is—' before the law, under that order of things in which Melchisedec was a priest.'[1] The words of this verse, taken by themselves, are certainly very dark, and apparently inexplicable. Some have supposed that these words do not refer to the comparison between the Aaronical priests and Mel-

---

[1] Cappellus and Peirce consider ὧδε as = ' in the Jewish republic, or State,' and ἐκεῖ as = ' in the place where Abraham met Melchisedec.'

chisedec, but to that between the Aaronical priesthood and our Lord Jesus Christ, "the High Priest of our profession:" "Here," on earth, "dying men receive tithes," *i.e.*, are priests; "but there," in heaven, "He is a Priest of whom it is testified that He never dies." This is plainly quite arbitrary and unsatisfactory. Others have supposed, that though Melchisedec is spoken of, the Apostle speaks of him as sustaining the person of Christ, as representing Christ, of whom he was a figure. But it is quite plain, that though many things may be predicated of persons who are types of Christ which cannot be predicated of them as types of Christ, yet nothing can be predicated of them as types of Christ which cannot be predicated of them personally. What is said of them as types of Christ may be true in a higher sense in reference to Christ, but it must be true of them in a lower sense; and, indeed, it is this that fits them for being types of Christ.

There can be no reasonable doubt that the words before us are the statement of an argument for the superiority of Melchisedec to the Aaronical priesthood; and in this point of view, let us inquire into its meaning and estimate its force. " Here men who die receive tithes." To " receive tithes," is here just equivalent to—' to be a priest.' ' Here men who die are priests;' or, ' under the Mosaic economy the priests are men who die.' The natural, obvious meaning of "men who die" is, 'mortal men.' But I apprehend there is evidence enough that the Apostle is using the phrase in a peculiar sense. He had said before, that Melchisedec, as a priest, was " without beginning of days or end of life," and " abides a perpetual priest;" *i.e.*, 'his priesthood did not, like the priesthood of Aaron, commence and terminate at a fixed period, but he was a priest as long as he lived.' Now it is in reference to this statement that he here remarks, ' the Levitical priests are *dying* priests.' They have "beginning of days, and end of life." They are not priests till thirty; they cease to be priests at fifty—that is the termination of their priestly life. But " here he receiveth tithes, of whom it is testified that he liveth."

Many have supposed that the words, "it is testified of him that he liveth," merely mean, that we have no account of Melchisedec's death. We read that he lived, but we never read that he died. This certainly savours more of rabbinical trifling than anything else. What bearing has it on the Apostle's argument?

What kind of a reasoner would he be who should say, 'Melchisedec is a greater priest than Aaron, or any of his sons; for, though he is no doubt dead, we have no account of his death?' In this he is but on a level with the greater part of the priests, of whose death we have no record. I apprehend the meaning of the Apostle's words is: 'Under the law the priesthood was temporary; but before the law the priesthood was perpetual. Here he receiveth tithes, of whom it is testified that he liveth, or abideth a priest continually.'

It may be asked, Where is this testified of Melchisedec? No such testimony is to be found in the 14th chapter of Genesis; but, if I mistake not, such a testimony is found in the 110th Psalm, to which the Apostle is referring, and from which he proceeds to argue: "Thou art a priest for ever, after the order of Melchisedec;"—*i.e.*, I apprehend, not, 'Thou shalt be a priest after the order of Melchisedec, and Thou shalt be a priest after that order for ever;' but, 'Thou shalt be a perpetual priest, after the order of Melchisedec.' Melchisedec was a priest all his life, and Thou shalt be a priest all Thy life. It is testified in these words that Melchisedec is a living, not a dying priest—a priest, not during a part, but during the whole, of his life. The Apostle's argument, then, is this: 'Melchisedec is superior to the Aaronical priesthood; for their priesthood is temporary and limited—they die as priests before they die as men. But Melchisedec, while he continued to live, continued to minister.'

In the 9th and 10th verses the Apostle brings forward, more distinctly, a statement which was implied in what he had already said of Abraham's acknowledging the priesthood of Melchisedec; but the more distinct enunciation of which was peculiarly fitted to promote his object—the showing that Melchisedec, as a priest, was superior to the order of Aaron. Ver. 9. "And, as I may so say, Levi also"—rather, 'even Levi'[1]—"who receiveth tithes, paid tithes[2] in Abraham. 10. For he was yet in the loins of his father when Melchisedec met him."

"As I may so say" is just equivalent to—'Indeed, I may go further: I may assert with truth, that Melchisedec was as much honoured as if Levi'—*i.e.*, plainly, the whole Levitical tribe—

---

[1] καί being intensive.

[2] It deserves notice that the Apostle does not say, δεκάτην ἔδωκεν, but, as Ebrard says, "purposely makes use of the passive δεδεκάτωται."

'had done him homage.'[1] The argument may at first seem more fanciful than solid. It certainly does not follow that a remote ancestor of mine was more honourable than a man of high rank, though his remote ancestor had given the most decided manifestations of his acknowledgment of the superiority of my remote ancestor. But the cases are not parallel. We have seen that the Apostle is speaking of official, and sacred official dignity. All the sacred dignity which belonged to the Israelitish people was concentrated in their ancestor, and derived from him. Abraham was the priest of his family—the prophet of his family—the king of his family. Aaron and his sons derived all their honour from Abraham; and therefore, when Abraham did homage to Melchisedec, they in effect did so too.

2. *The Prediction, that a Perpetual Priest was to arise, after the Order of Melchisedec, is a proof of the Inferiority of the Priesthood that was to be superseded, and of the Superiority of the Priesthood that was to supersede.*

The paragraph which follows is the development of another, and an equally satisfactory, argument for the superiority of the priesthood of Christ to that of Aaron, which is folded up in this ancient oracle. Inasmuch as this divine oracle declares that, even after the institution of the Levitical priesthood, in the Messiah there was to be raised up a perpetual Priest, not after the order of Aaron, but after another order,—it follows that the priesthood of Aaron was inadequate to the attainment of the great purposes of the priesthood, and, of course, was inferior to that priesthood by which it was to be superseded, and the per-

---

[1] ὡς ἔπος εἰπεῖν—a phrase used by writers, especially orators—" ad emollienda durius et audacius enuntiata." Some have considered it as = κεφάλαιον ἐπὶ 'τοῖς λεγομένοις, viii. 1; but this is not used except when a long statement has preceded, not when a new statement is introduced. Theophylact's note is good : τὸ δὲ ὡς ἔπος εἰπεῖν, ἢ τοῦτο σημαίνει, ὅτι καὶ ἐν συντόμῳ εἰπεῖν, ἢ ἀντὶ τοῦ ἵν' οὕτως εἴπω. Ἐπειδὴ γὰρ τόλμημα ἐδόκει τὸ εἰπεῖν, ὅτι ὁ Λευΐ, μήπω εἰς γένεσιν παραχθείς, ἐδεκατώθη παρὰ τοῦ Μελχισεδέκ, ἐκόλασε τοῦτο. "When he says ὡς ἔπος εἰπεῖν, he either means, ' that I may speak briefly,' or ' that I may speak *thus*.' As it seemed somewhat too bold to affirm that Levi, before he was brought into the world, paid tithes to Melchisedec, he thus corrects or qualifies it." Peter's ἐξὸν εἰπεῖν, Acts. ii. 29, is a similar mode of expression.

petual endurance of which proves its efficacy. Such is the Apostle's argument in this paragraph. Let us examine it somewhat more minutely.

Ver. 11. "If therefore perfection were by the Levitical priesthood (for under it the people received the law), what further need was there that another priest should rise after the order of Melchisedec, and not be called after the order of Aaron?"

The particle *therefore*[1] does not here indicate that what follows is an inference from what had just been stated. It is merely a particle of transition: the same particle in the beginning of chapter ix. is rendered, *then verily*. It intimates a transition to another argument bearing on the same general point—the superiority of Christ's priesthood to the Aaronical, and rising out of the same divine oracle.

The clause translated, "for under it the people received the law," is plainly parenthetical. It will lead to the more easy and distinct apprehension of the Apostle's meaning, if we, in the first instance, attend to the statement of the argument, without reference to the parenthesis. "If then perfection were by the Levitical priesthood, what further need was there that another priest should arise after the order of Melchisedec, and not be called after the order of Aaron?"

The passage in the 110th Psalm plainly intimates, that in the Messiah there was to arise a priest, long after the institution of the Levitical priesthood; and that He was not to belong to that order, but to another order,—even "the order of Melchisedec." Now, this divine declaration obviously implies in it, that the Levitical priesthood was incapable of securing the great general designs of the priesthood; for if it had, there would have been no necessity for a priest of another order being raised up—there would have been no necessity for the Messiah being a priest, or a priest of a different order from that of Aaron. The Apostle's question is just equivalent to a strong declaration: 'The prediction that the Messiah was to be a priest, and a priest after the order of Melchisedec, is a plain proof that perfection is not by the Levitical priesthood.'

But what are we to understand by the phrase, "if perfection were by the Levitical priesthood?" I apprehend it is just equivalent to—'If the Levitical priesthood were perfect—if it were

[1] οὖν.

adequate to gain all the ends for which the priesthood was designed.' But the question returns on us, What were these ends? In what does the perfection of a priesthood consist?

Some consider the "perfection" here spoken of as referring to expiation; others, to quieting the conscience and giving peace to the mind; others, to sanctification, in the systematic sense of that word—spiritual transformation of character; others, to true, permanent, everlasting happiness. I am disposed to think that the word is intended to comprehend all these ideas. The grand end of the priesthood was to *bring men to God*—to make them partakers of His favour, and image, and happiness, in all the extent of their nature, and during the whole eternity of their being; and in order to this, guilt must be expiated—the salvation of the sinner must be made compatible with, and illustrative of, the perfections of the divine character, and the principles of the divine government—the conscience must be tranquillized—the heart must be purified, that man may be capable of that happiness which consists in a participation of the divine blessedness.

The imperfection of the Levitical priesthood in this point of view, might be clearly demonstrated by a reference to the nature and design of its services,—and this the Apostle most satisfactorily does in the sequel; but here he argues to its imperfection from the simple fact, that long after its establishment, the Messiah, a priest not belonging to this order at all, but to another order, was to arise. God does nothing in vain. If the Levitical priesthood could have attained the great ends of priesthood, the Messiah had not been a priest, or, at any rate, not a priest "after the order of Melchisedec;" there would have been no need for this. It is plainly assumed in this argument, that the Messiah— the person to whom the oracle in the 110th Psalm refers—was not to be a priest after the order of Aaron. The whole force of the argument depends on the justness of this assumption; and accordingly, I apprehend, the principal object of the remaining part of the paragraph is to establish this.

But before going further, it will be necessary that we attend to the meaning and design of the parenthetical clause—" for under it the people received the law." The meaning which these English words naturally convey is: "The Israelitish people were subjected to the Levitical priesthood previously to their being placed under that economy commonly termed the Law.' But this cannot be the Apostle's meaning, for two very plain reasons: first, it is not true; for the Israelites were placed under the law as an economy previously to the appointment of the Levitical priesthood; and secondly, though it were true, it has no bearing on the Apostle's object. Commentators have seen this difficulty, and have fallen on different schemes for removing it. Some render it, 'the people received the law on account of the priesthood;' or, in plainer words, they were rendered a peculiar people, and placed under the law, that they might serve God according to the Levitical ritual. But this, though true, is not the natural meaning of the words, and does not seem to have any connection with the Apostle's argument. We use no improper freedom with the words when we render them, '*for the people were subjected to a law in reference to that priesthood;*'[1] *i.e.*, everything with respect to that priesthood was settled by divine positive appointment. It was restricted to a particular tribe, and it was regulated by a variety of carnal commandments —precepts having a reference to external and perishable things.

The remark, I apprehend, is introduced for the purpose of clearing the ground—if I may use the expression—for the proof that the priest mentioned in the 110th Psalm is not, and cannot be, of the Levitical order. None can be a priest of the Levitical order who does not in all things correspond to the description given in the law respecting the priesthood, to which the Israelitish people were subjected; and that this is not the case with regard to the person spoken of in the 110th Psalm, the Apostle clearly shows in the 13th and 14th verses, as we shall soon have an opportunity of seeing.

But before he enters on the evidence that He who is spoken of in the 110th Psalm is not, and cannot be, a Levitical priest, he makes an observation by the way, in the 12th verse, respecting the change of the priesthood being a clear evidence of the law being changed also. Ver. 12. "For the priesthood being changed, there is made of necessity a change also of the law."

These words, viewed as a general principle, would express a sentiment not consistent with truth. A complete change may

---

[1] ἐπί with the dative is often used as == ' in reference to:' Mark vi. 52; John xii. 16; Luke xxiii. 38; Rev. x. 11, xxii. 16; Heb. xi. 4. Winer, § lii. c. v. Carpzov renders it, "Populus vi legis ei subjectus erat."

take place with regard to the ecclesiastical arrangements of a people without any alteration in its civil constitution. It was otherwise, however, with the Israelitish people. The Levitical priesthood was so interwoven with the whole polity, that the extinction of that priesthood was equivalent to a dissolution of that economy. That is obviously true; but I do not think it is the truth which the Apostle here states. The law he is speaking of throughout the whole of this paragraph, is the law of the priesthood to which the Israelitish people had been subjected; and his assertion is just this: 'If a person, by divine appointment, fill the office of the priesthood who does not answer to the description given of a priest in the law—if he belongs not to the class to which, by that law, the priesthood is restricted, it is perfectly plain that He who enacted the law has annulled it. Jesus Christ's being a Priest, is a clear proof that the Mosaic law about the priesthood is abrogated.'

This is an important remark, naturally growing out of the Apostle's statement, and bearing too on his general object,—yet as obviously made by the way, and not forming any part of the illustration of the particular argument in which he is engaged. In a modern work, the remark we have been illustrating would have been a foot-note.

The Apostle returns to state the evidence that He to whom the oracle in the 110th Psalm refers, is not—cannot be—a priest of the Levitical order. According to the law respecting the priesthood to which the Israelitish people were subjected, none but the descendants of Aaron, who was of the tribe of Levi, could be priests. But whether we consider what is said of the Messiah in the Old Testament, to whom the Jews admitted the passage in the 110th Psalm to refer, or what we know of Jesus Christ, in whom all Christians consider it as having been accomplished, it is equally evident that the person spoken of in that Psalm could not be a Levitical priest; for, says the Apostle, as to the first of these things—ver. 13,—" For He of whom these things are spoken pertaineth to another tribe, of which no man gave attendance at the altar."

These words, "He of whom these things are spoken," or, "He to whom these things are spoken,"—plainly referring to the words of the divine oath, "Thou art a Priest for ever, after the order of Melchisedec,"—are just a descriptive appellation of the

Messiah. The Messiah, as every Jew knew, was to belong to a tribe of which none "gave attendance at the altar,"—even to the tribe of Judah. "To give attendance at the altar" is equivalent to priesthood. Now, that was confined by law to the family of Aaron, and the tribe of Levi. "And thou shalt bring Aaron and his sons unto the door of the tabernacle of the congregation, and wash them with water. And thou shalt put upon Aaron the holy garments, and anoint him, and sanctify him; that he may minister unto Me in the priest's office. And thou shalt bring his sons, and clothe them with coats: and thou shalt anoint them, as thou didst anoint their father, that they may minister unto Me in the priest's office: for their anointing shall surely be an everlasting priesthood throughout their generations. Thus did Moses: according to all that the Lord commanded him, so did he."[1] But it had been distinctly intimated by the prophets that Messiah was to descend from the family of David, and, of course, from the tribe of Judah,—a tribe which, though distinguished by royal honours, was, with the rest of the tribes with the exception of Levi, excluded from the honours of the priesthood.

The passages of prophetic Scripture which show that the Messiah was to descend from David, and consequently could not be a Levitical priest, are numerous. It is enough to quote two or three of them: "And when thy days be fulfilled, and thou shalt sleep with thy fathers, I will set up thy seed after thee, which shall proceed out of thy bowels, and I will establish His kingdom." "For unto us a Child is born, unto us a Son is given; and the government shall be upon His shoulder: and His name shall be called Wonderful, Counsellor, The mighty God, The everlasting Father, The Prince of Peace. Of the increase of His government and peace there shall be no end, upon the throne of David, and upon his kingdom, to order it, and to establish it with judgment and with justice from henceforth even for ever. The zeal of the Lord of hosts will perform this." "And there shall come forth a rod out of the stem of Jesse, and a Branch shall grow out of his roots: and the Spirit of the Lord shall rest upon Him, the spirit of wisdom and understanding, the spirit of counsel and might, the spirit of knowledge and of the fear of the Lord; and shall make

---

[1] Exod. xl. 12–16.

Him of quick understanding in the fear of the Lord: and He shall not judge after the sight of His eyes, neither reprove after the hearing of His ears: but with righteousness shall He judge the poor, and reprove with equity for the meek of the earth: and He shall smite the earth with the rod of His mouth, and with the breath of His lips shall He slay the wicked. And righteousness shall be the girdle of His loins, and faithfulness the girdle of His reins." "But thou, Bethlehem Ephratah, though thou be little among the thousands of Judah, yet out of thee shall He come forth unto Me that is to be ruler in Israel; whose goings forth have been from of old, from everlasting."[1]

The conclusion to be drawn from the fact here stated is plainly this: Messiah's priesthood, being clearly different from the Levitical priesthood, must supersede it, and thus prove that the law of priesthood has been essentially altered; and, superseding the Levitical priesthood, it must be a priesthood of superior dignity.

But not only does it appear from prophecy that the Messiah, to whom the prediction refers, was not to be of the tribe of Levi; it appears also from indubitable evidence that Jesus Christ, in whom the prediction was fulfilled, was, according to ancient prophecies, not of the tribe of Levi, but of Judah. Ver. 14. "For it is evident that our Lord sprang out of Judah; of which tribe Moses spake nothing concerning priesthood."[2]

The fact of Jesus Christ being a lineal descendant of David, and, of course, sprung from Judah, is established by the genealogies recorded by the Evangelists Matthew and Luke, and is spoken of by the Apostle as something universally acknowledged and incapable of being called in question. The sum of the argument is this: 'Jesus Christ, the Messiah, is, according to the ancient oracle, a priest. He is plainly not a Levitical priest, for He belongs to another tribe. His priesthood indicates that the Levitical high-priesthood is superseded, for, by the law on which it rests, it was exclusive; and therefore His priesthood is superior to that which it supersedes.'

The Apostle proceeds to bring forward another argument, founded on the words of the oath, that the Messiah is not, and

---

[1] 2 Sam. vii. 12; Isa. ix. 6, 7, xi. 1–5; Micah v. 2.

[2] ἀνατέταλκεν. Perhaps Num. xxiv. 17 was in the writer's mind,— ἀνατελεῖ ἄστρον ἐξ Ἰακώβ.

cannot be, a Levitical priest. Ver. 15. "And it is yet far more evident: for that after the similitude of Melchisedec there ariseth another priest, 16. Who is made, not after the law of a carnal commandment, but after the power of an endless life. 17. For He testifieth, Thou art a Priest for ever, after the order of Melchisedec."

This passage, like many others, is greatly obscured by the division of the verses;—the Apostle's argument not resting entirely or chiefly on the fact that the priest mentioned in the oath, to be raised up, was to be "after the order of Melchisedec," but on the fact that He was to be a *perpetual* priest, after that order.

The first question here is, What is it that "is evident?"—what is it that the Apostle is proving? It is not that there was to "arise another priest, after the order of Melchisedec,"—*that* is not what he intends to prove,—but the evidence of what he intends to prove. What he is proving—and proving from the passage in the 110th Psalm—is, that the Messiah was not to be a Levitical priest; and his argument is, 'The priest spoken of in the Psalm was not to be like the Levitical priests, "after the law of a carnal commandment, but after the power of an endless life."'

"The law of a carnal commandment" is plainly the law of the Levitical priesthood. It was a law, all whose details referred to *carnal, i.e.*, to external and perishable, things. It referred to natural descent, to corporeal qualifications, to external observances, to bodily purifications, in one word, to "things seen and temporal;"[1] and the priesthood corresponded to—was according to—its law. But the priesthood of the person mentioned in the 110th Psalm was not to be constituted in correspondence with this law, but in correspondence with "the power of an endless," or indissoluble, "life." The person spoken of is not a mortal man, but "the King eternal, immortal, and invisible," who sits on the throne of heaven, at the right hand of His Divine Father; and His priesthood has a correspondence to His

---

[1] Feebleness and mortality are the properties of $\sigma\acute{\alpha}\rho\xi$; and it is likely that the mutable, perishing character of the Mosaic economy, as opposed to the power of an endless life, was intended to be suggested. Livy, speaking of certain laws, calls them "leges mortales, ut ita dicam, et temporibus ipsis mutabiles:" xxxiv. 6.

immortal life. He is not like the Levitical priests, who " could not continue, by reason of death;" but as His life is endless, so is His priesthood. The law of His priesthood is not a dead letter, a powerless statute; it is a living, energetic, immutable, everlasting decree—the oath of God.

That the passage in the 110th Psalm warrants the argument the Apostle grounds on it is plain. The priest there mentioned is the Psalmist's "Lord," who lives and reigns for ever and ever; and He is "after the order of Melchisedec"—a perpetual priest—a priest as long as He lives—a priest during His life, which is an endless one. And that the argument is a good one to prove that the Messiah is not a Levitical priest, but a priest of a higher order, is equally so; for their priesthood was temporary and limited, whereas His is unlimited and perpetual.

The only thing in the passage that requires further to be noticed, is the introductory phrase, "*It is yet far more evident.*" Perhaps the comparative is here used for the superlative, as in chap. iii. 3; and the words may be equivalent to—' It is, further, very evident :' or, it may be intended to indicate—which is the truth—not that what is here stated is itself a clearer proof of our Lord's not being a Levitical priest than the fact referred to above, that He was not of the priestly tribe, but that the proof here stated is one which is more clearly and evidently deducible from the passage in the 110th Psalm, from which he is arguing. It may be inferred that the priest mentioned there is not a Levitical priest, inasmuch as this is not stated, and inasmuch as He is said to be a priest of another order; but it is expressly asserted that He is a perpetual priest, which clearly proves Him not to be of the order of Levi. It is plain, then, that the Messiah, who is in this ancient oracle represented as a priest, was not to be a Levitical priest; and that His priesthood necessarily implies the abolition of the Levitical priesthood, and, of course, its own infinite superiority.

This is expressed by the Apostle in the two verses that follow. Vers. 18, 19. "For there is verily a disannulling of the commandment going before, for the weakness and unprofitableness thereof. For the law made nothing perfect, but the bringing in of a better hope did; by the which we draw nigh unto God."

Here, even more than in the three preceding verses, the sense is greatly obscured by the division into verses. These two verses form but one sentence. The words, "For the law made nothing perfect," are parenthetical: the supplement *did* is obviously unnecessary. The whole sentence should be read thus: "For verily there is a disannulling of the commandment going before, for the weakness and unprofitableness thereof (for the law"—or, that law—"made nothing perfect); but there is a bringing in of a better hope, by the which we draw nigh unto God."

I apprehend the Apostle, in these words, has still in view the passage in the 110th Psalm. 'In this passage,' as if he had said, 'you have an intimation of the disannulling of the commandment going before;' that is, plainly, of the law of the Levitical priesthood, which preceded the coming of the Messiah. 'You have an intimation that that commandment, and the priesthood founded on it, would be abolished, on account of its weakness and unprofitableness—on account of its incapacity of gaining the great ends of the priesthood. (For, indeed, that law made nothing perfect. It did not make a perfect priest; it did not make perfect expiation; it did not afford perfect peace of conscience; it did not give real, far less perfect, sanctification. If it had, it would have been permanent.[1]) But in the passage so often referred to, the announcement of another and superior kind of priesthood necessarily implies its abolition' (ver. 11).

But in this passage there is not only the "disannulling of the commandment going before, for the weakness and unprofitableness thereof;" but there is "the bringing in of a better hope." There is a declaration of a perpetual priest, "after the order of Melchisedec"—a priest, the perfection of whose atonement and the prevalence of whose intercession are proved by the perpetuity of His office. There is not only an intimation that the "weak and unprofitable" priesthood is to be put down, but the announcement that a powerful and efficient priesthood should take its place; and therefore a ground laid for the hope of those bless-

[1] "The law in every respect opened up and imposed a number of problems without solving any of them. It set up in the decalogue the ideal of a holy life, but it gave no power to realize that ideal. By the law of sacrifice it awakened the consciousness of the necessity of an atonement; but it provided no true, valid offering for sin. In the institution of the priesthood it held forth the necessity of a representation of the sinner before God; but it gave no priest able to save men $εἰς\ τὸ\ παντελές$. In short, it left everything unfinished."—EBRARD.

ings which could be obtained only through the mediation of such a High Priest.

"By which hope,"[1] adds the Apostle, "we draw nigh to God"—we get near God, "entering" by faith and hope "within the vail." It is by the hope grounded on the only begotten of God being our perpetual High Priest that Christians draw near to God with filial confidence: ch. iv. 14-16, and x. 19-22. Such is the Apostle's second argument for the superiority of our Lord's priesthood, taken from the passage in the 110th Psalm.

3. *The Superior Solemnity of the Institution of the Priesthood of our Lord a Proof of its Superiority to the Levitical Priesthood.*

A third argument is brought forward in the 20th, 21st, and 22d verses. The superiority of the priesthood of Christ to the Aaronical priesthood is argued from the fact, that He was constituted a priest by a divine oath, while they were constituted priests without a divine oath. Let us examine this additional argument.

Ver. 20. "And inasmuch as not without an oath He was made priest: 21. (For those priests were made without an oath; but this with an oath by Him that said unto Him, The Lord sware, and will not repent, Thou art a Priest for ever, after the order of Melchisedec:) 22. By so much was Jesus made a surety of a better testament."

The first thing to be done here, is to fix the proper construction of the sentence. It is quite plain that the 21st verse is parenthetical. The 20th verse is obviously elliptical. Our translators have supplied the ellipsis by the words, *He was made a priest.* Though it comes materially to the same thing, perhaps it might have been better to have supplied it from the concluding clause of the sentence—" was made a surety." "Inasmuch as Jesus Christ was made a surety not without an oath, but by an oath, insomuch was He made the surety of a better testament;"—*i.e.*, in general terms, the dignity of the station

---

[1] This confirms the view we took of the meaning of the close of the 6th chapter. The hope there, as well as here, is the hope resting on the declaration, confirmed by the oath of God, that the Messiah was to be a perfect, perpetual High Priest.

bears a proportion to the solemnity of His appointment to it. The parenthetical verse is obviously intended for the more distinct statement and proof of the fact on which this argument proceeds,—to wit, that the constitution of our Lord's priesthood was attended with the solemnity of a divine oath, while the constitution of the Levitical priesthood was not attended with any such solemnity.

To bring out satisfactorily the meaning of the Apostle, it will be proper that we attend, first, to the fact or principle which the Apostle establishes : '" Jesus Christ is made the surety of a better testament" than that of which the Aaronical priesthood were made sureties, and of " a testament as much better," as is indicated by the presence of a divine oath in the one case, and the absence of it in the other ;'—then to the facts or principles by which he establishes this : ' The Levitical priests were made priests without an oath, but He was made a priest by an oath ;'—and finally, to the force of the argument which he grounds on these facts and principles for the superiority of our Lord's priesthood to that of the order of Aaron.

The fact or principle which the Apostle is establishing is, that Jesus has been made the " surety of a far better testament" than that of which the Levitical priests were made sureties. There are two words in the statement of this fact which require some explication—" testament" and " surety."

The word rendered here " testament"[1] is the same which is so often in this Epistle, and in other parts of the New Testament, rendered " covenant." It is a word which is of more comprehensive meaning than our word ' covenant,' which properly signifies a bargain, an agreement between different parties on certain terms. It signifies a constitution, an arrangement,

---

[1] Διαθήκη in classic Greek has, among other significations—such as ' covenant, league, bargain, institution'—the signification of ' testament,' but there is no evidence that it ever has this meaning in the New Testament. It is plainly the synonym of the Hebrew בְּרִית, which never means ' testament.' Indeed, it is very doubtful if testaments were known among the ancient Jews. Sureties have no place in a testament. Translators and commentators would not likely have given the sense of testament to διαθήκη here, had they not been looking forward to ch. ix. 16. " But," with Ebrard, " we interpret the passage reading the Epistle straight onward, and not in the reverse way. We will deal with the subsequent passage in its own place."

a dispensation or economy. It is the word ordinarily employed to denote the two divine arrangements or economies under which God has placed His Church, and here plainly describes that order of things introduced by the Messiah; and that order of things is stated to be a better order of things than that to which the Levitical priesthood belonged.

The word rendered "surety" is a word which nowhere else occurs in the New Testament.[1] A "surety," or sponsor, is one who stands in the room of another, and acts for him when he cannot act for himself. In both the economies under which God placed His Church there were such *sureties*,—persons who stood between God and His people, persons who acted in their name and for their behalf. Such was the place which the priests of the order of Aaron occupied in the former economy; such is the place which Jesus occupies in the new economy. To be the "surety" or mediator of a divine covenant or economy in reference to fallen men, is the same thing as to be a priest, who does for man what man cannot do for himself.[2]

The statement that "Jesus Christ is the Surety," or Mediator, "of a better covenant," obviously implies that there is another covenant, that that other covenant is a good one, and that there were sureties of that other good covenant. The other covenant referred to is plainly the Mosaic economy—the order of things commonly called "the Law"—what the Apostle terms "the first covenant," and "the old covenant."

This covenant or economy was good. It must have been so, for it was divine. It was well fitted to answer all the important purposes for which it was intended, though it was not adequate to the purposes which are served by the new and "better covenant" or economy—purposes which it was never intended to serve.

That economy or covenant had a "surety," or mediator— one who stood in the room, and acted in the name, of the people

---

[1] The word occurs twice in the apocryphal writings: Ecclus. xxix. 15, 16; 2 Mac. x. 28. The noun ἐγγύη occurs, Ecclus. xxix. 18, 19; and the verb ἐγγυᾶσθαι, in the LXX.; Ecclus. xxix. 17. It signifies 'a sponsor.' It seems not unlikely that the use of the term ἐγγίζειν (ver. 19) suggested the word ἔγγυος. Instead of ἔγγυος, the classical writers use ἐγγυητής or ἐξέγγυος.

[2] Some consider ἔγγυος as referring to God, as Schlichting, Grotius, Olshausen, and Ebrard. In appointing His Son the Mediator of the covenant, He gives *security* that all its promises will be fulfilled.

in their transactions with God; and that "surety," or mediator, was plainly the Aaronical high priest.

While these truths are plainly implied in the Apostle's statement, the truth directly asserted is, that Jesus is the Surety or Mediator of a better covenant or economy than that of which the Aaronical high priest was the surety. The economy to which He as a Surety or High Priest belongs, is a far better one than that to which the Aaronical high priest belonged as a surety; and the character of the priesthood depending on the character of the economy, it follows, of course, that He as a High Priest is far superior to Aaron or any of his sons.

It would be out of place here to enter into a particular illustration of those circumstances in which the superiority of the New Covenant to the Old consists; these will come under consideration by and by. All that the Apostle does here, is to argue that that covenant must be better than the covenant which preceded it, inasmuch as its Surety or Mediator was constituted with much greater solemnity than the sureties or mediators of that covenant. The fact, then, which the Apostle establishes is this, that the economy under which Jesus Christ is Surety or Mediator, is superior, and very far superior, to that economy under which the Levitical high priest was surety or mediator.

Let us now turn our attention to the facts or principles by which the Apostle supports this statement. These are to be found in the parenthetical statement contained in the 21st verse: "Those priests were made without an oath; but this with an oath by Him that said unto Him, The Lord sware, and will not repent, Thou art a Priest for ever, after the order of Melchisedec."

"Those priests were made without an oath."[1] The refer-

---

[1] Michaelis renders: "The priests γεγονότες, 'that were;' intimating that they, and the economy they belonged to, had no legitimate being, no existence as a divine institution. The Levitical priests were among the things which were." He considers it as a phrase similar to the following: Rom. vi. 17, "We thank God that *ye were*—ἦτε—the servants of sin;" and Dan. ii. 1, "His sleep had been upon him," *i.e.*, had now departed. The sublime Γέγονε, in Rev. xxi. 6 :—"They have been," says Jehovah, of the heavens and the earth when they have passed away and no place has been found for them. "I am the A and the Ω, the beginning and the ending." What a stoop from this height to notice Virgil's beautiful expression !—

———— "*Fuimus* Troes, fuit Ilium et ingens
Gloria Teucrorum."

ence here is to the original appointment of the Aaronical priesthood. That took place by an immediate revelation of the divine will to Moses: "Take thou unto thee Aaron thy brother, and his sons with him, from among the children of Israel, that he may minister unto Me in the priest's office, even Aaron, Nadab and Abihu, Eleazar and Ithamar, Aaron's sons."[1] But it was unaccompanied with any other solemnity.

"But this" Priest, "the High Priest of our profession," was made a priest "with an oath"—a divine oath, as appears manifestly from the passage so often referred to. The precise and full import of this divine oracle we are incapable of ascertaining. It is one of the subjects which, by their vastness and strangeness, oppress and confound the mind. In reading these words, we feel as if, like Paul, we were "caught up into the third heavens, and heard things which it is impossible" in mortal language intelligibly to explain. Our thoughts are turned back through the course of eternal ages; and we seem to witness—though the minuter parts of the sublime scene are hid in excess of brightness—that awfully important transaction among the eternal and independent Three in One, from which originates the whole scheme of our redemption, and which, according to the different aspects in which our feeble faculties consider it, is termed "the counsel of peace," or the decree of mercy. The general meaning, however, is abundantly apparent. God has, in the most distinct and solemn manner, declared it to be His unalterable determination that Jesus Christ shall be "a Priest for ever, after the order of Melchisedec."

It only remains now that, on this part of the Apostle's argument, we attend to the force of these facts as proofs that Jesus Christ is made the "Surety," or Mediator, "of a much better covenant" than that of which the Levitical high-priesthood were sureties or mediators; or, in other words, that He, as a High Priest, had inconceivably the superiority over them. The force of the argument lies, we apprehend, chiefly in two things. The oath of God marks both the importance and the perpetuity—the immutability—of the order of things to which it refers.

It marks the importance of the economy. No wise or good man interposes his oath in a matter of trivial consequence. If he voluntarily gives his oath, it is a plain proof that he considers

---

[1] Exod. xxviii. 1.

the matter as one of importance. That economy must then be a high and holy one indeed with regard to which Jehovah swears; and this circumstance must elevate it far above every other economy, though divine in its origin, that is not distinguished by this highest conceivable mark of its importance in the estimation of " Him who alone hath wisdom."

But the oath of God marks not only the importance, but the stability, of the economy in reference to which it is made. God is never represented in Scripture as swearing to anything but what was fixed and immutable. Thus He swears to Abraham that "all the nations of the earth should be blessed in his seed;"[1] and to the rebellious Israelites, that " they should not enter into His rest;"[2] and to David, that "his seed should endure for ever, and his throne to all generations."

The Levitical high-priesthood, and the economy to which it belonged, were divinely appointed, but they were not confirmed by oath. The law in reference to them was divine, and of course obligatory till repealed by the same authority which established it; but it was repealable—it has been repealed. But it is otherwise with the priesthood of our Lord, and the economy to which it belongs. Jehovah has pledged His power, and faithfulness, and being, that He shall be " a Priest for ever, after the order of Melchisedec." Such is the third argument for the superiority of our Lord as a Priest above the Aaronical priesthood, derived from the ancient oracle in the 110th Psalm.

4. *The Superior Permanence of our Lord's Priesthood proves its Superiority to the Levitical Priesthood.*

But the Apostle has not yet exhausted all the evidence which the passage contains of this interesting truth. He goes on to state a fourth argument, which is substantially this: ' From this ancient oracle it is plain that the Messiah was to continue for ever a Priest, whereas the Jewish high priests were continually changing in consequence of their being subject to the law of mortality.' This is stated in the 23d and 24th verses. 23. " And they truly were"—are become—"many priests, because they were not suffered to continue by reason of death: 24. But this man, because He continueth ever, hath an unchangeable priesthood."

[1] Gen. xxii. 16–18.     [2] Deut. i. 34–36.

By the law there could not be more than one high priest at a time; but, being a mortal man, his life as an individual was not commensurate with the whole duration of the priesthood. Death cut short his pontificate, and his place was occupied by a successor; so that, by the law of succession, the Jewish high priests had "become many." The Jews reckon about a hundred of them from Aaron to Phineas, the last of them, who perished in the destruction of the temple by the Romans. This constant change of priests, occasioned by death, showed "the weakness and unprofitableness" of the Jewish priesthood; that it was of a temporal and worldly nature, subject to the law of mortality, and did not extend its influence to the concerns of "the world to come;" and that all that depended on it was in a state of imperfection and mutability.

"But this" person to whom the ancient oracle refers, "because He continues ever, hath an unchangeable priesthood."[1] He to whom the Psalmist refers is not a mortal man, but "the only begotten Son," who sits and reigns along with His Father. He is "the first and the last, and the Living One;" and though He died, He "now lives for evermore," having the keys of death and of the unseen world. And "because He ever lives," He has no successor as a priest. The reason for a succession of priests does not here exist. "They could not continue by reason of death." He never dies—" death has no more dominion over Him;" therefore He never ceases to officiate as a High Priest.

From the perpetual endurance of our Lord's priesthood the inspired writer draws an inference highly illustrative of its superiority to the Levitical priesthood: Ver. 25. "Wherefore He is able also to save them to the uttermost that come unto God by Him, seeing He ever liveth to make intercession for them." "He ever lives to make intercession for those who come to God through Him;" *i.e.*, 'He ever officiates as a Priest in reference to those who employ Him as a Priest.'

To "come to God" through Christ, is just to expect and seek

---

[1] $ἀπαράβατος$—' a not-passing-away, a not-transmissible priesthood.' It is so, as Carpzov says, both *subjectively*, as the Priest never dies, and *objectively*, as the priesthood is unique—the first and the last of its kind. Of His priesthood may be said what Daniel says of His kingdom—' His atonement is an everlasting atonement, which shall not pass away, and His priesthood that which shall not be destroyed.' Dan. vii. 14.

the favour, and image, and enjoyment of God through the mediation of Christ Jesus, on the ground of His atonement, through the medium of His intercession. Now, "Jesus ever lives to make intercession for these." Some would understand the words, "make intercession," as just equivalent to—'interpose favourably in their behalf;' but we are rather disposed to understand the word in its full extent and peculiarity of meaning—'to interpose favourably in their behalf by presenting prayer to God in their behalf.' The only begotten of God, though naturally His Father's equal, in the economy of grace is His Father's servant; and all the blessings conferred on Him and His chosen people are conferred by the Father as sustaining the majesty of the Godhead. It is in consequence of the expressed will of the God-man, Christ Jesus, that the energies of the Divinity are exerted in the salvation of men.

Our High Priest "ever lives" thus to intercede for us; and the inference the Apostle draws is, "He is able to save to the uttermost." The phrase, "to the uttermost," taken by itself, may refer either to degree or duration. The context fixes its meaning here. "To the uttermost" is just equivalent to—'always, for ever.' 'He is able to save His people for ever, for He ever liveth to make intercession for them.' The justness of the deduction will be obvious, if we consider that if His atoning sacrifice had not been satisfactory, there would have been no room for His intercession at all; and if His sacrifice has been all-efficacious, and if "He ever lives" to follow up that sacrifice by intercessions which must be all-prevalent, is it not a fairly deduced inference—"He is able to save for ever them that come unto God by Him?"

### § 6. *The Superiority of our Lord's Priesthood to the Levitical Priesthood proved from His Superior Qualifications.*

The fifth argument for the superiority of our Lord's priesthood to that of the order of Aaron, which is contained in the verses following, though plainly suggested by, is not so completely grounded on, this ancient oracle as those which have been already illustrated. It may be thus stated: 'To fit a person for the successful discharge of the office of a priest for mankind, certain qualifications are absolutely necessary. These qualifications are wanting in the Aaronical high-priesthood, while they are to be found in absolute perfection in Jesus Christ, "the High Priest of our profession."' It follows, of course, that as a High Priest He is far their superior. Such is the substance of the argument which is stated more in detail in the passage which now lies before us for explication.

Vers. 26–28. "For such an High Priest became us, who is holy, harmless, undefiled, separate from sinners, and made higher than the heavens; who needeth not daily, as those high priests, to offer up sacrifice, first for His own sins, and then for the people's: for this He did once, when He offered up Himself. For the law maketh men high priests which have infirmity; but the word of the oath, which was since the law, maketh the Son, who is consecrated for evermore."[1]

The Apostle's argument goes on the principle that men (the pronoun *us* being equivalent, not to '*us* Christians,' but to '*us* men') need a high priest, and a high priest possessed of certain qualifications. Every kind of high priest will not suit their circumstances. The high priest they need—the high priest who alone can effectually be their surety, and gain for them the great end of bringing them to God—must be "holy, harmless, undefiled, separate from sinners, and made higher than the heavens."

He must be *holy*. The word "holy" in the Scriptures very generally signifies separation from a common to a religious purpose. Thus the nation of Israel was holy—the tribe of Levi was still more holy—the family of Aaron was peculiarly holy—the temple and all its furniture were holy. No doubt the high priest whom the circumstances of man called for must be thus *holy*—he must, by divine appointment, be set apart to perform the functions of his office; "for no man can" legitimately "take this honour to him except he be chosen of God, as was Aaron." The original word before us, however, is not that which is ordinarily employed to signify separation from a common to a religious purpose, but one which denotes moral qualities. It signifies moral excellence generally, when used alone; and when used with other words descriptive of particular forms of moral excellence, it signifies moral excellence in reference to God,—piety.

[1] γάρ. '*Now* Jesus is an ever living, immutable, endlessly powerful priest: for we needed such a High Priest. Had He not been this, He could not have been a fit High Priest for us.'

This is, I apprehend, its meaning here. The priest we need is one who is really and perfectly pious—one who "loves the Lord with all his heart, and strength, and soul, and mind," and who shows that he does so by a corresponding conduct.

He must also be *harmless*. This word is, I apprehend, descriptive of moral excellence in reference to men. Our high priest must be one who has never violated the laws either of justice or of mercy, who "loves his neighbour as himself."

He must still further be *undefiled*. The precise meaning of this term is not very easily fixed. Viewed in connection with the two that precede it, I am disposed to consider it as descriptive of moral excellence in reference to the individual himself—free from every tendency to intemperance and impurity.

Our high priest also must be " separate from sinners." This phrase seems explicatory of the three that precede it. By his perfect piety, justice, benevolence, and personal purity, he must be " separated from sinners;" *i.e.*, he must not be a sinner—he must not belong to that class of moral beings. The general sentiment conveyed by these four epithets is plainly this : ' The high priest we need must be absolutely innocent, morally perfect ;'—a sentiment which necessarily implies in it that he cannot be merely a man of our own order, " for all have sinned"—all are depraved. Ungodly, unrighteous, impure " sinners," are the appropriate epithets of all the race of Adam.

But absolute perfection of character is not the only requisite in a high priest suited to our circumstances: he must be possessed also of dignified station, of high authority, of unlimited power. He must be " made higher than the heavens." He must be one " higher than the heavens." The phrase is peculiar. It nowhere else occurs in Scripture ; but its meaning is obvious enough. He must occupy a place of the highest honour and power. And he must be one "*made* higher than the heavens." These words plainly imply that his elevation above the heavens is something conferred on him. It intimates that our high priest must be beneath the heavens in order to the discharge of some of the functions of his office, and that, in consequence of the successful discharge of them, he must be exalted far above all heavens for the successful discharge of other functions, and for gaining the grand object, the ultimate end, of his office.

The priest we require is one who, being thus "holy, harmless, undefiled, separate from sinners, and made higher than the heavens, needs not to offer up sacrifice for himself" at all, for he has no sins of his own to expiate; and he needs not *often* to offer up sacrifices for our sins, for his being " made higher than the heavens" proves that complete expiation has already been made. Such is the high priest who "becomes us."

The phrase " who becomes us" is equivalent to—' whom we need, who is necessary for us,'—just as our Lord's declaration to John, "It becomes us to fulfil all righteousness," is equivalent to—'it is necessary that we should fulfil all righteousness.'

Nor is it difficult to see that " *such* an high priest" is necessary. A morally imperfect high priest could not successfully perform the function of expiation for others. The person who interposes with God in the room of another must himself be on good terms with Him. He must deserve so well of the divine moral government as to make it wise and just on his account to bestow blessings on those who deserve them not. For this purpose, high dignity of nature and absolute perfection of character were necessary. And as a priest so completely immaculate was necessary for us, so it was not less necessary that he should be "made higher than the heavens"—exalted to high dignity and authority, as this was equally requisite to the proof of the completeness of the expiation made by his sacrifice, and for gaining the ultimate end of his priesthood—"the bringing of those" for whose benefit he acts "to God," in all the extent of meaning which belongs to that word—the making them perfectly holy and perfectly happy. Such is the high priest we need, and such are the grounds on which we need such a high priest.

Now, the Apostle shows that the Jewish high priests were not possessed of these qualifications. Many of them were men notorious for their crimes; all of them were " sinners;" and however dignified might be their situation, it could not be said of any of them that they were "made higher than the heavens." That they were not "holy, harmless, undefiled, and separate from sinners," is plain from the fact that they had " *daily* to offer up sacrifice, first for themselves." Some interpreters render the word " daily," ' on a certain day'[1]—supposing the reference to be to the great day of atonement. It seems plain, however,

---

[1] As a similar phrase in John v. 4 (κατὰ καιρόν) is rendered "at a certain season."

from the Jewish writers, that every day there were sacrifices offered for the priests, of whom the high priest was the head—the subordinate priests being merely his substitutes, performing services which it was impossible for him to overtake. This was a plain acknowledgment that they themselves were "sinners," and of course were destitute of that complete innocence, that absolute moral perfection, which was requisite in a high priest such as our circumstances required. And as their "daily offering sacrifice for themselves" proved that they were not "holy, harmless, undefiled, and separate from sinners," so their "offering *daily* sacrifices for the sins of the people" intimated that these expiatory sacrifices were not perfect—"did not take away sin." "For," as the Apostle afterwards argues, "then would they not have ceased to be offered? because that the worshippers once purged should have had no more conscience of sins. But in those sacrifices there is a remembrance again made of sins every year."[1]

The inadequacy of the Jewish high priests to the attainment of the ends for which we need a high priest is further stated in these words: "For the law maketh men priests who have infirmity." These words have commonly been understood as if they merely meant—'The law of Moses constitutes men who have infirmity priests.' I rather think the words, 'having infirmity,' refer not to their nature as men, but to their official character as priests. 'The law constitutes *men* priests; and in consequence of this, the priests constituted by the law are priests "having infirmity."' The legal priesthood is a mere *human* priesthood; and therefore it is an infirm—a weak, an inefficacious priesthood. That this is the meaning of the passage, seems plain from the antithesis between *men* and *the Son*—between *priests having infirmity*, and *a priest consecrated or perfected for evermore*. "The law made *men* priests;" *i.e.*, 'the priests constituted under the law were but mortal, sinful men,' and therefore not "holy, harmless, undefiled, and separate from sinners." And as it made *men*—mere mortal men—priests, it could not constitute an efficient priesthood. These *men*—these mere human priests—were "priests having infirmity." Weakness and unprofitableness were the character of their priesthood, so far as the expiation of moral guilt and the obtaining of

[1] Heb. x. 2, 3.

spiritual salvation were concerned. Their expiations, their intercessions, their benedictions, all had this character of weakness. They were not "such high priests as became us."

But Jesus, "the High Priest of our profession," is "such a High Priest as became us." He is all we need; for He "is holy, harmless, undefiled, separate from sinners, and made higher than the heavens." He is absolutely innocent—absolutely perfect, free of hereditary and personal guilt—free of original and acquired depravity. And He has been "made higher than the heavens." He has been "highly exalted, and received a name above every name which can be named, either in this world or that which is to come." He has "sat down on the right hand of the Majesty in the heavens; principalities and powers, thrones and dominions, having been made subject to Him." By His spotless purity and absolute perfection He was fitted for offering an acceptable sacrifice; and His high exaltation is a proof that the sacrifice He offered has indeed been acceptable.

And being thus "holy, harmless, undefiled, separate from sinners, and made higher than the heavens, He needeth not daily, as those high priests, to offer up sacrifice, first for His own sins, and then for the people's: for this He did once, when He offered up Himself." To a careless reader these words might seem to imply that Christ "offered up sacrifice for His own sins," as well as "for the sins of His people, once." But on a more careful inspection, we shall find that the division of the proposition is clear and explicit: (1) 'Our great High Priest is under no necessity of offering daily sacrifice for His own sins;' (2) 'He is under no necessity of offering daily sacrifice for the sins of His people.' The twofold proof of this twofold assertion is divided also with much distinctness into two clauses, each commencing with the particle "for." The proofs, however, according to a common usage in Hebrew composition, of which frequent traces are found in the New Testament, are arranged in an inverted order: the second assertion is first proved. 'He needs not to offer daily for the sins of the people, for this He did once for all, when He offered up Himself.' 'He needs not to offer daily for His own sins, for He is not, like the Levitical priests, a mere man, and an inefficient priest, but He is the Son of God, and as a priest, accomplished, perfect for ever.'

The non-necessity of offering for His own sins is first asserted and last proved, in order to give prominence to the grand distinction between Him and the legal high priests. He DID once for all offer sacrifice for the sins of His people : He never *did*, never *could*, never *will*, offer sacrifice for His own sins, because He is the Holy One of God.[1]

"He does not need daily"—*i.e.*, again and again[2]—"to offer up expiatory sacrifices for His people. He did this once when He offered up Himself." The sacrifice He offered was "Himself," cheerfully and perfectly doing all and suffering all the will of God; and this sacrifice being perfect, needs not to be repeated—it is *once for all*. It at once rendered unnecessary all other sacrifices and its own repetition; and His being "made higher than the heavens" is the evidence that its repetition is unnecessary. "He needs not to offer for His own sins; for the word of the oath, which was since the law, maketh the Son, who is consecrated for evermore."

"The word of the oath" is either, by a Hebraism, equivalent to 'the matter of the oath'—a circumlocution for the oath—or, 'the oracle respecting the oath,' referring to the verse of the 110th Psalm so often alluded to.[3] The last is, we think, the just interpretation. This oath is said to be "since the law."[4] The 110th Psalm was written long after the giving of the law. This is referred to apparently for the purpose of suggesting the thought, that the priesthood mentioned in that oracle, being inconsistent with the continuance of the Levitical priesthood, was intended to supersede it.

This word of the oath "*maketh* the Son." The expression

---

[1] Bishop Jebb.

[2] This seems to be the meaning. The attempts to make the strict meaning, 'daily, every day,' agree with the facts are failures. The reference cannot be to the daily offering of incense by the high priest, for that was not θυσία. Nor is the supposition that the high priest might sometimes voluntarily take part in the daily burnt-offering more satisfactory. Nor can καθ' ἡμέραν mean *die statuto*, on an appointed day every year—the great day of atonement. It must either be, that the high priest is viewed as, in the person of the ordinary priests, performing the daily sacrifice, or the phrase must be explained as Bengel does. The whole force of the illustration lies, not on the interval between the repetition of the sacrifice, but on the repetition itself.

[3] ὁ λόγος ὁρκωμοσίας = ἡ ὁρκωμοσία λεγομένη.

[4] In the Syr. and Vulg. "since the law" is connected with λόγος.

is elliptical: it is equivalent to—'maketh the Son a priest,' *i.e.*, 'declares that the Son is constituted a priest.' It is not unusual to represent that as done which is only declared to be done. Isa. vi. 9. "Go, tell this people, Hear ye indeed, but understand not;" 10. "Make the heart of this people fat,"—'declare that it is so.' Heb. viii. 13. "He has made the first old,"—'He has superannuated it—declared it to be old and overdated.' Those constituted priests by the law were *men*—mere men. He who is constituted priest by "the word of the oath" is "*the Son.*" The Apostle had stated that the person spoken of in Ps. cx. is the same as He who is spoken of in the 2d Psalm: chap. v. 5, 6. The Jews generally referred both passages to the Messiah.

Our High Priest "does not need to offer sacrifice for Himself," for He is "the Son"—"the Holy One of God." The divinity of our Lord's person puts personal guilt and depravity, as attached to Him, beyond the limits of possibility. As it is plain that the Jewish high priests are not "such high priests as become us," inasmuch as, being mere men when consecrated high priests, they are infirm, imbecile, inefficient high priests; so it is equally plain that Jesus Christ is "such a High Priest as becomes us," inasmuch as, being "the Son of God" when constituted a priest, He is a perfected priest "for evermore." The priest spoken of in the 110th Psalm is a priest who has finished the work of expiation; for He is represented as in "the heaven of heavens," on "the right hand" of God. The oracle refers to our Lord in His exalted state.

The words translated "*consecrated* for evermore," might have been more literally rendered, "perfected for evermore." It is the same word which occurs both in ch. ii. 10, "made perfect through suffering," and in ch. v. 9, "having been made perfect." The priest to whom the 110th Psalm refers is an accomplished priest—a priest who, being in heaven, in "the heaven of heavens," makes it evident that He has obtained all the merit, and, in consequence of this, all the legitimate power and authority, which are requisite for fully gaining all the objects to obtain which we guilty depraved men stand in need of a high priest.

Chap. viii. 1, 2. "Now of the things which we have spoken this is the sum: We have such an High Priest, who is set on the right hand of the throne of the Majesty in the heavens; a minister of the sanctuary, and of the true tabernacle. which the Lord pitched, and not man."

From the circumstance of these words forming the commencement of a new chapter, the greater part of readers, and the greater part of commentators, have taken it for granted that there is here a break in the Apostle's illustration or argument[1]—that he completes one argument or illustration in the words which immediately precede, and enters on a new subject, or on another branch of the same subject, in the passage now before us.

It does not appear to me possible, after having turned the subject in my mind with all the attention that I am capable of, on this principle to make out a clear, satisfactory train either of argument or illustration in these verses. I have been led, therefore, to consider them, not as the commencement of a new argument or illustration, but as the conclusion of the argument and illustration commenced in the 26th verse.

It is to be borne in mind that the high-priesthood of Jesus Christ is the great subject of discussion in the section of the Epistle of which these words form a part; and that, after having shown the reality of our Lord's high-priesthood by two arguments—the one derived from His legitimate investiture with this office, the other from His successful discharge of its functions—the Apostle proceeds to show the pre-eminent excellence and dignity of our Lord's high-priesthood. He, with much ingenuity, deduces four arguments for the superiority of our Lord's priesthood to that of Aaron and his sons from the ancient oracle recorded in the 4th verse of the 110th Psalm: "The Lord hath sworn, and will not repent, Thou art a priest for ever, after the order of Melchisedec." A fifth argument suggested by, though not so wholly grounded on, this ancient oracle, is entered on in the 26th verse of the preceding chapter, and is prosecuted, if we mistake not, down to the middle of the 6th verse of this chapter, where a new argument for the superiority of our Lord to the Aaronical priests obviously commences, the substance of which is this—'The superiority of our Lord's priesthood above that

---

[1] To use the words of a very learned and judicious scholar (Valcknaer), "The places where an improper insertion of punctuation marks has destroyed the graceful and skilfully integrated structure of the divine epistles of Paul are almost innumerable."

of Aaron and his sons is evident from the superior excellence of the covenant with which His priesthood is connected, to the covenant with which their priesthood was connected.' The substance of the argument contained in the paragraph which I have thus marked as beginning with the 26th verse of chap. vii., and terminating at the middle of the 6th verse of chap. viii., may be thus expressed: 'To fit a person for the successful discharge of the priesthood in reference to man, certain qualifications are necessary. These qualifications are wanting in the Aaronical priesthood: they are to be found in the highest perfection in Christ Jesus. Of course, Jesus Christ, as a high priest, is far their superior. We—that is, *men*—need a high priest "holy, harmless, undefiled, made higher than the heavens." The Jewish high priests do not answer to this description: Jesus Christ does. In Him we Christians have such a high priest; and the conclusion is, He has received a more excellent ministry.' In this way, I apprehend, everything hangs well together, and the Apostle's argumentative illustration appears complete and satisfactory. Indeed, the recurrence of the phrase, "*such* a high priest," "*such* a high priest became us," "we have *such* a high priest," seems intended for the express purpose of showing that the train of thought is continuous. 'The priest we need is one of absolute moral excellence—such a one as is not to be found among the sons of men—holy or pious, harmless, just and benevolent, undefiled, humble, chaste, temperate; and he must also be one of superhuman dignity and power—"made higher than the heavens." The Jewish high priests were not possessed of these qualifications: not of the first kind of qualifications, for they "needed daily to offer up sacrifices for their own sins;" not of the second, which implies the perfection of their sacrifices, for the imperfection of these sacrifices for the people is manifest from their constant repetition, and they must continue on earth to repeat them daily. The Jewish priests constituted by the law were mere men, and being mere men, they were *infirm* priests: weakness and unprofitableness were the characteristics of their ministry. But the priest spoken of in the ancient oracle is *the Son*, a being of a superior order; and being so, as a priest He is not infirm and imperfect—He is accomplished—perfected for evermore.' "Now," says the Apostle at this point of the argument, " WE have such a High Priest."

The prefatory clause, "Of the things which we have spoken this is the sum," though full of difficulty if considered as the commencement of a new paragraph, is easily explained on the principle of interpretation we have been led to adopt. "The things which we have spoken" refer, I apprehend, to the whole discussions respecting the priesthood of Christ, beginning at the 14th verse of the 4th chapter, and reaching down to the 18th verse of the 10th chapter. 'Of all that has been said, and of all that is to be said about the priesthood of Christ, this is the *sum*.' The word translated *sum* is used to signify either the substance of a statement—an abridged, compressed view of it—or the chief, the most important topic in a statement. It matters very little which view you take of it here. It is equally true, that the fact that Jesus Christ is such a high priest as we need, is the substance, and the principal topic, of the statements made by the Apostle in reference to His high-priesthood. The remark, which is substantially, though not formally, parenthetical, is intended to mark the supreme importance of the principle: " In Christ Jesus we have such a High Priest as becomes us."

The Apostle proceeds to expatiate on the glories of our High Priest. He is one "who is set on the right hand of the Majesty in the heavens," and He is "a minister of the sanctuary, and of the true tabernacle, which the Lord pitched, and not man."

"The Majesty in the heavens," like the similar phrase in the 1st chapter, ver. 3, "the Majesty on high," is an appellation of the Divinity—'the Majestic One;' and to be "set on the right hand of this Majestic One," is just to be elevated to communion with God in reigning—to be exalted to reign along with God. The 110th Psalm explains it. To Him respecting whom Jehovah has sworn, "Thou art a Priest for ever, after the order of Melchisedec," He has also said, "Sit Thou at My right hand till I make Thine enemies Thy footstool." Our High Priest is one who "has all power in heaven and in earth," —according to whose will all the energies of Omnipotence go forth, either in the production of external events, or in the diffusion of inward influence.

I cannot doubt that there is here an implied contrast between the Jewish high priests and our great High Priest. They at distant intervals, and for a short season, were allowed to approach to and stand before the emblematical throne of God. He sits permanently in the divine presence,—nay, He sits on the divine throne, "at the right hand" of its august, majestic occupant.

He is also "a minister of the sanctuary,[1] and of the true tabernacle, which God hath pitched, not man." These words imply that 'He is not a minister of the sanctuary—the figurative tabernacle—which man pitched; but He is a minister of the sanctuary—the true tabernacle—which God has pitched.' The words, "the true tabernacle," are obviously explicatory of the word "sanctuary." Our High Priest is now "a minister"—properly, a public functionary,[2]—acting, as the high priest did, in the name of His people in "the sanctuary," *i.e.*, in the holy place, the residence of the Divinity—the place where He peculiarly manifests His perfection and presence. "The true tabernacle" is equivalent to that reality of which the tabernacle under the law was a figure. The tabernacle was the place where Jehovah emblematically dwelt. The place where Jesus now is as a public functionary, is the place where Jehovah really dwells. It is a "tabernacle not pitched by man, but by God." It is "not made with hands, eternal in the heavens." These statements are plainly intended, and admirably calculated, to bring before the mind the infinite superiority of Jesus Christ as a priest to Aaron and his sons.

But how did He enter into this sanctuary? The high priests under the law entered into their sanctuary after having offered a sacrifice; and so also did the great "High Priest of our profession." Ver. 3. "For every high priest is ordained to offer gifts and sacrifices: wherefore it is of necessity that this man have somewhat also to offer."

No attentive reader can help being sensible that these words, taken by themselves, do not convey a distinct, complete, satisfactory meaning. The statement is obviously elliptical; and the following seems to me the most probable way of supplying the ellipsis: 'We have a High Priest who has entered into the

---

[1] Oecumenius among the ancients, and Schulzius among the moderns, consider τῶν ἁγίων as masculine, not neuter; and translate the whole phrase, 'the minister of the saints—the functionary, as high priest, of the true people of God.' But the common is without doubt here the true exegesis.

[2] λειτουργός.

heavenly sanctuary, the true holy of holies. Every high priest is appointed to offer up sacrificial gifts in order to his entrance into the earthly sanctuary: it was necessary, as the antitype must correspond to the type, that this illustrious Priest should have somewhat to offer, for the purpose of opening His way into the true sanctuary.' His being there is the proof at once that an expiatory sacrifice has been offered, and that that sacrifice has been effectual. And what was this "somewhat" which it was necessary that He should offer in order to His entering into the true sanctuary? We have but to look back a little to find the answer. It was "Himself," "holy, harmless, undefiled, separate from sinners." His perfect, cheerful obedience to the preceptive part of the divine law, and His perfect, cheerful submission to the sanctioning part of it, opened for Him, as a High Priest, His way into that true holy place, where in the presence of God He acts as a public functionary in the name of His redeemed ones.

It is plain that He could not have the sacrifices prescribed by the law to offer, for He did not belong to that class of persons to whom the offering of these was by law restricted; but He had a better sacrifice. "Wherefore, when He cometh into the world, He saith, Sacrifice and offering Thou wouldest not, but a body hast Thou prepared Me: in burnt-offerings and sacrifices for sin Thou hast had no pleasure: Then said I, Lo, I come (in the volume of the book it is written of Me) to do Thy will, O God. Above when He said, Sacrifice, and offering, and burnt-offerings, and offering for sin Thou wouldest not, neither hadst pleasure therein (which are offered by the law); then said He, Lo, I come to do Thy will, O God. He taketh away the first, that He may establish the second. By the which will we are sanctified, through the offering of the body of Jesus Christ once for all. And every priest standeth daily ministering, and offering oftentimes the same sacrifices, which can never take away sins: but this man, after He had offered one sacrifice for sins, for ever sat down on the right hand of God; from henceforth expecting till His enemies be made His footstool."[1]

Our High Priest is no more on earth, He is in heaven; and His absence, so far from being any cause of suspicion that we have not a High Priest—for we see Him not ministering as a

[1] Heb. x. 5-13.

Priest in an earthly tabernacle—is the necessary result of His being what He is, and of His having done what He has done. Vers. 4, 5. "For," says the Apostle, "if He were on earth, He should not be a priest, seeing that there are priests that offer gifts according to the law; who serve unto the example and shadow[1] of heavenly things, as Moses was admonished of God when he was about to make the tabernacle: for, See (saith He) that thou make all things according to the pattern showed to thee in the mount."

This is a passage which has greatly perplexed interpreters. Without going into a particular account of the different plausible explications which have been given of it, I shall shortly state what appears to me its probable meaning: further than that I cannot go.

It seems an answer to the suggestion of the unbelieving Jews: 'But you have no high priest on earth;' and the reply is, substantially—'No, we have not; and it is far better that we have not. If we had, He could not be the high priest we need. His ministry is a far higher ministry than that of any earthly priest; and the covenant, in the blessings of which connection with *Him* interests us, bears a proportion in the value of its blessings to the dignity of His ministry.' If Jesus Christ, the High Priest whom we acknowledge, were still on earth—were continuing on earth after having offered His sacrifice, He could not be a priest, or rather, He could not have been by way of eminence, PRIEST; He could not have been the Priest the Apostle is speaking of—the Priest after the order of Melchisedec; He could not have been the Priest who became us, who must be made higher than the heavens; He could not have been the Priest constituted by the word of the oath—the Son perfected for evermore; for the legal priests, who remain on earth after their sacrifice, are not such priests as become us—"they only serve unto the example and shadow of heavenly things."[2]

These words are generally, I believe, misunderstood. They

[1] ὑπόδειγμα, here = *copy, representation*, and the same idea is expressed in σκιά, but in a still stronger form. The shadow of a body represents not even a proper image of it, but only the colourless contour; and such a representation did τὸ κοσμικὸν ἅγιον, in which the Levitical high priest ministered, give of τὰ ἐπουράνια.

[2] Not 'a heavenly tabernacle,' but 'heavenly things;' "not," as Ebrard says justly, "heavenly *localities*, but heavenly *relations* and *facts*."

are considered as equivalent to—'who serve the purpose of being an example or shadow of heavenly things—who are types of something heavenly.' The words are, literally, 'who do service, or who officiate as priests, to, or in that which is, a type or shadow of the heavenly sanctuary.' It is the earthly tabernacle or temple which is here spoken of as "a type or shadow of heavenly things." And in support of this statement, the Apostle quotes the words of Jehovah to Moses: Exod. xxv. 40, xxvi. 30. Some interpreters have supposed, that to Moses in the mount God made a full revelation of the spiritual meaning of the tabernacle and its ordinances. Certainly we have no evidence of this.[1] All that these words imply is—God, by exhibiting to Moses a pattern after which the tabernacle was to be built, and repeatedly and strictly charging him to adhere to that pattern, intimated that some recondite meaning was shadowed forth; and that therefore it was necessary to be very exact in fashioning the tabernacle according to that divine model, which precisely corresponded to something else, not then to be made manifest.

The priests who remain on the earth are but typical priests, ministering in the typical sanctuary; and our High Priest would not have been "such a High Priest as became us," if He, like them, had continued on earth. Having offered the real sacrifice, He entered into the real heaven. Ver. 6. "But now hath He obtained a more excellent ministry;" *i.e.*, they, having offered typical sacrifices, minister in the typical sanctuary, the tabernacle which man has pitched; but He, having offered the real sacrifice, ministers in the sanctuary, the true tabernacle, which God has pitched.

Is He not then altogether "such a High Priest as became us," having "by the sacrifice of Himself completely purged our sins," and being "able to save us to the uttermost, seeing He ever liveth to make intercession for us?" And is He not far superior to Aaron and all his sons?

---

[1] "The force of the author's reasoning depends in no wise on whether Moses understood the typical signification of the tabernacle or not. Enough that Moses did not make or invent the plan of the tabernacle. Enough that God gave him the plan,—God, who knew well the symbolical signification of this plan. That the plan for the tabernacle was given by God, in this circumstance lies the nerve of the argument; for this reason is the Mosaic tabernacle a reflection of *heavenly* thoughts, ideas, relations."—EBRARD.

§ 7. *The Superiority of the Priesthood of Christ to the Levitical Priesthood proved from the Superiority of the Covenant with which it is connected.*

The argument for the pre-eminent excellence of our Lord's high-priesthood, on which the Apostle enters in the words which follow, may be thus stated : 'Jesus Christ, as a public functionary, is far superior in dignity to Aaron or any of his sons, for the covenant or economy in which He acts as a public functionary is of a far higher order than the covenant or economy in which they acted as public functionaries.'

Ver. 6. "But now hath He obtained a more excellent ministry, by how much also He is the Mediator of a better covenant, which was established upon better promises."

The Apostle has shown that Jesus Christ is in every point of view "*such* a High Priest as becomes us"—*such* a Priest as we need. He has offered in Himself an all-efficacious sacrifice; and on the ground of that sacrifice He has been invested with " all power in heaven and earth," to follow out the benevolent object of His obedience to the death, in the salvation of His redeemed people. In these points of view He is far superior to the Aaronical priests, who were not such high priests as became us. "He has obtained a more excellent ministry." As a public religious functionary, He occupies a higher place than they; and the measure of His superiority here referred to, is the superior excellence of the economy or order of things with which He as a High Priest is connected. "He is the Mediator of a better covenant" than that of which the Jewish high priest was mediator.

I have already had occasion to state that the word here, and generally in the New Testament, rendered *covenant*, is a word of much more comprehensive meaning than the English term by which it is translated. It signifies an arrangement, a constitution, an order of things, an economy.

The peculiar order of things under which the Jewish people were placed in consequence of the transactions at Sinai, is what the Apostle calls the "first covenant;" and of this the Jewish high priests were the mediators. They interposed between God and that people. By sacrifice and intercession they did what, according to the principles of that economy, was necessary for securing its advantages to those placed under it.

"The second" covenant is the order of things which was introduced by Jesus Christ. Of this covenant He is the Mediator. He interposes between God and those in reference to whom this covenant is established. By His sacrifice and intercession He does what, according to the principles of this economy, is necessary for securing its advantages to those placed under it.

The covenant of which Jesus Christ is the Mediator, is "a better covenant." The superiority of. the covenant with which Jesus Christ is connected as a Mediator, Surety, or Priest, to the covenant of which Aaron and his sons were mediators, sureties, or priests, has been inferred by the Apostle from the circumstance of His being constituted a High Priest "with an oath," while they were constituted high priests "without an oath"—the oath of God at once proving the importance and the immutability of the institution which it sanctions. Here the Apostle goes into a statement of the nature of the blessings secured by this covenant, as a proof of its superiority to the former covenant, and of the superiority of its Mediator to the mediators of the former covenant. It is "a better covenant," for it is "established on better promises."

The word translated *established*, properly signifies, 'has been the subject of legislation—has been established by law.' It is the same word that is employed in reference to the Levitical priesthood, chap. vii. 11 : "The people received a law in reference to it." It does not appear to me that the Apostle here means to say that the covenant of which Christ is the Mediator is established *on* promises ; for the promises are rather built on the covenant, than the covenant on the promises. He asserts, I apprehend, that this covenant has been established by law in reference to[1] better promises.

The word "promise" very often in this Epistle means the blessing promised. It does not matter much whether you understand it in this sense here, or in its primary signification. The meaning is materially the same.

The "first covenant," to which the Aaronical priesthood be-

---

[1] ἐπί, after words of speech or writing, etc., signifies sometimes *concerning, in reference to*: Gal. iii. 16, ἐπὶ πολλῶν—ἐφ' ἑνός.

longed, was established by law at Sinai, and it had a reference to a variety of promised blessings. The promises referred to the earthly Canaan, with all its advantages as a good, and large, and fertile country—"a land flowing with milk and honey;" and the quiet and peaceful enjoyment of these advantages under the special protection of God, while they abstained from idolatry, and continued to observe the law as delivered by Moses. A summary of the promised blessings in reference to which the first covenant was established by law, may be found in Deut. xxviii. 1–13.

The covenant to which the priesthood of Christ refers has been also established by law. It has been promulgated by divine authority. The truth with regard to it "has been spoken by the Son of God, and confirmed to us by those who heard Him; and God has borne witness with signs, and miracles, and gifts of the Holy Ghost, according to His own will." This covenant is established by law with a reference to the bestowment of promised blessings on men. These promised blessings are spiritual in their nature, and eternal in their duration; they are blessings suited to man as an intelligent, moral, religious, guilty, depraved, unhappy, immortal being, and therefore are of an incalculably higher nature than any blessings which refer merely to the enjoyments of the present life.

That the blessings of the covenant of which Christ is Mediator are superior to those of the covenant of which the Jewish high priests were mediators, the Apostle shows in two ways: first, by adverting to the general principle, that the superseding of the one by the other necessarily involves in it the superiority of the superseding economy, and the imperfection of the superseded economy; and then by bringing before the mind, in a quotation from the prophet Jeremiah, a condensed statement regarding the nature of the blessings which are to be enjoyed under the covenant of which Christ is Mediator.

Ver. 7. "For if that first covenant had been faultless, then should no place have been sought for the second." Every work of God is perfect, viewed in connection with the purpose which He means it to serve. In this point of view, the "first covenant" was faultless. But when viewed in the light in which the Jews generally considered it, as a saving economy, in all the extent of that word, it was not "faultless." It could not expiate moral guilt; it could not wash away moral pollution; it could not justify, it could not sanctify, it could not save. Its priesthood were not perfected—they were weak and inefficient; its sacrifices "could not take away sin," make perfect as concerning the conscience, or procure "access with freedom into the holiest of all." In one word, "it made nothing perfect." Had it been "faultless," had it served all the purposes of a saving economy—a restorative dispensation, there would have been no room for another institution.

But the Apostle shows clearly, from a passage which he quotes from the prophecy of Jeremiah, that God, plainly intimating the imperfection of the "first covenant," had declared that He would establish a new and perfect covenant; and by the enumeration of the blessings promised in that covenant, he shows that it is indeed "a better covenant, established in reference to better promises." Vers. 8-13. "For, finding fault with them, He saith, Behold, the days come, saith the Lord, when I will make a new covenant with the house of Israel, and with the house of Judah: not according to the covenant that I made with their fathers in the day when I took them by the hand to lead them out of the land of Egypt; because they continued not in My covenant, and I regarded them not, saith the Lord. For this is the covenant that I will make with the house of Israel after those days, saith the Lord; I will put My laws into their mind, and write them in their hearts; and I will be to them a God, and they shall be to Me a people: and they shall not teach every man his neighbour, and every man his brother, saying, Know the Lord: for all shall know Me, from the least to the greatest. For I will be merciful to their unrighteousness, and their sins and their iniquities will I remember no more. In that He saith, A new covenant, He hath made the first old. Now that which decayeth and waxeth old is ready to vanish away."

The words, "finding fault," do not appear to me to refer to God's finding fault with the Israelites, but to His finding fault with, or declaring imperfect, the Mosaic economy; for that is the point which the Apostle is establishing. The words may, and I apprehend ought, to be rendered, "But finding fault, He says to them."

The passage here quoted is taken from Jeremiah, where it stands thus: "Behold, the days come, saith the Lord, that I

## CHRIST A PRIEST OF A SUPERIOR COVENANT.

will make a new covenant with the house of Israel, and with the house of Judah; not according to the covenant that I made with their fathers, in the day that I took them by the hand, to bring them out of the land of Egypt (which My covenant they brake, although I was an husband unto them, saith the Lord); but this shall be the covenant that I will make with the house of Israel; After those days, saith the Lord, I will put My law in their inward parts, and write it in their hearts; and will be their God, and they shall be My people. And they shall teach no more every man his neighbour, and every man his brother, saying, Know the Lord: for they shall all know Me, from the least of them unto the greatest of them, saith the Lord: for I will forgive their iniquity, and I will remember their sin no more."[1]

As the quotation does not exactly correspond either with the Hebrew text or with the Greek version of the LXX., in common use when the Apostle wrote, it is probable that he quoted from memory,—the inspiring Spirit preventing him from in any degree misrepresenting the meaning of the sacred oracle. The only variation of importance is that found in the last clause of the 9th verse, when compared with the last clause of the 32d verse of the 31st chapter of Jeremiah. The true account of this variation seems to be this, that our translators have given to the word in Jeremiah its most ordinary signification; whereas it would appear, from the Apostle sanctioning the version of the LXX. in this instance, that it ought to have been understood in a less common meaning.[2]

Before looking particularly into the meaning of the different clauses of this prediction, and inquiring how it is fitted to serve the Apostle's purpose, of showing that the covenant of which Christ is Mediator is established on "better promises" than the Sinaitic covenant, and that therefore Jesus "has obtained a more excellent ministry" than the Levitical priests, it will be proper for us to attend to the general meaning and design of the passage where it originally occurs in the prophecies of Jeremiah. It has been considered by many interpreters as

---

[1] Jer. xxxi. 31-34.

[2] *Vide* Heinrichs and Ernesti. It deserves notice, that Gesenius, who in the earlier editions of his Heb. Lexicon rendered the words, "although I was an husband to them," in his later renders it, "and I rejected them." The LXX. have here given a correct version, and the Apostle has adopted it.

a mere accommodation, referring originally, not to the state of things under the Messiah, but to the state of things immediately after the return from the Babylonian Captivity. But if the principles laid down in the introductory remarks be sound, this cannot be admitted; for the Apostle's argument certainly implies, that in these words there is a description of the order of things under the Messiah. Others consider it as a prediction referring to the new economy generally, and that the phrases, " house of Israel," and " house of Judah," are to be understood mystically of the true Israel, whether Jews or Gentiles. But it seems to me quite plain, that the words are a prophecy of that general conversion of the Jews to Christianity which we are warranted to look for from many Old Testament predictions, and from the express declaration of the Apostle, that a period is coming when " all Israel shall be saved." It may indeed be said, How does the passage, in this view, answer the Apostle's object? The answer is easy. The covenant which in the last days of the Christian dispensation the Jews generally are to be brought under, is substantially the same covenant which, ratified in the blood of Jesus, has been, during the course of eighteen centuries, diffusing its blessings to an innumerable multitude of individuals, of every kindred, and people, and tongue, and nation.

" Behold, the days come"—*i.e.*, a period will arrive—" when I will make a new covenant with the house of Israel, and with the house of Judah,"—when I will bring the Jewish people under a new order of things—when I will establish a new economy among them. This is termed " a new covenant,"— plainly in contrast to the old covenant under which they had been placed at Mount Sinai.

This " new covenant" was not to be " according to the covenant made with their fathers;" *i.e.*, it is to be entirely of a different kind. Into that covenant they were brought as natural descendants of Abraham, Isaac, and Jacob; into this they will be brought by walking in the steps of these patriarchs' faith. That covenant was external and temporary; this is spiritual and eternal.

This " new covenant" is to be so different from the old, because they with whom that covenant was made " continued not in it, and Jehovah regarded them not," or was weary of them; and in consequence of their breach of His covenant, rejected them from being His people. According to an ordinary usage in prophecy, the words are uttered as if at the period when their fulfilment is to take place.

It was a proof of the faultiness of the first covenant, that it did not secure that those under it should conform themselves to its requisitions, and thus it did not secure them in the possession of those privileges, as the peculiar people of God, which depended on their conforming to these requisitions. " But this is the covenant that I will make with the house of Israel; After those days, saith the Lord, I will put My law in their inward parts, and write it in their hearts." ' I will not only give them a revelation of My will, but I will make them understand and believe that revelation, and live under its influence.[1] They shall have My laws among them, not only written in an external revelation, but, through the influence of the Holy Ghost, engraved on " the fleshly tables of the heart." '

" I will be to them a God,"—i.e., ' I will bestow upon them every blessing which such beings as men can expect from such a being as God ;' " and they shall be My people,"—" a people formed for Myself, that they may show forth My praise."

The words in the 11th verse are not to be understood absolutely, but comparatively. They intimate, that under that covenant there shall be a striking contrast to the ignorance which characterized the great body of those who were under the Old Covenant; that the revelation of the divine will shall be far more extensive and clear under the new than under the old economy; and that there shall be a correspondingly enlarged communication of the enlightening influences of the Holy Spirit.

They probably also are intended to suggest the idea, that that kind of knowledge which is the peculiar glory of the New Covenant is a kind of knowledge which cannot be communicated by brother teaching brother, but comes directly from Him —the Great Teacher, whose grand characteristic is this, that whom He teaches, He makes apt to learn.

---

[1] Some interpreters consider διάνοια as referring to the intellect, and καρδία to the will and affections. This is an undue refinement. The expressions are synonymous. Καρδία is often in the N. T. used in reference to the mind or intellect: Rom. i. 21 ; Eph. i. 18 ; and in the LXX. διάνοια is the translation of לב, Gen. xvii. 17.

The only other blessing mentioned, is full, free, irreversible pardon of sin. Under the Old Testament there were some sins which could not be expiated; and the expiation which was made, was, like everything under that economy, imperfect or temporary. But under the New Covenant the proclamation is, "Be it known unto you, that through this man is preached to you the forgiveness of sins; and by Him all who believe are justified from all things, from which ye could not be justified by the law of Moses."

Now, are not the promised blessings in reference to which the New Covenant, of which Jesus Christ is the Mediator, is established, incomparably better than the promised blessings in reference to which the Old Covenant was established? What is the body to the soul? What is Canaan to heaven? What are sacrifices, and lustrations, and all the pomp of the Levitical service, to the service of an enlightened mind, a pacified conscience, and a purified heart? The New Covenant is a better covenant than the Old; and the Mediator of the New Covenant has received "a more excellent ministry" than the mediators of the Old.

In the 13th verse the Apostle, as it were by the way, draws an inference from the language in which the prophet speaks of the New Covenant, as to the abrogation of the Sinaitic covenant. The terming of this order of things *new*, implies that the former order was become *old—antiquated;* for why have a new covenant, if the original one can serve the purpose? The *New* Covenant has been introduced. The former is now *old;* and, as *old*, is about to vanish away.[1] It had done two things: it had served its purpose as a figure, and as a schoolmaster; and it had also clearly showed that it could not serve the grand purpose of a saving economy; and therefore it was removed out of the way—an honourable end was put to it, in all its requisitions having been fulfilled in Christ. Christ redeemed those of His people who were under that covenant from its curse, by becoming a curse in their room, that the blessing of Abraham might come on the Gentiles, and that the New Covenant might be established, which proclaims that forgiveness and the Spirit may be obtained through believing.

---

[1] Ἐγγὺς ἀφανισμοῦ, 'just about to vanish.' In a very few years it did expire, with the flames which consumed the holy city and the holier temple —vanished into vapour and invisibility.

§ 8. *The Superiority of our Lord's Priesthood to the Levitical Priesthood proved from a comparison between them.*

In the prosecution of his argument respecting the superiority of Jesus Christ to the Aaronical high-priesthood, the Apostle is led to observe that He has received " a more excellent ministry"—He is a more dignified public functionary—than Aaron or any of his sons. This statement is at once an inference from the fact which he had just established, that Jesus is "such an High Priest as became us"—as our circumstances required—which neither Aaron nor any of his sons was, and it is the announcement of a principle, to the further illustration and proof of which he is about to proceed. He not only asserts the fact, that as a public functionary Jesus Christ is superior to Aaron and his sons, but he furnishes us with a measure by which we may estimate the degree of that superiority. His ministry or public function is as much superior to that of Aaron and his sons, as the covenant, or economy, or dispensation, or order of things of which He is the Mediator, is superior to that of which they were the mediators.

According to a principle of composition which obtains extensively in the New Testament, that which is last mentioned in an enumeration of particulars is first discussed. The Apostle, before proceeding to illustrate the nature and kind of this superiority of public function as high priest, establishes the truth of what he had said as to the measure of this superiority,— ' Jesus is the Mediator of a better covenant, established by law in reference to better promised blessings.' And he does this in two ways: first, by pressing the general principle, that the mere circumstance of one economy or covenant superseding another, under the wise and benignant administration of the divine government, is a proof of the imperfection of the superseded economy, and the superiority of the superseding economy; and then by showing, from a quotation from an ancient prophet, what was the true nature of the blessings promised under that economy of which Jesus is the Mediator. In this way he clearly establishes the fact, that the covenant or economy of which Jesus was Mediator is inconceivably superior to that of which Aaron and his sons were the mediators; and that, if this is to be the measure of the superiority of His public function to theirs, it is great indeed.

He now, I apprehend, in the paragraph on the illustration of which we are about to enter, proceeds to show directly the superiority of our Lord's ministry to that of Aaron and his sons, by contrasting the acts in which their respective ministries consisted, and the place in which these acts were respectively performed. The facts with regard to the ministry of Aaron and his sons are stated in the first ten verses of the ninth chapter. The facts with regard to the ministry of Jesus Christ are stated in the 11th and 12th verses; and the whole of what follows, from the 13th verse of this chapter down to the 18th verse of the 10th chapter, with which the section respecting the priesthood of Christ—and indeed the whole doctrinal part of the Epistle—concludes, is occupied with showing how these facts clearly prove that Christ Jesus has indeed received " a more excellent ministry."

### (1.) *General Comparison.*

Having made these general remarks, we are now prepared to enter on the more close investigation of the Apostle's particular statements. Chap. ix. 1. "Then verily the first covenant had also ordinances of divine service, and a worldly sanctuary." The object of the Apostle is to show that Jesus, the Mediator of the New Covenant, has " a more excellent ministry" than Aaron and his sons, who were the mediators of the Old Covenant. The first thing to be done in prosecuting such an object, is to show what kind of ministry Aaron and his sons had; and this is precisely what the Apostle does in the first ten verses of this chapter.

### 1. *Facts with regard to the Levitical Priesthood.*

The particles *then verily, also,* are mere particles of transition. You will observe that the word *covenant* is marked as a supplement. It is not in the original text. Some interpreters supply the word ' tabernacle,'—which word, indeed, appears in some of the MSS.; but there can scarcely be any doubt that our translators are right in the way in which they have filled up the ellipsis.[1] In the preceding verse the word *first* appears by

---
[1] Chrysostom very well says, ἡ πρώτη—τίς; ἡ διαθήκη.

itself; and there can be no doubt that it there refers to the first covenant. If the reference had been different here, it would have been marked by the insertion of another term. Besides, to insert the word *tabernacle* instead of *covenant*, would be to make the Apostle repeat the same thing without any obvious reason in the second verse, which he had already said in the first.

"The first covenant had ordinances of divine service,"—literally, 'ordinances of ministry;' *i.e.*, according to a Hebraism, an ordained or divinely appointed ministry—a divinely instituted set of public religious functions to be discharged by those who were its mediators. By changing the word, which is the same in the original, from " ministry" into " divine service," the connection of the Apostle's thoughts is obscured. A mere English reader does not see how these two statements hang together: 'Jesus, the Mediator of the New Covenant, has received a more excellent ministry than Aaron and his sons, who were the mediators of the Old Covenant. The Old Covenant had ordinances of divine service.' But the coherence of the thoughts is at once perceived when the statement is made *thus*: 'The Old Covenant had indeed a divinely appointed ministry; but that ministry was far inferior to that which Jesus has obtained.'

The Old Covenant had not only a divinely instituted set of public religious functions to be performed by its mediators, the Jewish high priests, but it had also a divinely appointed place in which these functions were to be performed. This is termed in the passage before us, "a worldly sanctuary." As to the word "sanctuary" there can scarcely be a difference of opinion. It indicates the place sanctified—that is, set apart, appropriated by divine appointment—for the performance of the ordained public functions of the high priest under that economy.

There is more difficulty in the descriptive epithet prefixed, "a *worldly* sanctuary."[1] Some interpreters understand by it, a

[1] It was not uncommon among the Jews to give a plural designation to the sanctuary of God: Ps. lxxiii. 17, "Till I went to the sanctuary,"—literally " sanctuaries;" lxxiv. 7, lxviii. 35; Lev. xxi. 33. The Romans have a similar usage. Thus Virgil:—

"——— Adytis hæc tristia dicta reportat."—*Æn.* ii. 115.
"Æternumque adytis effert penetralibus ignem."—*Æn.* ii. 297.

richly adorned sanctuary; others, a sanctuary which is emblematical of the mundane system; others, a sanctuary celebrated all over the world. I am disposed to think that the word translated *worldly* is here equivalent to 'earthly,'[1] and is employed in contrast with the terms "the *true*," "the *heavenly*," which are applied to that sanctuary in which " the High Priest of our profession" now officiates. The ideas which the word used in this sense conveys, are, material and perishing. There seems to be a peculiar emphasis in the word *had*.[2] The first covenant *had* these things, but it has them no longer. Its appointed set of functions have no divine authority, and its "worldly sanctuary" has lost even that species of holiness which once belonged to it. It was never anything but " a shadow," and it is now but the shadow of a shade.

According to the principle of composition already referred to, the Apostle, instead of proceeding to describe the instituted order of ministry, and the sanctuary or place of ministry, in the order he had mentioned them, begins with the sanctuary, and then goes back to the ministry. The sanctuary is described in the 2d, 3d, 4th, and 5th verses; the ministry, in the 6th, 7th, 8th, 9th, and 10th verses.

Let us attend to the description of the "earthly sanctuary," in which the Jewish high priests performed their ministry. "A tabernacle was made." The Apostle here plainly speaks of the Levitical institution as originally established by Moses, of which we have a particular account in the Book of Exodus. The sanctuary was a tabernacle or tent, thirty cubits, or forty-five

---

[1] ἐπίγειον, χειροποίητον, ταύτης τῆς κτίσεως, as opposed to σκηνὴ ἀληθινή, ἅγιον ἀληθινόν, ἐπουράνιον: ch. viii. 2, 5, ix. 23, 24. Hyperius explains it very well: " mundanum duntaxat, *i.e.*, externum, temporale, carnale, et nequaquam spirituale." It finds its explication in the antithesis, τὰ ἐπουράνια. It signifies the same thing as ἐπὶ γῆς, ch. viii. 4, with this difference, that in κ. lies not merely the locality, but the quality. The exegesis which gives it the signification of κόσμιος, 'adorned'—or 'for the whole world,' or 'a type of the world'—is plainly quite unsatisfactory. " The Old Testament sanctuary was an integral part of this world, which exists as a world separated from God, and in which, therefore, even when what was heavenly appeared, it must needs take the form of the limited, the particular—*i.e.*, under the distinction *fanum* and *profanum*. In this is involved at once the material, local, external, and emblematic character of the Old Testament ἅγιον, and at the same time also its imperfection."—EBRARD.

[2] εἶχε, not ἔχει.

feet, in length, ten cubits, or fifteen feet, in breadth, and the same in height,—forming an oblong square. This tabernacle was divided by a vail into two parts of very unequal size. The Apostle describes both of these apartments; the first of which was called "the holy place," in which was the candlestick, or lamp, or chandelier, for giving light to the tabernacle. It weighed a talent of beaten gold, and was all of one piece. From its shaft proceeded six branches, three on each side, and one in the middle, with a lamp on the top of each, containing pure olive oil. These lamps were trimmed and supplied with oil by the officiating priests every morning and evening: Exod. xxv. 31–39, xxvii. 20. Here also was "the table," which was formed of shittim wood, and stood on the north, as the candlestick on the south, of the tabernacle. It was two cubits, or three feet, in length, one cubit, or a foot and a half, in breadth, and a cubit and a half, or two feet three inches, in height, and was covered over with pure gold: Exod. xxv. 23–26. Here also was "the shewbread,"—literally, "the presentation of loaves." These loaves were twelve in number, according to the number of the twelve tribes of Israel. They were placed on the golden table in two piles, each containing six loaves. The loaves were of considerable size, and were formed of fine flour. Every Sabbath day fresh loaves were presented, and the stale ones, when removed, formed a part of the food of the priests, which was required to be eaten in the holy place: Lev. xxiv. 3–9. This was "called the sanctuary," or rather, "the holy place," in contrast with the inner apartment, which was termed "the holy of holies," and of which the Apostle proceeds to give us a description.[1]

"After," or behind, "the second vail was the tabernacle which is called the holiest of all." The first vail refers to the curtains which hung over the entry into the tabernacle from the court before it. The second vail was that which separated the two apartments within the tabernacle from each other. It was a large curtain, of various colours, and of curious workmanship. The apartment beyond this, which was a perfect square, was termed "the holiest of all," as there dwelt the emblem of Divinity enshrined in glory. To this most sacred apartment

[1] Josephus, Ant. iii. 6, says, "the whole temple was called the holy place; but the prohibited area within the four where men might go was called the holy of holies."

belonged "*the golden censer.*"[1] Interpreters have been very much perplexed with this word. It is a word which may signify anything which holds incense, or on which incense is laid. Some translate it, "the golden altar of incense;" but the golden altar of incense was in the holy place, not in the holy of holies. The ordinary censers were made of brass, but that which the high priest used when "he went into the holiest of all," we are informed by Jewish writers, was made of gold: Lev. xvi. 12, 13. "The holiest of all" may be said to have had this, either because, after the high priest had come forth, he might place it under the vail, so as that he could easily reach it when it was required for the next annual solemnity, or because, though generally laid up in the repository of holy vessels, it belonged solely to the service of the holy of holies, and was there whenever the high priest officiated.

Within this most sacred of places was "the ark of the covenant overlaid round about with gold." This ark or chest was three feet nine inches in length, two feet three inches in breadth, and the same in height. It is termed "the ark of the covenant," because it contained the two tables of stone on which were engraven the ten commandments, the sum and substance of the covenant under which Israel was placed. It was a rich and beautiful piece of workmanship, being overlaid round about with gold: Exod. xxxvii. 2. "In it," or rather 'by it,' "was the golden pot that had manna." It is expressly said, 1 Kings viii. 9, 2 Chron. v. 10, that there was nothing in the ark save the two tables of stone which Moses put there at Horeb. The book of the law was to be "put in the side of the ark,"[2] that is, in a repository attached to the ark. In like manner, the golden pot, containing an omer of manna, was placed near the ark, "and Aaron's rod which budded." Of the history of this miraculous rod we have an account in Num. xvii. 2-11. In the ark were "the two tables of the covenant," *i.e.*, the two tables of stone hewn by Moses, and on which were divinely

---

[1] θυμιατήριον. Calmet calls this passage "maxima totius epistolæ difficultas." Ebrard well remarks, "If there existed no greater difficulties in it than this, then the Epistle to the Hebrews is one of the easiest books in the New Testament." The whole of Ebrard's exposition deserves to be read.

[2] Deut. xxxi. 26.

engraved the ten commandments. These are called "the tables of the covenant,"[1] because they contained the words of the covenant with Israel; and "the tables of the testimony of witness,"[2] because they attested the covenant—were a standing evidence of what God had required of and promised to His people; and because they were deposited in the ark, it is called "the ark of the testimony."[3]

Over this sacred chest were "the cherubim of glory shadowing the mercy-seat."[4] The cherubim were emblematical representations of the angels as the attendants and ministers of Jehovah. Much learning and labour have been bestowed in endeavouring to discover the precise form of these emblematical representations, but without success. We know they were represented with wings, which, being outstretched, "shadowed the mercy-seat." They are called "cherubim of glory," either from the bright resplendency of the representations, being formed of gold, or rather from their being connected with the Shekinah, the visible glory of Jehovah. Their wings overshadowed, and their faces looked down towards, the mercy-seat.

"The mercy-seat," or propitiatory, was the lid of the ark of the covenant. The name in Hebrew is taken from a word which signifies both to cover and to expiate or appease. It was by the sprinkling of the blood of the sacrifice of atonement on this golden lid that the work of expiating the sins of the congregation of Israel was completed. On this mercy-seat the visible emblem of the Divinity rested as on a throne, and from thence Jehovah gave forth all His oracles: Exod. xxv. 22. Hence He is said to "sit between the cherubim;"[5] and prayers are addressed to Him, as dwelling there, to bestow favours on His people.

Such is the account the Apostle gives us of the sanctuary in which the ministry of the Old Covenant was performed. He concludes his account with these words: "of which things we cannot now speak particularly;"—*i.e.*, I apprehend, 'of which things the object I have in view does not require, nor indeed

---

[1] Deut. ix. 9.      [2] Exod. xxxi. 18, xxxii. 15.
[3] Exod. xxv. 22.
[4] For an account of these ornaments, Exod. xxv. 17-22, xxxvii. 6-9, may be consulted.
[5] Ps. xcix. 1.

admit of, my entering into a more particular description.'[1] I do not think that we have any right to say that the Apostle here refers to the mystical meaning of these things in the tabernacle. That, generally speaking, the Levitical service was a type and a shadow, there can be no doubt. That everything in in it was emblematical, is much more than Scripture warrants us to assert; and to presume to give a mystical meaning when Scripture has given none, is to intrude into things which God has not revealed to us.

It were an easy thing to entertain you by the hour with the dreams of the philosophical Jews on this subject. I might tell you that they considered the whole tabernacle as an emblem of the universe, the first tabernacle being the emblem of earth, and the second of heaven—that the seven lamps are emblems of the seven planets—that the shew-bread was an emblem of the productions of the earth by which men are supported; and I might lay before you the almost equally unsupported fancies of pious and learned Christian divines, who have allowed imagination to occupy the place of reason in interpreting what, if they be emblems, are many of them unexplained emblems. I might thus amuse you, but I am afraid I could not thus edify you.

I shall direct your attention to a few passages of Scripture which may throw some light on some of these emblems. The golden candlestick seems explained, Rev. i. 12, 13, 20; the golden censer, Rev. viii. 3, 4; the mercy-seat, Heb. iv. 16; the cherubim, probably 1 Pet. i. 12. To carry further the explication of these emblems, real or supposed, than the word of God warrants us, is in reality to add to the divine revelation; and he who requires men to receive such explication, in effect lays claim to inspiration; and he who yields obedience to such a claim, exalts a mere fallible fellow-mortal to the level of prophets and apostles. There are other ways of adding to divine revelation—scarcely less dangerous, in some points of view more dangerous because less suspected—than by conjoining books of human composition with those Scriptures "which are given by inspiration of God."[2]

---

[1] λέγειν κατὰ μέρος is = the more common Greek expression, λέγειν καθ' ἕκαστον; it is opposed to λέγειν ἐν κεφαλαίῳ—' to speak briefly, summarily.'

[2] Archibald M'Lean, that man " mighty in the Scriptures," as Robert Hall characterized him to me, says, with his usual good sense, " As the

## COMPARISON WITH THE LEVITICAL PRIESTHOOD.

In the paragraph which follows we have an account of the general nature and various parts of that ministry which the Levitical priesthood performed in this sanctuary. Ver. 6. "Now when these things were thus ordained, the priests went always into the first tabernacle, accomplishing the service of God: 7. But into the second went the high priest alone once every year, not without blood, which he offered for himself, and for the errors of the people."

The words, "when these things were thus ordained," refer to the original arrangements respecting the sanctuary, or place in which the Levitical priesthood were to exercise their ministry. It is just equivalent to—'when the tabernacle, consisting of two apartments, had been prepared, and the furniture appropriate to each had been placed in it.'

When this had been done, the Levitical priesthood performed their divinely appointed ministry in it in the following manner: —" The priests"—*i.e.*, the sons of Aaron generally—" went into the first," or outer, "tabernacle *always*," or continually,—*i.e.*, often, regularly, every day as occasion required,—as contrasted with " the high priest entering alone once a year into the second" or inner sanctuary, "accomplishing the service of God,"—*i.e.*, performing the acts of appointed ministration which belonged to them. These appointed acts of ministration were such as the following:—sprinkling the blood of the sin-offerings before the vail which divided the holy place from the most holy, trimming and supplying the lamps of the golden candlestick, burning incense on the golden altar, and changing the loaves of presentation on the golden table. These acts of ministration were performed by the ordinary priests, as the substitutes of the high priest, according to a regular order, though the division into courses does not seem to have taken place till towards the close of David's reign.

While the first tabernacle was thus open to the priests generally every day, for the performance of these acts of ministrations, "into the second tabernacle," or holy of holies, none of them were permitted to enter, or even to look. " The high

Apostle here declines giving a particular explanation of these things, I must be excused from attempting it." Men far more " unskilled in the word of righteousness" have not been so forbearing. But " fools do rush in where angels fear to tread."

priest *alone*"—not only none entering with him, but none being in the sanctuary when he entered the adytum—and he only "*once* every year"—*i.e.*, on one day in every year, viz., on the tenth day of the seventh month, the great day of atonement for the sins of the whole nation of Israel during the preceding year—was allowed to go into the immediate presence of the emblem of Jehovah the God of Israel, "which dwelt between the cherubim." On that day the high priest seems to have entered thrice : first, with the censer of burning coals and incense, that the cloud thus produced might cover the mercy-seat, and intercept his view of the Shekinah or visible divine glory, lest he should die; then with the blood of the bullock which had been offered " for his own sins" and that of his house or family—*i.e.*, the whole priesthood—to sprinkle it seven times before the mercy-seat; and lastly, with the blood of the goat which had been offered "for the sins of the people," to sprinkle it also seven times before the mercy-seat: Lev. xvi. 1-19. A fourth entrance is mentioned in the Mishna, for the purpose of bringing out the censer.

When the high priest entered into the holy place, he entered "not without blood." These words convey two ideas,—that he entered *with blood*, and that he could not enter lawfully without blood. His object in entering was to finish the expiation of the sins of himself and his house, and of the whole house of Israel; and this could not be done without sacrificial blood. It was not enough that the piacular victim should be presented and slain, and have its blood poured out at the door of the tabernacle of the congregation. The atonement was not completed till a portion of the blood was sprinkled seven times before the mercy-seat. This blood was offered or presented to God " for the priest himself, and for the errors of the people ;" or rather, ' for his own errors, and for those of the people.' "Errors" is here a general name for sins, for in every sin there is involved error; and we know that on the great day of atonement expiation was made not only for what are ordinarily termed "sins of ignorance," but for all sins, with the exception of those for which the law of Moses furnished no means of atonement : Num. xv. 30, 31.

Before proceeding to describe further the nature and particular acts of the ministry of the Levitical priesthood, whether performed by the ordinary priests or by the high priest, the Apostle notices, by the way, the mystical meaning of the fact which he had just stated,—that none but the high priest, and he only once a year, was permitted to enter into the holy of holies. Ver. 8. "The Holy Ghost this signifying, that the way into the holiest of all was not yet made manifest, while as the first tabernacle was yet standing: 9. Which was a figure for the time then present."

The whole of the Levitical ritual was of divine appointment. It was in consequence of the inspiration of the Holy Spirit—in consequence of communications made to him by God, through His Spirit, that the tabernacle was erected and its services established by Moses. It was emblematical; and the true meaning of these emblems was an intimation of the divine will, just as really as if this meaning had been expressed by words. The phrase, "the Holy Ghost this signifying," is just analogous to a declaration in reference to the Lord's Supper to this effect: The Lord Jesus thus signifying that He died in our room, for our salvation; and that "whosoever believeth in Him shall not perish, but have everlasting life." But in both these cases, and indeed in all such cases, we are to recollect that we are not out of our own imaginations to assign a meaning to emblems, and then say, 'The Holy Ghost signifies this;' but we are to "hear what God the Lord has spoken," and receive His interpretation of His own emblem. Had not the Apostle made the statement contained in the text, I might have conjectured as to the meaning of the emblem referred to, but I durst not have said, 'The Holy Ghost signified this.'

But what was the mystical meaning of the exclusion, not only of the people, but of the ordinary priests, from "the holiest of all," and the admission of even the high priest only once every year? It was, "that the way into the *holiest of all* was not made manifest, while the first tabernacle continued standing." "The first tabernacle" has, by many judicious interpreters, been considered as descriptive both of the holy place and the most holy place—of the whole Levitical sanctuary, as contrasted with the true sanctuary of which it is a figure; and that it is termed "the *first* sanctuary" much in the same way as the Sinaitic covenant is called "the *first* covenant." We are disposed to think that the phrase is used just in the same way as in the 2d and 6th verses, as signifying the outer sanctuary, from which the people were excluded, and into which, but no farther, were the priests themselves allowed to enter. That "first tabernacle"—both as being shut up by a vail from the sight and entrance of the people, and also as being divided by the second vail from the holy of holies, into which only the high priest once a year entered—formed the essential part of the emblem, the meaning of which the Apostle here explains. Remove "the first tabernacle," and the vail which divided it from the holy of holies, and the emblem is destroyed. By "the first tabernacle" having a "standing," I understand its continuing to be a separate apartment from the holy of holies,—which it ceased to be on the death of Christ; for then the vail was rent asunder, and the two apartments became as it were one. While "the first tabernacle" continued as originally constructed, there was no entrance at all into the holiest of all, the place of the emblematic presence of the propitiated Divinity, for the great body of the people, who were not allowed to draw nearer than the vail or door of the sanctuary,—no entrance into "the holiest of all" for the great body of the priests, for they were allowed to go no farther than the vail which divided the holy place from the holy of holies,—no entrance into "the holiest of all" even for the high priest, except "once a year," with incense and with blood.

Such was the emblem; and the meaning was, that while this emblem remained, " the way into *the holiest of all* was not made manifest." " The *holiest of all*" here obviously signifies that of which the second tabernacle was the emblem. Now it may be considered as emblematical either of a state or a place. To be in the holy of holies is to be near to the reconciled Divinity—to be in a state of favour and fellowship with Him—to be in a place where His favour and fellowship, in all their transforming and blissful influences, are enjoyed. When it is said, then, that " the way into the holiest of all was not made manifest," the meaning is, not that under that dispensation none could enjoy the favour and fellowship of God (He led many into the holy of holies, but it was by a way which they knew not), but, that the method by which guilty and depraved men are brought to the enjoyment of that favour and fellowship, the perfection of which is to be found only in heaven, was not then clearly revealed. Dark intimations were given, but no distinct revelation. Christ—" Christ crucified," we know, is the way; and on His dying, " the Just

One in the room of the unjust," the emblem, being no longer significant, was destroyed by the miraculous rending of the vail, and an intimation given that now "the way into the holiest of all was made manifest."[1]

And thus "the first tabernacle" was "a *figure*"—an emblematical representation of the truth—"for the time *then* present." You will notice the word *then* is a supplement. By "the time present," I do not apprehend the Apostle means the period of the Old dispensation, but the period of the New. The words may be literally rendered, 'until the present time'—the present time being the same period which in the 10th verse is called "the time of reformation." The particle translated *for* often signifies *until*: Matt. x. 22; Luke xii. 19; John xiii. 1; Acts iv. 3; 2 Tim. i. 12; Gal. iii. 23, 24.[2] "The first tabernacle" was an emblematical representation till the commencement of the new order of things, when "the way to the holiest of all" being "made manifest," the emblem which intimated that it "was not yet made manifest" was destroyed, as no longer expressive of the truth.

Returning from this short digression as to the emblematical meaning of a particular part of the Levitical institution, the Apostle resumes the prosecution of his leading object in the paragraph, which is to illustrate the nature of the ministry of the Levitical priesthood, that by way of contrast with it, it might become evident that Jesus had "obtained a more excellent ministry." Ver. 9. "In which were offered both gifts and sacrifices, that could not make him that did the service perfect, as pertaining to the conscience; 10. Which stood only in meats and drinks, and divers washings, and carnal ordinances, imposed on them until the time of reformation." The grammatical construction of this passage is difficult. Stuart construes it thus: "Oblations and sacrifices are offered which cannot fully accomplish what is needed for the conscience of him who performeth the services, being imposed (with meats and drinks, and divers washings—ordinances pertaining to the flesh) only until the time of the reformation." The words *in which*, according to the

---

[1] On reviewing this exegesis, I feel disposed to say, with Abresch on another occasion, "Perhaps this may seem too subtle, and I would not wish to dispute with anyone about it."

[2] The LXX. render עַד *εἰς* and *ἕως*, Exod. xvi. 23, 24; Lev. xxv. 22.

reading which is followed,[1] may be considered as referring either to "the first tabernacle," or the period during which it had a "standing"—the period from its establishment down to what the Apostle calls "the present time," or "the time of reformation." In the first case, it is *during which period;* in the latter, it is *in which tabernacle*. The meaning is materially the same. In "the first tabernacle," during this period, "both gifts and sacrifices were offered,"—*i.e.*, both unbloody and bloody oblations were presented to God; but these religious ministrations "could not make him that did the service perfect, as pertaining to the conscience."

"Him that did the service," or the worshipper, does not refer solely to the priest, but to the person in whose room the priest officiated in presenting these oblations. It may refer to the priest, but only to him when offering oblations "for himself." These services "could not make the worshipper perfect, as pertaining to the conscience." To "perfect" a worshipper, is to fit him for acceptable, and delightful, and advantageous intercourse with God. These services, when performed according to the due order, "perfected" the worshipper as to the flesh for the meantime—enabled and authorized him to enjoy the privileges of the Sinaitic covenant; but they could not perfect him in reference "to the *conscience*." "The conscience" here refers to man as a spiritual, reasonable being, accountable to God, the moral Governor of the world. These services could not remove guilt, nor the disquieting sense of guilt, and fear of punishment; nor could they produce real holiness. They could not enable us to feel towards God as our Father and Friend; they could not fit and dispose us to intercourse and fellowship with Him; they were not services in "the holiest of all," nor had they any tendency to lead forward into the presence of a reconciled Divinity.

The imperfect nature of these services is further illustrated in the words which follow, which seem to contain a reason why they "could not make the worshipper perfect, as pertaining to the conscience."—" *Which stood*." You will observe these words are a supplement; and, I apprehend, an unnecessary one—the meaning seems clearer without it. "In which tabernacle were offered both gifts and sacrifices which could not make perfect,

---

[1] ὄν, the text. rec. and Griesb., or ἥν, the reading followed by our translators, and marked by Griesb. as probable.

as pertaining to the conscience, him who worshipped, in meats and drinks, and divers washings, and carnal ordinances imposed until the time of reformation." The religious services consisted "in meats and drinks." This does not at all refer to the distinction of meats into clean and unclean, or to the restrictions under which Nazarites lay as to the use of strong liquors. It refers to the sacrifices and libations, which consisted of flesh and bread—of blood and wine. The sacrifices are expressly termed the meat, or food, of God's house, and were connected with drink-offerings, which were of wine: Lev. iii. 16, xxi. 17; Exod. xxix. 40, 41; Num. xv. 5, 7, 10. The "divers washings," or baptisms, refer to the ablutions to which on various occasions both the priests and the people had to submit, to cleanse them from ceremonial pollutions, and fit them for taking a part in the service of Jehovah as the God of Israel.

These services are described as "*carnal ordinances*,"—institutions which possessed that general character of externality and materiality, which was the distinguishing feature of the whole economy. They cleansed the body from ceremonial defilement, but not the soul from moral guilt. These services were "imposed," authoritatively enjoined by God on the Israelites. The word seems intended to convey the idea that these injunctions were burdensome, lay heavy on those on whom they were imposed. And indeed, when we consider their number, variety, and frequency, with the much attention, and labour, and expense which they required, we need not wonder that Peter (Acts. xv. 10) should describe them as "a burden which neither they nor their fathers were able to bear."[1]

It was, however, only a temporary institution. It was added till the Seed should come in reference to whom the promises were made. They were "imposed" only "till the time of reformation"—till the Messiah should come and "restore all things"—till the period appointed, and which had now arrived, when "in Christ there should be a new creation"—when "by the sacrifice of Himself" He was to put an end to the Aaronical priesthood and the Levitical economy, and on the ground of a completed expiation introduce a spiritual order of worship, more acceptable to God, and at once more pleasing and advantageous

---

[1] Theophylact very happily says, "since the law was a heavy yoke, he naturally spoke of them as being 'imposed'."

to men. Such is the Apostle's account of the ministry of the Levitical priesthood, compared with which he declares that Jesus Christ "hath received a more excellent ministry." That it is more excellent, nothing more is necessary to evince, than merely to state in what it consists.

### 2. *Contrasted Facts respecting our Lord's High-priesthood.*

The words which follow contain the description of the ministry of Jesus Christ as "the Mediator of the new and better covenant," as contrasted with the ministry of Aaron and his sons, the mediators of the former covenant. Vers. 11, 12. " But Christ being come an high priest of good things to come, by a greater and more perfect tabernacle, not made with hands, that is to say, not of this building ; neither by the blood of goats and calves, but by His own blood, He entered in once into the holy place, having obtained eternal redemption for us." These words naturally call our attention to two things : The official character with which our Lord is invested, and the ministry which He has performed in that official character. His official character : He is " come a High Priest of good things to come." His ministry in that official character : He has "obtained eternal redemption for His people;" He has entered into the holy place ;" He has done so " through a greater and more perfect tabernacle ;" He has done so " not by the blood of goats and of calves, but by His own blood ;" and He has done so " once for all."

Let us then, first, turn our attention for a little to the official character with which our Lord is here represented as invested : " Christ being come a High Priest of good things to come." Our Saviour receives a great variety of appellations from the inspired writer of this Epistle. Sometimes He is termed "Jesus" —sometimes " Christ"—sometimes " Jesus Christ"—sometimes " the Son"—sometimes " the Son of God." These appellations are all significant, and by no means used indiscriminately. The attentive reader may almost in every case discern a reason why the particular appellation employed is used in preference to any other. It is easy to do so in the case before us. " Christ" is here equivalent to the Messiah, the name under which the great Deliverer was made known to the ancient Church, and whom they expected to " come and restore all things." The sum of the statement in the text is—'The Messiah having come[1] in the character in which He was promised, has done all that it was predicted He should do.'

The character in which Christ came, according to the prophecies which went before concerning Him, was that of "*the High Priest of good things to come.*" "*Good things to come*" is a descriptive appellation of that economy of which Jesus Christ is High Priest, and of which the law, the economy of which Aaron and his sons were the high priests, was a "shadow." It receives this appellation as a salutary system, a system of blessings, not so much, if at all, because its best blessings are future blessings—blessings to be enjoyed in a future world, but, conformably to the Jewish mode of speaking on this subject, in which the state of things under the Messiah was termed "the coming world," or "the world to come," the peculiar benefits of that state are termed "the coming good things." The phrase describes that economy of which the two great characters are truth and grace, and which "came by Jesus Christ"—the "good things to come."[2] The Messiah, when He came, was not a High Priest after the law—not a High Priest offering carnal sacrifices and obtaining temporal benefits. He was a High Priest of a new, a higher, a better economy. He offered a more valuable sacrifice; He obtained more important blessings. Of this economy He is the "High Priest;" *i.e.*, He transacts with God as to the religious interests of those who are the subjects of His economy. He makes expiation for their sins; He intercedes for them with God; He is the Author of eternal salvation to them. Such is the official character which belongs to our Lord. He has "come the High Priest of good things to come."

Having made these cursory remarks on the character with which the text represents our Lord as invested, I proceed, secondly, to the illustration of what I have principally in view: —The ministry which in this official character our Lord has accomplished. The Apostle's account of His ministry is con-

[1] παραγενόμενος, following after—viz., the Levitical High Priest of the ceremonial régime; he himself being the High Priest who should make the true expiation. It has been supposed that there is in the word π. an allusion to Ps. xl. 8, "Lo, I come." This passage seems to have been already before the Apostle's mind, though its illustration does not occur till ch. x. 7.

[2] Kuinoel's note is good : "These good things are described as μέλλοντα ('to come'), because at that time, when the Levitical worship was running its course, they were future, reserved for the 'time of reformation' (v. 10)."

tained in these words: "He has entered into the holy place, by"—or rather, through—"a greater and more perfect tabernacle, that is not of this building; by the blood, not of goats and calves, but by His own blood, having obtained eternal redemption for us."

His ministry consists of two parts, the one rising out of the other—the "obtaining eternal redemption for His people," and the "entering into the holy place;"—the one corresponding to the offering of the sacrifice of atonement, the other to the entering into the holy of holies to present the blood of that sacrifice before the mercy-seat.

(1.) The first great act of our Lord's ministry as the "High Priest of good things to come," is the "obtaining eternal redemption for His people." The high priests under the law obtained a temporary deliverance for those in whose room they acted, by presenting an appointed victim in their place to the displeased Divinity: the "High Priest of good things to come" obtained an everlasting deliverance for those in whose room He acted, by presenting Himself in their room, according to divine ordination, "a sacrifice and an offering." The Jewish high priest obtained a temporary deliverance by making a ceremonial and imperfect expiation: the "High Priest of good things to come" obtained an everlasting deliverance by making a real and an absolutely perfect expiation. In plain words, Jesus Christ has done all and suffered all which was necessary to make the complete deliverance of all His people from evil, in all its forms, and in all its degrees, for ever and ever, not merely consistent with, but gloriously illustrative of, all the perfections of the divine character, and all the principles of the divine government. He has "finished transgression, made an end of sin, and brought in an everlasting righteousness." "His blood cleanseth from all sin." "In Him there is redemption through His blood, the forgiveness of sins."

The efficacy of the sacrifice of Christ thus to "obtain eternal redemption," by making complete expiation, is traced by the Apostle to the dignity of His person—giving infinite value to the offering of His immaculate nature, His perfect obedience, and His piacular sufferings. It was because "*through the eternal Spirit* He offered Himself to God," that His spotless and unblemished sacrifice was available to the perfect expiation of the sins and the eternal redemption of the souls of all in whose place

He stood, and for whose benefit He acted as the "High Priest of good things to come."

(2.) The second great act of our Lord's ministry as the "High Priest of good things to come," is His "entering into the holy place." When the Jewish high priest on the great day of atonement had finished the first part of his ministry, in obtaining deliverance for the people by the expiation of their sins, he went into the holy of holies, with the blood of atonement, to present before God evidence of the completed expiation, and to make intercession for the people, if not really, yet emblematically by burning incense. The whole of what he did in the holy place, as well as the going into it, is pointed out by the phrase, "entering into the holy place." When the Messiah, as the "High Priest of good things to come," had finished on the cross His expiatory sacrifice, He entered into the true holy place, to present, as it were, to God the evidence of the completeness of the atonement He had made, and to follow it up by a never-ceasing interposition in behalf of His people, founded on His all-perfect atoning sacrifice. All this is included in His "entering into the holy place."

By "the holy place" into which our great High Priest has entered, we are to understand "the heaven of heavens," the place where the Divinity most remarkably manifests His excellence, or communicates His blessings to unfallen and restored intelligent beings, as appears from ver. 24. When our Lord entered into heaven, He entered in His public character as a fully accomplished High Priest, "having been made perfect through suffering." His very entrance there was a proof of the perfection of His sacrifice; and additional evidence of this delightful truth is to be found in the place which He occupies there, and in the manner in which He is employed there. When He "entered into the holy place," it was not to stand ministering before the throne, but it was to sit down at the right hand of Him who sitteth on it. "All power in heaven and on earth" is conferred on Him; and all this power He employs for completing the salvation of those whom He has redeemed by His own blood. The following is the description given by the prophetic Spirit of the high and beatific state of Messiah the royal Priest, when He had entered into the holy place :—" The King shall joy in Thy strength, O Lord; and in Thy salvation how greatly shall He rejoice! Thou hast given Him His heart's desire, and hast not withholden the request of His lips. Selah. For Thou preventest Him with the blessings of goodness: Thou settest a crown of pure gold on His head. He asked life of Thee, and Thou gavest it Him, even length of days for ever and ever. His glory is great in Thy salvation: honour and majesty hast Thou laid upon Him. For Thou hast made Him most blessed for ever: Thou hast made Him exceeding glad with Thy countenance."[1] He is, indeed, represented as *interceding for* His people there; but there is nothing humiliating in the intercession of our great High Priest. It is just another way of expressing this idea, that it is in consequence of His expressed will that every exertion of divine power, directly or indirectly, connected with the salvation of men, whether in producing external event or inward influence, is put forth.

Into this glorious place and state the " High Priest of good things to come" entered " by a greater and more perfect tabernacle, that is not of this building." By the tabernacle here described some very judicious commentators have understood our Lord's human nature; and they have explained the phrase, entering by this tabernacle, as equivalent to—' entering through means of services performed in this tabernacle.' There can be no doubt that the human nature of our Lord may with much propriety be termed the tabernacle or temple which the Divinity inhabits; and it was by services performed by Christ in human nature that " He entered into the holiest of all." But, without extreme harshness, I do not see how the figure can be thus explained here. The allusion does not seem to be to the priest entering the holiest of all in consequence of services done in the holy place, but to his passing through the holy place in order to his entrance into the holiest of all. Nowhere in this Epistle is, I apprehend, the human nature of Christ compared to the tabernacle. Besides, this would introduce tautology; for, ver. 12, it is said, He entered " by His own blood." The meaning of the inspired writer may, I think, be thus stated :—Our Lord offered His sacrifice on the earth, as the Jewish high priests did without the tabernacle; and having offered His sacrifice on the earth, He passed through the visible heavens, as they passed through the outer tabernacle, into the heaven of heavens, of

[1] Ps. xxi. 1-6.

which the most holy place was an emblem. He entered into the holy place through the visible heavens, which are represented in the Old Testament Scriptures as the tabernacle of Jehovah—His outer court, throughout which are scattered displays of grandeur and beauty worthy of the antechamber of the great King, the Lord of hosts,—a tabernacle certainly greater, more magnificent, more perfect, more highly finished, than the Mosaic tabernacle, with all its curious embroidery and costly ornaments,—a tabernacle formed immediately by the hand of God, who " in the beginning stretched out the heavens as a curtain."

The tabernacle through which Christ entered into the holy place is said " not" to be " of this *building*," or of this creation, or establishment. The words are plainly intended to complete the antithesis. He obtained, not temporal, but eternal redemption for His people; and having done so, entered not into the material holy of holies, but into the immediate presence of God; and in doing so, He passed not through the outer tabernacle erected by Moses, but through the visible heavens.

The following is the history of this glorious event:—" And He led them out as far as to Bethany; and He lifted up His hands, and blessed them. And it came to pass, while He blessed them, He was parted from them, and carried up into heaven."[1] What took place after He rose above the sight of mortal eye, and the hearing of mortal ear, sacred history does not tell us. But " the Spirit of prophecy is the witness of Jesus," and this is His testimony: " God is gone up with a shout, the Lord with the sound of a trumpet. Sing praises to God, sing praises: sing praises unto our King, sing praises." " The chariots of God are twenty thousand, even thousands of angels: the Lord is among them, as in Sinai, in the holy place. Thou hast ascended on high, Thou hast led captivity captive: Thou hast received gifts for men; yea, for the rebellious also, that the Lord God might dwell among them."[2] We cannot doubt that the whole of the attendant cherubim in the holy of holies, if not awed into reverent silence, put forth their choicest melodies when the great " High Priest of good things to come" sat down on the heavenly throne, sprinkled with His own blood, on the right hand of Jehovah, who liveth for ever and ever.[3]

[1] Luke xxiv. 50, 51.   [2] Ps. xlvii. 5, 6; lxviii. 17, 18.
[3] Michaelis considers the outer sanctuary as the Church on earth, in

It is still further stated, that when He thus entered into the true holiest of all, it was "not through the blood of goats and calves, but through His own blood." The reference here does not seem to be to the priest entering with blood in his hand, but to the fact of his entering into the holy place in consequence of the shedding of the blood of the bullock and the goat as sin-offerings for himself and for the congregation. It was on the ground of the expiation made that he entered into the holy place. It is on the ground of the all-perfect expiation made by the blood of the Redeemer that He enters the true holy place. It was because He "humbled Himself, and became obedient unto death, even the death of the cross," that He was "highly exalted, and received a name that is above every name." The perfection of His atonement is the ground of His exaltation, and of His unbounded saving power. "He is able to save to the uttermost," for "He ever lives to make intercession" for His people; and He ever lives, because He once "died, the just for the unjust, that He might bring men to God."

The only other circumstance mentioned in reference to our Saviour's entrance into the holy place, is that He "entered *once*," *i.e.*, once for all—not once every year, but once for all. A new year brought new guilt; and this guilt required a new sacrifice, and a new entrance into the holy place. But by His one sacrifice He obtained eternal redemption for His people; and the expiation being complete, the entrance into the holiest of all was final—once and for ever.

The Jewish high priest had to come out, that he might again perform the work of expiation. But our great High Priest comes no more out to perform the ministry of atonement. That is over, completely over. He will indeed come forth. "Behold, He cometh in clouds, and every eye shall see Him." But "when He comes the second time, it will be without a sin-offering." It will be not to expiate the sin that has been done already; it will be to consummate the salvation of "all who look for Him." May every one of us, while He proclaims, "Behold, I come

---

which Christ acted the part of a priest not only, as he says, for three years and a half of His ministry, but during the whole period of His humbled ἐνσάρκωσις. This is an exegesis that deserves examination. It is quite consistent with making the visible heavens the vail which divides the holy from the holy of holies.

quickly," be enabled to respond from the heart, " Even so come, Lord Jesus."

(2.) *More Particular Comparison, referring to the comparative Efficacy of the two Priesthoods.* Chap. ix. 13–x. 18.

The proposition which the Apostle is occupied with proving and illustrating in the paragraph of which these verses form a part, is that laid down by him in the sixth verse of the preceding chapter: ' Jesus Christ, " the High Priest of our profession," has received a more excellent ministry than Aaron or any of his sons.' The religious functions which He performs as a High Priest, are of a far higher order than the religious functions which they performed as high priests. To prepare the way for satisfactorily proving this proposition, he gives a succinct account, first of the ministry of Aaron and his sons as high priests, and then of the ministry of Jesus Christ as a High Priest. In merely making these statements, the immeasurable superiority of His function to theirs becomes very evident.

But there are two points of superiority on which the inspired writer dwells, as of peculiar importance. The *efficacy* of the priestly function of Jesus Christ is higher in its *kind*, and more complete in its *degree*. To the illustration of these, I apprehend, the whole of the remaining part of the section, which ends with the 18th verse of the next chapter, is devoted, with the exception of the passage from the 15th to the 24th verse, which I consider is parenthetical,—a digression for the purpose of meeting the Jewish prejudice, that the Messiah was not to die, by showing that His death as a sacrifice was absolutely necessary for the ratification of the covenant of which He is the Mediator.

The principle, that the ministry of our Lord is superior to the ministry of the Aaronical high priests, inasmuch as its efficacy is of a much higher kind than theirs was, is stated and proved in the 13th and 14th verses.

The principle, that the ministry of our Lord is superior to the ministry of the Aaronical high priests, inasmuch as its efficacy is much more complete in its degree, as appears from the contrast between their constantly recurring services, and His " offering of Himself once for all," is stated and proved at considerable length, from the 25th verse of this chapter down to the 18th verse of the next chapter, which terminates the doctrinal part of the Epistle.

Our attention is to be devoted, first, to the former of these proofs of the superiority of the ministry of Jesus Christ as a Priest to Aaron and all his sons.

1. *The Efficacy of our Lord's Priesthood is of a higher kind than that of the Levitical Priesthood.*

Vers. 13, 14. " For if the blood of bulls and of goats, and the ashes of an heifer sprinkling the unclean, sanctifieth to the purifying of the flesh; how much more shall the blood of Christ, who through the eternal Spirit offered Himself without spot to God, purge your conscience from dead works, to serve the living God?"

The superiority of the ministry of Jesus Christ to that of Aaron and his sons, as manifested in the superior kind of efficacy which belongs to it, is the great subject of these words. That superiority is both asserted and proved. The assertion is thus made :—" The blood of bulls and goats, and the ashes of an heifer sprinkling the unclean, sanctifieth to the purifying of the flesh." " The blood of Christ, who through the eternal Spirit offered Himself without spot to God, purges the conscience from dead works, to serve the living God." The argument is thus stated :—" For if the blood of bulls and of goats, —how much more." Let us endeavour first to ascertain the meaning of the statement, and then we will be prepared for inquiring into the force of the argument.

The statement respecting the nature of the efficacy belonging to the ministrations of Aaron and his sons is contained in these words :—" The blood of bulls and of goats, and the ashes of an heifer sprinkling the unclean, sanctified to the purifying of the flesh." The services of the law are sometimes spoken of by divines as if they had been utterly, and in every sense, inefficacious. This is, however, by no means an accurate representation. For the purpose served by the ministry of our great New Testament Priest,—the so expiating all moral guilt as to lay a secure foundation for its forgiveness, and for the sanctification and final salvation of him who had contracted it,—they were indeed altogether inefficacious. To gain this end they never were intended; and therefore it is not to be wondered at if they were in no degree fitted for a purpose they were not meant to serve. But they were intended to serve a purpose; and they were well fitted to serve that purpose—they actually did serve it. If they had not had efficacy of some kind, they would have been altogether unfit for being emblems of the all-efficacious ministry of Jesus Christ.

What were the nature and extent of the efficacy which belonged to these services, is distinctly stated in the words now under consideration. " The blood of bulls and goats" is obviously just equivalent to—' the blood of animals offered as sacrifices for sin, according to the law of Moses.' The phrase, "the ashes of an heifer," refers to a remarkable ceremonial usage, of which we have a particular account in the 19th chapter of the Book of Numbers. A red heifer, or young cow, without blemish, upon which never yoke had come, was to be taken without the camp, slain in the presence of the priest, who was to sprinkle of her blood with his finger seven times before the tabernacle of the congregation; the carcase was then to be burnt entire, and into the midst of the fire which consumed it were to be thrown by the priest cedar wood, hyssop, and scarlet wool. When the carcase was completely consumed, the ashes were to be collected and preserved. On a person's contracting that ceremonial defilement which arose from touching a dead body, a portion of these ashes was to be mixed in running water, and a clean person, dipping a bunch of hyssop in the mixture, was to sprinkle it on him that was unclean.

Now the sprinkling of the blood of an animal offered as a sacrifice for sin, or the sprinkling of this mixture of the ashes of the burnt heifer and pure running water, on a person who was ceremonially polluted, and therefore excluded from mingling with his brethren in the solemnities of divine service, and indeed in the ordinary intercourse of life, " sanctified to the purifying of the flesh," *i.e.*, it removed ceremonial defilement. The person thus sprinkled according to the due order, might lawfully mingle with the congregation of the Lord. These sprinklings " sanctified" such a person. By his ceremonial pollution he had been excluded for a season from the holy people, the people set apart for the service of God —he had become common or unclean; but by these sprinklings he was anew separated or devoted to the service of God, so far as "the purifying of the flesh" was concerned. "The purifying of the flesh" does not mean the cleansing of the body—for sprinkling with blood and ashes rather soiled than purified,—but it means external, ceremonial purification, as opposed to spiritual, real purification. This, then, was the nature of the efficacy which belonged to the ministry of Aaron and his sons: It removed ceremonial pollution; it produced ceremonial sanctification; it relieved the Israelites from the inconveniences connected with being excluded from the society of the external Jewish Church, and from the observance of its ordinances, and obtained for them the advantages connected with restoration to the enjoyment of that society, and to the observance of these ordinances. This was the kind of efficacy which belonged to the ministry of Aaron and his sons. The fact of the efficacy of these sacrifices for their appointed purpose is strongly stated, Lev. vi. 2-7: "If a soul sin, and commit a trespass against the Lord,—he shall bring his trespass-offering unto the Lord, a ram without blemish out of the flock, to the priest; and the priest shall make an atonement for him before the Lord; and it shall be forgiven him, for anything of all that he hath done, in trespassing therein."

But the ministry of our Lord as a High Priest was "a more excellent ministry;" for its efficacy was of a far superior nature. "The blood of Christ, who through the eternal Spirit offered Himself without spot unto God, purifies the conscience from dead works, to serve the living God."

The first thing that here requires consideration is the statement, that "Christ through the eternal Spirit offered Himself without spot to God." "Christ offered Himself to God;" *i.e.*, Christ took the place of sinners, and did and suffered in their room what to the infinitely wise, and holy, and just Governor of the world seemed necessary and sufficient to make their pardon and salvation consistent with, and illustrative of, the perfections of His character, and the principles of His moral administration. He presented Himself, having done all and suffered all the requisitions of the law on Him as the substitute of sinners, in the precise manner, with the precise temper in which the law required this to be done,—He presented Himself, having "finished the work given Him to do," having done the whole will of His Father,—He presented Himself as the victim of His elect people. And " He offered Himself *without spot*." Not only was the obedience and the satisfaction, viewed by themselves, complete, but He who yielded them was completely free from sin. Indeed, there are little more than two ways of expressing the same truth; for what He offered was *Himself*,—all that He was, all that He had done,—that entire, most willing subjection to the law man had violated, both in its precept and sanction, which He had yielded from the moment of His incarnation to the moment of His death. The offering was completed on the cross, but it did not commence there. To the absolute sinlessness, to the complete perfection of the victim thus offered, the Apostle often refers. On this circumstance the sacred writers place peculiar stress; for without it the sacrifice would have been altogether in vain. Had Christ been a sinner in any respect or degree—had His flesh been sinful flesh—had His humanity been, strictly speaking, fallen humanity,—He would have been utterly disqualified for achieving the great work of our salvation: He would have needed for Himself that blessing which He came to confer on others. The Levitical law made persons priests who had to offer sacrifice for themselves as well as for those for whose benefit they officiated; but our High Priest is " holy, harmless, undefiled." " He needed not to offer first for His own sins;" for He had no sins of His own to offer for. He was manifested to take away sin, and " in Him was no sin." " We are redeemed with the precious blood of Christ, as of a lamb without blemish and without spot." Otherwise He would not have been such a priest or victim as became us—as we needed.

When Christ thus "offered Himself to God without spot," He did so " through the eternal Spirit." The phrase " eternal[1] Spirit" occurs nowhere else in the New Testament. The phrase has been variously explained. Some refer it to the Holy Spirit, personally dwelling in our Lord; or to divine influence, guiding all His thoughts and feelings, words and actions; or to the declarations in the ancient prophets respecting Him: 'He offered Himself under the guidance and influence of the Holy Spirit,

---

[1] Some codd. read ἁγίου in place of αἰωνίου; but the weight of evidence, direct and indirect, external and internal, is in favour of the *textus receptus*.

or according to the declarations of the Holy Spirit, who is eternal.' Others refer it to our Lord's divine nature. This was "the Spirit of holiness," according to which He is declared to be the Son of God—the Spirit by which He lived, even when put to death in the flesh—the Spirit by which, when "manifested in the flesh," He was "justified."[1] According to either mode of interpretation, the statement is true; for Christ may be said to have "offered Himself without spot unto God" both through the Holy Ghost and through His divine nature.[2] We are disposed, upon the whole, to coincide with those numerous learned and judicious interpreters who adopt the latter mode of interpretation. Had it not been for our Lord's divine nature, He could not have yielded acceptable and effectual substituted obedience and satisfaction. A mere creature can never yield more obedience than it owes for itself; and a mere creature has no right, were the thing practicable, to make a sacrifice of its own happiness to obtain the happiness of another. It was the living God manifested in flesh who was both our High Priest and victim; and He stamped His own glory on the propitiation for our sins, both on the priestly act and on the ransom offered.

[1] Others consider it as referring to the strong impulse of His own mind or spirit, in the same way as they explain what is said of Simeon (Luke ii. 27), $\mathring{\eta}\lambda\theta\epsilon\nu\ \dot{\epsilon}\nu\ \tau\tilde{\omega}\ \pi\nu\epsilon\dot{\nu}\mu\alpha\tau\iota\ \epsilon\dot{\iota}\varsigma\ \tau\dot{o}\ \dot{\iota}\epsilon\rho\acute{o}\nu$. Besides other objections, this exegesis does not account for the use of the epithet $\alpha\dot{\iota}\omega\nu\acute{\iota}o\nu$. Others consider it as = 'eternal life'—'endowed with immortal life, having $\delta\dot{\nu}\nu\alpha\mu\iota\nu\ \zeta\omega\tilde{\eta}\varsigma\ \dot{\alpha}\kappa\alpha\tau\alpha\lambda\dot{\nu}\tau o\nu$.' Others refer it to our Lord's exalted state as opposed to a state of *mortal flesh*. This is inconsistent with the *usus loquendi*, and, like the former, goes on the supposition of Christ's expiatory oblation being made in heaven. Others consider it as = 'having eternal power' or efficacy as a victim. The words will not bear this; and if they could, it would be a taking for granted the very thing to be proved. Others consider it as stating that He offered Himself not according to the short-lived, external letter of the Mosaic law, but according to its true meaning—its 'ever-living spirit;' but this is certainly to bring a sense into the words which otherwise could never have been brought out of them. The choice among all these modes of interpretation is confined to two: that which considers the 'eternal Spirit' as designating the Holy Ghost, and that which considers it as designating our Lord's divine nature.

[2] A very ingenious defence of the first of these views is to be found in the *Christian Magazine* for 1803, vol. vii. It is from the pen of my esteemed colleague, the late Professor Duncan, and shows how early his attention had been directed to the critical study of the sacred writings.

Now the Apostle asserts that "the blood" of this spotless sacrifice of Himself, which Christ offered to God, "purges the conscience from dead works, to serve the living God." "The blood" of this sacrifice is just the sacrifice itself, which was consummated in the shedding of the blood, or death, of the victim. The effects of the sacrifice of Christ may be considered either in reference to God, or in reference to the sinner. The blood of Christ, viewed as *shed*, renders the salvation of the sinner consistent with the perfections of the divine character, the principles of the divine government, the declarations of the divine word. The blood of Christ, viewed as sprinkled on the believing sinner, relieves his mind from the constraints, and terrors, and jealousies, and pollutions of guilt, and enables him to serve God without fear, with filial love and holy joy. These two effects of the sacrifice of Christ are closely connected. The second depends on the first. The blood must be shed in order to its being sprinkled. It is to the last of these effects that there is a direct reference in the passage before us. "The blood of Christ," sprinkled on the conscience, "purges" or purifies it "from dead works, to serve the living God."

*Dead works*, as I endeavoured to show when explaining the 1st verse of the 6th chapter, are *sins*, which receive this appellation either because they deserve death, or are the works of those who in a spiritual sense are dead—or, like dead men, produce pollution, which must be cleansed. Indeed, the somewhat remarkable phrase, "*dead* works," seems to have been suggested to the Apostle's mind by what he had said about the purifying power of lustration by the sprinkling of a liquor in which the ashes of a heifer had been mingled. This removed the external pollution contracted by having touched a *dead* body; but the blood of Christ, applied to the conscience, removed the spiritual pollution contracted by sinful deeds, the source of a much deeper, deadlier pollution than contact with a dead body could produce. These dead works pollute and defile the conscience, and render men utterly unfit for the spiritual service of God. "The conscience" here is just the man as a spiritual being, capable, from the constitution of his nature, of the spiritual service of God. Sin makes man hateful in God's sight—the object both of judicial displeasure and moral disapprobation. But this is not all: conscious guilt unfits a man for acceptably serving God. The essence of the service which God requires of His intelligent creatures is love. The man whose conscience is polluted with unpardoned guilt cannot love. He knows he has offended God; he knows he deserves punishment; he does not, he cannot, love the Being whom he regards as his enemy; he cannot seek his enjoyment in communion and fellowship with Him. Nothing can fit man for the service of God but what purifies the conscience from the pollution produced by these "dead works;" and nothing can do this but the blood of the sacrifice of Jesus Christ.

"The blood of Christ sprinkled on the conscience purges it from dead works." "The blood of Christ sprinkled on the conscience" is a highly figurative expression, but its meaning is not obscure: it is just expressive of a man's knowing and believing the truth respecting the sacrifice of Jesus Christ. This is the only way in which, according to man's rational and moral nature, the blood of Christ can be *applied* to him—in which Christ's sacrifice can have a cleansing power over him. When the truth on this subject is understood and believed by the sinner, the immediate consequence is, just in the degree in which the truth is understood and believed, that the conscience is pacified and purified—the terrors and jealousies of guilt are removed. He is sweetly constrained to love Him who "spared not His Son, but delivered Him up" for his salvation. What has satisfied, and what he sees has satisfied, all the demands of divine justice, satisfies the demands of his awakened conscience; and now he comes to God "in Christ reconciling the world to Himself, not imputing to men their trespasses." He "comes boldly to the throne of grace." He finds happiness in communion with God, and walks at liberty, keeping His commandments. His obedience becomes the obedience of the heart. Till the heart is thus "sprinkled from an evil conscience" by the blood of Christ—till it is freed in some measure from the fear of wrath, and reconciled to God—sinners are not, they cannot be, possessed of that faith, and love, and holy confidence, and filial freedom, which are necessary to the acceptable service of God.

Such is the statement of the Apostle respecting the superior kind of efficacy which belongs to the ministry of Christ as a High Priest, above that which belonged to the ministry of Aaron and his sons as high priests. Their ministry was effectual for removing ceremonial defilement, and fitting men for ceremonial worship: His is effectual for removing the impurities of the conscience, and for fitting men for spiritual worship.

We are now prepared for attending to the force of the Apostle's argument; for he not only asserts this superiority, but he proves it. His argument runs thus: " If the blood of bulls and of goats, and the ashes of an heifer sprinkling the unclean, sanctifieth to the purifying of the flesh; how much more shall the blood of Christ, who through the eternal Spirit offered Himself without spot to God, purge your conscience from dead works, to serve the living God?" The force of the Apostle's argument may be brought out, I think, in the two following propositions:—(1.) The ministry of Christ has all to give it efficacy for its purposes which the ministry of Aaron and his sons had to give it efficacy for its purposes; and (2.) The ministry of Christ has much to give it efficacy for its purposes which the ministry of Aaron had not. Let us attend to these propositions in their order.

(1.) The ministry of Christ has all to give it efficacy for its purposes which the ministry of Aaron and his sons had to give it efficacy for its purposes. Now what was it that gave the ministry of Aaron and his sons its efficacy? What was it that made "the sprinkling of blood and of the ashes of an heifer" effectual for the purpose of "sanctifying to the purifying of the flesh?" The answer is easy: viz., divine appointment. Now He who appointed these things to purify the flesh, appointed the blood of Christ to purify the conscience. His blood is the blood of Christ, the *Anointed One*—the divinely appointed Saviour. The Father sent Him to be the Saviour of the world. "He made to meet on Him the iniquities of us all." He "sets Him forth a propitiation." He "made Him sin for us, that we might be made the righteousness of God in Him." If, then, the appointment of God gave efficacy for ceremonial purification to "the blood of bulls and goats, and the ashes of an heifer," will not the same divine appointment equally give efficacy for the purification of the conscience to the blood of the appointed victim of human transgressions? This is a good argument, and it is implied in the words before us, but this does by no means exhaust their meaning; for the argument is not, "If the blood of bulls and of goats sanctifieth to the purifying of the flesh, *even so*," but "*how much more* shall the blood of Christ purge your conscience from dead works!"

This leads me to the second proposition. (2.) The ministry of Christ has much in it to give it efficacy which the ministry of Aaron and his sons had not. The whole of the efficacy of their ministry arose from divine appointment. Without *that* it would have been an empty, an impious show—no more efficacious than the sacrifices of the heathen; but in consequence of this divine appointment, it was efficacious for its own purposes, notwithstanding the weaknesses and faults of those who exercised it. The efficacy of our Lord's ministry depends, no doubt, on its divine appointment; but its efficacy was by no means solely owing to its divine appointment. Had it not been divinely appointed, it could not have been efficacious; or rather, it never could have existed. Aaron's ministry was efficacious just because it was appointed. Christ's ministry was appointed because in its own nature fitted to be efficacious. The obedience, sufferings, and death of a Divine Person in human nature, were in their own nature fitted to gain all the ends which were contemplated by the Divine Being in this most wonderful of all the divine dispensations. We have redemption in Him, because He is "the first begotten," *i.e.*, prince, "of the whole creation"—because by Him we are created. "His blood cleanseth from all sin," for it is the blood of Him who is God's own Son. He purged our sins by his sacrifice, because He who offered the sacrifice was "the brightness of the Father's glory, and the express image of His person;" and the sacrifice by which He purged our sins was the sacrifice of Himself. The divinity of our Lord's nature gave a transcendent worth and efficacy to His sacrifice. "The divine act of the assumption of human nature by the eternal Word communicated its own dignity and value to all the mediatorial acts of the incarnate Saviour. The union then formed was constant and invariable. Though it was impossible that the divine nature could be subject to suffering, it was the Mediator in His whole person who acted for the salvation of men; and all He did for this purpose was impressed with the essential dignity and moral value of His divine perfection."[1] Such is the Apostle's statement and argument respect-

[1] Pye-Smith's "Four Discourses on the Sacrifice and Priesthood of Jesus Christ," 4th edit., pp. 68, 69, condensed.

ing the superior kind of efficacy which belongs to the ministry of Christ as our High Priest.

The paragraph which follows (vers. 15–24) must be numbered among the passages which mistranslation has rendered obscure : " And for this cause He is the Mediator of the new testament, that by means of death, for the redemption of the transgressions that were under the first testament, they which are called might receive the promise of eternal inheritance," etc. It is impossible for a mere English reader to make a satisfactory sense out of these words. What meaning can he attach to the phrase, " mediator of a testament ? " In a testament or last will we have a testator, and legatees, and an executor or executors; but who is the mediator of a testament ? It is an expression just as anomalous as the testator of a covenant.[1]

It is difficult to see how the new economy or covenant can be called a testament. The only point of resemblance is, that death in it, as in the case of a testament, was necessary in order to the enjoyment of its benefits; though even here the leading idea is not expressed,—" the death of the testator " not being the procuring cause of the legacies, but merely the condition of obtaining possession of them. But if the new economy were repre-

[1] It is mortifying, but instructive, to find so sensible a man as Limborch, in defence of a false interpretation, writing such absurdity as this : " διαθήκη testamentum est, ultimæ voluntatis testatio, qua quis bonorum suorum hæredes post mortem suam instituit. Institutioni interdum adduntur quædam conditiones, quas testator hæredi suo præscribit. Si conditiones testator addit, per figuratum loquendi modum, ipsi quasi *actus quidam mediatorius*, cujus interventu hæreditas ad hæredem devolvitur, tribui potest, et testamentum aliquam habet similitudinem cum fœdere." If a testament is to be viewed as a διαθήκη, then the μεσίτης is not the testator, but the *executor*. There cannot be a doubt that διαθήκη stands as the expression of the idea conveyed by the Hebrew בְּרִית, which never signifies a testament,—and as little, that the proper meaning of the Greek word is, ' arrangement, disposition, disposal.' I can understand how interpreters who hold that the Apostles adopted the rabbinical modes of exposition can explain διαθήκη of a testament; but how persons who hold that they reasoned like men at once of sense and integrity—still more, like men inspired by the Spirit of wisdom and holiness, can be satisfied with such an exegesis, I confess myself utterly incapable of comprehending. I do not wonder to find it in such writers as Böhme and Kuinoel, but I confess I both wonder and deplore when I meet with it in such a writer as Moses Stuart. I do not know to what I would not submit sooner than, holding the inspiration of the Apostle, admit that he reasons as Mr Stuart represents him as reasoning.

sented as a testament, the testator would be God the Father, not Jesus Christ, for it is God who blesses us with "heavenly and spiritual blessings in Christ Jesus;" and even supposing that Jesus Christ was considered as the testator, it is plain that His resurrection destroys the propriety of the figure.

It is, if possible, still more difficult to attach any consistent idea to the term "testament" as descriptive of the first covenant, or Mosaic economy. It was a law imperatively enjoined, not a disposition of benefits which might be accepted or refused. Besides, who was the testator here? and how was the testament confirmed by his death? and what is the meaning of transgressions of the old will, to atone for which the maker of the new will died?

Besides, it is impossible to see the force of the Apostle's reasoning. He is obviously accounting for the death of Christ—dignified and exalted as He was—by showing that it was absolutely necessary to the gaining of the great object for which He was constituted the High Priest and Mediator of the new economy. Now it requires but little perspicacity to see that there is no force in such an argument as the following: 'The New Covenant may be considered as a testament, inasmuch as its blessings cannot be enjoyed without the death of Christ. Now, as a testament, in order to be valid, requires that the testator should be dead, therefore it was necessary for Christ to die.' That is the argument as it stands in our translation; an argument which, taking for granted in the premises what it proposes to prove, obviously proves nothing. Setting his inspiration out of the question altogether, the author of the Epistle to the Hebrews was obviously a person of too clear a mind to argue in this way.

Now all this perplexity, in which an intelligent English reader of this paragraph must feel himself involved—and the more intelligent and inquisitive he is, he will be the more perplexed—arises out of a mistranslation of a very few words. The word translated "testament" in this paragraph, is the same that in the preceding context is rendered "covenant;" and not only in the preceding context, but wherever it occurs in the New Testament, except in the following instances, in every one of which it ought to have been rendered "covenant:" Matt. xxvi. 28; Mark xiv. 24; Luke xxii. 20; 1 Cor. xi. 25; 2 Cor. iii. 6, 14; Heb. vii. 22; Rev. xi. 19. The substitution of the word "covenant"—understanding by that, 'arrangement, economy, order of things'—in the room of the word "testament," with a few slight changes which necessarily rise out of that substitution, gives distinctness of meaning and conclusiveness of argument to a passage which, as it stands in our version, appears to me altogether inexplicable.[1]

Let us now proceed to a somewhat more minute inspection of the various parts of this paragraph. But before doing so, it will be requisite to say a word or two as to the design of this paragraph, and the manner in which it is introduced.

The Apostle is proving that Jesus Christ, as a High Priest, has received a more excellent ministry than Aaron or his sons. He has described in succession their ministry and His. He has, in the words immediately preceding the subject of exposition, shown that His ministry excels theirs in the kind of efficacy which it possesses: theirs was efficacious to remove ceremonial defilement, and to fit for external worship; His is efficacious to remove moral defilement, and to fit for spiritual worship. And in the paragraph which follows the verses under consideration, he shows that His ministry excels theirs in the completeness of its efficacy: theirs requiring to be continually repeated; His being performed once for all. The paragraph before us comes in between these two proofs of the superiority of our Lord's ministry. It is a

[1] It were very uncandid not to admit that the method of exegesis adopted by us has its difficulties, and that these are by no means of a light nature. They are chiefly two, and both rising out of the *usus loquendi*. The word διαθέμενος, and the phrase ἐπὶ νεκροῖς, must be interpreted in a way not forbidden by their native import, but unauthorized by any scriptural or classic example, with the exception of a passage from Appian, De Bello Civ. lib. ii., quoted by Peirce, of a use of διαθέμενος in a sense somewhat similar to that which our plan of interpretation gives it. But these difficulties appear to be like the dust in the balance when weighed against those which are involved in the ordinary hypothesis. Ebrard's note is very valuable, and throws new light on the use of the word διαθέμενος. He considers διαθ. as meaning the person with whom God makes a διαθήκη. In every such case there was a covenant burnt-offering. God enters into covenant with sinners only as persons for whom atonement has been made, persons who have in the representative victim died. "Without the shedding of blood there can be no remission," and where there is no remission there can be no interest in the διαθήκη. "The sinner under the condemning and reigning power of sin *cannot* have fellowship with God; there must be death for sin, and by it death to sin, in order to his personally enjoying covenanted blessings."

kind of digression, but a digression closely connected with, naturally rising out of, the argument. It is intended to meet the Jewish prejudice which may be expressed in the question, 'But why did this great High Priest die?' and the substance of the paragraph is just this: 'Death, and the death of a person so illustrious, was, in the nature of things, absolutely necessary to the gaining of the great ends of that new and better covenant of which Jesus Christ, our great High Priest, is the Mediator.'

We are now prepared for entering on the particular exposition of the different clauses of the paragraph under consideration. Ver. 15. "And for this cause He is the Mediator of the new testament (covenant), that by means of death, for the redemption of the transgressions that were under the first testament (covenant), they which are called might receive the promise of eternal inheritance." I shall endeavour, first, distinctly to point out the true construction of this somewhat complicated sentence, and then inquire into its meaning.

The phrase, "for this cause," may either be considered as looking backward or forward. If it look forward, the meaning is—'Jesus Christ is the Mediator of the New Covenant for this cause, viz., that by means of death, for the redemption of the transgressions that were under the first testament, they which are called might receive the promise of eternal inheritance.' If it look backward, as we believe it does, the meaning is—'Because the blood of Christ, who through the eternal Spirit offered Himself without spot to God, purges the conscience from dead works, to serve the living God, while the blood of bulls and goats, and the ashes of an heifer sprinkling the unclean, could only sanctify to the purifying of the flesh; for this reason, Christ is the Mediator,' etc. The great object of the New Covenant is, that "the called might receive the promise of eternal inheritance." In order to this, there must be a "redemption of the transgressions under the first covenant;" in order to this redemption, death—and death, too, of a particular kind—must take place; and it is because the death of Christ is such a death as was necessary—His blood, when He offered Himself, having the power of "purifying the conscience"—that "He is the Mediator of the New Covenant." This seems to me the Apostle's train of thought. Let us examine its various parts, and their mutual connection and dependence.

The grand ultimate object of the New Covenant, so far as men are concerned, is, that "the called may receive the promise of eternal inheritance." "They who are *called,*" or "the *called ones,*" is a descriptive appellation of the true spiritual people of God, borrowed, like so many others, from a denomination given to the Israelites as the external people of God. The appellation originates in the *call* of Abraham. He was effectually 'called by God to leave his native country, to go into a distant land, in which he and his posterity were to enjoy peculiar blessings. His natural posterity are termed God's *called ones,* Isa. xlviii. 12, because invited and led by God into the possession of peculiar privileges. In the New Testament it is transferred to the true spiritual people of God—the spiritual descendants of Abraham, whether they were his natural descendants or not. They are often termed "the called"—"the called of Christ Jesus;" and the phrase in its complete form appears in 1 Thess. ii. 12: "Called unto the kingdom and glory of God."

The great design of the New Covenant is, that these chosen and called ones, these spiritual Israelites, "might obtain the promise of eternal inheritance"—literally, 'of the eternal inheritance.' To "obtain the promise of the eternal inheritance," is not to have the eternal inheritance promised to them. The word 'promise' is often equivalent to—the blessing promised. To "inherit the promises," is to enjoy the blessings promised. The patriarchs to whom the promises were made, are said to have "died, not having received the promises;" *i.e.*, not having received the promised blessings. "The promise of the Spirit" is equivalent to—'the promised Spirit;' and, in like manner, "the promise of the eternal inheritance" is equivalent to—'the promised eternal inheritance.'[1] The great design of the New Covenant was, that the spiritual Israel might obtain the promised eternal inheritance. The design of the first covenant was, that Israel according to the flesh might obtain the earthly and temporary inheritance of Canaan, and enjoy there a variety of privileges, all bearing the external, temporary character of the economy to which they belonged. But the inheritance into which the New Covenant is intended to bring the spiritual Israel, is an "eternal inheritance." It is that of which Canaan and its privileges were types and emblems. It is that state of

---

[1] ἡ αἰώνιος ἐπηγγελμένη κληρονομία.

holy happiness, rising out of the enjoyment of the divine favour and fellowship, into which a man enters by believing, and which will be consummated in the heavenly world. This is the "inheritance incorruptible, undefiled, and that fadeth not away," which in its most perfect form "is laid up in heaven," but on the partial enjoyment of which "they who are called" enter even here below on their believing, and which they enjoy just in proportion to their faith.

Now, in order to the called obtaining this promise, there must be a "redemption of the transgressions which were under the first covenant." "The transgressions under the first covenant" does not appear to be equivalent to—'the sins which were committed against, or during the continuance of, the Mosaic economy.' The scope of the passage leads me to consider it as equivalent to—'the sins which remained unexpiated under that covenant—the transgressions which its expiatory sacrifices could not make atonement for.' That first covenant had a set of expiatory sacrifices which were effectual for removing ceremonial guilt and pollution, and securing the enjoyment of the earthly and temporary inheritance; but they had no efficacy in removing moral guilt and defilement, and therefore the transgressions which exclude men from the "eternal inheritance" remained under that covenant unexpiated. "It was not possible that the blood of bulls and of goats could take away sin." But God can "by no means clear the guilty"—He cannot admit man, viewed as guilty, into the possession of the "eternal inheritance;" therefore, if man is to obtain that inheritance, there must be a "redemption of the transgressions" which remained unexpiated "under the first covenant."

"The redemption of transgressions" is a strangely sounding phrase, but its meaning is not obscure. It is the paying the ransom of—*i.e.*, the penalty incurred by—these transgressions. Perhaps it might be rendered, 'redemption from the transgressions which remained unexpiated under the first covenant,'—deliverance from guilt, or liability to punishment, in consequence of an adequate ransom being paid. The redemption from transgressions could only be in consequence of the expiation of transgressions.

Now, in order to this expiation of transgressions, which the first covenant could not expiate, death was necessary; and death, too, of a particular kind. "Christ is Mediator of the New Covenant, that by means of death, for the redemption of the transgressions that were under the first testament, they which are called might receive the promise of eternal inheritance." The meaning of this clause may, I apprehend, be thus given: 'that a death having taken place, which expiated the transgressions which the first covenant could not expiate.' The Apostle's principles are these: 'Without the shedding of blood there can be no remission; and the dignity of the blood shed must correspond to the value of the remission granted. The death of a bull, or a heifer, or a goat, or a lamb, may suffice for obtaining remission of ceremonial guilt, but it will not suffice for the remission of moral guilt. The remission of moral guilt is necessary to the called obtaining the inheritance; and therefore such a death must intervene as lays a solid foundation for the granting of this remission.'

Now the death of Christ is such a death. He, the Christ, the divinely appointed, the divinely qualified Redeemer—He has paid the ransom of the sins for which the first covenant could make no atonement; He has "offered Himself unspotted"— an all-perfect sacrifice; He has done so "through the eternal Spirit"—His divine nature, which imparts infinite value to His sacrifice; and the blood of that sacrifice can do what the blood of bulls and goats could never do—it can " purge the conscience from dead works, to serve the living God." And thus the death of the incarnate Only-begotten, which appears at first sight so unaccountable as to make us doubt the reality of the whole economy of which it makes a part, is seen to be indeed "the wisdom of God" in a mystery. It is this which makes Him the successful Mediator of the New Covenant; it is thus that He secures for those who are interested in this covenant the ineffable blessing of the promised "eternal inheritance."

The meaning of this verse is now, I trust, clearly evident. 'Because the blood of Christ, who through the eternal Spirit offered Himself without spot to God, can purge the conscience from dead works, to serve the living God, while the blood of bulls and goats could only sanctify to the purifying of the flesh; therefore, for this cause, He is the Mediator of the New Covenant, that such a death being undergone as expiated the transgressions which the sacrifices of the first covenant could not expiate, the true spiritual people of God might obtain the spiritual and eternal happiness which had been promised to them.'

We are not to conclude from this passage that none under the law were saved. We are only to conclude that all who were saved were so not by the legal expiations, but by the fore-appointed propitiation of the Son of God: Rom. iii. 25.

In the words which follow, the Apostle proceeds to show how death, and how such a death as that of Christ Jesus, was necessary in order to Jesus Christ's being the successful Mediator of the New Covenant. That death was necessary, he shows from the 16th to the 22d verse; that such a death—the death not of irrational animals, but of a person of the highest dignity—was necessary, he shows in the 23d and 24th verses. Let us examine his illustrations somewhat more particularly.

Vers. 16, 17. " For where a testament is, there must also of necessity be the death of the testator. For a testament is of force after men are dead: otherwise it is of no strength at all while the testator liveth."

I have endeavoured to prove that the word " testament" in the whole of this paragraph should have been rendered *covenant*, in the sense not of a bargain, but of an arrangement, economy, order of things; and that, of course, a number of other slight changes in our version, corresponding to this and rising out of it, are necessary to bring out the meaning of the inspired writer. The word translated " testator" must have a rendering corresponding to the word " covenant." The radical meaning of the word " covenant" is something arranged or established; and the word rendered *testator*, viewed in reference to a covenant, is the person or thing that establishes or ratifies the covenant—that makes it what it is, an established, fixed, effective arrangement. The Apostle's assertion then is, 'Where a covenant is, there must also of necessity be the death of that which ratifies it, or gives it force.'

This plainly cannot be considered as a general statement respecting all covenants or arrangements. We know that it was customary among some nations to confirm their leagues by killing an animal, an emblematical action, imprecating a similar fate on either of the parties who should violate the league. But it is not easy to see how this custom can be made to bear on the illustration of the passage before us. Besides, we have no evidence that the practice was universal with respect to leagues either between states or individuals; and far less have we evidence that the death of the sacrificial victim was necessary to the validity of every arrangement to which the word rendered "covenant" may be applied.

We apprehend the Apostle is speaking, not of covenants in general—not of "men's covenants," as he speaks in the Epistle to the Galatians,[1] but of divine covenants—of covenants having the same general nature as that of which Jesus Christ is the Mediator—arrangements made and revealed by God for bestowing blessings on mankind in their fallen state. This is the only principle of interpretation which gives distinctness to the Apostle's statements, and force to his arguments. And it gives both, as, we trust, will appear by and by.

Where there is a divine covenant, the object of which is the communication of benefits to fallen men, there must be of necessity the death of that which ratifies it, or the sacrificial victim. "For a covenant is of force *over the dead*." That is the literal rendering of the words translated, *after men are dead*. The meaning is, 'A covenant is confirmed when the sacrificial victims have been slain: otherwise it has no force while that which ratifies it liveth.'[2] Or, as it may be rendered, 'Since the ratifier has no efficacy while he lives.' It is not the life, but the death of the victim, which confirms the covenant. Such is the general meaning of the words. The death of Christ was necessary to His being the successful Mediator of the New Covenant; for in every such covenant it is necessary that the ratifier, the sacrificial victim, should die. For such covenants become valid *over the dead*, *i.e.*, by the slaughter of the sacrificial victims; since the ratifier, the sacrificial victim, has no efficacy as a ratifier while he lives. Let us now examine the sentiments which these words convey, and the argument which they embody.

The words contain two statements: the first a statement of fact—'Such covenants as that of which Christ is Mediator have always been ratified by the death of victims;' the second a statement of the reason of this fact—'It not only is so, but there is a necessity that it should be so.' Let us attend to these in their order.

[1] Gal. iii. 15.
[2] Covenants with God were made ἐπὶ θυσίαις, Ps. l. 5.

The statement of fact is, that such covenants have always been ratified by death; *i.e.*, the enjoyment of the benefits secured by them has been suspended on the death of sacrificial victims. The Apostle mentions only another of these covenants, viz., the Sinaitic one; but we apprehend the statement holds in all its extent. In the case of the arrangement or covenant revealed to Adam after his fall, there is reason to believe there was ratification by sacrifice. The only satisfactory account of the skins of the animals which formed by divine appointment the clothing of our first parents after the fall is, that they were the skins of animals slain in sacrifice,—a fact which, if admitted, gives great significancy to Jehovah *thus* clothing man—covering his nakedness. The covenant made with Noah seems, with at least equal plainness, to have been ratified by sacrifice. The covenant with Abraham was confirmed by the death of sacrificial victims; and, as the Apostle more fully states, the covenant at Sinai was thus ratified.

But the Apostle not only states that it was so, but that it must be so. " Where there is a covenant, there must of necessity be the death of that which ratifies it." Some have supposed that the force of these words is no more than this :—' Since in all covenants of this kind there has been ratification by the death of sacrificial victims, there must be so in this case also,'—resolving the necessity entirely into divine appointment. This does not seem to be the natural meaning of the words; and there is much in the Bible that leads us to assert a necessity of another kind—a necessity which occasioned the divine appointment. When God, the holy and righteous God, bestows benefits on men, who have violated His law, and deserve His displeasure, He must do it in a way which is worthy of His holiness and His justice,—He must do it in a way which shows that He hates sin, while He bestows benefits on the sinner. While in bestowing favours He shows Himself " the Lord God, merciful and gracious," in bestowing only on the ground of a sacrifice offered, a victim suffering death, He shows Himself to be Him " who will by no means clear the guilty" without satisfaction to the injured honours of His character and government. Why were the victims sacrificed at the confirmation of the first covenant, but to show that blessings could not be conferred on fallen men without a display of God's displeasure at sin, and His determination to punish it? Why did Jesus Christ die as a propitiatory victim? It was "to declare the righteousness of God in the remission of the sins which are past, through His forbearance"—to declare His righteousness in continuing to pardon sin—to make it evident that "He was just, while justifying the ungodly sinner believing in Jesus." Under the New Covenant the sacrificial victims which were under the Old were to have no place; for they were not fitted to answer the end of sacrificial victims there—they had no adequate proportion in their dignity and value to the worth of the blessings which it promises and secures; therefore under it God had declared that "He desired not" such "sacrifices and offerings." But a sacrificial victim was absolutely necessary, and a sacrificial victim of dignity corresponding to the value of the blessings of the New Covenant; and therefore the Only-begotten comes forward, saying, "Lo, I come to do Thy will;" and that will was the expiation of the sins of His people by the offering of His body once for all.

The sum and substance, then, of the Apostle's argument is just this:—' The death of Jesus Christ, who is the Son of God, was absolutely necessary to the obtaining for His people the blessings of that New Covenant of which He is the Mediator; for the perfections of the divine character, the rights of the divine government, require that in all arrangements for bestowing blessings on fallen man there should be the death of a sacrificial victim corresponding in dignity to the value of the blessings bestowed. Without such a death no such arrangement can be carried into effect.'

The Apostle goes on to illustrate at some length the general principle, that "where there is a covenant, there must of necessity be the death of that which ratifies it," by referring to the history of the original promulgation of the first, or Sinaitic covenant. Ver. 18. "Whereupon neither the first (testament) covenant was dedicated without blood."

The word *dedicated* is obviously equivalent to 'ratified or confirmed.'[1] The first covenant was not ratified without the shedding of the blood of piacular victims. The manner in which this ratification took place is particularly described in the 19th

---

[1] Chrysostom explains ἐγκεκαίνισται, βεβαία γέγονεν: and Theophylact's note is, τί δέ ἐστι τὸ ἐγκεκαίνισται; τοῦτ' ἔστι, τὴν ἀρχὴν τῆς συστάσεως καὶ τῆς βεβαιώσεως ἔλαβεν.

verse :—" For when Moses had spoken every precept to all the people according to the law, he took the blood of calves and of goats, with water, and scarlet wool, and hyssop, and sprinkled both the book and all the people." The Apostle here refers to Exod. xxiv. 3, 7, 8. There are some circumstances in the Apostle's account which are not in Moses' narrative ;—such as, that the blood was " the blood of calves and goats,"—that it was mingled "with water,"—and that it was sprinkled by means of an instrument formed of " scarlet wool and hyssop." These particulars the Apostle might easily gather from the law, in its prescriptions of the manner of performing similar ceremonial purifications : Lev. iv. 23, ix. 3; Num. vii. 16, 17. However he obtained the information, we are sure it is correct; for " all Scripture is given by the inspiration of the God" of perfect knowledge and absolute veracity. " The book"[1] was probably laid on the altar and sprinkled along with it.

There are two things which particularly deserve notice here. In order to the ratification of the covenant, the blood of the propitiatory victims is first shed and then sprinkled ; intimating that by a propitiatory sacrifice expiation must be made for sin ; and that the merits of this propitiatory sacrifice must be transferred as it were to the individual, in order to the benefits of the covenant being enjoyed. The corresponding truths in reference to the New Covenant are highly important, and, I trust, familiar to all your minds.

While Moses thus sprinkled the blood of the victims, he announced the meaning and design of the solemn ceremony by proclaiming,—ver. 20—" This is the blood of the covenant which

---

[1] Some interpreters connect αὐτό τε τὸ βιβλίον with λαβών, not with ἐρράντισε, and place a point after βιβλίον. They urge that we do not read in Exodus that the book of the law was sprinkled,—that there seems an impropriety in sprinkling what was perfectly holy. But neither do we read anything of some other things mentioned here. The Vulgate, the Syriac, and Arabic versions give the meaning, that the book was sprinkled. In covenants, both parties were sprinkled with blood. This mode of exegesis makes the expression very harsh and unnatural. The particle καί, before πάντα τὸν λαόν, being found in all the MSS., cannot be expunged ; nor is it redundant, as has been suggested, for it is closely connected with the particle τε which precedes. It is very true what Schmid remarks, " The construction of the word βιβλίον with λαβών is so harsh and difficult, that you should certainly be hesitant about it, seeing that the nature of the subject-matter does not compel you to follow it."

God hath enjoined unto you;" *i.e.*, 'This is the blood, by the shedding of which the covenant which God has established with you is confirmed.' These words are plainly alluded to by our Lord in the institution of the Lord's Supper: "This is My blood of the New Covenant"—'This represents My blood, by the shedding of which the New Covenant is confirmed.' The meaning of Moses' words is, 'By such shedding of blood, often to be repeated, according to the due order, you are secured of the blessings promised in this covenant.' The meaning of our Lord's words is, 'By the shedding of this blood once for all ye are secured of the blessings promised in the New Covenant.'

In the verses which follow, the Apostle goes on to remark, that not only was the covenant solemnly ratified by the shedding of blood at its promulgation, but that also at the setting up of the tabernacle, and the commencement of the Levitical service, a similar shedding of blood and sprinkling took place; and that, during the whole continuance of that economy, almost everything was purged or sanctified by blood, and that remission of guilt could only, according to the principles of that economy, be obtained by the shedding of blood. Vers. 21, 22. "Moreover, he sprinkled likewise with blood both the tabernacle, and all the vessels of the ministry. And almost all things are by the law purged with blood; and without shedding of blood is no remission."

The 21st verse seems to refer to what took place at the first consecration of the tabernacle and its vessels; and the general principle involved in these ceremonial services is—Expiation of sin is necessary to acceptable worship of God; and this can only be obtained by the shedding of blood. The 22d verse seems to refer to what took place during the whole course of the Mosaic economy, with a particular reference to the solemn purifications which took place on the great day of atonement. The Apostle says, "almost all things," for there were exceptions. Some things were purified by fire, others with water, others with water mixed with the ashes of the red heifer: Num. xxxi. 23, xix. 2–10; Lev. xvi. 28. The great lesson taught was, "without shedding of blood there is no remission;" *i.e.*, blood must be shed in order to the enjoyment of the blessings promised in the covenant. Such is the Apostle's illustration and proof of the necessity of the death of Christ.

But the Apostle's assertion is not only, In order to the ratification of the New Covenant, death was necessary; but such a death as should be effectual to the expiation of the sins for the expiation of which the former covenant made no provision; and this is the idea which he develops in the two verses which follow.

Ver. 23. "It was therefore necessary that the patterns of things in the heavens should be purified with these; but the heavenly things themselves with better sacrifices than these. 24. For Christ is not entered into the holy places made with hands, which are the figures of the true; but into heaven itself, now to appear in the presence of God for us." The general principle involved in these words is, plainly, that in expiation the victim must correspond in dignity to the nature of the offences expiated, and the value of the blessings secured. "The blood of bulls and of goats, and the ashes of an heifer," may expiate ceremonial guilt, and secure external, temporary blessings; but in order to the expiation of moral guilt, and the attainment of spiritual and eternal blessings, a nobler victim must bleed.

"Things in the heavens" and " heavenly things" are plainly expressions of the same import. What is the precise meaning of these two synonymous terms, may perhaps be best learned by endeavouring to ascertain what those objects are which the Apostle calls their "patterns," or types; and then by inquiring of what those objects were the patterns and types.

It is plain that "the patterns of the things in the heavens" are just the things which were purified by the blood of animals slain in sacrifice under the first covenant: the Israelitish people, the book of the law, the tabernacle, and the vessels of ministry. Now what answers to these under the New Covenant? Of what were these the patterns and types? Of what were the Israelitish people the pattern? Let the Apostle Paul answer the question: "We are the circumcision, and worship God in the spirit, who rejoice in Christ Jesus, and have no confidence in the flesh." Let the Apostle Peter answer it. "Ye are," says he, addressing Christians, "a chosen generation, a royal priesthood, a holy nation, a peculiar people." Having thus found out of what the Israelitish people were a type or pattern, there is little difficulty in finding out that of which the book of the law, and the tabernacle, and the vessels of ministry were the types or patterns. What in the New Covenant answers to the book of the law? It is plainly the revelation of mercy—the testimony of God concerning His Son—the promise of eternal life through Him. And as to the tabernacle and the vessels of ministry, they plainly were types or patterns of favourable intercourse and fellowship with God, and the means of maintaining it. These are all termed *heavenly things*, in opposition to the *earthly things* of the Mosaic dispensation. The people of God have their citizenship in heaven; their affections are there already; and there is to be their everlasting abode. The revelation of mercy—the promise of eternal life—has a principal reference to the heavenly state; and communion and fellowship with God, as enjoyed here, is the earnest of heaven—as enjoyed hereafter, is the essence of heaven. Such is, I apprehend, the meaning of the phrases, "things in heaven," or "heavenly things," and their "patterns" or types.

The Apostle makes a double assertion respecting these "patterns of heavenly things," and "the heavenly things themselves." He asserts that "the patterns of heavenly things were purified by these" things, *i.e.*, by the shedding and sprinkling of the blood of the sacrificial victims, and that "the heavenly things were purified by better sacrifices than these;" and he asserts that both of these things were "necessary." He here, as in the preceding part of the digression, makes first a statement of fact, and then of the reason of the fact.

"The patterns of the heavenly things" were purified by the shedding and sprinkling of the blood of the legal sacrifices. The Apostle uses one word, *purified*, in reference to all "the heavenly things," and all "the patterns of the heavenly things;" but it is quite plain that that word must be modified in its meaning by the nature of the things to which it is applied. Men, a divine revelation, and religious privileges, cannot be *purified* in the same sense. Let us inquire what the blood of the legal sacrifices did in reference to the Israelitish people, what it did in reference to the book of the law, what it did in reference to the tabernacle and the vessels of ministry; and then what the blood of the better sacrifice did in reference to the spiritual people of God, in reference to the revelation of mercy, and in reference to the great privilege of the new economy—favourable intercourse with God. And if we can attain to clear, distinct views on these points, we shall understand what is meant by the purification of "the patterns of heavenly things," and the purification of "the heavenly things themselves." "The patterns of things in the heavens" were purified by the legal sacrifices.

What did they effect for the Israelitish people? They expiated their ceremonial guilt; they freed them from that punishment to which their violation of the law exposed them, and which, had not these sacrifices been offered, would have been inflicted on them; and, freeing them from ceremonial guilt, qualified them for ceremonial service.

What did the sprinkling of blood on the book of the law effect? It ratified the law. On the ground of the blood shed, all the promises in that book were sure to all who complied with the conditions on which they were suspended.

What was the effect of the sprinkling of the blood on the tabernacle and vessels of ministry? On the ground of the blood shed, these might be lawfully employed by the Israelites, according to the appointed order, as the medium of favourable intercourse with Jehovah as their God, propitiated by sacrifice. Such seems to me the import of the purification of "the patterns of heavenly things" by the shedding and sprinkling of the blood of the legal sacrifices.

We should not experience much difficulty in unfolding the meaning of the corresponding assertion as to "the heavenly things themselves." They are purified by "better sacrifices than these." We are not to suppose, from the use of the plural number, that "the heavenly things" are purified by a plurality of sacrifices. One great object of the Apostle in this Epistle is, to assert the unity of the sacrifice of Christ, to which all purifying efficacy under the new economy is exclusively ascribed. It has been very justly remarked by Dr Pye Smith, that the plural form, "superior sacrifices," appears to be used as a declaration of the general truth, that though for a temporal and ceremonial cleansing, animal sacrifices had served; yet, for a real, holy, spiritual, and eternal effect, sacrifices of intrinsic worth and transcendent excellence would be found necessary. The sequel points out the application of this general proposition to the particular case before us.[1] "The heavenly things" are purified

---

[1] Kuinoel's note is worth quoting: "The words 'with better sacrifices' are to be explained of Christ's sacrifice. The plural is put for the singular. Thus change of number is common even with secular writers; Longin. de sub. xxiii. 2; Eurip. Hec. 265—προσφάγματα de una victima:

by the sacrifice of Christ, which was a better sacrifice than the Levitical sacrifices. That it was an infinitely better sacrifice, is plain to any person who considers for a moment the design of a sacrifice. Was not the voluntary submission of the Only-begotten of God, in the room of sinners, to all the demands of the holy law of God, an inconceivably more satisfactory and striking demonstration of the excellence of that law, and the evil of violating it, than all the sacrifices of the Mosaic law afforded—than the sacrifices of any, or of all, the creatures of God could have afforded?

But what is meant by "the heavenly things" being purified by this sacrifice? What effect has this sacrifice on those who are the people of God according to the New Covenant? The blood of Christ, as shed, expiates their sins—*i.e.*, renders their pardon and salvation consistent with, and illustrative of, the perfections of the divine character, and the principles of the divine government,—and as sprinkled, "purges the conscience from dead works, to serve the living God"—*i.e.*, when the truth in reference to it is understood and believed, it quells the jealousies of guilt, and fits the man for spiritual, affectionate worship.

What effect had the blood of this sacrifice on the revelation of mercy, which, under the new economy, answers to the book of the law under the old? It ratified it. It is because this blood was shed that it is absolutely certain that "whosoever believeth in Christ Jesus shall not perish, but have everlasting life." The promise of eternal life is yea and amen in the blood of Christ.

It only remains here, that we ask what effect the blood of this sacrifice had in reference to that of which the tabernacle and

v. Porson. ad Eurip. Orest. 1051. But the author of the epistle used the plural because he had used the plural when speaking of the purification of the earthly tabernacle, and because of the superiority of Christ's sacrifice, which exceeded all other sacrifices in its power and efficacy." Dr Pye Smith's opinion was forestalled by Carpzov, who says, after mentioning the exegesis adopted by Kuinoel: "I would prefer to expound this passage thus : that the apostle should be said to be stating in general terms in this section what he later (v. 25) defines more exactly and explains in detail (a thing that he quite often does in this epistle, e.g. iii. 4, v. 1, viii. 3). By a defect of language, it comes about that we may talk in general terms about something of which there is only a single instance. Therefore, the excellent material which learned commentators have brought together upon this verse concerning the offering and sacrifice of Jesus Christ could more conveniently have been kept for other verses."

the vessels of ministry under the law were a pattern. That effect was favourable communion with God, and the means of enjoying it. It is the shedding and sprinkling of this blood that makes it right in God to admit man to this fellowship, and which fits him for the enjoyment of it both on earth and in heaven. Such seems to me to be the meaning of the purifying the heavenly things by a sacrifice superior to those offered up under the law.

But the Apostle not only asserts the purification of " the patterns of heavenly things," and of " the heavenly things themselves," by appropriate sacrifices, but he asserts the necessity of such purification : " It was necessary that the patterns of things in the heavens should be purified with these." Some interpreters apprehend that all that is meant is—' It was necessary, because God so appointed it.' This is true; but it does not seem to me to exhaust the Apostle's meaning, if it even partially unfold it, which I think doubtful. As to " the patterns of things in the heavens," there appears to me to have been a double necessity—a necessity arising out of the general nature of such arrangements, which the Apostle has explained in the preceding context, and a necessity arising out of the typical nature of this particular arrangement.

Every divine arrangement for conferring benefits on fallen man must carry along with it an assertion of the violated rights of the divine law; and the nature of this assertion must correspond to the nature of the blessings to be conferred. There was an obvious propriety that an arrangement having for its object the bestowal of temporal, temporary blessings as the reward of external obedience, should be attended with an assertion of the violated rights of the divine law of a kind far inferior to that which attended the arrangement which has for its object the communication of spiritual and eternal blessings.

There was also a necessity arising out of the particular character of the Mosaic covenant as typical. If it was to represent the way of salvation through Christ, it was absolutely necessary that there should be the shedding and the sprinkling of blood for purification. So much for the necessity of " the patterns of things in the heavens" being purified with blood.

But the Apostle goes on to assert that it was *necessary* that " the heavenly things themselves should be purified by better sacrifices than these." The ground of that necessity is obvious.

The reality must excel the shadow; and the assertion of the rights of the divine government must correspond to the importance of the blessings conferred on sinners, just as the price paid must correspond to the value of the article purchased.

The 24th verse—" For Christ is not entered into the holy places made with hands, which are the figures of the true; but into heaven itself, now to appear in the presence of God for us"—with which this interesting digression closes, seems introduced for the purpose of bringing this idea fully before the mind: 'For Christ's priesthood does not belong to the typical order of things, but to the real order of things of which it was a shadow.'[1] It is as if he had said, ' I speak of heavenly things, for Christ's priesthood has a reference to heavenly things. His priesthood has nothing to do with the earthly tabernacle and animal sacrifices; He has not entered, like the Aaronical high priest, into the material holy places in the tabernacle or temple raised by human agency, which were figures of the true (holy places). The holy places were among the figures of the heavenly things; and they represented *heaven*, both as a state and a place—a state of most friendly and intimate communion—a place where the glories of the reconciled Divinity are manifested with peculiar lustre. Into heaven, both as a state and a place, our great High Priest has entered.' It is, however, as appears from the concluding words, chiefly to heaven as a place that the Apostle refers. He is entered " into heaven itself"—into the real heaven—there " to appear in the presence of God." There in His glorified human nature, bearing plain marks of former degradation and suffering—" a Lamb as it had been slain"—He appears[2] before the throne of God *for us*, as our Representative, as our Advocate, making intercession on the ground of His all-perfect atonement.[3]

[1] ἀντίτυπα is here used in the very opposite way to that in which we use the word 'antitypes,' borrowed from it. Antitype with us is the thing signified by the type; antitype here is the type itself: ἀντίτυπα and ὑποδείγματα are plainly synonyms.

[2] τῷ προσώπῳ τοῦ Θεοῦ, just a translation of the Heb. לִפְנֵי אֱלֹהִים.

[3] νῦν. Having made an all-perfect atonement, He *now*, henceforward and for ever, makes appearance for us as our advocate, no more to come out to offer sacrifice.

2. *The Efficacy of the Priesthood of our Lord is more perfect in degree than that of the Levitical Priesthood.*

In the next verse the Apostle proceeds to the enunciation of another proof that Jesus Christ has received a more excellent ministry than Aaron or any of his sons; viz., that the efficacy of His ministry is not only higher in its nature, but more complete in its degree—theirs requiring to be continually repeated, His being performed once for all.

Let us proceed to consider the manner in which the Apostle illustrates this theme. Ver. 25. "Nor yet that He should offer Himself often, as the high priest entereth into the holy place every year with blood of others; 26. (For then must He often have suffered since the foundation of the world;) but now once in the end of the world hath He appeared, to put away sin by the sacrifice of Himself."

It is impossible to read with attention the 25th verse without perceiving that it is elliptical, that is, that some words are wanting to complete the sense. Some have proposed to complete the sense by borrowing the words, "it was necessary," from the 23d verse, thus—"Neither was it necessary that He should offer Himself often." The principal objection against this mode of supplying the ellipsis is, that it does not suit the proper meaning of the particle rendered "that," which is, 'in order that,' or 'so that.' The most natural and satisfactory way of completing the sense is, to repeat the words from the previous verse: "Nor did He enter into heaven itself, the true holy place, that," in order that, "He should offer Himself often." This makes the whole sentence run easily, and gives a clear, connected, consistent sense: Christ is not entered into the material holy place, nor is He entered into the true holy place with the intention of offering Himself often.

We are not to think of Christ's "offering Himself" as something which He does in heaven, as Grotius does—something which He does after He has entered into the true holy of holies. The Apostle obviously identifies His offering Himself with His suffering. The Apostle's meaning will become distinctly obvious if we attend to the usages under the Mosaic economy to which he is alluding—to that part of the ministry of the Aaronical high priest with which he is contrasting the ministry of Jesus Christ. The high priest offered sacrifice by shedding the blood of the sacrificial victim, and laying it on the altar. This was what is properly called, offering the sacrifice. The sacrifice was offered without the tabernacle, though the blood of the sacrifice was carried into the holy of holies, and presented before the emblem of the divine presence. After having offered the sacrifice, the high priest went with its blood—not his own blood, but the "blood of others"—into the holy of holies. But when he entered, it was not that he might permanently remain there; it was that, having finished his ministry on that occasion, he might go forth, and again, as the season returned, offer sacrifice, and again enter into the holy place. And thus the life of the high priest was spent in a succession of offerings and entrances into the holy place.

But it is not so with "the great High Priest of our profession." He has offered His sacrifice, and He has entered into the holy place; but He has not entered for the purpose of coming forth again to offer another sacrifice—His sacrifice will never be repeated. That it will never be repeated may be inferred from the circumstance of its being so long in being offered. The design of the sacrifice of Christ is the expiation of moral guilt. Without expiation there can be no pardon. Multitudes of men had been pardoned and saved from the introduction of sin into the world—" since the foundation of the world." If repetitions of Christ's sacrifice were necessary for this purpose, as repetitions of the Mosaic sacrifices were for the remission of continually recurring violations of the first covenant, then, on the same principle that these repetitions should take place now, they ought to have taken place at proper intervals, like the Mosaic sacrifices, ever since, by the introduction of sin, which was very soon after "the foundation of the world" (the phrase occurs in a similar way, Luke xi. 50), such a sacrifice became necessary. But we know that no such thing did take place; we know that "the remission of all the sins that are past, through the forbearance of God," took place on the ground of the foreappointed propitiation in the blood of Christ; and we know also, that all the sins which have been committed, or shall yet be committed, which shall be forgiven, will be forgiven on the ground of the same propitiation.

Instead of offering a constantly recurring series of sacrifices throughout the whole course of the period during which the sins to be expiated were committed, Christ has " now once in the end of the world appeared, to take away sin by the sacrifice of Himself." Christ never appeared as a Priest in our world till He was " manifested in flesh"—till " in the fulness of time God set Him forth, made of a woman, made under the law."

The period of our Lord's appearance is termed " the end of the world"—literally, ' in the conclusion of the ages.' This is plainly here an allusion to the Jewish mode of speaking which I have repeatedly had occasion to advert to in the course of this exposition. They spoke of the age before the law, the age under the law, and the age after the law. These are the "times," or "ages," so often spoken of in Scripture. The age under the Messiah is the last of these ages, and is often termed "the latter times." At the conclusion of the patriarchal and Mosaical ages —" in the last of the ages, He was manifested once," for the first and the only time, " for the purpose of *taking away sin*."

" Sin" here plainly means guilt; and the "taking away of sin" is the expiation of guilt—the complete expiation of the guilt of all the sanctified or separated ones. The object of His appearance was to do and suffer all that was necessary to render the pardon, and consequent salvation, of all the " many sons" whom He was to " bring to glory," consistent with, and gloriously illustrative of, all the perfections of the divine character, and all the principles of the divine government. It was to " finish transgression, and to make an end of sin."

And this great end was to be obtained not by the sacrifice of animal victims, but " by the sacrifice of Himself." He was to remove their guilt or liability to punishment by taking it upon Himself, and in their room doing what they were bound to do, suffering what they deserved to suffer. The sacrifice of Christ, is just the uniform, cheerful, persevering, perfect obedience to all the preceptive part, and submission to the sanctionary part, of the divine law, violated by the sins of men.

This most important truth, in reference to Christ's not entering the holy place with an intention of coming back again to offer Himself in sacrifice, is illustrated by a reference to a somewhat analogous arrangement in reference to mankind. Vers. 27, 28. " And as it is appointed unto men once to die, but after this the judgment; so Christ was once offered to bear the sins of many: and unto them that look for Him shall He appear the second time, without sin, unto salvation."

The force of these words—" It is appointed unto men once to die, but after this the judgment; so Christ was once offered to bear the sins of many: and unto them that look for Him shall He appear the second time, without sin, unto salvation"—seems to me to be this: By the divine ordination, rising out of the sin of man, men die once, and but once. They indeed come back again out of their graves; but that is not that they may again die, but that they may be judged. And the analogical points in the case of our Lord are: He offered Himself once as the victim of the sins of His people. He will indeed return to the world again, but it will not be to offer a sacrifice; it will be for a totally different purpose—it will be to complete the salvation of all who "look for Him." Death is something which, according to the law of nature, can be undergone but once. If Lazarus, the son of the widow of Nain, and some others, underwent it twice, they are exceptions to the general law. When men die, they do not die that they may return to life, and then die again: they die that their bodies may remain in the grave, and their souls in the separate state, till the appointed period for the general resurrection; and then they shall return to life, not to die, but to be judged. "For we must all stand before the judgment-seat of Christ." "God hath appointed a day in which He will judge the world, by the Man whom He has ordained; and of which He has given assurance to all men, in that He has raised Him from the dead." The judgment here has often been interpreted of that judgment of every individual which has been supposed immediately to follow death. But the observations made are sufficient to show that it refers to the general judgment, as this alone supports the analogy which is here plainly stated: 'As men die but once; and when they return to life, it is not to die, but to be judged: so Christ offered Himself but once; and when He returns, it is not to offer sacrifice, but to confer salvation on His people.' There is an analogy stated between man's dying once and Christ's offering Himself once—between man's coming back to life, not to die, but to be judged, and Christ's returning to our world, not to die as a victim, but to reign as a Saviour.

The last of these analogies is more strongly expressed in the original than in our translation—" So Christ, having been once offered to bear the sins of many, shall appear the second time, without sin, to them who look for Him for salvation." Christ was offered as a sacrificial victim for the purpose of " bearing the sins of many." The " many" here are the same as the " many sons"—His " brethren"—those who should be " heirs of salvation," for every one of whom, " by the grace of God, He tasted death."[1] To bear their sins, is just to be charged with their guilt or obligation to punishment, and to undergo the consequence of being thus charged with their guilt. God " made to meet on His head," as the great sacrificial victim, " the iniquity of them all." The consequence was, " exaction was made, and He became answerable. It pleased the Lord to bruise Him; He put Him to grief; and His soul was made an offering for sin." Now, having offered *Himself* a sacrifice, and having thus presented an offering of infinite value, " He has entered into the holiest of all, into heaven itself"—as men, having once died, go into the separate state; and there He will abide till the mystery of God be finished. He will no more return to our world to suffer and die. He will indeed appear again, as men who have once died will live again; but as they will live again, not again to die, but to be judged, so He will appear again, not to expiate the sins, but to complete the salvation, of His people.

" Christ will appear a second time" in our world. This is very plainly stated in Scripture. " This same Jesus," said the angels to the disciples while " they stood gazing up into heaven," after their Lord had disappeared in the clouds, " who is taken up from you into heaven, shall so come in like manner as ye have seen Him go into heaven." This coming is very often spoken of in the New Testament, represented as one of the grand objects of the Christian's hope; and the time of its arrival is represented as the period of their complete deliverance.

When He is a second time manifested in our world, He

---

[1] To say that πολλοί is $=$ πάντες, is to make a very questionable statement. Nothing almost in the New Testament seems plainer to me, than that in one sense Christ gave Himself a ransom for all, and in another and higher sense gave Himself for the Church. The declaration, that He died with a special reference to those who are actually saved, does in no degree interfere with the declaration, that He died with a general reference, " the just for the unjust."

shall be "without sin." In one sense He was "without sin" when He appeared the first time. "Without sin" has often been interpreted, 'without a sin-offering'—'not as a sin-offering, not for the purpose of again presenting Himself in sacrifice.' That is substantially the meaning; but I rather think "sin" is here used as it is in the preceding clause of the verse: to "bear the sins of many," is to bear their guilt. When He came the first time, the sins of all His people, the sins of the whole world, were laid on Him; but now He will come *without sin*. He has borne, and borne away these sins by His one sacrifice—"He has put away sin." There is no more remaining to be borne by Him —He appears not for expiation, but for salvation.¹

"He will appear to them that look for Him for salvation." These words obviously admit of various constructions, which bring out various meanings. They may signify, 'He will appear to them that look for Him, for salvation.' He will be manifested to *them*, and not to others. But we know that, when "He comes in clouds, every eye shall see Him." We apprehend the meaning is, 'He will come for salvation to those who look for Him, or who expect Him.' "They who look for Him" is not a designation peculiar to those of Christ's people who shall be on the earth at the time He comes the second time. It is the general character of all His true people. They "look for the blessed hope, and the glorious appearing of the great God their Saviour." To this grand event their hopes look forward, as the consummation of their blessedness. For the *grace* is to be brought to them at His coming. They "know that when He who is their life shall appear, they also shall appear with Him in glory." His manifestation is to be their manifestation as "the sons of God." When He appears, it will be "for their salvation;" *i.e.*, for their complete and eternal deliverance from evil in all its forms and degrees, and for their being made happy, according to all their various susceptibilities of happiness, up to their largest capacity of enjoyment, and during the entire eternity of their being.

Such is the fact as to the unity of the sacrifice of our Lord Jesus Christ. How this contrasts with the multiplicity of the sacrifices of the Aaronical high priests, and how this multiplicity

¹ χωρὶς may refer to the phrase ἀνενεγκεῖν ἁμαρτίας—thus: χωρὶς τοῦ ἀνενεγκεῖν ἁμαρτίας—'not again to take away sin, without suffering again the penalty for sin.'

shows the imperfection of their ministry, and this unity shows the perfection of His, the Apostle proceeds to show in the verses which immediately follow, which are most closely connected with those which we have illustrated, and which should not have been divided from them by the commencement of a new chapter.

In the verses which follow we have the corresponding statement respecting the imperfection of the ministry of Aaron and his sons as sacrificing priests, as evinced by its continual repetition. Chap. x. 1. "For the law having a shadow of good things to come, and not the very image of the things, can never with those sacrifices, which they offered year by year continually, make the comers thereunto perfect."[1]

The particle *for* seems here merely a particle of transition and connection, equivalent to—' moreover, furthermore.' "The law" here plainly signifies the Mosaic institute generally—the order of things established at Mount Sinai. This system is said to have "had a shadow of good things to come, but not the very image of the things." In explaining the 11th verse of the ninth chapter, I had occasion to illustrate the phrase, "good things to come." It does not mean generally, future benefits; still less does it refer solely to benefits to be enjoyed in a future state. It is a denomination of the blessings of the New Covenant—the blessings to be enjoyed under the Messiah. With a reference to the period under the law, the Messiah is termed, " He who was to come ;"[2] the period of His administration is termed, "the age" or "world to come ;"[3] and the peculiar blessings which are to result from His administration, " good things to come."[4] Perfect expiation of moral guilt, moral purification, free and favourable intercourse and fellowship with God—these are among the "good things to come."

Of these benefits the law is said by the Apostle to have had " a shadow, but not the very image." Many good interpreters consider the expression, "very image of the things," as equivalent to "the good things to come" themselves; and view the Apostle as saying, 'The legal institutions were not the good

---

[1] The natural order seems to be—ὁ γὰρ νόμος, κ.τ.λ., οὐδέποτε δύναται τελειῶσαι τοὺς προσερχομένους ταῖς αὐταῖς θυσίαις ἃς προσφέρουσιν κατ᾽ ἐνιαυτὸν εἰς τὸ διηνεκές.

[2] ὁ μέλλων.   [3] αἰὼν μέλλων.   [4] μέλλοντα ἀγαθά.

things promised under the Messiah, they were merely a typical representation of them;' and they suppose that in these words the Apostle is assigning the reason why the sacrifices of that law could not make a perfect expiation. They think the force of the Apostle's statement may be thus given : ' Since the legal sacrifices were only typical, they could not, however frequently repeated, expiate sin.' This no doubt brings out a good sense, but it is to me very doubtful if it be the sense of the Apostle. I can nowhere find evidence that the phrase, " image" or "likeness" of a person or thing, ever signifies the person or thing itself. " Shadow" and "image" seem to me equally expressive of pictorial representations, though of different degrees of distinctness. The word *shadow* is used by artists to denote the first rude outline which they take of an object which they mean to represent; the word *image*, of the completed picture or statue. The Apostle's meaning seems to be, ' The Mosaic institute contained in it a rude sketch, but not by any means a complete picture, of the blessings to be enjoyed under the Messiah.'

There are two truths contained in this statement, in reference to the Mosaic institute, considered as typical, which are of high importance. The first, that the *whole* of the Mosaic institute was not typical; and the second, that what was typical was imperfectly typical. Many good men have taken for granted, and acted on the assumption, that every part of the Mosaic institute had a typical meaning, and have often quoted the passage before us as a proof of this general principle. But what the Apostle says is, not that the law, taken in all its extent, *was* a shadow, but that the law *had* a shadow,—that in some of its institutions there was a typical representation of persons, and events, and privileges belonging to a coming dispensation. What that portion of the Mosaic institutions is which has such a typical meaning, we are not at liberty to conjecture. We are not warranted to consider anything as typical but what is distinctly stated in Scripture to be so.

The second truth is an equally important one. Even in those institutions which are unquestionably typical, because declared to be so in Scripture, we are not to look for an entire correspondence between the type and the antitype. What was typical was imperfectly typical. The representation was that of a rude sketch, not of a completed picture. The law would have had not merely "a shadow," but "the very image" of the "good things to come," if there had been *one*, not *many* high priests—if there had been one, not many sacrifices—if there had been one, not many entrances into the holy place—and if by this one offering and entrance into the holy place the Israelites had been delivered from all the evils threatened, and secured in all the privileges promised, under the first covenant, all the days of their life. There would have been then a complete correspondence: the one would have been a finished figurative representation of the other. But the Apostle's assertion is, 'Even what was typical was imperfectly typical.' And the remark is made apparently by the way, to suggest the idea to those who were in danger of thinking too highly of that economy, that it not only cannot obtain the blessings which Christianity offers, but it is but a very imperfect representation of them. It seems stated not so much, if at all, for the purpose of accounting for the inefficacy of the Mosaic sacrifices, as for the purpose of accounting for the discrepancies which he had stated, and was about to state, between the type and the antitype.

This "law," then, which in some of its institutions had a typical, but still only an imperfectly typical, representation of the benignant realities of a better dispensation, "could never with those sacrifices, which they"—*i.e.*, the Levitical priests—"offered year by year continually, make the comers thereunto perfect." This is just one of the cases in which the representation is a shadow, not an image. There are sacrifice, and expiation, and purification. There is the shadow, but there is not the image; for there is not one sacrifice, but many,—there is not complete and permanent expiation and purification, but imperfect and temporary expiation and purification. In these words there is an implied and an express statement.

The implied statement is, 'The law had a series of annual sacrifices, which continued as long as the law itself existed.' The law had many other sacrifices beside the sacrifice offered on the great day of atonement, to which there is here a reference; but the Apostle particularly mentions this series of sacrifices, because offered by the high priest personally, and viewed with peculiar veneration by the Jewish people. If it could be made out that "*these* sacrifices could not take away sin," they would never for a moment suppose that sacrifices which they themselves viewed as of inferior efficacy could produce this effect.

The express statement is, that "the law," by these frequently repeated annual sacrifices, "could not make the comers thereunto perfect." The phrase, *comers*, is just equivalent to 'worshippers.' The phrase in its complete form is, 'comers to God.' 'The law could not make those who approached to God perfect.' To perfect a worshipper, is to accomplish him as a worshipper. Now, what is necessary to fit a being like guilty and depraved man for the acceptable and comfortable worship of God? Perfect expiation must be made, complete pardon bestowed, the conscience must be quieted, and the heart purified,—this is necessary in order to the accomplishing of the worshipper as a worshipper—this is necessary to the bringing of him to God.

By some good interpreters the word *continually* is connected with this clause, thus: "The law could not make the worshippers continually"—*i.e.*, permanently—"perfect." It could not afford complete, and therefore it could not afford permanent expiation; and, of course, it could not afford permanently, any more than completely, those blessings which rise out of expiation.

That the frequently repeated expiations under the law could not make the worshippers under it perfect, the Apostle proves by two arguments: the first drawn from their frequent repetition, the second drawn from the nature of the case. The first argument is stated in the second and third verses; the second in the fourth verse. Let us attend to them in their order.

Vers. 2, 3. "For then would they not have ceased to be offered? because that the worshippers once purged should have had no more conscience of sins. But in those sacrifices there is a remembrance again made of sins every year."

There can be little doubt that the Jews considered the annual recurrence of the sacrifices of expiation on the great day of atonement as one of the glories of their economy. And so it was, when viewed in reference to the ends which it was intended to serve. But when they considered this circumstance as one of the things which gave them reason to trust in that economy as a method of justification, they plainly fell into the mistake of taking that for a proof of strength which was in reality an evidence of weakness. Had any one of these sacrifices completely expiated the guilt of the Israelitish people, there never had been another; or had any number of these sacrifices served the purpose, then there had been an end of presenting them.[1] But the institution was a series of sacrifices, to be offered annually as long as the law continued unrepealed.

The reason why, if they had made those who approached to God perfect, they would have ceased to be offered, is clearly given by the Apostle in the second clause of the verse: "For the worshippers once purged should have had no more conscience of sins." "Once purified;" *i.e.*, having had their sins once fully expiated. Some may perhaps think, that as men are continually contracting new sins, the repetition even of a perfect sacrifice might be necessary to expiate them. But this plainly could not be necessary with respect to God, if one sacrifice had made full satisfaction, so as to be of perpetual efficacy; nor would such a repetition be necessary in respect of the conscience of the individual, if that one sacrifice were, on satisfactory evidence, believed to be sufficient to obtain continued pardon.

"When the Apostle says that worshippers whose sins have been completely expiated would have no more conscience of sin, he does not mean that they would have no more consciousness of having sinned, 1 John i. 8; nor does he mean that they would be insensible of the evil and demerit of their sin; nor does he mean that they would no more have occasion for repentance, confession of sin, and application to the throne of grace for mercy through that perfect sacrifice which expiated their sins and quieted their consciences. But what he means is this, that had the sacrifices of the law procured a real and everlasting remission of sins, and had the worshippers believed they had such an efficacy, they would have had no more uneasiness of conscience on account of the sins for which atonement had been made, as if that atonement were not sufficient, or as if a further atonement were necessary to discharge them from the guilt of sin before God; but might have rested fully assured that God required no further satisfaction for sin, nor

---

[1] This is very strongly stated in the question in the beginning of the verse. In many excellent codd., instead of ἐπεὶ ἄν, is read ἐπεὶ οὐκ ἄν, and the latter has been adopted in the English version. Theophylact and Œcumenius intimate that it should be read as a question,—κατ' ἐρώτησιν ἀνάγνωθι. This reading is preferred by the most judicious editors—Mill, Griesbach, Matthiæ, Knapp, Schott, Vater.

any more offering for that purpose. Of course the repetition of sacrifices would have ceased."[1]

But this was not the case; "for," says the Apostle, "in these annual sacrifices there was a remembrance again made of sins every year." The offering of these sacrifices was an acknowledgment that the offerers were yet sinners, whose sins had not been expiated.[2] From the confession offered by the priest on the great day of atonement, there seems to have been an acknowledgment not only of the sins of the past year, which had been contracted since the last sacrifice was offered, but also of former sins, as if they had been but imperfectly expiated.

It has been a question with interpreters, whether the "remembrance of sins" here spoken of refers to God or to the offerers. It is plain from the passage just referred to, that the Israelites were required on these occasions to remember their sins; but I am strongly disposed to think that the Apostle's idea is, that these divinely instituted repeated sacrifices for sin were an intimation from God that He had not yet received an adequate atonement—that, so far as former sacrifices went, their sins were yet remembered or marked against them; whereas, on the other hand, as we shall see more fully by and by, the divine appointment, that the sacrifice of Christ is never to be repeated, is an intimation that God "is well pleased for His righteousness' sake," and that the sins of those who are interested in this atonement shall never be remembered against them. Such is the Apostle's first proof that the law could not take away sin, drawn from the fact of the continued repetition of these sacrifices.

His second argument, drawn from the nature of the thing, is contained in the 4th verse. "For it is not possible that the blood of bulls and of goats should take away sins."

---

[1] M'Lean.

[2] The Apostle here applies to the annual sacrifices of atonement what Moses says of a particular sacrifice, Num. v. 15 : "It is an offering of memorial, bringing sin to remembrance." Philo, in his book De Vita Mosis, L. iii., says, Θυσίαι καὶ εὐχαὶ οὐ λύσιν ἁμαρτημάτων, ἀλλ' ὑπόμνησιν ἐργάζονται—"Sacrifices and prayers do not abolish sins, but recall them to remembrance." To this the state of things after the atonement is opposed : καὶ τῶν ἁμαρτιῶν αὐτῶν οὐ μὴ μνησθῶ ἔτι. A state of full salvation cannot exist, or be known, without the existence and knowledge of the remission of sins : Luke i. 77.

To "take away sin" is to expiate guilt.[1] How was this impossible? Some say, because God has not appointed it to be so. This is the truth, but by no means the whole truth. It was impossible, because the shedding of the blood of animals was no adequate manifestation of the displeasure of God against sin— no effectual means of vindicating the honours of His violated law and contemned authority—no appropriate means for transforming the sinner's character. There is the less necessity for my dwelling on this subject at present, as I have had repeated opportunities of stating what appears to me to be truth on it, and shortly before, in illustrating the Apostle's assertion, "It was necessary that the patterns of the things in the heavens should be purified with these sacrifices; but the heavenly things themselves with better sacrifices than these."

The Apostle now proceeds to show, from an ancient oracle in the Psalms in reference to the Messiah, that the doctrine he had been teaching, respecting the inefficacy of the multiplied sacrifices under the law, and the efficacy of the one sacrifice of the Messiah, was clearly witnessed to by the Old Testament Scriptures.

Vers. 5-10. "Wherefore, when He cometh into the world, He saith, Sacrifice and offering Thou wouldest not, but a body hast Thou prepared Me: in burnt-offerings and sacrifices for sin Thou hast had no pleasure: Then said I, Lo, I come (in the volume of the book it is written of Me) to do Thy will, O God. Above, when He said, Sacrifice, and offering, and burnt-offerings, and offering for sin, Thou wouldest not, neither hadst pleasure therein (which are offered by the law); then said He, Lo, I come to do Thy will, O God. He taketh away the first, that He may establish the second. By the which will we are sanctified, through the offering of the body of Jesus Christ once for all."

The connecting particle, "wherefore," is equivalent to—'in accordance with these statements.' "When He cometh into the world, He saith." These words are equivalent to—' The Messiah, in an ancient oracle, which refers to His incarnation, is represented as using the following language : " Sacrifice and offering Thou wouldest not, but a body hast Thou prepared Me: in burnt-

---

[1] Grotius grossly misinterprets when he represents ἀφαιρεῖν ἁμαρτίας as = " bring sin to an end—put a stop to sinning."

## COMPARISON WITH THE LEVITICAL PRIESTHOOD. 439

offerings and sacrifices for sin Thou hast had no pleasure: then said I, Lo, I come (in the volume of the book it is written of Me) to do Thy will, O God.'"

To prepare us for perceiving the force of the Apostle's argument three things are necessary:—first, to apprehend the principles on which it proceeds; secondly, to account for the difference which exists between his quotation and the prophetic oracle as it stands in the Old Testament Scriptures; and thirdly, to affix a distinct meaning to the words of the oracle as quoted by the Apostle.

As to the principles on which the argument proceeds, they are plainly these:—Jesus Christ is the Messiah: this ancient oracle refers to the Messiah; and therefore it may legitimately be applied to Jesus Christ. With regard to the first of these principles, it was admitted by those to whom he was writing. It was the admission of this principle that made them what they were —professedly Christian Hebrews. As to the second, admitting the inspiration of the Apostle, no doubt can be entertained respecting its truth. He, a man who "spake as he was moved by that Spirit" under whose influence the oracle was originally uttered, declares that it refers to the Messiah. But it is not necessary to rest the matter here. What is said here can be true of none but the Messiah; and all that is said here is true of Him. Most certainly David could not say that God did not require of him sacrifice and offering, or that in his time there was to be an end put to these oblations; nor could he say that he came to do that will of God which all these sacrifices could not accomplish. None but the Messiah could say this.

There are two plans of interpreting the 40th Psalm, on either of which the Apostle's application of the portion of it here quoted to the Messiah may satisfactorily be explained. The Psalm has by some very learned and judicious interpreters been considered as a Psalm written by David, in his own person, thanking God for a remarkable deliverance, and requesting further deliverance from distresses in which he was still involved; and they consider the passage from the 5th to the 10th verse to include that "new song" of which he speaks as put in his mouth, and which refers to the Messiah. Other interpreters, equally learned and judicious, consider the whole Psalm as prophetic, and, like a number of other Psalms, wholly spoken in the person of the Messiah. To the last, as the simplest mode of interpretation, I certainly am disposed to give the preference.

The only objection of apparent weight to this mode of interpretation arises from the language employed in the 12th verse: "Mine iniquities have taken hold upon me, so that I am not able to look up: they are more than the hairs of mine head; therefore my heart faileth me." It may be said, How can this be applied to Him who "knew no sin," "in whom was no sin," but who "was holy, harmless, undefiled, and separate from sinners?" This difficulty is not so formidable as at first sight it appears. "Iniquity" is often, in Scripture language, equivalent to guilt, liability to punishment. Thus the iniquities of the congregation were laid on the sacrificial victim, and so became its iniquities as that it bore the punishment due to them. In like manner God "made to meet" on the head of His incarnate Son, as the victim of a world's transgressions, "the iniquities of them all;" and "exaction was made, and He became answerable." God made "Him, who knew no sin," sin in our room; so that the Messiah, contemplating the number and heinousness of those sins, the obligation to expiate which was laid on Him, might well exclaim, "Innumerable evils have compassed Me about." The difficulty may be disposed of in a somewhat different way. The word translated "iniquity" not unfrequently signifies punishment as well as guilt: thus, Gen. iv. 13, xix. 15; 2 Kings vii. 9; Job xxi. 19. In this case, "mine iniquities" is a phrase just equivalent to—'my penal afflictions.'

The third principle—that this ancient oracle may legitimately be applied to Jesus Christ—so obviously results from the two former, that it is unnecessary to say one word in illustration of it. These are the principles on which the Apostle's argument proceeds.

The next thing to be done, is to inquire into the apparent discrepancy between the Apostle's quotation and the ancient oracle as it stands in the Old Testament Scriptures. The differences are merely verbal, with the exception of one. What in the Psalm, as it stands in the Old Testament, is, "Mine ears Thou hast opened," is in the Apostle's quotation, "a body hast Thou prepared Me." The Apostle's quotation is made from the Greek translation of the Bible then in use, where the words are found just as he quotes them. But the question still occurs, How comes it that what in the original Hebrew is, "Mine ears Thou hast opened," is in the Greek version, and in the Apostle's quotation, "a body hast Thou prepared Me?" There are but two ways in which this difficulty can be removed: either by showing that the two translations, widely as they differ in words, agree in meaning; or by admitting that there has been a change made either on the Hebrew or the Greek text since the Epistle was written. Learned and judicious interpreters have supported both these modes of reconciliation.

In support of the first hypothesis it has been urged, that whether you suppose the words, "Mine ears hast Thou opened," to refer to the Israelitish usage of boring the ears of a slave who refused to accept of his freedom, as an emblem that he was voluntarily a perpetual servant, or whether you interpret it, as you must do the parallel passage—plainly referring to the Messiah—Isa. l. 5, the meaning is, 'Thou hast made Me Thy servant;' and that, as the assumption of human nature was absolutely necessary, and actually took place, in order to the Son of God, as His servant, doing His will for the salvation of men by offering Himself as a sacrifice, the expression, "a body Thou hast prepared Me," is very nearly equivalent to—'Thou hast fitted Me for being Thy servant.' This is very ingenious; but it would suppose one of two things, neither of which is true: either that the Greek translator distinctly understood the doctrine of the incarnation and its design ; or, that he wrote under the inspiration of the Holy Ghost.

We are reduced, then, to the necessity of supporting the second way of removing the difficulty—that a change has taken place either in the Hebrew or Greek text since the Apostle made the quotation. That the change has not taken place in the Greek text, seems plain from this fact, that a part of the Apostle's argument rests on the very word *body*, ver. 10. We come, then, to the conclusion, that a change has taken place in the Hebrew text, owing probably to the mistake of a transcriber (and a very slight mistake, from the similarity of the letters, would have produced the exact change which has taken place), and that originally in the 40th Psalm the assertion was, "a body hast Thou formed for Me," or "prepared for Me."[1]

[1] See Dr Pye Smith's Scrip. Test., 5th Ed., vol. i., p. 208.

Let us now inquire into the meaning of this sacred oracle.[1] It consists of two parts: one referring to the Levitical sacrifices; the other, to the sacrifice of the Messiah.

That which refers to the Levitical services runs thus:— "Sacrifice, and offering, and burnt-offerings, and offering for sin, Thou wouldest not—Thou hast had no pleasure in them." It would serve no good purpose to distinguish nicely between these different kinds of sacrifice. The meaning is just—the whole Levitical service. When it is said, God "would not," and "had no pleasure in" these services, the meaning is, not that He did not appoint them, nor that, when properly performed, He did not approve of them; but the meaning is,— None of these—not all of them together—could accomplish that which by way of eminence was the will of God—that in which He had pleasure[2]—the expiation of human guilt, the attainment of human salvation. They could not so satisfy His justice as to lay a foundation for the honourable exercise of mercy; and probably also the idea is meant to be conveyed, that now that the Messiah was coming into the world, they were to cease, and in no point of view henceforward could their presentation be agreeable to God. Such is the meaning of that part of the oracle which refers to the Levitical sacrifices.

That which refers to the sacrifice of Messiah is as follows:— "A body hast Thou prepared Me. Then said I, Lo, I come (in the volume of the book it is written of Me) to do Thy will, O God."

'When it appeared, after a long course of ages, that the Levitical sacrifices could not accomplish the will of God, then He sent forth the Messiah, who was His Son, in human nature; and He, having "the form of a servant," voluntarily came forward—appealing for the evidence of His divine mission and its purpose to the Old Testament prophecies—to do what the sacrifices under the law could not do, to accomplish the benignant will of God respecting the salvation of mankind.' Such is the meaning of the second part of the ancient oracle.

We are now prepared to attend to the Apostle's reasoning

---

[1] Peirce's long note, and Moses Stuart's interpretation of this difficult passage, in the 20th Excursus, added to his Commentary, deserve a careful perusal.

[2] חָפֵץ.

from this oracle. Vers. 8, 9. " Above, when He said"—or rather, 'Having in the beginning of the oracle said'—" Sacrifice, and offering, and burnt-offerings, and offering for sin, Thou wouldest not, neither hadst pleasure therein (which are offered by the law); then said He"—or, 'He then says'—"Lo, I come to do Thy will, O God. He taketh away the first, that He may establish the second." That is, 'In these words He plainly intimates that the Levitical sacrifices were inefficacious for doing the will of God, and that the work of the incarnate Saviour was completely efficacious.'

The Apostle adds, for the purpose of more clearly explaining what *the will of God* referred to in the prophetic oracle meant, —ver. 10—" By the which will"—according to which benignant good pleasure of God—" we are sanctified, through the offering of the body of Jesus Christ once for all."

The will of God was completely fulfilled in Christ's offering His body once for all for the sanctification of His people. The *sanctification* of Christ's people does not mean exclusively or primarily the making them inherently holy;—it means the expiation of their sins, leading to the remission of their sins, the quieting of the conscience, the purifying of the heart, and thus to the consecrating of them to God as " a peculiar people." This was done by the one offering of the body of Christ; *i.e.*, by what He did and suffered in their nature, and in their room. In this way the will of God was accomplished. He was glorified in man's salvation. Justice was satisfied, and mercy had free course. This was the work the law could not do, but which God has done by the incarnation and sacrifice of His Son. This was the work given Christ to do: John x. 17, 18, xiv. 31. This was the leading design for which He came into our world: Matt. xx. 28 ; 1 Tim. i. 15. And it is on the ground of His having thus completely done the will of His Father that He is invested with unlimited dominion, and crowned with supreme honours: Phil. ii. 9, 10. Such is the Apostle's corroborative argument, deduced from the Old Testament Scriptures, for the inefficacy of the numerous Levitical sacrifices, and for the efficacy of the one sacrifice of the Messiah. Let us learn more and more highly to prize every part of the Holy Scriptures, and see that in our own experience we know it to be " profitable for doctrine, reproof, correction, and instruction in righteousness."

Let us all endeavour to turn to experimental and practical use that very important passage of Old Testament Scripture, which we have just seen explained by an infallible commentator; and let the *one* all-perfect and efficacious sacrifice of the incarnate Only-begotten be the sole ground of our hope before God; and let us rest on it as indeed a foundation broad enough and strong enough to sustain the hopes and the happiness of all, however guilty and depraved, who really build on it.

The paragraph which follows forms the conclusion of the doctrinal part of the Epistle to the Hebrews. Vers. 11–14. "And every priest standeth daily ministering, and offering oftentimes the same sacrifices, which can never take away sins: but this man, after He had offered one sacrifice for sins, for ever sat down on the right hand of God; from henceforth expecting till His enemies be made His footstool. For by one offering He hath perfected for ever them that are sanctified."

These verses seem to me to be just a summing up of the argument arising out of the contrast between Aaron and his sons and Jesus Christ as sacrificing priests, as to the efficacy of their respective ministries;—theirs proved to be incomplete by its perpetual repetition; His proved to be perfect by its being performed once for all. The connective particle "and" is equivalent to—'and thus.' The expression, "every priest," has by some interpreters been supposed to refer to the Levitical priests universally. We rather think the reference is to the Levitical high priests universally. The comparison throughout is between Christ and the high priest, who is often by way of eminence called "the priest." It is not true that every Levitical priest offered sacrifices daily : there were only a comparatively small portion of the priests engaged every day in performing sacrifices. But it may be said in truth of the high priest—who was the head of the priesthood, whose substitutes all the inferior priests were, who of course might be said to do what they did—that he offered sacrifices every day. This seems to me the just mode of interpreting the phrase "daily," though here, as well as in chap. vii., some good expositors suppose the reference is to the great day of atonement, as if it were *regularly, on a certain day*. The phrase, "*every* priest," is plainly intended to suggest the idea that there were many of them—a succession of them, showing that their work could not be completed at once.

Every Aaronical high priest " stood ministering." Some have supposed these words just equivalent to—' continued ministering ;' but I cannot help thinking that standing, as the posture of ministry, and ministry incompleted, is contrasted with sitting down, as the posture of Him who has finished His work.[1]

They not only "stand ministering," but "stand ministering daily." They had ministered yesterday; but to-day they must minister again, and again they must minister to-morrow and the next day—so long as the legal dispensation continues. Every day they begin afresh, as if nothing had yet been done.

They "stand ministering daily, offering often the same sacrifices." They do the same thing over and over again, and make no progress towards complete expiation; for those sacrifices, however frequently offered, "cannot take away sin"—cannot expiate guilt.

They could not satisfy the demands of the divine justice—they could not quiet the conscience nor purify the heart of the worshippers. The phrase is very significant. Let them be offered however frequently, and with whatever cost, punctually and solemnly, they could never, by any means, or at any time, expiate sin, or procure its pardon. This is the one side of the contrast: 'A long succession of priests, in the posture of servants whose work is not finished, offering daily the same sacrifices, none of which, not all of which put together, could expiate sin.'

Now for the opposite side of the contrast. Vers. 12, 13. "But this man, after He had offered one sacrifice for sins, for ever sat down on the right hand of God; from henceforth expecting till His enemies be made His footstool."

The word *man* is a supplement, though not marked as such. If any supplement was requisite, 'Priest' or 'High Priest' would have been more appropriate; but I rather think that it would have been more emphatic just to have rendered it literally: "But HE"—there was no mistaking the reference—that illustrious

---

[1] Theophylact admirably remarks: "standing is a sign of ministering, sitting, as Christ does, a sign of being ministered to." Valcknaer observes on this remark, "This is an excellent observation of the old theologians which Theophylact has preserved. Having first occupied themselves with allegorical and fanciful trivialities, Christians began eventually, following the lead of Chrysostom in particular, to seek out the true sense of Scripture, i.e. the literal sense."

personage of whom the Apostle had been speaking,[1]—"He having offered one sacrifice for sins." He did not " stand ministering daily, offering oftentimes the same sacrifice;" He came forward and once laid on the divine altar Himself as a sacrifice for sins; He presented Himself, doing and suffering all that divine justice required, as the victim of His people's transgressions. This series of active and passive obedience—of labour and suffering—terminated in His death. "It is finished," said the accomplished High Priest; and instead of continuing standing, again to offer sacrifice, He "sat down on the right hand of God." The phrase, "for ever," may be construed either with the words, "sacrifice for sins," or with the words, "sat down on the right hand of God." It does not matter much which mode of construction is adopted. In the first case the meaning is, 'Having offered one sacrifice for sins for ever,' *i.e.*, of perpetual efficacy, 'He sat down,' etc.; in the other it is, as our translators have rendered, 'He sat down for ever,' etc.

To "sit down at the right hand of God," is to reign along with God. Having finished His expiatory work, Christ no longer stands at the altar; "entering within the vail," He sits down on the throne of mercy, at the right hand of the Father, who is propitiated by His blood. He does not cease to be a Priest, but henceforward He is "a Priest upon His throne." And invested with unlimited power and dominion, He sits on the throne of God, "henceforth expecting till His enemies be made His footstool." He no more descends from the throne to take His place at the altar of sacrifice. The work of expiation is over for ever. Nothing now remains to the accomplishment of the great ends of His priesthood, but that in this state of glory and dignity He "wait till His enemies be made His footstool;" *i.e.*, till by the exertion of the divine power, which is put forth at His expressed will, every obstacle in the way of the complete salvation of the children whom the Father has given Him be removed. He returns no more to earth to offer sacrifice. That is utterly unnecessary. "For by one offering He has perfected for ever them that are sanctified."

The "sanctified," or separated, or consecrated ones, are the

---

[1] Instead of αὐτός, many MSS. read οὗτος. Griesbach considers the reading as "haud contemnenda;" and the cautious Knapp has given it a place in the text.

same persons who in other parts of the Epistle are represented as those who shall be "heirs of salvation"—the "many sons" of God to be "brought to glory"—the "brethren" of the Messiah. This is not the only passage in the Epistle where the chosen people of God receive this appellation. "Both He that sanctifieth"—the Consecrator—"and they who are sanctified"—the consecrated—"are all of one."[1]

"By His one offering He perfected for ever them that are sanctified." Here, as in the foregoing verse, the word "for ever" admits of a double construction: 'by one offering for ever,' *i.e.*, by one offering of perpetual efficacy; or, 'by one offering He has for ever perfected them that are sanctified.' To "perfect" means, as we have already seen, to accomplish in the character referred to. To accomplish the devoted—the consecrated ones, is to expiate their guilt—to lay a foundation for their complete and everlasting pardon, for the quieting of their consciences, and for the purifying of their hearts—for making them complete as the peculiar people of Jehovah, His "purchased possession."

The Apostle closes his argument, and along with it the doctrinal part of the Epistle, by showing the bearing which a passage formerly quoted by him has on the complete efficacy of the one sacrifice of the Messiah, by which the New Covenant was ratified. Vers. 15-18. "Whereof the Holy Ghost also is a witness to us: for after that He had said before, This is the covenant that I will make with them after those days, saith the Lord; I will put My laws into their hearts, and in their minds will I write them; and their sins and iniquities will I remember no more. Now, where remission of these is, there is no more offering for sin."

"Whereof" is a supplement, and not a necessary one. "The Holy Ghost also testifies to us." The testimony of the Holy Ghost is that formerly quoted from Jer. xxxi. 31. "For after He had said." To complete the sense, the words must be supplied,—'He then adds,' ver. 17. The Apostle's argument rests entirely on the quotation in the 17th verse. This is a proof that the New Testament writers sometimes, in their quotations, for the sake of connection, bring forward portions of Scripture on which they do not intend to ground an argument.

[1] Heb. ii. 11.

The force of the words in the 16th verse may be more accurately given, thus: 'Having given them My laws, I will write them on their hearts and minds.' Under the first covenant He gave His people His laws, but He wrote them on tables of stone, not on "the fleshly tables of the heart," as under the New Covenant.

The manner in which this divine oracle bears on the perfection of the Messiah's sacrifice, is very distinctly stated by the Apostle in the 18th verse:—" Now, where remission of these is, there is no more offering for sin."

The remembrance of sin by God is equivalent to the sentence of condemnation remaining in force; the not remembering of sin by Him is equivalent to remission or pardon. Pardon can be dispensed only on the ground of expiation. If there is perfect pardon, there must have been perfect expiation; and if there be perfect expiation, what more need can there be for sacrifice for sin, the only end of which is expiation? Thus does the Holy Spirit, by declaring that under the New Covenant there is complete pardon, testify that in the one sacrifice by which that covenant was ratified there was complete expiation.

"And here," to use the language of Dr Owen, "are we come to a full end of the dogmatical part of this Epistle, a portion of Scripture filled with heavenly and glorious mysteries,—the light of the Church of the Gentiles—the glory of God's people Israel—the foundation and bulwark of faith evangelical." In closing my illustrations of this most interesting part of the inspired volume, I must, along with that great and good man, "with all humility, and sense of my own weakness and utter disability for so great a work, thankfully own the guidance and assistance vouchsafed me in the interpretation of this Epistle." In the course of it, darkness has often been made light in my own mind, and crooked things straight. New and more satisfactory, clearer and more extensive views of the divine economies, have opened themselves to my inquiries, and, I trust, a deeper conviction has been lodged in my heart of the inappreciable excellence—of the absolute perfection of the Christian salvation, and of that divinely inspired volume which contains an account of it. If these effects have in any degree been produced on the minds of my readers, to God be all the glory.

It may be proper, now that we have finished the doctrinal part of the Epistle, shortly to mark its general outlines.

The design of the Epistle is to establish the pre-eminence of Christianity above Judaism; and this design is prosecuted by showing in succession that Jesus Christ, who is the sum and substance of Christianity as well as its Author, is superior to the three great objects of Jewish veneration—the angels, Moses, and the Aaronical high-priesthood.

The first section is devoted to the illustration of the superiority of Jesus Christ to the angels. It commences with the 4th verse of the first chapter, and closes at the end of the second chapter. In the latter part of the first chapter, by Scripture quotations the Apostle shows that Jesus Christ is essentially superior to the angels, having received " a more excellent name than they;" and that He is officially superior to them, as " having been made much better than they." In the commencement of the second chapter, he employs these truths as motives to stedfastness; and in the close of that chapter, meets, and satisfactorily answers, the objection to the dignity of Christ Jesus founded on His sufferings and death, showing that these were absolutely necessary to the gaining of the full end of His mission.

The second section, which is devoted to the illustration of the superiority of Christ to Moses, begins at the beginning of the 3d chapter, and reaches down to the 13th verse of the 4th chapter. The Apostle here shows that Jesus Christ resembles Moses in being set over the whole family of God, and in being faithful in the discharge of the duties which rise out of so important a trust; but is superior to Moses, as He is the Founder of the family over which He is placed, and is not a servant temporarily placed over the family, but the Son permanently set over a family in which He has a natural interest—over which He has a natural superiority. And he improves this truth by warning them against trifling with the authority of Christ, lest they should exclude themselves from richer blessings, and expose themselves to severer evils, than their ancestors did by trifling with the authority of Moses.

The third section, which is devoted to the illustration of the superiority of Jesus Christ to the Aaronical priesthood, commences with the 14th verse of the 4th chapter, and ends with the paragraph we have just been explaining. It is occupied with proving, first the reality, and then the pre-eminence, of the priesthood of our Lord Jesus Christ.

The object of the Apostle is to demonstrate the reality and the pre-eminence of His high-priesthood—that in HIM we Christians have a High Priest, and a *great* High Priest. The reality of our Lord's high-priesthood is argued from His having been legitimately invested with the office, and from His having successfully performed its functions. The pre-eminence of our Lord's high-priesthood is not discussed in a general way, but with a particular reference to the Aaronical high-priesthood, the object of peculiar veneration to the Jews. The proof may be divided into two parts. The first, which branches out into a variety of arguments, is derived from the ancient oracle respecting the Messiah in the 110th Psalm: "The Lord hath sworn, and will not repent, Thou art a Priest for ever, after the order of Melchisedec." The second part of the proof is contained in the illustration of this principle:—' Jesus Christ hath received a more excellent ministry than Aaron or any of his sons—the functions He performs as High Priest are far superior to those which they performed.' The superiority of one office or function to another, or of the person who fills the one or performs the other, must depend on one or on both of the following circumstances: the superior importance of the object in view, or the superior degree of completeness and certainty with which that object is attained. This is the principle which lies at the foundation of the Apostle's argument; and after giving a succinct account of the ministry, first of Aaron and his sons, and then of Jesus Christ, "the High Priest of our profession," he clearly shows that His ministry had a far higher object than theirs, and that it much more completely gains this object than theirs gained its very inferior object. He shows that both a higher kind and a higher degree of efficacy belongs to His ministry than to theirs:—a higher kind of efficacy—their ministry serving only to remove ceremonial guilt and defilement, and fit for external worship; His ministry removing moral guilt and pollution, and fitting for spiritual worship:—a higher degree of efficacy: theirs only imperfectly gaining its comparatively unimportant object, which was proved by its frequent repetition; His completely gaining its inconceivably important object, which was proved by its being performed "once for all."

Mingled with the illustration of these arguments are a number of digressions. The first and longest of these commences immediately after the close of the proof of the reality of our Lord's high-priesthood, at the 11th verse of the 5th chapter, and reaches down to the end of the 6th chapter. Its object is to place in a clear point of light the criminality and danger of listlessness and inattention to Christian truth, as naturally leading to apostasy, and all its fearful results.

# PART II

## PRACTICAL

§ 1. *General Exhortation to Perseverance, and Warning against Apostasy.* Chap. x. 19-xii. 29.

THE preceding part of this Epistle has been chiefly occupied with stating, proving, and illustrating some of the grand peculiarities of Christian doctrine; and the remaining part of it is entirely devoted to an injunction and enforcement of those duties which naturally result from the foregoing statements. The paragraph, vers. 19-23, obviously consists of two parts:—a statement of principles, which are taken for granted as having been fully proved; and an injunction of duties, grounded on the admission of these principles. "Having therefore, brethren, boldness to enter into the holiest by the blood of Jesus, by a new and living way, which He hath consecrated for us through the vail, that is to say, His flesh; and having an High Priest over the house of God; let us draw near with a true heart, in full assurance of faith, having our hearts sprinkled from an evil conscience, and our bodies washed with pure water. Let us hold fast the profession of our faith without wavering (for He is

faithful that promised)." The principles stated are these:—
First, " We have boldness to enter into the holiest by the blood
of Jesus;" and secondly, We have a great " High Priest over
the house of God." The duties enjoined are,—" drawing near,"
and " holding fast the profession of our faith," or rather, hope.

The first principle which the Apostle takes for granted as
having been sufficiently proved, is thus expressed in our version:
—" Having therefore, brethren, boldness to enter into the
holiest by the blood of Jesus, by a new and living way, which He
hath consecrated for us through the vail, that is to say, His flesh."

It is not often that there is reason to complain of our translation, that it is not sufficiently literal. It is often so literal as
to be obscure, if not unintelligible. But in the passage before
us there is ground for such a charge. The words, literally rendered, run thus:—" Having therefore, brethren, boldness, or
confidence, in reference to the entrance into the holiest, by the
blood of Jesus—or by blood, of Jesus,—by which entrance[1] He
has opened, or consecrated, for us a new and living way,—
through the vail, that is, of His flesh."[2]

The first question which here suggests itself is, What are
we to understand by the entrance of the holiest? whose entrance is it that is referred to? and what is the nature of this
entrance? It has been common to consider the entrance into
the holiest here as the entrance of believers; and that entrance
has been explained of the thoughts, affections, and devotions of
Christians being fixed on and addressed to a reconciled Divinity,
by which they have all that intercourse of mind with God which
is compatible with a state in which the capacities of the soul are
confined by its union to an earthly body. But to this mode of
interpretation there are very strong objections. Throughout
the whole of this Epistle, the true holy of holies is heaven; and
to enter into this true holy of holies, is just to go to heaven.
Besides, it is plain that the principle which the Apostle states
here is one which he had already illustrated. Now, what the

---

[1] $ἥν$ may be $= καθ' ἥν$.

[2] Most justly has Valcknaer remarked, "Few seem to understand this
passage." Εἰς is expressive of a direction of mind towards an object; $παρ$-
$ῥησία$ $εἰς$, ' boldness in reference to:' Matt. xxvi. 10; Acts ii. 25; Rom. iv.
20, xvi. 19, etc., etc. Παῤῥησία and παῤῥησιάζεσθαι are generally construed with the same prepositions as πίστις and πιστεύειν.

Apostle has been illustrating, is neither that Christians have a present spiritual access to God in heaven, nor that they shall have a future real, bodily entrance into heaven; but that Christ, as our High Priest, has really and bodily gone into heaven, the antitype of the holy of holies.[1] I cannot doubt, then, that the entrance here mentioned is the entrance of Jesus Christ, and that the true meaning of the whole phrase is, ' the entrance of Jesus into the holiest by His own blood.'

A few additional remarks on the construction of the passage are necessary, to open the way to our distinct and satisfactory apprehension of its meaning. The words, "by a new and living way, which He hath opened for us," are, literally, " by which entrance He has opened, or consecrated, for us a new and living way,"—and are, I apprehend, parenthetical. The phrase, " through the vail," connects with " the entrance into the holiest through the blood of Jesus ;"—it is a further description of this entrance. The entrance of Jesus by His own blood into the holiest through the vail, is just what is described, chap. ix. 11, 12.

The concluding explicatory clause, " that is, His flesh," has commonly been supposed to refer to the words which immediately precede it—" the vail ;" and has been considered as teaching that Christ's body was the antitype of the vail which divided the holy from the most holy place, and that the rending of that vail was emblematical of His death. To this mode of interpretation there are, however, great objections. Throughout this Epistle, as the holy of holies is evidently the heaven of heavens, so the holy place—the tabernacle and its vails—seems as plainly to be the visible heavens, through which our High Priest entered into the heaven of heavens. Besides, though the rending of the vail, taken by itself, and its consequence, the laying open of the holy of holies, may be considered as a fit emblem of the death of Christ, yet the figure does not hold in the point referred to : the high priest left the vail behind when he entered,—Christ carried " His flesh," His human nature, along with Him to heaven.

I am disposed to consider the words, " that is, of His flesh,"

[1] The οὖν refers back to what immediately precedes, but especially to chap. ix., where it was shown that Christ has entered into the true holy of holies.—THOLUCK.

as referring to the entrance of our Lord into the holy place,—the word 'entrance' being understood, thus: "that is, the entrance of His flesh;" just as the word 'tabernacle' is understood in the parallel passage,—" a greater and more perfect tabernacle, that is, not the tabernacle of this building." The passage without the parenthesis would read thus:—" Having then, brethren, boldness in reference to the entrance of Jesus by His own blood into the holiest of all, through the vail, that is, the entrance of His flesh."

Having thus endeavoured to ascertain the true construction of this somewhat involved and difficult passage, let us shortly illustrate the glorious truths which it unfolds:—Jesus Christ, our great High Priest, has entered into the holiest; He has done so by His own blood; He has done so through the vail; He has done so bodily; and He has consecrated this entrance for us, a new and a living way. You will observe that these are just the great truths which the Apostle had been stating and illustrating in the preceding section.

Jesus has "entered into the holiest," *i.e.*, into heaven. He is "a great High Priest passed into the heavens,"—a "High Priest set on the right hand of the Majesty in the heavens,"—"He is entered in into the holy place,"—" not the holy places made with hands, but into heaven itself."[1]

He has entered in "with blood," with His own blood; *i.e.*, His entrance into heaven as our High Priest is the result of the all-perfect expiation of our sins, which He effected by the shedding of His own blood. "When He had by Himself purged our sins, He sat down on the right hand of the Majesty on high." "For the suffering of death, He was crowned with glory and honour." "As the Captain of salvation, He was made perfect through suffering." "Having been made perfect through the things which He suffered, He is become the Author of eternal salvation to all who obey Him." "He is entered in, not by the blood of goats and calves, but by His own blood." "After He had offered one sacrifice for sins, He for ever sat down on the right hand of God."[2]

He has entered "through the vail;" that is, through the visible heavens, of which the tabernacle and its vails, as concealing the holy of holies from general inspection, as necessary

[1] Heb. iv. 14, viii. 1, ix 12, 24.  [2] Heb. i. 3, ii. 9, 10, v. 9, ix. 12, x. 12.

## GENERAL EXHORTATION AND WARNING. 457

to be gone through in order to enter it, were emblematical. Our " great High Priest is passed through the heavens." " He is entered into the holy place, through a greater and more perfect tabernacle than the tabernacle of this building."[1]

He has entered bodily into heaven. His entrance is the entrance of His " flesh," or body, *i.e.*, of Him as embodied; just as to " present our bodies living sacrifices," means, ' present ourselves as embodied beings.' Our Lord's entrance is not a metaphorical entrance; it is as real as that of the high priest, which was its emblem. The same God-man Jesus who died on the cross, ascended up through these heavens, far above them, into the heaven of heavens; and there, in human nature, as the representative of His people, He appears in the immediate presence of God.

The only other principle contained in these words is that expressed in the parenthetical clause. This bodily entrance into the holiest by His own blood, through the visible heavens, " He has consecrated for us, a new and living way." The word " consecrate" literally means, ' opened up;' and it matters very little whether you understand it in its primary or secondary sense. The idea which the Apostle here expresses is the same as that brought forward in the 20th verse of the 6th chapter, where Jesus is represented as entering as our " Forerunner"[2] within the vail. The general meaning is plainly this :—' By His bodily entrance through these visible heavens into the heaven of heavens, on the ground of His atoning sacrifice, He has secured that in due time all of us who are His people shall also, through that blood, bodily pass through these heavens into the heaven of heavens.' When He went away He said to His disciples, " In My Father's house are many mansions : if it were not so, I would have told you. I go to prepare a place for you. And if I go and prepare a place for you, I will come again, and receive you unto Myself; that where I am, there ye may be also."[3] He is gone to glory through His own blood, that through that blood He may bring the whole company of the " many sons to glory." Through the power of His atonement it is secured that they shall all, like Him, be raised from the dead, and, like Him, be taken up to heaven. These " vile bodies" being changed, " and made like unto His glorious body,"

[1] Heb. iv. 14, ix. 11, 12.    [2] Πρόδρομος.    [3] John xiv. 2, 3

they "shall be caught up to meet Him in the air," and go with Him to the heaven of heavens.

This mode of entering heaven, which Christ has opened for us, is "a new and a living way." His entrance to heaven is our way of entering it; and it is a new way—a way totally different from that in which innocent man would have entered heaven—a way belonging to the New Covenant, in which all things are new—a way which man could never have opened up, and newly proclaimed in the doctrine of Christianity. "A living way" seems equivalent to 'a life-giving way—the way of life to life,' in all the extent of meaning which belongs to that peculiarly emphatic term. To have followed the Jewish high priest into the holy place would have been *death*.

Now, concerning this "entrance of our Lord Jesus into the holiest," we have "boldness." This is the same word which in chap. iii. 6 is termed "confidence," and chap. iv. 16, "boldness." It properly signifies 'freedom of speech,' but often is used for that state of firm belief and assured confidence which leads to freedom of speech and determination of action.[1] Here it is, I apprehend, expressive of that state of mental confidence which naturally springs from the knowledge and faith of the truths here referred to. 'Having confidence of mind in reference to our spiritual interests; knowing and being sure, as we are, that Christ as our High Priest has gone bodily to heaven, and that in due time, through His death and exaltation, we shall be taken bodily to heaven also.' This, then, is the first principle which the Apostle takes for granted as having been already abundantly established.

The second is, that "we have a great Priest over the house of God." The word "having" is very properly repeated here to make out the sense. Perhaps the whole phrase, "having boldness," or confidence, should have been repeated. "The house of God" may signify either the family of God, or the temple of God. It is plainly used in the first sense in the beginning of the 3d chapter. Though I cannot speak with perfect conviction on the subject, I think it probable that it here means the temple of God—the celestial temple.[2] We

[1] Eph. iii. 12; Heb. iii. 6, iv. 16; 1 John ii. 28, iii. 21, iv. 17, v. 14.

[2] Comp. x. 19, viii. 1, 2, ix. 24, vii. 25, iv. 16. ἐπί used as ch. iii. 6.

know that our Lord Jesus, as our High Priest, is gone to heaven; and we know also, that *there* He is over the temple of God—that everything with respect to the acceptable mode of worship is committed to Him.

The truth here stated, like those formerly referred to, is spoken of as one already established. The greatness of Christ Jesus as a Priest is the grand subject of the third and principal section of the Epistle; and that He is over the celestial temple, is distinctly asserted in the 1st verse of the 8th chapter.

On the foundation of these principles, the Apostle proceeds to exhort the Hebrews to " draw near with a true heart, in full assurance of faith," and to " hold fast the profession of their faith without wavering; for He is faithful that promised."

Since these things are so, and since we have abundant evidence that they are so, " let us," says the Apostle, " draw near with a true heart, in the full assurance of faith, having our hearts sprinkled from an evil conscience, and having our bodies washed with pure water. Let us hold fast the profession of our faith without wavering; for He is faithful who hath promised."

To " draw near" is the same as to " come to God"—to " come to the throne of grace;" and is expressive of worshipping God as a reconciled Divinity. The language in which this idea is expressed is borrowed from the Jewish ritual. In all their religious exercises they looked towards, and in many of them they approached towards, the emblem of Jehovah's favourable presence in the holy of holies. " Let us draw near" is just equivalent to—' let us worship God as the God of peace—let us draw near to Him as propitious to us.'

And let us do so " with a true heart." This phrase seems to me very nearly synonymous with our Lord's description of acceptable worship, John iv. 24 : " In spirit and in truth."[1] " Let us draw near to God "—not by mere bodily service, but by the exercise of the mind and heart—not figuratively, but really —" with a true heart,"—with the mind enlightened with the truth, and with the heart made *true, sound, upright*, through the influence of this truth; not under the influence of the " evil

---

[1] It is the Heb. בְּלֵב שָׁלֵם, rendered ἀληθινὴ καρδία by the LXX., Isa. xxxviii. 3, and καρδία τελεία, 1 Kings viii. 61, xi. 4, xv. 3. Theophylact thus explains it: ἀδόλου, ἀνυποκρίτου πρὸς τοὺς ἀδελφοὺς, ἀδιαστάκτου, μηδὲν ἀμφιβαλλούσης, μηδὲν ἐνδοιαζούσης περὶ τῶν μελλόντων καὶ διὰ τοῦτο μικροψυχούσης.

heart of error and unbelief," which leads men away from God, but under the influence of the heart of truth and faith, which, by uniting the mind and heart of man to the mind and heart of God, gives real fellowship with Him.

Christians are exhorted thus to draw near to God, " in the full assurance of faith." " The full assurance of faith" is just equivalent to—' the fullest and most assured belief.' The question naturally occurs, The full and most assured belief of what? And the answer is easy : The full and assured belief of that respecting which we have confidence—that Christ as our High Priest has bodily passed through these heavens into the heaven of heavens by His own blood, thereby proving the perfection of His atoning sacrifice, and the efficacy of his intercession ; and thus securing that in due time we shall also enter in a similar way into the heavens; and that in heaven, whither He has entered as our Forerunner, He is a great High Priest over the celestial temple, having everything connected with the acceptable worship of God committed to His management. We ought to draw near to God with this full assurance, because we have the most abundant evidence that these things are true, and because it is the assurance of these things which enables us to draw near. It is the faith of the truth respecting the reality and efficacy of the sacrifice of Jesus Christ, and the hope that rises out of that faith, that enable us to *draw near* to *Him*, from whom, but for this faith and hope, had we just views of His holiness and justice and power, we would seek shelter, if possible, under rocks and mountains.

It is a just and important remark of Dr Owen, respecting the meaning of the phrase, " assurance of faith,"—" The full assurance of faith here respects not the assurance that any have of their own salvation, nor any degree of such assurance ; it is only the full satisfaction of our souls and consciences of the reality and efficacy of Christ's priesthood to give us acceptance with God, in opposition to all other ways and means thereof, that is intended." " Let us draw near in the full assurance of faith," is just—' Let us worship God in the firm faith of these truths.'

The two following clauses have, in later times, very generally been considered as both referring to the exhortation, "let us draw near," and as descriptive of the qualifications of an acceptable worshipper. "Having the heart sprinkled from an evil conscience, and the body washed with pure water," has been considered as just equivalent to such phrases as—"being purified from all filthiness of the flesh and of the spirit,"—"being sanctified in the whole man, soul, body, and spirit;" and the Apostle has been supposed to teach the important truth, that the worship of men living habitually in the indulgence either of internal or external sin cannot be acceptable. I cannot but take a somewhat different view of the matter. This is no doubt an important truth, but it has no particular bearing on the Apostle's argument. The construction of the original text induces me, along with many of the most learned both of ancient and modern expositors, to connect the phrase, " and having our bodies washed with pure water," not with the exhortation, " let us draw near," but with the exhortation, "let us hold fast our profession; thus: "Let us draw near, having our hearts sprinkled from an evil conscience; and having our bodies washed with pure water, let us hold fast the profession of our faith."

The words, "having our hearts sprinkled from an evil conscience," appear to me not so much intended to state that we must be holy in heart if we would acceptably worship God, as to bring forward the truth, that "having a heart sprinkled from an evil conscience, through the full assurance of faith," we may, and we ought, to draw near to God as the God of peace. "An evil conscience" is a conscience burdened and polluted with the sense of unpardoned guilt. A man who has offended God, and knows this, and who has no solid ground of hope of pardon, is totally unfit for affectionate fellowship with God. His mind is a stranger to confidence and love—it is full of jealousy, and fear, and dislike. The man must get rid of this "evil conscience" in order to his coming to God. This is expressed by the Apostle by the "heart being *sprinkled* from this evil conscience." The "evil conscience" occupies the same place, as a bar in the way of spiritually drawing near to God, as ceremonial defilement did in the way of ceremonially drawing near to God; and as ceremonial defilement was removed by the sprinkling of the blood of the ritual expiatory sacrifice, so the "evil conscience" is removed by what he terms the sprinkling of the blood of Christ. That which in the New Covenant corresponds to the sprinkling of the blood, is " the faith of the truth as it is in Jesus," by which the sinner is delivered from the jealousies of guilt, and the tormenting fear of divine vengeance. The words, then, are just equivalent to—'Having obtained freedom from those jealousies and fears which arise out of unpardoned guilt, and keep us at a distance from God,—having obtained freedom from these by the faith of these truths, let us draw near to God.' There is an allusion to the consecration of Aaron and his sons, whose garments were sprinkled with blood that they might enter into the sanctuary. Christians are invited, sprinkled *inwardly*—on the conscience with the blood of the only effectual atoning sacrifice,—not only into the sanctuary, but into the holy of holies, where God is, and where the *Forerunner* is also.

It must be evident to every person who has attentively considered and distinctly understood what has been said, that the Apostle's exhortation naturally rises out of and is strongly enforced by the principles on which it is grounded. 'Since we have the most satisfactory evidence that Christ Jesus has bodily gone through these visible heavens into the heaven of heavens, on the ground of His own meritorious, expiatory death, thus proving at once the perfection of His sacrifice and the prevalence of His intercession; and since He has thus secured that all we, believing in Him, shall in due time enter into the heaven of heavens in the same way,—let us worship Jehovah as the God of peace, with enlightened minds and upright hearts, in the assured faith of these truths, by which we are delivered from those jealousies and fears which a guilty conscience produces, and which prevent us from approaching Jehovah as the propitiated Divinity, reconciling the world to Himself, not imputing to men their trespasses.'

It must be equally plain that the Apostle meant his readers to draw the conclusion—' How much better is the way of drawing near to God which is thus opened up than the way of drawing near to Him by the ritual of Moses, and how foolish as well as criminal would it be to abandon the former and revert to the latter!' The Jews, on the ground of the entrance of their high priest through the tabernacle and its vails into the material holy place by the blood of animal sacrifices, though they had no reason to hope they were ever to be allowed to go into the holiest, were yet encouraged tremblingly to approach towards the emblem of the reconciled Divinity, having their bodies purified from ceremonial defilement by the sprinkling of "the blood of bulls and goats." But we Christians have the most satisfactory evidence that our High Priest has passed through these heavens into the heaven of heavens by His own blood, and has secured that in due time we shall follow Him; and through the faith of this truth, our consciences are freed from those jealousies and fears which prevent spiritual intercourse with God, and therefore we can, and we ought, in the spiritual institutions of our holy faith, to cultivate affectionate and childlike intercourse with Jehovah as our Father, because His Father —as His God, and therefore our God.

The Apostle's second exhortation is in these words: "And having our bodies washed with pure water, let us hold fast the profession of our faith without wavering." The great body of MSS. read, "profession of our hope," which seems to be the true reading. It does not, however, materially alter the sense. "The profession of our hope" is just equivalent to—'the hope we profess, the acknowledgment we have made of our hope.' "Let us hold this fast;" *i.e.*, 'let us not abandon it. Let us not be induced by any worldly motive to apostatize from the faith of Christ, and thus abandon that hope of entering at last into the true holy place by the blood of His sacrifice, of which we have made a solemn acknowledgment.'

That solemn acknowledgment was made when they submitted to baptism; and to this, I apprehend, the Apostle refers when he says, "having your bodies washed with pure water." Some have supposed that the allusion is to the divers washings or immersions under the law, by which both the priests and the people were purified for approaching God in worship, and that the Apostle, as it were, says, 'As you have the substance of which the sprinkling of blood was an emblem, so you have also the substance of which the washing of water was an emblem.' I have already, however, stated to you what appear to me satisfactory reasons for considering the words before us as standing in connection, not with the injunction, "let us draw near," but with the injunction, "let us hold fast." And if this mode of connection is adopted, there can scarcely be any doubt that the reference is to Christian baptism. Submitting to Christian baptism by a Jew was a renunciation of Judaism—

it was a public and solemn acknowledgment of his hope in Christ. It was a declaration that he considered himself as *one* with Christ—as having died with Him, been buried with Him, been raised with Him,—and of his expectation of a personal resurrection and ascension entirely on the ground of what He did and suffered, "the Just One in the room of the unjust." That this was the import of a person's submitting to baptism, seems plain from the words of the Apostle: "Know ye not, that so many of us as were baptized into Jesus Christ were baptized into His death? Therefore we are buried with Him by baptism into death; that like as Christ was raised up from the dead by the glory of the Father, even so we also should walk in newness of life. For if we have been planted together in the likeness of His death, we shall be also in the likeness of His resurrection: knowing this, that our old man is crucified with Him, that the body of sin might be destroyed, that henceforth we should not serve sin." "For as many of you as have been baptized into Christ have put on Christ. There is neither Jew nor Greek, there is neither bond nor free, there is neither male nor female: for ye are all one in Christ Jesus. And if ye be Christ's, then are ye Abraham's seed, and heirs according to the promise."[1] The substance, then, of the Apostle's exhortation seems to be,— 'Having in your baptism made a solemn acknowledgment of your hope of eternal life through Christ Jesus, hold fast the hope which you have acknowledged, in opposition equally to the threats of persecutors and the sophistical reasonings of false teachers.'

He adds a very powerfully persuasive motive in the words which follow: "For He is faithful who has promised." God, to give the "heirs of salvation" "strong consolation," has confirmed by an oath that declaration in reference to the everlasting priesthood of Jesus Christ, on which all their hope depends; and He cannot lie—He cannot deny Himself. He can as soon cease to exist as cease to be faithful to His promise. "He is not a man, that He should lie; nor the son of man, that He should repent." And He has proved His faithfulness in accomplishing the promise with regard to our great High Priest. He has brought Him—according to His promise, that "He would not leave His soul in the separate state, nor suffer His Holy One to see corruption,"—He has "brought Him from

[1] Rom. vi. 3–6; Gal. iii. 27–29.

the dead;" and He will in due time fulfil all the promises which He has made to His people, bringing them again from the dead, and giving them that "kingdom prepared for them before the foundation of the world." A consideration of the faithfulness of the Promiser is the principal means of strengthening faith in the promise.

Vers. 24, 25. "And let us consider one another to provoke unto love, and to good works: not forsaking the assembling of ourselves together, as the manner of some is; but exhorting one another: and so much the more, as ye see the day approaching." For the purpose of mutually confirming each other in the hope of the Gospel, the Apostle exhorts the Hebrew Christians to "consider one another, to provoke unto love and good works." Christians are not merely to be concerned about their improvement and safety as individuals, but as members of one body they are to seek to promote each other's best interests. They are to "consider each other." They are to attend to each other's wants, infirmities, temptations, and dangers, and to administer suitable assistance, advice, caution, admonition, and consolation. In this way they are to stir up each other "to love." The word "provoke" is ordinarily used in a bad sense, but here it is just equivalent to 'excite.' They are to act the part which is calculated to call forth in one another's bosoms the workings of that peculiar affection which all Christians have to each other. By doing offices of Christian kindness, they are to excite Christian love in return. They are required to excite each other "to good works;" *i.e.*, I apprehend, to the "labour of love."[1] They are to "do good to all as they have opportunity," and "especially to those of the household of faith."

Such a course was calculated at once to confirm their own faith and that of their brethren. The faith of the truth, and that holy love which it produces, act and react on each other. Accordingly, the Apostle exhorts the Hebrew Christians to be regular in attending on the stated meetings for instruction and worship: "Not forsaking the assembling of yourselves together."[2] It is by means of the public assemblies or churches

---

[1] Heb. vi. 10.

[2] ἐπισυναγωγήν,—perhaps in contradistinction to συναγωγὴν, the name for the ordinary Jewish religious assemblies, as if the ἐπις. superseded the σ.

of the saints that the visible profession of Christ's name is kept up in the world; and the exercises in which Christians there engage — reading, preaching the word, prayer, the Lord's Supper—are all well calculated to strengthen their faith and hope. "Some"[1] of the Hebrew Christians had become negligent in attending to this duty. The Apostle calls on his readers, instead of imitating the conduct of these persons, to "exhort one another." His meaning may be, to exhort one another to attend on these assemblies; or, generally, as chap. iii. 12, 13, to exhort one another to be "stedfast and unmoveable, always abounding in the work of the Lord."

He adds à powerful motive: "And so much the more, as ye see the day approaching." "The day" here referred to seems plainly the day of the destruction of the Jewish State and Church. That day had been foretold by many of the prophets, and with peculiar minuteness by our Lord Himself: "And He said, Take heed that ye be not deceived: for many shall come in My name, saying, I am Christ; and the time draweth near: go ye not therefore after them. But when ye shall hear of wars and commotions, be not terrified: for these things must first come to pass; but the end is not by and by. Then said He unto them, Nation shall rise against nation, and kingdom against kingdom: and great earthquakes shall be in divers places, and famines, and pestilences; and fearful sights and great signs shall there be from heaven. But before all these, they shall lay their hands on you, and persecute you, delivering you up to the synagogues, and into prisons, being brought before kings and rulers for My name's sake."[2] He assures His followers that in that awful destruction they should be preserved. But this security was only to be expected in attending to His cautions, and persevering in faith, and hope, and holiness: "Take heed that ye be not deceived: for many shall come in My name, saying, I am Christ; and the time draweth near: go ye not therefore after them." "Take heed to yourselves, lest at any time your hearts be overcharged with surfeiting, and drunkenness, and cares of this life, and so that day come upon you unawares." "But he that shall endure unto the end, the same shall be saved."[3] These events were now very near; and

---

[1] καθὼς ἔθος τισὶν, by *meiosis* for πολλοῖς.  [2] Luke xxi. 8–12.
[3] Luke xxi. 8, 34; Matt. xxiv. 13.

the harbingers of their coming were well fitted to quicken to holy diligence the Hebrew Christians, that they might escape the coming desolation. But the Apostle, to impress on their minds still more strongly the infinite importance of perseverance in the faith and profession of the Gospel, lays before them a peculiarly impressive view of the complete and "everlasting destruction" which awaits the final apostate in a future state.

Vers. 26, 27. "For if we sin wilfully after that we have received the knowledge of the truth, there remaineth no more sacrifice for sins, but a certain fearful looking for of judgment and fiery indignation, which shall devour the adversaries."[1]

The first point which here requires our attention is the description of the persons of whom the Apostle is speaking. That description consists of two parts. They are such as "have received the knowledge of the truth;" and such as, "after having received the knowledge of the truth, sin."

They are such as "have received the knowledge of the truth." By *the truth*, we are, without doubt, to understand Christianity, which is not only truth as opposed to falsehood and error, but—what we apprehend, probably, was chiefly in the Apostle's view—is truth, or reality, as contrasted with the shadows of the Mosaic economy. The truth, the reality, of which the shadow was given by Moses in the law, "came by Jesus Christ." The Gospel makes known to us the real High Priest, the real sacrifice, the real holy place. To "receive the knowledge of this truth," is not only to be furnished with the means of obtaining a knowledge of Christian truth, but actually to apprehend its meaning and evidence in some good measure, so as to make a credible profession of believing it. To "receive the knowledge of the truth," seems just the same thing as the "being enlightened," which is spoken of in the 6th chapter.

Now, it is taken for granted that persons who "have received the knowledge of the truth" may *sin*. The persons who are here described are persons who, "after they have received

---

[1] Vers. 26-31. These are awfully impressive words. As a learned interpreter (Carpzov) remarks, in language suggested by a noble passage of Jerome—"We hear Paul, not speaking, but casting forth Periclean thunderbolts, and we tremble. A fearsome prospect of judgment, a fury of wrath, the everlasting ruin of death, a disastrous fall into the hands of the living God (every word a thunderbolt)—this is what awaits those who, after gaining knowledge of the truth, deliberately sin."

the knowledge of the truth, *sin*." The word *sin* here is plainly used in a somewhat peculiar sense. It is descriptive not of sin generally, but of a particular kind of sin,—apostasy from the faith and profession of the truth, once known and professed. "The angels that sinned" are the apostate angels. The apostasy described is not so much an act of apostasy as a state of apostasy. It is not, 'If we have sinned, if we have apostatized;' but, 'If we *sin*, if we apostatize, if we continue in apostasy.'

They are described as not only habitually sinning, or as continuing in a state of apostasy, but as doing this *wilfully; i.e.*, obstinately, determinedly, in opposition to all attempts to reclaim them. The contrast implied in the use of the word "wilfully" does not seem so much between sins committed in ignorance and sins committed knowingly, as between a temporary abandonment of the faith and profession of the Gospel, under the influence of fear, or some similar motive, and a determined, persevering, final apostasy. The character here described, then, is that of a man who has at one time obtained such a knowledge of the meaning and evidence of the Gospel as to induce him to make an open profession of Christianity, but who has as openly abandoned its profession, and lives in a state of determined apostasy.

With regard to such a person, the Apostle declares that "there remains no more sacrifice for sins." The persons immediately referred to were Jews. When they became Christians, they gave up the legal sacrifices for sin; but then, in the one sacrifice of Christ they found what infinitely more than supplied the deficiency. But, renouncing the sacrifice of Christ, what are they to do? There is no salvation without pardon—no pardon without a sacrifice for sin. In apostatizing from the faith of Christ, they have renounced all dependence on His sacrifice: and there is no other. They may return to the legal sacrifices, but these "never could take away sin;" and now that the substance is come, of which they were but the shadow, they are no longer useful even for the subsidiary purpose they once served. Jesus is the High Priest promised in the ancient oracle. It is vain to look for another; and it is equally in vain to look for His appearing a second time to offer sacrifice. To the apostate, then, "there remaineth no more sacrifice for sins."

The Apostle's assertion is not, 'If a person apostatize, there is no hope of his obtaining pardon through the one sacrifice of Christ;' but it is, 'If a person persevere in apostasy, putting away from him the one sacrifice of Christ, there is not, there cannot be, for him any other sacrifice for sin.' The apostate must perish, not because the sacrifice of Christ is not of efficacy enough to expiate even his guilt, but because, continuing in his apostasy, he will have nothing to do with that sacrifice which is the only available sacrifice for sin.

Instead of another sacrifice for sin remaining for the apostate, so that, though he give up Christ, he may yet be saved, there remains for him nothing "but a certain fearful looking for of judgment and fiery indignation, which shall devour the adversaries." The word "judgment" here, as in many other places, is equivalent to 'punishment,' to which the sinner is doomed or adjudged: James ii. 13; 2 Pet. ii. 4. When it is said that "there remains" for the apostate "a fearful looking for" of this punishment, the meaning does not seem to be that every apostate is haunted by a dreadful anticipation of coming destruction; for, though this has been the case with some apostates, it is by no means characteristic of all apostates: the meaning is, the apostate has nothing to expect but a fearful punishment.[1] He has no reason to hope for expiation and pardon, but he has reason to fear condemnation and punishment.

The epithet *certain* here, does not denote either an assured expectation, or the certainty of the punishment. It is used in the same way as in the expressions, 'a *certain* man,' 'a *certain* place,' 'a *certain* occurrence.' It is intended to suggest the idea that the punishment to be expected by the apostate is a punishment of undefined, undefinable magnitude—something that is inexpressible, inconceivable. We cannot exactly say what it is; we can only say that a certain awful punishment awaits him, the nature and limits of which cannot be fully understood by any created being. As a sinner, he is exposed to the wrath of God. He obstinately refuses to avail himself of the only "covert from this" fearful "storm," and therefore he must meet it in all its terrors. It must break on his unsheltered head. And "who knows the power of His anger?" The extent of infinite power must be measured, the depths of infinite wisdom must be

---

[1] Equivalent to ἐκδοχὴ κρίσεως φοβερᾶς.

fathomed, ere that awful question can be resolved. We can only say, "According to His fear, so is His wrath." The most dreadful conception comes infinitely short of the more dreadful reality. We can only say of it, 'It is a certain fearful punishment which the apostate has to expect.'

This punishment is further described as "fiery indignation." There remains for the apostate, *indignation* or wrath, even the wrath of God. God is angry with him for all his sins, and especially for the sin of apostasy; and this "wrath of God abideth on him." He is exposed to the fearful effects of God's moral disapprobation and judicial displeasure; and having renounced the sacrifice of Christ, he has nothing to save him from these. The displeasure of God is termed "fiery indignation," or 'indignation of fire,' to represent in a striking manner its resistless, tormenting, destroying efficacy.

It will prove its power in "devouring the adversaries." "The adversaries" here, are, I apprehend, primarily the unbelieving Jews. The Apostle does not say here, as he does elsewhere, "those that believe not,"—"those who obey not the Gospel of Christ;" but, "*the adversaries.*" The appellation is peculiarly descriptive. The unbelieving Jews were actuated by a principle of the most hostile opposition to Christ and Christianity: "Who both killed the Lord Jesus and their own prophets, and have persecuted us; and they please not God, and are contrary to all men."[1] The "fiery indignation" of God is to "devour" these adversaries, and along with them the apostates from the faith of Christ.

It is not improbable that here, as in the passage just quoted from the Epistle to the Thessalonians, there is a reference to the awful judgments which were about to befall the unbelieving Jews, and in which the apostates were to have their full share; but the ultimate reference seems to be to the great "day of wrath and revelation of the judgment of God," when "the Lord Jesus shall be revealed from heaven, with His mighty angels, in flaming fire, taking vengeance on them that know not God, and obey not the Gospel of our Lord Jesus Christ," who "shall be punished with everlasting destruction from the presence of the Lord, and from the glory of His power." Such was the punishment which awaited the apostate of the primitive age, and mate-

[1] 1 Thess. ii. 15.

rially the same is the punishment which awaits the apostate of every succeeding age.

In the verses which follow we have at once an illustration of the certainty and severity of the doom which awaits the apostate, and a vindication of the justice of that doom. Vers. 28, 29. "He that despised Moses' law died without mercy under two or three witnesses: of how much sorer punishment, suppose ye, shall he be thought worthy, who hath trodden under foot the Son of God, and hath counted the blood of the covenant, wherewith he was sanctified, an unholy thing, and hath done despite unto the Spirit of grace?"

The general sentiment obviously is—'If their punishment shall exceed in severity that of the despiser of Moses' law as much as their crime exceeds his in heinousness—and strict justice requires and secures this,—then it will be severe indeed.' Let us proceed now to examine these dreadful words somewhat more minutely.

The person with whom the apostate is compared, is "the despiser[1] of Moses' law." In every violation of a law there is an implied contempt of the law and the lawgiver. But "the despiser of Moses' law" is plainly not every violator of that law; since for many of its violations there were expiatory sacrifices. "The despiser," or *annuller*, "of Moses' law," is the person who acts by the law of Moses the part which the apostate does by the Gospel of Christ, who renounces its authority, who determinedly and obstinately refuses to comply with its requisitions. I cannot help thinking that the Apostle has probably a peculiar reference to the person who, having violated the law of Moses, refuses to have recourse to the appointed expiations. But whatever there may be in this, "the despiser of Moses' law" is the person who treats Moses as if he were an impostor, and refuses, obstinately refuses, to submit to his law as of divine authority.

Now, such a person under the Mosaic economy, whether a native Jew or a sojourner in the Holy Land, was doomed to death. He "died without mercy under[2] two or three witnesses;" *i.e.*, when the crime was satisfactorily proved, he was capitally

---

[1] ἀθετήσας.

[2] ἐπί,—expressive of the condition on which their condemnation and punishment depend; = the Heb. עַל־פִּי: Deut. xvii. 6, xix. 15.

punished; and it was particularly enjoined, that in such cases no pardon nor commutation of punishment should be allowed. The highest punishment man can inflict on man was in such cases uniformly to be inflicted. The best illustration of this statement of the Apostle is to be found in the law to which he refers. " If thy brother, the son of thy mother, or thy son, or thy daughter, or the wife of thy bosom, or thy friend, which is as thine own soul, entice thee secretly, saying, Let us go and serve other gods, which thou hast not known, thou, nor thy fathers; namely, of the gods of the people which are round about you, nigh unto thee, or far off from thee, from the one end of the earth even unto the other end of the earth; thou shalt not consent unto him, nor hearken unto him; neither shall thine eye pity him, neither shalt thou spare, neither shalt thou conceal him: but thou shalt surely kill him; thine hand shall be first upon him to put him to death, and afterwards the hand of all the people."—" If there be found among you, within any of thy gates which the Lord thy God giveth thee, man or woman, that hath wrought wickedness in the sight of the Lord thy God, in transgressing His covenant, and hath gone and served other gods, and worshipped them, either the sun, or moon, or any of the host of heaven, which I have not commanded; and it be told thee, and thou hast heard of it, and inquired diligently, and, behold, it be true, and the thing certain, that such abomination is wrought in Israel; then shalt thou bring forth that man or that woman, which have committed that wicked thing, unto thy gates, even that man or that woman, and shalt stone them with stones, till they die. At the mouth of two witnesses, or three witnesses, shall he that is worthy of death be put to death; but at the mouth of one witness he shall not be put to death. The hands of the witnesses shall be first upon him to put him to death, and afterward the hands of all the people: so thou shalt put the evil away from among you."[1] The justice of this law would be very readily admitted by those to whom the Apostle refers, and must be evident to every person who acknowledges the divine legation of Moses. These, then, are the principles which lie at the foundation of the Apostle's argument, that " the despiser of Moses' law" was doomed to certain death, and that it was just that he should be thus doomed.

[1] Deut. xiii. 6-9, xvii. 2-7.

He now goes on to describe the conduct of the apostate in such language as to make it plain that he is far more deeply criminal than " the despiser of the law of Moses," and thus to prepare the way for the conclusion to which he wishes to bring his readers, that he shall most certainly be far more severely punished. The apostate is one who has " trodden under foot the Son of God." The general idea is—' He has treated with the greatest conceivable contempt a personage of the highest conceivable dignity.' "The despiser of Moses' law" trampled under foot Moses as a divine messenger—the servant of God; but the apostate " tramples under foot" Jesus, who is a divine Person—" the Son of God." " Trampling under foot the Son of God" may be considered as referring generally to the dishonour done to Jesus Christ by apostasy. It is a declaration that He is an impostor,—a declaration that His Gospel is "a cunningly devised fable." But I cannot help thinking that there is a peculiar reference to the dishonour done to Christ Jesus as the great sacrifice for sin by the apostate. The sacrifice He offered was Himself. Now the apostate, in declaring that in his estimation Jesus Christ had offered no sacrifice for sin, as it were tramples on that sacred body, by the offering of which " once for all" Christ Jesus made expiation for the sins of His people. Instead of treating His sacrifice as it ought to be treated—as something of ineffable value, inconceivable efficacy—he treads it under foot as vile and valueless.

He " accounts the blood of the covenant, wherewith he was sanctified, an unholy thing." " The blood of the covenant" is obviously the blood of Christ; and it receives this name, because by the shedding of this blood the New Covenant was ratified, as the Old Covenant was by the shedding of the blood of animal sacrifices.

Interpreters have differed as to the reference of the clause, " by which he was sanctified,"—some referring it to Christ, and others to the apostate. Those who refer it to Christ explain it in this way,—' By His own blood Jesus Christ was consecrated to His office as an intercessory Priest.' Those who refer it to the apostate consider the Apostle as stating, that in some sense or other *he* had been sanctified by the blood of Christ. I cannot say that I am satisfied with either of these modes of interpretation. I do not think that Scripture warrants us to say that any man who finally apostatizes is sanctified by the blood of Christ in any sense, except that the legal obstacles in the way of human salvation generally were removed by the atonement He made; and though I have no doubt that by His bloodshedding our Lord was separated, set apart, sanctified, consecrated, and fitted for the performance of the functions of an interceding High Priest, I cannot distinctly apprehend the bearing which such a statement has on the Apostle's object, which is obviously to place in a strong light the aggravations of the sin of the apostate. I apprehend the word is used impersonally, and that its true meaning is, 'by which there is sanctification.' It is just equivalent to—' the sanctifying blood of the covenant.' The word "sanctify," as I have had occasion fully to show in the course of this exposition, is used in a somewhat peculiar sense in the Epistle to the Hebrews. It signifies, when used in reference to men, to do what is necessary and sufficient to secure them, who are viewed as unclean, favourable access to the holy Divinity. When the blood of Jesus Christ, by which the New Covenant is ratified, is called sanctifying blood, the meaning is, that that blood shed expiates sin—renders it just and honourable in God to pardon sin, and save the sinner; and that this blood sprinkled (*i.e.*, in plain words, the truth about this blood understood and believed), "purges the conscience from dead works," removes the jealousies of guilt, and enables us to serve God with a true heart. This is the peculiar excellence of the blood of Christ. It, and it alone, thus sanctifies.[1]

Now the apostate accounts this "blood of the covenant, by which," and by which alone, "there is sanctification, an unholy thing;" *i.e.*, a common thing, not a sacred thing,—and not only an unconsecrated thing, but a polluted thing. The apostate, instead of accounting the blood of Christ, by which the New Covenant is ratified, possessed of sanctifying virtue, looks upon it as a common, vile, polluted thing,—the blood not only of a mere man, but the blood of an impostor, who richly deserved the punishment he met with,—blood which not merely had no tendency to sanctify, but blood which polluted and rendered doubly hateful to God all who were foolish enough to place their

---

[1] It was with great satisfaction I found Professor Moses Stuart had come to the same conclusion as to the meaning of this phrase, translating —" the blood of the covenant, by which expiation has been made."

hopes of expiation and pardon on its having been shed in their room, and for their salvation.

The apostate is still further described as " doing despite to the Spirit of grace." " The Spirit of grace" is a Hebraism for 'the gracious, the kind, the benignant Spirit.' It has been supposed that this phrase is borrowed from Zech. xii. 10. But "the spirit of grace" there being joined with " the spirit of supplication," seems descriptive, not of the Holy Spirit personally, but of the temper He forms—' a grateful, prayerful temper.' By " the gracious Spirit," I understand that divine Person who, along with the Father and the Son, exists in the unity of the Godhead; and He is termed " the Spirit of grace," or " the gracious Spirit," to bring before our minds the benignant object of all His operations in the scheme of mercy. This benignant Spirit the apostate is represented as " doing despite to,"—as treating with indignity and insult. That Holy Spirit dwelt in " the man Christ Jesus." By that Holy Spirit numerous and most striking attestations were given to the truth of His doctrine. " God bare witness by gifts of the Holy Ghost, according to His own will." When a man in the primitive age apostatized, he necessarily joined with the scribes and Pharisees in ascribing to diabolical agency what had been effected by the influence of the Holy Ghost; than which, certainly, a greater indignity, or more atrocious insult, could not be offered to that divine Person. There can be little doubt that the person described here belongs to the class described in the 6th chapter, who are said to have been "made partakers of the Holy Ghost;" *i.e.*, to have been themselves in the possession of the supernatural gifts of the Spirit, as well as the subjects of His common operations. And certainly for such persons to ascribe the benignant operations of the Holy Ghost on themselves to infernal agency, was the most outrageous and malicious indignity of which human nature is capable.

Such, then, is the crime of the apostate. He treats with the greatest conceivable indignity two divine Persons—the Son and the Spirit of God; he " tramples under foot" Him whom angels adore; he counts polluted and polluting that which is the sole source of sanctification; he repays benignity with insult—the benignity of a divine Person with the most despiteful insult. His punishment, then, must be inconceivably severe, and absolutely certain.

This sentiment is stated by the Apostle far more energetically in the heart-appalling question that follows, than it could have been by any direct assertion : " Of how much sorer punishment, suppose ye, shall he be counted worthy ? If he that despised," etc. In one point of view the despiser of the law and the apostate from the Gospel seem to stand on a level. They both wilfully renounce a sufficiently accredited divine revelation ; but the aggravations attending the apostate's crime are numerous and great. " The despiser of Moses' law" despised indeed a holy man—a divine messenger ; but the apostate despises the Son and Spirit of God, and acts towards them in a far more malicious and insulting manner than the contemner of Moses' law did towards that legislator. If the one deserved death, does not the other deserve damnation—destruction, "everlasting destruction, from the presence of the Lord, and from the glory of His power ?" And if the punishment of " the despiser of Moses' law" was absolutely certain, can the punishment of the contemner and despiser of God's Son and Spirit be in any degree doubtful ? The justice of God requires that the punishment of the apostate be awfully severe, and indubitably certain.

In the two verses which follow we have a further illustration of the awful severity and the absolute certainty of the punishment of the apostate, from the circumstance, that the declaration that a God of infinite power will punish them is made by a God of infinite veracity. Ver. 30. " For we know Him that hath said, Vengeance belongeth unto Me, I will recompense, saith the Lord. And again, The Lord shall judge His people." The quotations are made from the prophetic song of Moses,— " To Me belongeth vengeance and recompense ; their foot shall slide in due time : for the day of their calamity is at hand, and the things that shall come upon them make haste. For the Lord shall judge His people, and repent Himself for His servants, when He seeth that their power is gone, and there is none shut up, or left,"[1]—and refer to the punishments which God would inflict on the wicked Israelites at their latter end. The meaning of the words is plainly,—' I *Myself* will punish them, and the punishment shall bear the impress of My omnipotence.'

The appositeness of the second quotation may not at first

[1] Deut. xxxii. 35, 36.

## GENERAL EXHORTATION AND WARNING. 477

sight appear so plainly. It may seem a promise rather than a threatening. It is indeed a promise, and not a threatening; and I apprehend, that both in the place where it originally occurs and in the passage before us, it is brought forward for the purpose of comforting the minds of those who continued stedfast in their attachment to their God,—assuring them that while He punished rebels and apostates, He would watch over their interests, and protect them from dangers which threatened to overwhelm them. In the prophetic writings generally, the punishment of the enemies of God and the deliverance of His people are closely connected. The same event is very often vengeance to the former and deliverance to the latter. This was the case with the fearful events which were impending over the impenitent and apostate Jews, and to which, in the whole of this passage, I think it highly probable that the Apostle has an immediate reference. The words admit, however, of another interpretation. The word *judge* is not unfrequently used as equivalent to 'punish,' or 'take vengeance:' Gen. xv. 14; 2 Chron. xx. 12; Ezek. vii. 3. In this case it is equivalent to—' Beware of supposing that the relation you think you stand in to God will protect you. "Judgment will begin at the house of God." "You only have I known of all the families of the earth; therefore will I punish you for your iniquities." Whoever escapes, you shall not escape:' Matt. xi. 21-25; Luke xii. 47, 48.

The words, "We know HIM that hath said," are just a very emphatic manner of saying, ' We know His power to destroy: and we know also that "His word is quick and powerful, sharper than a two-edged sword." We know that "He is not a man, that He should lie; nor the son of man, that He should repent: hath He said, and shall He not do it? or hath He spoken, and shall He not make it good?"'

The same sentiment, as to the omnipotence of God to punish, is very strikingly repeated in the 31st verse. "It is a fearful thing to fall into the hands of the living God."[1] "Who knows the power of His wrath? According to His fear, so is His wrath." The scriptural description of the final punishment of the enemies of God is enough to make the ears of every one

---
[1] ἐμπεσεῖν εἰς τὰς χεῖρας is a Hebraistic mode of expression,—נָפַל בְּיַד. In classic Greek it would be—*i.* ὑπὸ τὰς χεῖρας. Ζῶντος, 'powerful, ever-living.'

that heareth it to tingle. Well may we say, with our Lord,—
" Be not afraid of them that kill the body, and after that have
no more that they can do: but I will forewarn you whom ye
shall fear: Fear Him, which, after He hath killed, hath power
to cast into hell; yea, I say unto you, Fear Him."[1] Such is
the doom, the certain doom, of the man who lives and dies an
apostate. Let none despair. It is not the act of apostasy, it
is the state of apostasy, that is certainly damnable. Let all beware of being " high-minded." " Let them fear, lest a promise
being left them, any man should seem to come short of it."
Let them guard against every approach to apostasy. The
grand preservative from apostasy is to grow in " the knowledge of our Lord and Saviour Jesus Christ;" and to " add to
our faith virtue, knowledge, temperance, patience, godliness,
brotherly-kindness, and charity."[2] It is in doing these things
that we are assured that we shall " never fall," and that " so an
entrance shall be ministered to us abundantly into the kingdom
of our Lord and Saviour Jesus Christ."

To apprehend distinctly the meaning, to feel fully the force,
of the exhortations contained in the paragraph which follows, it
is necessary that the circumstances of those to whom they were
originally addressed should be before the view of the mind.

This Epistle was written a few years before the final destruction of the Jewish civil and ecclesiastical polity by the
Romans. This was a season of peculiar trial to the Christians
in Judea. Christianity was now no longer a new thing. Its
doctrines, though they had lost nothing of their truth and importance, no longer were possessed of the charm of novelty;
and their miraculous attestations, though to a reflecting person
equally satisfactory as ever, were from their very commonness
less fitted than at first to arrest attention, and make a strong
impression on the mind. The long-continued hardships to
which the believing Hebrews were exposed from their unbelieving countrymen, were clearly fitted to shake the stability of their
faith, and to damp the ardour of their zeal. Jesus Christ had
plainly intimated to them, that ere that generation had passed
away He would appear in a remarkable manner, for the punishment of His enemies, and the deliverance of His faithful followers. The greater part of that generation had passed away,

---

[1] Luke xii. 4, 5.  [2] 2 Pet. i. 5-7.

## GENERAL EXHORTATION AND WARNING.

and Jesus had not yet come, according to His promise. The scoffers were asking, with sarcastic scorn, " Where is the promise of His coming ?" and " hope deferred" was sickening the hearts of those who were " looking for Him." The " perilous times" spoken of by our Lord had arrived. Multitudes of pretenders to Messiahship had made their appearance, and had " deceived many." Many of the followers of Jesus were offended—many apostatized, and hated and betrayed their brethren. " Iniquity abounded, and the love of many," who did not cast off the Christian name, " waxed cold."

In these circumstances, it was peculiarly necessary that the disciples of Christ should be fortified against the temptations to apostasy, and urged to perseverance in the faith and profession of the Gospel. This is the grand object of this Epistle, and every part of it is plainly intended and calculated to gain this object. The whole of the doctrinal part of the Epistle is occupied in showing the pre-eminent excellence of Christianity, by displaying the matchless glory of Christ; and the greater portion of the practical part of the Epistle is employed in stating and enforcing the exhortation to remain "stedfast and unmoveable" in their attachment to their Lord, in their belief of the doctrines, the observance of the ordinances, and the practice of the duties of their " most holy faith."

In the preceding context the Apostle has most impressively urged on their minds the peculiar advantages to which their new faith had raised them as to favourable and delightful intercourse with God, and the fearful consequences of apostasy, as irresistible arguments to "hold fast their profession;" and in the passage which lies before us for interpretation, in order to gain the same end, he calls on them to recollect their past experience in reference to Christianity,—to reflect on all they had suffered for it, and on all which it had done for them under their sufferings,—and to pause and ponder before, by apostasy, they rendered useless all the labours and sorrows they had endured, and blasted all the fair hopes which they had once so fondly cherished, and which had enabled them to bear, not only patiently, but joyfully, all the trials to which they had been exposed. Vers. 32–34. " But call to remembrance the former days, in which, after ye were illuminated, ye endured a great fight of afflictions ; partly, whilst ye were made a gazing-stock both by reproaches and afflictions; and partly, whilst ye became companions of them that were so used. For ye had compassion of me in my bonds, and took joyfully the spoiling of your goods, knowing in yourselves that ye have in heaven a better and an enduring substance."

The period to which the Apostle wishes to recall their minds is that which immediately followed their illumination, or, in other words, their obtaining the knowledge of the truth. That state of ignorance and error in which they were previously, is figuratively represented as a state of darkness; and when, by the statement of Christian truth and its evidence, they were delivered from ignorance and error, they are said to have been enlightened.

On their being enlightened, they had to " endure a great fight of afflictions." It is not improbable that the Apostle refers to the severe and general persecution which followed the death of Stephen, and with which, as he had taken a very active part in it himself, he was intimately acquainted; and to that which took place not long afterwards by Herod, when "he slew James, the brother of John, with the sword." The variety and severity of the trials to which at that period Jewish believers were exposed, are very strikingly expressed in the phrase, "great fight of afflictions." It is not improbable that, in using the word *endure*, the Apostle meant to convey the idea, not only that they had been exposed to these varied and severe trials, but that they had worthily sustained them—they had *endured* the fight. They had persevered till the conflict was finished, and they had come off conquerors. That is plainly the meaning of the word when the Apostle James says, "Behold, we count them happy who endure."

In these afflictions they had been involved both personally and by their sympathy with their suffering brethren. They "endured a great fight of afflictions, partly, when they were made a gazing-stock,"—made public spectacles, as malefactors, who in the theatres were often made, in the presence of the assembled people, to fight with each other, or with wild beasts. This was literally the case with some of the Christians, though I do not know that any of the Hebrew Christians were thus treated. The idea is—'set up as objects of the malignant and scornful notice of the public.' This they were by the "reproaches" which were cast on them. These reproaches were of two kinds: false charges were brought against them, and their faith and hope were ridiculed—their character and conduct as Christians held up to scorn. By "afflictions," as distinguished from "reproaches," we are to understand sufferings in person, such as torture of various kinds. And as many of the Hebrew Christians had been "made gazing-stocks" by personally undergoing their trials, so also had they become so by avowing themselves "the companions of those who were so used." Genuine Christians feel towards one another as brethren; and when they see their Christian brethren suffering for the cause of Christ, they naturally, though not directly, attach themselves to, take part with, their suffering brethren, and thus come in for a share of the public scorn which is poured on them.

The Apostle particularly notices one instance in which they "became companions of those who were thus used:" "For ye had compassion of me in my bonds." Supposing these words to be the genuine reading, they seem to refer to the kind attention shown to Paul by some of the Hebrew Christians when in *bonds* at Jerusalem and Cesarea.[1] But, according to the best critics, the true reading is—"for ye had compassion on those who were bound," or "on the prisoners."[2] Those among the Hebrew Christians who were not themselves imprisoned, became companions with them by sympathizing with them, owning them as their brethren, and doing everything which lay in their power to alleviate their sufferings.

The Apostle, having noticed the sufferings to which they had been exposed in their reputation and persons, and by sympathy with their suffering brethren, now calls to their mind the sufferings they had sustained in their property, and the manner in which they had borne them. They were "spoiled of their goods,"—they were unjustly deprived of their property; and when they were so, instead of repining, or thinking of retaining their property by giving up their religion, they "took the spoiling of their goods joyfully." They were as it were glad that they had this means of showing their attachment to Christ

---

[1] Comp. Phil. i. 13, 16; Col. iv. 18.

[2] Besides the external evidence for δεσμίοις, there is internal evidence also. Συμπαθεῖν δεσμοῖς is a strange and unprecedented expression: μνημονεύειν τῶν δεσμῶν is quite another thing.

and His cause—they counted themselves honoured in being called on to make such a sacrifice.

This mode of feeling did not arise from stoical apathy, or from enthusiastic feeling: it arose from their persuasion that the religion which called on them to sacrifice their worldly property secured them in a far more valuable property. In some of the most ancient MSS. the words, " in heaven," are wanting. On the supposition that they do not form a part of the original text, the meaning is—" Ye took joyfully the spoiling of your goods, knowing that in yourselves you had a better and enduring substance;" *i.e.*, 'You cheerfully parted with your external property, because you knew that your most valuable and permanent property was within you. They could not take from you the love of God—the comforts of the Holy Ghost—the hope of eternal life. If they could have taken these from you—and these you would cast from you if you renounce Christianity—they would have made you poor indeed; but whatever else they might take from you, if they left you these, you knew that you were *rich*, rich for ever.'

If the words, " in heaven," be considered as belonging to the text, then the meaning is somewhat different. 'Ye took joyfully the spoiling of your goods, knowing in yourselves'—*i.e.*, being fully persuaded—' that whatever the world may think, this is the truth, that in heaven there is laid up for you[1] true and abiding substance.'[2] Worldly wealth scarcely deserves the name of *substance*: it is, like all things worldly, unsubstantial; and it is, like all things worldly, fading and shortlived. But celestial wealth is real substance, and permanent as real. " Moth and rust do not" there " corrupt: thieves do not" there " break through, nor steal." The man who is fully persuaded that he has in heaven this substance will not grieve very much at the loss of worldly substance in any circumstances; but when the giving up of the latter is required in order to the obtaining of the former, he will show that he counts it but as the dust in the balance, and will " joyfully take the spoiling of his goods."

---

[1] ἑαυτοῖς, which is the true reading, expresses peculiar property—' that as *your own* you have,' etc.

[2] The natural order of the words seems to be—κρείττονα ὕπαρξιν καὶ μένουσαν ἐν οὐρανοῖς; but μένουσαν, as expressing the chief idea, is placed behind. Their worldly substance had been found anything but μένουσα.

## GENERAL EXHORTATION AND WARNING.   483

Such, then, are the things which the Apostle wishes the Hebrew Christians to "call to remembrance."

It is easy to see how the calling of these things to remembrance was calculated to serve his purpose—to guard them from apostasy, and establish them in the faith and profession of the Gospel. It is as if he had said, 'Why shrink from suffering for Christianity now? Were you not exposed to suffering from the beginning? When you first became Christians, did you not willingly undergo sufferings on account of it? And is not Christianity as worthy of being suffered for as ever? Is not Jesus the same yesterday, to-day, and for ever? Did not the faith and hope of Christianity formerly support you under your sufferings, and make you feel that they were but the light afflictions of a moment? and are they not as able to support you now as they were then? Has the substance in heaven become less real, or less enduring? and have you not as good evidence now as you had then that to the persevering Christian such treasure is laid up? Are you willing to lose all the benefit of the sacrifices you have made, and the sufferings you have sustained? and they will all go for nothing if you endure not to the end.' These are considerations all naturally suggested by the words of the Apostle, and all well calculated to induce them to "hold fast the profession of their faith without wavering."

Accordingly, he adds, ver. 35, "Cast not therefore away your confidence, which has great recompense of reward." The "confidence" of the Christian Hebrews is just a general name for the open, consistent, fearless adherence to Christianity amid all the difficulties they had been exposed to. This they were to hold fast, and not to cast away. If they shrunk from the contest, and became cowards, this was to cast it away. Instead of casting it away, they were to hold it fast—to continue "stedfast and unmoveable," in nothing moved by their adversaries; for it "has great recompense of reward;"—*i.e.*, a steady, uniform, persevering adherence to Christ will be abundantly rewarded. The sufferings, however great, "were not worthy to be compared with the glory which was to be revealed." Faithful is He who hath said, "Blessed are ye when men shall revile you, and persecute you, and shall say all manner of evil against you falsely, for My sake. Rejoice, and be exceeding glad; for great is your reward in heaven."

But then the reward can be obtained only by holding fast this confidence—by adhering steadily and perseveringly to Christ and His cause. It is "he who endures to the end that shall be saved." This is the sentiment contained in the 36th verse: "For ye have need of patience, that, after ye have done the will of God, ye might receive the promise."

The word "patience" properly signifies 'perseverance;'[1] and the phrase, "ye have need of perseverance," is just equivalent to—'ye must persevere,' "that, having done the will of God, ye may receive the promise." "The promise" here is the blessing promised; to receive the promise, is to obtain the promised blessing.[2] Now the only way of obtaining the promised blessing is to persevere in doing the will of God. It is by "adding to faith, virtue; and to virtue, knowledge; and to knowledge, temperance; and to temperance, patience; and to patience, godliness; and to godliness, brotherly-kindness; and to brotherly-kindness, charity;"—it is in doing these things that we are secured that "we shall never fall," and it is thus that there "will be ministered to us abundantly an entrance into the everlasting kingdom of our Lord and Saviour Jesus Christ."

The Apostle encourages the Christian Hebrews to persevere, from the consideration that their Lord's promise to appear in their behalf was inviolably faithful, and would soon be accomplished. Ver. 37. "For yet a little while, and He that shall come will come, and will not tarry."

In these words there is an allusion to words employed by the prophet Habakkuk; but it is a mere allusion.[3] "He that shall come," or 'He that is coming,' was an appellation given by the Jews to the Messiah. It is here used plainly in reference to some "promise of His coming." It cannot refer to His first coming in the flesh, for that was already past. It cannot refer to His second coming in the flesh, for that is even yet future,

---

[1] ὑπομονή: Luke xxi. 19; 1 Thess. i. 3; Matt. x. 22, xxiv. 13.

[2] Τὴν μεγάλην μισθαποδοσίαν, ver. 35; τὴν ὕπαρξιν ἐν οὐρανοῖς, ver. 34; ἐπαγγελία, res promissa, Heb. vi. 15, ix. 15, xi. 39.

[3] Habakkuk's words (ii. 3, 4), according to the LXX., are: ἐὰν ὑστερήσῃ, ὑπόμεινον αὐτὸν, ὅτι ἐρχόμενος ἥξει καὶ οὐ μὴ χρονίσῃ. Ἐὰν ὑποστείληται, οὐκ εὐδοκεῖ ἡ ψυχή μου ἐν αὐτῷ, ὁ δὲ δίκαιος ἐκ πίστεώς μου ζήσεται. The writer uses the words of the prophet as the vehicle of his own ideas.

after the lapse of nearly eighteen centuries; whereas the coming here mentioned was a coming just at hand. But though these are the only comings of the Son of God in the flesh, they are by no means the only comings that are mentioned in Scripture. There are particularly two comings mentioned in the New Testament: His coming in the dispensation of the Holy Spirit; and His coming for the destruction of His Jewish enemies, and the deliverance of His persecuted people. The first is referred to in John xiv. 18, 19: "I will not leave you comfortless; I will come to you. Yet a little while, and the world seeth Me no more; but ye see Me: because I live, ye shall live also." The second, in Matt. xxiv. 27: "For as the lightning cometh out of the east, and shineth even unto the west; so shall also the coming of the Son of man be." It is to the last of these that there is a reference in the passage before us. Jesus Christ had promised, that when He came to execute vengeance on His enemies of the Jewish nation, His friends should not only be preserved from the calamity, but obtain deliverance from their persecutions: "When these things begin to come to pass, then look up, and lift up your heads; for your redemption draweth nigh."[1] This coming was to take place before that generation passed away. More than thirty years had already elapsed; and within eight or nine years—" a little while"—the prediction was accomplished. It is as if the Apostle had said, 'Hold out but a little longer, and the coming of the Lord, both as showing the fearful doom of His enemies and His faithfulness in reference to the promise made to His friends, will free you from your present temptations to apostasy.'

The Apostle concludes this paragraph by asserting at once the necessity of faith—continued faith—in order to salvation, and the certainty of apostasy leading to destruction. The words in the 38th verse are also an allusion to the words of Habakkuk, but they do not seem quoted in the way of argument: "Now, the just shall live by faith: but if any man draw back, My soul shall have no pleasure in him." The words, "The just by faith shall live," may either mean, 'The just or righteous man shall live by faith as the influencing principle of his conduct,'—as the Apostle says, "The life I live in the flesh, I live by the faith of the Son of God;" or

[1] Luke xxi. 28.

they may signify, "The man who is just by faith, shall live," *i.e.*, shall be saved, shall obtain eternal life. The passage is quoted and reasoned from by the Apostle in two passages: Rom. i. 16, 17, "For I am not ashamed of the Gospel of Christ: for it is the power of God unto salvation to every one that believeth; to the Jew first, and also to the Greek. For therein is the righteousness of God revealed from faith to faith: as it is written, The just shall live by faith." And Gal. iii. 11, "But that no man is justified by the law in the sight of God, it is evident: for, The just shall live by faith." In both these passages, the words are to be understood in the last of these senses; and though either of them will afford a suitable meaning in the place before us, I think it most likely that the Apostle uses them in the same way as in other places of his writings. It is the man justified by believing that is saved; and the man justified by believing is not the man who *has* believed merely, but the man who continues believing: that is the man who "shall live"—who obtains true, permanent happiness.

"But if any man draw back, My soul shall have no pleasure in him." The word, *any man*, is a supplement, and has been added to prevent any inference unfavourable to the perseverance of the saints from being drawn from this passage. It is not right, however, to add to the word of God, even to defend truth.[1] If the man "justified by faith" were to "draw back," God's "soul could have no pleasure in him." This is in no way inconsistent with the doctrine of the perseverance of the elect, which appears to us very plainly taught in Scripture. If God has "chosen them in Christ before the foundation of the world," and "predestinated them to the adoption of children to Himself"—if He has "called them according to His purpose," and if they are really "washed, and sanctified, and justified in the name of the Lord Jesus, and by the Spirit of our God"—if there is "an inheritance laid up in heaven for them," and if they are "kept to it by the power of God, through faith unto salvation"—if there be an inseparable connection between being foreknown and predestinated, and being called, and justified, and glorified,—then it is evident that they must "persevere" in faith and holiness "unto the end," and at last "receive the end of their faith, even the salvation of their souls." But it should never be forgotten that

---

[1] Bloomfield's long note here deserves to be consulted.

the Scripture doctrine of the perseverance of the elect is one thing, and the application of it to individuals quite another thing. No elect person can know that he is an elect person till he believe the Gospel; or that he shall "persevere unto the end," but while he is actually persevering in faith and holiness. The question is not, whether the elect shall persevere; that is a clearly revealed truth; but the question is, Am I among the number? This I cannot know but by believing, and persevering in believing, and in the necessary results of believing: adding to my faith virtue, knowledge, temperance, patience, godliness, brotherly-kindness, and charity. Yet it is perfectly consistent with this for me to believe that if I "draw back," God's "soul will have no pleasure" in me; and the faith of this is just one of the appropriate means to prevent my drawing back.

"But," says the Apostle, in the spirit of Christian charity, which "hopeth all things," on the principle that the Hebrew Christians were what they professed to be—ver. 39. "We are not of them who draw back to perdition"[1]—among those who, having apostatized, shall perish; "but of them who believe to the saving of the soul,"[2]—*i.e.*, who believe straightforward till the soul is saved—who continue to the end, and, continuing to the end, are saved. This passage, though containing some things peculiar to the state of the Hebrew Christians, is in its substance plainly applicable to Christians in all countries and in all ages.

The Apostle now, for the illustration and enforcement of his exhortation, brings forward a great variety of instances, from the history of former ages, in which *faith* had enabled individuals to perform very difficult duties, endure very severe trials, and obtain very important blessings. The principles of the Apostle's exhortation are plainly these: 'They who turn back, turn back unto perdition. It is only they who persevere in believing that obtain the salvation of the soul. Nothing but a persevering faith can enable a person, through a constant continuance in

[1] Ἡμεῖς οὐκ ἐσμὲν ὑποστολῆς εἰς ἀπώλειαν. Many interpreters supply υἱοί or τέκνα; but this is not necessary. We do not belong to the apostasy—the apostates doomed to destruction.

[2] Ἡμεῖς ἐσμὲν πίστεως εἰς περιποίησιν ψυχῆς. We belong to *the faith*—the believers, destined to obtain "the salvation that is in Christ with eternal glory." Kypke considers the phrase as = ἡμεῖς οὐκ ἐσμὲν (ἐξ) ἀ.—ἀλλ' (ἐκ) π., and considers οἱ ἐκ πίστεως, Gal. iii. 7; τὸν ἐκ π., Rom. iii. 26; οἱ ἐξ ἐριθείας, Rom. ii. 8, as parallel modes of expression.

well-doing, and a patient, humble submission to the will of God, to obtain that glory, honour, and immortality which the Gospel promises. Nothing but a persevering faith can do this; and a persevering faith can do it, as is plain from what it has done in former ages.'

The Apostle's illustration of the efficacy of faith in enabling the believer to perform duty, endure trial, and obtain blessings, is prefaced by a remark or two explicatory of the sense in which he employs the word *faith* in this discussion. Chap. xi. 1. " Now faith is the substance of things hoped for, the evidence of things not seen."

Faith is in the New Testament employed sometimes to signify the act or state of the mind which we call belief, and sometimes the object of the mind in this state or act—the thing believed. It is here obviously employed in the first sense, as equivalent to 'believing.' Now what, according to the Apostle, is faith, or believing? It is " the substance of things hoped for, the evidence of things not seen." I have always felt it difficult to attach distinct ideas to these English words. They have generally been considered as intended to express the following sentiment:—' Faith gives, as it were, a real subsistence in the mind to things hoped for; it makes evident things which are not seen—it gives a present existence to things future, a visible form to things unseen. A promise is made of future good—a revelation of something not discoverable by sense or reason. To the unbeliever the promised good, the revealed truths, are an unsubstantial vision—mere creatures of the imagination; to the believer they are substantial realities.' This is no doubt truth; but I cannot help thinking these ideas are rather put into the words than brought out of them.[1] Taking the English words in their ordinary meaning: Believing a promise respecting future good, is not the substance of that good; nor is believing a revelation with respect to things unseen, the evidence on which I believe. The act of faith or believing, the object of faith or truth in reference to what is future or unseen, and the ground of faith, or evidence, are obviously three completely distinct things; and without the greatest confusion of thought, one of them cannot be mistaken for any of the two other.

[1] Kuinoel says of this exegesis, "A subtle interpretation which cannot be commended for straightforwardness."

The word translated "substance" occurs only five times in the New Testament, and all these instances are in the writings of the Apostle Paul. In one case, Heb. i. 3, it is translated *person;* but that passage is plainly altogether inapplicable to the illustration of the phrase before us. In the other three places where it occurs—2 Cor. ix. 4, xi. 17; Heb. iii. 14—it is translated *confidence;* and that, too, is the reading in the margin in the present instance. I have little doubt that that word expresses the Apostle's idea. 'Faith, or believing, is a confidence respecting things hoped for.' The word translated "evidence" is derived from a verb which signifies 'to convince;' and its natural and most obvious meaning is, 'conviction.' It occurs only in one other place in the New Testament—2 Tim. iii. 16, where I think there is little doubt that its meaning is 'conviction.' "All Scripture is profitable for doctrine, for reproof,"—rather, 'for conviction,' *i.e.*, for teaching men what is true, and for showing them that it is true. This, I apprehend, is its meaning here: 'Faith is a conviction in reference to things not seen.' This, then, is the Apostle's account of faith: 'It is a confidence respecting things hoped for; it is a conviction respecting things not seen.' A promise is made respecting future good. I am satisfied that He who promises is both able and willing to perform His promise. I believe it; and in believing it, I have a confidence respecting the things which I hope for. A revelation is made respecting what is not evident either to my sense or my reason. I am satisfied that this revelation comes from One who cannot be deceived, and who cannot deceive. I believe it; and in believing it, I have a conviction in reference to things which are not seen. Faith in reference to events which are past, is belief of testimony with regard to them; faith in reference to events which are future, is belief of promises with regard to them.

This "confidence respecting things hoped for," founded on a divine promise—this "conviction respecting things unseen"—is the grand spring of dutiful exertion, and dutiful submission; it is this, and this alone, that can induce a man to persevere in doing and suffering the will of God, till in due time the promised blessing is obtained. That it had been so in past ages, is the proposition which the Apostle is about to prove and illustrate by a numerous induction of particular instances; and he introduces them by remarking generally, that by this faith the ancient saints had been enabled to do, and suffer, and obtain, so as to have their names, and services, and trials, and attainments honourably recorded in the Book of God. Ver. 2. "For by it the elders obtained a good report."

*For* is here obviously a mere connective particle, equivalent to *moreover*. The words do not contain in them any reason for what is stated in the previous verse. The word "elders" is used both in the Old and New Testament as a title of office; but here it is plainly equivalent to 'ancients,' and refers to the same persons who are called "the fathers"[1] in the first verse of the Epistle. By means of their faith these good men performed actions, sustained trials, and obtained blessings, of which we have an account in the Book of God. Thus on account of their faith they are favourably testified of by God, or have "obtained a good report." The reference does not seem to be chiefly, if at all, to the high opinion entertained of them by their descendants, but to the honourable record which God has given of them, and to which the Apostle is about more particularly to turn his attention.[2] We would have naturally expected that the Apostle should now immediately proceed to bring forward one of these ancients, as an illustration of the efficacy of faith in enabling men to do duty, sustain trial, and obtain blessings. But instead of this, he interposes an observation, the object of which seems to be, to illustrate by an example what he meant by faith being "a conviction in reference to things not seen."

Ver. 3. "Through faith we understand that the worlds were framed[3] by the word of God; so that things which are seen were not made of things which do appear." The particular manner of the creation of the world is an object of faith. It is one of the unseen things. We did not witness it. Reason might perhaps have discovered, what when discovered it can satisfactorily prove, that the world was created, and created by God; but how the world was created, whether out of nothing or out of pre-existent materials, reason could say nothing. God has given us a revelation on this subject, and our knowledge rises out of our belief of that revelation. It is because we be-

---

[1] πατέρες.

[2] Ebrard considers the words as = ' were testified to in reference to their faith,' *i.e.*, as being believers. This is probably the true exegesis.

[3] καταρτίζειν, parare, creare, = ποιεῖν. Ps. lxxiii. 16.

lieve what we find written in the first chapter of Genesis, that we know that "in the beginning" God created the universe by merely commanding it to be. The concluding clause of this verse is very obscure : "So that the things which are seen were not made of things that do appear."[1] This, then, is an illustration of what faith is, viewed as a "conviction in reference to things not seen." I know that God created the world out of nothing; but how do I know? I did not see it; but God has told me so in a well-accredited revelation, which I believe; and by believing it, or by faith, "I understand that the worlds were framed by the word of God."[2]

The Apostle now proceeds to give us an account of the efficacy of faith in enabling men to perform duties, endure trials, and obtain benefits, as exemplified in the experience of some of

---

[1] Many interpreters, following the Vulgate, Chrysostom, Theodoret, Theophylact, and Œcumenius, think that μὴ ἐκ φαινομένων stands for ἐκ μὴ φαινομένων. Chrysostom's words are, δῆλόν ἐστι ὅτι ἐξ οὐκ ὄντων τὰ ὄντα ἐποίησεν ὁ Θεός, ἐκ τῶν μὴ φαινομένων τὰ φαινόμενα, ἐκ τῶν μὴ ὑφεστώτων τὰ ὑφεστῶτα. In support of these views, they assert that such transpositions are common in the best writers, and that the Hebrews were in the habit of calling a thing not existing, לֹא נִמְצָא, οὐχ εὑρισκόμενον; and they quote as a parallel passage, 2 Macc. vii. 28, οὐκ ἐξ ὄντων ἐποίησεν αὐτά (viz., the heaven and the earth, and all things in them). On the other hand, Beza, Schmid, Storr, Schulz, Böhme, Winer, and Kuinoel, consider this transposition as arbitrary, and think that the particle μὴ should be connected with γεγονέναι. The meaning in this case is, 'The world exists by the will of God; so that it is not formed of pre-existent matter, but called into being, when there was nothing but God.' We have the same sentiment, 2 Macc. vii. 28, ἀξιῶ σε, τέκνον, ἀναβλέψαντα εἰς τὸν οὐρανὸν καὶ τὴν γῆν, καὶ τὰ ἐν αὐτοῖς πάντα ἰδόντα, γνῶναι, ὅτι οὐκ ἐξ ὄντων ἐποίησεν αὐτὰ ὁ Θεός, καὶ τὸ τῶν ἀνθρώπων γένος οὕτως γεγένηται. Calvin, usually so judicious in his interpretations, for the sake of an ingenious notion, as Tholuck justly says, departs from the prevalent and correct explanation. He connects ἐκ with the verb, forces on τὰ βλεπόμενα the signification of 'mirror,' and translates, "fide intelligimus aptata esse secula verbo Dei, ut non apparentium (the τὰ ἀόρατα of Rom. i. 20) specula fierent."

[2] Rational as the doctrine is, I apprehend no man ever held it who did not owe it to revelation. Thales, Plato, Aristotle, and other eminent philosophers, indulged in visionary speculations about the creation of the world, very different indeed from the view which "He who made it, and revealed His work to Moses," has given. The opinions of the ancient philosophers may be reduced to two. They either thought that the world had existed from eternity, or that its materials were eternal, which the Divinity at some very remote period had put into order.

those ancients of whom God in His word has, on account of their faith, given a favourable testimony. The first individual in whose history the Apostle finds an illustration of the beneficial efficacy of believing is Abel. Ver. 4. "By faith Abel offered unto God a more excellent sacrifice than Cain, by which he obtained witness that he was righteous, God testifying of his gifts; and by it he, being dead, yet speaketh."

The history to which the Apostle refers is to be found Gen. iv. 1-5: "And Adam knew Eve his wife; and she conceived, and bare Cain, and said, I have gotten a man from the Lord. And she again bare his brother Abel. And Abel was a keeper of sheep, but Cain was a tiller of the ground. And in process of time it came to pass, that Cain brought of the fruit of the ground an offering unto the Lord. And Abel, he also brought of the firstlings of his flock, and of the fat thereof. And the Lord had respect unto Abel, and to his offering: but unto Cain, and to his offering, He had not respect. And Cain was very wroth, and his countenance fell." Both Cain and Abel offered sacrifice; but Abel offered a more excellent sacrifice. It has been supposed by many interpreters, that the word translated *more excellent*[1]—properly signifying, 'fuller, larger, more abundant'—refers to Abel's offering an expiatory sacrifice, in addition to the eucharistic sacrifice, which alone Cain presented. It has been thought by others that the Apostle's meaning is, that the sacrifice of Abel was in itself a more valuable one, consisting of animals, than that of Cain, which consisted of vegetables. We are rather disposed to think that the meaning is, generally, 'Abel's sacrifice was a better, a more valuable, a more availing sacrifice, than Cain's.' It better answered the end of a sacrifice, which is to be acceptable to God. How it was so, will appear by and by.

It was by faith that Abel offered a more acceptable sacrifice than Cain. Faith throughout the whole of this chapter is the belief of a divine revelation. It is plain, then, that a revelation had been made both to Cain and Abel respecting the duty of offering sacrifice, and the acceptable method of performing that duty. Though we have no particular account of the institution of sacrifice, the theory of its originating in express divine appointment is the only tenable one. The idea of expressing re-

[1] πλείονα.

ligious feelings, or of expiating sin, by shedding the blood of animals, could never have entered into the mind of man. We read that God clothed our first parents with the skins of animals; and by far the most probable account of this matter is, that these were the skins of animals which He had commanded them to offer in sacrifice.[1] We have already seen, in our illustrations of the ninth chapter, ver. 16, that all divine covenants, all merciful arrangements in reference to fallen man, have been ratified by sacrifice. The declaration of mercy contained in the first promise seems to have been accompanied with the institution of expiatory sacrifice. And expiatory sacrifice, when offered from a faith in the divine revelation in reference to it, was ac-

---

[1] "It is easy to be demonstrated," says Hallett, "that sacrifices owed their original to the will and appointment of God. The Apostle says, as Moses said before him, that Abel's sacrifice was acceptable to God. But it would not have been acceptable if it had not been of divine institution, according to that plain, obvious, and eternal maxim of all *true* religion, Christian, Mosaic, and natural, 'In vain do they worship GOD, teaching for doctrines the commandments of men,' Mark vii. 7. If there be any truth in this maxim, Abel would have worshipped God in vain, and God would have had no respect to his offering, if his sacrificing had been merely a commandment of his father Adam, or an invention of his own. The divine acceptance, therefore, is a demonstration of a divine institution."— "Anything that has been answered to the argument for the divine institution of sacrifice, taken from this passage, is," as Dr M'Crie remarks, "extremely futile. The words of Episcopius are self-contradictory, and even ridiculous : " Abel, by faith alone, directed by no divine command, i.e. by the impulse of right reason alone, judged that God must be worshipped with the best that he had in his flock." *Instit. Theol.* lib. i. cap. viii. § 3. That must be fancy, not faith, which has a respect to no precept or word of God. Is it then the same thing to act from faith and from the dictates of right reason ? This is not only glaringly untheological, but unphilosophical also. Nor is the attempt of the learned Spencer to elude the force of this argument more successful. He describes the faith of Abel to have been a firm persuasion, deeply fixed in his mind, as to the favourable disposition of God to men, which caused him to form his conduct by the rules of piety. He adds, that he and the rest of the patriarchs offered sacrifice 'from a certain pious simplicity of mind (ex pia quadam simplicitate).' But the Apostle does not speak of any general persuasion which influenced Abel's worship; but he asserts that faith was specially exercised by him in the act of offering this sacrifice, and that it was this which rendered it more excellent than Cain's. As to this *pia simplicitas*, it is degrading to the patriarchs to impute it to them, although this is often done by persons who, boasting of their own superior light, have become 'vain in their imaginations.'"—PHILISTOR. *Christian Magazine for* 1803, vol. vii., pp. 407, 408.

ceptable to God, both as the appointed expression of conscious guilt and ill desert, and of the hope of mercy, and as an act of obedience to the divine will.

It would appear that this revelation was not believed by Cain, that he did not see and feel the need of expiatory sacrifice, and that his religion consisted merely in an acknowledgment of the Deity as the author of the benefits which he enjoyed. Abel, on the other hand, did believe the revelation. He readily acknowledges himself a sinner, and expresses his penitence and his hope of forgiveness in the way of God's appointment. Believing what God had said, he did what God had enjoined;—he brought the sacrifice God had appointed, and offered it in the way in which He had appointed it to be offered. What was the extent of Abel's knowledge of the nature and design of expiatory sacrifice, we cannot tell. All that we know, and all that is necessary for the Apostle's argument, is this: Abel, believing what God revealed, did what God commanded, and obtained evidence that God was pleased with him and his services; while, on the other hand, Cain, not believing what God had revealed, did not do what God had commanded, and instead of receiving evidence that God was pleased with him, had a clear demonstration that He was displeased with him.[1]

On account of this faith thus influencing his conduct, Abel "obtained witness that he was righteous." "The Lord had respect unto Abel and his offering." To be righteous, is just to be an object of the approbation of the Supreme Judge. How God manifested His approbation of Abel, and disapprobation of Cain, we cannot tell. It is not an improbable conjecture, that it was in a manner similar to that in which He testified His approbation of Elijah and his sacrifice, of Abram and his sacrifice, and of Aaron's sacrifice on his entering on the priest's office: Gen. xv. 17; Lev. ix. 24; 1 Kings xviii. 3. Abel's sacrifice was probably consumed by fire from heaven, while Cain's remained untouched. At the same time, though a probable conjecture, this is but a conjecture. It is enough that we know that he did receive a distinct testimony of the approbation of God. "God testifying of his gifts;" *i.e.*, 'God making it manifest that his gifts were acceptable to Him, while his brother's gifts were not acceptable.'

[1] δι' ἧς, i.e., πίστεως, not θυσίας.

The concluding clause of the verse is somewhat obscure: "And by it he, being dead, yet speaketh;" *i.e.*, I apprehend, 'By or on account of his faith,' manifested in his sacrifice. Following a different reading from that adopted by our translators, some render the words, 'and on account of this, he is yet spoken of.' This, though a truth, is one which has no direct bearing on the Apostle's object. Besides, the reading followed by our translators is admitted by the best critics to be the genuine one.

But what are we to understand by these words, "On account of his faith," or, "by means of his faith, he, though dead, yet speaketh?" It has been common to suppose that this just means, that Abel still speaks to us by his example, as recorded in Scripture—still speaks to us of the importance and efficacy of faith. But this is not at all peculiar to Abel; it is equally true of all the persons who are mentioned in this chapter. Besides, in whatever the Apostle states in reference to these elders, he obviously alludes to what is testified of them in Scripture. I therefore cannot at all doubt that the Apostle refers to the subsequent part of Abel's history, as detailed in the fourth chapter of the Book of Genesis: "And He said, What hast thou done? the voice of thy brother's blood crieth unto Me from the ground."[1] And this conviction is strengthened by noticing the way in which the Apostle contrasts the blood of Christ—called by him "the blood of sprinkling"—with "the blood of Abel," chap. xii. 24. 'On account of his faith, manifested in his sacrifice, though dead, he yet spoke;'[2] *i.e.*, God manifested His regard to him by the punishment He inflicted on his murderer. The earth would not cover his blood. His blood was precious in God's sight; and He proved it to be so by not allowing him who shed it to escape unpunished. His faith, manifested by his sacrifice, drew down upon him, both while living and dead, proofs that he was the object of the divine favourable regards. Such

---

[1] Gen. iv. 10.

[2] From Philo it appears that the Jews were struck with the representation of Abel, though dead, speaking by his blood to God: ζῇ δὲ τὴν ἐν Θεῷ ζωὴν εὐδαίμονα, μαρτυρεῖ δὲ τὸ χρησθὲν λόγιον, ἐν ᾧ φωνῇ χρώμενος καὶ βοῶν—εὑρίσκεται. "He," *i.e.*, Abel, "lives in God a happy life; for the sacred Scripture gives testimony of him, in which he is found using a voice," *i.e.*, 'speaking and crying.'

is the first of the Apostle's illustrations of the importance and efficacy of faith.

The second example of the power of faith is that of Enoch. Ver. 5. "By faith Enoch was translated that he should not see death; and was not found, because God had translated him: for before his translation he had this testimony, that he pleased God."

To the illustration of this paragraph, two things are necessary. We must first attend to the Apostle's account of the high privilege which Enoch obtained—he "was translated;" and then to the Apostle's proof that it was "by faith" that he obtained this privilege.

The account we have of the strange transaction referred to, in Gen. v. 24, is in these words: "Enoch was not, for God took him."[1] The Apostle quotes from the Septuagint, and by his quotation sanctions the view that version gives of the words. Enoch, instead of dying like other men, was in some miraculous manner carried bodily to heaven; some change taking place, no doubt, on his body, and that of Elijah, similar to that which is to take place on the bodies of the saints that are found alive at the end of the world, to fit them for the celestial state; for we know that "flesh and blood cannot inherit the kingdom of God, neither can corruption inherit incorruption." This is all the information the Scriptures give us with respect to Enoch's translation; and it were worse than a waste of time to bring forward the baseless conjectures which men, anxious to be wise beyond what is written, have advanced on the subject.

Let us now attend to the Apostle's proof that it was "by faith" that Enoch obtained this distinguished privilege. That proof is brought forward in the following words: "For before his translation he had this testimony, that he pleased God." Ver. 6. "But without faith it is impossible to please Him: for he that cometh to God must believe that He is, and that He is a rewarder of them that diligently seek Him."

The words, "before his translation," etc., are obviously equivalent to—'for in the sacred history, before we read of his translation, we read of his being the object of the peculiar favour of God. His translation is there represented as the consequence of

---

[1] לָקַח, the same word used in reference to Elijah, 2 Kings ii. 3.

this peculiar favour of God; and this peculiar favour he could not have enjoyed, had he not been a believer, for to the enjoyment of this peculiar favour faith is absolutely necessary.' This is the Apostle's argument. Let us look at its various parts, that we may distinctly see that it is fairly drawn from the passage of Old Testament history from which it is deduced.

In our version of Genesis we read nothing of Enoch's pleasing God. We read, " Enoch walked with God," which is a literal version of the Hebrew text. The expression, " walked with God," has commonly been considered as descriptive of Enoch's character as a singularly pious man, who, realizing the divine presence, habitually thought and felt, spoke and acted, as under the eye of God. I am rather disposed to consider it as descriptive of Enoch's privilege: he was beloved of God, and, as an evidence of it, he was admitted to intimate and delightful intercourse with Him. He was a prophet, to whom God made communications of His will; and it is not at all unlikely that, as in the case of Moses, sensible proofs might be given to his cotemporaries that he was in a remarkable degree the object of the divine regard. I am induced to take this view of it, because I find the two most ancient versions of the Scriptures (the Syriac and Greek) rendering the phrase, " walked with God," " pleased God," not only here, but in Gen. vi. 9, where the same phrase again occurs in reference to Noah;[1] and the Apostle sanctions this interpretation by reasoning from it. This, then, is the first step in the Apostle's argument, to prove that " by faith Enoch was translated." The Scriptures testify that Enoch was the object of the divine peculiar regard previously to his translation, and represent that translation as an expression of this peculiar regard.

The second step is, Faith, or believing, is absolutely necessary in order to any man's being the object of the peculiar regard of Jehovah. " Without faith it is impossible to please God." These words admit of two different interpretations, according as you explain the reference of the phrase, " to please God." They may either signify, ' without believing the truth about God, it is impossible to enjoy His favour;' or, ' without believing the truth about God, it is impossible to possess that character, or to prosecute that course of conduct, which

[1] *Vide* Gen. xvii. 1, xxiv. 40; Ps. lvi. 13, cxvi. 9.

only can meet with His approbation.' Both are truths. The last is the view most commonly taken of the assertion here; but I am inclined to consider the first as probably expressing the Apostle's idea. The only way in which guilty men, who have forfeited God's favour, can regain it, is through the faith of the truth respecting Him. "By the deeds of the law no flesh living can be justified." If Enoch enjoyed the divine favour, it must have been through believing.

The Apostle confirms his assertion, that without believing, it is impossible to be well-pleasing to God, by adding, " for every one that cometh to God must believe that He is, and that He is the rewarder of them who diligently seek Him." " To come to God," is here plainly equivalent to—' to be the object of His kind regards.' No one can draw near to Him with acceptance, as to a Father and a Friend, who does not " believe that He is, and that He is the rewarder of them who diligently seek Him." To " believe that God is," is something more than to believe that there is a God. There are many who believe that there is a First Cause, whom they call God, whose notions of the character of God are not only greatly defective, but greatly erroneous. These persons believe that there exists a being whom they call God; but their faith is not the faith of the truth. There really exists no such being in the universe as the being they conceive of: he is a mere creature of their own minds. To " believe that God is," is to believe in the existence of such a Being as God's works and word declare Him to be: it is to believe the truth with regard to Him. No person can be the object of the complacency of God who does not credit the revelation He has made to him of Himself.

There is particularly one truth about God which must be believed by all who would approach to Him with acceptance, and that is, that " He is the rewarder of all who diligently seek Him;"—in other words, that He is merciful, and disposed to pardon and save all who seek Him,—that is, who in the way of His appointment, by believing His word and hoping in His mercy, seek their happiness in Him. The faith of the truth about God, as disposed to pity, pardon, and save all, even the most guilty of the children of men, who come to Him in the way of His appointment—that is the faith by which, in every age of the world, men have been justified. The degree of information respecting the details of the method of salvation has been very different in different ages; but the great truth, through the faith of which men are interested in that method of salvation, has never varied. It is, " that God is, and that He is the rewarder of them who diligently seek Him."

This, then, is the Apostle's argument, and it is plainly a good one: ' Enoch is a glorious illustration of the efficacy of faith in obtaining benefits. He obtained a most important benefit—translation to heaven without tasting of death; and it was through believing that he obtained this benefit. The Scriptures represent him as before his translation an object of the peculiar divine favour; and they represent his translation as a manifestation of this peculiar favour. But none but a believer can be an object of the divine peculiar favour. It is by faith, and faith alone, that a man can be justified.'

The concluding part of the 6th verse is valuable, as giving us a further illustration of the Apostle's description of faith in the first view. To believe the truth with regard to the character of God, is " conviction with regard to things unseen," " for no man hath seen God at any time;" and to believe " that He is the rewarder of them who diligently seek Him," is " confidence respecting things hoped for." It is also useful for confuting two very absurd tenets which have been adopted by some men. There are men, even professed Christians, who maintain the innocence of error,—who say it is of no consequence what men believe, if they but live well. That is just equivalent to saying that it is of no consequence to " please God"—to be an object of His complacency and kind regard; for " without faith it is impossible to please God." There are others who affirm, that in serving God we ought to have no respect to the " recompense of reward." But the Apostle states it as forming a necessary part of that truth which must be believed in order to our pleasing God, " that He is the rewarder of those who diligently seek Him."

This passage has often been abused for the purpose of proving that the heathen, who have no written revelation, are not in such deplorable circumstances as the friends of missions represent them. They have the means of knowing that " God is, and that He is the rewarder of them who diligently seek Him;" and if they believe this, they, like Enoch, will please

God, and though they should not, like him, be translated, yet when they die they will certainly go to heaven. That the heathen have to a certain extent the means of knowing that "God is," is plain from the first chapter of the Romans; but the Apostle, who asserts this truth, asserts also, that in consequence of the depravity of man's nature, these means are not improved, and therefore but increase their guilt and deepen their condemnation; and that, in fact, the heathen world " by wisdom knew not God," but, on the contrary, " did service to them who by nature are no gods." The views of every heathen are not only necessarily very defective, from the imperfection of the means of knowledge, but, as experience teaches, they are uniformly greatly erroneous. The god or gods in whose existence they believe, is not the true God. With regard to the second article of that faith which the Apostle represents as necessary to please God, " that He is the rewarder of them that diligently seek Him," that is what no man without an express revelation could ever discover. It is very consonant with reason to believe that God will make innocent and obedient creatures happy; but as to whether God will be reconciled to sinners, and make them ultimately happy, or in what way He is to be sought for this purpose, it is plain that unenlightened reason can give no information. The faith here spoken of must be founded on a supernatural revelation of the true character of God, and of His purposes of mercy towards a lost world. It was through the faith of the revelation made in his time on this subject, that Enoch was accepted of God; it is through the faith of the revelation now made to us, that we are to be accepted of God. It is not my purpose to enter into the general question of the salvability of the heathen; but I think it must be evident to every careful reader, that that doctrine receives no support from the passage before us. It would be a strange thing indeed, if in an Epistle, the great object of which is to show the supreme importance of the faith of the Gospel, we should meet with a declaration that men may be saved without knowing anything about the Gospel.

The third example of the efficacy of faith which he brings forward, is that afforded by the history of Noah. Ver. 7. "By faith[1] Noah, being warned of God of things not seen as yet,

---

[1] πίστει must be construed, not with χρηματισθείς, but with κατεσκεύασε: δι' ἧς must not be referred to κιβωτόν, but to πίστει.

moved with fear, prepared an ark to the saving of his house; by the which he condemned the world, and became heir of the righteousness which is by faith." Let us first shortly attend to the facts of the case; and then consider the illustration which they afford of the efficacy of faith in enabling to perform duties, to endure trials, and to obtain blessings.

The facts are these: " Noah was warned of God of things not seen as yet;" in consequence of this, he was "moved with fear," and built an ark; he obtained the salvation of his family; " he condemned the world, and he became an heir of the righteousness that is by faith."

The first fact is, " Noah was warned of God of things not seen as yet." The approaching deluge was the event of which Noah was warned. The circumstances of that event are termed " things not seen *as yet ;*" because, though in their own nature sufficiently apprehensible by the senses, they were *then* unseen, because future, and because nothing in the appearance of nature indicated their approach. We have a particular account of the warning in Gen. vi. 12–18 : " And God looked upon the earth, and, behold, it was corrupt : for all flesh had corrupted his way upon the earth. And God said unto Noah, The end of all flesh is come before Me ; for the earth is filled with violence through them : and, behold, I will destroy them with the earth. Make thee an ark of gopher-wood : rooms shalt thou make in the ark, and shalt pitch it within and without with pitch. And this is the fashion which thou shalt make it of ; The length of the ark shall be three hundred cubits, the breadth of it fifty cubits, and the height of it thirty cubits. A window shalt thou make to the ark, and in a cubit shalt thou finish it above; and the door of the ark shalt thou set in the side thereof ; with lower, second, and third stories shalt thou make it. And, behold, I, even I, do bring a flood of waters upon the earth, to destroy all flesh, wherein is the breath of life, from under heaven ; and every thing that is in the earth shall die. But with thee will I establish My covenant : and thou shalt come into the ark, thou, and thy sons, and thy wife, and thy sons' wives with thee."

The second fact refers to the influence which this warning had on the mind and conduct of Noah. He was " moved with fear," and he " prepared an ark." When it is said that Noah was " moved with fear," we are not to suppose that he was in any degree afraid that he or his family were to perish in the approaching deluge. He had precisely the same reason for expecting his deliverance, and that of his family, along with a small remnant of all species of living creatures, that he had for expecting the destruction of the rest of mankind and the animal tribes. It is easy, however, to see how Noah was "moved with fear." An evil of such tremendous magnitude, inflicted on account of sin, placed in a very striking light the irresistible power, the immaculate purity, the inflexible justice of God, and was fitted to fill the mind with reverence and godly fear. Besides, Noah knew that he and all his family were sinners, and deserved to perish along with the rest of their race; and he knew also, that though, if the ark was prepared, according to the divine appointment, all was safe; it was equally true, that if the ark was not prepared, he and they must perish in the general ruin. The very idea of this must have excited a salutary terror, and operated as a powerful motive to diligence in the building of the ark. When we consider the size of the ark,—especially when connected with the collection of the various animals, which from the history seems to have been Noah's work,—the undertaking, in any circumstances, must have been an arduous one; and when we consider the difficulties which must have arisen out of the state of sentiment and feeling of the great body of mankind, it may well be considered as one of the most extraordinary examples of difficult duty which the world has ever witnessed. The testimony of God on this subject is this—adding, after a particular detail of the commands laid on Noah,— "Thus did Noah; according to all that God commanded him, so did he."

The third fact stated by the Apostle is, that Noah thus obtained the deliverance of his family. He "built an ark to the saving of his house." "House," here, is plainly equivalent to 'family.' The words, "to the saving of his house," taken by themselves, may either signify what was the design of Noah in building the ark, or what was the result of his building the ark. In the first case, they are equivalent to—'he built an ark that his family might be saved;' in the second case, they are equivalent to—'he built an ark, and thus his family was saved.' Both are truths; but it is the last of these truths which serves the Apostle's object—the illustration of the efficacy of faith. By building the ark, Noah obtained the salvation of his family. " And all flesh died that moved upon the earth, both of fowl, and of cattle, and of beast, and of every creeping thing that creepeth upon the earth, and every man : all in whose nostrils was the breath of life, of all that was in the dry land, died. And every living substance was destroyed which was upon the face of the ground, both man, and cattle, and the creeping things, and the fowl of the heaven; and they were destroyed from the earth: and Noah only remained alive, and they that were with him in the ark."[1] When " all flesh" had died, "Noah remained alive, and they that were with him in the ark."

The next fact stated is, " He condemned the world." These words have generally been supposed to refer to that tacit condemnation which Noah, by his conduct, in obeying the divine commandment, and preparing for the coming deluge, as it were pronounced on an ungodly world.[2] But as it is said that " by faith" (for I apprehend there can be no doubt the reference is to faith in the relative " which," and not to the ark, as some have supposed; for it was by the same thing, whatever it was, that he " condemned the world" and " became the heir of the righteousness of faith ;" and certainly it was not by the ark that he was justified) " he condemned the world," I am disposed to consider the words as referring to the same fact which Peter, in his second Epistle, ii. 5, refers to, when he calls Noah " a preacher of righteousness." I think we are warranted from the declaration here, as explained by that in the Epistle of Peter, to conclude, that the warning Noah received from God he publicly proclaimed,—remonstrated with the men of his age on their wickedness, called them to repentance, and denounced, on their continuing in sin, the awful sentence of a common and universal destruction.

The last fact stated is, that Noah "became," or *was*, " an heir of the righteousness which is by faith." " The righteousness by faith" is just the justification by believing; and to be

---

[1] Gen. vii. 21-23.

[2] The following passage from Ecclesiasticus has been referred to for illustration :—κατακρίνει δὲ δίκαιος καμὼν τοὺς ζῶντας ἀσεβεῖς, καὶ νεότης τελεσθεῖσα ταχέως πολυετὲς γῆρας ἀδίκου. " The dead just man condemns the living ungodly; and the finished youth swiftly condemns the protracted old age of the wicked."

"an heir of the righteousness of faith," is just to participate in the blessing of justification by believing—to be justified by believing. In this part of his statement, I apprehend the Apostle refers to two passages in the book of Genesis: the first, ch. vi. 8, "Noah found favour in the sight of the Lord;" and the second, ch. vi. 9, "Noah walked with God;" which, as the Apostle has explained it in the preceding context, is equivalent to—'Noah was well-pleasing to God,'—Noah was a justified person—a person treated by God as if he had been righteous, as an object of His peculiar favour; and, as the Apostle has shown, if he was so, it must have been through believing.

These are the facts of the case. Let us now see how they illustrate the efficacy of faith for enabling to perform duties, to endure trials, and to obtain blessings.

It has been supposed by some, that the Apostle means to say that it was *by faith* that Noah was "warned of God of things not seen as yet;"—that is, that the warning given to Noah was a proof of God's peculiar regard to Noah; and that this token of peculiar regard, like every other, was bestowed on him as a believer. But I rather think that the phrase, "by faith," is intended to refer to "moved by fear, prepared an ark;" the warning being considered as the revelation which was the subject of that faith through which Noah performed his difficult duties, endured his severe trials, and obtained the glorious reward. Had the warning not been believed, Noah would not have been "moved with fear"—he would not have "prepared an ark." He would have continued, like the unbelieving generation among whom he lived, careless and disobedient. But believing, as he did, the warning in all its extent, he could not but be "moved with fear"—he could not but set about "preparing the ark." Noah believed the whole testimony. It was a declaration of universal destruction, with the exception of himself and his family, and a declaration that even they could be saved only by the "preparing of an ark." Had Noah believed merely that "the end of all flesh was come before God," he would indeed have been filled with fear, but that fear would not have moved him to prepare an ark. It was the faith at once of the coming general destruction and the particular way of escape which produced the effect of his prosecuting the laborious and difficult work of preparing the ark.

As it was by faith that Noah prepared the ark, so it was by faith that he obtained the salvation of his family. That privilege was connected in inseparable union with a preceding duty, which preceding duty could not have been performed without faith. Had not the ark been prepared, Noah and his family could not have been saved; and had not Noah believed, the ark would not have been prepared. You see, then, how the salvation of Noah's family was the result of his faith.

It was by faith also that he " condemned the world." The revelation which he believed furnished him with the great subject of his condemnatory addresses; and it was the faith of this revelation that enabled him, in defiance of their scorn, to tell them the truth. He believed, and therefore spoke.

It was by faith also that " he became an heir of the righteousness which is by faith." This scarcely requires any illustration. The language of the Apostle is not in reality, what it is in appearance, tautological. When he says, Noah by faith " became heir of the righteousness which is by faith," he just means, that Noah by his own personal faith obtained an interest in that method of justification, in which no man can obtain an interest but by believing.[1]

This example of Noah is thus admirably fitted to serve the Apostle's purpose. Faith enabled Noah to perform very difficult duties. It enabled him to make the laborious preparations, which must have occupied many years, for the approaching deluge; it enabled him to do his duty, and to persevere in doing it, amid many difficulties and discouragements; it enabled him fearlessly, though alone, as " a preacher of righteousness," to pronounce the sentence of condemnation on a guilty world, though in doing so he must have exposed himself to cruel mockings, and very probably to imminent hazards. Faith enabled Noah to endure very severe trials. The conviction, that without building the ark he and his family must perish, and if it were prepared they were safe, rendered powerless the shafts of ridicule. He endured, as seeing what was yet invisible. Faith enabled him to obtain most important benefits,—the deliverance of his family, and a personal interest in the justification that is by believing.

---

[1] The phrase, ἡ κατὰ πίστ. δικ., is plainly the same thing as ἡ δικ. ἐκ πίστ., Rom. i. 17, ix. 30, x. 6; and διὰ πίστ., Rom. iii. 22, Phil. iii. 9; or simply δικ. πίστ., Rom. iv. 13.

The example is the more instructive, as it naturally, and almost necessarily, brings before the mind the fearfully destructive efficiency of unbelief. The world that perished had materially the same message delivered to them as that which Noah received. Had they repented, there is no reason to doubt that the fearful infliction would not have taken place. Noah believed, and feared, and obeyed, and was saved. They disbelieved, and mocked, and were disobedient, and perished.

Faith and unbelief are the same things still. The believer, like Noah, has been " warned of God of things not seen as yet." He has heard that " all have sinned," and that God cannot " clear the guilty," and " the wicked must be turned into hell;" and he has heard also, that " God hath set forth His Son a propitiation through His blood," and that " whosoever believeth shall not perish, but have everlasting life ;" and that by the believer seeking " glory, honour, and immortality," eternal life shall assuredly be obtained. Like Noah, he believes the divine warning; he is filled with fear at the display which these truths give of the power, and holiness, and justice of God; he sees that everlasting destruction is his inevitable portion, unless he avail himself of the only way of escape, and that, availing himself of this way of escape, he is secure of everlasting happiness; and believing this, he " flees for refuge to the hope set before him,"—and he continues fleeing for refuge; and in the way of God's appointment, the way of faith and holiness, he seeks perseveringly, and he obtains assuredly, " the end of his believing, even the salvation of his soul." He believes the whole of the divine testimony. If he believed only the first part of it, he would despair; if he believed only the last part of it, he would presume. But believing both, he both fears and hopes; and under the combined influence of fear and hope, he performs duty, endures trials, and ultimately obtains the promised blessing.

The unbeliever, like the ungodly world in the days of Noah, hears the divine testimony, but will not receive it. Hell excites no fears—heaven no desires. He continues in impenitence and disobedience, till down comes the thunderbolt. He is conveyed into the regions of hopeless punishment, and learns, too late, how criminal and dangerous it is, under the influence of " an evil heart of unbelief," to " depart from the living God."

## GENERAL EXHORTATION AND WARNING. 507

The fourth example of the efficacy of faith is derived from the history of Abraham, the father of the Hebrew nation. Vers. 8-10. "By faith Abraham, when he was called[1] to go out into a place which he should after receive for an inheritance, obeyed; and he went out, not knowing whither he went. By faith he sojourned in the land of promise, as in a strange country, dwelling in tabernacles with Isaac and Jacob, the heirs with him of the same promise: for he looked for a city which hath foundations, whose builder and maker is God."

Of the facts referred to in the 8th verse, we have an account in the beginning of the 12th chapter of the book of Genesis. " Now the Lord had said unto Abram, Get thee out of thy country, and from thy kindred, and from thy father's house, unto a land that I will show thee: and I will make of thee a great nation, and I will bless thee, and make thy name great; and thou shalt be a blessing: and I will bless them that bless thee, and curse him that curseth thee: and in thee shall all families of the earth be blessed. So Abram departed, as the Lord had spoken unto him; and Lot went with him: and Abram was seventy and five years old when he departed out of Haran."[2]

Though in the Mosaic history the account of this call is not given till after the account of the death of Terah in Haran, yet it is plain from the speech of Stephen that it took place in Mesopotamia, previously to his leaving that country along with his father. The call consisted of two parts,—a command and a promise. The command was, " Get thee out of thy country, and from thy kindred, and from thy father's house, unto a land that I will show thee." The promise was partly implicit,—" I will give thee this land for an inheritance;" and partly explicit, —" I will make of thee a great nation, and I will bless thee, and make thy name great; and thou shalt be a blessing: and I will bless them that bless thee, and curse him that curseth thee: and in thee shall all the families of the earth be blessed."

---

[1] Theodoret supposes that καλούμενος Ἀβραάμ refers to the change of the patriarch's name from Abram to Abraham. Some MSS. and versions read ὁ καλούμενος; but the whole context shows that the reference is to what is usually termed "the call" of Abraham,—his being divinely commanded to leave his native country, and go into a land to be pointed out to him.

[2] Gen. xii. 1-4.

Abraham believed that both the command and the promise came from God; and therefore he obeyed the command, and expected the fulfilment of the promise. His faith was "confidence in reference to things hoped for;" it was "conviction in reference to things not seen as yet." Had Abraham not believed that the call came from God, or had he not believed that God was at once able and disposed to perform His promises, he would have disregarded the call, and continued in Mesopotamia; but because he believed, he obeyed. It was his faith which led him to break asunder those very strong bands which bind men to their country and their kindred, and to undertake a journey of unknown length, and difficulty, and danger,—towards a country of which he knew nothing, but that God had said to him, "I will show it thee." "He went forth, not knowing whither he went." He proceeded in the direction which the divine call pointed out; and he went onward till the same divine call directed him to stop.

This certainly was a very remarkable manifestation of the power of faith in enabling a man to perform a difficult duty. It is difficult for us to form a distinct conception of it, as no case strictly analogous can occur among us. But let us suppose a person, previous to the discovery of America, leaving the shores of Europe, and committing himself and his family to the mercy of the waves, in consequence of a command of God, and a promise that they should be conducted to a country where he should become the founder of a great nation, and the source of blessings to many nations; and we have something like what actually took place in the case of Abraham.

The object for which this instance of the power of faith is brought forward is obvious, and it is well fitted to serve that object. Nothing but faith could have enabled Abraham to act as he did. Faith made what would otherwise have been impossible, easy. God was calling the Hebrew Christians to break through bands as strong as those which bound Abraham to Mesopotamia, in abandoning Judaism, and to take a course in a determined attachment to Christianity, the consequences of which were as apparently hazardous, and as completely unknown to them and beyond their control, as the circumstances of Abraham's journey from Mesopotamia to Canaan. Nothing could enable them to do this but faith—a full persuasion that the command to embrace Jesus of Nazareth as "the end of the law for righteousness," and the promise of eternal life as the gift of God to all who did so, equally came forth from God. And while nothing could enable them to do this but such a faith, such a faith would make these otherwise impracticable duties easy. This would prevent them from "turning back to perdition," and would enable them to "press onward to the mark, for the prize of the high calling of God in Christ Jesus."

And it is equally true now as it was then. Nothing but the faith of the Gospel can induce a man to abandon the world and commence a pilgrimage towards heaven. And wherever there is the faith of the Gospel, there will be such an abandonment— there will be the commencement and the prosecution of such a pilgrimage. If Abraham had continued in Mesopotamia, or stopped short of Canaan, it would have been a proof that he did not believe the divine testimony; and whatever men may profess, if they continue to love the world, and become "weary in well-doing," it is clear evidence that they have not believed the Gospel.

We have another instance of the power of faith in enabling to persevere in a course of duty, while the blessing promised is not immediately conferred, brought before our minds in the next verse. This, too, is taken from the history of Abraham. Ver. 9. "By faith he sojourned in the land[1] of promise, as in a strange country, dwelling in tabernacles with Isaac and Jacob, the heirs with him of the same promise."

When Abraham came into the land of Canaan, the promise which was implied in what was said to him at his call in Mesopotamia, was given him in the most explicit language: "The Lord appeared unto Abram, and said, Unto thy seed will I give this land."[2] Hence that country received the appellation, "the land of promise," or the promised land. But that promise was not immediately, was not soon, fulfilled. Abraham did not obtain possession of it, nor did his posterity, till nearly five centuries after. To use the language of Stephen, "God gave him no inheritance in it, no, not so much as to set his foot on: yet

---

[1] εἰς γῆν for ἐν γῇ. Such a use of εἰς with a noun of place is not unfrequent. Bretschneider's Lex. εἰς, 5, c.
[2] Gen. xii. 7.

He promised that He would give it to him for a possession, and to his seed after him, when as yet he had no child."[1] Had Abraham not been a persevering believer—had he not continued to "account Him faithful who had promised"—he would not have continued in Canaan in such circumstances, a pilgrim and sojourner, dwelling in tents, and having no certain or abiding dwelling-place. He would have returned to the country from which he had come out, and where his relations had possessions and fixed places of abode; or he would have gone into some other country, where, with the property he had, he might have procured for himself an inheritance. But because Abraham believed that in due time the promise would be fulfilled, he preferred dwelling in a tent in Canaan to dwelling in a palace anywhere else. He goes into Egypt during the time of famine; but it is to sojourn, not to settle. He sends Eliezer to obtain a wife for Isaac into Mesopotamia, and takes an oath of him, that even in the case of his not succeeding in getting one of his kinswomen as a wife to Isaac, he was not to take Isaac back again to the land of his ancestors. He continued, along with Isaac and Jacob—to whom as well as to Abraham the promises were made, and who are therefore called "heirs with him of the same promise,"—to live in Canaan, though not put in possession of it. Though the promise was long in being fulfilled, he did not doubt but it would be in due time fulfilled; and therefore he determined that he and his posterity should continue in the land to which the promise referred.

It is equally easy here, as in the former case, to see the object the Apostle had in view in bringing forward this particular exemplification of the power of faith, and to see how well fitted it is for gaining that end. Nothing but continued faith could have enabled Abraham to continue a pilgrim and a sojourner in Canaan, waiting for the fulfilment of the promise. Continued faith did enable Abraham to do so. Nothing but continued faith could enable the Christian Hebrews to continue "stedfast and unmoveable" in the profession and practice of Christianity during that season of privation and suffering, of undefined length, which might intervene before the full accomplishment of the promises which had been made to them. Per-

[1] Acts vii. 5.

severing faith would enable them to do this. He who continues believing will "endure to the end," and "be saved."

The words which follow in the 10th verse seem to contain the reason why Abraham continued to sojourn in the land of promise. Ver. 10. "For he looked for a city which hath foundations, whose builder and maker is God."

These words have been supposed by some very learned interpreters to refer to the literal Jerusalem, the metropolis of the Holy Land, when it became the possession of the descendants of Abraham. They consider the Apostle as saying, 'The reason why Abraham continued to live in Canaan, though he had no inheritance there, though he and his family had to live in moveable tents, was, that he expected that in due time, in that country, a stable city would be erected for them by the remarkable providence of God—that the whole territory should be peopled by his descendants, not as wandering tribes, but as the inhabitants of towns and cities, having Jerusalem built on the rocky mountains as its metropolis.' This is ingenious, but it is not satisfactory. We have no reason to believe that any revelation was made to Abraham as to the building of Jerusalem. The "city which has foundations" seems plainly the same city mentioned in the subsequent context as a city prepared for them by God, in the better, the heavenly country and the description, "whose builder and maker is God," which seems nearly equivalent in meaning to the expression respecting the true tabernacle, "which, it is said, God pitched, not man," seems to exclude the workmanship of man, and points it out to us as not a literal but a figurative expression, indicating not an earthly, but a heavenly city. The Apostle's assertion then is, that Abraham "looked for a city which has foundations, whose builder and maker was God." What does it mean?

The land of promise is in the Scriptures the emblem of the heavenly inheritance, and the earthly Jerusalem of the residence of the saints there. They are represented as dwelling in a glorious city, with Jehovah in the midst of them as their King. To denote the stability, the immutability, and the eternity of this state of happiness, the heavenly city is said to "have foundations." It is not a collection of tents or tabernacles, which have no foundations, and which are easily removed, but it is a city built on the everlasting hills of Paradise.

It is not unlikely that Psalm lxxxvii. 1 was in the Apostle's mind: "His foundation is in the holy mountains." The travelling tent, pitched in the evening and struck in the morning, finely contrasts with the "city which has foundations"—firmly builded. And to denote its divine origin and transcendent excellence, it is termed a city "whose builder and maker is God." It is thus opposed to all earthly cities, which are built by man's hands, just as the Apostle distinguishes the heavenly sanctuary from the earthly by describing it as being "made without hands," and as he distinguishes the resurrection body from the "earthly house of this tabernacle," as "a house not made with hands, eternal in the heavens."

According to the Apostle, then, Abraham expected true, permanent happiness from God in a future state. This expectation must have been founded on a revelation made to him, and believed by him. Our Lord teaches us that the promise of immortality and the resurrection is implied in the promise, "I will be a God to thee;" and there is nothing improbable in the supposition, that the patriarchs may have had clearer revelations of a future state made to them than any that are recorded in Scripture. If we admit the inspiration of this Epistle, it is plain, however we may explain it, that Abraham did cherish an expectation of permanent and perfect happiness in a future world.

All that remains to be explained, is the connection in which the words in the 10th verse stand to the preceding statement. If the word *for* be understood in its most usual sense, as expressing the reason of a previous assertion, then the meaning is—'Abraham's expectation of permanent, perfect happiness in heaven, enabled him patiently to submit to all the inconvenience of a state of pilgrimage in Canaan during the period which was to elapse before that land became the inheritance of his posterity.' If the word *for* be understood, as it often must, as merely connective, as equivalent to 'moreover,' then the meaning is—'Abraham's expectation that God would in His own time fulfil the promise, that Canaan was to be the inheritance of his posterity, induced him to continue in that country, though but a pilgrim and sojourner. But Abraham had higher expectations than this. He not only expected for his posterity a secure settlement in Canaan, but he expected for

## GENERAL EXHORTATION AND WARNING. 513

himself an everlasting abode in heaven.' It matters very little in which of these two ways the connection is explained.[1]

The great practical truth intended to be taught us by this passage of Scripture is, that it is the faith of the Gospel, producing the expectation of eternal life, that can alone enable a person cheerfully to submit to all the privations and sufferings connected with the Christian life, and induce him, "by a patient continuance in well-doing, to seek," so as to obtain, "glory, honour, and immortality."

The design of the paragraph which follows, is to show, from the history of Abraham, that faith is not only efficacious in enabling men to perform difficult duties and to endure severe trials, but also to obtain important blessings. Vers. 11, 12. "Through faith also Sara herself received strength to conceive seed, and was delivered of a child when she was past age, because she judged Him faithful who had promised. Therefore sprang there even of one, and him as good as dead, so many as the stars of the sky in multitude, and as the sand which is by the sea-shore innumerable." The substance of this statement is—'Through believing, Abraham and Sarah, though arrived at a time of life when, according to the ordinary course of nature, it was not to be expected that they would have any children, became the founders of a family numerous as the stars of heaven, or as the sand along the sea-shore.' This blessing was conferred on them as *believers*. It was as the gracious reward of their faith that they obtained this high honour.

Some learned interpreters have supposed that it is Abraham's faith alone that is spoken of in this paragraph, and that the Apostle's intention is to say, 'As the reward of Abraham's faith, Sarah became fruitful, and brought him a son, from whom sprang innumerable descendants.' The words, however, certainly seem

---

[1] Wakefield's note on these verses does credit to his taste. "Nowhere will you find words of more choice elegance. Παροικεῖν means to reside temporarily ; κατοικεῖν, to have as one's fixed abode. In that country, therefore, they lived as temporary residents ('strangers'), and always in tents; they were inhabitants of a sure home in another's country; they were soon to leave the former land, but would never leave the latter as long as they lived. And their movable tents, pitched on the face of the ground ('earthly'), to be shifted hither and thither as occasion arose, are elegantly contrasted with the city established upon foundations (see Is. xxxviii. 12, LXX). And τεχνίτης is he who executes the design of a building ; δημιουργός, he who builds it. Hence our translators should have rendered, as they quite easily could have done—'whose *contriver* and builder is God'."

more naturally to refer to Sarah's faith. The facts of the case seem to have been these :—Jehovah appeared to Abraham, and promised that he should have a son by his wife Sarah. The promise was afterwards repeated in the hearing of Sarah, who laughed at it within herself as a thing incredible, considering the advanced age of herself and her husband; and afterwards, through fear, she denied that she laughed; so that she was in the first instance guilty both of unbelief and of falsehood. But when she found that the hidden reasonings of her heart had been detected by the divine Messenger—when she heard Him put the silencing question, "Is anything too hard for the Lord?" and received from Him new assurances that she certainly would become a mother,—she perceived that the promise was the word of Him who was able to do as He had said, however inconsistent with the ordinary course of nature; and she no longer laughed at the promise, but believed it, reckoning that He who had promised was faithful. As the gracious reward of her faith, Sarah obtained strength to lay the foundation of a race or family; for so the words may be, and so we apprehend they ought to have been rendered.[1] The meaning of the whole verse is—' To Sarah the believer God gave the high honour of being the mother of His peculiar people.'

The connective particle *therefore* seems to me equivalent to —' for this cause ;' *i.e.*, Because of faith, through means of believing, "there sprang of one, and him as good as dead,"—or in reference to these things, dead,—" so many as the stars of the sky in multitude, and as the sand which is by the sea-shore innumerable." It is not necessary to enter into a minute examination of these words. The general sentiment is, plainly, ' Abraham and Sarah, through believing, obtained a high honour, an important privilege,—the honour and privilege of being the founders of the holy nation,—an honour and privilege, the attainment of which

---

[1] καταβολή signifies 'foundation,' ch. iv. 3, ix. 26 ; σπέρμα signifies ' a family—offspring,' ch. ii. 16, ver. 18 *inf.* The Latins says, "fundare domum" or "familiam." Euripides, Herc. Fur. 1261, uses the verb καταβάλλομαι in this sense. This is the exegesis of Ernesti, C. F. Schmid, Cramer, Böhme, and Kuinoel. It is greatly preferable to scarcely decent interpretations of many critics. The manner in which some critics contrive to introduce discussions of an indelicate kind into works of Scripture interpretation, a fault by no means uncommon, is exceedingly revolting to every rightly constituted mind. "A lewd interpreter is never just."

at the time it was promised to them was highly improbable—was all but impossible, which nothing but faith in God could have led them to expect, which without faith in God they would never have obtained.'

It is not difficult to see how this statement was calculated to gain the Apostle's object. God had made promises to the Christian Hebrews, the fulfilment of which seemed to involve as great difficulties at least as the fulfilment of the promise made to Abraham. The language of Abraham's example to them was, "Fear not, only believe." All the blessings and honours included in the salvation that is in Christ with eternal glory— all these will assuredly be yours, if ye continue to "count Him faithful who has promised." Whatever difficulties, whatever apparent impossibilities, lie in the way, like Abraham, "be strong in faith, and give glory to God;" be fully persuaded that "what He has promised He is able to perform;" be fully persuaded that "He cannot deny Himself;" "against hope, believe in hope,"—*i.e.*, confidently expect what but for the divine promise it would have been folly, it would have been presumption, to have expected. Abraham did so, and his hope did not make him ashamed. "Go ye and do likewise," and your hope shall not make you ashamed nor confounded, world without end.

But let us never forget that it was God's testimony and promise which Abraham believed, and not a figment of his own imagination. Let us take heed that it is God's testimony and promise that we believe—let us take heed that we really *believe* it—let us take care to cherish no hope but what that testimony and promise warrant; and then it is impossible for us to believe too firmly, or to hope too confidently.

The importance of *persevering* faith is plainly an idea which the Apostle wished to impress on the minds of those to whom he was writing; and to gain this object, he turns their attention to the instructive fact, that the ancient saints of whom he had been speaking continued believers as long as they continued in this world. They lived believing, and they died believing. Vers. 13–16. "These all died in faith, not having received the promises, but having seen them afar off, and were persuaded of them, and embraced them, and confessed that they were strangers and pilgrims on the earth. For they that say such things declare plainly that they seek a country. And truly, if they had been mindful of that country from whence they came out, they might have had opportunity to have returned: but now they desire a better country, that is, an heavenly: wherefore God is not ashamed to be called their God; for He hath prepared for them a city."

The expression, "all these," does not refer to the whole of the ancient saints mentioned in the previous context, for Enoch never died at all; and though Abel and Noah died, and died in faith, yet from the 15th verse it is plain that the expression refers only to the whole of the persons last mentioned as sojourners in the land of Canaan, Abraham and Sarah, Isaac and Jacob. "They all died *in faith;*" *i.e.*, they all died believers—they all died expecting the fulfilment of the divine promises. They had lived in this faith, and they died in it. They had not indeed "received the promises," *i.e.*, the promised blessings. They had not received the inheritance of Canaan—they had not received the blessings connected with the coming of that illustrious descendant of Abraham, " in whom all the nations of the earth were to be blessed;" but they saw these blessings "afar off," *i.e.*, they knew that at a future period—with regard to some of them a distant period—the promise would certainly be fulfilled. They "were persuaded of them." These words are not to be found in the most valuable MSS., or in any of the ancient versions or commentators, and are probably a comparatively modern interpolation. They add nothing to the sense. They merely give the meaning of the previous figurative expression, they "saw them afar off,"[1] and they "embraced them." They were not only persuaded of the truth and certainty of the promises, but also of the goodness of the things promised. The blessings promised were the objects of their desire, esteem, and affection; and in consequence of this—in consequence of their placing their chief affection on objects which they knew they were never to enjoy in this world—they "confessed that they were strangers and pilgrims on the earth." Abraham did so when he wished to purchase, not an inheritance for himself living, but a sepulchre

---

[1] The ἐπαγγελίαι, the promised blessings, are represented as coasts which the seafaring man descries at a distance. Virgil has a similar expression:

" Quum procul obscuros colles humilemque videmus
 Italiam."—*Æn.* iii. 522, 523. THOLUCK.

for himself and his family when dead: "I am a stranger and a sojourner with you: give me a possession of a burying-place with you, that I may bury my dead out of my sight."[1] Jacob made the same confession to Pharaoh. He represents his own life and the life of his fathers as a pilgrimage: "And Jacob said unto Pharaoh, The days of the years of my pilgrimage are an hundred and thirty years: few and evil have the days of the years of my life been, and have not attained unto the days of the years of the life of my fathers, in the days of their pilgrimage."[2] This confession meant more than that they had not yet obtained the earthly inheritance. Long after Israel had entered into Canaan we find David saying, "Hear my prayer, O Lord, and give ear unto my cry; hold not Thy peace at my tears: for I am a stranger with Thee, and a sojourner, as all my fathers were." "I am a stranger in the earth; hide not Thy commandments from me."[3] We find him using this expression not only for himself, but for the whole congregation of Israel: "For we are strangers before Thee, and sojourners, as were all our fathers: our days on the earth are as a shadow, and there is none abiding."[4]

That the confession, that "they were strangers and sojourners," implied more than that they had not obtained that inheritance which they yet firmly believed their posterity would obtain, is plain from what follows: Ver. 14. "For they that say such things declare plainly that they seek a country."

They who confess that they are "pilgrims and strangers on the earth," and do so as long as they continue on the earth, by doing so, plainly[5] intimate that they are seeking a country which is not on earth.

The word rendered "country" is very expressive. It is exactly rendered by a word lately borrowed from the German, and scarcely yet fully naturalized in our language, *fatherland*—a country where a man's father dwells, which he possesses as his own, and in which his children have a right to dwell with him. Thus it is exactly opposed to a strange or foreign land. That it was not their earthly fatherland that they were seeking,

---

[1] Gen. xxiii. 4.  
[2] Gen. xlvii. 9.  
[3] Ps. xxxix. 12, cxix. 19.  
[4] 1 Chron. xxix. 15.  
[5] ἐμφανίζουσιν—'they did not conceal it.' This is the word used by the LXX., Isa. iii. 9, to render לֹא כִחֵדוּ.

is plain. Abraham at God's command had renounced that; "and indeed," ver. 15, "if they had been mindful of that country from whence they came out, they might have had opportunity to have returned."

The country of Terah, their father, where their natural relations had possessions, was Chaldea; and if it had been it that they were seeking, they might easily have returned to it. From the call of Abraham to the death of Jacob was a space of 200 years. During this period they might easily have returned to Chaldea. The distance was no obstacle. There does not seem to have been any external obstruction. But they gave clear evidence that they were not disposed to return. Abraham takes an oath of his servant that he will not endeavour to induce Isaac to return to that land. Jacob indeed went thither; but there he would not stay, and through innumerable dangers returned to Canaan. 'No,' says the Apostle; 'they were indeed seeking a country, but it was a better country, even a heavenly one.' They looked for true happiness in a future state. They expected the complete fulfilment of the promise, "I will be thy God," in heaven.

"Wherefore," or *for this cause,* "God is not ashamed to be called their God; for He hath prepared for them a city." God had "prepared for them a city;" *i.e.,* in plain terms, 'God had secured for them immutable, eternal happiness in heaven;' and because He had done so, He "was not ashamed to be called their God." The idea here, I apprehend, is not the condescension on the part of God in taking the name of the God of the patriarch, but the inconceivable glory and blessedness of that final state which He has prepared for them. It is a glory and happiness worthy of God to bestow on those who are the objects of His peculiar love. In preparing *such* a city for them, and in bringing them to it, He fully answers all the expectations which His calling Himself their God, and calling them His people, could awaken in their minds. When "brought home to glory," every one of His people will be disposed to say, 'Now I understand what is meant by the promise, "I will be thy God." He has done all that He said; He has done more than it ever could have entered into my mind to conceive. He has no reason to be ashamed when he calls Himself *my God.*'

These remarks of the Apostle (vers. 13–16), though in some

measure a digression, are well fitted to gain his great object. It is as if he had said, 'The grand ultimate object of the faith and hope of the patriarchs was not Canaan, nor the blessings of the external economy to be established there; it was substantially the very same object which Christianity more clearly holds out to our faith and hope—spiritual, eternal happiness in the enjoyment of God in heaven.' Religion is materially the same thing in all countries and ages. Are we in possession of it?

Another very striking illustration of the efficacy of faith in enabling to sustain a very severe trial, to perform a very difficult duty, and to obtain a very important blessing, is contained in the paragraph which follows, vers. 17-19. The passage of Old Testament history referred to is one of the most interesting in the sacred volume. "And it came to pass after these things, that God did tempt Abraham, and said unto him, Abraham. And he said, Behold, here I am. And He said, Take now thy son, thine only son Isaac, whom thou lovest, and get thee into the land of Moriah; and offer him there for a burnt-offering upon one of the mountains which I will tell thee of. And Abraham rose up early in the morning, and saddled his ass, and took two of his young men with him, and Isaac his son, and clave the wood for the burnt-offering, and rose up, and went unto the place of which God had told him. Then on the third day Abraham lifted up his eyes, and saw the place afar off. And Abraham said unto his young men, Abide ye here with the ass; and I and the lad will go yonder and worship, and come again to you. And Abraham took the wood of the burnt-offering, and laid it upon Isaac his son; and he took the fire in his hand, and a knife; and they went both of them together. And Isaac spake unto Abraham his father, and said, My father: and he said, Here am I, my son. And he said, Behold the fire and the wood; but where is the lamb for a burnt-offering? And Abraham said, My son, God will provide Himself a lamb for a burnt-offering: so they went both of them together. And they came to the place which God had told him of; and Abraham built an altar there, and laid the wood in order, and bound Isaac his son, and laid him on the altar upon the wood. And Abraham stretched forth his hand, and took the knife to slay his son. And the Angel of the Lord called unto him out of heaven, and said, Abraham, Abraham. And he said, Here am I. And He said, Lay not thine hand upon the lad, neither do thou anything unto him: for now I know that thou fearest God, seeing thou hast not withheld thy son, thine only son, from Me. And Abraham lifted up his eyes, and looked, and behold behind him a ram caught in a thicket by his horns: and Abraham went and took the ram, and offered him up for a burnt-offering in the stead of his son. And Abraham called the name of that place Jehovah-jireh: as it is said to this day, In the mount of the Lord it shall be seen. And the Angel of the Lord called unto Abraham out of heaven the second time, and said, By Myself have I sworn, saith the Lord; for because thou hast done this thing, and hast not withheld thy son, thine only son: that in blessing I will bless thee, and in multiplying I will multiply thy seed as the stars of the heaven, and as the sand which is upon the sea-shore; and thy seed shall possess the gate of his enemies: and in thy seed shall all the nations of the earth be blessed; because thou hast obeyed My voice."[1] Such is the inspired narrative.

Let us now attend to the Apostle's inspired annotations. "By faith Abraham, when he was tried, offered up Isaac: and he that had received the promises offered up his only begotten son, of whom it was said, That in Isaac shall thy seed be called: accounting that God was able to raise him up, even from the dead; from whence also he received him in a figure."

The whole of the Apostle's statements are reducible to the following propositions:—Abraham sustained a very severe trial;

[1] Gen. xxii. 1-18.—The audacity of the German neological interpreters is amusingly displayed in the manner they dispose of this narrative. "The Canaanites, among whom Abraham was living, were in the habit of sacrificing human beings, especially children. One day the patriarch, who was convinced that human sacrifices were offensive to God, had heard that his neighbour had appeased God with human victims. A dream brought back to him his waking thoughts in the manner that we read of in Gen. xxii, and strongly confirmed his conviction that God hates sacrifices of that sort. He told his dream to the members of his household. The story was spread by word of mouth, and came to take the form that the things that had happened in his dreams had really happened; and in this form it was consigned to writing."—GREVERUS, *in Comm. Misc. Syntag.*, Oldenburg, 1794, p. 94. Whatever Abraham did, there is no doubt this interpreter dreamed, when he wrote this; and unless men are themselves under the influence of the πνεῦμα κατανύξεως, Rom. xi. 8, they will but laugh at such dreamers and such dreams.

Abraham performed a very difficult duty; Abraham obtained a very important blessing; and it was through believing that he did all this. It was his faith which enabled him thus to suffer, thus to act, and thus to obtain.

Abraham sustained a very severe trial. "He was *tried.*" In these words the Apostle obviously refers to the first verse of the 22d chapter of Genesis. The words used, both in Genesis and in the passage before us, signify, either 'to put to trial,' or 'to tempt,' *i.e.*, to solicit to sin; and in order to know which of these two senses it bears in any particular passage, it is necessary to inquire what is the character of the agent who occasions the trial or temptation, and the objects which he has in view. Wherever God is represented as tempting men—as in the case before us—the word is to be understood in the sense of trial. "Let no man," says the Apostle James, "say, when he is tempted"—*i.e.*, plainly, to commit sin—"that he is tempted of God: for God cannot be tempted of evil, neither tempteth He any man." He never deceives any man's judgment; He never corrupts any man's affections; He never does anything that can make Him chargeable with the blame of men's sins. In the case before us, Abraham was not solicited to sin; but a trial was made of the reality and of the strength of his principles of faith and obedience.

When we speak of God's trying men, we are not to suppose that He needs to discover by experiment what is their real character. He knows what is in them before the trial, He knows beforehand what will be the effect of the trial; but He thus makes men's characters known to themselves and to their fellow-men, for ends worthy of His own infinite wisdom, righteousness, and kindness. It also deserves to be noticed that the means which God employs to prove His people are fitted to improve them. The means He employs to discover the good that is in them are calculated to increase and perfect it; the means He employs to discover the evil that is in them are calculated to lessen and destroy it. The means of Abraham's trial was the command recorded in the 2d verse of the 22d chapter of Genesis. The commandment was given apparently in such a manner as left Abraham no room to doubt that it was the commandment of Jehovah. Without this, there had been no sufficient ground for faith, or for the trial of faith.

This trial of faith was perhaps as severe as ever was experienced. He is commanded to do a thing for which no reason could be assigned but the will of Him who gave the command. He is commanded to do what was most abhorrent to natural, and to innocent, praiseworthy, natural feeling. He must not only consent to the death of a son, but he must with his own hand put him to death; and he must do this, not while his mind is warm and agitated by the divine communication, but after an interval of some days, during the whole of which the revolting deed, in all its horrors, must be before his mind. And then such a son!—the son of his old age—a son just at that time of life when the opening faculties and affections made him an object of peculiar fond regard to a father—a son, too, we have reason to believe, of the most amiable dispositions and most engaging manners. He is commanded to do what is, apparently, equally inconsistent with the divine command and the divine promise. The sacredness of human life was a principle very distinctly stated in the revelation made to man after the deluge: "I will require the life of man of the hand of his brother. Whosoever sheddeth man's blood, by man shall his blood be shed." The apparent incongruity between such a statute and a command to put to death a human being who had been guilty of no crime, was well fitted to try the reality and strength of Abraham's faith. Besides, God had promised to Abraham a numerous posterity, through whom the most important blessings were to be communicated to mankind at large; and it had been distinctly stated to him, that "in Isaac his seed should be called;" *i.e.*, that the posterity in reference to whom these glorious predictions had been given forth, were to be the descendants of Isaac. Isaac had yet no children; and his death at this period, in any circumstances, seemed to lay the gravestone on Abraham's hopes, rendering the accomplishment of them altogether impossible. It is quite natural to suppose also that such thoughts as the following would suggest themselves to his mind:—' How will Sarah bear this awful bereavement? Isaac's death in any circumstances would probably bring down her grey hairs in sorrow to the grave. How will it be possible for me to inform her of this awful mandate, or, more dreadful still, of that awful mandate having been executed? What effect will this apparently most unnatural action have on the minds of the surrounding inhabitants, who know not Jehovah? Must they not account me a monster, and my Divinity a demon?'

Such was the trial to which Abraham was exposed. But he sustained the trial. He yielded obedience to the apparently unreasonable and hard command. He performed the difficult and all but impracticable duty. He "offered his son," says the Apostle.[1] We know that he did not actually slay his son and burn his body; but he laid him on the altar, his hand was lifted up to inflict the fatal blow, and the sacrificial pile was prepared and ready to be lighted up. The sacrifice on the part of Abraham was essentially offered up. Whatever inward workings of natural affection there may have been, however strange and unaccountable the command may have appeared to him, Abraham seems never for a moment to have hesitated. He rises early in the morning which succeeded the night when the divine communication was made to him, makes the necessary preparations, commences his journey, and loses no time in reaching the spot which he believed destined for the fearful sacrifice; and even there, there is no trace of hesitation, or even reluctance to execute the will of Jehovah in the immolation of a child inconceivably dear to him. Never was a human being, perhaps, called to a more difficult duty; and never, perhaps, was any duty performed in a spirit of more perfect submission of mind and heart to the will of God.

But Abraham is represented as not only sustaining a very severe trial, and performing a very difficult duty, but as obtaining a very important blessing. He receives his son from the dead as "in a figure."[2] It seems to me not probable that the

---

[1] προσενήνοχεν, 'showed himself ready to offer:' John viii. 27, xiv. 17; Acts xxi. 13. The word, like our English word *offer*, has a general meaning, as well as the particular meaning of *present in sacrifice*. It is well rendered by C. F. Schmid, "he led him forward like a victim to sacrifice." As Salvian says, "as far as the action of his heart was concerned, he sacrificed him."—*De gubern. Dei*, lib. i.

[2] ὅθεν may be rendered either *unde* or *quare*: 'whence'—that is, ἐκ νεκρῶν—or ' for which reason,' διὰ πίστιν, manifested in his readiness to obey. In the first sense it occurs, Matt. xiv. 7; Acts xxvi. 19, = ἐξ οὗ ; in the second, Heb. ii. 17, iii. 1, vii. 25, viii. 3, ix. 18. The words, αὐτὸν καὶ ἐν παραβολῇ ἐκομίσατο, are among the δυσνόητα, 2 Pet. iii. 16. They admit, and as a matter of course they have received, a great variety of interpretation. Most consider the words, ἐν παραβολῇ, as meaning, 'in a similitude,'

Apostle, in showing the influence of faith, not only in enabling men to sustain trials and perform duties, but also to obtain benefits, would neglect to avail himself of the very striking illustration afforded by this very remarkable event. In Abraham's estimation, and in his own, Isaac was as it were already dead, and God as it were restored him from the dead. Isaac's restoration to Abraham in these circumstances must have been felt as a greater blessing than his bestowal at first, especially when connected, as it was, with a most gracious declaration of the divine approbation, and a renewal of the " exceeding great and precious promises" which had been formerly made to him.

Now the Apostle's assertion is, that it was *by faith*, or through believing, that Abraham sustained this trial, performed this duty, and obtained this benefit. Let us inquire into the nature and extent of this influence of faith.

It was faith which enabled him to sustain the trial. Had he not believed that God is infinitely wise, and powerful, and faithful, and good; and had he not believed that the command to offer up his son came from God, as well as the promise that in him should his seed be called,—had he not believed this, it is obvious that he could not have sustained the trial to which he was exposed; and it is equally obvious that a sufficiently

---

'as it were;' but they explain this similitude variously. Some refer it to his having received Isaac ἐκ τῆς νεκρᾶς μήτρας Σάῤῥας,—from a mother as good as dead. But the words seem to refer to something subsequent to his offering Isaac—the reward of his offering him. Others consider it as saying that he received Isaac as a type of his great descendant, who was to be really offered, and really to rise from the dead. We should need a new revelation to assure us that this is the meaning. Others, as an image or type of the resurrection of the dead generally. This is equally unsupported; it is entirely arbitrary. Others have considered ἐν παραβολῇ as = 'in circumstances of great danger,'—as if it were παρ' ἐλπίδα; but this is not satisfactorily supported, though I find, to my surprise, Tholuck adopting this view. Others consider ἐν παραβολῇ as equivalent to—'with an oracular declaration,' and suppose the reference to be to the declaration made by God to Abraham, Gen. xxii. 12, 16–18; and consider the use of the word παραβολή as applied to Balaam's oracles, Num. xxiii. 7, 18, xxiv. 3, 15, 20, as supporting this view of it. This is ingenious, but too ingenious to be satisfactory,—*arguta*, not *simplex*. By far the simplest and most satisfactory interpretation adopted, is that which considers the words as = 'he received him *as it were*,' quodammodo—not actually, but ἐν παραβολῃ, ἐν ὁμοιώματι—'from the dead.'

firm faith in these truths was quite adequate to produce the effects which we know were produced.

It was this which enabled him to perform a duty so peculiarly difficult. Had he been weak in faith, he would have doubted whether two revelations, apparently inconsistent, could come from the same God, or, if they did, whether such a God ought to be trusted to or obeyed. But being strong in faith, he reasoned in this way : 'This is plainly God's command. I have satisfactory evidence of that ; and therefore it ought to be immediately and implicitly obeyed. I know Him to be infinitely wise and righteous, and what He commands must be right. Obedience to this command does indeed seem to throw obstacles in the way of the fulfilment of a number of promises which God has made to me. I am quite sure God has made these promises. I am quite sure that He will perform them. How He is to perform them, I cannot tell. That is His province, not mine. It is His to promise, and mine to believe—His to command, and mine to obey—His to bestow blessings, and mine to receive them; but I am persuaded that, sooner than let these promises fail of accomplishment, God will reanimate the ashes of my Isaac, and that in him, though offered up as a burnt-offering, my seed shall yet be called.' He was persuaded "that God was able even to raise him from the dead." You thus see how it was through believing that Abraham performed this very difficult duty.

It is equally plain that it was through believing that Abraham obtained the great blessing of receiving his beloved Isaac, as "in a figure," from the dead. This important favour was conferred on Abraham as the gracious reward of his believing. It was indeed the reward of his submission and obedience ; but that submission and obedience were the result of his believing.

The bearing which this statement has on the Apostle's object is direct and obvious. The Christian Hebrews were exposed to severe trials, called to difficult duties, and they had promises made to them which, if they "consulted with flesh and blood," they must have supposed were not very likely ever to be performed. How are these trials to be endured, these duties to be performed, these benefits to be obtained ? Look to Abraham. Are your trials more severe than his ? are your duties more difficult than his ? are the blessings you look for less likely to be conferred on you than the blessings which were promised to him, and which in due time were all performed to him? How did he sustain the trial? how did he perform the duty? how did he obtain the blessing? By believing. "Go ye and do likewise." Without faith, any trial becomes insupportable, any duty becomes impracticable. With faith, no trial is insupportable, no duty is impracticable; nay, every trial, every duty, is easy. Of such infinite importance is it that we believe, and persevere in believing. A very natural practical reflection from what has been said is, that Christians should not be afraid of trials, nor backward to submit to them, when God calls them to it. Abraham's trial, though as severe a one as any saint ever met with, was meant in kindness, and in effect was conducive both to his spiritual improvement and to his true happiness. Who would not willingly endure Abraham's trial to obtain Abraham's reward? Trials are necessary to the saint in the present state. There is a 'need be' that we be "in heaviness through manifold trials." Yet ought Christians "to count it all joy when they are brought into manifold trials, knowing that the trying of faith worketh patience," or rather perseverance. "Tribulation worketh patience; patience, experience; and experience, hope." "No chastisement for the present is joyous, but grievous; but it yieldeth the peaceable fruits of righteousness to those who are exercised thereby." "The trial of our faith, which is more precious than that of gold, will be found to glory and honour at the coming of our Lord Jesus Christ." Let us never forget, however, that, in order to our trials being useful to us, they must be endured in faith. "Our afflictions will work out for us a far more exceeding and an eternal weight of glory, if"—but only if—"we look not at the things which are seen and temporal, but at the things which are unseen and eternal." No spiritual child of Abraham need expect an exemption from trials—from severe trials. These are not to be courted, but neither are they to be sinfully shunned. They are to be submitted to in a humble dependence on Him who supported and strengthened Abraham, and who says to all His people in their trials, "My grace is sufficient for you; My strength shall be made perfect in weakness." A firm faith in this will carry us through the severest trials triumphantly; and "we shall be made more than conquerors through Him that loves us."

We have three new witnesses brought forward to the importance of faith, in the 20th, 21st, and 22d verses—Isaac, Jacob, and Joseph. " By faith Isaac blessed Jacob and Esau concerning things to come. By faith Jacob, when he was a dying, blessed both the sons of Joseph; and worshipped, leaning upon the top of his staff. By faith Joseph, when he died, made mention of the departing of the children of Israel; and gave commandment concerning his bones."

The general principle contained in these statements seems to be this: Faith enabled Isaac, and Jacob, and Joseph to do what otherwise they could not have done—to pronounce prophetic benedictions on their posterity, which in succeeding ages were accurately accomplished. Now, fully to apprehend the meaning and design of the Apostle's statements, it will be necessary that we first attend to the facts to which he refers—to what Isaac and Jacob did; then show how it was through believing that they did what they did; and, lastly, point out the manner in which this illustrates the importance of faith, and serves the Apostle's object—the placing in a clear point of light the necessity of the Hebrew Christians persevering in the faith of the Gospel, notwithstanding all the temptations to apostasy to which they were exposed.

The facts to which the Apostle refers in the 20th verse are recorded in the 27th chapter of the book of Genesis. " And it came to pass, that when Isaac was old, and his eyes were dim, so that he could not see, he called Esau his eldest son, and said unto him, My son. And he said unto him, Behold, here am I. And he said, Behold now, I am old, I know not the day of my death. Now therefore take, I pray thee, thy weapons, thy quiver and thy bow, and go out to the field, and take me some venison; and make me savoury meat, such as I love, and bring it to me, that I may eat; that my soul may bless thee before I die. And Rebekah heard when Isaac spake to Esau his son. And Esau went to the field to hunt for venison, and to bring it. And Rebekah spake unto Jacob her son, saying, Behold, I heard thy father speak unto Esau thy brother, saying, Bring me venison, and make me savoury meat, that I may eat, and bless thee before the Lord before my death. Now therefore, my son, obey my voice, according to that which I command thee. Go now to the flock, and fetch me from thence two good kids of the goats; and I will make them savoury meat for thy father, such as he loveth. And thou shalt bring it to thy father, that he may eat, and that he may bless thee before his death. And Jacob said to Rebekah his mother, Behold, Esau my brother is a hairy man, and I am a smooth man: my father peradventure will feel me, and I shall seem to him as a deceiver; and I shall bring a curse upon me, and not a blessing. And his mother said unto him, Upon me be thy curse, my son; only obey my voice, and go fetch me them. And he went, and fetched, and brought them to his mother: and his mother made savoury meat, such as his father loved. And Rebekah took goodly raiment of her eldest son Esau, which were with her in the house, and put them upon Jacob her younger son. And she put the skins of the kids of the goats upon his hands, and upon the smooth of his neck. And she gave the savoury meat and the bread, which she had prepared, into the hand of her son Jacob. And he came unto his father, and said, My father. And he said, Here am I; who art thou, my son? And Jacob said unto his father, I am Esau thy first-born; I have done according as thou badest me: arise, I pray thee, sit and eat of my venison, that thy soul may bless me. And Isaac said unto his son, How is it that thou hast found it so quickly, my son? And he said, Because the Lord thy God brought it to me. And Isaac said unto Jacob, Come near, I pray thee, that I may feel thee, my son, whether thou be my very son Esau or not. And Jacob went near unto Isaac his father; and he felt him, and said, The voice is Jacob's voice, but the hands are the hands of Esau. And he discerned him not, because his hands were hairy, as his brother Esau's hands. So he blessed him. And he said, Art thou my very son Esau? And he said, I am. And he said, Bring it near to me, and I will eat of my son's venison, that my soul may bless thee. And he brought it near to him, and he did eat: and he brought him wine, and he drank. And his father Isaac said unto him, Come near now, and kiss me, my son. And he came near, and kissed him: and he smelled the smell of his raiment, and blessed him, and said, See, the smell of my son is as the smell of a field which the Lord hath blessed: therefore God give thee of the dew of heaven, and the fatness of the earth, and plenty of corn and wine: let people serve thee, and nations bow down to thee: be lord over thy brethren, and let thy mother's sons bow down to thee: cursed be every one that curseth thee, and blessed be he that blesseth thee. And it came to pass, as soon as Isaac had made an end of blessing Jacob, and Jacob was yet scarce gone out from the presence of Isaac his father, that Esau his brother came in from his hunting. And he also had made savoury meat, and brought it unto his father, and said unto his father, Let my father arise, and eat of his son's venison, that thy soul may bless me. And Isaac his father said unto him, Who art thou? And he said, I am thy son, thy first-born, Esau. And Isaac trembled very exceedingly, and said, Who? where is he that hath taken venison, and brought it me, and I have eaten of all before thou camest, and have blessed him? yea, and he shall be blessed. And when Esau heard the words of his father, he cried with a great and exceeding bitter cry, and said unto his father, Bless me, even me also, O my father! And he said, Thy brother came with subtilty, and hath taken away thy blessing. And he said, Is not he rightly named Jacob? for he hath supplanted me these two times: he took away my birthright; and, behold, now he hath taken away my blessing. And he said, Hast thou not reserved a blessing for me? And Isaac answered and said unto Esau, Behold, I have made him thy lord, and all his brethren have I given to him for servants; and with corn and wine have I sustained him: and what shall I do now unto thee, my son? And Esau said unto his father, Hast thou but one blessing, my father? bless me, even me also, O my father! And Esau lifted up his voice, and wept. And Isaac his father answered and said unto him, Behold, thy dwelling shall be the fatness of the earth, and of the dew of heaven from above; and by thy sword shalt thou live, and shalt serve thy brother; and it shall come to pass, when thou shalt have the dominion, that thou shalt break his yoke from off thy neck."[1] Thus " Isaac blessed Jacob and Esau concerning things to come;" *i.e.*, he pronounced a prophetic benediction[2]—for that is the import of the original word —first on Jacob, and then on Esau, in reference to events which were to take place in future ages. The blessing pronounced on Jacob runs in these terms (vers. 28, 29): " God give thee of the dew of heaven, and the fatness of the earth, and plenty of corn and wine: let people serve thee, and nations bow down to thee:

---

[1] Gen. xxvii. 1–40.   [2] εὐλογεῖν.

be lord over thy brethren, and let thy mother's sons bow down to thee: cursed be every one that curseth thee, and blessed be he that blesseth thee." The blessing pronounced on Esau runs thus: "Behold, thy dwelling shall be the fatness of the earth, and of the dew of heaven from above; and by thy sword shalt thou live, and shalt serve thy brother; and it shall come to pass, when thou shalt have the dominion, that thou shalt break his yoke from off thy neck." Both these prophetic benedictions respecting "things to come" were in due time fully and minutely realized. Such are the facts of the case as to Isaac.

Now the question naturally occurs, How was it *by faith* that Isaac pronounced these benedictions? The answer to that question is: A revelation was made to the mind of Isaac by God respecting the events which were to occur to his descendants in future times. Isaac firmly believed this revelation; and it was his faith in this revelation that led him to utter these prophetic benedictions. In ordinary circumstances, no wise man will be very minute or very confident in his statements respecting future events. But we see Isaac, believing the divine revelation, speaking with perfect confidence and with great minuteness "concerning things to come;" and we see also the event justifying the confidence with which he spoke. Though the events were, some of them, of a very improbable kind,—such as that the children of one who was but a stranger and sojourner, having no property but a burying-place, were to be numerous and powerful nations,—yet Isaac, believing that the revelation came from God, and having no doubt respecting the power and the faithfulness of the Revealer, unhesitatingly uttered the prediction.

There is indeed a difficulty connected with this subject, that is likely to suggest itself to the reflecting mind, arising out of the circumstance, that Isaac conceived that he was pronouncing a benediction on Esau when he uttered Jacob's blessing. The difficulty is more apparent than real. The revelation made to Isaac's mind was, that the events to which that benediction refers were to take place respecting the posterity of the individual who was now before him. That was Jacob, though Isaac supposed him Esau. And that this was the truth, is plain from the fact, that when Isaac discovered his mistake, he does not say, 'The blessing was originally intended for Esau, and therefore will be his, though through my mistake it was pronounced over his brother;' but he says, "I have blessed him, and he shall be blessed;"—plainly intimating two things: that in the revelation made to him, the reference was to the person before him; and that in uttering it, he merely declared the will and determination of Him "whose counsel shall stand, and who will do all His pleasure." The whole transaction is a striking proof of what the Apostle says, "The prophecy of old time came not by the will of man, but holy men spake as they were moved by the Holy Ghost." Isaac had too firm a faith in the unalterableness of the divine determinations to suppose for a moment that his private affection could transfer the superior blessing from his younger to his elder son.

The next inquiry that suggests itself is, How does this statement, that "by faith Isaac blessed Jacob and Esau concerning things to come," subserve the Apostle's object—the impressing on the minds of the Hebrew Christians the importance and necessity of their persevering in faith in order to their performing their duties, enduring their trials, and obtaining their inheritance as Christians? It plainly illustrates this general principle: 'Faith can enable a man to do what nothing else could enable him to do. What but faith in a divine revelation could have enabled Isaac, or any man, to utter predictions referring to distant ages, which predictions were in due time accurately fulfilled?' The Hebrew Christians were called on to act, and suffer, and expect, in a way which nothing but faith could enable them to do. They were required to "deny themselves, take up their cross, and follow Christ;" they were required to "forsake father, and mother, and houses, and lands;" they were required to "cut off right hands, and to pluck out right eyes;" and they were called on, amid all this, to cherish an unsuspecting dependence on the divine peculiar kindness, and an unclouded hope of glory, honour, and immortality. To do all this, was really, in a moral sense, as far out of their power as the prediction of future events, in a physical sense, was out of the power of Isaac. But as a faith in the revelation made to Isaac enabled him to do what otherwise he could not have done, so a faith in the revelation made to them would enable them to do what otherwise they could not have done. If they, knowing who and what Jesus Christ is—knowing His power, and His wisdom, and His faithfulness—firmly believed what He has said, that "whosoever believeth in Him shall not perish, but have everlasting life;" that whosoever denies Him shall be denied by Him, and whosoever confesses Him shall be confessed by Him, in the presence of His Father and the holy angels; that "it is the Father's good pleasure to give His people the kingdom,"—if they firmly believed this revelation, they would be enabled to do things as far exceeding the unassisted powers of man as predicting future events is—they would be brought under "the powers of the world to come," and be enabled to act, and to suffer, and to hope as "seeing the God that is invisible," and the world that is "unseen and eternal."

And as Isaac could not possibly have without faith prophetically blessed his children "concerning things to come," so neither could they without faith persevere in doing and suffering the will of God, and in looking for the mercy of God unto eternal life. Such, so far as I have been able to apprehend, is the force of the fact stated in the 20th verse, as affording an illustration of the importance of faith, and suggesting a motive to the Hebrew Christians to persevere in believing.

The next facts brought forward are quite of the same kind: —" By faith Jacob, when he was a dying, blessed both the sons of Joseph; and worshipped, leaning upon the top of his staff." " Jacob, when a dying," or drawing near death—when on his deathbed—like his father Isaac, under the influence of the Spirit of prediction, uttered prophetic benedictions respecting his posterity.

It is the ingenious conjecture of a learned interpreter, that the words, " of Joseph," did not originally belong to this verse, but were introduced by an early transcriber from the beginning of the next verse; and that the statement made by the inspired writer is, " Jacob, when dying, blessed each of his children." This certainly agrees with what we know to be the fact. He pronounced prophetic benedictions on all his children, which in the future history of their descendants were remarkably realized. He called his sons to him, and said, " Gather yourselves together, that I may tell you what shall befall you in the last days." You have a record of these prophetic benedictions in the 49th chapter of Genesis. And these were given " when a dying," in the strictest sense of the word; for "when he had made an end of commanding his sons, he gathered up his feet into the bed, and yielded up the ghost, and was gathered to his people."

At the same time, this, though an ingenious conjecture, is but a conjecture. The fact, as it is stated by the Apostle, agrees also with the history; and the mere circumstance of our thinking it more likely that he should refer to the blessing of all his children than to the blessing of Joseph's children, is no sufficient reason, in opposition to the uniform testimony of MSS. and versions, to conclude that there has been a change in the text. Considering, then, the present reading as correct, the facts referred to are these, recorded in the 48th chapter of Genesis. When Joseph heard that his father was sick, he went to visit him, along with his sons Manasseh and Ephraim. The history of their benediction cannot be so well told as in the words of the inspired historian :—" And Israel beheld Joseph's sons, and said, Who are these? And Joseph said unto his father, They are my sons, whom God hath given me in this place. And he said, Bring them, I pray thee, unto me, and I will bless them. (Now the eyes of Israel were dim for age, so that he could not see.) And he brought them near unto him; and he kissed them, and embraced them. And Israel said unto Joseph, I had not thought to see thy face; and, lo, God hath showed me also thy seed. And Joseph brought them out from between his knees, and he bowed himself with his face to the earth. And Joseph took them both, Ephraim in his right hand toward Israel's left hand, and Manasseh in his left hand toward Israel's right hand, and brought them near unto him. And Israel stretched out his right hand, and laid it upon Ephraim's head, who was the younger, and his left hand upon Manasseh's head, guiding his hands wittingly; for Manasseh was the first-born. And he blessed Joseph, and said, God, before whom my fathers Abraham and Isaac did walk, the God which fed me all my life long unto this day, the Angel which redeemed me from all evil, bless the lads; and let my name be named on them, and the name of my fathers Abraham and Isaac; and let them grow into a multitude in the midst of the earth. And when Joseph saw that his father laid his right hand upon the head of Ephraim, it displeased him: and he held up his father's hand, to remove it from Ephraim's head unto Manasseh's head. And Joseph said unto his father, Not so, my father: for this is the first-born; put thy right hand upon his head. And his father refused, and said, I know it, my son, I know it: he also shall become a people, and he also shall be great; but truly his younger brother shall be greater than he, and his seed shall become a multitude of nations. And he blessed them that day, saying, In thee shall Israel bless, saying, God make thee as Ephraim, and as Manasseh. And he set Ephraim before Manasseh."[1]

The words which the Apostle adds regarding Jacob, "and worshipped, leaning on the top of his staff," have by some been supposed merely to describe the circumstances in which the benediction of Ephraim and Manasseh was given. But we apprehend they refer to a different fact altogether, in which the power of faith was illustriously displayed. The fact referred to is recorded in the 47th chapter of Genesis. "And the time drew nigh that Israel must die: and he called his son Joseph, and said unto him, If now I have found grace in thy sight, put, I pray thee, thy hand under my thigh, and deal kindly and truly with me; bury me not, I pray thee, in Egypt: but I will lie with my fathers; and thou shalt carry me out of Egypt, and bury me in their burying-place. And he said, I will do as thou hast said. And he said, Swear unto me. And he sware unto him. And Israel bowed himself upon the bed's head."[2]

To remove the appearance of discrepancy which exists between the words of Moses and of Paul, it is but necessary to remark, that the word translated, to *bow himself*, often signifies 'to worship,' as bowing a person's self is an ordinary token or sign of religious worship; and that the word rendered "bed" by our translators in Genesis, and "staff" here, is a word which, according to the manner in which it is pointed, has the one or other of these significations.[3] The question is between the accuracy of the Masoretic punctuation, and the version of the LXX. and the Apostle's quotation.

[1] Gen. xlviii. 8-20.      [2] Gen. xlvii. 29-31.

[3] Great respect is due to the Masoretic punctuation, as generally the record of the ancient interpretation of the Hebrew Scriptures; but, as Mr Stuart justly remarks, "that the present vowel-points of the Hebrew do not in *every* case give the most probable sense of the original, will not appear strange to any one who reflects that they were introduced after the fifth century of our present era. All enlightened critics of the present day disclaim the idea that they are authoritative."

The reference does not seem to me to be so much to the fact taken by itself, as in connection with the other facts with which it is related in the sacred narrative. The words were intended to bring the whole scene before the mind, and in this way are equivalent to—'Jacob, when dying, by faith expressed an earnest desire to be buried in the land of promise; and on receiving satisfactory assurance that this wish would be complied with, testified his firm confidence in the promise—a belief in which excited this desire—by worshipping, bending over his staff, which was necessary to support his now enfeebled frame.'[1]

These are the facts: now let us see how it was *by faith* that Jacob did these things. The whole of the illustrations respecting Isaac's benediction of his sons, are plainly equally applicable to Jacob's benediction of his sons or grandsons. A revelation was made to Jacob's mind respecting their future fortunes; he believed it; and his faith in this revelation enabled him to do what otherwise he could not have done—predict what was to happen to his descendants through a long series of generations. With regard to the second fact: it plainly was Jacob's faith in the promise that Canaan was to be the inheritance of his posterity, and in the other promises connected with this, that led him to wish to be buried there, and not in the land of Egypt. The ordering that he should take enfeoffment of it, as it were, by his dead body, was a very strong expression of his full persuasion that in due time his posterity should, according to the

---

[1] The fact is mentioned not only as a picturesque one, bringing the whole scene before the mind of the reader, but as intimating that even in the last extremity of human feebleness Jacob "continued strong in faith, giving glory to God." It is scarcely credible how much absurdity has been taught about this act of worship. Some of the Fathers, Schoetgen says, have "pie magis quam docte" written on this subject: really we cannot help thinking their piety and learning on the subject much on a level. Hear the drivelling nonsense which flows from the pen of one of them :—" Did not Jacob the patriarch, when he was about to bless his sons, raise himself a little from the bed on which he was lying, and, leaning on the top of his staff, which signified the precious cross, and, putting his hands into the form of a cross, so pray for their good fortune and happiness ?"— GRIGENTIUS SEPHRENENSIS, *in disputatione cum Herbano Judæo*. A likely method indeed this to convert the Jews! Others insist that there was a cross on the top of the staff, and that the patriarch worshipped it. Surely men were given up to "strong delusions," who could believe this.

divine promise, possess it as an inheritance; and the pious expression of his satisfaction at obtaining security that this would be done, was a very becoming manner of testifying his full confidence in the divine promise.

The manner in which the first of these facts is calculated to serve the Apostle's purpose has been already explained. The manner in which the last of them does so may be thus stated: 'Faith enabled Jacob, when dying in Egypt, at a distance from Canaan, when all his family were in Egypt, and when there was nothing that looked like their returning to Canaan, firmly to expect, and to give clear evidence of his expecting, the fulfilment of the promise respecting that land being the inheritance of his posterity. Nothing but *faith* could have enabled him to do so. Faith, and nothing but faith, can enable you, amid events which seem to make the fulfilment of the promises made to you all but an impossibility, firmly to expect their accomplishment, and exhibit satisfactory evidence that you hold fast that confidence which has great recompense of reward.'

The next fact brought forward refers to Joseph, and is nearly of the same kind as those which we have just been illustrating. Ver. 22. "By faith Joseph, when he died"[1]—*i.e.*, when on his deathbed—"made mention of the departing of the children of Israel; and gave commandment concerning his bones." There are two facts stated here respecting Joseph. Of both we have the record in the 50th chapter of Genesis: "And Joseph said unto his brethren, I die; and God will surely visit you, and bring you out of this land unto the land which He sware to Abraham, to Isaac, and to Jacob. And Joseph took an oath of the children of Israel, saying, God will surely visit you, and ye shall carry up my bones from hence."[2] Joseph predicted the exodus of the children of Israel. He believed the promises made to Abraham, Isaac, and Jacob, that Canaan should be the possession of their posterity; he believed the promise made to Jacob immediately before he came into Egypt,—"And He said, I am God, the God of thy father: fear not to go down into Egypt; for I will there make of thee a great nation. I will go down with thee into Egypt; and I will also surely bring thee up again: and Joseph shall put his hand upon thine eyes;"[3]

---

[1] τελευτῶν: the complete expression, τελ. βίου.
[2] Gen. l. 24, 25.   [3] Gen. xlvi. 3, 4.

—and it is not at all unlikely that a direct revelation had been made to himself on the subject. As a proof of his faith in the divine promises, "he gave commandment concerning his bones;" —he took an oath of his brethren, that they should convey his remains to the land of promise.

We have already, by anticipation, said all that is necessary to show how these things were done by faith, and how their being done by faith is an illustration of the importance of faith, and in this way well fitted to serve the Apostle's purpose, as a motive to the Hebrew Christians to believe, and to persevere in believing—to live believing, and to die believing. Many of these displays of faith which have come under our review, have been given towards the close of life, or in the article of death. It is a question of deep interest to us all, Have we a faith which will support us amid the frailties of age, amid the debilities or the agonies of dissolving nature? We all profess faith now: the hour which is to try whether we possess it or not is fast approaching. The reality and the strength of our faith must by and by—God only knows how soon—be put to a severe trial. Ah! how many, who thought they had faith in health, find they have none in sickness; and how many, who thought their faith strong, find then that it is indeed but "as a grain of mustard-seed!" Let us now, by seeking clear, distinct, extended views of Christian truth and its evidence, "lay up a good foundation for the time to come, that we may lay hold on eternal life." Nothing but the faith of the Gospel can enable a rationally thinking man to enter with composure and delight into the unseen world. It is the faith of the Gospel, and that alone, which can enable the expiring mortal to exult in the dissolution of "the earthly house of this tabernacle," and say, "O death, where is thy sting? O grave, where is thy victory?"

In the paragraph which follows, we have a further illustration of the importance of faith, drawn first from the conduct of Moses' parents, and then from the conduct of Moses himself. The illustration drawn from the conduct of Moses' parents is contained in the 23d verse: "By faith Moses, when he was born, was hid three months of his parents,[1] because they saw he

---

[1] Πατέρες is used for both parents, as Euripides uses βασιλεῦσι for **Admetus** and his queen.

was a proper child; and they were not afraid of the king's commandment." Here, as in the preceding illustrations, I shall first attend to what Moses' parents did; then show how they did it by faith; and then point out the bearing of this illustration on the Apostle's great object—the fortifying of the believing Hebrews against the temptations to apostasy to which they were exposed.

The facts, as we learn from the 2d chapter of Exodus, were these :—Some time before the birth of Moses, the king of Egypt, alarmed at the rapid multiplication of the Israelites, issued an edict that every male child born among them should be put to death. On Moses being born, his parents, Amram and Jochebed, instead of complying with this atrocious enactment, concealed him for three months; and while they showed by concealing him that in one sense they were afraid of the king's commandment—as they knew, if they were discovered, that both his life and theirs would have been sacrificed to the tyrant's resentment,—yet they were not so afraid of the king's commandment as to purchase security, as it is to be feared too many did, by becoming to a certain degree accessory to the murder of their children. The remarkable beauty of the child, which is noticed by Stephen, and particularly described by Josephus, is here represented as having had its influence over the minds of his parents, in rendering them solicitous for his preservation: "They saw that he was a *proper*"[1]—rather, beautiful—" child."

But, though not insensible to the force of such natural principles, their conduct is chiefly to be traced to a higher principle. It was by faith that they did all this. A considerable number of good expositors consider this as just equivalent to—' In the exercise of trust in God, they acted in this way. They knew that, in endeavouring to protect their infant child, they were but doing their duty; and they, trusting in the divine righteousness and benignity, expected that they would be protected in the discharge of this duty.' This is, however, to depart from the meaning which the Apostle has given to the word "faith," as "confidence respecting things hoped for, conviction respecting things unseen," founded on an express revelation of the divine

---

[1] A child not maimed or sickly, but who looked well and likely to live: = the Heb. טוֹב רֹאִי, 1 Sam. xvi. 12; ἀγαθὸς τῇ ὁράσει, LXX. Stephen represents him as ἀστεῖος τῷ Θεῷ, Acts vii. 20.

will. I have no doubt that the word has here the same meaning as in the other parts of the chapter, and that the Apostle's statement is, that it was Moses' parents believing a divine revelation that enabled them to act as they did. But the question naturally occurs, What revelation of the divine will did they believe? It is highly probable, not only that they were acquainted with the divine, frequently repeated, promises respecting the numerous posterity of Abraham, Isaac, and Jacob, and their possession of Canaan as an inheritance, and with the divine oracle respecting their deliverance in the fourth generation from that country in which they were to suffer so many hardships; but I cannot help thinking that there is a reference to a more particular revelation, made to the parents of Moses themselves. We have no account of any such revelation being made in the book of Exodus; but we know that many events, and many events of importance, took place which are not recorded in Scripture. We know that, at the time this Epistle was written, it was the common faith of the Jews that such a revelation had been made. Josephus, in his "Antiquities of the Jews," Book ii. chap. v., expressly states, that a divine communication was made to Amram during the pregnancy of Jochebed, that the child about to be born was to be the deliverer of his nation from Egyptian tyranny. There is nothing in Scripture inconsistent with this. Though we have no account in Scripture of an express revelation made as to sacrifice, we conclude, from its being said that it was "by faith Abel offered a more excellent sacrifice than Cain," that such a revelation was made; and on the same principle, I cannot help considering the Apostle as here giving sanction to the commonly received belief of the Jews on this subject, and stating that it was the faith of Moses' parents in this revelation that led them to act as they did, in preserving their infant's life at the risk of their own.

In this view of the matter, everything is plain. Had Amram and Jochebed not believed the divine declaration, it is probable that they would have acted as many others did, and, fearing the king's commandment, have secured their own lives by allowing the birth of their infant son to be known, which would have led to his destruction; but believing that the declaration came from God, and believing His power and faithfulness, they took a course which to the eye of sense seemed full of hazard, but which, through their believing, they knew to be the path of security as well as of duty.

The bearing of this on the Apostle's object is direct and obvious. The Hebrew Christians were required to follow a course full of difficulties and hazards; but if, like Amram and Jochebed, they believed that it was a course prescribed by God, and prescribed, too, as the means of the accomplishment of "exceeding great and precious promises," their faith would raise them above the influence of fear, and make what seemed at first impossible, not only practicable, but easy.

Though it is not particularly mentioned, there can scarcely be any doubt that it was under the divine direction that Moses' parents not only concealed him for three months, but at the expiration of this period had recourse to the plan which they adopted, by preparing for the infant deliverer of Israel a little ark of bulrushes, and laying him among the flags by the side of the Nile. The Jewish historian already referred to expressly says, that in doing so, they determined rather to entrust the care of the child to God than to depend on their own concealment of him, whereby both themselves and the child should be in imminent danger; but they believed that God would in some way for certain procure the safety of the child, in order to secure the truth of His own predictions. Whether we consider the conduct of the parents of Moses as the consequence of a belief in a second express revelation, or of such believing reasonings on the former revelation, it is a very striking demonstration of the power of faith. When constrained by the necessity of circumstances, or called by an express declaration of the divine will, they place their infant—peculiarly dear to them from the hazards they had already run for him, and the important interests which were bound up in his life—in circumstances of apparently great danger, assuredly believing that "He was faithful who had promised," and that Moses was as safe in the ark of bulrushes on the banks of the Nile, as he could have been in his mother's bosom, in some peaceful cottage far removed beyond the power of the cruel Egyptian king.

If the first part of the history strikingly illustrates the power of faith in enabling men to sustain severe trials and perform difficult duties, the sequel of it equally illustrates its power in enabling them to obtain important benefits. The expectations of

## GENERAL EXHORTATION AND WARNING. 541

Amram and Jochebed, founded on their faith in a divine revelation, were not disappointed. Moses' life was preserved, and he was brought into the circumstances most favourable for his being trained up for the important work to which he was destined. The faith of Amram and Jochebed was richly rewarded, when they saw their son enjoying all the advantages of the most accomplished education which Egypt could supply, and, through the wonderful providence of Jehovah, that power which had meditated his destruction, employed for his welfare, and, in being so employed, preparing the means of its own overthrow.

The history of Moses' infancy, as an illustration of the faith of his parents, is thus admirably fitted to serve the Apostle's object. It illustrates his general principle: 'Persevering faith will do what nothing else can: it will enable you to do and suffer all the will of God, and, after having done so, to receive the promise.' You may be called to trials and duties as difficult and severe as those of Amram or Jochebed,—you may be called to what will expose your life, and what may be dearer to you than your life, to extreme danger; but a faith in the Gospel will prevent you from shrinking from the task assigned you—will support you while engaged in it, while He in whom you believe will render even these difficulties and hazards the very means of securing for you the great end of your faith, and the great object of your hope—the salvation of your souls.

We are now to direct our attention to the still more remarkable display of the importance of faith afforded by the conduct of Moses himself. Ver. 24. "By faith Moses, when he was come to years, refused to be called the son of Pharaoh's daughter; 25. Choosing rather to suffer affliction with the people of God, than to enjoy the pleasures of sin for a season; 26. Esteeming the reproach of Christ greater riches than the treasures in Egypt: for he had respect unto the recompense of the reward."[1] We shall first attend to the account of Moses' conduct, and then show how his conduct was influenced by his

---

[1] In some codd. the following words are inserted between verse 23 and verse 24: πίστει μέγας γενόμενος Μωϋσῆς ἀνεῖλεν τὸν Αἰγύπτιον, κατανοῶν τὴν ταπείνωσιν τῶν ἀδελφῶν αὐτοῦ. Mill considers the words as genuine; but they are not by any means sufficiently supported. The repetition of πίστει M. μ. γ. is very unlike the concinnity of the writer of the Epistle to the Hebrews. It seems to have been added by some transcriber from Acts vii. 24.

faith. We shall first inquire what he did, and then show that it was by faith that he did it.

"When he came to years, he refused to be called the son of Pharaoh's daughter;" he "chose rather to suffer affliction with the people of God, than to enjoy the pleasures of sin for a season;" and he "esteemed the reproach of Christ greater riches than the treasures of Egypt." The phrase, "when he was come to years," literally signifies, 'when he became great;' and, taken by itself, might refer to that elevated station in society to which Moses was raised in the Egyptian court. It seems, however, plainly contrasted with the phrase, "when he was born," in the 23d verse, and is just equivalent to, 'when he arrived at maturity.'[1] "He refused to be called the son of Pharaoh's daughter." On Moses being found by this princess in the ark of bulrushes on the banks of the Nile, moved with compassion, she seems to have resolved immediately to take charge of the infant; and accordingly the charge she gave to his mother, who providentially became his nurse, was, "Take this child, and nurse it for me, and I will give you your wages." It might very probably then be her intention to educate him as her slave, or for some of the ordinary professions; but, on his being brought back by his mother, she was so much delighted with the beautiful child, that she resolved to adopt him as her own,—"he became her son;" and as a memorial of the remarkable circumstances of his coming under her protection, she called him Moses, which in the Egyptian language, signifies 'out of the water.' It has been supposed by some that the king of Egypt had no other child than the daughter mentioned in the book of Exodus; that she had no children; and that Moses, as her adopted son, might be considered as the heir apparent to the Egyptian crown. This appears not very probable; at any rate, it is not certain. It is obvious, however, that the adopted son of the daughter of the king of Egypt, then one of the richest, most populous, and civilised nations in the world, must have occupied a very dignified station in society, and possessed in no ordinary measure worldly wealth and honours. During childhood and youth he bare the name of "the son of Pharaoh's daughter," and enjoyed the secular advantages which were connected with so honourable a title.

[1] וַיִּגְדַּל is used in the same way, Exod. ii. 11.

## GENERAL EXHORTATION AND WARNING. 543

But "when he was come to years"—arrived at mature age—"he refused to be called the son of Pharaoh's daughter." It is quite possible that the Apostle may refer to some particular fact in Moses' history, known when he wrote, but now forgotten. There may have been some public occasion on which the continued enjoyment of the honours connected with this title by Moses might be suspended on his doing something which would have amounted to a renunciation of the religion of his forefathers, and which led him openly to renounce the dignified situation he had so long occupied. This may have been the case, but the words before us do not warrant us to say that it was so. They merely intimate that he voluntarily renounced the honours and advantages connected with the title of "the son of Pharaoh's daughter." He saw his kinsmen enslaved and oppressed; he knew that by renouncing all connection with them, he might retain that situation of ease, and affluence, and honour which he possessed; he saw that, if he identified himself with them, he must renounce his wealth and his dignities; and he unhesitatingly made his choice. He gave up the name of an Egyptian prince and took in its room that of an Israelitish bondman.

When he was grown, he went out to his brethren, and looked on their burdens; and burning with indignation at the unjust treatment which one of them received from an Egyptian, executed summary vengeance on the oppressor. That act was a renouncing for ever of the name of "the son of Pharaoh's daughter." "He chose rather to suffer affliction with the people of God, than to enjoy the pleasures of sin for a season." By "the people of God" we are to understand the Israelites, now in Egypt. They were "chosen out of all the families of the earth" to be the depositaries of the true religion, to enjoy peculiar privileges, and to serve important purposes in the development of the grand scheme of divine mercy for the salvation of mankind. The number of genuine saints among them at the period referred to seems to have been small; but almost all the saints on the earth were to be found among them, and as a people—as the descendants of Abraham, Isaac, and Jacob—they were in covenant with God. This "people of God" were, at the period referred to, "suffering affliction." Of these afflictions we have an account in Exod. i. 13, 14, and ii. 23: "And the Egyptians made the children of Israel to serve with rigour. And they made their lives bitter with hard bondage, in mortar, and in brick, and in all manner of service in the field: all their service, wherein they made them serve, was with rigour." "And it came to pass, in process of time, that the king of Egypt died: and the children of Israel sighed by reason of the bondage, and they cried; and their cry came up unto God, by reason of the bondage." Moses was originally one of this people, and in the perils of his childhood shared in their afflictions. By the remarkable care of Providence, he had been for a season separated from them, and placed in circumstances of security and ease. But when he arrived at mature age, he voluntarily preferred casting in his lot with the afflicted people of God to the continued enjoyment of the honours and pleasures of the Egyptian court. These are termed "the pleasures of sin." Many of the pleasures of a court life are usually in their own nature sinful pleasures. But here, I apprehend, the idea intended to be conveyed is this. The pleasures of the Egyptian court, even such of them as were innocent in themselves—and we have no reason to think that Moses ever indulged in any other—were sinful pleasures in his case. He could not continue to enjoy them without in effect renouncing his connection with the people of God, and his interest in those blessings which were secured to them by the divine covenant. If he continued to enjoy them, he could not have discharged the duties of that office to which he was destined, as the deliverer of the people of God, and must have been implicated in the guilt of their Egyptian oppressors. The sinful pleasures which Moses renounced are termed "pleasures for *a season;*" *i.e.,* temporary—liable to innumerable interruptions in this life, and unavoidably ending with it. He chose rather to endure for a season the afflictions of the people of God, than to enjoy for a season the pleasures of an ungodly world.

The same general truth is represented in a different way in the next clause: "He esteemed the reproach of Christ greater riches than all the treasures of Egypt." I believe every attentive reader of the Bible has felt some difficulty in satisfactorily explaining to himself this passage. He to whom the appellation "Messiah, Christ, or Anointed" belongs, did not appear in our world till more than 1500 years after the days of Moses. The Son of God indeed existed from eternity, but He did not become the Christ till He assumed human nature. The great

GENERAL EXHORTATION AND WARNING. 545

Deliverer had indeed been promised, but He had not been promised under the name of the Messiah.

"The reproach of Christ" is a phrase of which, when taken by itself, the most natural meaning is, 'the reproach which Christ Himself suffered;' and if we depart from this primary sense, the next meaning which the words suggest is, 'reproach endured on account of Christ.' It does not seem possible to make sense of the passage, adopting either of these meanings. I shall very shortly state what appear to me the only two probable interpretations which have been given of the passage, leaving my readers to make their choice between them. I cannot say either of them is entirely satisfactory to my own mind.

The word "Christ" is by some interpreters considered as referring not to our Lord Jesus Christ, the anointed—*i.e.*, the divinely chosen and designated—Deliverer, but to the Israelitish people, the divinely chosen and designated people. There can be no doubt that the patriarchs of that people are termed God's christs, or anointed ones, Ps. cv. 15; and in Hab. iii. 13, it seems highly probable that the Israelitish people are termed God's anointed: "*with* Thine anointed;" rather, 'to save Thine anointed,' or 'for the salvation of Thine anointed.' In this case "the reproach of Christ" is nearly synonymous with the "afflictions of the people of God," just as "the treasures of Egypt" correspond with "the pleasures of sin for a season."

The second mode of interpretation goes on the principle, that "the reproach of Christ" is equivalent to—'reproach similar to that which Christ sustained;' just as in 2 Cor. i. 5 the phrase, "sufferings of Christ," is equivalent to—'sufferings similar to those which Christ endured.' In the first case the meaning is, 'Moses willingly took part in the contempt and reproach to which the oppressed Israelites were exposed;' in the second, the meaning is, 'Moses, the deliverer of Israel, willingly submitted to reproaches similar to those which were heaped on Jesus Christ, the Saviour of man.' It does not matter much which of the two modes of interpretation you adopt. In both cases the words express a truth, and an appropriate truth. At the same time, I confess that I lean to the first mode of interpretation.[1]

[1] I think it not improbable that there is a particular reference to "circumcision," the mark of belonging to the χριστός λαός, or χριστοῦ λ.,—that

Moses' voluntary preference of the abject state of the Israelites to the elevated station he held in Pharaoh's court, is very emphatically described as his "esteeming their reproach greater riches than all the treasures of Egypt." The idea intended to be conveyed, we apprehend, is this—he counted it more his interest to be poor and reproached with the Israel of God, than to be wealthy and honoured with the ungodly Egyptians.

Such was the estimate Moses formed, and his conduct corresponded with it. He took a decided part with them, the consequence of which was that he was obliged to abandon all the comforts of a courtly life, to flee into the deserts of Arabia, and remain there in obscurity for a considerable number of years; and on his return to Egypt, for the purpose of delivering his countrymen, he identified himself with them, and exposed himself to great difficulties and dangers by doing so. Now what was it that induced Moses to think and act in this way? What made him "refuse to be called the son of Pharaoh's daughter?" What led him to " choose rather to suffer affliction with the people of God, than to enjoy the pleasures of sin for a season?" What made him "esteem the reproach of Christ greater riches than the treasures in Egypt?" It was faith, says the Apostle. "By faith Moses, when he was come to years, refused to be called the son of Pharaoh's daughter; choosing rather to suffer affliction with the people of God, than to enjoy the pleasures of sin for a season; esteeming the reproach of Christ greater riches than the treasures in Egypt: for he had respect unto the recompense of the reward." Now there are here two questions: What did Moses believe? and how did his belief influence his judgment, his choice, and his conduct?

It is not very easy to say what was the extent of Moses' belief, for we do not know exactly the extent of the revelation made to him. It is not improbable that revelations were made to the patriarchal Church of which we have no record; but in speaking of Moses' faith, we must confine ourselves to what we know from Old Testament history was made known to him,

---

σημεῖον having a peculiar reference to the Messiah. This distinction excited contempt and ridicule among foreigners. How the Roman poets laugh at the *Verpi!* Mart. vii. 82; Catullus xlv.; Juvenal xiv. 104. On the other hand, the præputium, uncircumcision, is termed in Scripture "the reproach of Egypt," ὀνειδισμὸν Αἰγύπτου, Josh. v. 9.

or to what, from the statements in the passage before us, we have ground to conclude was made known to him. Moses, then, like his parents, believed the promises made to Abraham, Isaac, and Jacob, as to Israel being God's peculiar people, as to their ultimately being a numerous and prosperous nation, and as to Canaan being their inheritance. He believed also the prediction of their deliverance from the land in which they were for a long term of years to endure severe oppression, and that God would judge, or punish, their oppressors. He believed, I doubt not, the divine intimation given to his parents respecting his being the deliverer of Israel; and if, as is not improbable, a similar revelation was made directly to himself, he believed that.

Still further, it seems plain from the passage before us, that Moses believed a revelation which had been made respecting a future state of rewards in another world: "*he had respect,*" we are told, "*to the recompense of the reward.*" This is one of the passages which lead me to think that plainer revelations of a future state were made to the patriarchs than any that are recorded in the Old Testament Scriptures. "The recompense of reward" cannot refer to the possession of Canaan, for Moses was never to enter into that country. The meaning seems to be this—'Moses expected that all the sacrifices he made in the cause of God and His people would be far more than compensated in a future state;' and this expectation could only be grounded on a corresponding revelation. Such was the faith of Moses.

Now it is not difficult to perceive how this faith led Moses to judge as he judged, to choose as he chose, to act as he acted. If Moses really believed that Israel was the peculiar people of God, whom He had promised to protect, and bless, and deliver; and if he believed that Jehovah was infinitely powerful, and wise, and faithful; was it not the natural and the necessary consequence of this, that he should seek to identify himself with them? If he really believed that Jehovah would certainly punish their Egyptian oppressors, and that the time of righteous retribution was fast approaching, was not the natural consequence of this to renounce all connection with them, and to consider the highest and most honourable situation among them as the very reverse of desirable? If he really believed that God had appointed him to be the agent in effecting the deliverance of Israel, was not this sufficient to make him leave the court of Pharaoh, and interfere for the protection and defence of his oppressed brethren? And if he really believed that in a future world Jehovah would abundantly recompense him for all the sacrifices, and losses, and sufferings to which he might be exposed, was it not natural for him to prefer affliction with the Israelites to ease and pleasure with the Egyptians, and to count it his true interest to be poor and despised with the former, rather than affluent and honoured with the latter? In all this there is no mystery. It is the rational account of Moses' conduct: it is impossible to account for it in any other way. Had Moses had no faith on these subjects, or an opposite faith, his judgment, and choice, and conduct would have been different. He would have gladly been "called the son of Pharaoh's daughter;" he would have chosen rather to enjoy "the pleasures of sin for a season," than to "suffer affliction with the people of God;" he would have accounted "the treasures of Egypt" greater riches than "the reproach of Christ;" for, not believing, he could not have "had respect to the recompense of reward."

None of the exemplifications of the importance of believing, brought forward by the Apostle, is better fitted to serve his purpose than that which we have been considering. The Hebrew Christians were called on to part with an honour which they were accustomed to value above all other dignities. They were excommunicated by their unbelieving brethren, and denied the name of true children of Abraham. Their unbelieving countrymen were enjoying wealth and honour. The little flock they were called on to join were suffering affliction and reproach. Like Moses, they were called on to make great sacrifices, submit to great privations, endure severe sufferings. Now, how is this to be done? 'Look at Moses. Believe as Moses believed, and you will find it easy to judge, and choose, and act as Moses did. If you believe what Christ has plainly revealed, that "it is His Father's good pleasure to give" His little flock, after passing through much tribulation, "the kingdom;" if you are persuaded that, according to His declaration, "wrath is coming to the uttermost" on their oppressors, you will not hesitate to separate yourselves completely from your unbelieving countrymen in a religious point of view, at whatever expense,—you will "come out from among them, and be separate,"—you will at all hazards connect yourselves with the suffering people of God, fully persuaded that "faithful is He who hath promised." "Every one that hath forsaken houses, or brethren, or sisters, or father, or mother, or wife, or children, or lands, for My name's sake, shall receive an hundred-fold, and shall inherit everlasting life."[1]

The practical bearing of the passage is not confined to the Hebrew converts, or to the Christians of the primitive age. In every country, and in every age, Jesus proclaims, "If any man would be My disciple, he must deny himself, he must take up the cross and follow Me." No man can do this but by believing. Believing, every man may, must do this. The power of the present world can only be put down by "the power of the world to come;" and as it is through *sense* that the first power operates on our minds, it is through *faith* alone that the second power can operate on our minds. Some find it impossible to make the sacrifices Christianity requires, because they have no faith. Multitudes find it difficult to make them, for they have little faith. If we have faith, we shall find such sacrifices practicable; if we have strong faith, we will find them easy. They must be made; otherwise our Christianity is but a name, our faith is but a pretence, and our hope a delusion.

The verses which follow bring before our mind other illustrations of the importance and efficacy of faith, derived from the history of Moses. The first of these is contained in the 27th verse. "By faith he forsook Egypt, not fearing the wrath of the king: for he endured, as seeing Him who is invisible." Here we shall follow the general plan we have adopted in reference to these illustrations :—Attend first to the facts, and then to the Apostle's account of these facts; inquire first what Moses did, and then show how it was by faith that he did what he did.

Now, what did Moses do ? "He left Egypt;" he "did not fear the wrath of the king;" and "he endured." Moses twice left Egypt—once as a solitary fugitive, and once as the leader of the hosts of the Israelitish people. It has been a question among expositors, to which of these events does the Apostle refer. This appears to us a question of no very difficult solution. Whether it was by faith that Moses left Egypt when he fled

[1] Matt. xix. 29.

into Midian, is a point not very easily determined; but certainly, when he left Egypt on that occasion, it could not have been said that he " did not fear the wrath of the king;" for fear of the king was obviously the principal cause of his flight. When Moses found that his slaughter of the Egyptian was known, he "feared." And "when Pharaoh heard of it, he sought to slay Moses;" "and Moses," we are told, "fled from the face of Pharaoh, and dwelt in Midian." It plainly, then, cannot be to this leaving of Egypt that the Apostle refers: it must be to his second leaving of Egypt. Now, as this was the closing act of a long, closely connected series of events, there can be little doubt that it is in this point of view that the Apostle considered it; and therefore, in order to bring the illustration fully before the mind, we must take a hurried view of these antecedent events.

Moses left the land of Midian, where he was comfortably settled, and for forty years had enjoyed the advantages of the tranquillity of the pastoral life; returned to Egypt for the purpose of effecting the deliverance of his countrymen from servitude, and leading them towards Palestine, their promised inheritance; and, after a long struggle with the unbelief of his countrymen, and the obstinacy of the Egyptian king, which was overcome by a series of the most wonderful miracles, ultimately succeeded in his hazardous and apparently hopeless enterprise.

In thus "forsaking Egypt," he "did not fear the wrath of the king." The king was very much enraged at Moses, and no doubt wished above all things to destroy him, and seemed to have it completely in his power to realize his wish. But Moses discovered no fear. He prosecuted his object till he gained it, unterrified by all Pharaoh's threats; and having left Egypt, though followed by Pharaoh and his embattled hosts, yet still he remained unmoved. "Fear not," said he to the terrified Israelites,—" fear ye not, stand still, and see the salvation of God."

It is also stated that Moses "endured." The word, we apprehend, is expressive of Moses' firm, determined perseverance in the course of conduct which he had adopted, notwithstanding all the difficulties he met with in it, from the unbelief of his countrymen, and from the policy and power of the Egyptian king. The whole statement in reference to Moses' conduct is this: Neither the terrors of the wrath of the king of Egypt, nor the disgust which the ingratitude, and unbelief, and waywardness of his countrymen were calculated to produce, prevented him from prosecuting the great object which he had in view till he brought it to a prosperous issue. Such was the conduct of Moses.

Now, to what are we to attribute it? The Apostle's answer is, To his faith. "By faith he forsook Egypt, not fearing the wrath of the king: for he endured, as seeing Him who is invisible." And here, as formerly, there are two questions which call for resolution: What did Moses believe? and how did his faith influence his conduct? The answer to these two questions will be most satisfactorily given, not in a separate, but in a combined form.

Moses believed the revelations made to him respecting the deliverance of the children of Israel, the part he was to act in that deliverance, and the assistance Jehovah would afford him in accomplishing it. What these revelations were, you will find by consulting the book of Exodus. "Now Moses kept the flock of Jethro his father-in-law, the priest of Midian: and he led the flock to the back-side of the desert, and came to the mountain of God, even to Horeb. And the Angel of the Lord appeared unto him in a flame of fire out of the midst of a bush; and he looked, and, behold, the bush burned with fire, and the bush was not consumed. And Moses said, I will now turn aside, and see this great sight, why the bush is not burnt. And when the Lord saw that he turned aside to see, God called unto him out of the midst of the bush, and said, Moses, Moses. And he said, Here am I. And He said, Draw not nigh hither: put off thy shoes from off thy feet; for the place whereon thou standest is holy ground. Moreover He said, I am the God of thy father, the God of Abraham, the God of Isaac, and the God of Jacob. And Moses hid his face; for he was afraid to look upon God. And the Lord said, I have surely seen the affliction of My people which are in Egypt, and have heard their cry by reason of their taskmasters; for I know their sorrows. And I am come down to deliver them out of the hand of the Egyptians, and to bring them up out of that land unto a good land and a large, unto a land flowing with milk and honey; unto the place of the Canaanites, and the Hittites, and the Amorites, and the Perizzites, and the Hivites, and the Jebusites. Now therefore, behold, the cry of the children of Israel is come unto Me: and I have also seen the oppression wherewith the Egyptians oppress them. Come now therefore, and I will send thee unto Pharaoh, that thou mayest bring forth My people, the children of Israel, out of Egypt." "And they shall hearken to thy voice: and thou shalt come, thou and the elders of Israel, unto the king of Egypt, and ye shall say unto him, The Lord God of the Hebrews hath met with us: and now let us go, we beseech thee, three days' journey into the wilderness, that we may sacrifice to the Lord our God. And I am sure that the king of Egypt will not let you go, no, not by a mighty hand. And I will stretch out My hand, and smite Egypt with all My wonders which I will do in the midst thereof: and after that he will let you go."[1] Had Moses not believed that this revelation came from God, or had he not believed that Jehovah was at once powerful and faithful, able and disposed to do what He had said, Moses would have remained in Midian, where he seems to have been very comfortably settled; but, firmly believing that this revelation did come from God, and that He was both able and willing to do what He had said, Moses could not but leave Midian, and deliver the message with which he was entrusted, both to his kinsmen and to the Egyptian king. The reception he at first met with from the Israelites was powerfully calculated, both in itself and as a begun fulfilment of the divine oracle, to encourage him. On the message being delivered, and the signs performed, "the people believed; and when they heard that the Lord had visited the children of Israel, and that He had looked upon their affliction, they bowed their heads and worshipped."[2] But subsequent events were in their own nature fitted to discourage him; and indeed, had it not been for his faith, would certainly have induced him to abandon his enterprise in despair. When he delivered his message to Pharaoh, he met with a direct and most insolent refusal. "Thus saith the Lord," said Moses, "the God of Israel, Let My people go, that they may hold a feast to Me in the wilderness." Pharaoh's impious reply was, "Who is the Lord, that I should obey His voice to let Israel go? I know not the Lord, neither will I let Israel go." Instead of

[1] Exod. iii. 1–10, 18–20.  [2] Exod. iv. 31.

procuring Israel's release, this interference brought on them a double weight of oppression, which drew forth from them cutting reproaches against Moses, and even imprecations of divine vengeance on him. And here Moses' faith seems to have begun to fail him; for he "returned unto the Lord, and said, Lord, wherefore hast Thou so evil-entreated this people? why is it that Thou hast sent me? For since I came to Pharaoh to speak in Thy name, he hath done evil to this people; neither hast Thou delivered Thy people at all."[1] A new revelation was made to him for the strengthening of his faith. "Then the Lord said unto Moses, Now shalt thou see what I will do to Pharaoh: for with a strong hand shall he let them go, and with a strong hand shall he drive them out of his land. And God spake unto Moses, and said unto him, I am the Lord: and I appeared unto Abraham, unto Isaac, and unto Jacob, by the name of God Almighty; but by My name Jehovah was I not known to them. And I have also established My covenant with them, to give them the land of Canaan, the land of their pilgrimage, wherein they were strangers. And I have also heard the groaning of the children of Israel, whom the Egyptians keep in bondage; and I have remembered My covenant. Wherefore say unto the children of Israel, I am the Lord, and I will bring you out from under the burdens of the Egyptians, and I will rid you out of their bondage; and I will redeem you with a stretched-out arm, and with great judgments. And I will take you to Me for a people, and I will be to you a God; and ye shall know that I am the Lord your God, which bringeth you out from under the burdens of the Egyptians. And I will bring you in unto the land, concerning the which I did swear to give it to Abraham, to Isaac, and to Jacob; and I will give it you for an heritage: I am the Lord."[2] And though after this the people of Israel "hearkened not to him for anguish of spirit and cruel bondage;" and though Pharaoh continued obstinate, amid all the miraculous judgments inflicted on him and his people; yet Moses, believing the divine declarations, persevered. Had he not believed, he must have soon given up the undertaking as hopeless; but believing, he found even in Pharaoh's obstinacy, which had been predicted, encouragement to persevere. The state of exasperation into which Pharaoh was thrown by such repeated and dreadful

[1] Exod. v. 22, 23.     [2] Exod. vi. 1-8.

calamities, was well fitted to fill with terror such an unprotected individual as Moses; but believing that "God was for him," he "did not fear what man could do to him." At last, overwhelmed by the fearful infliction of the sudden death, in one night, of all the first-born in the land of Egypt, Pharaoh gave an extorted consent to the departure of the Israelites out of Egypt; and Moses, at their head, "forsook Egypt." The undertaking in which Moses thus engaged, was one which nothing but faith could have induced any rational man to enter on. The endless difficulties of conducting such a prodigious multitude of men, women, children, and cattle, through waste solitudes, or the territories of hostile tribes, towards a country already in the possession of numerous and powerful nations, must have appeared altogether insurmountable. But Moses, by faith, entered on this apparently desperate enterprise, because he believed that Jehovah had promised, and that He was both able and willing to perform Hi promise, "to bring them in unto the land, concerning which He had sworn to give it to Abraham, to Isaac, and to Jacob."

He persevered in the course prescribed to him " as one who saw Him who is invisible." These words admit of two modes of interpretation: Either, 'his faith had the same effect on him as if the unseen Deity, with every conceivable emblem of His power, and wisdom, and faithfulness, had become an object of bodily vision;' or, 'he endured as one who saw'—*i.e.*, by the eye of faith, the only way in which He can be seen—'the invisible Divinity.' Either mode of interpretation gives a good sense, but we apprehend the latter is the Apostle's meaning. The expression naturally leads the mind back to the declaration in the first verse. His faith was "confidence respecting things hoped for, conviction in reference to things not seen." Without such faith, Moses could not have done, and suffered, and obtained as he did; with such faith, the discharge of the duties enjoined on him, though very difficult—the enduring of the trials assigned him, though very severe—the attainment of the blessings, though very valuable and apparently unattainable, became natural and easy.

The bearing of this illustration on the Apostle's great object is direct and obvious: 'What faith did for Moses, faith can do for you; what nothing but faith could do for Moses, nothing but faith can do for you.' The Hebrew Christians were placed in circumstances somewhat analogous to those of Moses. They were required to "come out and be separate" from their unbelieving countrymen. The difficulties that lay in the way of renouncing Judaism were, though of another nature, scarcely less formidable than those which lay in the way of Moses leaving Egypt; and, like him, in abandoning Judaism they had to commence a course of indefinitely long and severe labour and trial, previously to their obtaining a permanently secure and happy settlement in the heavenly Canaan. What could enable them to make such sacrifices, to put forth such exertions, to submit to such privations, to encounter such opposition, and to persevere in doing so, amid all those circumstances which had an obvious tendency to damp their ardour and shake their resolution? Faith, and nothing but faith.

In the word of the truth of the Gospel it had been distinctly stated to them that Jesus Christ was the divine Deliverer promised to the fathers—that "His blood cleanses from all sin" —that "all power in heaven and on earth" belongs to Him— that "whosoever believeth in Him shall not perish, but have everlasting life"—that, to be His disciples, men must "deny themselves, take up their cross, and follow Him"—that "He will never leave and never forsake His people"—that "His grace shall be made sufficient for them," and that He "will perfect His strength in their weakness"—that He will "make all things work together for their good"—that He "will confess before His Father and the holy angels" those who "confess Him before men," and "deny before His Father and the holy angels" those who "deny Him before men"—and that "to him who overcometh He will give to sit with Him on His throne, even as He also hath overcome, and is set down with His Father on His throne."

Now, if these truths were not believed, it could not be expected that they would "forsake father, and mother, and sisters, and brothers, and houses, and lands, for Christ's sake and the Gospel's,"—it could not be expected that they should enter on and prosecute a course of conduct directly opposed to all the strongest inclinations of unchanged human nature.

But if they really did believe these truths—if by the eye of faith they habitually contemplated the invisible God, the unseen Saviour, and the great realities of the eternal world,—would not the fear of God extinguish all other fear—the love of the Saviour neutralize the power of all opposing affections—the majestic glories of eternity make all earth-born glory grow dim or disappear, shrink to a thing of nought,—nay, would not the very afflictions and trials they met with, when viewed as a verification of the declarations of the Saviour, operate as a confirmation of their faith, that He whose declaration, that "in the world they should have tribulation," had been fulfilled, would be found equally true to the other connected declaration, "In Me ye shall have peace?" Under the influence of an enlightened faith, the very circumstances which to the unstable prove the occasion of apostasy, are found, as evidences of the faithfulness of the Saviour, and the truth of His declarations, the means of attaching the Christian the more closely to the cause of his Lord and Saviour.

The duties and difficulties, the trials and privations of Christians, are substantially the same in all countries and in all ages; and nothing can enable them to conduct themselves properly in reference to these but faith. Looking away from what is seen and temporal to the God who is invisible, the Saviour who is unseen, the world which is eternal,—that, and that alone, will enable us to brave dangers before which the stoutest heart, unsupported by the faith of the Gospel, must quail, and make the feeblest of us "more than conquerors" over the most powerful of our spiritual foes. Believing "the exceeding great and precious promises" of God, and the power and faithfulness of Him who has given them, the Christian remains "stedfast and unmoveable" amid all the storms of temptation which threaten to shake his attachment to Christ and His cause. Isa. xl. 28-31.

We come now to the last of these displays of the importance of faith, drawn from the history of Moses.

Ver. 28. "Through faith he kept the passover, and the sprinkling of blood, lest he that destroyed the first-born should touch them." Let us here, as in former cases, attend first to the facts, and then to the Apostle's account of the facts; or, in other words, inquire first what Moses did, and then show that it was by faith that he did what he did. The facts are—"Moses kept the passover, and the sprinkling of blood;" and he did so, "*in order that* the destroyer *might not*"—or, "*so that* the destroyer *did not*—touch them;" for the words will admit either rendering.

The phrase rendered, "kept[1] the passover," taken by itself, may either signify—'*instituted*,' or '*observed* the passover.' In one of the old English versions it is rendered—" he ordained the passover, and the sprinkling of blood." It was not so much Moses, however, as Jehovah, that ordained these religious observances. The phrase here employed is the same as that used by our Lord, when He says, Matt. xxvi. 18, "I will *keep* the passover at thy house with My disciples." "Keep" is perhaps not the best word which might have been employed: it suits very well with the word "passover," but it does not suit so well with the phrase, "sprinkling of blood." "Observe" applies equally well to both. 'Moses observed the passover, and the sprinkling of blood.' The facts referred to are narrated at large in the 12th chapter of the book of Exodus. The following is a brief summary of them :—A short time before the departure of Israel from Egypt, Moses gave warning both to Pharaoh and to the Israelites, that at midnight on the fourteenth day of the month Abib, all the first-born both of man and of beast were, by a miraculous visitation of Heaven, suddenly to die. He predicted also that this dreadful infliction of divine wrath would not only make the Egyptians consent to the departure of the children of Israel, but make them anxiously urge their departure. And, as a means of protecting the first-born of the children of Israel from the general desolation, he commanded every family to set apart a male lamb or kid of the first year, on the tenth day of the month; and on the fourteenth day of the month this lamb or kid was to be slain, in the evening; its blood was to be sprinkled, by means of a bunch of hyssop, on the doorposts and lintels of their house; and the flesh, having been roasted, was to be eaten with unleavened bread and bitter herbs; while, with girt loins, and sandals on their feet, and staff in hand, they stood ready to commence their march from Egypt towards the land of promise. The event exactly corresponded with Moses' prediction; and he and the children of Israel, according to the divine appointment, "observed the passover, and the sprinkling of blood." That is, they sacrificed the lambs and kids, and prepared all their carcases, according to the divine ap-

---

[1] πεποίηκε.

pointment, and with their blood sprinkled the door-posts and lintels of their dwellings.

This service received the name of "the passover," because, while Jehovah visited in wrath every house of the Egyptians, He passed over the houses of the Israelites, and did not suffer the destroyer to come into their houses to smite them. This fact is referred to in the concluding part of the verse. Moses "observed the passover, and the sprinkling of blood, lest he who destroyed the first-born should touch them."

The appellation, "destroyer[1] of the first-born," seems to be descriptive of some angelic agent employed by Jehovah in the execution of this awful judgment. No doubt Jehovah Himself must be considered as the grand primary agent; for "can there be evil in a city," or land, "and He has not done it?" but in the words, "The Lord will pass over the door, and will not suffer the destroyer to come in unto it to smite you," Jehovah and the destroyer are plainly distinguished from each other. Some interpreters would explain this by saying, that the ancient Jews were accustomed to ascribe all remarkable phenomena to the agency of invisible beings; and that all that is meant, is just that, by some means or other, the first-born of man and beast in Egypt suddenly died. It appears to us the far more rational mode of interpretation to consider the words as bearing their plain meaning, and as intended to teach us that one of those "angels who excel in strength" was employed by Him, whose will they do, and to the voice of whose word they dutifully listen, to execute the richly deserved, though awfully severe, judgment which He had denounced against the Egyptians.[2]

For this destroyer "not to touch" the Israelites, is obviously equivalent to—'not to injure, hurt, or destroy them.' The phraseology very probably is intended to suggest the idea of the perfect ease with which this angelic agent performed his dreadful office. His *touch* was fatal.

The words, "Moses observed the passover, and the sprinkling of blood, lest he who destroyed the first-born should touch them," may either be understood as expressing the *object* which Moses had in view in observing the passover and the sprinkling of

[1] מַשְׁחִית of the Hebrew.

[2] 2 Kings xix. 35 ; 1 Chron. xxi. 12, 15 ; 2 Chron. xxxii. 21 ; Ecclus. xlviii. 21 ; Isa. xxxvii. 36.

blood, or the *event* of his doing so. In the first case they are equivalent to—' Moses observed the passover, and the sprinkling of blood, in order that the destroyer of the first-born might not touch them.' In the second case they are equivalent to—' Moses observed the passover, and the sprinkling of blood, so that he who destroyed the first-born did not touch them.' Both are truths, and both are truths which directly bear on the Apostle's object. If I were required to choose between the two interpretations, I would probably prefer the second; as in this case the facts brought forward are a proof not only of faith enabling a man to do what otherwise he could not have done, but also of its enabling a man to attain what otherwise he could not have attained. So much, then, for the facts stated by the Apostle in this verse: "Moses observed the passover, and the sprinkling of blood."

Let us now inquire into the account which the Apostle gives of these facts. The following questions naturally present themselves to the mind: What made Moses observe the passover, and the sprinkling of blood? How came he to know that the children of Israel were to depart from Egypt on the fourteenth day of the month Abib? How came he to know that the proximate cause of their leaving Egypt was to be the sudden and simultaneous death of the first-born both of man and beast throughout that country? How came he to consider the sacrifice of a lamb or kid, the eating of it roasted, and the sprinkling of its blood on the door-posts and lintels, as a preservative for the Israelites from the destruction which walked in darkness?

The only satisfactory answer to all these questions is that given by the Apostle. It was by faith Moses did these things. Divine revelations were given him on these subjects; and he believed these revelations, and he acted accordingly. Without such revelations, or without a faith in these revelations, he could not have done as he did; with such revelations, and with a faith in them, he could not but act as he did. The deliverance of Israel from Egypt could not have been foreseen by human sagacity. It was, at the time Moses intimated that it would take place on a certain day, less probable than when he first entered on his enterprise. Even supposing the event to be of a kind which human sagacity could have predicted as at no great distance, could human sagacity have enabled him to fix the precise day? could it have enabled him to say what was to be the immediate cause of effecting so unlikely an event? and even supposing him possessed of all necessary information on these points, would it ever have entered into his mind to have encumbered the Israelites, on the very eve of their departure, with such an operose religious ceremony as the passover and the sprinkling of blood, or to have considered such rites as in any degree calculated to protect the Israelites from a calamity so general that not one family in Egypt was free from it? The only satisfactory account—and it is a satisfactory one—is this: By faith Moses did all this. God revealed to Moses that Israel was to be delivered on the fourteenth day of the month Abib—that the universal destruction of the first-born among the Egyptians was to be the proximate cause of their deliverance—that the appointed way of securing the Israelites from the general calamity was the passover and the sprinkling of blood; and Moses believed these revelations, and, believing them, spoke and acted accordingly.

Such appears to me to be the meaning of the declaration in the text, "By faith Moses kept the passover, and the sprinkling of blood, lest he that destroyed the first-born should touch them." I am aware that many excellent men have attached a very different meaning to these words. Misapprehending the design of the Apostle in the whole of this discussion,—supposing that it is his object to prove the doctrine of justification by faith in Christ Jesus, instead of to illustrate the importance and power of faith in a divine revelation,—they have considered the statement in the text as equivalent to—'Moses observed the passover and the sprinkling of blood by faith, looking through these rites as emblems of the atoning sacrifice of Jesus Christ, and the manner of that sacrifice becoming effectual for the salvation of the individual sinning.' That sacrifice, and especially the sacrifice of the passover, was a divinely intended emblem of the manner in which our guilt was to be expiated, and our salvation obtained, by the obedience to the death of the incarnate Son of God, is most clearly taught in the Holy Scriptures. But how far Moses and the other Old Testament saints were aware of this emblematical reference, is another question, and one by no means so easily resolved. What were the precise views entertained by the true Israel respecting the offices of the Messiah and the work of redemption—respecting the import and reference of expiatory sacrifice, is indeed among the most curious and intricate questions in theology. We know that they were saved, as we are, through the atonement; and we know also that they were saved by faith. We know, to use the language of a great writer, that "the cross of Christ, considered as the meritorious basis of acceptance, the only real satisfaction for sin, is the centre round which all the purposes of mercy to fallen men have continued to revolve. Fixed and determined in the counsel of God, it operated as the grand consideration in the divine mind on which salvation was awarded to believers in the earliest ages, as it will continue to operate in the same manner to the latest boundaries of time."[1] We know, too, that it was through believing that in every age the individual sinner obtained a personal interest in the blessings secured by that atonement; but that faith must have corresponded to the revelation made. We have no evidence that any revelation was made to them of the precise manner in which the salvation of a sinner is to be made compatible with the perfections of God, the honour of His law, and the great ends of His moral administration. In offering sacrifice, the believing Israelite recognised his guilt, his just exposure to destruction, and his exclusive reliance on divine mercy. "The way into the holiest was not made manifest" to them. I do not know if the circumstances of the ancient Church have ever been more accurately—they cannot be more beautifully—described, than in the words of the author whom I have just quoted:—"Exposed to dangers from which they knew of no definite mode of escape, and placed on the confines of an eternity feebly and faintly illumined, they had no other resource besides an implicit confidence in mysterious mercy."

But apart from these general considerations altogether, I apprehend that in the object of the Apostle, which we have endeavoured to bring distinctly out in the course of these lectures, we have the most satisfactory evidence that the faith by which Moses observed the passover and the sprinkling of blood, was just the belief of the revelations which were made to him on these subjects.

[1] Robert Hall.

It only remains that we very shortly show the bearing which this statement has on the Apostle's great object, which is the importance, and necessity, and sufficiency of believing, and continuing to believe, in order to the discharge of the duties enjoined on the Christian, the sustaining of the trials allotted to him, the attainment of the blessings promised to him. Christians are called on sometimes to perform duties which must appear unreasonable and absurd to an unbelieving world, and for which they themselves can assign no reason but the will of Him who has appointed them. A Christian in a heathen country strictly observing the Lord's day, to the apparent material disadvantage of his worldly interests, is a case in point. How is he to be enabled to persevere in the performance of this duty, amid the temptations to neglect it to which he is exposed? Look to Moses and the children of Israel observing the passover and the sprinkling of blood. The Egyptians, no doubt, thought it a very strange and unaccountable thing for the Israelites to be, all of them, bedaubing the entrances of their houses with blood; and the Israelites themselves could give no reason but one for it—God had commanded it. Yet believing this, they observed the appointed rite. In like manner, faith in the divine origin of the Christian Sabbath, and in the threatenings and promises in reference to it, will induce a Christian, even amid very strong temptations to act otherwise, to remember the Sabbath day to keep it holy. A similar case in point might be taken from a small body of Christians in a heathen country observing the Lord's Supper. But further, Christians are called on also to expect very important ends by very strange means. They are called on to expect a complete change of state and character by means of the death of God's Son on a cross, and by means of their understanding and believing the truth respecting this death. This seems as irrational an expectation as that of obtaining security from the destroyer of the first-born by observing the passover and the sprinkling of blood. A firm faith that God had established a connection between these two things, led Moses and the Israelites to perform the commanded rites as the means of obtaining the promised security; and a belief that " God so loved the world as to give His only-begotten Son, that whosoever believeth in Him shall not perish, but have everlasting life," will enable the Christian to hold fast this confidence, that,

## GENERAL EXHORTATION AND WARNING. 563

believing the truth as it is in Jesus, he shall have peace with God, and victory over the world, and eternal life, through the blood of the Lamb.

The next illustration of the power of faith which the Apostle, following down the course of Israelitish history, brings forward, is that furnished by that people passing in safety through the Arabian Gulf, while their Egyptian pursuers, in attempting to follow them, were overwhelmed by its waters. Ver. 29. " By faith they passed through the Red Sea as by dry land; which the Egyptians assaying to do were drowned."

The facts of the case are narrated at large in the 14th chapter of the book of Exodus. " And the Lord spake unto Moses, saying, Speak unto the children of Israel, that they turn and encamp before Pi-hahiroth, between Migdol and the sea, over against Baal-zephon: before it shall ye encamp by the sea. For Pharaoh will say of the children of Israel, They are entangled in the land, the wilderness hath shut them in. And I will harden Pharaoh's heart, that he shall follow after them; and I will be honoured upon Pharaoh, and upon all his host; that the Egyptians may know that I am the Lord. And they did so. And it was told the king of Egypt that the people fled: and the heart of Pharaoh and of his servants was turned against the people, and they said, Why have we done this, that we have let Israel go from serving us? And he made ready his chariot, and took his people with him. And he took six hundred chosen chariots, and all the chariots of Egypt, and captains over every one of them. And the Lord hardened the heart of Pharaoh king of Egypt, and he pursued after the children of Israel: and the children of Israel went out with an high hand. But the Egyptians pursued after them (all the horses and chariots of Pharaoh, and his horsemen, and his army), and overtook them encamping by the sea, beside Pi-hahiroth, before Baal-zephon. And when Pharaoh drew nigh, the children of Israel lifted up their eyes, and, behold, the Egyptians marched after them; and they were sore afraid: and the children of Israel cried out unto the Lord. And they said unto Moses, Because there were no graves in Egypt, hast thou taken us away to die in the wilderness? wherefore hast thou dealt thus with us, to carry us forth out of Egypt? Is not this the word that we did tell thee in Egypt, saying, Let us alone, that we may serve the Egyptians?

for it had been better for us to serve the Egyptians, than that we should die in the wilderness. And Moses said unto the people, Fear ye not, stand still, and see the salvation of the Lord, which He will show to you to-day: for the Egyptians whom ye have seen to-day, ye shall see them again no more for ever. The Lord shall fight for you, and ye shall hold your peace. And the Lord said unto Moses, Wherefore criest thou unto Me? speak unto the children of Israel, that they go forward: but lift thou up thy rod, and stretch out thine hand over the sea, and divide it; and the children of Israel shall go on dry ground through the midst of the sea. And I, behold, I will harden the hearts of the Egyptians, and they shall follow them: and I will get Me honour upon Pharaoh, and upon all his host, upon his chariots, and upon his horsemen. And the Egyptians shall know that I am the Lord, when I have gotten Me honour upon Pharaoh, upon his chariots, and upon his horsemen. And the angel of God, which went before the camp of Israel, removed, and went behind them; and the pillar of the cloud went from before their face, and stood behind them. And it came between the camp of the Egyptians and the camp of Israel; and it was a cloud and darkness to them, but it gave light by night to these: so that the one came not near the other all the night. And Moses stretched out his hand over the sea; and the Lord caused the sea to go back by a strong east wind all that night, and made the sea dry land, and the waters were divided. And the children of Israel went into the midst of the sea upon the dry ground: and the waters were a wall unto them on their right hand, and on their left. And the Egyptians pursued, and went in after them to the midst of the sea, even all Pharaoh's horses, his chariots, and his horsemen. And it came to pass, that, in the morning-watch, the Lord looked unto the host of the Egyptians through the pillar of fire, and of the cloud, and troubled the host of the Egyptians, and took off their chariot-wheels, that they drave them heavily: so that the Egyptians said, Let us flee from the face of Israel; for the Lord fighteth for them against the Egyptians. And the Lord said unto Moses, Stretch out thine hand over the sea, that the waters may come again upon the Egyptians, upon their chariots, and upon their horsemen. And Moses stretched forth his hand over the sea, and the sea returned to his strength when the morning appeared; and the Egyptians fled against it; and the Lord overthrew the Egyptians in the midst of the sea. And the waters returned, and covered the chariots, and the horsemen, and all the host of Pharaoh that came into the sea after them: there remained not so much as one of them. But the children of Israel walked upon dry land in the midst of the sea; and the waters were a wall unto them on their right hand, and on their left. Thus the Lord saved Israel that day out of the hand of the Egyptians; and Israel saw the Egyptians dead upon the sea-shore. And Israel saw that great work which the Lord did upon the Egyptians; and the people feared the Lord, and believed the Lord, and His servant Moses." Such is the inspired historian's narrative: now for the inspired Apostle's commentary.

" By faith they"—*i.e.*, Moses and the Israelitish people—"passed through the Red Sea as by dry land." A revelation had been made to them, that they should safely pass along that strange pathway, which, by the arm of Jehovah, had been opened up for them through the waters of the Arabian Gulf. Had no revelation been made to them,—in which case there could have been no faith, there being nothing to believe,—or had the revelation not been believed by the Israelites, they durst not have ventured into the fearful chasm, but in all probability would have sought, by unqualified submission, to appease the fury of the tyrant from whose grasp they had escaped, as the more probable way of saving their lives. But believing the divine declaration, and no doubt having their faith strengthened by the miraculous division of the waters as they approached them (for it was natural for them to reason in this way: ' He who has divided the waters can keep them divided;—He has performed one part of His wonderful prediction; He will perform the other also. He cannot have done this great wonder to lure us to our doom, but to open a way for us to secure deliverance'), they entered the dried-up channel, and proceeded along that untrodden path, till they safely arrived on the opposite shore. Faith thus enabled the Israelites to do what otherwise they could not have done—obey the command of God, to attempt a passage of this arm of the sea through the midst of its waters. It enabled the Israelites also to obtain what otherwise they could not have obtained—a safe passage, and complete security from their Egyptian pursuers.

The question has often been put, Was the faith by which the Israelites passed through the Red Sea *saving faith*? I have no doubt that a number of the Israelites, as well as Moses, were believers of the comparatively dim revelation of that scheme of mercy of which we have the completed revelation, and through that faith obtained eternal life. I have as little doubt, however, that by far the greater part of them were in this sense of the word unbelievers; and, in consequence of their unbelief of this revelation, never entered into the heavenly rest, even as, on account of their unbelief of another revelation, they never entered into the rest of God in Canaan. It is equally obvious, I think, that the faith of the revelation made to Moses respecting the Israelites obtaining a safe passage through the Red Sea, was not what we ordinarily term saving faith; and there is nothing to make us think that the Israelites, in believing that revelation, understood that it had a typical reference, and in consequence believed that God would deliver them from spiritual dangers, of which the waves of the Arabian Gulf, furiously agitated by tempest, afforded but an imperfect emblem.

The Apostle's object is to show the power of real faith in God, whatever be its object. The nature and extent of that efficacy will depend on the nature and extent of the revelation believed. A faith in a revelation respecting the safe passage of the Red Sea enabled the Israelites fearlessly to entrust themselves in the strangely formed valley between two mountainous ridges of tumultuous waves, and to reach in safety the opposite shore. A faith in the revelation of salvation from guilt and depravity, and death and hell, will enable the Christian to perform all the duties, and endure all the difficulties, that are involved in obtaining complete possession of this salvation, and will in due time bring him into the enjoyment of all its blessings, in all their perfection.

A subject often receives much illustration by contrast. This mode of illustration is adopted here. The power of faith, in enabling the Israelites to pass through the Red Sea safely, is illustrated by the helpless, hopeless destruction of the infatuated Egyptians, who attempted to follow them. The Egyptians had no faith on this subject—they could have none. No revelation had been made to them; and even if the revelation had been made to them which was made to the Israelites, it is doubtful if they would have believed it. And if they had believed it, it would not have led them to follow the Israelites, but, on the contrary, would have prevented them. The same revelation, though equally firmly believed, will produce different effects on different individuals. A revelation that the Israelites were to be safely led through the Red Sea, though believed by an Egyptian, could be no ground of expectation that *he* was to be led safely through the Red Sea also. The revelation of a free and a full salvation to the guiltiest of the human race, believing in Jesus, though believed by a fallen angel, could be no ground of expectation that *he* was to be a partaker of this salvation.

The Egyptians, led not by faith in a divine revelation, but by their furious passions, followed the Israelites into the Red Sea. It was night, and, to the Egyptians, dark night. The chasm in the waters of the gulf was probably of very considerable width, extending very likely for some miles. The Egyptians were probably neither aware of the great miracle which had been wrought for Israel, nor of the extreme danger in which they had involved themselves. In darkness they were pursuing Israel. Where Israel went, they supposed they might follow; and it does not seem that they discovered their real circumstances till in the morning they found themselves in the midst of the sea. Then they said, "Let us flee from the face of Israel; for the Lord fighteth for them against the Egyptians."[1] But it was too late. Now had arrived the hour when much-enduring, long-despised divine forbearance was to be avenged for all the insults offered to it. It is difficult to say whether the historical or the poetical account of the fearful catastrophe is most picturesque and affecting. We have the first in Exod. xiv. 26-28: "And the Lord said unto Moses, Stretch out thine hand over the sea, that the waters may come again upon the Egyptians, upon their chariots, and upon their horsemen. And Moses stretched forth his hand over the sea, and the sea returned to his strength when the morning appeared; and the Egyptians fled against it; and the Lord overthrew the Egyptians in the midst of the sea. And the waters returned, and covered the chariots, and the horsemen, and all the host of

[1] Exod. xiv. 25.

Pharaoh that came into the sea after them: there remained not so much as one of them." We have the second in chap. xv. 4-11: "Pharaoh's chariots and his host hath He cast into the sea: his chosen captains also are drowned in the Red Sea. The depths have covered them: they sank into the bottom as a stone. Thy right hand, O Lord, is become glorious in power: Thy right hand, O Lord, hath dashed in pieces the enemy. And in the greatness of Thine excellency Thou hast overthrown them that rose up against Thee: Thou sentest forth Thy wrath, which consumed them as stubble. And with the blast of Thy nostrils the waters were gathered together, the floods stood upright as an heap, and the depths were congealed in the heart of the sea. The enemy said, I will pursue, I will overtake, I will divide the spoil; my lust shall be satisfied upon them; I will draw my sword, my hand shall destroy them. Thou didst blow with Thy wind, the sea covered them; they sank as lead in the mighty waters. Who is like unto Thee, O Lord, among the gods? who is like Thee, glorious in holiness, fearful in praises, doing wonders?"

The general truth taught by the ineffectual and ruinous attempt of the Egyptians is this: that they who attempt to do without faith, what believers successfully do by faith—those who attempt to obtain without faith, what believers succeed in obtaining by faith—will assuredly be disappointed. The believer obtains peace with God; but all the unbeliever's attempts to obtain solid peace will end in disappointment. Men are sanctified through the belief of the truth; but all attempts to make a person's self holy without believing, will assuredly end in disappointment. By believing, a man will make a consistent profession of Christianity amid all the temptations to which he may be exposed: a man who enters on a profession of Christianity without faith, is sure, sooner or later, to manifest its hollowness. Every persevering believer will certainly obtain the salvation of his soul as the end of his believing; but every man who is seeking genuine and permanent happiness without believing, will find himself at last, like the Egyptians, engulphed in the depths of destruction, when he hoped as a conqueror to set his foot on the shore of the celestial country.

The bearing of this illustration on the Apostle's object is direct and obvious. The Hebrew Christians were exposed to numerous and severe afflictions in the maintenance of their Christian profession, and submission to these was absolutely necessary in order to their progress towards the heavenly promised land. Faith alone could enable them—faith would assuredly enable them—to enter on and pass through these trials, however severe. Without faith, in the mere prospect of them, they may very probably return to spiritual Egypt; or, if they presumptuously plunge in, like the Egyptians, they are likely to be overwhelmed by them. Nothing but faith, persevering faith, can enable the Christian to pass safely through all the trials and dangers of the wilderness, uphold him amid the waves of the Red Sea of affliction and the swellings of the Jordan of death, and give him a sure and everlasting resting-place in the Canaan above.

The next illustration of the importance of faith, is that taken from the miraculous overthrow of the walls of Jericho. Ver. 30. "By faith the walls of Jericho fell down, after they were compassed about seven days."

The facts of this case are narrated at large in the book of Joshua: "And it came to pass, when Joshua was by Jericho, that he lifted up his eyes and looked, and, behold, there stood a man over against him, with his sword drawn in his hand: and Joshua went unto him, and said unto him, Art thou for us, or for our adversaries? And he said, Nay; but as captain of the host of the Lord am I now come. And Joshua fell on his face to the earth, and did worship, and said unto him, What saith my lord unto his servant? And the captain of the Lord's host said unto Joshua, Loose thy shoe from off thy foot; for the place whereon thou standest is holy. And Joshua did so. Now Jericho was straitly shut up because of the children of Israel: none went out, and none came in. And the Lord said unto Joshua, See, I have given into thine hand Jericho, and the king thereof, and the mighty men of valour. And ye shall compass the city, all ye men of war, and go round about the city once. Thus shalt thou do six days. And seven priests shall bear before the ark seven trumpets of rams' horns; and the seventh day ye shall compass the city seven times, and the priests shall blow with the trumpets. And it shall come to pass, that when they make a long blast with the ram's horn, and when ye hear the sound of the trumpet, all the people shall shout with a great shout; and the wall of the city shall fall down flat, and the people shall ascend up, every man straight before him. And Joshua the son of Nun called the priests, and said unto them, Take up the ark of the covenant, and let seven priests bear seven trumpets of rams' horns before the ark of the Lord. And he said unto the people, Pass on, and compass the city, and let him that is armed pass on before the ark of the Lord. And it came to pass, when Joshua had spoken unto the people, that the seven priests, bearing the seven trumpets of rams' horns, passed on before the Lord, and blew with the trumpets; and the ark of the covenant of the Lord followed them. And the armed men went before the priests that blew with the trumpets, and the rere-ward came after the ark, the priests going on, and blowing with the trumpets. And Joshua had commanded the people, saying, Ye shall not shout, nor make any noise with your voice, neither shall any word proceed out of your mouth, until the day I bid you shout; then shall ye shout. So the ark of the Lord compassed the city, going about it once: and they came into the camp, and lodged in the camp. And Joshua rose early in the morning, and the priests took up the ark of the Lord. And seven priests, bearing seven trumpets of rams' horns before the ark of the Lord, went on continually, and blew with the trumpets: and the armed men went before them; but the rere-ward came after the ark of the Lord, the priests going on, and blowing with the trumpets. And the second day they compassed the city once, and returned into the camp: so they did six days. And it came to pass on the seventh day, that they rose early, about the dawning of the day, and compassed the city after the same manner seven times: only on that day they compassed the city seven times. And it came to pass at the seventh time, when the priests blew with the trumpets, Joshua said unto the people, Shout; for the Lord hath given you the city. And the city shall be accursed, even it, and all that are therein, to the Lord: only Rahab the harlot shall live, she and all that are with her in the house, because she hid the messengers that we sent. And ye, in anywise keep yourselves from the accursed thing, lest ye make yourselves accursed, when ye take of the accursed thing, and make the camp of Israel a curse, and trouble it. But all the silver, and gold, and vessels of brass and iron, are consecrated unto the Lord: they shall come into the treasury of the Lord. So the people shouted when the priests blew with the trumpets: and it came to pass, when the people heard the sound of the trumpet, and the people shouted with a great shout, that the wall fell down flat, so that the people went up into the city, every man straight before him, and they took the city."[1]

The destruction of the walls of Jericho was obviously miraculous—produced immediately by the power of God. It may be asked, Then how was it "by faith?" Whose faith is referred to, and how did this faith influence the event? The faith referred to is plainly the faith of Joshua, believing the divine oracle uttered to him, and the faith of the people of Israel, believing the same oracle as reported to them by Joshua. How, then, faith influenced the event, is easily explained. The oracle distinctly declared that the manifestation of the divine power in a particular way was connected with certain actions to be performed by the children of Israel. They believed the oracle; because they believed the oracle, they performed the actions; and according to the oracle, the miraculous event took place. Suppose no oracle delivered, or suppose the oracle not to be believed—suppose Joshua or the people of Israel to have considered the appearance of the glorious personage, styling

---

[1] Joshua v. 13-15, vi. 1-20.—The Comment of a rationalist interpreter is worth recording, if but to prove what fearful $\sigma\tau\rho\epsilon\beta\lambda\omega\tau\alpha\iota$ of the divine word these men are: "*Doubtless*" (the confidence of men believing without evidence is generally proportioned to their confidence in disbelieving in the face of evidence. Neological interpreters do wonderful feats in both ways) "the facts are these. Joshua ordered his soldiers to go round the city for seven days, and to refrain from any attack on it. When, after this, the inhabitants were feeling safe, Joshua commanded his soldiers on the seventh day to assault that part of the city which was less fortified " (where did he find out that?) " and to attack its walls amid the blowing of trumpets and blood-curdling shouts; and we think this was done with such violence that the walls seemed to fall of their own accord. However true it may be that some things in this history are related with poetic licence, nothing of its serious import is reduced. For it makes no difference to faith, whether these things took place in a miraculous way, or by a sequence of events not known before."—DINDORF.

"To laugh were want of goodness and of grace,
But to be grave exceeds all power of face."

But ridicule and scorn are not the appropriate feelings. We "do well to be angry" at such unfair treatment of an ancient, still more an inspired writer; and our hearts should dissolve in pity for men who, endowed with strong intellects and extensive learning, and applying both to the study of the Scriptures for a lifetime, arrive only at such results as these.

himself "the captain of the Lord's host," to have been a mere delusion of the fancy: their conduct is altogether unaccountable. They are before one of the most strongly defended cities in the land of Canaan. They dig no trenches to preserve themselves safe. They stand not in battle-array to meet any sally on them by the garrison. They lay no formal siege, set no battering engines, raise no shouts to intimidate the inhabitants. But in solemn silence, in sacred procession, the whole armed men, following the ark and the priests, encircled the city once every day for six days. On the seventh day the strange procession compassed the devoted city six times in accustomed portentous silence, till at last, at a signal given by Joshua, the priests blew a united blast on their unmusical trumpets, and the people raised one shout of anticipated triumph, and by the power of God the walls of Jericho fell flat, and they marched at once on all sides into the heart of the city. On the supposition of the revelation being made and believed, all is natural. Joshua and the people of Israel could not have acted differently.

The general truth here is the same as that involved in the former instance. Faith, persevering faith, enabled Joshua and the Israelites to do what otherwise they could not have done, and by doing so, to obtain what otherwise they could not have obtained; and the bearing of this on the Apostle's object is not difficult to perceive or explain.

The Hebrew Christians were engaged in a cause, the success of which, in the estimation of human reason, was even more hopeless than the capture of Jericho by the Israelites. The final triumph of the religion of Jesus over Judaism and paganism, false philosophy and worldly power, which had been distinctly predicted, seemed very unlikely. The means—the only means they were warranted to employ, appeared very ill fitted to gain their object. The preaching of the Gospel, the prayers of the Church, the holy conversation of believers, and their patience under manifold and severe afflictions,—what Milton happily styles "the unresistible might of weakness,"—these were to be the means by which the powers of darkness were to be shaken, and the walls of adamant and iron, reaching even up to heaven, within which superstition had entrenched herself, levelled with the ground. "The Captain of the Lord's host" had uttered the following oracle:—"All power in heaven and earth is given unto Me. Go ye therefore, and teach all nations: and, lo, I am with you alway, even unto the end of the world." This believed, was quite enough to induce them to commence and continue, amid all discouragements, the use of the appointed means, till the promised end was gained. Nothing else could have induced them to do so.

And it is equally true still, that faith—that nothing else but faith—can carry forward the Christian Church in its predicted triumph over the world and hell. What is the reason that there has been so little missionary effort in the Christian Church, in comparison of what there ought to have been? and why has that little effort been so languid, interrupted, and ineffectual? What but the want of a sufficiently implicit persevering faith in the promises, leading to a correspondingly implicit and persevering obedience to the commandments, of the great "Captain of our salvation?"

Nor is it difficult to perceive that this has a bearing on the transactions of the inward life of every Christian. Every individual Christian, in "working out his own salvation," has to contend with the same enemies, as in doing his part in the great work of the propagation of Christianity throughout the world. The Apostle's words, Eph. vi. 12, which in their primary meaning refer to the difficulties of the apostolic ministry, are true when used in reference to every Christian. They have to "wrestle with flesh and blood;" but not only with flesh and blood, but " with principalities and powers, with the rulers of the darkness of this world, with spiritual wickedness in high places." Barriers more difficult to be broken down than the walls of Jericho, seem to stand between them and holiness and heaven. How are these enemies to be overcome? how are these barriers to be removed? Faith can do it; nothing but faith can do it. Let all the allurements and all the terrors of the world be laid before the Christian, and use their combined influence to draw him away from truth, and holiness, and God; and let, through means of believing, the awful and the delightful realities of the eternal world be brought before his mind, and "this will be the victory, even our faith" overcoming the world. O how false, and hollow, and worthless, and absurd, and detestable seem all the promises and all the threats of "the prince of this world," when by the ear of faith we hear the Prince of the universe proclaim, "Be of good cheer, I have overcome the world,"—"I am the First, and the Last, and the Living One,"—" Be faithful to death, and I will give you a crown of life,"—"To him that overcometh, will I give to eat of the hidden manna, and will give him a white stone, and in the stone a new name written, which no man knoweth saving he that receiveth it!" Then the Christian feels that greater indeed is " He who is in him, than he who is in the world." Difficulties vanish; great mountains become a plain; there is no propensity so strong but he finds it now possible to resist, almost delightful to mortify; and just in the degree in which he believes, can he "do all things through Christ strengthening him."

The last of those Scripture illustrations of the power of faith which the Apostle unfolds particularly, is drawn from the history of Rahab the Canaanitess. Ver. 31. " By faith the harlot Rahab perished not with them that believed not, when she had received the spies with peace." Here, as on former occasions, let us look first at the facts, and then at the Apostle's account of the facts: first to what Rahab did and obtained; and then to the influence of her faith in leading her to act as she acted, and in enabling her to attain what she attained.

The discreditable appellation given to Rahab in our version has appeared to some learned men not warranted by the original term. They consider it as properly signifying ' a hostess or innkeeper;' or, understanding the word in a figurative sense, interpret it as equivalent to ' idolater.'[1] I rather think our translators, in common with by far the greater part of other interpreters, have accurately expressed the truth; and that in the conversion of Rahab (for I apprehend we have good evidence of her spiritual conversion) we are furnished with a beautiful display of the sovereignty of divine grace, and the power of divine influence, through the faith of the truth, to elevate the most degraded, and purify the most depraved, forms of human character.

The facts stated in reference to Rahab are two. She " received the spies[2] in peace;" and she " perished not with them

---

[1] The word cannot be derived regularly from יון, ' to feed.' It comes obviously from זנה, ' to commit whoredom;' and though idolatry was spiritual whoredom in the Israelitish people, yet I do not know that an individual Jewish idolater is termed a whoremonger or adulterer, far less a Gentile who did not belong to the nation married to Jehovah.

[2] κατασκόπους. James calls them ἀγγέλους, ii. 25.

who believed not." When Joshua, previously to Israel's passing the Jordan, sent from Shittim two men as spies to Jericho, to bring him intelligence of the state of matters among the Canaanites, they were hospitably entertained by Rahab, to whose house they were providentially directed; and when sought for by order of the king of Jericho, they were concealed by her at the peril of her own life, and through her dexterity obtained a secure retreat. As a reward for this important service, when all the inhabitants of Jericho were put to the sword, Rahab and her family were preserved alive, and obtained a place among the peculiar people of God,—Rahab marrying Salmon, the prince of Judah, and thus becoming one of the ancestors of the Messiah. Such are the facts: now for the Apostle's account of these facts.

How came Rahab to act as she acted?—how came she to obtain what she obtained? It was by believing, says the Apostle. Had Rahab acted on the ordinary principles of human nature, she would immediately, on discovering who the Israelitish spies were, and what was their errand, have given information to the authorities of the city, that they might be apprehended; at any rate, when search was made for them, she never would have exposed her own life to imminent peril in order to save them. What was that principle which exceeded in force the love of country and the fear of death? It was faith. Hear Rahab's own confession of her belief: "And she said unto the men, I know that the Lord hath given you the land, and that your terror is fallen upon us, and that all the inhabitants of the land faint because of you. For we have heard how the Lord dried up the water of the Red Sea for you, when ye came out of Egypt; and what ye did unto the two kings of the Amorites, that were on the other side Jordan, Sihon and Og, whom ye utterly destroyed. And as soon as we had heard these things, our hearts did melt, neither did there remain any more courage in any man, because of you; for the Lord your God, He is God in heaven above, and in earth beneath."[1] Had Rahab not heard these things in reference to Jehovah as the God of Israel, or had she, like many of her countrymen, heard but not believed them, she could not have acted as she did; but having heard and believed them, she could not but act as she did. It

[1] Joshua ii. 9–11.

deserves notice that no direct revelation was made to Rahab, but she had credible evidence of the reality of the revelations which Jehovah had made of His power and regard for Israel, which laid a foundation for firm belief. The efficacy of faith as an operative principle does not depend on the divine revelation which is the subject of faith being made directly to the individual, but on the individual's being fully persuaded, on sufficient evidence, that such a revelation has been made.

But how was it by faith that Rahab perished not with her unbelieving countrymen? The answer is obvious: her deliverance was the reward of her treatment of the spies, which originated in her faith. Had she not believed, she would not have been delivered; had she remained an unbeliever, she must have perished among the unbelievers.

We are not to suppose that the whole conduct of Rahab in reference to the spies receives the approbation of the inspired writer, while he represents that conduct as an illustration of the power of faith. Rahab's falsehood cannot be justified, and is a proof that, if strong in faith in one way, she was weak in faith in another. All that the Apostle says—and we have seen how completely he is borne out by the history in what he says—is, 'Faith enabled Rahab to do what otherwise she could not have done, and to attain what otherwise she could not have attained.'

This illustration of the power, the necessity, the sufficiency of faith, was peculiarly fitted to come home to the business and bosom of the Hebrew Christians. They, like Rahab, were called on to do violence to their patriotic feelings, to separate themselves from their unbelieving kindred and country, and to follow a course which exposed them not only to "the spoiling of their goods," but to imminent hazard of their lives. Nothing but faith could enable them to act properly in these circumstances. If they really believed Jesus Christ to be the true Messiah, their Saviour and Lord—if they really believed His declarations, and promises, and threatenings: "He that loveth father, or mother, or sister, or brother, or houses, or lands, more than Me, is not worthy of Me;" "He that loseth his life shall find it; he that saveth his life shall lose it;" "He that continueth to the end shall be saved;"—if they really believed this, they would readily do all and suffer all that was required of them—they would submit to privations, expose themselves to dangers, and make sacrifices, from which otherwise they would have shrunk with terror; they would be content to have "their name cast out as evil" by their countrymen; and in this "patient continuance in well-doing," growing out of their believing, they would in due time attain to complete deliverance—"to glory, honour, and immortality." While, on the other hand, if they did not believe, they must fall before their temptations, and perish among their unbelieving countrymen.

And is not the illustration replete with instruction to professors of Christianity in every country and in every age? The terms of discipleship have never varied. "If any man will be My disciple, let him deny himself, take up his cross, and follow Me." All who would live godly must make sacrifices, and expose themselves to hazards. Faith, and nothing but faith, can enable persons cheerfully to make such sacrifices, to expose themselves to such dangers. Faith can do it; and, in the deliverance from the destruction which awaits the unbelievers, will in due time obtain for them a rich recompense for all they have hazarded and all they have lost in the cause of Christ.

Instead of prosecuting the course which he had begun, of particularly detailing the facts in which the power of faith manifested itself in the doings, and sufferings, and attainments of the Old Testament worthies, the Apostle, perceiving that this would have extended the Epistle beyond due limits, contents himself with barely enumerating the names of a number more of these believers, and in general terms describing the effects of their faith; intimating at the same time that there were many more besides those whom he mentions, who, in their actions and sufferings, in their lives and in their deaths, gave striking evidence to the power of believing in endowing man as it were with a supernatural strength, both for action and endurance. Vers. 32–38. "And what shall I more say? for the time would fail me to tell of Gedeon, and of Barak, and of Samson, and of Jephthae; of David also, and Samuel, and of the prophets: who through faith subdued kingdoms, wrought righteousness, obtained promises, stopped the mouths of lions, quenched the violence of fire, escaped the edge of the sword, out of weakness were made strong, waxed valiant in fight, turned to flight the armies of the aliens. Women received their dead raised to life again: and others were tortured, not accepting deliverance;

that they might obtain a better resurrection. And others had trial of cruel mockings and scourgings, yea, moreover of bonds and imprisonment: they were stoned, they were sawn asunder, were tempted, were slain with the sword: they wandered about in sheep-skins and goat-skins; being destitute, afflicted, tormented (of whom the world was not worthy): they wandered in deserts, and in mountains, and in dens and caves of the earth."

This is a very beautiful paragraph. It divides itself into two parts. Generally, it is an illustration of the power of faith; but the power of faith is viewed in two aspects—its power to enable men to do what otherwise they could not have done, and its power to enable men to suffer what otherwise they could not have suffered. We have an illustration of the first from the beginning of the 32d to the end of the first clause of the 35th verse; we have an illustration of the second from the beginning of the second clause of the 35th verse to the end of the 38th verse.

Let us examine, then, the Apostle's illustration of the power of faith to enable men to do what otherwise they could not have done. "And what shall I more say?" or, 'Why should I recite examples any longer? The point is already fully proved, clearly illustrated. Besides, time would fail me to recount all the examples recorded in Old Testament history of the power of faith. It would swell the Epistle to an inconvenient size.' He therefore contents himself with referring to a number of other illustrious individuals, who by faith had "obtained a good report;" and by turning to the Old Testament they could easily verify his reference, and see that in their actions the power of faith was not less strikingly manifested than in those which had been more particularly detailed.

The first person mentioned is Gideon. At a time when the worship of Baal prevailed to such an extent in Israel that the opposer of it was considered as a criminal worthy of death, Gideon cut down the grove dedicated to that idol, and overthrew his altar. What enabled Gideon to do this? It was faith. A revelation was made to him; he believed the revelation, and acted accordingly. "And it came to pass the same night, that the Lord said unto him, Take thy father's young bullock, even the second bullock of seven years old, and throw down the altar of Baal that thy father hath, and cut down the grove that is by it; and build an altar unto the Lord thy God upon the top of this rock, in the ordered place, and take the second bullock, and offer a burnt sacrifice with the wood of the grove which thou shalt cut down. Then Gideon took ten men of his servants, and did as the Lord had said unto him: and so it was, because he feared his father's household, and the men of the city, that he could not do it by day, that he did it by night."[1] Gideon, after collecting an army of thirty-two thousand men to fight against the Midianites and Amalekites, who at that time oppressed Israel, made proclamation, that every individual who was afraid of the approaching combat was at liberty to retire, and thus reduced his troops to ten thousand. He then subjected them to a very strange kind of trial, by bringing them to a pool of water and making them drink; dismissing such of them as lay down to drink, and retaining only such as, in a bending posture, lapped the water with their hands. His army was thus reduced to three hundred men; and these three hundred men he armed in a very extraordinary manner—with trumpets and with empty pitchers, and with lamps in these pitchers. By these most unlikely means Gideon obtained a complete victory, and delivered Israel out of the hands of their enemies.

Now how are we to account for Gideon's conduct, and for Gideon's success? There is but one way. He did all this "by faith." A divine revelation was given him; he believed, and acted accordingly. He used the means appointed by God, though in themselves utterly unfit for gaining the end; and it was to him according to his faith. Without such a revelation as he had, and without faith in that revelation, he could not have acted as he did; with such a revelation, and with faith in such a revelation, he could not but act as he did.

Barak is the next person mentioned as affording in his history an illustration of the power of faith. He, at a period when the Israelites were completely subjected to the oppressive yoke of Jabin, king of Canaan, raised a small band of ten thousand men, and at their head attacked Sisera, the commander of Jabin's numerous and well-appointed army, and completely discomfited him.

What was it that enabled Barak to undertake, and what was

[1] Judges vi. 25–27.

it that enabled him to succeed in, so apparently hopeless an enterprise? It was faith. A divine revelation was made to him through the medium of Deborah the prophetess; he believed it, and acted accordingly. Had no revelation been made, or had he disbelieved it, the attempt would never have been made.

The next illustration of the power of faith is taken from the very singular history of Samson. Samson performed many wonders. He tore a lion to pieces, as if it had been a kid; he burst asunder the strongest cords with which he could be bound, and, single-handed, slew a thousand of his enemies; he carried off the gates of Gaza and their posts on his shoulders; and he overturned the pillars by which the stately temple of Dagon was supported.

Now how did Samson do all these things? By faith. We are generally told, previously to any of his extraordinary feats, "The Spirit of the Lord came upon him." That is, I apprehend, a revelation was made to his mind that the divine power was to be put forth in connection with some exertion of his, so that he was to be enabled to do something far exceeding his natural powers. He believed this, and acted accordingly; and found that it was to him according to his faith.

Jephthah is next mentioned as an exemplification of the power of faith. At the time when the children of Israel were oppressed by the Ammonites, Jephthah, a man of low birth, with very inadequate means, effected their deliverance. How was this accomplished? It was through his believing. "The Spirit of the Lord came upon him;" *i.e.*, a revelation was made to him that he was to be the deliverer of Israel. He believed it, and acted accordingly.

David is next mentioned; but it were tedious to bring before you all the illustrations of the power of faith furnished by his eventful history. It is not improbable that the Apostle particularly refers to his victorious combat with the Philistian giant. David, a young man, unarmed but with a sling and a few pebbles, entered the lists with the veteran and well-accoutred gigantic champion of the Philistines, and gained the victory. These are the facts. What is the only rational account of them? David had received a divine revelation. This is plain from the confident manner in which he speaks: "This day will the Lord deliver thee into mine hand: and I will smite thee, and take thine head from thee; and I will give the carcases of the host of the Philistines this day unto the fowls of the air, and to the wild beasts of the earth; that all the earth may know that there is a God in Israel. And all this assembly shall know that the Lord saveth not with sword and spear: for the battle is the Lord's, and He will give you into our hands."[1] He believed it, and this accounts satisfactorily both for his conduct and for his success. Other instances of the power of faith will readily occur to the mind of every person intimately acquainted with David's history.

Samuel is the last of the ancients mentioned by name as exemplifying the power of faith. We cannot say certainly to what the inspired writer refers. It is possible that he refers to his anointing David to be king over Israel, notwithstanding the extreme danger to which this exposed him. A divine revelation was made to him; he believed it, and acted accordingly. His anointing Saul was another proof of the power of faith. But the event to which we are disposed to think it most probable, from its miraculous character, that the Apostle refers, is that recorded in 1 Sam. xii. 16-18: "Now therefore stand and see this great thing, which the Lord will do before your eyes. Is it not wheat-harvest to-day? I will call unto the Lord, and He shall send thunder and rain; that ye may perceive and see that your wickedness is great, which ye have done in the sight of the Lord, in asking you a king. So Samuel called unto the Lord; and the Lord sent thunder and rain that day: and all the people greatly feared the Lord and Samuel." A revelation was made to Samuel that the divine power was to be put forth in connection with certain words which he spoke. He believed that revelation; he spoke the words, and the event followed.

"The prophets" are then brought forward as exemplifying the power of faith. Appropriate instances will readily occur to every person familiarly acquainted with Old Testament history. Nathan reproving David; Micaiah denouncing Ahab's overthrow; Elijah fed by ravens—miraculously increasing the meal and the oil of the widow of Zarephath, and raising from the dead her son—bringing down fire from heaven to consume the sacrifice on Mount Carmel—withholding and bestowing rain by

---

[1] 1 Sam. xvii. 46, 47.

his prayers; Elisha performing similar wonders; Isaiah predicting Hezekiah's lengthened life, and the sudden destruction of the Assyrian army. These, and multitudes of other similar events in the history of the prophets, attest the power of faith. They are events of which no rational account can be given on any principle but this: A revelation of the divine will was made to them; they believed it, and this produced its appropriate effect. They were enabled to do what otherwise they could not have done.

The Apostle goes on to particularize some of the wonderful works which these men did, under the influence of faith, in the 33d and following verses.

The question has sometimes been put, Were all the persons here mentioned true saints? The question is rather a curious than a useful one. My answer to it is, Really I do not know. I am sure that some of them were; I hope all of them were. But all that is of importance for us to know is this, that all of them believed some divine revelation made to them, and that their faith of that revelation enabled them to do what otherwise they would not have been able to do. Their being brought forward here as illustrations of the power of faith, in no degree sanctions any pieces of their conduct which are inconsistent with the principles of truth and righteousness. Gideon's making an ephod out of the spoils of the Midianites; Jephthah's immolating his daughter, or devoting her to perpetual celibacy— for it seems difficult to determine which of these he did; Samson's taking a Philistian wife, and keeping company with a harlot; David's complicated sin in the matter of Uriah the Hittite;—none of these receive any sanction from the statement of the plain, well-supported fact, that all of these men, in consequence of their believing, were enabled to do things which otherwise they could not have done. These sins were proofs, not of faith, but of unbelief. In every one of them they acted without a divine revelation, or in opposition to a divine revelation. In reading Scripture history, let us recollect that the faults of good men are recorded to serve as beacons, not as guide-posts; that in copying any mere human character we must be cautious. There is but one *all*-perfect pattern. HE is "all fair; there is no spot in Him." He has "set us an example;" let us "follow *His* steps."

## GENERAL EXHORTATION AND WARNING. 583

The paragraph from vers. 33-38 naturally divides itself into two parts: the first, illustrative of the power of faith to enable men to accomplish successfully the most difficult enterprises; the second, illustrative of its power to enable men to sustain patiently the most severe trials. Let us examine these two divisions of the paragraph in their order.

The first reaches from the beginning of the 33d verse to the end of the first clause of the 35th verse. "Who" (*i.e.*, the ancient worthies referred to in the preceding verses) "through faith subdued kingdoms, wrought righteousness, obtained promises, stopped the mouths of lions, quenched the violence of fire, escaped the edge of the sword, out of weakness were made strong, waxed valiant in fight, turned to flight the armies of the aliens. Women received their dead raised to life again."[1]

They "subdued kingdoms." This refers, I apprehend, to Joshua and David. Joshua subdued the kingdoms in Canaan, and David subdued those which were around that country—such as Moab, Ammon, Edom, and Syria; and they both subdued these kingdoms through believing. God had clearly revealed, not merely that it was His purpose that these kingdoms should be subdued, but also that Joshua and David were to be instruments of their subjugation. They believed this divine revelation; their faith manifested itself by corresponding exertions; and God, according to His promise, and in reward of their faith, crowned their exertions with success.

They "wrought righteousness." To "work righteousness," sometimes means in Scripture, to 'live a holy life;' as in such passages as these:—"Lord, who shall abide in Thy tabernacle? who shall dwell in Thy holy hill? He that walketh uprightly, and worketh righteousness." "But in every nation he that feareth God, and worketh righteousness, is accepted with Him."[2] There can be no doubt that many of the persons re-

---

[1] This is a very admirable passage. Most justly does Carpzov remark, "With the skill of a Demosthenes he piles up examples of those who by faith alone stood their ground, and with great courage bore disasters, dangers, fire, bonds, torture, mockery, flogging, stoning, the sword's point, and even death. Here all the marks of the orator appear, ἀσύνδετα, delectus vocum, αὔξησις καὶ δείνωσις, πεῦσις καὶ ἐρώτησις, κλίμακες, ἀθροισμοί, σφοδρὸν καὶ ἐνθουσιαστικὸν πάθος, comparent."

[2] Ps. xv. 1, 2; Acts x. 35.

ferred to did live holy lives, and that their living holy lives was owing to their believing the truth with regard to the divine character and will; and that the enabling an entirely depraved being, such as all men naturally are, habitually to live a holy life, is one of the most remarkable exemplifications of the power of faith. Yet I apprehend the general scope of the passage leads us to interpret the phrase, "wrought righteousness," in a more restricted sense, as equivalent to—'carried the laws of justice into execution, executed judgment.' I think it not improbable that the Apostle had in his eye Phinehas and Elijah, who both of them, through believing, executed judgment—inflicted merited punishment on notorious offenders—in circumstances in which, had they not been believers, they durst not have done it. The particulars of the two cases may be read —the first, in Num. xxv. 7; and the second, 1 Kings xviii. 40. Or the phrase may signify, ' procured justice for the oppressed;' as many of the judges did, by executing righteous judgment on the oppressors.

They "received promises." The word "promise" in the New Testament is often used to signify the thing promised. "The promise of the Father," is that which the Father has promised; "the promise of the Spirit," is the Spirit who is promised —the promised Spirit; to "inherit the promises," is to enjoy the promised blessings. In the same way, in the passage before us, to "receive promises," is to obtain the blessings promised. Through believing, these elders who have "obtained a good report," obtained possession of the blessings promised to them. It was promised to Joshua that he should conquer Canaan; and through believing he obtained the conquest of Canaan. It was promised to Gideon that he should defeat the Midianites; and through believing he obtained their complete discomfiture. It was promised to David that he should be king over Israel; and through believing he obtained the kingdom. Great difficulties seemed to be in the way of these good men obtaining the blessings promised. Without believing, they could not have obtained them; by believing, they did obtain them.

There is no inconsistency between the declaration here, that these "received promises," and the declaration in the 39th verse, that they "did not receive the promise." They received the accomplishment of many particular promises made to them, but they did not receive the accomplishment of the promise—the promise of the Messiah, or of the "salvation with eternal glory" which is in Him.

They "stopped the mouths of lions." This has by some been referred to what Samson and David did when, unarmed, they each of them slew a lion. But the words seem rather to describe what took place in the case of Daniel, when cast into the den of lions for his fidelity to his God. God sent His angel to shut the lions' mouths, that they did not hurt him. And this was done by faith; for it is expressly stated, that this was done " because he believed in his God."

They "quenched the violence of fire." Some have supposed that the reference here is to Aaron running, under a divine impulse, in consequence of a revelation made by Moses, into the midst of the congregation at the time a plague was destroying the Israelites by thousands, and, by making an atonement for them, arresting its fatal progress. But these interpreters seem to have confounded two separate events—the destruction of the 250 men of the company of Korah by fire from heaven, the violence of which was not quenched; and the plague, which does not seem to have been fire from heaven, that on the succeeding day destroyed 14,700 of the people, on account of their impious murmurings. The reference is probably to what happened to the three young Israelites in Babylon, who refused to yield obedience to the edict of Nebuchadnezzar, requiring all to worship the colossal image which he had erected in the plain of Dura. They were cast into "a burning fiery furnace, seven times heated,"— in which they were not only preserved alive, but walked up and down in the midst of the flames; and on being taken out, it was found that the violence of the fire had indeed been quenched—that it had had no power over their bodies—that " not even the hair of their heads was singed, nor their coats changed, nor had the smell of fire passed upon them." It was by faith that the violence of the fire was quenched. A revelation had been made to their minds that God would preserve them alive in the fiery furnace. They believed it; and, believing it, they permitted themselves to be cast into it, and found that it was to them according to their faith. "Our God, whom we serve," said they, " is able to deliver us from the burning fiery furnace; and He will deliver us out of thine hand, O king. But if not,"—that is, even if it were otherwise, though no such deliverance awaited us,—" be it known unto thee, O king, that we will not serve thy gods, nor worship the golden image which thou hast set up."[1]

They "escaped the edge of the sword." To "escape from the edge of the sword," may be considered as a general phrase: 'to obtain deliverance in circumstances of extreme danger.' And in this case it is applicable to many incidents recorded in the Old Testament, of persons, through the faith of a divine revelation, obtaining such deliverances; as in the case of David when in Keilah, where, but for a divine revelation and faith in it, he must have fallen by the sword of Saul. You have the story at length in the 23d chapter of 1st Samuel. It is not unlikely, however, that there is a direct reference to the cases of Moses and Elijah. We find Moses saying, Exod. xviii. 4,—" The God of my father was mine help, and delivered me from the sword of Pharaoh." The flight of Moses from Egypt into Midian was probably the result of a divine revelation made to him, and believed by him. Elijah's life was in extreme danger when Jezebel threatened to slay him with the sword, as he had done the priests of Baal. But he "escaped the edge of the sword." He fled into the wilderness; and though we have no particular account of this being the result of a divine revelation, yet, as Elijah seems to have taken few steps of importance without direct divine instruction, it is highly probable that it was. This seems to us a more probably just interpretation of the phrase, "by faith they escaped the edge of the sword," than considering it as equivalent to—' God protected them because they believed in Him.'

"Out of weakness they were made strong." When weak, through faith they became strong. This may refer to such instances as Barak, and Gideon, and Jephthah, who in consequence of believing the divine revelation made to them, and acting on it, from weak, helpless individuals, became powerful leaders of mighty armies. But as the word " weakness" properly refers to bodily sickness or disease, the reference most probably is to the case of Hezekiah, who in consequence of his faith recovered from a mortal disease. You have the particulars of this case in 2 Kings xx., and in Isa. xxxviii. A revelation was made to Hezekiah by the prophet Isaiah, confirmed by a miraculous

[1] Dan. iii. 17, 18.

sign. Hezekiah believed it; it was to him according to his faith—" out of weakness he became strong."

They "waxed," or were made,[1] "valiant"—that is, strong—"in fight," or battle. In the case of many of the heroes mentioned above, their faith of the divine promise of success gave them a kind of preternatural courage and strength in battle—enabled them to achieve exploits to which otherwise they would have found themselves entirely unequal.

"Turned to flight[2] the armies of the aliens." Of this we have many examples in Old Testament history. Let two or three serve as a specimen. Josh. x. 1–10. Here we have "armies of the aliens;" here we have a divine revelation; Joshua believing it; and in consequence of his faith, "turning these armies of the aliens to flight." 2 Sam. v. 17–25. Here, too, we have "armies of the aliens;" a divine revelation made; David believing it; and in consequence of believing it, "turning these armies to flight." 2 Chron. xx. 1–26.

"Women received their dead raised to life again." The reference seems here plainly to the restoration to life of the Sareptan and Shunammite widows' sons by Elijah and Elisha: 1 Kings xvii. 22–24; 2 Kings iv. 36. It was "by faith" that these strange events were brought about. A revelation, made to the minds of the prophets and believed by them, led them to speak the word or do the action which by divine appointment was connected with the putting forth of the divine power to work the miracle. Such is the illustration of the power of faith to enable men successfully to accomplish the most arduous enterprises; and the conclusion to be drawn from it plainly is, There is no enterprise so difficult, but faith in a divine revelation promising success can enable a man cheerfully to undertake, steadily to prosecute, and prosperously to finish it.

The second division of the paragraph is an illustration of the power of faith to enable men patiently to endure the severest trials—to continue stedfast in their duty to God notwithstanding their being exposed to extreme suffering.

Ver. 35. "Others were tortured, not accepting deliverance; that they might obtain a better resurrection." "Others,"—*i.e.*,

---

[1] ἐγενήθησαν.

[2] ἔκλιναν is well rendered, "turned to flight." Thus Homer, Il. E. 37: Τρῶας ἔκλιναν Δαναοί.

another set of believers, persons different from those whose wonderful achievements and attainments have just been mentioned. The word translated "tortured," properly signifies to stretch upon an instrument called τύμπανον (the shape of which is not certainly known at present), for the purpose of giving the body an attitude of peculiar exposure to the power of cudgels or rods. It involves the idea of double suffering, from being stretched on this instrument of torture and beaten; and, as used here, it plainly signifies tortured to death in this way.[1] Perhaps the word may, without impropriety, be considered as signifying torturing to death in any way. There can be little doubt that, under the idolatrous kings of Israel and Judah, numbers of individuals were put to death for their steady attachment to the pure worship of Jehovah; but it is scarcely possible, I think, carefully to read the history of the persecutions under Antiochus Epiphanes without coming to the conclusion that it is to them the inspired writer directly refers.

There is no doubt, says the judicious Dr Owen, that the Apostle here refers to the story that is recorded in the sixth and seventh chapters of the second book of the Maccabees. For the words are a summary of the things and sayings that are ascribed to Eleazar, who was beaten to death when he had been persuaded or allured to accept deliverance by transgressing the law. And the same may be said of the mother and her seven sons, whose story and torments are there also recorded. The words of Josephus are—" They every day underwent great miseries and bitter torments; for they were whipped with rods, and their bodies were torn to pieces, and were crucified while they were still alive and breathed."[2] When they were thus tortured they would not accept of deliverance; *i.e.*, on the condition of their denying Jehovah and violating His law. When Eleazar was offered the means of escaping punishment, he replied, "It becometh not our age to dissemble. For the present time I should

---

[1] To this mode of torture Prudentius seems to refer in the 14th Hymn of his Peristephanon:

" Tundatur tergum crebris ictibus,
   Plumboque cervix verberata extuberet.
     \*     \*     \*     \*
   Pulsatur ergo martyr, illa grandine,
   Postquam inter ictus hymnum dixit plumbeos."

[2] Antiq. ix. 5.

be delivered from the punishment of men, yet should I not escape the hand of the Almighty, alive and dead."[1] When the youngest of the seven sons of the Jewish mother was assured by Antiochus, with an oath, "that he would make him both a rich and a happy man if he would turn from the laws of his fathers, and that also he would take him for a friend, and trust him with affairs," he obstinately refused; and when the king urged the mother to counsel the young man to save his life, her reply was, " I will counsel my son;" and turning to her son; she said, " Fear not this tormentor, but, being worthy of thy brethren, take thy death, that I may receive thee again in mercy with thy brethren."

The reason of their constancy amid tortures is given—" that they might obtain a better resurrection." The reference of the word "better" is not at once seen by an English reader. The first clause of the verse, literally rendered, is, " Women received their dead by *a resurrection*." These tortured saints refused deliverance that they might obtain a resurrection, and a better resurrection than that which restored these dead persons to a life in this world—even the resurrection to life eternal. It deserves notice that the hope of the resurrection is expressly stated by those who were tortured to death, and who would not accept of proffered deliverance, as the reason of their continuing constant unto death. "It is good," said one of those noble martyrs, when mangled, and tormented, and ready to die—" It is good, being put to death by men, to look for hope from God, to be raised up again by Him." " My brethren," said the youngest of them, " are dead under God's covenant of everlasting life;" and the mother bore all her sufferings with a good courage, because of the hope which she had in the Lord.

Ver. 36. " Others had trial of cruel mockings and scourgings, yea, moreover of bonds and imprisonment." " Mockings" refer to the scorn, derision, and buffetings which the victims of persecution experienced. " Scourgings" refer to another mode of inflicting stripes than that referred to in the former verse. Micaiah and Jeremiah are instances of persons who were tried by " bonds and imprisonment," and who stood the trial—remained " stedfast and unmoveable."

---

[1] Afterwards, too, he said, Δυνάμενος ἀπολυθῆναι τοῦ θανάτου, σκληρὰς ὑποφέρω κατὰ τὸ σῶμα ἀλγηδόνας μαστιγούμενος, κατὰ ψυχὴν δὲ ἡδέως διὰ τὸν αὐτοῦ (ΤΟΥ ΚΥΡΙΟΥ) φόβον ταῦτα πάσχω. 2 Macc. vi. 30.

Ver. 37. "They were stoned, they were sawn asunder, were tempted, were slain with the sword." Sawing asunder was a most cruel method of inflicting death, in use in very early times —2 Sam. xii. 31—and still employed, it is said, in the Burman Empire. Tradition teaches that Isaiah the prophet was put to death in this horrible manner by Manasseh. The instances mentioned in this verse are not recorded in the Old Testament, but were doubtless all of them realities, and often repeated under the dreadful persecution of Antiochus Epiphanes.

The phrase, "they were tempted," has occasioned much difficulty to interpreters.[1] It does seem strange that a word expressive of suffering in general should be introduced in the midst of words descriptive of particular kinds of suffering. The word does not seem used in its general sense of trial, but of temptations to forsake their religion, presented to them in the midst of their sufferings, of which we have already had an instance. This seems to have been a common practice. Not only life, but wealth and honour, were frequently proffered in the midst of tortures most agonizing to the human frame, in order to tempt the martyrs to forsake their religion. Such temptations, in such circumstances, were among the severest trials of faith; and to enable them to rise above them, was one of faith's noblest triumphs.

Others of these ancient believers, who were not deprived of life, were yet exposed to numerous and great inconveniences. They had to abandon their own habitations, and, destitute of the ordinary accommodations of human civilised society, lived in the wilderness like wild beasts. "They wandered about in sheep-skins and in goat-skins, in deserts, and in mountains, and in dens and caves of the earth, destitute, afflicted, and tormented."[2] These

---

[1] Some consider it as an interpolation, inserted by mistake, in consequence of the preceding word being twice written. Others suppose that the original reading was—ἐπυρώθησαν, ἐπυράσθησαν, ἐπρήσθησαν—all signifying, 'they were burned;' or ἐπηρώθησαν, 'they were mutilated;' or ἐπράσθησαν, 'they were sold as slaves;' or ἐσπειράσθησαν, or ἐσπειράθησαν, 'they were tortured and killed by being tied to the spokes of wheels put in motion;' or ἐπάρθησαν, 'they were transfixed.' But all this is conjecture, and the best critics keep the word in the text.

[2] Mountains, waste places, and caves, are spoken of in Scripture as the usual places of refuge in times of affliction: Matt. xxiv. 16; 1 Sam. xxii.; 2 Sam. xxiv.; Judges vi. 2; 1 Sam. xiii. 6; Isa. ii. 19.

words need no explanation; and the best commentary on them is just the history of the persecutions which the people of God, in various ages, have undergone. It is a striking fact, that these words are just as descriptive of what the Christian Church has undergone since the Apostle wrote, as they were of what the Jewish Church had undergone before he wrote.

The parenthesis in the beginning of the 38th verse is peculiarly beautiful: "Of whom the world was not worthy." Their persecutors thought them not worthy of the world; but the truth was, the world was not worthy of them. The world could not bear a comparison with them in respect of worth. They were of a character far elevated above the rest of the world. "To tell the great, the mighty, the wealthy, the rulers of the world, that they are not worthy of the society of the poor, destitute, despised wanderers whom they hunt and persecute as the offscouring of all things, fills them with indignation. There is not an informer or apparitor but would think himself disparaged by it. But they may esteem it as they please. We know that this testimony is true, and the world shall one day confess it to be so."

The great truth which the Apostle means to bring before the mind by these statements is: 'Faith can enable men to endure the severest sufferings. It was faith that enabled these holy confessors to suffer all this patiently, cheerfully, perseveringly. Nothing but faith could have done this.' The application to the Hebrews is plain and obvious: 'You have much to do, you have much to suffer, as Christians. Faith can—nothing but faith can—enable you to do and suffer it all.' The truth is one of importance to *us* as well as to *them.*

The Apostle concludes his historical illustrations of the importance of faith in the remarkable words, vers. 39, 40, "And these all, having obtained a good report through faith, received not the promise: God having provided some better thing for us, that they without us should not be made perfect."

The words, "*all these,*" have by some interpreters been considered as referring only to the whole of those who are represented as having suffered under the influence of faith; and they have supposed that they are here spoken of in contrast with those who *acted* under the influence of faith. The latter class, by faith, obtained promises; the former, though they have obtained a good report through faith, received not the promise.

While Gideon, and Barak, and Jephthah, and Samson, and David, and Samuel, by their heroic deeds, performed under the influence of faith, obtained possession of blessings that had been promised to them, those who, when exposed to the fierce persecutions of the Syro-Macedonian king, through faith endured tortures of the most exquisite kind, died without obtaining such blessings. On carefully looking at the passage, however, it must appear that the statement of such a contrast could in no way serve the Apostle's purpose; and the contrast stated is not between two different classes of the ancient worthies—between the working believers and the suffering believers, but between believers under the ancient economy and believers under the new economy. All those persons to whose history the Apostle in the preceding part of the chapter has referred, as an illustration of the power of faith,—all those whose names are honourably recorded in the book of God, either expressly on account of their faith, or on account of achievements which originated in faith,—"all these received not the promise."

These words, taken by themselves, may either signify, 'had not the promise *made* to them,' or, 'had not the promise *fulfilled* to them.' Those interpreters who take the first view of these words explain them thus: 'Those ancient believers had a number of promises made to them; but there was one promise, which by way of eminence may be called *the* promise—the promise of the resurrection and of an immortal life of happiness,—that promise was not given to them—they obtained it not. "Life and immortality have been brought to light by the Gospel." This better thing has been provided for us.' This is, however, by no means satisfactory; for it is quite evident, from the statements made in the preceding part of this chapter, that the promise, "I am the Lord thy God," included the promise of the resurrection and immortal happiness, and was understood by these ancients to include this promise. The promise, no doubt, is more fully unfolded, and expressed in much plainer terms, under the new than it was under the old economy; but the promise of eternal life, though forming no part of the law, was yet given to the people of God both before the law and under the law. To "receive the promise," must be understood as signifying, to receive the promised blessing, just as to "inherit the promises" is to possess the promised blessings.

But what is the promised blessing which none of these Old Testament worthies, though renowned for their faith, received? The great blessing promised to the ancient Church was the Messiah, and salvation, in all the extent of that word, through Him. It was promised to them that "the seed of the woman should bruise the head of the serpent;" that "in Abraham's seed all the families of the earth should be blessed;" that to them "a Son should be born, a Child given, whose name should be Wonderful, Counsellor, the Mighty God;" that Israel should be " saved in the Lord with an everlasting salvation." Now, this blessing, which is indeed a congeries of blessings, these ancient believers did not receive while they lived. They died before the Messiah became incarnate, and suffered, and died, and rose again; and of course they could not enjoy those blessings which originate in that fuller and clearer revelation of the truth respecting the salvation of the Messiah, and that correspondingly enlarged communication of divine influence which were the natural consequences of that great event. On their death, indeed, they entered into a state free from sin, and fear, and suffering; but still they "received not the promise." They waited in heaven, some of them for some thousands of years, expecting the revelation of the mystery of mercy; but till that took place they could not have the full knowledge and enjoyment of the promised blessing. We have no reason to think that the departed spirits of good men knew more of the plan of redemption than the angels did, who had to learn from the dispensations of God to the Church this "manifold wisdom of God." On the finishing of the great work given to the incarnate Son to do, and on His taking possession of His mediatorial throne, a prodigious accession must have been made to the happiness of the spirits of the ancient believers. But even yet they have not fully received the promise. The promise of a glorious resurrection, and an immortal restored life in their glorified bodies, remains yet unperformed. This is not matter of enjoyment, but of expectation. Their "flesh rests in hope," and their spirits, looking forward to the glorious consummation, breathe out the words, "How long, O Lord, how long!" Thus did all these ancient worthies, though celebrated for their faith, not receive the promised blessing.

One would have naturally expected a declaration of an

opposite kind: 'All these, having obtained a good report through faith, did receive the promise. After all the difficulties and trials, labours and sufferings, to which they were exposed, they at last obtained in the promised blessing a rich recompense for them all.' And this might have been justly enough said; for all true believers under the former economy did, immediately on death, obtain blessings which more than compensated for all their toils and sorrows; and further, such a statement would have been well fitted to support the Christian Hebrews amid their trials. But the statement contained in the text is equally true—that these excellent men, notwithstanding their faith, were not immediately, nor soon, put in possession of the great blessing promised to them. And its statement was well fitted also to prevent the Christian Hebrews from casting away their confidence, and to induce them to persevere, though the promised blessing might be long in being conferred on them.

Some have supposed that the intended practical application of the Apostle's remark may be thus expressed:—' These ancient believers persevered in their attachment to Jehovah and His cause in life and in death, though the great object of their faith, and hope, and desire, was not bestowed on them. How much stronger is the obligation, how much greater the encouragement, to perseverance in your case, who have received the promise! How easy it is to continue to believe in a well attested past fact, in comparison with continuing to believe in a future event, which is in itself very improbable, and for which they had no ground of expectation but the divine promise! How much more are your circumstances calculated to facilitate perseverance than theirs!'

There is force in this arguing; but we do not think that it is the argument suggested by the Apostle's train of thought. It is quite plain that he represents the enjoyment of the promised blessing as yet future, even with regard to the Christian Hebrews: "Ye have need of patience, that, after ye have endured the will of God, ye may obtain the promise."[1] It is as if he had said, 'Let not the fact, that the great object of your expectation is something yet future—something which you are never to enjoy in this world—something which, in all its extent, you are not to enjoy till the time of the consummation of all things,—

[1] Heb. x. 36.

let not this prevent you from persevering. All these elders, who through faith obtained a good report, and are now entered on the inheritance of the promised blessing,—all these, during the whole of their lives on earth, and many of them for ages after their death, did not obtain the promised blessing.'

That this is the practical bearing of the passage, will, I trust, become more apparent as we proceed with the illustration of the 40th verse, which is certainly one of the most difficult in the whole Epistle :—" God having provided some better thing for us, that they without us should not be made perfect."

" God has provided some better thing for *us*." There can be no doubt that the pronoun *us* refers to saints under the Christian economy. For them God has " provided some better thing." The question naturally occurs, Better than what ? And the answer ordinarily returned is, Better than what the saints under the Old Testament economy enjoyed. *They* did not receive the promise, *i.e.*, the promised blessing : *we* have received it. The Messiah is come, and we are blessed with heavenly and spiritual blessings in Him. " Blessed," says our Lord, " are the eyes which see the things which ye see ; for verily I say unto you, that many prophets and righteous men have desired to see the things which ye see, and have not seen them, and to hear the things which ye hear, and have not heard them." " The mystery which was kept secret from former ages and generations, is now made manifest." The true atonement for sin has been made, and clearly revealed. " The way into the holiest has been made manifest." The influence of the Holy Spirit has been more copiously dispensed. Life and immortality have been illuminated by the Gospel. A rational, spiritual, and easy system of worship, has taken the place of the complicated, and burdensome, and carnal ordinances of the law. The Church has passed from a state of minority, subjected to tutors and governors—a state of pupillage, into a state of mature sonship. All this is truth, and important truth ; but still I doubt if it is the truth here stated. The promise here spoken of does not seem to be directly and principally the promise of the Messiah, or of the blessings of His reign to be enjoyed in this world ; but " the promise of eternal inheritance,"—a promise, the full accomplishment of which the saints under the new economy do not obtain in the present state, any more than the saints under the ancient economy,—a promise, the full accomplishment of which they are to obtain after a patient enduring of the will of God. These " better things" which God has provided for us, or foreseen concerning us, are to be enjoyed when we and our elder brethren are together perfected.

The answer to the question, What is the reference of the word " better" in the clause before us ?—with what are the things provided for Christians by God compared ?—which we would be disposed to give is this: The comparison is not between what the saints under the old economy enjoyed and what saints under the New Testament economy enjoy on earth, but between what the saints under the new economy enjoy on earth, and what they are ultimately to enjoy in heaven. ' God has provided something better for us than anything we can attain in the present state, just as He had provided something better for them than anything they could attain in the present state. The ultimate object of their faith and hope lay beyond death and the grave, and so does ours.'

The good things provided for us by God are thus described by the inspired writers :—" We know that when the earthly house of our tabernacle is destroyed, we shall have a building of God, a house not made with hands, eternal in the heavens." When we are " absent from the body," we shall be " present with the Lord." " We know that them who sleep in Jesus, God will bring with Him." " When He who is our life shall appear, we shall appear with Him in glory." " When He shall appear, we shall be like Him ; for we shall see Him as He is." " We look for the Saviour from heaven, who shall change these vile bodies, and fashion them like unto His own glorious body." " And so shall we be for ever with the Lord." " For this mortal shall put on immortality, and this corruptible shall put on incorruption ; and then shall be brought to pass that saying, Death is swallowed up in victory." These are the things provided for Christians by God, inconceivably better than anything they can enjoy here below.

But it may be said, ' These things are not provided *exclusively* for Christians; they are equally provided for the ancient believers. We readily admit this ; but we do not think that there is anything in the Apostle's language that would lead us to consider the good things spoken of as the exclusive possession of

Christians. Indeed, the Apostle does not seem to be here pointing out a contrast, but a resemblance, in the circumstances of Old Testament and New Testament believers: ' Old Testament believers did not obtain the promise in the present state, and neither do New Testament believers; for God has provided for them better things than any bestowed on them here below. We, as well as our elder brethren, must die in faith as well as live in faith. We must live believing, and die believing.'

It now only remains that we turn our attention to the concluding clause of the sentence, " that they without us should not be made perfect." Some connect the words with the first clause, considering the second as a parenthesis; thus: " All these, having obtained a good report through faith, received not the promise, that they might not without us be perfected." We consider them as equally connected with both clauses. Their meaning, I apprehend, would be brought out somewhat more distinctly by a very slight change in their order, which the original certainly warrants, if it does not demand: " that they, not without us, might be made perfect." God has so arranged matters, that the complete accomplishment of the promise, both to the Old Testament and New Testament believers, shall take place together; they shall be made perfect, but not without us; we and they shall attain perfection together.

The Old Testament saints died without receiving the promised blessing; but their faith was not therefore of no avail. In due season they shall be perfected; *i.e.*, the promise, in its full extent, shall be performed to them. And as God has provided for us, too, " better things" than any we enjoy here below, when they are perfected we shall be perfected along with them.

To " be made perfect," is, I apprehend, just the same thing as to " receive the promise," or to enjoy the " better things" provided for us. This exactly accords with the representations in other parts of Scripture. The whole body of the saved are together to be introduced into the full possession of the " salvation that is in Christ Jesus with eternal glory." There is to be " a gathering together unto the Lord Jesus at His coming." They are to be presented " a glorious Church," perfect and complete, " without spot, or wrinkle, or any such thing." As one assembly, they are to be invited to enter into " the kingdom prepared for them from the foundation of the world." They are to be " caught up together to meet the Lord in the air; and so are they to be for ever with the Lord."

Such views were well fitted to encourage the Christian Hebrews to persevere in believing,—to live by faith, to die in faith. ' The ancient believers lived and died without obtaining the great promised blessing, and so must you; but the promised blessing, in all its extent, will in due time be conferred on you both. They shall be perfected, and so shall you.'

Such is the interpretation of this very difficult passage which appears to me most probable. It is an interpretation which gives meaning and coherence to every part of the statement; the meaning given is in accordance with the doctrine of the Scriptures generally, and bears directly on the particular object which the Apostle has in view, the impressing on the mind of the Hebrews the importance of persevering faith.

At the same time, as in a number of points it is not the common mode of interpretation, it may be proper to state, in as few words as possible, how this passage is ordinarily explained. " The ancient worthies persevered in their faith, although the Messiah was known to them only by promise. We are under greater obligations than they to persevere; for God has fulfilled His promise respecting the Messiah, and thus placed us in a condition better adapted to perseverance than theirs. So much is our condition preferable to theirs, that we may even say, Without the blessing we enjoy, their happiness could not be completed." This is excellent sense, but I cannot bring it out of the Apostle's words.

The particular use to be made of the great truth which we think taught in them, that the great object of our hope, as well as that of the ancient believers, is yet future, is abundantly obvious; and the Apostle has in another of his Epistles very clearly pointed it out. If " our life is hid with Christ in God," and if we are not to appear in glory till we appear along with Him, ought we not supremely to " seek the things which are above, where Christ sitteth at God's right hand,"—" set our affections on the things above, and not on the things which are on the earth,"—" mortify our members which are on the earth,"—" mortify the flesh, with its affections and lusts?" Habitually " looking for and hasting to the coming of our Lord Jesus," which is to be the gathering together of all His chosen people, may we all of us in that day find mercy of the Lord; and along with the venerable assembly of patriarchs and prophets, the goodly fellowship of the ancient believers, with the glorious company of the apostles, with the noble army of the martyrs, and the holy catholic Church of God throughout all the earth, obtain the " salvation that is in Christ with eternal glory."

The words which follow, in ch. xii. 1, 2,—" Wherefore, seeing we also are compassed about with so great a cloud of witnesses, let us lay aside every weight, and the sin which doth so easily beset us, and let us run with patience the race that is set before us, looking unto Jesus, the Author and Finisher of our faith; who, for the joy that was set before Him, endured the cross, despising the shame, and is set down at the right hand of the throne of God,"—contain the practical improvement of the Apostle's long and eloquent historical proof and illustration of the power of persevering faith, to enable men to do whatever God commands, however difficult,—to endure whatever God appoints, however severe,—and to obtain whatever God promises, however great and glorious, strange, and apparently unattainable. They are substantially an exhortation to the Hebrew Christians to a steady, active, persevering discharge of Christian duty, notwithstanding all the privations and sufferings, dangers and difficulties, to which this might expose them. Fully to apprehend their meaning and feel their force, it will be necessary that we attend in succession to the principle on which the exhortation proceeds, to the duty which it enjoins, to the means which it prescribes for facilitating its performance, and to the manner in which it requires this duty to be performed.

The principle on which the exhortation is founded is, " We are surrounded by a great cloud of witnesses;" the duty enjoined is, " running perseveringly the race set before us;" the means prescribed for facilitating the performance of this duty are, " the laying aside every weight, and especially the laying aside the sin that does most easily beset us;" and the manner in which this duty is to be performed is, " looking to Jesus, the Author and Finisher of our faith, who, for the joy that was set before Him, endured the cross, despising the shame, and is set down at the right hand of the throne of God."

The paragraph is highly rhetorical; and its meaning will

be but imperfectly understood—its force and beauty will be utterly lost to us—if we do not distinctly apprehend, and steadily keep in view, those historical facts or ancient customs from which the inspired writer borrows his imagery, and in allusion to which he fashions his language.

Some learned interpreters have considered the imagery and language as borrowed from the march of the Israelites through the deserts of Arabia towards the promised land; and that the divinely recorded experience of the faithful under the Old Testament dispensation, guiding the steps and cheering the hearts of Christians in their journeyings through the wilderness of this world towards the heavenly Canaan, is here represented under the emblem of that cloud of glory which marshalled the way for the hosts of Israel through untrodden paths to the good land promised to their fathers. The suggestion is ingenious, but not at all satisfactory. It applies only to the first clause of the paragraph; and even in reference to it, the analogy does not hold, for the cloud of glory did not encompass the camp of Israel—it went before them; and valuable as the recorded experience of the saints undoubtedly is, it could very imperfectly serve to the spiritual Israel the purpose which the cloud of glory served to Israel after the flesh. It is to the word and Spirit of the great God our Saviour, and not to the experience of men, however holy, that we look primarily for direction and consolation amid the perplexities and sorrows of our pilgrimage.

The reference is not to Jewish history, but to Grecian custom; and the Hebrew Christians are not here represented as journeying through a " waste, howling wilderness" towards a fertile country, but as engaged in running a race, the gaining of which would crown them with rich rewards and unfading honours. The allusion is here, as in many other parts of the Apostle's writings,[1] to those public agonistic or gymnastic games, which among the Greeks had less the character of a frivolous amusement than that of a grave civil institution, or a solemn religious ceremony. The most imposing form of this singular custom was perhaps that presented at Olympia, a town of Elis, where games were celebrated in honour of Jupiter once every five years. An almost incredible multitude, from all the

[1] *E.g.*, 1 Cor. ix. 24; Phil. iii. 12; 1 Tim. vi. 12; 2 Tim. iv. 7, 8.

states of Greece and from the surrounding countries, attended these games as spectators. The noblest of the Grecian youths appeared as competitors. In the race, to which there is an allusion in the paragraph before us, a course was marked out for the candidates for public fame, and a tribunal erected at the end of the course, on which sat the judges—men who had themselves in former years been successful competitors for Olympic honours. The victors in the morning contests did not receive their prizes till the evening, but, after their exertions, joined the band of spectators, and looked on while others prosecuted the same arduous labours which they had brought to an honourable termination. By keeping these few facts in your memory, the meaning and force of the Apostle's language will be much more readily and distinctly perceived.

The first thing to which our attention is to be directed, is the principle on which the Apostle's exhortation proceeds, "We are surrounded with a great cloud of witnesses." He takes this for granted, as already proved. The words are a brief summary of what he had stated at length in the preceding chapter, expressed in language suited to the figurative view which he is giving of the character and duty of the Hebrew Christians. The *witnesses* here referred to are plainly the worthies under the former dispensations, mentioned or referred to in the preceding context.

The word "witness" has two meanings: 'a person who gives testimony,' and 'a spectator.' The word is applicable to the elders, who for their faith are honourably mentioned in Scripture, in the first of these senses. Their recorded achievements, and sufferings, and attainments, attest in the most satisfactory way the power of faith, its necessity, and its sufficiency for all the purposes of duty and trial. And had it been simply said, 'Seeing we have so many witnesses to the power and importance of persevering faith, let us persevere in believing,' we should at once have said, this is the meaning of the expression. But when we look at the whole passage in its connection, we cannot help seeing that the word is used here in its second sense. These venerable men are represented as the spectators of the exertions of the Christian Hebrews.

These witnesses are represented as surrounding the Christian racers, as, in the course appointed for them, they "run that they may obtain." It has been supposed by many that these words teach us that the departed spirits of holy men are acquainted with what is going on in the Church below, and take a deep interest in the labours and trials of those who, after their example, are through persevering faith seeking for the full possession of the promised blessings. It may be so, it not improbably is so; but the words do not teach any such doctrine. They obviously, as I have already said, are just a summary of the statements contained in the 11th chapter; and certainly there is no such statement made there, as that "the spirits of the just made perfect" are spectators of the labours and trials of their younger brethren still on the earth.

The whole paragraph is figurative; and, in accordance with the principal figure—that which represents the Hebrew Christians as racers—the ancient worthies whose actions are recorded in Scripture are represented as spectators; their deeds, and sufferings, and triumphs, as recorded in Scripture, being calculated to have the same influence on the minds of the believing Hebrews, as the interested countenances and encouraging plaudits of the surrounding crowd had on the minds of the Grecian combatants. The solitary Christian, in the exercise of faith, finds that, under the influence of that divine principle, he is not solitary. The inspired history is converted as it were into a glorious amphitheatre, from which, while he treads the arena, or courses along the stadium, a countless host of venerable countenances beam encouragement, and ten thousand times ten thousand friendly voices seem to proclaim, 'So run that ye may obtain: we once struggled as you now struggle, and you shall conquer as we have conquered. Onward! onward!'

The Apostle speaks of a *cloud* of such witnesses. The word is expressive of their great number. It is common, I apprehend, in all languages to describe a vast assembly under the figure of a cloud.[1] We find instances of this use of the phrase both in the Old and New Testament. "Who are these"—says the prophet Isaiah, referring to the prodigious numbers of converts in the latter days, when, to use another figure, "nations shall

---

[1] Virgil, Æn. vii. 793, speaks of "nimbus peditum." Livy, xxxv. 49, speaks of "peditum equitumque nimbus." Herodian viii. 105 : νέφος τοσοῦτο ἀνθρώπων. Euripides, Phœniss. 1321: νέφος πολεμίων. Homer, Il. ψ. 133 : νέφος πεζῶν. Diodorus Siculus, iii. 28 : νεφέλη, i.q. νέφος ἀκρίδων.

## GENERAL EXHORTATION AND WARNING. 603

be born in one day,"—"Who are these that fly as a cloud, and as the doves to their windows?"[1] And Ezekiel, speaking of Gog and Magog, whose number is to be as the sand of the sea, says, "Thou shalt be like a cloud to cover the land."[2] And the Apostle Paul, in the Epistle to the Thessalonians, speaking of the joyful events of the time of the consummation of all things to the people of Christ, says, they who have been raised, and they who have been changed, shall be "caught up together *in clouds*," not 'in *the* clouds,'—*i.e.*, in prodigious numbers,—"to meet the Lord in the air." The number of the holy men who, in consequence of their experience being recorded to us in the Bible, are as it were present with us, cheering and encouraging us, is very great. The Apostle particularizes a great many, and then says, "But what shall I say more?"—or, 'why should I go on to multiply examples?'—"for the time would fail me," etc.

The peculiar mode of the Apostle's statement deserves notice. It is not, '*Ye* are surrounded,' but "*we*;" not, 'Do *ye* run,' but "let *us* run." He here speaks "according to the wisdom given to him,"[3] and admonishes Christian teachers, that their duties and those of their hearers are substantially the same; that they need the motives they urge on others; and that they are then most likely to be successful in impressing truth on others, when they show that they feel strongly their own individual interest in it.

The particle *also* is in our version unfortunately placed. As it stands, it conveys the idea—'The ancient worthies were surrounded with a cloud of witnesses, and so are we;' which certainly is not what he intends to communicate. The particle, unless it is simply an expletive, which is not unfrequently the case, ought either to be connected with the particle which precedes it, and the two rendered, 'And therefore;' or with the succeeding clause, "let us run the race that is set before us." 'They ran the race set before them; let us also run the race set before us.'

The force of the connective particle "wherefore," or 'therefore,' is sufficiently plain. 'Since such a multitude of great and good men, by the recorded triumphs of their persevering faith,

---

[1] Isa. lx. 8.     [2] Ezek. xxxviii. 9, 16.

[3] We prefer this view to Carpzov's, who says, "More rhetorum, facundus scriptor ac θιόπνευστος, ἡμεῖς scripsit, ut 2 Cor. ix. 4, ἡμεῖς, ἵνα μὴ λέγωμεν ὑμεῖς."

cheer us on as if they were spectators of our labours and trials, *let us run the race set before us.*'

These words bring before our mind the second point to which we proposed to turn your attention—the duty which the Apostle enjoins. The language is figurative, but it is not obscure. The whole of Christian duty is represented as a race—a race set before them, which they must run, and "run with patience." The principal ideas suggested by this figurative view of Christian duty are the following: It is active, laborious, regulated, progressive, persevering exertion.

The duties of the Christian are of a kind that call for the *vigorous* exertion of all the faculties of his nature, both intellectual and active. The Christian life is a race, in which the powers of movement require to be fully put forth. Christianity does not consist, as too many seem to think it does, in abstract or mystical speculation, enthusiastic feeling, and specious talk. It no doubt does interest the understanding and the heart; but it proves the hold it has of both by unlocking the sources of activity which they contain, and making them flow forth abundantly in useful exertion. It leads the man to "deny ungodliness and worldly lusts, and to live soberly, and righteously, and godly;" "to do justly, to love mercy, to walk humbly with his God."

Christianity is *laborious* as well as active exertion. The angels never tire in their race, but it is otherwise with even the most thoroughly sanctified of the children of God in the present state. In their but imperfectly renewed natures, as well as in external circumstances, they have numerous causes which tend to check the rapidity and regularity of their movement. "Without are fightings, within fears." They are in danger of stumbling and falling; their attention is in danger of being called off by surrounding objects; and through continued exertion they are apt to become "weary and faint in their minds." To represent the Christian life as an unvaried scene of pleasurable employment, is equally to contradict the declarations of Scripture and the lessons of experience. There is pleasure, higher pleasure than aught that the world can afford, even in the most laborious parts of Christian duty, if performed under the influence of Christian principle; but there is toil and difficulty also. It is no easy matter to "flesh and blood" to deny self, to take up the cross, to follow Christ, to cut off the right hand, to pluck out the right eye, to "mortify our members which are on the earth," to "crucify the flesh, with its affections and lusts."

Christian duty, still further, is *regulated* exertion. A man may make active and laborious exertion by running up and down in various directions, but this is not to run a race. The racer must keep to the course prescribed; he must "run the race set before him," else his exertions, however active and laborious, will serve no good purpose. Christian duty must be regulated by the law of Christ. It consists not merely in doing, but in doing what Christ has commanded; not merely in suffering, but in suffering what Christ has appointed.

*Progression* is another idea suggested by the figurative representation here given of Christian duty. A man may be very active and laborious without moving from the spot where he stands, but this is not a race. The Christian must make progress; he must grow in knowledge, and faith, and humility, and usefulness, and universal holiness; he must, to use the language of one Apostle in reference to himself, "forget the things which are behind, and reach forth towards those which are before, and press toward the mark"—or along the prescribed course—" for the prize of the high calling of God in Christ Jesus;" or, to borrow the language of another Apostle in prescribing the duty of Christians, he must "add to his faith virtue, and to virtue knowledge, and to knowledge temperance, and to temperance patience, and to patience godliness, and to godliness brotherly-kindness, and to brotherly-kindness charity."

Finally, Christian duty is here represented as *persevering* exertion. This idea is suggested by the very term *race;* for no race is won in which the runner does not continue running till he reach the goal. But it is still more distinctly brought out in the exhortation, "Run with patience the race set before you."

*Patience*[1] properly signifies that temper which enables us to bear long-continued privation or suffering without murmuring, and to maintain a quiet, contented mind, while promised and expected blessings are long in being bestowed on us. This is a most valuable temper, but it is not exactly the temper which best suits the running of a race. That requires *ardour* rather than

---

[1] ὑπομονή.

*patience.* The truth is, the word here, and in many other passages of the New Testament, rendered "patience," properly signifies 'perseverance.' To "run with patience" is to run perseveringly, to persevere in running, just as "the patience of hope" is persevering hope. Christian duty is not to be thought of as having any limit but the limits of life. We must "be faithful to the death" if we would "obtain the crown of life;" we must "endure to the end" if we would "be saved." It is in continuing to "add to our faith virtue, knowledge, temperance, patience, godliness, brotherly-kindness, and charity," that we are assured "we shall never fall, but *so* an entrance shall be ministered to us abundantly into the everlasting kingdom of our Lord and Saviour Jesus Christ."

From these remarks, the meaning of the Apostle's exhortation to the Hebrew Christians, "Run with patience the race set before you," appears to be—'Persevere in the active discharge of all the duties enjoined on you as Christians, notwithstanding all the difficulties and dangers to which this may expose you. Hold fast the faith of Christ, and live under its influence. Let neither the allurements nor the terrors of the world induce you to turn from your course, or to slacken your pace. Beware of yielding to the influence of spiritual languor; but, trusting in the Lord, renew your strength; run, and be not weary; walk, and be not faint.'

The third topic to which these words call our attention, is the means which the Apostle prescribes for facilitating compliance with the exhortation, to persevere in running the race set before the Hebrew Christians. They must "lay aside every weight,[1] and the sin that did most easily beset them."

The language in the first of these clauses is figurative, and is borrowed from the practice of the Olympic racers laying aside all superfluous clothing, and disencumbering themselves of everything which could impede their movements as they pressed toward the mark for the prize. The meaning is, that Christians should immediately abandon and most carefully avoid everything, either in opinion, or disposition, or conduct, which tends to prevent the ready, persevering discharge of the duties enjoined on them. For the persevering performance of Christian duty, everything

---

[1] ὄγκος is properly "swelling;"—everything that increased the size and weight of the body, and was an encumbrance to free motion.

in itself sinful must be abandoned and avoided.[1] Christians are sometimes apt to think that they scarcely stand in need of being exhorted to abstain from what is obviously criminal; but such a thought springs from their not being sufficiently aware of the power of "sin that dwells in them,"—from their not believing with sufficient firmness that "in them, that is, in their flesh, dwells no good thing." He who knows them better than they do themselves has thought it proper to give to them such exhortations as the following:—"Take heed to yourselves, lest at any time your hearts be overcharged with surfeiting, and drunkenness, and cares of this life."[2] "Let us cast off the works of darkness, and let us put on the armour of light." "Let us walk honestly, as in the day; not in rioting and drunkenness, not in chambering and wantonness, not in strife and envying." "Put off, concerning the former conversation, the old man, which is corrupt according to the deceitful lusts.—Wherefore, putting away lying, speak every man truth with his neighbour: for we are members one of another.—Let him that stole steal no more: but rather let him labour, working with his hands the thing which is good, that he may have to give to him that needeth. Let no corrupt communication proceed out of your mouth, but that which is good to the use of edifying, that it may minister grace unto the hearers.—Let all bitterness, and wrath, and anger, and clamour, and evil-speaking, be put away from you, with all malice." "Mortify therefore your members which are upon the earth; fornication, uncleanness, inordinate affection, evil concupiscence, and covetousness, which is idolatry."[3] False views, depraved dispositions, immoral actions, have obviously a direct and powerful influence in impeding the Christian in his Christian race. His principal danger is perhaps, however, from another kind of weight—the indulging in an undue degree, affections, and the prosecuting with an undue degree of intensity, pursuits which are not in

---

[1] Chrysostom explains ὄγκον as = τὸν ὕπνον, τὴν ὀλιγωρίαν, τοὺς λογισμοὺς τοὺς εὐτελεῖς, πάντα τὰ ἀνθρώπινα. "Sleep, negligence, low and abject thoughts, all human business."—Theophylact's exposition is: τὸ βάρος τῶν γηΐνων πραγμάτων, καὶ τῶν ἐπ' αὐτοῖς φροντίδων. "The weight of worldly businesses, and anxious thoughts about them."

[2] Luke xxi. 34.

[3] Rom. xiii. 12, 13; Eph. iv. 22, 25, 28, 29, 31; Col. iii. 5.

themselves sinful; nay, which may be not only innocent, but praiseworthy. It is our duty to love father and mother, sister and brother; but if we love them more than Christ, we are unfit for the Christian course. It is our duty to be "diligent in business;" but if we embark in worldly pursuits, however just and honourable, with an undue ardour—if we devote to them too many of our thoughts, and too much of our time, we are subjecting ourselves to a load under which we shall move heavily, if we move at all, in the spiritual race. Indeed, every earthly inclination—every earthly pursuit, however innocent in itself, when it interferes with the cultivation of Christian dispositions and the practice of Christian duties, becomes a weight which must be laid aside. There are certain habits in reference to religion itself which form great encumbrances to the persevering discharge of Christian duty. A fondness for what is curious and new in religion—a disposition to "intrude into things not seen," because not revealed—a giving heed to doctrines which minister questions rather than godly edifying—a turning aside unto vain janglings,—this appears to me one of the weights which Christians of the present as well as of the apostolic age need to lay aside, if they would so run as to obtain. The great enemy of our souls does not care much what it is that keeps us from prosecuting our Christian course, if we are but kept from prosecuting it; and when he can so far delude us as to make us believe that we are prosecuting that course when we are either standing still or proceeding in another direction, he considers his object as gained in the best possible way.

There is one general principle which may be laid down on this subject. Whatever tends to bring us more under the influence of present, sensible objects, is a weight which must impede our progress towards heaven. Hence the necessity of guarding against the love of the world in all its varied forms, so strongly stated by our Lord and His Apostles: "Take heed, and beware of covetousness." "Love not the world, neither the things of the world." The language of the Apostle in the clause before us, places in a very forcible point of view the extreme folly of Christians allowing themselves to be unduly attached to worldly pursuits. An Olympic racer binding himself with a heavy load, which greatly retarded his progress, rendered doubtful his success, and could be of no use to him when he reached the goal, is but a feeble figure of the incongruous folly of a worldly-minded professor of Christianity.

But in order to their running the Christian race, they must not only "lay aside every weight," but also, or especially, " the sin that does so easily beset them." This sin, whatever it is, is considered as the burden or encumbrance of which it was especially desirable that they should get and keep rid. Interpreters have found much difficulty in fixing the precise import of the word which is rendered in our translation by the circumlocution, "*which so easily besets.*"[1] It occurs nowhere else in the New Testament, and it occurs in no classical Greek author. Etymology, analogy, and the context, are therefore the only means we have of ascertaining its signification. Some expositors render it 'perilous, full of danger,' and consider it as referring to the peculiarly hazardous nature of the sin of apostasy, into which the Hebrew Christians were in peculiar danger of falling. The hazards connected with that sin are strikingly depicted in the beginning of the 6th and the end of the 10th chapter. Others, rendering the word 'the well-surrounded sin,'[2] consider the Apostle as referring to the frequent occurrence of this sin at this period, according to our Lord's prophecy, that "when iniquity abounded, the love of many should wax cold," and guarding them against committing the well-patronized sin—following the multitude in deserting the Saviour.

Upon the whole, we are disposed to prefer the sense given by our translators to both of these. It equally suits the etymology of the word,—which may with as much regard to the analogy of the language be rendered, *which readily surrounds*, as *which is well surrounded;* the epithet is very descriptive of the sin to which, we apprehend, he refers; and in this case there is an allusion—which is not the case in either of the other modes of interpretation—to the leading figure of the paragraph. This sin is compared to a loose garment which readily comes round the limbs of the racer, and, entangling him, diminishes his speed, retards him in his course. So much for the meaning of the word. Now for its reference.

Many good divines have supposed that there is no reference

[1] εὐπερίστατον.
[2] Sin in this case is to be considered as personified—as a θαυματαποιός, who has crowds of worshippers and admirers around him.

to any particular sin; but that it is a caution to the Hebrew Christians individually to be particularly on their guard against that sin to which, from constitution or circumstances, they are peculiarly liable. That there is in every individual a predominant tendency to some one form of immoral disposition or habit, is more than I am prepared to admit. At the same time, there can be no doubt that, from the constitution of the body or of the mind, and from the circumstances in which individuals are placed, there are certain sins into which they may more readily fall than others. The young are in most danger from the love of pleasure; the middle-aged, from the love of influence and power; the old, from the love of money. One has a tendency to be parsimonious, another to be profuse. Riches and poverty have their respective temptations; and even the desirable middle lot is not without them; and a great deal of practical religious wisdom consists in carefully marking these tendencies and temptations, and guarding against them. While I have no doubt that this general truth is very fairly deducible from the passage before us, I apprehend that the Apostle refers to that sin to which, from the peculiar circumstances in which they were placed, the Hebrew Christians were especially liable.

What that sin was, it is not difficult to discover. It is the sin, to guard them against which is the great object of the whole of the Epistle—the yielding to the "evil heart of unbelief, in departing from the living God." Their former prejudices in favour of Judaism, the privations and sufferings to which their profession of Christianity exposed them, the numerous instances of those who "went back and walked no more with Jesus,"—all these powerfully operated, along with those depraved principles which are common to human nature in all circumstances, to shake the constancy of their faith. While they ought to watch against everything which might impede their progress, it was peculiarly their duty to guard against what would assuredly prevent them from ever reaching the goal, by turning them aside from the course altogether.

We, my brethren, are not exposed to the same temptations as the Hebrew Christians to *open* apostasy; but that inward apostasy from Christ which consists in unbelieving thoughts and feelings, is a sin that easily besets Christians in all countries and ages, and is indeed the bitter and abundant source of all their sins and all their sorrows. We live by faith—we walk by faith—we run by faith—we fight by faith. Without faith we cannot run at all; and if our faith wax feeble, our pace will be slackened. There is no prayer the Christian needs to put up more frequently than, "Lord, increase my faith; help my unbelief." Whatever darkens our views or shakes our confidence with respect to any of the great principles of our Christian faith, cuts the very sinews of dutiful exertion, so that it becomes very difficult, or rather altogether impossible, to persevere in running "the race that is set before us."

It only remains now that we turn our attention to the manner in which the Apostle calls on the Hebrew Christians to perform the duty enjoined on them. They are to persevere in running the race set before them, "looking to Jesus, the Author and Finisher of their faith; who, for the joy that was set before Him, endured the cross, despising the shame, and is set down at the right hand of the throne of God."

The first thing to be done here, is to inquire into the meaning of the appellation here given to our Lord, "The Author and Finisher of our faith." You will notice that the word *our* is a supplement. The Apostle's expression is, "the Author and Finisher of faith," or rather, "of the faith." The ordinary meanings of faith are two—'believing,' and 'what is believed.' Understanding the word in its first sense, Jesus may be considered as "the Author and Finisher of faith," as He by His Spirit enables men first to believe, preserves them believers, and increases their faith, till that, like every other part of the Christian character, is made perfect in heaven. Understanding the word in its second sense, Jesus Christ is "the Author and Finisher of the faith," *i.e.*, of the Christian religion. He is the Introducer and Perfecter of it. He is at once its Author and its subject—" the Alpha and Omega, the beginning and the ending, "the *all in all* of it. Both of these modes of interpretation bring out a good meaning, but neither seems to bring out a meaning particularly appropriate to the Apostle's object.

I cannot help thinking that *the faith* here is a general name for 'the faithful,' or believers; just as the *circumcision* is for the circumcised, the *uncircumcision* for the uncircumcised, the *captivity* for the captives; or, to refer to analogous modes of expression from later times, the *League*, in French history, for the

Leaguers; or, to come nearer home, *Dissent* for Dissenters, *the Secession* for the Seceders. The word translated *author* occurs in application to our Lord in three other passages of Scripture: "The *Prince* of life, Acts iii. 15; "A *Prince* and a Saviour," Acts v. 31; "The *Captain* of salvation," Heb. ii. 10. The proper signification is 'leader'—one who goes before and conducts others, and who thus by example shows them how to proceed. This, we apprehend, is its meaning here: 'Jesus, the Leader, and as the Leader, the Exemplar, of the faith.'[1] Jesus, who has run the race before us, and "set us an example, that we should follow His steps."

The word rendered *finisher* or *perfecter*, is, I apprehend, equivalent to—'rewarder.' The Apostle never loses sight of the principal figure, the Olympic stadium; and Jesus is here represented as one who, Himself having gained the highest honours of the race on a former occasion, sits now on an exalted throne, near the goal, as judge of the competitors, and with garlands in His hand to crown the victors.[2] He is the Rewarder of the faithful, or believers. "Be faithful to death," says He, " and I will give thee a crown of life." "To him that overcometh will I give to sit with Me on My throne, even as I also overcame, and am set down with My Father on His throne."

The words that follow seem to me illustrations of these two appellations here given to our Lord. He is the Leader and Exemplar of the faithful; for " He endured the cross, despising the shame," and He did this " for the joy that was set before Him." The Man Christ Jesus lived a life of faith when here below; He "looked not at the things which were seen and temporal, but at the things unseen and eternal." He believed that His own exaltation and the salvation of His people would certainly be the result of His doing and suffering the will of God; and therefore He "endured the cross." He patiently and perseveringly did and suffered all the will of God. "He became obedient to death, even the death of the cross." And He " de-

---

[1] ἀρχηγοὶ τῆς κακίας, 1 Macc. ix. 61, are "examples of wickedness." Lachish is represented by Mic. i. 13 as ἀρχηγὸς ἁμαρτίας, " the exemplar of sin." Cicero calls Cato (de Fin. iv. 16), " Omnium virtutum auctor"— the example, or pattern, of every virtue.

[2] τελειωτὴς was the name of the βραβεύς, who judged the competitors and conferred the prizes.

spised the shame;" *i.e.*, the ignominy to which He was exposed, never in the slightest degree induced Him to shrink from the discharge of duty,—not that He did not count ignominy an evil, for "reproach broke His heart,"—but that no evil could shake His determination to "finish the work which the Father had given Him to do."

As our Leader and Exemplar He thus acted, "*for* the joy which was set before Him." This clause admits of two different interpretations, according to the meaning you affix to the particle *for*. The proper signification is, *instead of;* but it is not unfrequently used to signify *on account of*. If we understand it in the first way, the meaning is, that Jesus, our Leader and Exemplar, voluntarily gave up a state of glory and enjoyment in order to endure the cross, and despise the shame. "Being in the form of God, He emptied Himself, and took on Him the form of a servant." In this case, the exhortation, to "look to Jesus" as our Exemplar, is nearly parallel to that in Phil. ii. 5, "Let this mind be in you, which was also in Christ Jesus," etc. The only objection to this mode of interpretation is, that the epithet, "set before Him," does not seem so well to suit our Lord's pre-existent glories, as His mediatorial honours laid before Him, held up to Him as the reward of His mediatorial labours.

If we understand the particle *for* in the second way, as equivalent to—' for the sake of,' the meaning is, that the anticipated glories of that state to which Jesus was to be raised on His finishing the work given Him to do, animated Him to a persevering performance of the duties and endurance of the evils connected with its performance. This is a true and scriptural sentiment also. Our Lord believed the promises made to Him: He believed that He was to "be exalted, and extolled, and made very high"—that He was to "see of the travail of His soul, and be satisfied"—that "His soul should not be left in the separate state, nor His body see corruption"—that "God would show Him the path of life;" and, believing this, He "did not fail, nor was He discouraged;"—He persevered, amid inconceivable difficulties and sufferings, till He could say, "It is finished."

We are disposed to prefer the latter mode of interpretation, as it presents Jesus as an example of the very duty which the

Apostle is here enjoining on the Hebrews—the persevering, under the influence of faith, in doing the will of God, notwithstanding all the dangers and difficulties in which this may involve us. Such is the Apostle's illustration of the appellation, "the Leader or Exemplar of the faithful.' As the *Finisher*, the *Perfecter*, the Rewarder of the faithful, "He is set down on the right hand of the throne of God;" *i.e.*, He is exalted to a state of the highest honour and authority. "All power in heaven and in earth" is given to Him, and therefore He is able abundantly to reward those who continue faithful to the death; and His being so gloriously rewarded, is satisfactory evidence that in due time they shall be rewarded also.

Now, in running with perseverance the race that is set before them, Christians are to "look to Jesus Christ" as their Leader and Exemplar, their Perfecter and Rewarder; *i.e.*, they are habitually to make the truth respecting Him in these characters the subject of their believing contemplation. It is as if he had said, 'The record of the labours, and sufferings, and triumphs of Old Testament believers, may and ought to be a source of instruction, motive, and encouragement to you amid your difficulties and trials; but the record of the unparalleled labours, and sufferings, and glories of your Lord and Saviour is the grand source of instruction, motive, and encouragement.' A firm habitual faith of what Christ has done for them, and of what He will do for them, is at once necessary and sufficient to make Christians, in opposition to every conceivable difficulty and temptation, persevere in running "the race set before them." If they "become weary and faint in their minds," it is because they do not "consider Him." If they neglect their duty, it is because they forget their Saviour. How infinitely important, then, is the knowledge of the truth in reference to *our Lord!* All our comfort, all our holiness, depends on this. Let us, with the Apostle, count all things loss for this excellent knowledge. Let those who are destitute of it seek above all things to obtain it. "It is more precious than rubies; and all the things that can be desired are not to be compared to it." Seek, then, this wisdom; and with all your seeking, seek this understanding; and let those who know the Lord follow on to know Him.

In the paragraph which follows, the Apostle's object plainly is, to guard the Hebrew Christians against the **temptations to** apostasy which naturally arose out of that state of suffering in which their profession of Christianity involved them. And the first consideration which he brings forward for this purpose, is derived from the sufferings to which the Son of God patiently submitted, while working out the salvation of His people. Ver. 3. " For consider Him that endured such contradiction of sinners against Himself, lest ye be wearied and faint in your minds."

The connective particle translated *for*, is here, as in many other places, equivalent to 'moreover.' The Hebrew Christians were in danger of " becoming weary and faint in their minds." The language is figurative, but not obscure. Scripture is generally the best interpreter of Scripture; and a passage in the book of Revelation, ch. ii. 2, throws much light on that now before us. "I know," says our Lord to the church of Ephesus, "thy works, and thy labour, and thy patience"—rather, thy perseverance.—" Thou hast borne, and hast patience"—or rather, hast persevered—" and for My name's sake hast laboured, and not fainted." To faint and be weary, is just the reverse of persevering labour and suffering for the name of Christ.[1] It is, under the depressing and discouraging influence of severe and long-continued trials, to abandon, either partially or totally, the duties which rise out of the Christian profession. Severe and long-continued privations and sufferings on account of our connection with Christ, try the reality and the strength of our attachment to Him.

To such privations and sufferings the Hebrew Christians were exposed; and that they might not yield to their influence, the Apostle turns their minds to the multiplied, severe, and long-continued sufferings of our Lord, and His patient and persevering endurance of them. He was exposed to worse sufferings than they were, and yet He never became weary or faint in His mind. This is the great truth he brings forward as a preventive and antidote to spiritual weariness and faintness.

Jesus Christ was exposed to " the contradiction of sinners

---

[1] Some connect ταῖς ψυχαῖς ὑμῶν with κάμητε. It is better to connect with ἐκλυόμενοι. Κάμνω is often used in reference to mental fatigue, without any qualifying phrase, which is not the case with ἐκλύομαι. At ver. 5 indeed it is used simply; but then the full expression had been employed immediately before.

against Himself." The word rendered *contradiction*, in its strict sense, refers to contumelious language; but it is here, as in other places, used as equivalent to ' opposition,'—ill usage generally.¹ Jesus Christ was opposed, by words and actions, on the part of " sinners," *i.e.*, by the wicked Jews who were His cotemporaries. The whole of our Lord's history is a commentary on these words. They ridiculed Him as a low-born, low-bred, fanatical madman; they branded Him as " a glutton and wine-bibber"—" a friend of publicans and sinners"—an impostor—a seditious person—an impious usurper of divine honours—a person in league with apostate spirits; and their conduct corresponded with their language. They laid snares for His life; and after, through the treachery of one of His disciples, He was put into their hands, they treated Him with the most contumelious scorn and barbarous cruelty.²

The Apostle not only states that our Lord was exposed to this opposition from sinful men, but that He *endured* it. That expression not merely intimates that He suffered this, but it describes how He suffered it. He "endured this contradiction:" He patiently bore it; He did not "become weary or faint in His mind." His purpose of " finishing the work given Him to do" was never shaken. He *endured*—endured to the end.

The Apostle's exhortation, " Consider³ Him that endured such contradiction of sinners against Himself," contains more in it than a careless reader is apt to suppose; and everything contained in it is calculated to serve his purpose, to prevent the Christian Hebrews from yielding to the dispiriting influence of the calamities to which they were exposed. " Consider Him who endured," etc. ' Recollect His relation to God and His relation to you. Remember that He was the only-begotten and well-beloved Son of God,—the brightness of His glory, and the express image of His person. If *He* suffered, should *you*,

¹ It is = the Heb. רִיב, Hos. iv. 4, and מָרַד, Isa. lxv. 2, LXX. *Vide* John xix. 12; Tit. ii. 9.

² The expression is ἀντιλογία εἰς αὐτόν. In some codd., for αὐτόν we read αὐτούς. This is obviously a gloss, arising from supposing that εἰς αὐτόν was superfluous, and that εἰς αὐτούς expressed the idea—' in opposition to their own true interests.' The genuineness of the text. recep. is undoubted.

³ ἀναλογίσασθε, cogitate, instituta comparatione.

creatures, sinners, wonder that you suffer, or murmur when you suffer? Remember that He is your Lord and Teacher; and is it not enough that the disciple should be as his teacher, and the servant as his lord? Remember that all His sufferings were for you; and will you shrink to suffer for Him? Consider not only Him who suffered, but what He suffered. Consider Him who endured such contradiction of sinners against Himself. Think how numerous, how varied, how severe, how complicated, how uninterrupted, how long-continued, were His sufferings. What are your sufferings in comparison of His? And then consider not only what He suffered: think of the temper in which He suffered,—how meek in reference to men—how submissive in reference to God! and by this consideration learn not to allow your sufferings to produce, on the one hand, resentment towards men, nor, on the other, discontent towards God. And especially, let the thought, that He *endured* all this—that notwithstanding all this, He stood steadily to His purpose of saving you, at whatever price—excite in you an invincible resolution also to *endure*,—to suffer no affliction to shake your attachment to Him; but, as every reproach, and insult, and injury but made Him the more set His face as a flint, let your afflictions but rouse into more energetic vigour all the principles of Christian obedience; and knowing that He suffered for you, and what He suffered for you, and how He suffered for you,—and knowing how well He deserves that you suffer for Him, and has, in suffering for you, set you an example, that ye should follow His steps,—instead of being weary and faint in your minds, let tribulation work perseverance, and perseverance experience, and experience hope.' Such, and so powerful, is the first consideration which the Apostle brings forward to counteract the influence of affliction on the minds of the Christian Hebrews to produce a partial or total abandonment of Christian duty.

The second consideration is drawn from the fact, that the sufferings to which they had yet been exposed were by no means so severe as they might have been—so severe as they might yet be—so severe as the sufferings not only of Christ, but of many confessors in former ages, had been. Ver. 4. "Ye have not yet resisted unto blood, striving against sin."

The Hebrew Christians were engaged in a contest. They were "striving against sin." "Sin" has, by some very good interpreters, been considered as equivalent to 'sinners,' referring to their unbelieving countrymen. We think it more natural to consider the words as figurative. *Sin* is personified, and is represented as the combatant with which the Hebrew Christians were contending. The various afflictions to which they were exposed in consequence of their attachment to the cause of Christ, may be viewed as the means which sin employs in order to subdue them, or as the evils to which they are exposed in the prosecution of their warfare.

Now, in "striving against sin"—in resisting the attempts made to induce them to apostatize—they had sustained temporal loss in a variety of forms. They had lost the good opinion of their countrymen. Their "names had been cast out as evil." They had been reviled and calumniated. They had, some of them, been "spoiled of their goods." They had "endured a great fight of afflictions," having been made " a gazingstock by reproaches and afflictions." Some of them had even fallen as martyrs, such as Stephen, and James the brother of John. But at the period when this Epistle was written, none of them were called to lay down their life for the cause of truth and righteousness. The force of the Apostle's admonition may be thus expressed:—'Your sufferings, though numerous and severe, are not such as to excuse weariness or faintness of mind. You have not yet been called to part with life.[1] Many believers under a former dispensation were called on to make this sacrifice, and they cheerfully made it. When tortured even to death, they refused deliverance on the condition of apostasy; and will you abandon the cause of truth before you are exposed to such a trial? Jesus, the great Leader and Rewarder of the faithful, resisted to blood. He would not abandon your cause, though it should cost Him His life; and will ye abandon His cause, merely because it exposes you to reproach and poverty?'

The words seem also to intimate, that not yet called on to resist to blood in their combat with sin, it was quite possible that they might soon. And in this view of the matter, there is an appeal made to the principle of honourable shame. When they became Christians, they were told plainly at what hazard they

---

[1] μέχρι αἵματος = μέχρι φόνου sive θανάτου, 2 Mac. xiii. 14. Αἷμα, like the Heb. דם, often signifies a violent death: 2 Sam. iii. 28; Matt. xxiii. 30, xxvii. 24.

became so: they were not inveigled into the profession of that religion by false representations of ease and worldly comfort. They were told, that if they would live godly in Christ Jesus, they must lay their account with suffering persecution; and that losing even their life for Christ's sake was by no means an impossible or an improbable event. 'Now what sort of soldiers are you, if the minor hardships of warfare so dispirit you as to make you think of abandoning your standard before you have received a wound, in a cause of which you are not worthy to be defenders if you are not ready to shed the last drop of your blood!' The Christian soldier should be thankful when his trials are not extreme ones. To use Dr Owen's words, whatever befalls us on this side blood is to be looked on as a fruit of divine tenderness and mercy. In taking on them the profession of the Gospel, the Christian Hebrews had engaged to bear the cross in all the extent of that expression. They were not yet called on to redeem their pledge in all its extent; but that very circumstance rendered their conduct the more blameable and shameful, if they refused to give what was much less than they had promised. It is of great importance, if we would remain faithful in times of trial, that we habitually keep in mind the worst evils we can be exposed to. This will preserve us from being shaken or surprised by the less evils which may befall us, and make us feel that, instead of murmuring that the burden laid on us is so heavy, we have reason to be thankful that it is not heavier.

The third consideration brought forward in the following verses is founded on the nature and design of the afflictive dispensations to which they were exposed. Their afflictions were not, as their enemies insisted, and as their unbelieving hearts were but too apt to suspect, intimations that they were the objects of the divine displeasure,—tokens that God disapproved of their connecting themselves with Jesus of Nazareth and His followers,—but were indeed tokens of His parental love, and means used by Him for disciplining them for that higher state of being, and that nobler order of enjoyment, which Jesus had died on earth to procure for them, and gone to heaven to prepare for them. This is the subject of the Apostle from the 5th down to the 13th verse.

The words in the beginning of the fifth verse ought, we apprehend, to be read interrogatively: "And have ye forgotten the exhortation which speaketh unto you as unto children? My son, despise not thou the chastening of the Lord, nor faint when thou art rebuked of Him: for whom the Lord loveth He chasteneth, and scourgeth every son whom He receiveth." The afflictions which befell the primitive Christians in consequence of their attachment, were to many of them stumblingblocks. With their Jewish prejudices, this was the very reverse of what they expected. The peculiar people of God, the followers of Messiah, were, in their estimation, entitled to anticipate a very different lot. This mode of thinking naturally led them to entertain doubts that they had done wrong in embracing Christianity; that, instead of being the favourites of Heaven, they were the objects of divine displeasure; and that the best thing they could do was to revert to their old creed, by means of which they would obtain security from the evils which so severely pressed on them.

The Apostle meets this tendency to apostasy by showing them the true nature and design of the afflictive dispensations to which they were exposed. And he does so by appealing to those Scriptures which they admitted to be " given by inspiration of God," and which were " profitable for doctrine, for reproof, for correction, and for instruction in righteousness." It is as if he had said, ' Surely these afflictions could never have made you weary and faint in your minds if you had understood and habitually remembered the words of God in the Old Testament Scriptures, in which, as a wise and kind Father, He represents affliction as a necessary discipline for the spiritual improvement of His children.'

There are two very important general remarks which are naturally suggested by the manner in which the Apostle introduces this quotation. The first is, that the Old Testament Scriptures are intended for our instruction as well as for the instruction of those to whom they were originally addressed. The exhortation contained in the book of Proverbs speaks to the Christians of the primitive age. "Whatsoever things were written aforetime, were written for our learning." There is need of wisdom in drawing from the Old Testament Scriptures the instruction they are intended to give *us;* but, directly or indirectly, every part of these holy writings is intended to instruct us.

The second general remark is, that the true way of being

preserved from going wrong, is to look at everything in the light of the Holy Scriptures. Afflictions, which, when considered by themselves, may be considered as a temptation to apostasy, when viewed in the light of God's word, will be found to be an argument to stedfastness. If, in consequence of their afflictions, the Hebrew Christians were in danger of " becoming weary and faint in their minds," it was because they had forgotten the scriptural view of the nature and design of afflictions, and of their duty under afflictions.

The passage quoted is from the book of Proverbs, ch. iii. 12: " For whom the Lord loveth He correcteth, even as a father the son in whom he delighteth." The quotation is made from the LXX., the version in common use at the time the Epistle was written. Though not a literal rendering of the Hebrew text, it yet gives its meaning with sufficient accuracy; and this is one out of very many instances in which it is evident that the writers of the New Testament, in quoting the Old, frequently quote in a general way, keeping close to the meaning, though by no means to the words.

The view given of the nature of affliction is contained in the 6th verse, as connected with the address, *My son*. "Whom the Lord loveth He chasteneth, and He scourgeth every son whom He receiveth." The general truth is, Affliction, in some form or other, is allotted by God to every individual whom He regards with peculiar favour, as the necessary means of promoting their spiritual improvement; and is therefore to be considered as a proof of His parental love. The doctrine is not, that in every case affliction is a proof of God's fatherly love to the individual afflicted; but, that every child of God may expect affliction, and that to him affliction is a proof of his heavenly Father's kind regard.

The exhortation founded on this view of the nature and design of affliction is, " Despise not thou the chastening of the Lord, neither faint when thou art rebuked of Him." The Hebrew Christians were not to despise the chastisements of the Lord; they were not to count them of little value. ' Instead of spurning them from you, regard them as important blessings. They are chastisements,—discipline, intended, calculated, necessary for your real welfare; they are not the strokes of an enemy, but the rod of a Father; they are the chastisement of the Lord, the greatest, the wisest, the best of beings, who can do nothing without a reason, nothing without a good reason—nothing in caprice, nothing in cruelty. Treat them not, then, as common, valueless things.'

And while you thus regard them, "faint not when you are rebuked of Him." To faint when we are rebuked of God, is, under the influence of despondency, to sink into a state of criminal inaction—to become unfit for the discharge of our active duties. Now Christians should not thus faint under afflictions; for they are the rebukes of a Father—of One who loves them, and who rebukes them, not to depress, but to excite them. Let our afflictions rouse our spiritual energies. The thought that we need rebuke, and that He who rebukes is infinitely wise and good, should equally prevent us from sinking into a state of desponding, helpless inactivity. In this case we directly contradict the design of God in these dispensations, which is to quicken and animate us.

The words which follow are the Apostle's amplification of the argument against apostasy contained in the words of the inspired Israelitish sage, and his application of it to the circumstances of those to whom the Epistle was addressed. Vers. 7-11. "If ye endure chastening, God dealeth with you as with sons: for what son is he whom the father chasteneth not? But if ye be without chastisement, whereof all are partakers, then are ye bastards, and not sons. Furthermore, we have had fathers of our flesh which corrected us, and we gave them reverence: shall we not much rather be in subjection unto the Father of spirits, and live? For they verily for a few days chastened us after their own pleasure; but He for our profit, that we might be partakers of His holiness. Now, no chastening for the present seemeth to be joyous, but grievous: nevertheless afterward it yieldeth the peaceable fruit of righteousness unto them which are exercised thereby." The substance of his statements may be summed up in the following propositions:—Afflictions are so far from being proofs that those who are visited with them are objects of the divine displeasure, that an entire freedom from them would be a ground of doubt whether the individual was an object of the divine peculiar favour. The character of Him from whom these afflictions come, and the design for which they are sent, should induce us dutifully to receive, and patiently to bear them. The consequences of these afflictions, when thus endured, are so advantageous, that they more than compensate the pain they occasion to us during their continuance.—To the consideration of these truths, peculiarly suited to the circumstances of the believing Hebrews, but full of interest to Christians in all countries and in all ages, let us now turn our attention.

The first of these principles is contained in the 7th and 8th verses. " If ye endure chastening, God dealeth with you as with sons : for what son is he whom the father chasteneth not? But if ye be without chastisement, whereof all are partakers, then are ye bastards, and not sons."

The words, " if[1] ye *endure* chastening," have by many good interpreters been considered as equivalent to—'if ye patiently and perseveringly submit to the afflictions laid on you.' There is no doubt that the phrase, taken by itself, may signify this; but it seems plain, from its being opposed, not to impatient suffering, but to exemption from suffering, that the Apostle's intention is to express merely the fact of being afflicted, not to describe the manner in which the affliction is received. ' If ye meet with affliction, God deals with you as with *children.*' We cannot conclude that when we meet with affliction, therefore we are the children of God—the objects of His peculiar favour; for affliction is the common lot of man; in that respect, "one event happens to the righteous and the wicked;"— but neither can we conclude that we are His enemies, the objects of His judicial displeasure. The Apostle's sentiment is, ' Afflictions, however severe, are no proofs that we are not God's children.'

"For what son is there whom the father chastens not?" This question presents in a very lively manner, the reason, along with the proof that afflictions are not necessarily wrathful inflictions, why we are not to conclude from our afflictions merely that

---

[1] There is a various reading here worth noticing. A number of good MSS., and some of the ancient versions and Fathers, read, instead of ε παιδείαν, εἰς παιδείαν, and connect it with what goes before—παραδέχεται εἰς παιδείαν. Ὑπομένετε. The ordinary reading is, however, preferable. Παιδεύειν is not exactly = μαστιγοῦν or κολάζειν : the word signifies, in its primitive sense, 'to educate ;'—this is its classic signification. It then came to signify, ' correction,' as a part of education—' discipline.' In Greek the allusion to the paternal relation is retained, which is not the case in our word ' chastisement.'

we are not the children of God. Every son among men stands in need of chastisement in some form or degree; and every wise and kind father will inflict chastisement when he sees it to be necessary for the good of his son. The most endearing of all the relations in which God is pleased to reveal Himself to His people, that of a Father, thus leads them to expect afflictions. There is none of them but stand in need of discipline; and He who condescends to call them children, and Himself their Father, means all that these words convey, and certainly loves them too well to withhold those chastisements which in His infinite wisdom He sees to be absolutely necessary and most fitted for promoting their spiritual improvement.[1]

But this is not all. Not only is it true that affliction is no proof that we are not the children of God, but the want of affliction would be a ground of doubt whether the individual exempted was a member of God's spiritual family. " But if ye be without chastisement, whereof *all*"—*i.e.*, all the children— " are partakers, then are ye bastards, and not sons."

The allusion here, is either to spurious children whom an adulterous wife attempts to impose on her husband, and whom he refuses to take care of as his children; or to illegitimate offspring, who usually—though certainly most criminally—are almost entirely neglected, so far as parental superintendence and discipline are concerned, by their father. 'If ye were free of affliction, that, instead of being a proof of your being the objects of God's peculiar regard, would be the very reverse.'

The words do not necessarily imply that any human being is a stranger to affliction. They only assert that, were any human being in these circumstances, it would be a proof, not of his being an object of the divine peculiar favour, but of his being an outcast of His family. They, however, suggest the

---

[1] There is a remarkable passage in Seneca, which almost tempts one to believe that he had seen the passage before us. After representing a good man as " the offspring of God," he goes on to say: " That mighty parent, inflexible in his demand for virtue, trains up his offspring with some hardness, as stern fathers do. And therefore when you see good men, whom the gods accept, toiling and sweating and climbing rough paths, and bad men wallowing in a stream of pleasures: consider that we like forwardness in our slaves, but self-restraint in our sons, and that we encourage the pertness of the former, but restrain the latter with a more painful discipline, and draw the same conclusion about God. He does not keep a good man in luxury, he does not bring him up in ease, but tests him, toughens him, and makes him ready for himself."—SENECA, *de providentia*, cap. i. *ad fin.*

truth—and, I apprehend, were intended to suggest the truth—that a life of comparative freedom from afflictions, being unfriendly, in the present state, to our religious and moral improvement, is by no means to be considered by itself as an indication of the peculiar regard of God. In all ages, the remarkable prosperity of individuals obviously and decidedly irreligious has attracted attention. Not that the irreligious are uniformly, or usually, remarkably prosperous—the reverse is the truth,—but that they are occasionally so; and where it is so, their prosperity, instead of being a blessing to them, is a curse: just as the illegitimate child, deprived of the advantage of parental discipline, and left in many cases to the unrestrained influence of his appetites and passions, finds his liberty his ruin. "Wherefore do the wicked live, become old, yea, are mighty in power? Their seed is established in their sight with them, and their offspring before their eyes. Their houses are safe from fear, neither is the rod of God upon them. Their bull gendereth, and faileth not; their cow calveth, and casteth not her calf. They send forth their little ones like a flock, and their children dance. They take the timbrel and harp, and rejoice at the sound of the organ. They spend their days in wealth, and in a moment go down to the grave. Therefore they say unto God, Depart from us; for we desire not the knowledge of Thy ways. What is the Almighty, that we should serve Him? and what profit should we have, if we pray unto Him?" "For I was envious at the foolish, when I saw the prosperity of the wicked. For there are no bands in their death; but their strength is firm. They are not in trouble as other men; neither are they plagued like other men. Therefore pride compasseth them about as a chain; violence covereth them as a garment. Their eyes stand out with fatness: they have more than heart could wish. They are corrupt, and speak wickedly concerning oppression: they speak loftily. They set their mouth against the heavens; and their tongue walketh through the earth."[1]

Remarkable prosperity should produce gratitude, but it should not produce exultation. On the contrary, it should excite fear and caution, lest we should be among those whose portion is in the present state, and whose prosperity will destroy them.

[1] Job. xxi. 7–15; Ps. lxxiii. 3–9.

The statement contained in these two verses seems a deduction from the quotation from the book of Proverbs. God chastens whom He loves; He scourges His sons. Of course, "when ye endure chastening, God deals with you as with sons." He chastens *all* whom He loves; "He scourges *every* son whom He receives." It follows, "If ye be without chastisement, of which all the children are made partakers, then are ye bastards, and not sons."

The second proposition to which we were to give our attention is, The character of Him from whom these afflictions come, and the purpose which they are intended to answer, should induce us dutifully to receive and patiently to bear them. This is contained in the 9th and 10th verses.

There is a very striking contrast between our human and divine fathers. "We have had fathers of our flesh"—*i.e.*, we have had natural parents; they chastened us—they had a right to do so from their relation, and they did so; they restrained us—they "corrected us;" and we did not rebel against them—"we gave them reverence." Now, if it was reasonable and right in us to submit to *their* chastisement, must it not be much more obviously reasonable and right to submit to the chastisement of the Father of our spirits? *i.e.*, as I apprehend, not so much the Creator of our immortal minds, who "breathed into our nostrils the breath of life," and thus made us "living souls," which is true, but our spiritual Father, as opposed to our natural fathers,—He to whom we are indebted for spiritual and eternal life. "Shall we not much rather be in subjection to Him?"

To be in subjection to our spiritual Father is a phrase of extensive import. It denotes "an acquiescence in His sovereign right to do what He will with us as His own; a renunciation of self-will; an acknowledgment of His righteousness and wisdom in all His dealings with us; a sense of His care and love, with a due apprehension of the end of His chastisements; a diligent application of ourselves unto His mind and will, or to what He calls us to in an especial manner at that season; a keeping of our souls by persevering faith from weariness and despondency; a full resignation of ourselves to His will, as to the matter, manner, times, and continuance of our afflictions;"[1]—in one word, a

---

[1] Owen.

"lying passive in His hand, and having no will but His." This is to be subject to "the Father of our spirits."[1] And surely, if our natural relation to our earthly parents, and the favours they are the instruments of conferring on us, make it fitting that we should submit to them, surely the spiritual relation in which we stand to our heavenly Father, and the infinitely more valuable and numerous blessings of which He is the Author, make it proper that we should be subject to Him.

A strong additional motive to this subjection is contained in the concluding clause—" *and live.*" To *live,* here, is equivalent to—' to be happy.' Subjection to "the Father of our spirits," when He chastens us, is the only way, and the sure way, to true happiness. There is an inward satisfaction in a childlike submission to divine. chastisement—a conscious union of mind and will with God, fellowship with "the Father of our spirits"—which is far superior to any earthly pleasure; and it is in a patient suffering, as well as in a persevering doing, of the will of God, that His children in due time arrive at "glory, honour, and immortality," and receive, in its most perfect form, "eternal life."

A further argument for submission to the chastisements of our spiritual Father is derived from His object in these chastisements, as contrasted with the object which our natural fathers had in their chastisements. "For they verily for a few days chastened us after their own pleasure; but He for our profit, that we may be made partakers of His holiness." Our earthly fathers restrained us and corrected us " for a few days,"[2] —a short season—the season of infancy, childhood, and early youth; and they did so "after their own pleasure,"[3] or as it seemed good to them.

There are many parents who, in inflicting chastisement, are guided just by the impulse of the moment, and have no direct reference to the ultimate welfare of the child; and even the

---

[1] As Num. xvi. 22, xxvii. 16, אֱלֹהֵי הָרוּחֹת לְכָל־בָּשָׂר, ὁ Θεὸς τῶν πνευμάτων καὶ πάσης σαρκός. Proclus terms the Demiurgus τῶν ψυχῶν Πατήρ. Plat. Theol. lib. vi. cap. iii.

[2] πρός joined to nouns of time is = *ad,* or *per:* Gal. ii. 5; Luke viii. 13; John v. 35; 2 Cor. vii. 8. *Their* chastisement has a reference to our brief sojourn on earth—at best, ὁ ἡ.; *His,* to our everlasting state.

[3] κατὰ τὸ δοκοῦν, pro arbitrio suo. In many cases parents act on the principle, " Sic volo, sic jubeo, stat pro ratione voluntas."

wisest and kindest human parent, in chastising his child, may not only mistake as to the kind and measure of chastisement that is best fitted for promoting his child's moral improvement, but may be to a very considerable degree arbitrary in his corrections—more influenced by natural irritation than by a reasonable wish to do his child good.

But our heavenly Father never chastises His children except "for their profit." His object is uniformly their real advantage; and the form, the degree, the duration of the affliction, is all ordered by infinite wisdom so as best to gain this object. He " does not afflict willingly," *i.e.*, arbitrarily, nor grieve without cause. All the afflictions of His people are intended and are requisite for promoting their highest interest. Kind, wise intention does not always in an earthly parent secure the employment of the best means to realize that intention; but in God they are always united in the highest degree.

> " Parents may err, but He is wise,
> Nor lifts the rod in vain."

The concluding words are commonly considered as stating in what the "profit" of God's children, which is His object in their afflictions, consists. It consists in their becoming " partakers of His holiness." The holiness of God consists in His mind and will being in perfect accordance with truth and righteousness. And to become "partakers of His holiness," is just to have the mind brought to His mind, the will brought to His will : to think as He thinks—to will as He wills—to find enjoyment in that in which He finds enjoyment. This is man's profit. This is the perfection of his nature, both as to holiness and happiness. This is *to live*—to live the life of angels, to live the life of God; to partake of His holiness is to "enter into *His* joy." And this is the design of God in all the afflictions of His people—experimentally to convince them of the vanity of the creature, and the absolute necessity and sufficiency of God in order to true happiness.

I am not quite sure but this clause is to be considered as opposed to the clause, " for a few days," and ought, as it may be rendered, " *till*[1] we become partakers of His holiness."

[1] There is no doubt this is a signification of the preposition εἰς: Gal. iii. 24, εἰς Χριστόν, until Christ. *Vide* note on εἰς τὸν καιρὸν τὸν ἐνεστηκότα, sup. ch. ix. 9.

God's chastening will never entirely cease till its end be gained. So long as we are here below, we need chastening, and we shall receive it. The great transforming process, in which chastisement holds an important place, will go on till it is completed in our being made "partakers of His holiness"—till we have no mind different from the mind of God, no will different from the will of God—till, according to our measure, we be holy as He is holy, and perfect as He is perfect. And then, the end of chastisement being gained, it will cease for ever; and as the mature, the fully grown, the thoroughly educated children of God, we shall live for ever in our Father's house above, in the eternal enjoyment of that happiness which He has secured for us by the obedience to the death of His own Son, and for which He has prepared us by the influence of His Spirit and the discipline of His providence. Oh! who would not submit patiently, thankfully, to discipline, necessary, fitted, intended, certain—if endured in a childlike spirit—to produce so glorious a result?

We proceed now to the illustration of the third of these propositions:—The consequences of these afflictions, when dutifully sustained, are so advantageous, that they more than compensate the pain which they occasion during their continuance. This is plainly stated in the 11th verse: "Now, no chastening for the present seemeth to be joyous, but grievous: nevertheless afterward it yieldeth the peaceable fruit of righteousness unto them which are exercised thereby."

One of the excellences of Christian morality is its suitableness to the essential principles of our nature. There is nothing impracticably rigid in its principles. It makes war with nothing in human nature but with its depravity. It proves itself the work of Him who at once is intimately acquainted with, and who tenderly pities, the innocent weakness of humanity—one who "knows our frame, and remembers that we are dust." The principles of Christian morality in reference to affliction are striking illustrations of these remarks. Fortitude, and patience, and resignation under affliction are required, but not apathy to affliction. The stoical philosophy, the purest of all the ethical systems of the Grecian schools, required its followers to account pain no evil, and to be equally joyful in the deepest adversity and in the highest prosperity. It has been justly observed, this is either *absurdity*, or it is a mere play upon words.

The Apostle admits that it is of the very nature of affliction to produce pain and sorrow. "No chastisement"—*i.e.*, no affliction—"for the present"—*i.e.*, while it continues—"*seemeth to be*." These words are not intended to intimate that the pain produced by affliction is merely apparent, not real; they suggest the idea—'Afflictions are thought and felt by those who bear them to be not joyous, but grievous.' They produce painful, not pleasurable emotions; they are intended to do so; they cannot serve the purpose for which they are sent without doing so. There is a necessity not only that we be occasionally and "for a season in manifold tribulations" or trials, but "in heaviness," through means of these manifold tribulations or trials.

There are men who seem to think it a point of mental courage and hardihood, when visited with affliction, to keep off a sense of it. They count it pusillanimity to mourn or be affected with sorrow on account of them. This is neither natural nor Christian. Reason and revelation equally condemn all such attempts, as calculated to counteract the great design of affliction. There is no pusillanimity in acknowledging that we feel the strokes of an almighty arm. It is the truest wisdom of a creature to humble itself "under the mighty hand of God." If we are among His people, He will mercifully compel us to acknowledge that His chastisement is not a thing to be despised or made light of. He will—O how easily can He do it?—continue or increase our affliction, or bring upon us other afflictions, till He break the fierceness and tame the pride of our spirits, and bring us like obedient children to be subject to "the Father of our spirits."

But while the Apostle admits that the afflictions of Christians are, during their continuance, "not joyous, but grievous," he at the same time teaches, that "afterwards they yield the peaceable fruit of righteousness to them who are exercised by them." Let us first attend to the phraseology, which is somewhat peculiar; and then, shortly illustrate the important and encouraging sentiment which it conveys.

The language is obviously figurative. "The peaceable fruit of righteousness." The phrase, "fruit of righteousness," taken by itself, most naturally signifies, 'the effects of righteousness—the fruits which righteousness, whatever that word signifies, produces.' But here you will notice that it is chastisement or affliction that is represented as producing the fruit. Whatever is meant by the "fruit of righteousness," is plainly represented as the effect of affliction. The phrase, "fruit of righteousness," seems to be a phrase of the same kind as "the first fruits of the Spirit;" *i.e.*, the influences of the Spirit tranquillizing, and purifying, and blessing the soul, which are the commencement of the celestial blessedness. The "fruit of righteousness" is not some effect of righteousness, but it is righteousness itself considered as the effect of affliction. Chastisement produces fruit, and that fruit is righteousness. *Righteousness* is here, I apprehend, to be understood as just equivalent to a frame of mind and a course of conduct corresponding to what is right; it is the same thing as becoming "partakers of God's holiness."

This fruit is termed "peaceable fruit." *Peace*, according to the Hebrew idiom, is equivalent to happiness or prosperity. "The peaceable fruit" is just equivalent to—'the salutary, useful, happy fruit.' Affliction produces the happy result of promoting spiritual improvement, making men more holy.

And it produces this happy result "to those who are exercised with it." The expression, "exercised with it," is a word borrowed from the gymnastic games. It describes those persons who, divested of the greater part or the whole of their clothing, were trained by a variety of hardships and exercises for the race or combat. The Apostle's idea seems to be this, that afflictive dispensations of Providence, when viewed and treated as divinely appointed means of disciplining men for the service of God, promote the spiritual improvement of those who are visited with them, which is a most salutary result, and more than compensates the pain which they occasion while they continue.

These salutary fruits are produced *afterwards*. The salutary effect may not be immediately produced.[1] Like the production of fruit, it may be gradual; but such will, in good time, be the result of all sanctified affliction.

Having thus explained the phraseology, and brought out the Apostle's meaning—namely, that afflictions, when viewed and treated as divinely appointed means for disciplining us for God's service, however painful while they continue, will ultimately pro-

---

[1] ὕστερον seems used in contrast with πρὸς ὀλ. ἡμ. above. '*Afterwards*, when the few days of life are gone by, the fruits of God's chastisement will be enjoyed.'

duce the salutary effect of bringing our minds, and hearts, and conduct into a completer correspondence with the perfect rule of righteousness, the divine will, in other words, will promote our spiritual improvement, let us briefly illustrate this principle.

And here let it be distinctly understood that it is not affliction taken by itself that is represented as producing this effect: it is affliction understood to be, and treated as, the chastisement of the Lord. The natural effect of affliction on an unsanctified mind, is either to irritate or depress; in either case, instead of promoting, it hinders spiritual improvement. That, however, arises entirely from the ignorance, and unbelief, and obstinacy of the person afflicted. And even with regard to Christians, it is true that it is just in the proportion as they regard and improve affliction as the chastisement of the Lord, that affliction will promote their spiritual interests.

Affliction, rightly considered, is calculated to impress on the mind the evil of sin generally, our own sinfulness, the vanity of the world, the importance of an interest in the divine favour, the value of a good conscience, the blessedness of a well-grounded hope of eternal life. In the time of ease and prosperity, the mind is naturally thoughtless and inconsiderate; the realities of the spiritual and eternal state are in some measure forgotten; the enjoyments of life supply, as it were, the place of the happiness which arises from a good conscience and peace with God. But sanctified affliction makes us see things as they really are; leads to serious self-inquiry; prevents us from saying, "Peace, peace, when there is no peace;" fixes the mind on the things which concern our everlasting interests, and excites an anxiety to remove everything which interferes with or endangers them. Prosperity not only produces inconsideration, but pride. It is said of the wicked, that "because their strength is firm, and they are not in trouble as other men, pride compasseth them about as a chain."[1] Even Christians are in danger of feeling in some measure this malignant influence of long-continued prosperity; they are in danger of being elated with, and glorying in, their enjoyment—of forgetting the Giver in the gift—of overestimating the value of such blessings, and underrating their dangers. In such cases afflictions are excellent and necessary correctives. They make us feel our own meanness, wretched-

[1] Ps. lxxiii. 4-6.

ness, frailty, and folly; they tend to wean the affections from the "things which are on the earth,"—to lead us to seek for happiness in growing conformity to the will of God,—in one word, to "look not at the things which are seen and temporal, but at the things which are unseen and eternal." It is in this way that "our afflictions work for us a far more exceeding and an eternal weight of glory;" it is in this way they improve our character, and increase our happiness; it is in this way they fit us for more actively doing and more patiently suffering the will of God; it is in this way they make death less dreadful and heaven more desirable, and thus prepare us for both.

In the 12th and 13th verses, the Apostle points out the use which the Christian Hebrews should make of the considerations which he had brought forward in reference to their afflictions. "Wherefore lift up the hands which hang down, and the feeble knees; and make straight paths for your feet, lest that which is lame be turned out of the way; but let it rather be healed."

In the first part of this sentence there is obviously a reference to Isa. xxxv. 3, "Strengthen ye the weak hands, and confirm the feeble knees;" and in the second part, to Prov. iii. 26, "For the Lord shall be thy confidence, and shall keep thy foot from being taken;" but it is merely an allusion. For the hands to hang down, and the knees to be feeble, are figurative expressions to denote a tendency to abandon the discharge of Christian duty. To "lift up the hands" and "the feeble knees" —to support them, as it were, by bandages bracing them—is a figurative expression for, 'Be active and persevering in the discharge of duty; rouse yourselves and each other to this activity and perseverance.' "Make straight paths for your feet;"[1]—*i.e.*, 'Proceed straight forwards in the discharge of Christian duty, notwithstanding all difficulties; beware of turning aside in any degree that may lead to abandonment of the right way altogether; proceed straight onwards;'—" lest that which is lame

---

[1] Καὶ τροχιὰς ὀρθὰς ποιήσατε τοῖς ποσὶν ὑμῶν. These words form a hexameter verse. It not rarely happens that writers in prose unconsciously express their ideas in what corresponds to the artificial rules of rhythm. T. ò. do not mean paths that have no windings in them, for it is no easy matter to make such paths straight; but the words denote smooth, in opposition to rough, and filled with obstructions and stumblingblocks. In this way the phrase occurs in the LXX., Prov. iv. 11, 12, xi. 5, xii. 15.

be turned out of the way." The word rendered, "turned out of the way," may with equal propriety be rendered, 'be dislocated:' 'Proceed straight onward; for if you go into bye-paths, the joints which are already lame may be dislocated, and you prevented from prosecuting the course altogether.' The meaning of that is, 'Beware of moving, even in a slight degree, from the path of duty; for that may end in final apostasy.' On the contrary, let what is lame "rather be healed"—let the feeble joint be bandaged and strengthened: *i.e.*, in plain words, 'By turning your minds to the truths which I have been pressing on your attention, let every disposition to halt in or abandon the onward way of well-doing be removed.'

The force of the connective particle is obvious. 'For these reasons,—since your great Leader endured such contradiction of sinners; since your sufferings are not so severe as those of many who have gone before you; since it is so far from being true that your sufferings are proofs that God does not love you, that an entire exemption from these sufferings would have given you ground to doubt if you belonged to His family; since these afflictions come from your spiritual Father, and are intended for your spiritual benefit; since, in one word, however painful at present, they certainly will, if rightly received by you, promote your spiritual improvement,—surely you ought not to abandon the cause of Christ. On the contrary, you should persevere with increasing determination and ardour, removing and disregarding all obstacles which obstruct your progress, and keeping straight forward, as the only way of reaching the mark for the prize of the high calling of God in Christ Jesus.'

The exhortation seems so expressed as to point out the duty of the Hebrew Christians not only to themselves, but to each other. We are to use the statements furnished us by the Apostle not only for our own special improvement, but also for that of our brethren. Let us all take care not to be the cause of stumbling to our brethren. The best way of doing this is by making "straight paths for our own feet." The fear of offending or making to stumble a brother, must not make us neglect our duty.

It seems universally agreed among expositors that the practical part of the Epistle to the Hebrews divides itself into two parts: the first consisting of a general exhortation to perseverance in the faith, profession, and practice of Christianity, notwithstanding all the difficulties and dangers in which this might involve them; and the second embracing a variety of particular exhortations suited to the circumstances of the Hebrew Christians at the time this Epistle was written.

There is not the same harmony of opinion as to where the first of these divisions terminates, and the second commences. In the judgment of some interpreters, the 13th verse of this chapter closes the first division, and the second opens at the 14th. It appears to me more probable that the first division reaches to the close of this chapter, and the second commences with the beginning of the following one. The comparative view of the two economies, the Mosaic and the Christian, and the impressive warning with which this chapter closes, form a most appropriate termination to the hortatory discourse commencing with the 19th verse of the tenth chapter, to "hold fast the profession of their hope without wavering," and seem plainly to mark the conclusion of one of the divisions of the Epistle.

This is not a mere question of arrangement—it has an important bearing on the interpretation of the passage which lies before us; as, on the supposition that it forms a part of the general exhortation to stedfastness, the particular duties here enjoined must be considered as urged with a peculiar reference to their circumstances, as exposed to temptations to apostasy, and under obligations to resist these temptations. The Apostle had placed before their minds the fearful consequences of apostasy; he had also presented them with abundant evidence, that persevering faith, as it was absolutely necessary, was completely sufficient, to enable them to perform all the duties enjoined on them, to undergo all the trials allotted to them, and to obtain all the blessings promised to them as Christians. He had shown them that the afflictions to which they were exposed on account of their Christian profession, instead of operating as temptations to apostasy, ought to be felt as motives to perseverance; and in the words which follow, he instructs them as to the course of conduct which in their circumstances they ought to follow, in order to their continuing "stedfast and unmoveable" in the faith, and profession, and practice of the religion of Christ.

Taking this general view of the paragraph, let us proceed to examine somewhat more minutely its various parts. Ver. 14.

"Follow peace with all men, and holiness, without which no man shall see the Lord."

It is the duty of Christians to be at peace among themselves, to be on their guard against all alienation of affection towards each other; and there can be no doubt that the maintenance of this brotherly-kindness is well fitted to promote stedfastness in the faith and profession of the Gospel. But in the words before us there seems to be a reference not so much to the peace which Christians should endeavour to maintain among themselves, as that which they should endeavour to preserve in reference to the world around them. They are to "follow peace with all men."

They live amidst men whose modes of thinking, and feeling, and acting are very different from—are in many points directly opposite to—theirs. They have been fairly warned, that "if they would live godly in this world, they must suffer persecution." They have been told that "if they were of the world, the world would love its own; but because they are not of the world, but Christ has chosen them out of the world, therefore the world hateth them." "In the world," says their Lord and Master, "ye shall have tribulation." But this, so far from making them reckless as to their behaviour towards the men of the world, ought to have the directly opposite effect. If the world persecute them, they must take care that this persecution has in no degree been provoked by their improper or imprudent behaviour. They must do everything that lies in their power, consistent with duty, to live in peace with their ungodly neighbours. They must carefully abstain from injuring them; they must endeavour to promote their happiness. They must do everything but sin in order to prevent a quarrel.

This is of great importance, both to themselves and to their unbelieving brethren. A mind harassed by those feelings which are almost inseparable from a state of discord, is not by any means in the fittest state for studying the doctrines, cherishing the feelings, enjoying the comforts, or performing the duties of Christianity; and, on the other hand, the probability of our being useful to our unbelieving brethren is greatly diminished when we cease to be on good terms with them. As far as lies in us, then, if it be possible, we are to "live peaceably with all men."

But while the Christian Hebrews were, by a harmless, kind, and useful behaviour towards their unbelieving neighbours, to cultivate peace with them, they were never to forget that there was something more valuable still—something which must not be sacrificed even to secure peace, *i.e.*, holiness. "Follow peace with all men, and holiness, without which no man shall see the Lord;" *i.e.*, 'Endeavour to live at peace with all mankind, so far and no further than that is compatible with the holiness without which no man can see the Lord.'

The proper meaning of the word *holiness* is 'devotedness to God.' Christians "are not their own; they are bought with a price;"—they have been consecrated to God "by the washing of regeneration, and the renewing of the Holy Ghost." They have voluntarily devoted themselves to Him. Holiness is that temper of mind and that course of conduct which correspond to this state and character.

To "follow holiness," is to live like persons devoted to God, as the God and Father of our Lord and Saviour Jesus Christ; to make it evident that we are His, and are determined to serve Him; that to promote His interests and to advance His glory are our great objects in life.

Without this spiritual devotedness to God we shall never "see the Lord." By the Lord, I apprehend we are here to understand our Lord Jesus Christ; and by seeing Him, we understand, the being with Him where He is, and beholding His glory—the enjoyment of the celestial happiness, the essence of which consists in more intimate knowledge of, more complete conformity to, more intimate fellowship with, Jesus Christ. Without sincere, habitual devotedness to God through Christ Jesus, we can never attain the heavenly happiness; and that for two reasons: (1.) Such is the unalterable determination of God; and (2.) this unalterable determination of God is not an arbitrary arrangement, but corresponds with the nature of things. A person not sanctified, not devoted to God, is entirely unfit for the celestial enjoyments. It is equally true that we must be like Him in order to our seeing Him as He is, and that the seeing Him as He is shall make us more and more like Him.

We must, then, at all events "follow holiness;" at all hazards we must act the part of persons sincerely and entirely devoted to God. If, in consistency with this, we can live in peace with all men, it is so much the better; but if peace with men cannot be purchased but at the expense of devotedness to God, then we must—we must willingly—submit to the inconveniences arising from having men to be our enemies, knowing that it is infinitely better to have the whole world for our enemies and God for our friend, than to have the whole world for our friends and God for our enemy.

The whole exhortation seems to us equivalent to—' Beware of unnecessarily provoking the resentments of the men of the world. If possible, live at peace with them; but never act a part inconsistent with your character as persons devoted to God in order to secure yourselves from their persecutions: if you do, you will act a very unwise part, for you will shut yourselves out from the enjoyment of the celestial blessedness.'[1]

As a further means of preventing apostasy, the Apostle exhorts the Christian Hebrews to watch over each other with a holy jealousy. Vers. 15-17. " Looking diligently lest any man fail of the grace of God; lest any root of bitterness springing up trouble you, and thereby many be defiled; lest there be any fornicator, or profane person, as Esau, who for one morsel of meat sold his birthright. For ye know how that afterward, when he would have inherited the blessing, he was rejected: for he found no place of repentance, though he sought it carefully with tears."

The natural order in explaining such a passage as that now before us, is to attend, first, to the evils against which the Apostle exhorts the Hebrew Christians to guard; and then to the manner in which they are to guard against them. The evils to be guarded against are: " any man's failing of the grace of God"—" any root of bitterness which should trouble and defile them"—"any profane" or sensual "person" rising up among them, who should for present enjoyment sacrifice future happiness.

The Hebrew Christians are exhorted to guard against " any

---

[1] " ' Follow peace with all men' (*i.e.*, Do not think it necessary to enter on hostile aggressions against any man, not even the heathen Romans), ' and holiness, without which no man shall see the Lord ;' *i.e.*, but at the same time do not so mix yourselves up with them as to lose that purity, ἁγιασμόν, which is to Christians what ceremonial holiness was to the Jews."—STANLEY.

man's failing of the grace of God." Here two questions meet us: What is the grace of God? and what is it to fail of the grace of God?

The grace of God, in the language of systematic theology, is either *divine influence*, or the *effect* of divine influence. In the Scriptures, the grace of God is the divine kindness, or some effect of the divine kindness. In the passage before us, I apprehend, the grace of God, or this grace of God, refers to that effect of divine favour or kindness mentioned in the preceding verse: seeing the Lord—obtaining the celestial blessedness, which consists in the knowledge of, conformity to, and fellowship with, Christ. And to fail of this grace of God, is just to come short of heaven.

Now, the Hebrew Christians were to watch over each other, lest any of them should, by not following holiness, by not cultivating devotedness to God, fail of attaining that state of perfect holy happiness in the immediate presence of the Lord, which is the prize of our high calling.[1]

They were to watch particularly "lest any root of bitterness springing up should trouble them, and thereby many be defiled." The Apostle's language is figurative, and borrowed from a passage in Deuteronomy: "Lest there should be among you man, or woman, or family, or tribe, whose heart turneth away this day from the Lord our God, to go and serve the gods of these nations; lest there should be among you a root that beareth gall and wormwood."[2]

"A root that beareth gall and wormwood," is just another name for a secret apostate, a false-hearted professor of the true religion; or, as Moses expresses it, "a man or woman whose heart turneth away from the Lord our God." For such a root to "spring up," is for such individuals to manifest their apostatizing tendencies by their words or their conduct. When circumstances call these forth—as when persecution for the word's sake arises—then such persons trouble the Church. Their false doctrines and their irregular conduct trouble their

---

[1] This seems more satisfactory than interpreting χάρις Θεοῦ, 'religio Christiana;' and is certainly juster than the utterly untenable Arminian interpretation of this as well as Gal. v. 4, to lose finally the peculiar favour of God, once possessed.

[2] Deut. xxix. 18.

brethren, not only by producing grief and regret, but also in many cases by introducing strife and debate, and all the innumerable evils that rise out of them. And by this means "many are defiled." The " root of bitterness" has as it were a power of contaminating the plants in the neighbourhood of which it puts forth its bitter leaves and brings forth its poisonous fruits. A false-hearted professor, introducing false doctrines, or sinful practices, is very apt to find followers. "Evil communications corrupt good manners;" and " a little leaven," when allowed to ferment, will go far to "leaven the whole lump." "Profane and vain babblings increase unto more ungodliness."[1]

But they were to guard not only against speculative irreligion and error, to which I apprehend there is a direct reference in the words just explained, but also against practical ungodliness and immorality. They are to "look diligently, lest there be among them any fornicator, or profane person, like Esau, who for a morsel of bread sold his birthright." Esau is not in the Old Testament represented as a fornicator, but the Jewish interpreters with one consent accuse him of incontinence; and his marrying two Canaanitish wives against the will of his pious parents, certainly does not speak favourably either for his continence or piety.

It is strange that *fornicators* and *profane* persons should be in any way connected with a Christian church. They certainly have no business there. In a Christian church, where anything approximating to primitive discipline prevails, they will not be allowed to remain when they appear in their true colours. But it would appear that at a very early period such persons did find their way into the Christian Church; and it is deeply to be regretted that such persons are still to be found in her communion—persons who, while they make a profession of Christianity, are secretly the slaves of impurity, lightly regard the promises and threatenings of religion, and, where they think themselves safe, can speak contemptuously of its doctrines and laws. Esau was such a person; and he manifested

---

[1] " ' Lest any root,' etc. ; ' lest there be any profane,' etc. : *i.e.*, lest any of you, for the sake of his temporary gratification, should go after heathen customs ; lest any of you, for the sake of his temporary gratification in the sacrificial feast, fall into the sins by which these feasts are so often accompanied. 1 Cor. viii. 13, vi. 13."—STANLEY.

his character by relinquishing all claim and title to the privileges connected with primogeniture, for a trifling and temporary enjoyment. You have an account of the facts referred to in the 25th chapter of Genesis, vers. 29, etc.

The case of Esau is introduced not only for the purpose of the awfully impressive warning which follows, but also to suggest this thought to the Christian Hebrews: 'Beware of permitting sensual and profane men to find their way into, or to retain their place in, your society; for whenever the temptation occurs, they will act like Esau: they will openly apostatize; to avoid present suffering, or to obtain present enjoyment, they will make shipwreck of faith and a good conscience.' Such are the evils against which the Apostle exhorts the Hebrew Christians to guard.

The means which he recommends them to use for this purpose is to *look diligently*. The word rendered "looking diligently"[1] is the same which in 1 Pet. v. 2 is translated "taking the oversight," and from which the word usually employed to designate the rulers of the Church is taken—bishops, or overseers. A careful discharge of their official duties on the part of the elders, is one of the best safeguards of the Christian Church against the evils here referred to. But it seems plain that the Apostle is not here addressing the elders among the Hebrew Christians in particular, but the whole brotherhood; and of course he does not refer principally, if at all, to official superintendence, but to the common care and oversight which all the members of a Christian church should exercise in relation to each other. The relation in which the members of a Christian church stand to each other, gives rise, like every other relation established by God, to a set of corresponding duties; and this duty of mutual superintendence is one of the most important. Every member of such a society should consider himself as his "brother's keeper;" and recollecting that not only the best interests of the individual but of the society are concerned—that his own interests, and, what is of highest consideration, the interests of his Lord and Master, are concerned—every member of a Christian church should "look earnestly lest any" of his brethren "fail of the grace of God." If he discovers anything in his opinions, or temper, or language, or conduct which endangers his final salvation, he ought to attend to our Lord's rule,

[1] ἐπισκοποῦντες.

by first speaking to the individual by himself; then, if this does not serve the purpose, by speaking to him in the presence of one or two of the brethren; then, if this does not serve the purpose, by bringing the matter before the assembly appointed for that purpose, that is, according to our views of Church discipline, the assembly of the elders. In this way a constant watch should be kept "lest any man fail of the grace of God;" "lest any root of bitterness spring up;" "lest there be any profane" or sensual "person," who in the day of trial will abandon his profession.

I am afraid that a great deal of that impurity of Christian communion which is one of the worst characters of the Christianity of our times, and produces such deplorable results in many ways, is to be traced to a neglect of this mutual superintendence. I do not mean to exculpate those who are officially overseers; but it must be obvious that all their attempts, however honest, to secure purity of communion will be of but little avail, if they are not seconded by the brotherly oversight of the members themselves. This is a duty very plainly commanded in the passage before us; and this is by no means the only passage of Scripture where it is enjoined. See Heb. iii. 13; 1 Thess. v. 14; 1 Cor. xii. 24, 25.

The words in the 17th verse are obviously intended to strike terror into the minds of those who might be induced, like Esau, to sacrifice spiritual privileges for worldly advantages; and the general idea is, 'A time will come when you will bitterly, but in vain, regret your foolish choice and conduct.' Esau did so. When he found that, by the overruling providence of God, the blessings connected with primogeniture were given to Jacob, he earnestly sought to inherit the blessing; and when he was told it was impossible, he still sought, even with tears, to make his father repent, or change his mind. But in vain. He had despised and sold his birthright, and must take the consequences.[1]

[1] Schoetgen's note is excellent. "The word μετάνοια here does not mean repentance in the theological sense, but a change of mind and purpose. Isaac had blessed Jacob. Esau wanted him to withdraw the blessing, and sought that goal with tears. But he had not yet repented of his evil deeds and inconstancy, for he was a 'profane person', and threatened his brother Jacob with death." The Jews, who are often wise beyond what is written, say he afterwards became a true penitent. We shall be glad to find it so. "The word μετάνοια does not signify repentance, as if this was denied to Esau, but Isaac's withdrawal of Jacob's blessing, which he sought in vain."—HUTCHINSON, *Not. ad Cyropædiam*, lib. i.

In like manner, the profane and sensual professor of Christianity, who for present enjoyment gives up the promised inheritance in heaven, will one day regret, and vainly regret, his choice: Luke xiii. 25–28. He will "find no room for repentance;" *i.e.*, no means of altering the divine determination, that the man who prefers earth to heaven while here, must, when he leaves earth, go to hell and not to heaven. This passage, rightly interpreted, throws no obstacles in the way of a sinner who has made and long persisted in a foolish choice, making a wise one now. "*Now* is the accepted time; *now* is the day of salvation." If you wish to inherit the blessing, you may; but there is only one way in which you can—the way of faith, repentance, and obedience. Eternal life is yours if you choose it, not otherwise. Eternal life is the gift of God through Jesus Christ our Lord; and nothing but an obstinate refusal to receive it shall exclude any man who hears the Gospel from its enjoyment.

The words which follow, vers. 18–28, form the concluding paragraph of the general exhortation, to hold fast the faith and profession of Christianity, in opposition to all temptations to return to Judaism, grounded on the demonstration of the immeasurable superiority of the former to the latter, which had been presented to them in the doctrinal part of the Epistle. It opens with a very striking comparative view of the two economies, the *Mosaic* and the *Christian*; and the general sentiment intended to be conveyed is plainly this: 'From the Sinaitic dispensation —rigid in its requisitions, terrible in its sanctions, severe and unbending in its whole character—it is in vain to look for salvation; but the Christian economy, "full of grace and of truth," reveals a propitiated Divinity, and unites earth with heaven. How wise is it to seek security from the terrors of Sinai in the peace and serenity of Sion! How foolish to abandon the perpetual sunshine, the unfading verdure, the undisturbed tranquillity of Sion, for the murky clouds, and lurid lightnings, and angry thunders, and barren wastes of Sinai!' Let us proceed to examine somewhat more minutely this comparative view of the two economies.

Vers. 18–21. "For ye are not come unto the mount that might be touched, and that burned with fire, nor unto blackness, and darkness, and tempest, and the sound of a trumpet, and the voice of words; which voice they that heard entreated that the word should not be spoken to them any more: (for they could not endure that which was commanded, And if so much as a beast touch the mountain, it shall be stoned, or thrust through with a dart: and so terrible was the sight, that Moses said, I exceedingly fear and quake.)"

The particle *for* does not connect these words with what immediately precedes, but with the general design of the section. It is equivalent to—'moreover,' or, 'another reason for your holding fast your profession is to be found in the contrast existing between the law and the Gospel.' The general sentiment is, 'Ye are not under the law, which was a rigid and severe economy.'

That sentiment is, however, very rhetorically expressed. That economy was established at Sinai. The assembled congregation of Israel were there placed under that order of things. To be under that economy is here figuratively represented as being of the congregation of Israel at Sinai at the giving of the law; and the severe character of that economy is indicated by a most graphic description of the terrific natural and supernatural phenomena by which its establishment was accompanied. Instead of saying in simple words, 'Ye are not under the law, that severe and wrathful economy,' he says, 'Ye are not of the congregation of Israel who came to Mount Sinai, and from its cloud-capt summit received, amid clouds, and darkness, and thunder, and lightnings, a fiery law.'

There can be no doubt that the mountain here referred to is Mount Sinai in the desert of Arabia. It is termed "the mount which might be touched." Some interpreters have suspected that the negative particle has been omitted, and that the Apostle's expression originally was, 'the mount that might not be touched,' referring to the injunction quoted in a succeeding verse; but this is a conjecture which receives no support from any MS. or version. Others have connected this word, as well as the word "burned," with the clause, "with fire:" 'the mount which was touched and burned with fire'—*i.e.*, 'struck by lightning;' but this is a sense which the words do not naturally suggest.[1] The Apostle's meaning is, that they were not come to the material,

---

[1] In that case, ὄρει would have either preceded ψηλαφωμένῳ, or followed κεκαυμένῳ.

tangible mountain, Sinai,[1] but to the immaterial, spiritual mountain, Sion. Before examining particularly the phraseology in which the Apostle describes the awful solemnities which attended the giving of the law, it will serve a good purpose to bring before your mind the Mosaic history of these transactions. "In the third month, when the children of Israel were gone forth out of the land of Egypt, the same day came they into the wilderness of Sinai. For they were departed from Rephidim, and were come to the desert of Sinai, and had pitched in the wilderness; and there Israel camped before the mount. And Moses went up unto God, and the Lord called unto him out of the mountain, saying, Thus shalt thou say to the house of Jacob, and tell the children of Israel; Ye have seen what I did unto the Egyptians, and how I bare you on eagles' wings, and brought you unto Myself. Now therefore, if ye will obey My voice indeed, and keep My covenant, then ye shall be a peculiar treasure unto Me above all people: for all the earth is Mine. And ye shall be unto Me a kingdom of priests, and an holy nation. These are the words which thou shalt speak unto the children of Israel. And Moses came, and called for the elders of the people, and laid before their faces all these words which the Lord commanded him. And all the people answered together, and said, All that the Lord hath spoken we will do. And Moses returned the words of the people unto the Lord. And the Lord said unto Moses, Lo, I come unto thee in a thick cloud, that the people may hear when I speak with thee, and believe thee for ever. And Moses told the words of the people unto the Lord. And the Lord said unto Moses, Go unto the people, and sanctify them to-day and to-morrow, and let them wash their clothes, and be ready against the third day: for the third day the Lord will come down in the sight of all the people upon Mount Sinai. And thou shalt set bounds unto the people round about, saying, Take heed to yourselves, that ye go not up into the mount, or touch the border of it: whosoever toucheth the mount shall be surely put to death: there shall not an hand touch it, but he shall surely be stoned, or shot through; whether it be beast or man, it shall not live: when the trumpet soundeth long, they shall come up to the mount. And Moses went down from the mount unto the people, and sanctified the people; and

---

[1] αἰσθητός, ἐπίγειος, in contrast with πνευματικός, νοητός, οὐράνιος.

they washed their clothes. And he said unto the people, Be ready against the third day: come not at your wives. And it came to pass on the third day, in the morning, that there were thunders and lightnings, and a thick cloud upon the mount, and the voice of the trumpet exceeding loud; so that all the people that was in the camp trembled. And Moses brought forth the people out of the camp to meet with God; and they stood at the nether part of the mount. And Mount Sinai was altogether on a smoke, because the Lord descended upon it in fire; and the smoke thereof ascended as the smoke of a furnace, and the whole mount quaked greatly. And when the voice of the trumpet sounded long, and waxed louder and louder, Moses spake, and God answered him by a voice. And the Lord came down upon Mount Sinai, on the top of the mount: and the Lord called Moses up to the top of the mount; and Moses went up. And the Lord said unto Moses, Go down, charge the people, lest they break through unto the Lord to gaze, and many of them perish. And let the priests also, which come near to the Lord, sanctify themselves, lest the Lord break forth upon them. And Moses said unto the Lord, The people cannot come up to Mount Sinai: for Thou chargedst us, saying, Set bounds about the mount, and sanctify it. And the Lord said unto him, Away, get thee down, and thou shalt come up, thou, and Aaron with thee: but let not the priests and the people break through to come up unto the Lord, lest He break forth upon them. So Moses went down unto the people, and spake unto them. And God spake all these words, saying, I am the Lord thy God, which have brought thee out of the land of Egypt, out of the house of bondage. Thou shalt have no other gods before Me. Thou shalt not make unto thee any graven image, or any likeness of anything that is in heaven above, or that is in the earth beneath, or that is in the water under the earth: thou shalt not bow down thyself to them, nor serve them: for I the Lord thy God am a jealous God, visiting the iniquity of the fathers upon the children unto the third and fourth generation of them that hate Me; and showing mercy unto thousands of them that love Me, and keep My commandments. Thou shalt not take the name of the Lord thy God in vain: for the Lord will not hold him guiltless that taketh His name in vain. Remember the Sabbath day, to keep it holy.

Six days shalt thou labour, and do all thy work: but the seventh day is the Sabbath of the Lord thy God: in it thou shalt not do any work, thou, nor thy son, nor thy daughter, thy man-servant, nor thy maid-servant, nor thy cattle, nor thy stranger that is within thy gates: for in six days the Lord made heaven and earth, the sea, and all that in them is, and rested the seventh day: wherefore the Lord blessed the Sabbath day, and hallowed it. Honour thy father and thy mother; that thy days may be long upon the land which the Lord thy God giveth thee. Thou shalt not kill. Thou shalt not commit adultery. Thou shalt not steal. Thou shalt not bear false witness against thy neighbour. Thou shalt not covet thy neighbour's house, thou shalt not covet thy neighbour's wife, nor his man-servant, nor his maid-servant, nor his ox, nor his ass, nor anything that is thy neighbour's. And all the people saw the thunderings, and the lightnings, and the noise of the trumpet, and the mountain smoking: and, when the people saw it, they removed, and stood afar off. And they said unto Moses, Speak thou with us, and we will hear: but let not God speak with us, lest we die." "And ye came near, and stood under the mountain; and the mountain burned with fire unto the midst of heaven, with darkness, clouds, and thick darkness." "These words the Lord spake unto all your assembly in the mount, out of the midst of the fire, of the cloud, and of the thick darkness, with a great voice; and He added no more: and He wrote them in two tables of stone, and delivered them unto me. And it came to pass, when ye heard the voice out of the midst of the darkness (for the mountain did burn with fire), that ye came near unto me, even all the heads of your tribes, and your elders; and ye said, Behold, the Lord our God hath showed us His glory, and His greatness, and we have heard His voice out of the midst of the fire: we have seen this day that God doth talk with man, and he liveth. Now therefore why should we die? for this great fire will consume us: if we hear the voice of the Lord our God any more, then we shall die. For who is there of all flesh that hath heard the voice of the living God speaking out of the midst of the fire, as we have, and lived? Go thou near, and hear all that the Lord our God shall say; and speak thou unto us all that the Lord our God shall speak unto thee, and we will hear it, and do it. And the Lord heard the voice of your words, when ye spake unto me; and the Lord said unto me, I have heard the voice of the words of this people, which they have spoken unto thee : they have well said all that they have spoken. Oh that there were such an heart in them, that they would fear Me, and keep all My commandments always, that it might be well with them, and with their children for ever! Go say to them, Get you into your tents again. But as for thee, stand thou here by Me, and I will speak unto thee all the commandments, and the statutes, and the judgments, which thou shalt teach them, that they may do them in the land which I give them to possess it."[1]

With the facts of the case before us, we will find little difficulty in explaining the language used by the Apostle in reference to them. Indeed, the greater part of his description is borrowed from the Mosaic history. The words rendered, "that burned with fire," according to our translation, are a further description of Mount Sinai. They may with equal propriety be rendered, 'the burning fire :' 'Ye are not come to the material mountain of Sinai, nor to the burning fire,'—a prodigious, supernatural burning, which is called in Deuteronomy "the great fire of God," and which reached up to heaven, from the midst of which came forth the voice of Him who "is a consuming fire." The "blackness and darkness" describes the lurid, murky state of the atmosphere; the "tempest," the violent agitation of the clouds by sudden gusts of wind. "The sound of a trumpet" refers either to thunder, or to some supernaturally produced noise more resembling the piercing sound of a trumpet, and, from its unnatural sound, more terrific than thunder. "The voice of words" is the articulate voice pronouncing, from the midst of the unearthly fire, the law of the ten commandments; and so awfully impressive was that voice, that when it ceased, the Israelites earnestly requested Moses to intercede with God that they might hear it no more.[2]

The Apostle notices in a parenthesis, that the prohibition,

---

[1] Exod. xix. 1–xx. 19 ; Deut. iv. 11, v. 22–31.

[2] The description of Philo is very graphic, and strikingly resembles that of the inspired writer. Πάντα δ', ὡς εἰκὸς, τὰ περὶ τὸν τόπον ἐθαυματουργεῖτο, κτύποις βροντῶν μειζόνων ἢ ὥστε χωρεῖν ἀκοὰς, ἀστραπῶν λάμψεσιν αὐγοειδεστάταις, ἀοράτου σάλπιγγος ἠχῇ πρὸς μήκιστον ἀποτεινούσῃ καθόδῳ νεφέλης, ἣ κίονος τρόπον τὴν μὲν βάσιν ἐπὶ γῆς ἠρήρειστο, τὸ δὲ ἄλλο σῶμα πρὸς αἰθέριον

under a very severe penalty, of even touching the mountain, greatly alarmed the people of Israel. "They could not endure that which was commanded." These words have by some been referred to what goes before, as if it had been meant to state, that the reason why the children of Israel desired to hear no more " the voice of words," was that they could not endure the laws which it had promulgated. But not only does what follows require that these words should be viewed in reference to it, but it is obvious from the history that it was not the *law*, but the manner of its promulgation, which alarmed them. "They could not endure that which was commanded;" *i.e.*, it affected them with intolerable terror. If even an irrational animal was to be put to death in a manner which marked it as unclean, something not to be touched, what might rational offenders expect as the punishment of their sin? and if the violation of a positive institution of this kind involved consequences so fearful, what must be the result of transgressing the moral requisitions of the great Lawgiver?

Another circumstance mentioned by the Apostle as strikingly illustrating the terrific character of the giving of the law, is that Moses was agitated with fear, even to trembling. "So terrible was the sight, that Moses said, I exceedingly fear and quake." The fact here referred to is not recorded in the Mosaic history. It is indeed said, Exod. xix. 16, that "all the people in the camp trembled"—a declaration including Moses. The fear mentioned by Moses, Deut. ix. 19,—"For I was afraid of the anger and hot displeasure wherewith the Lord was wroth against you to destroy you"—was on a different occasion. The particular fact to which the Apostle refers, like others mentioned by him in his writings, seems to have been preserved by tradition, of which, indeed, traces are to be found in the rabbinical writings.[1] Of the truth of the fact here asserted by an inspired writer, we can have no doubt. Moses, who had witnessed so

ὕψος ἀνέτεινε, πυρὸς οὐρανίου φορᾷ καπνῷ βαθεῖ τὰ ἐν κύκλῳ συσκιάζοντος. "All things, as was meet (in the presence of the Deity), were preternatural and prodigious: deafening peals of thunder, most vivid coruscations of lightning, the sound of an invisible trumpet issuing from a distant cloud, like a lofty pillar resting on the earth, and its head in the height of heaven, and a thick smoky cloud, produced by the force of celestial fire, darkening the surrounding atmosphere."

[1] *Vide* Capell. *in loc.*, et Wetstein, Gal. iii. 19.

many remarkable displays of the divine power and majesty—who above every other mere human being had been accustomed to intercourse with God,—even he was constrained, by the overwhelming terror of the scene, to exclaim, "I exceedingly fear and quake."[1]

The circumstances of the giving of the law were in accordance with its genius as a divine economy. The people of Israel in a "waste, howling wilderness," standing in speechless terror at the foot of a rugged mountain enveloped with black clouds, now agitated by tempest, and now partially illuminated by flashes of lightning; while from the midst of a devouring fire, towering above the summit of the mountain, and flaming up to heaven, an unearthly trumpet uttered its spirit-quelling notes, and the voice of Jehovah proclaimed the statutes of that all-perfect law, which forbids sin in all its forms and degrees, and requires the unreserved submission of the mind and heart, and the undeviating obedience of the whole life,—were a striking emblem of the situation of all under that dispensation which was then established—a dispensation of which the leading features were strongly marked in these circumstances.

The material mountain is an emblem of its earthly and sensible character: the clouds and darkness, of its obscurity; and the tempest and flaming fire, the fearful trumpet, and yet more awful voice, of the strictness of its precepts, and of the severity of its sanctions;—the holiness and the justice of Jehovah being plainly revealed, while but a very dim and imperfect manifestation was made of His grace and mercy.

The Apostle's statement, then, is equivalent to—'The law—the Mosaic economy—is a system, the leading characters of which, marked in the circumstances of its establishment, are externality, obscurity, and severity; and you as Christians are not under this economy.'

He then goes on to describe the Christian economy in the same highly rhetorical manner, under the emblem of a spiritual mountain and city, whose names are borrowed from the mountain and city dedicated to the divine service in the Holy Land—Sion and Jerusalem; where is the spiritual temple of

---

[1] The Apostle seems to refer to some well-founded tradition, as Stephen seems to do when he represents Moses as ἔντρομος γενόμενος at the burning bush, Acts vii. 32.

Jehovah, the Judge, the God of all; where "Jesus, the Mediator of the New Covenant," ministers; where the host of angels, and the congregation of the first-born redeemed from among men, hold their holy and joyful assembly. And the fact of the Hebrew Christians being under this economy is represented by their coming to this holy hill and city, and joining this august convocation.

If this idea is distinctly apprehended, it will at once put an end to the question, whether the passage before us refers to the state of the Christian Church on earth or in heaven. It is plainly a description of the whole economy—an economy which extends both to earth and to heaven, and which, beginning in time, will continue throughout eternity. The general sentiment is, 'In becoming Christians you have joined a holy and happy society, at the head of which is the Father of spirits, and next to Him Jesus, the Captain of our salvation, and under them the whole host of holy angels, and the whole family of redeemed men, whether on earth or in heaven.' Let us examine somewhat more minutely the particular expressions.

"Ye are come to Mount Sion, and to the city of the living God, the heavenly Jerusalem." The literal Mount Sion was a beautiful hill on the south-east side of Jerusalem, on one of the eminences of which stood the temple: Ps. xlviii. 2. The name is plainly here used figuratively. The Sion here spoken of is a spiritual mountain, as contrasted with the mountain which could be touched—the mountain which is spiritually[1] called Sion, on which the Lamb stands with the hundred forty and four thousand who have His Father's name written in their foreheads. The literal Jerusalem was the divinely appointed metropolis of the Holy Land, the seat of government and religion. Jerusalem's "foundations were in the holy mountains," and "as a city, was builded compact together." "Thither the tribes went up, the tribes of the Lord, unto the testimony of Israel, to give thanks to the name of the Lord. For there are thrones of judgment, the thrones of the house of David." Jerusalem, like Sion, is here used figuratively for the heavenly Jerusalem. As the people of Israel, pilgrims in a wilderness, without fixed dwelling-place, trembling at the foot of a precipitous mountain covered with clouds and darkness, are an em-

---

[1] $\pi\nu\epsilon\nu\mu\alpha\tau\iota\kappa\tilde{\omega}\varsigma$, Rev. xi. 8.

blem of those under the law, the same people, dwelling safely in stable habitations, in the magnificent and delightfully situated city Jerusalem, enjoying all the advantages of a pure religion and a stable government, are an emblem of those who possess the privileges of the Gospel economy.

The emblem is highly significant. It marks the economy to which they belong, as one which brings them into close and delightful fellowship with God. They do not stand at the foot of the mountain, while Jehovah dwells on its summit amid the thick darkness and the devouring fire; but they come even to His seat, they dwell in His presence, they have constant access to Him. It marks, too, the permanence of that economy. They dwell not in tents, but in "a city which has foundations, whose builder and whose maker is God." These appear to me the leading ideas: 'Ye are brought into a state of permanent, favourable intercourse with Jehovah; ye are become citizens of heaven.' All that follows is an expansion of that idea.

By coming to Mount Sion and the New Jerusalem, they of course mingle with the inhabitants of this divine city. These are of two kinds: angelic and human. "Ye are come," says the Apostle, "to an innumerable company of angels." A careful reader of the original text will see that the following word, "the general assembly," does not refer to the first-born, but to the angels. The words, literally rendered, are, "Ye are come to myriads, the general assembly, of angels." Angels are unembodied spiritual intelligences, holding a higher place than man in the scale of being. Those of them who kept their first abode are described in Scripture under the names of seraphim and cherubim—'burning ones, powerful ones,'—"principalities and powers," "thrones and dominions." They dwell in God's presence; they "do His commandments, hearkening to the voice of His word." Vast numbers of these holy beings were on Mount Sinai at the giving of the law: Deut. xxxiii. 2. The law was given by the ministration of angels. But the Israelites did not come to them. They were at the bottom of the hill in darkness, while the angels surrounded Jehovah in the inaccessible light. "But," says the Apostle, "ye are come to myriads, to the general assembly, of angels." The word rendered "general assembly" properly signifies a solemn festal convocation, such as was held by the Greeks at their public religious games. The general idea is, 'You are brought into intimate relation with the whole host of holy unembodied spirits.' By the mediation of Jesus Christ, the Apostle informs us that it is the purpose of God, " in the dispensation of the fulness of times," which is just the Gospel economy, to " bring together into one" holy society " things on earth and things in heaven." Christians come to angels, not by sensible intercourse, but by spiritual relation. On our being reconciled to God, we are reconciled to all His holy creatures. They love us—we love them. We engage in substantially the same religious services; we have the same joys. Even in the present state, they, though unperceived by us, minister to our welfare; and in due time the barriers in the way of immediate intercourse will be removed, and, equal to the angels of God, we shall mingle with them in an unreserved interchange of thought and feeling.

But angels are not the only citizens of the New Jerusalem. We come to "the church of the first-born, whose names are written in heaven." The word rendered *church* is by no means of so definite a meaning as that English word is. It designates any assembly, whether sacred or civil. Here, I apprehend, it refers to the whole body of truly good men on earth, viewed as one great assembly. Many consider it as referring to the sacred assembly of the upper world; but they are afterwards described as " the spirits of just men made perfect;" and in the other places of Scripture where persons are described as having their " names written in heaven," or " in the book of life," they are always spoken of as being on earth. The people of God are termed " the first-born " in allusion to what is said of Israel: "Israel is My son, My first-born." It marks them as dedicated to the service of God, and the heirs of the " inheritance incorruptible, undefiled, and that fadeth not away." And by their names being written in heaven, or enrolled in the celestial album, we apprehend we are to understand that the persons referred to are genuine Christians—men who have not only been admitted to external communion, whose names are not merely enrolled in the books of the visible Church, but who have been admitted to fellowship by the Great Head of the Church, and their names inscribed in His book of life. The idea is, 'In becoming Christians ye become connected with the whole body of the faithful, an innumerable company out of many a kindred, people, and tongue. Every good man is your brother.'

But, what is greater and more glorious still, you come "to God the Judge of all." These words ought to be rendered, "to the Judge the God of all." Christians approach, they draw near, the Judge. The Israelites stood afar off, but the Christian draws near—draws near with boldness—to the Judge; for he knows that He is "God in Christ, reconciling the world unto Himself, not imputing their trespasses unto them." "The God of all;" *i.e.*, the God of all the citizens of Sion—He "of whom all the family in heaven and in earth are named." When it is said He is their God, it means, He acknowledges them with favour and approbation: Eph. iv. 6; Rom. iii. 29; Heb. viii. 10, xi. 16; Rev. xxi. 3, 7.[1]

They come also to "the spirits of just men made perfect;" *i.e.*, to the disembodied spirits of departed holy men, who, having finished their course, have obtained their reward. They who by the faith of the truth become the subjects of the new economy, " sit down with Abraham, and Isaac, and Jacob," and all the prophets, and Apostles, and martyrs, and confessors, " in the kingdom of their Father."

> "One family, we dwell in Him;
> One Church, above, beneath;
> Though now divided by the stream—
> The narrow stream of death."

We are bound together by the tie which binds us to one God and one Saviour. We think along with them; we feel along with them. They love us; we love them. It may be the intercourse on their side with us even here is more intimate than we are aware of; and yet a little while, and the whole family will be assembled in their Father's house, never more to go out for ever.

Still further, Christians "come to Jesus the Mediator of the New Covenant, and to the blood of sprinkling, which speaks better things than that of Abel." It may seem strange that Jesus and His atoning blood should be mentioned last; but it is easy to account for it; for it is by our coming to Him that we are led to the spiritual Sion, and introduced to Sion's God and

---

[1] Tholuck remarks: "I do not think that God is here mentioned as κριτής to enhance the idea of terror, but to point out God as the legislative Head—the fountain of that *law* which binds together the ' civitas cœlestis.' "

Sion's citizens. We have already explained at large the meaning of the phrases, "New Covenant," and "Mediator." Jesus is the person who, in the new and better economy, interposes between God and us, and does all that is necessary in order to our obtaining its advantages and blessings. We come not to the Aaronical priesthood, the mediator of the Old Covenant, but to "Jesus the Mediator of the New[1] Covenant," who is "such a Mediator and High Priest as becomes us; holy, harmless, and undefiled, made higher than the heavens,"—" who being the brightness of the Father's glory, and the express image of His person, has by Himself purged our sins, and is set down on the right hand of the Majesty on high; being made so much better than the angels, as He has obtained by inheritance a more excellent name than they,"—" worthy of more honour than Moses,"—having obtained a more excellent ministry than Aaron,"—" a Priest for ever, after the order of Melchisedec."

The sentiment in the last clause might have been expressed thus: " Who hath sprinkled us with His own blood;" but the Apostle prefers to speak of the blood of expiation separately. "The blood of sprinkling" is just the blood by the sprinkling of which the individual was so purified that he might lawfully approach unto God. " The blood of sprinkling" is just the obedience to the death of the Son of God. That blood shed expiates guilt, makes it a just thing in God to pardon sin; that blood sprinkled on the conscience—*i.e.*, the truth in reference to this expiation understood and believed—removes the jealousies of guilt, produces love to God, and enables the sinner to worship with acceptance and delight. They have such an interest in His atonement as enables them to "draw near with boldness to the throne of grace."

That blood " speaks better things than *that of* Abel."[2] The language is figurative, but not obscure. Abel's blood cried for

---

[1] The Apostle uses νέας instead of καινῆς. The one word is more full of meaning than the other. It conveys the idea of freshness—perpetual freshness and vigour. What is καινή may become παλαιά; but νέα and παλαιά are incongruous ideas.

[2] Griesbach considers the reading τὸ "Αβελ as equal to the T. R. In some MSS. τοῦ is found. 'Abel by his blood,' and 'the blood of Abel,' mean the same thing. The phrase, παρὰ τὸν "Αβελ, is just = ἢ τὸ αἷμα τοῦ "Αβελ λαλεῖ.

vengeance—for the infliction of punishment on the murderer; but the blood of Christ proclaims peace and salvation. The voice of Abel's blood drove Cain away from God; but the voice of Jesus' blood invites us, and, when sprinkled on the conscience, constrains us, to come near. It is a very unnatural interpretation to refer "the blood of Abel" to the blood of his sacrifice. His sacrifice, as *typical*, spoke the same things, though not so distinctly, as what is here termed "the blood of sprinkling." It spoke, though in enigmatical language, of atonement, and reconciliation, and pardon, and salvation.—Such is the contrast between the former and the latter dispensation. There, all is awful, terrible, and threatening; here, all is gracious, alluring, and animating. What folly to adhere to the former! what absolute madness to renounce the latter! It is impossible to conceive a more appropriate conclusion to the exhortation to perseverance than this comparative view, and the awfully impressive exhortation with which it is followed.

The words which follow—vers. 25-28—appear to me to be the conclusion of the body of the Epistle (the thirteenth chapter having much the appearance of a double postscript), and admirably comports with the place it holds. The Epistle commences with the declaration that the Gospel is the completed revelation of the divine will respecting the salvation of men,—a revelation made not by man or angel, but by the Only-begotten of God; and it closes with a solemn exhortation to beware of treating such a revelation in a manner unworthy of its character, as the ultimate manifestation of the mind of God, made by that Eternal Word of life who was in the beginning with the Father, and who has declared Him unto men. The first and the last paragraphs of the Epistle, properly so called, bind together as it were all the intervening statements, illustrations, and arguments. "God, who at sundry times spoke to the fathers by the prophets, hath in these last days spoken to us by His Son." "See, then, that ye refuse not Him that speaketh."[1]

The interpretation of the whole passage depends on the reference which we give to the phrase, *Him that speaketh.* By

---

[1] In reading such a passage as this, who does not feel the justice of the burning words of that accomplished scholar Burmann? "Who ever can read those divine letters of blessed Paul, rich with matter and sweetness of expression—who can read his holy sermons to the people, or to a Christian congregation, without being greatly moved in his mind? Who will not

some interpreters, the appellation has been considered as having a different reference each time it is used. They have supposed the Apostle's meaning to be, 'Beware of neglecting or despising the warning of him who now speaks to you,' *i.e.*, of the Apostle himself; 'for if they escaped not who neglected or despised him who spoke on earth'—*i.e.*, Moses, or, as some strangely think, Abel,—'how shall we escape if we neglect or despise Him who speaks from heaven?' *i.e.*, Jesus Christ. Others refer the phrases, "Him that speaketh," and "Him that speaketh from heaven," to Jesus Christ; and "him that spake on earth" to Moses. It appears to us far more simple and natural to consider the phrase, "Him that speaketh," as referring to the same person in all the three instances; and that the person referred to is *God*, as the Author of all revelation. "God, who at sundry times, and in divers manners, spake to the fathers by the prophets," and who "now in these last days speaks to us by His Son," who is "the brightness of His glory, and the express image of His person," and "who, having purged our sins by Himself, is set down on the right hand of the Majesty on high." "He who speaketh" is the general appellation; and "He that speaketh on earth" and "He that speaketh from heaven," or "He speaking on earth" and "He speaking from heaven," are not two different speakers, but the same speaker speaking in different circumstances.[1] These remarks, distinctly understood, will carry light throughout the whole paragraph.

When God is here termed "He that speaketh," the idea intended to be conveyed is, Christianity is a divine religion: the declarations of the Apostles are a revelation of the will of God. It is precisely the same sentiment which is more fully expressed in the beginning of the second chapter: 'A great salvation has been made known to us: it began to be spoken by the Lord; it has been confirmed by them who heard Him; and God has borne testimony, both by signs and wonders, and divers miracles,

be drawn into a state of utter amazement, and cry, O marvellous power of speech! O rich river of eloquence! O how worthy of God himself, how fit for God, is his speech!"—*Orat. de eloquentia et poetica*, p. 25.

[1] Carpzov justly remarks: "On Mount Sinai the same 'voice of words', the same 'word', shook the earth as will remove the heavens in due time. The words of Haggai ii. 7, invoked in v. 26 and taken there as referring to God the Father, indicate that the reference here also is to God, and no other subject should be supplied for the verb."

and gifts of the Holy Ghost, according to His will.' Christ is to be considered as the Messenger of His Father. God spoke by Him. He was the Prophet of whom Jehovah spoke to Moses when He said, "I will put My words in His mouth, and He shall speak unto them all that I command Him. And it shall come to pass, that whosoever will not hearken unto My words, which He shall speak in My name, I will require it of Him." The " voice from the most excellent glory," proclaiming, "This is My beloved Son, hear ye *Him*," declared the words of Jesus the voice of God; and His declaration was, " The words which I speak are not Mine, but His that sent Me." And in the same manner, the doctrine of the Apostles was the voice of God ; for, says our Lord, " He that heareth you, heareth Me ; and he that heareth Me, heareth Him that sent Me." To " refuse Him that speaketh," then, is just not to attend to, not to believe, not to obey the Christian revelation, as the voice of God.

Against this sin the Apostle cautions the Hebrews : " See," then, " that ye refuse not Him that speaketh." ' Beware of inattention, unbelief, and disobedience in reference to the Christian revelation. Consider that it is a divine revelation—a divine revelation on the most important of all subjects—a divine revelation of the completest form—a divine revelation by the most exalted of messengers; and consider all this, see that ye neglect and despise it not.'

The exhortation is enforced by a fact and an argument. The fact is, " They who refused Him speaking on earth escaped not ;" the argument is, " If they escaped not who refused Him speaking on earth, much more shall not they escape who refuse Him speaking from heaven." Let us attend to these in their order.

The fact is, " They who refused Him speaking on earth escaped not." God " speaking on earth" seems to me nearly equivalent to—' God making a revelation of His will by means of men ; God speaking to the fathers by the prophets.' The phrase includes—it probably directly refers to—the revelation of the divine will by Moses ; but I do not see any reason to limit it to that particular revelation. " They who refused God speaking on earth did not escape ;" they met with " a just recompense of reward," and especially " they that despised Moses' law died without mercy." " With many of them," says the Apostle, " God was not well pleased"—the reason was, they refused Him speaking to them,—"and they were overthrown in the wilderness." The Old Testament history is full of illustrations of this statement, that " they who refused God speaking on earth did not escape." Many of them were punished in a most exemplary manner on earth, and such of them as died impenitent are suffering the vengeance of eternal fire.

The fact is in itself sufficiently alarming; but it lays a foundation for a still more alarming argument. " If they who refused Him speaking on earth did not escape, much more shall not we escape," says the Apostle, " if we turn away from Him speaking from heaven." As for God to speak on earth, is to speak—reveal His will, by the instrumentality of men; so, for God to speak from heaven, is to reveal His will by the instrumentality of a divine Person—His own Son,—one who, even when on earth, was in heaven, and who, in His glorified human nature, is now " at the right hand of the Majesty on high." The revelation referred to is the Christian revelation, the completion of which was given by our Lord after His ascension from earth to heaven. The Apostles had the mind of Christ. He came by them " preaching peace to them who were afar off," as well as " to them who were nigh." There is a double argument in the Apostle's words: ' If they were punished because they refused Him, we will be punished if we refuse Him,—if they were punished who refused Him speaking on earth, much more will we be punished if we refuse Him speaking from heaven.' The superior dignity of the Messenger, and the superior importance of the message, which the employment of such a Messenger necessarily implies, make it equitable, and that, under the government of a righteous God, makes it certain, that our punishment will be more severe than theirs. What must be the measure of the severity, if it corresponds to the value of the salvation rejected, and the dignity of the Saviour despised! Let us recollect that these awful words are not less applicable to us than to those to whom they were originally addressed. God speaks to us from heaven; for He speaks to us by His Son. In this precious book we have the voice of God in heaven; and His merciful exhortation is still, " After so long a time, To-day, if ye will hear My voice, harden not your hearts." " Now is the accepted time; now is the day of salvation."

We enjoy privileges of incalculable value, in having the Christian revelation,—of incalculable value, when we contrast our circumstances with the Jews under the law, and still more when we contrast them with those of the heathen nations. But if we "refuse Him who speaks," we will have reason to envy throughout eternity the comparatively tolerable doom of the disobedient Jew and the wicked heathen. "How can we escape, if we neglect so great salvation?"

It has sometimes occurred to me, that the Apostle, in the words now before us, carries forward the imagery of the preceding paragraph, and that he contrasts God speaking from the material mountain Sinai, and establishing a carnal and temporary economy, and God speaking from the spiritual mountain Sion, and establishing a spiritual and everlasting economy. This limits the reference of the words, "speaking on earth," to what took place at Sinai, and "speaking from heaven" to the revelation made by God through Jesus Christ, exalted to heaven, when the new economy was established. In this case the force of the argument is,—'If those who disobeyed Jehovah, speaking on earth respecting an earthly and temporary economy, were punished, surely much more will they be punished who disobey Him speaking from heaven, respecting a spiritual and everlasting order of things.' This view of the passage seems best to harmonize with what follows, in which the different effects of the voice of God on earth and the voice of God in heaven are very graphically described.

With regard to the voice of God on earth, it is said that it "shook the earth."[1] I cannot doubt that the language here was suggested by the fact, that at the giving of the law the mountain of Sinai and its neighbourhood were shaken by an earthquake. At the same time, as the material mountain is plainly emblematical of the external economy which was established then, the shaking of the earth is emblematical of the change which took place in the establishment of that economy. Shaking is emblematical of change; shaking the earth, of external change. A most important change took place at the giving of the law. The external state of the Jewish people was most materially altered,—high and important privileges were conferred on them; but great and glorious as was the change, it did

---

[1] Οὗ ἡ φωνὴ τὴν γῆν ἐσάλευσε τότε, is a complete elegiac verse.—CARPZ.

not extend to heaven. The *promise*—the economy which God, immediately after the fall, had established in reference to man's spiritual and eternal interests—remained unchanged. The economy established at Sinai, *viewed by itself*, was a temporal and temporary covenant with a worldly nation, referring to temporal promises, an earthly inheritance, a worldly sanctuary, a typical priesthood, and carnal ordinances.

The voice in heaven produces more extensive and more permanent effects. It shakes both earth and heaven—effects a change both on the external and spiritual circumstances of those who are under it; and it effects a permanent change, which is to admit of no radical essential change, for ever. The Apostle, according to the wisdom given to him, does not in plain direct terms assert the complete abolition of the Mosaic economy, and the establishment of a spiritual and perpetual order of things in its room; but he refers to an ancient oracle, in which the extent and nature of the change which was to take place on the coming of the Messiah are described; and thus in the least offensive manner introduces an important doctrine, to the reception of which the prejudices of the Jews opposed very powerful obstacles.

"But now He hath promised." The word *now* does not denote the period when the promise was made, but the period to which the promise refers, which was *now*, opposed to *then*, when the law was established. It is equivalent to—' But with regard to the present period, which is the commencement of a new order of things, He has promised, saying.' This use of the word *now* in the Apostle's writings is common: Rom. iii. 21, xvi. 26. The passage referred to is Hag. ii. 7, "And I will shake all nations, and the Desire of all nations shall come: and I will fill this house with glory, saith the Lord of hosts;"—a passage admitted by the Jews to refer to the coming of the Messiah.

"To shake heaven and earth," is in Scripture often expressive of a very great change. Here, however, the meaning is obviously more definite; it is a shaking heaven and earth as contrasted with a shaking earth only. Some interpreters consider these words as referring to events yet future,—the changes which will usher in the consummation of all things; but it is plain the Apostle considers the shaking as past, and as having produced its effect in the establishment of "a kingdom which cannot be moved." Some interpreters would refer these words to the miraculous changes, both in the visible heavens and in the earth, by which the commencement of the Christian dispensation was distinguished; others, to the political and ecclesiastical changes which it produced. We think it much more natural to understand the words as equivalent to—' I will make a great change, not only in the external, but in the spiritual state of the Church.' The *earth* was shaken; *i.e.*, the external form and state of the Church was completely altered. But that was not all: the heavens were shaken; a clearer and more extensive revelation of spiritual truth was made,—a more abundant and powerful dispensation of divine influence was given. The whole system of the Church was put into a new order. He who sits upon the throne saith, " Behold, I make all things new."

But the Apostle refers not only to the extent of the change, but also to its permanence, especially as that permanence, established as it is by change, involves in it the entire abrogation of the state of things whose place the new economy occupies. The ancient oracle not only indicates the extent, but the permanence of the change; "for," says the Apostle, "this word," or oracle, " *Yet once more,*"—the Apostle quoting only the first words, while he plainly refers to the whole passage, though his argument is more particularly grounded on the words, " Yet *once more,*"—" this word, *Yet once more,* signifieth the removing of those things that are shaken, as of things that are made, that those things which cannot be shaken may remain." The general idea is: The language intimates that this shaking of the heaven and earth of the Church is to be the last shaking; and, of course, that nothing in her constitution henceforward remains of a perishable kind—or that can be shaken; all is permanent and immovable. The order of things now introduced is not, like that which preceded it, to give way to another. The things which are shaken are removed. The things shaken are the earth and the heaven of the Church; that is, the external and the spiritual state of things: they are to be so shaken as to be removed; a complete change is to take place. The law was *added* to the promise as a temporary appendage, and did not abrogate it; but the Gospel takes the place of the law, and thus abolishes *it*. The law was but a change on *the earth* of the Church, and left *the heaven*, which was regulated by *the promise*, unshaken, unchanged; but the Gospel reaches both *the earth* and *the heaven* of the Church, and " old things pass away, and all things become new."

The clause, " as of things which are made," is considerably obscure. The " things that are shaken"—the state of the heaven and the earth of the Church under the former economy—" are removed, as things which are made." " Things that are made ;" what is the meaning of this ? Some have considered these words as equivalent to—' frail, perishing things,' as things of a corporeal and created kind generally are : ' The heavens and the earth of the Church under the old economy were like the material heaven and earth : they were to perish. But the new heavens and earth, which were to be the result of this ultimate shaking, were to endure for ever.' They consider the Apostle's idea as the same as that of the prophet, when he says, in reference to the very same event, " Lift up your eyes to the heavens, and look upon the earth beneath ; for the heavens shall vanish away like smoke, and the earth shall wax old like a garment, and they that dwell therein shall die in like manner : but My salvation shall be for ever, and My righteousness shall not be abolished."[1] The only difficulty here is in getting these ideas out of the word *made*. Others, with much less probability, have explained the word as equivalent to—' destined, or doomed ;' and others, as equivalent to—' fashioned so as to make a great show ;' and others have, without any sufficient reasons, suspected a slight change in the text, and that the word originally written by the Apostle was one which signifies *labouring*,[2] like a ship tossed in the waves, ready to go to pieces ; or to vary the figure, and use the words of the Apostle, " become old, and ready to vanish away." Admitting the first mode of interpretation, the words, " that those things which cannot be shaken may remain," are equivalent to—' so that those things which cannot be shaken may remain ;' *i.e.,* the declaration in the passage, that the change referred to is to be the ultimate change in the state of the Church, is an intimation that the things which remain unchanged by it are to remain unchanged for ever.

I cannot help thinking that the words, " as of things which are made," are not to be viewed as a separate clause, but as most intimately connected with what follows. " Things which were made, in order that the things which cannot be shaken

[1] Isa. li. 6.     [2] πεπονημένων for πεποιημένων.

might remain," is the description of the heavens and earth of the Church under a former dispensation. They were made not to continue; they were made in reference to a system which was to continue; and when they had served their purpose, they passed away. Just as, in building a bridge across a wide ravine or mighty river, there is a cumbrous and unsightly mass of scaffolding and enginery erected, till the work is completed and the key-stone fixed; and then there is a shaking among the scaffolding, till it gives way, and is entirely removed. It seems a work of entire destruction; but it is but the removal of what was never anything better than necessary preparation—what, now that the end is gained, is unsightly encumbrance.[1] And now the work of art, which had been but obscurely seen when rising to perfection, bursts on the delighted eye, self-supported,—

> "—— Like the cerulean arch we see,
> Majestic in its own simplicity."

Everything in the new dispensation is solid. We have not the emblem of Divinity, but God Himself; not a typical expiation, but a real atonement; not bodily purifications, but spiritual holiness: all is spiritual, all is real, all is permanent. How happy is the individual who is interested in this new and better economy! The living during the period of this economy does not secure an interest in its blessings; the belonging to a visible society called a church does not secure an interest in its blessings. He who belongs to this new creation must himself become "a new creature;" he "must be born again;" he must be "transformed, by the renewing of his mind." Faith in the truth as it is in Jesus is the only way in which we can be introduced into this new and better world, and be made participants of its high and holy blessings. Just in the degree in which we understand and believe the truth do we become participants of these blessings. And now "may the God of our Lord Jesus Christ, the Father of glory, give unto you the spirit of wisdom and revelation in the knowledge of Him: the eyes of your understanding being enlightened; that ye may know what

---

[1] A similar meaning is brought out by connecting μείνῃ with τὰ σαλ., not with τὰ μὴ σαλ.; thus, "The removal of the things which were made, *that*—for the purpose that—they might wait for the things that cannot be shaken,—remain until these came, or were established, and no longer."— BAULDRY, quoted by Carpzov.

is the hope of His calling, and what the riches of the glory of His inheritance in the saints, and what is the exceeding greatness of His power to us-ward who believe, according to the working of His mighty power, which He wrought in Christ, when He raised Him from the dead, and set Him at His own right hand in the heavenly places, far above all principality, and power, and might, and dominion, and every name that is named, not only in this world, but also in that which is to come; and hath put all things under His feet, and gave Him to be the head over all things to the Church, which is His body, the fulness of Him that filleth all in all."[1]

The concluding words of the chapter contain in them an account of the practical improvement which the Apostle wished the Hebrew Christians to make of the view he had given them of the glories of the Gospel economy. Vers. 28, 29. "Wherefore, we receiving a kingdom which cannot be moved, let us have grace, whereby we may serve God acceptably with reverence and godly fear: for our God is a consuming fire."

To "receive a kingdom," is to be invested with royalty—to be made a king; and to "receive a kingdom which cannot be moved," is permanently to be invested with royalty—to be made a king for ever. From the connective particle, *wherefore*, it is plain that to receive an immovable kingdom is but another mode of expressing what is meant by "coming to Mount Sion," etc. It is another figurative mode of expressing the privileges and honours which, under the new economy, men obtain by the faith of the truth as it is in Jesus.

It is a common thing in Scripture to represent the privileges and honours of Christians under the figure of a kingdom. The figure is, however, not always employed in the same way. Very frequently the whole of the new economy is represented as a kingdom: "the kingdom of God"—"the kingdom of heaven." Of this kingdom Messiah is the Prince, and true Christians are the subjects. When a man believes the Gospel, he enters into this kingdom, and becomes a partaker of its numerous and invaluable rights and privileges. At other times the blessings enjoyed by Christians are represented under the figure of a kingdom; and in this case they are represented, not as subjects, but as kings—possessors of royalty. They are "a royal priest-

[1] Eph. i. 17-23.

hood;" they "reign in life by Christ Jesus;" they are "kings and priests." It is plainly in the last way that the figure is employed in the passage before us. "We," says the Apostle—that is, obviously, we Christians—" have received a kingdom"—have been invested with royalty—have been made kings.[1]

Royalty is the most exalted form of human life. The kingly state is the most dignified known on earth; and, however mistakenly, men have been accustomed to consider royal happiness as the consummation of mortal blessedness. When the Apostle says, then, "We have received a kingdom," he means, in plain words, we have obtained happiness and honour, of which the most dignified and happy state known among men affords but an imperfect representation. And who that knows the truth on this subject, and is capable of rightly appreciating the value of things, can hesitate as to the justness of the Apostle's representation? To enjoy the peculiar favour of, to be admitted to familiar intercourse with, the greatest and best of beings; to be associated with angels and "the spirits of just men made perfect;" to have the inheritance of the world; to be secured that everything in the universe is ours, so far as it is necessary to promote our true happiness; to be loved and esteemed by all the wise, and holy, and benignant beings in the universe,—surely this is real dignity, true happiness. This is royalty indeed; and "this honour"—this felicity—" have all the saints."

But they not only receive a kingdom, but "a kingdom which cannot be moved;" they not only are made kings, but "they shall reign for ever and ever." The privileges conferred on them are indefeasible privileges, they never can be taken from them. Jehovah said to Israel, when at Sinai He constituted them His people, "Ye shall be to Me a kingdom of priests;" but the kingdom bestowed on them was a kingdom which could be moved. It was shaken; it was removed. The royal, sacred dignities of Israel after the flesh are no more; they have passed away with the economy out of which they originated. But it is otherwise with the kingdom of which we Christians, by the belief of the truth, become possessors. The blessedness and the honour arising from the favour, the image, and the fellowship of Jehovah, are substantial and real. The vicissitudes of time cannot affect them; over them death can have no power; and

[1] Οὗτος γὰρ παραλαβὼν βασιλείαν, 2 Mac. x. 11.

eternity will but develop their excellence and demonstrate their indestructibility. Well then might the Apostle say, "We have received a kingdom which cannot be moved." We have been made kings unto God, and we shall reign for ever and ever. We have obtained, through the faith of the truth, privileges and honours of the very highest kind; and they are stable as the throne, endless as the years, of Him who has conferred them.

Privilege and duty are closely, are indissolubly connected. The more valuable the privilege, the stronger the obligation to gratitude and obedience to Him who has graciously conferred it. This is a principle which pervades the whole of the Apostle's writings; and we find him applying it here when he says, "Wherefore, we having received"—*i.e.*, since we have received —"a kingdom which cannot be moved, let us have grace, whereby we may serve God acceptably with reverence and godly fear: for our God is a consuming fire."

The exhortation, "let us have grace," has been variously interpreted. Grace, in the language of systematic theology, is divine influence; and it is common to understand the exhortation as if it were—'Let us seek divine help, which is necessary in order to our acceptably serving God, and which we shall obtain if we seek it.' This is good enough sense, but it is impossible to bring it out of the Apostle's words. It gives to the word *grace* a sense which it is very doubtful if it ever has in Scripture; and to the phrase, *have grace*, a meaning which it is certain it never has. *Grace* in Scripture signifies the free favour of God. That is its primary and proper signification; but it is often used to denote particular manifestations of the divine favour,—in other words, divine benefits. It has been supposed that here it refers —as in the passage, "We beseech you that ye receive not the grace of God in vain"—to that remarkable manifestation of the divine favour, that invaluable divine benefit, the revelation of mercy; and that the word *have* is here—as it is apparently in some passages of Scripture, 1 Tim. i. 19, iii. 9; Rev. vi. 9— equivalent to *hold;* and that the Apostle's exhortation is, 'Let us hold fast that divine favour, the revelation of mercy, by means of which we have obtained the kingdom which cannot be moved; let us continue stedfast in the faith, notwithstanding all the temptations to apostasy to which we are exposed, by which continued faith alone we can serve God acceptably.'

This also gives a good sense, but it is not the sense which the words naturally suggest.¹

The phrase translated *have grace* is idiomatical (like the Latin *ago gratias*), and is used to signify, 'to be grateful, to express gratitude.' Of this use of the phrase we have a number of instances in the New Testament. Luke xvii. 9, "Doth he *thank*?"² literally, 'Does he have grace?' 1 Tim. i. 12, "I *thank*;"³ literally, 'I have grace.' 2 Tim. i. 3, "I *thank*;" literally, 'I have grace.' This, I apprehend, furnishes us with the key to the expression. 'Let us be thankful; let the reception of blessings so invaluable excite a corresponding gratitude.' "Having received a kingdom which cannot be moved, let us be thankful."

*Gratitude* is, as it were, the soul and the sum of the Christian's duty. Where it is absent, no duty can be performed aright; where it is present in due energy, every duty will be performed aright. The duty which the Apostle enjoins on the Hebrew Christians he himself habitually performed. Who can read his Epistles without being struck with the deep, habitual gratitude which he discovers to Jesus Christ, and to God as the God and Father of Jesus Christ? "I thank God," exclaims he, "through Jesus Christ our Lord." "Thanks be to God, who giveth us the victory through our Lord Jesus Christ." "Thanks be to God for His unspeakable gift."⁴ How frequently, how affectionately, does he urge this duty on Christians! "Give thanks always to God and the Father in the name of Jesus Christ."⁵ "Give thanks to the Father, which hath made us meet to be partakers of the inheritance of the saints in light; who hath delivered us from the power of darkness, and hath translated us into the kingdom of His dear Son." The Apostle's exhortation, then, is, 'Let us be grateful to Him who has conferred on us blessings so rich and honours so high—who has given us a kingdom, a kingdom which cannot be moved.'

Let us be grateful, "that we may serve God acceptably." The words, "whereby we may serve God acceptably," are parenthetical, and contain the reason why we should cultivate gratitude to Him who has conferred on us such benefits. We ought to serve Him. Our service will be of no use if it is not accept-

---

¹ It would, I apprehend, require the article: τὴν χάριν, instead of χάριν.
² μὴ χάριν ἔχει;   ³ χάριν ἔχω.
⁴ Rom. vii. 25; 1 Cor. xv. 57; 2 Cor. ix. 15.   ⁵ Eph. v. 20.

able; and it cannot be acceptable if it is not the result of gratitude, the expression of thankfulness. The word rendered "*serve*"[1] God, properly refers to religious worship. I do not think that it is here to be restricted to religious duties properly so called; but I apprehend it is used to express the idea, that every duty on the part of a Christian should have a religious character. Whatever he does should be in the name of the Lord Jesus, giving thanks to God the Father through Him. The presenting of himself a living sacrifice to God in all the duties of life, is "rational worship."[2] The Christian, though invested with royal dignity, must remember that there is a King of kings, and that his true honour, as well as duty, consists in serving Him. External acts of duty will serve no good purpose if they are not acceptable; *i.e.*, if they are not regarded with complacency by Him to whom they are performed. Now they will not be regarded with complacency by Him, unless they are the expression of gratitude. The only homage which is acceptable to Him is the homage of the heart—of the heart penetrated with gratitude for His "unspeakable gift," and of which the native language is, 'We love Him who hath so loved us.'

But while the Apostle calls on the Hebrew Christians to be thankful, seeing they have "received a kingdom which cannot be moved," he calls on them to be thankful "with reverence and godly fear." Their gratitude and its expressions were not to be of that light character which the reception of temporal and temporary blessings is calculated to excite, but of that grave, chastened, solemn, sublime character, which corresponds with the spiritual, heavenly, and eternal benefits that had been conferred on them. There is something awful in everything connected with God; and when Christians rejoice, they should "rejoice with trembling." When a Christian considers how the blessings which he enjoys were obtained, such a manifestation of the divine holiness and righteousness, as well as benignity, is brought before the mind, as, while it does not in the slightest degree impair his joy in the Lord and his confidence in His mercy, excites an overwhelming sense of His infinite majesty and purity, and induces him to say, "Who shall not fear Thee, and glorify Thy name? for Thou only art holy."

The ground of that holy fear, with which our grateful, joy-

---

[1] λατρευωμεν.   [2] λογικὴ λατρεία, Rom. xii. 1.

ful services to Him who has given us "a kingdom that cannot be moved" should be accompanied, is stated in the concluding verse of this chapter: "For our God is a consuming fire." Hence the necessity and propriety of "reverence and godly fear." The Apostle obviously refers to the words of Moses, Deut. iv. 24, where God is termed a *consuming fire*. The ideas intended to be conveyed seem to be absolute moral purity, connected with irresistible power. Our God is glorious in holiness, and inflexible in justice. He will "by no means clear the guilty," without complete satisfaction to the injured honours of law and government. He shows Himself "a consuming fire" in not sparing His Son when He took our place, but wounding and bruising Him even to the death, "the Just One in the room of the unjust;" and He shows Himself "a consuming fire" in punishing with peculiar severity those who neglect and despise the revelation of grace, reigning through righteousness unto eternal life. The God of the law and the God of the Gospel is the same God—unchanged, unchangeable. His mercy beams forth more gloriously in the Gospel than in the law, but His holiness is not obscured by the effulgence of His mercy. No, the displeasure of God against sin is more strongly marked in the sacrifice of His Son, than in all the hecatombs of victims which bled on the Jewish altars; and we may rest assured, that "if he who despised Moses' law died without mercy, he will be accounted worthy of much sorer punishment, who treads under foot the Son of God, treats as unclean the sanctifying blood of the covenant, and does despite to the Spirit of grace." The Gospel despiser, the impenitent apostate, will find that there is no wrath like the wrath of contemned, abused mercy, and that it is indeed "a fearful thing to fall into the hands of the living God." The belief of the infinitely energetic holiness of God, manifesting itself both in the sufferings of Christ and in the peculiarly sore punishment of the despiser and neglecter of the Gospel, is admirably fitted to produce that "reverence and godly fear," which is in perfect harmony with that grateful love which arises from the faith of the truth as it is in Jesus.

It is a just remark of a judicious expositor and divine, "God does not leave our compliance with the Gospel merely to the generosity and gratitude of the human heart; for, however noble these principles are, the hearts of believers themselves are not always under their vigorous influence. Indeed, the human heart is not so generous and grateful in this imperfect state as many imagine; and he must be a stranger to his own heart who does not feel this. We need to have our fears as well as our hopes stimulated, and the Gospel affords sufficient motives for both."[1] Let us then, in the careful study of the character of God, as manifested in the person, work, and doctrine of our Lord Jesus Christ, the great Revealer of Divinity, lay our minds and hearts open to all the motives, of whatever kind, which it suggests; and having obtained such high and holy privileges, and such "exceeding great and precious promises," let us "cleanse ourselves from all filthiness of the flesh and of the spirit, and perfect holiness in the fear of God."

§ 2. *Particular Exhortations.* Chap. xiii. 1–14.

This chapter may be considered as dividing itself into two parts,—the first being an exhortation to a variety of duties, the second being the conclusion of the Epistle. The duties enjoined are some of them *moral*, and others *religious*. The moral duties recommended are—the love of the brethren, and its appropriate manifestations in hospitality towards strangers and sympathy with sufferers; chastity; freedom from covetousness; contentment; a grateful recollection and pious improvement of the instructions and examples of their deceased pastors; and liberality and beneficence. The religious duties recommended are—fidelity to God; unshaken steadiness in the faith and profession of the Gospel, notwithstanding all the suffering and reproach to which it might subject them; thanksgiving; dutiful subjection to their pastors; and prayer for the Apostle and his brethren. The conclusion of the Epistle consists of three parts: a prayer to God; a request to his brethren; and a parting salutation and benediction. Let us examine these various parts as they lie in order.

The chapter begins with a recommendation of brotherly love. Ver. 1. "Let brotherly love continue."

The persons to whom this Epistle was addressed were at once *Jews* and *Christians;* and according as we view them in the one or other of these aspects, the phrases, "brotherly love,"

[1] M'Lean.

and the "continuance" of brotherly love, must be somewhat differently interpreted. The Jews had a peculiar regard to each other, as distinguished from the Gentile nations; and it was one of the charges which the unbelieving Jews brought against their Christian brethren, that they had become enemies to their nation. Now, the Apostle may be understood as saying, 'Give no occasion for this reproach. Show that in becoming Christians you have not ceased to be, in every good sense of the word, Jews—that the expansion of your philanthropy has not lessened the ardour of your patriotism. Let all the regard you ever had for your brethren, your kinsmen according to the flesh, continue; only let your mode of manifesting it correspond with the juster views which you have now obtained of their true interests.' Paul's "own brotherly love," in this sense, continued. What a striking expression of it have we in these words! Rom. ix. 1–5, x. 1.

But the persons whom he was addressing were not only *Jews*, but *Christians;* and as Christians they formed part of a spiritual brotherhood bound together by ties more intimate and sacred. They were all " the children of God by faith in Christ Jesus." They all stood in the relation of children to God; they had all been formed to the character of the children of God; and the faith of the truth, by which at once the relation was constituted and the character formed, naturally and necessarily led to mutual esteem and love. This is, we apprehend, the view the Apostle is here taking of the Christian Hebrews; and this peculiar affection with which genuine Christians regard each other, is that brotherly affection the continuance of which is the subject of the Apostle's exhortation. All true Christians are taught of God to love one another. " He who loves Him who begat, must also love those who are begotten of Him." He who does not love the children of God, is not himself a child of God.

The degree in which this love is felt depends on a great variety of circumstances. It obviously was felt in a very great degree in the earlier days of the primitive Hebrew Church: Acts ii. 44, 45, iv. 32, 34. To this the Apostle refers in chap. vi. 10, and x. 32, 33, 34: " Ye became companions of those who were made a gazingstock; and ye had compassion of me in my bonds." It is not unlikely that, owing to a variety of circumstances, the ardour of their first love had abated. "Iniquity," according to the Saviour's prophecy, "was abounding, and the love of many," both towards the Saviour and towards one another, "was waxing cold." The Apostle's exhortation is, "Let brotherly love continue." 'Persevere in that warm, disinterested affection towards each other as Christians, by which, after ye were illuminated, ye were so remarkably characterized.'

The instruction afforded by this exhortation is suited to Christians in all countries and in all ages. Love to the brotherhood is a duty wherever the brotherhood exists. From the impure state of Church communion, in consequence of which there are so many in external fellowship whom an enlightened Christian cannot regard as brethren in Christ, and from the division of the Christian Church into a variety of hostile factions, there are difficulties thrown in the way of the cultivation of this Christian virtue; but the obligation to cherish this disposition is in no degree diminished. Wherever you see the image of your Lord—wherever there is a consistent profession of the faith of Christ—there ought we to fix our Christian affections; and having fixed them, we are not easily to allow them either to abate or to be transferred. It is finely remarked by the illustrious divine to whom I have already more than once referred: "The love which is among His disciples is that whereon the Lord Christ hath laid the weight of the manifestation of His glory in the world. But there are only a few footsteps of it left in the visible Church, some marks that it hath been, and dwelt there of old. It is, as to its lustre and splendour, retired to heaven, abiding in its power and efficacious exercise only in some corners of the earth and secret retirements. Envy, wrath, selfishness, love of the world, with coldness in all the concerns of religion, have possessed the place of it. And in vain shall men wrangle and contend about their differences in opinions, faith, and worship, pretending to advance religion by an imposition of their persuasion on others: unless this holy love be again re-introduced among all those who profess the name of Christ, all the concerns of religion will more and more run to ruin. The very continuance of the Church depends secondarily on the continuance of this love. It depends primarily on faith in Christ, whereby we are built on the Rock and hold the Head. But it depends secondarily on this mutual love. Where this faith and love are not, there is no Church. Where they are, there is a Church materially, always capable of evangelical form and order."[1]

Having enjoined the continuance of brotherly love, the Apostle goes on to point out some of the ways in which the existence and continuance of this principle were to be manifested; and he particularly mentions the appropriate display of love to stranger brethren, and to suffering brethren. With regard to stranger brethren, he says, ver. 2, "Be not forgetful to entertain strangers: for thereby some have entertained angels unawares." With regard to suffering brethren, he says, ver. 3, "Remember them that are in bonds, as bound with them; and them which suffer adversity, as being yourselves also in the body." Let us attend to these commanded methods of displaying the love of the brotherhood in their order.

The duty enjoined in the 2d verse is repeatedly in the apostolical Epistles termed "hospitality," but is something considerably different from what is now ordinarily meant by that word. To be hospitable, in the common use of the term, is descriptive of the disposition and habit of liberally entertaining friends, relations, neighbours, or acquaintances. Where such entertainments proceed from genuine kindness, and are unstained by excess, where they do not occupy too much time, where they do not in their expense trench on the demands of justice and benevolence, they are at least innocent, and may serve a number of useful purposes. The Christian duty here enjoined is something totally different. It is the gratuitous and kind entertainment of Christian brethren who are "strangers." In the primitive age, Christians, in consequence of persecution, were often driven from their habitations and native countries, and Christian teachers travelled into strange lands to plant and water the churches. It was the duty of Christians to show the love of the brotherhood by receiving such persons into their houses, and supplying them with the necessaries and comforts of life. For his exemplary discharge of this duty, John pronounces an eulogium on "the well-beloved Gaius," 3 John 5-8. Besides, Christians travelling even on secular business were, in consequence of their Christianity, exposed to inconveniences among pagans of which we can form no very distinct concep-

[1] Dr Owen.

tion; and it was of much importance, both to their comfort and their improvement, that they should live with a Christian family. Accordingly, we find Phœbe, who seems to have gone from Corinth to Rome on business, commended to the kind attentions of the Roman Christians, that they should not only " receive her in the Lord as becometh saints," but that they should " assist her in whatsoever business she had need of them." The Apostle's injunction then is, 'Be ever ready, according to your ability, to receive into your houses, and entertain with kindness, such Christian strangers as, in the service of the Gospel, from the force of persecution, or in the ordinary course of business, stand in need of your hospitality.'

The motive which the Apostle employs to enforce this exhortation is drawn from the unlooked-for honour and advantage which in former times had arisen from the performance of a similar duty. "For thereby"—*i.e.*, by entertaining strangers—"some have entertained angels unawares." There is plainly here a reference to Abraham and Lot, who entertained angels hospitably in their houses, supposing that they were human strangers. It is quite possible that the same thing may have happened to other good men under the former dispensation. The force of the motive does not seem to lie in any probability that they might have the same honour, but in this general principle, that they might derive advantage from the exercise of hospitality greater than they anticipated; that they might have the honour and happiness of entertaining men distinguished for their Christian worth and excellence, and who, by the spiritual communications made by them, would far more than compensate for the external accommodations afforded them.

The circumstances of Christians are greatly changed in the course of ages, but the spirit of Christian duty remains unchanged. It is still the duty of Christians to open their houses as well as their hearts to their stranger brethren, especially to such as are occasional visitants on business connected with the kingdom of our Lord Jesus. I do not think it creditable to the state of Christian feeling among us, that ministers occasionally visiting our city on public business are in many cases under the necessity of seeking accommodation at their own cost, or at the expense of the public cause which they are promoting. I am persuaded wealthy Christians would find a rich reward in performing the duty of Christian hospitality. In entertaining such strangers, they would entertain occasionally men who have much of the spirit of angels. A more powerful recommendation of the duty than even that contained in the passage before us, is to be found in the words of our Lord at the great day, when He is to "come in His glory, and all the holy angels with Him." "Then will He say to those on His right hand, I was a stranger, and ye took Me in." And when they answer, "Lord, when saw we Thee a stranger and took Thee in?" He shall reply, "Inasmuch as ye did it to the least of these My brethren, ye did it to Me."

Another way in which the Christian Hebrews were to manifest their brotherly love, was by "remembering them who were in bonds, as bound with them; and them who suffer adversity, as being themselves in the body." "Those who were in bonds" are plainly the Christians who for their religion had been committed to prison. This was a very common occurrence in the primitive age. These were to be remembered by their brethren. They were to be often thought of with affection and interest; they were to be prayed for; they were to be visited; they were to be supplied with food and clothing and other comforts, and every lawful means employed to mitigate the rigour of their confinement and to obtain their liberty. Onesiphorus, whose conduct Paul mentions with so much gratitude, is an example of the mode of behaviour here recommended: "The Lord give mercy unto the house of Onesiphorus; for he oft refreshed me, and was not ashamed of my chain: but, when he was in Rome, he sought me out very diligently, and found me. The Lord grant unto him that he may find mercy of the Lord in that day: and in how many things he ministered unto me at Ephesus, thou knowest very well."[1]

They were to "remember those who were in bonds, as bound with them." The language is very emphatic. When Saul was persecuting the Church, Jesus called to him from heaven, "Saul, Saul, why persecutest thou *Me*?" and in answer to the question, "Who art Thou, Lord?" He replied, "I am Jesus whom thou persecutest." He considered Himself as bound and persecuted in those who were bound and persecuted in His cause. In like manner Christians are to sympathize with their

[1] 2 Tim. i. 16–18.

imprisoned brethren as if they themselves were in bonds. They are to make the same exertions for them that they would be disposed to make for themselves if they were in their circumstances.

But "bonds and imprisonment" are but one of the many evils to which Christians are exposed; and therefore the Apostle adds, "Remember them who suffer adversity, as being yourselves in the body." To "suffer adversity," when by itself, may signify every species of affliction, whether personal or relative, mental or bodily—sickness, pain, loss of relatives or property. At the same time, I think it probable that the Apostle had a direct and principal reference to afflictions undergone in the cause of Christ. To be reproached, turned out of secular employment, spoiled of goods, banished, or in any other way to be exposed to suffering on account of the profession of the Gospel, —all this is included in suffering adversity.

Now, such Christians were to be remembered by their more prosperous brethren, "as being themselves in the body." These words admit of two modes of interpretation. It may mean that they ought to sympathize with, comfort, and assist them, as being themselves members of the same mystical body with them, according to the Apostle's statement; "For as the body is one, and hath many members, and all the members of that one body, being many, are one body; so also is Christ. For by one Spirit are we all baptized into one body, whether we be Jews or Gentiles, whether we be bond or free; and have been all made to drink into one Spirit.—That there should be no schism in the body; but that the members should have the same care one for another. And whether one member suffer, all the members suffer with it; or one member be honoured, all the members rejoice with it. Now ye are the body of Christ, and members in particular."[1] Or it may mean—and, we rather think, does mean —'Pity them and help them; for ye too are yet in the body—ye too are liable to the same afflictions under which they now labour. Their situation may soon be yours.' Christians in our country and age are not exposed in the same degree to affliction on account of their religion; but there is still, and there ever will be, suffering on account of religion; and wherever this is to be found in any form, or in any degree, it ought to draw out the

[1] 1 Cor. xii. 12, 13, 25–27. This is Calvin's exegesis.

tenderest sympathies of their fellow-Christians. How admirably fitted is Christianity to improve at once the character and the situation of mankind! It is plainly calculated to make mankind happier, in the most afflicted conceivable situation, than without it they could be in the most prosperous conceivable circumstances.

A family is the elementary form of human society, the germ of nations and churches; and the relation in which families originate is the foundation of all other human relations. The institution which forms that relation must of course be of peculiar importance. That institution is of direct divine appointment, and is nearly coeval with the existence of the human race. In its primitive and only legitimate form, it is the union of one man and one woman for life; and just in proportion as it has preserved this form, has it served its purpose, in distinguishing man from the brute creation, in excluding the disorders of licentiousness, and in cultivating the best affections of the heart. It has been well said, that whatever there is of virtue, honour, order, or comeliness among men—whatever is praiseworthy and useful in all societies, economical, ecclesiastical, or political—depends on this institution; and that by all to whom children are dear, relations useful, and inheritances valuable, marriage should be accounted honourable.

Marriage, as an institution, has in every age received the approving sanction of every enlightened philosopher and every wise legislator; and the opinion of those who would banish or degrade it, has always been considered by sober thinkers as a sentiment indicative of a dark mind and a depraved heart, and which, if brought into action, would be found equally hostile to the worth and to the happiness of mankind. The Holy Scriptures stamp this important institution with the broad seal of the divine approbation. They lead us back to its commencement in Paradise; they inform us that a divine benediction rests on it; they borrow from it an image to illustrate the tender and intimate relation between Christ and His people; they unfold its duties and enforce them by the most cogent motives; they class its prohibition with the "doctrine of devils;"[1] and in the passage before us they pronounce it "honourable in all."

Ver. 4. "Marriage is honourable in all, and the bed undefiled: but whoremongers and adulterers God will judge."

[1] Jay.

At the period this Epistle was written, and among those to whom it was addressed, there seem to have prevailed a variety of mistaken notions respecting marriage, and some subjects closely connected with it. In the corrupt age of the Jewish as of the Christian Church, a false notion of the superior sanctity of a state of celibacy seems to have been entertained; and the opinion, which was universal apparently among the Pagans, seems also to have been common among the Jews, that if the marriage vow was not violated—if the seventh commandment was not broken in the letter—no harm was done, no moral guilt was contracted. Whether we view these words before us as an assertion or a precept, they seem to be directed against these false and dangerous opinions.

If, with our translators, we consider them a statement, their meaning appears to be—'Marriage is a state which itself is honourable among all classes of men; and the bed undefiled is honourable,'—*i.e.*, there is nothing morally degrading, there is nothing polluted, as the Jewish Essenes alleged, in the marriage relation, if its duties be strictly observed; on the contrary, it is worthy of respect,—'among all classes of men; but the unbridled indulgence of that principle of our nature which makes marriage a wise and benevolent institution, and for the proper regulation of which marriage is intended, is in a very high degree displeasing to God, and will draw down tokens of His righteous displeasure.'

This is excellent sense, but still, I apprehend, it is not just the meaning of the Apostle. I apprehend the words are a precept, and not a statement.[1] They stand in the midst of a set of moral precepts, and the sentence is constructed on precisely the same principles as the next verse, which cannot otherwise be rendered than as an injunction. We have, we are afraid, in the manner in which the words are rendered, an instance of the undue influence of the wish to obtain an argument against an enemy's doctrine. That the passage, rendered as a statement, contains in it a stronger and more direct condemnation of the detestable doctrine of the Roman Catholic Church respecting the celibacy of the clergy, and the peculiar sanctity of a state of celibacy, than when translated as a precept, seems to have been the true reason why the first mode of rendering has been preferred by our

---

[1] The word to be supplied is not ἐστί, but ἔστω.

own and by many other of the Protestant translators. Considered as a precept, which for the reasons already assigned we are disposed to do, the words are, "Let marriage be honourable among all, and let the bed be undefiled; for[1] whoremongers and adulterers God will judge:" *i.e.*, 'Let marriage be accounted a sacred and venerable thing, both by those who have and by those who have not entered into it. Let the purity of the marriage bed be equally respected by the married and the unmarried; for impurity of every kind is hateful in the estimation of God; and all its perpetrators will assuredly be subjected to the righteous judgment, and will as assuredly meet with the unqualified condemnation, of God.'

These words are not less applicable to us than they were to those to whom they were originally addressed. From the peculiarities of modern society, especially in large cities, peculiar facilities are afforded both for the commission and the concealment of the sins against which this divine injunction is particularly directed; and it is to be feared that even among the professors of Christianity there are persons who avail themselves of these facilities. If there be any such who may read these pages, in the name of God I assure them that their sin will find them out; and that, however they may cloke these abominations from the eye of man, they must one day be made manifest before the judgment-seat of Christ, and have their final doom determined by that law that declares that "no whoremonger nor unclean person hath any inheritance in the kingdom of God or of Christ." "Let no man deceive you with vain words; for because of these things cometh the wrath of God upon the children of disobedience."

The next moral precept refers to the repressing of covetousness, and the cultivation of contentment. Vers. 5, 6. "Let your conversation be without covetousness; and be content with such things as ye have: for He hath said, I will never leave thee, nor forsake thee. So that we may boldly say, The Lord is my helper, and I will not fear what man shall do unto me."

"Conversation," in modern English, signifies colloquial discourse. When our translation of the Scriptures was made, it is obvious that its meaning was more extensive. It plainly

---

[1] The Vulgate translates δὲ *enim;* Griesbach and Lachmann read γάρ instead of δέ.

then was equivalent to—'character and conduct.' "Let your conversation be such as becometh the Gospel of Christ," is plainly equivalent to—'Let your whole frame of sentiment, affections, and habits correspond to the revelation of mercy.' "Having your conversation honest among the Gentiles" is equivalent to—'Habitually conducting yourselves in such a manner as to impress even the unconverted heathen with sentiments of respect for you.' The word is plainly used in this extensive sense in the passage before us. "Let your conversation be without covetousness" is equivalent to—'Let your manners be without covetousness. Let not covetousness characterize your behaviour;' in other words, 'Be not covetous.'

The word generally rendered *covetousness* in the New Testament[1] is a term expressive of an undue regard for anything present and sensible, seen and temporal. The word here rendered "covetousness"[2] is of a more limited signification; it denotes one variety of the love of the world—the love of worldly wealth, the love of money. The injunction is, Be not inordinately fond of worldly possessions. This is an important Christian duty at all times; but it was peculiarly called for from the Hebrew Christians at the time this Epistle was written. A man could not become a Christian without exposing his worldly property to great hazards, and in many instances to certain loss. Important worldly advantages were to be gained by concealing or renouncing Christianity. A man under the powerful influence of the love of money was in danger of employing means for obtaining it inconsistent with his duty as a Christian—was in danger of "making sacrifices of faith and a good conscience" to retain it; and when deprived of it, was in danger of mourning its loss as if it were the loss of his happiness. The danger of this principle to a Christian is very graphically described by the Apostle, when he says, "They that will"—that are determined to—" be rich fall into temptation and a snare, and into many hurtful and foolish lusts, which drown men in destruction and perdition. For the love of money"—the same word as in the text—"is the root of all evil, which, while some have coveted after, they have erred from the faith, and have pierced themselves through with many sorrows." It is an evil against which Christians in every country and age ought carefully to

[1] πλεονεξία, ἐπιθυμία.  [2] φιλαργυρία.

guard; and never perhaps was there a country and an age in which it was of more importance to guard against it than our own.

In opposition to this love of money, so dangerous, so ruinous to a Christian, the Apostle enjoins the cultivation of contentment. "Be content with such things as ye have,"—literally, 'Be content with present things.'[1] "Godliness with contentment is great gain. For we brought nothing into the world, and it is certain we can carry nothing out; and having food and raiment, let us be therewith content." We are to be satisfied with food and raiment; and if we are not, "our conversation" is not "without covetousness." But it may be said, 'There are different kinds and qualities of food and raiment. The rich man and Lazarus had equally food and raiment; but the one was clothed in purple and fine linen, and fared sumptuously every day; the other was covered with rags, and fed with the crumbs from the rich man's table. What is to be the standard of contentment as to food and raiment?' The Apostle furnishes us with it in the words before us: "Be content with present things." Indeed, if we do not make this the standard of contentment, we will never be content at all. The Apostle himself admirably exemplified the virtue which he here recommends. "Not that I speak in respect of want: for I have learned, in whatsoever state I am, therewith to be content. I know both how to be abased, and I know how to abound: everywhere, and in all things, I am instructed both to be full and to be hungry, both to abound and to suffer need."[2] This contentment is not at all inconsistent with a duly regulated desire to improve our circumstances, and the use of the lawful means fitted for obtaining this purpose. It does not consist in a slothful neglect of the business of life, or a real or pretended apathy to worldly interests. It is substantially a satisfaction with God as our portion, and with what He is pleased to appoint for us. It is opposed to covetousness, or the inordinate desire of wealth; and to unbelieving anxiety—dissatisfaction with what is present, distrust as to what is future.

Numerous powerful motives to the repressing of covetous-

[1] τὰ παρόντα. "The resources which are available for the maintaining of life, however small—nature is content with a little."—CARPZ.
[2] Phil. iv. 11, 12.

ness and the cultivation of contentment might be brought forward, but the Apostle confines himself to one; but that one is a most cogent and persuasive one: "For HE hath said, I will never leave thee, nor forsake thee."[1] The passage quoted is a promise made to Joshua, on his being intrusted with the great work of bringing in God's chosen people into the inheritance of the Gentiles, Josh. i. 5. Similar promises are to be found in various parts of the Old Testament. These words have a direct reference to Joshua, but they lay a foundation for the faith of every saint. God stands in the same relation to all His people. The promise here quoted was really made to Joshua alone; but the Apostle argues on the obviously fair principle, that the unchangeable God will do like things in like cases. God promised to be constantly with Joshua amid all the difficulties and trials of his situation; and He will be with His people in every age, in all their difficulties and trials.

There is something peculiarly emphatic in the way in which he introduces the motive: "For HE hath said." It is somewhat similar to—"We know *Him* that has said," ch. x. 30. It is more emphatic than if it had been said—'God hath said.' HE has said; and His power is omnipotent, and His wisdom unsearchable, and His faithfulness inviolable. "*He* is not a man, that He should lie; neither the son of man, that He should repent: hath He said, and shall He not do it? or hath He spoken, and shall He not make it good?" And if HE be with us—if infinite power be our defence, and infinite wisdom our guide, and infinite love and excellence our portion—what need of covetousness, what ground of contentment! What would we have more than Divinity with us? What is all the wealth, and honour, and pleasure of the world, if He is not with us? If He leave us, what matters it what is left behind; and if He does not leave us, what matters who or what forsake us? Well may we without anxiety, and with sweet inward satisfaction, pass through floods and fires if He is with us. The one will not drown, the other will not consume us. "The floods will not overwhelm, the fires will not kindle on us." Yea, when we walk through the shadow of death, we need fear no evil; for still *He* is with us; His staff and His rod they will sustain us.

[1] This is perhaps the strongest negation in the Bible. There are five negative particles: οὐ μή—οὐδ' οὐ μή.

"So that WE may boldly say, The Lord is my helper, and I will not fear what man shall do to me." If HE has said, I will, never leave, WE may well say, What shall MAN do. The quotation here is from Ps. cxviii. 6. The best commentary on these word is to be found in the 8th chapter of the Epistle to the Romans: "If God be for us, who can be against us? He that spared not His own Son, but delivered Him up for us all, how shall He not with Him also freely give us all things? Who shall lay any thing to the charge of God's elect? It is God that justifieth; who is he that condemneth? It is Christ that died, yea rather, that is risen again, who is even at the right hand of God, who also maketh intercession for us. Who shall separate us from the love of Christ? shall tribulation, or distress, or persecution, or famine, or nakedness, or peril, or sword? (as it is written, For Thy sake we are killed all the day long; we are accounted as sheep for the slaughter.) Nay, in all these things we are more than conquerors through Him that loved us. For I am persuaded, that neither death, nor life, nor angels, nor principalities, nor powers, nor things present, nor things to come, nor height, nor depth, nor any other creature, shall be able to separate us from the love of God, which is in Christ Jesus our Lord."[1] "If God be for us, who can be against us?" God is for us, for He has not spared His Son; and He will continue for ever to be for us, for nothing can separate us from His love. What abundant consolation, what strong support, have Christians amid the evils of life! and how shameful is it when they allow either the hope of worldly good things, or the fear of worldly evils, so to influence their minds as to induce them to act a part inconsistent with their obligations to Him who has said, "I will never leave thee, I will never forsake thee!" Surely we should be ready to say, We will never leave Him, we will never forsake *Him*. But we must look to *Him* to enable us to form and to keep this resolution; for it is only by His not forsaking *us* that we can be secured from not forsaking *Him*.

The great design of the Apostle in the Epistle to the Hebrews, as I have frequently had occasion to remark since I commenced its exposition, is to fortify those to whom it is addressed against the numerous and powerful temptations to apostasy to which they were exposed, and to induce them to

[1] Rom. viii. 31-39.

continue "stedfast and unmoveable" in the faith of the truth as it is in Jesus, in the profession of that faith, and in the performance of the duties which rise out of that faith and profession. This leading object is scarcely ever for a moment lost sight of by the inspired writer. Everything of the nature of statement, argument, or motive throughout the Epistle, will be found to bear more or less directly on this point; and almost everything of the nature of injunction or exhortation will be found to have for its object, either directly the persevering faith and profession and practice of Christianity, or something that is fitted instrumentally to promote, *to secure* this persevering faith and profession and practice.

Among the motives which the Apostle employs, those derived from example hold a conspicuous place. The whole of the 11th chapter consists of a most persuasive recommendation of persevering faith, from the achievements it had enabled holy men under a former dispensation to perform, the trials it had enabled them to sustain, and the attainments it had enabled them to realize. In the passage before us, he brings the motive derived from example to bear on the minds of his readers in another, and, if possible, a still more impressive form. He brings before their mind the faithfulness even unto the death of those venerable men who in former years had presided among them, and calls upon them to go and do likewise.

Ver. 7. "Remember them which have the rule over you, who have spoken unto you the word of God; whose faith follow, considering the end of their conversation." To a careful reader of this passage, it must be plain that it refers, not to the present, but to the former, not to the living, but to the dead rulers of the Hebrew Church. The "conversation" or life of the persons spoken of had come to an end, and they were thus the proper objects of remembrance. In this case it would have been better to have rendered the words translated "them who have the rule over you"—a phrase which describes living pastors—simply, "your rulers,"[1]—an expression which merely designates the office, without fixing anything as to whether they now filled it or had formerly filled it.

To understand the divine injunction contained in this verse, it will be proper that we consider, first, the description here

[1] τῶν ἡγουμένων ὑμῶν.

given us of the persons in reference to whom a variety of duties are enjoined on the Hebrew Christians; and then, that we attend to these various duties that are enjoined in reference to these persons.

The persons in reference to whom the Apostle speaks, are described as their rulers, and as having spoken to them the word of God. There can be no doubt that the persons referred to were the *pastors*, or elders, or bishops of the Hebrew Church. These pastors are represented as at once *rulers* and *teachers*. In every orderly society there must be rulers; and our Lord Jesus, who is not the author of confusion, but of peace, in all the churches of the saints, among the gifts which He has bestowed on these churches, has included "governments," or rulers. The pastors, or bishops, or elders of the primitive Church had no arbitrary power over their brethren. The command of our Lord to the primitive rulers of His Church was, "Be not ye called masters;" and His command equally to the pastors and to the flock was, "Call no man master on earth." "The princes of the Gentiles," said our *one* Master in heaven, "exercise dominion over them, and they that are great exercise authority upon them; but it shall not be so with you."[1] But though they had no arbitrary power, they yet bare rule. Chosen by their brethren, they presided in their assemblies; they declared the will and executed the laws of the supreme and sole King of the Church; they reproved, they rebuked, they exhorted with all authority. They enjoined the believers to "observe all things whatsoever Christ had commanded them;" they reproved them when they neglected or violated His laws; and when any individual was obstinate and impenitent in transgression, they excluded them from the communion of the faithful. In all this they exercised no legislative authority: they had no power to enjoin new laws, to institute new ordinances, to invent new terms of communion. Their authority was entirely subordinate to the authority of Christ. Yet, within the limits He prescribed to them, they were *rulers*; and it was the duty of the brethren, who had chosen these pastors to be over them in the Lord, to obey them, and submit themselves to them.

There never has been any change introduced by Him who alone has the power of alteration in such a case, into the con-

[1] Matt. xx. 25.

stitution of His Church; and it is of equal importance that the office-bearers in a church should not aspire to a higher degree of authority, and should not be content with a lower degree of authority, than that which their Master has assigned them; and that the members of a church should equally guard against basely submitting to a tyranny which Christ has never instituted, and lawlessly rebelling against a government which He has appointed.

These pastors are represented as not only rulers, but as teachers. They "spoke the word of God" to them. Indeed, it was in a great measure as teachers that they were rulers and guides. They ruled and guided their brethren by declaring to them the will of God, and bringing to bear on their consciences the numerous and powerful motives which urge them to yield obedience to it. It does not seem that, in the primitive age, rulers were uniformly teachers. The Apostle speaks of "the elders who rule well, especially those who labour in word and in doctrine;" which seems to indicate that there were elders who ruled, and who ruled well, who yet did not labour in word and in doctrine. And this is our scriptural authority for that class of church officers commonly, though absurdly, called '*lay elders*.' The terms, 'clergy' and 'laity,' are not scriptural terms, and the ideas they are intended to express are not scriptural ideas. If the term, 'clerical,' or 'clergy,' be equivalent to—'vested with ecclesiastical office'—elected and ordained to rule in Christ's Church (and this is the least objectionable sense which can be given to the term)—the elders who only rule are as really clerical as the elders who both rule and teach. The individuals referred to by the Apostle, however, were obviously among those who both ruled and laboured in word and doctrine.

The manner in which the Apostle describes this last and most important part of their duty deserves our attention. "*They spoke the word of God*." They made plain to their brethren the meaning and evidence of the divinely inspired revelation of the will of God. It is very possible some of the persons referred to were inspired men; but the description is perfectly applicable to the duty of Christian teachers in all countries and ages, though uninspired. Their great business is just to "*speak the word of God*." The more Christian teachers realize this description in their mode of teaching, the more good are they likely to do. We who are teachers are in danger of indulging too much in speculations of our own about the things which are the subjects of the word of God; and those who are hearers are in danger of being so pleased with the exercise which this species of teaching gives to the imaginative and reasoning powers, as to consider it as the best species of teaching. But, in truth, it is only in the degree in which we "speak the word of God"—in which we clearly exhibit its meaning and evidence, in which we bring man's mind into contact with God's mind—that we discharge our duty to our Master, or promote the real spiritual improvement of our hearers. To have made a single doctrinal statement of Scripture better understood and more firmly believed—to have made a man in his conscience feel more strongly the obligation of a single religious or moral duty—is in reality doing more solid good than sending away an audience delighted and astonished with the ingenuity of the preacher's speculations, the force of his reasoning, the splendour of his imagery, and the resistless force of his eloquence. To "speak the word of God" is the grand duty of the Christian teacher. Such are the persons in reference to whom the Apostle enjoins a variety of duties—the deceased pastors of the Hebrew Church, men who had ruled them and spoken the word of God to them.

The duties he enjoins in reference to them are the following: They were to "remember" them; they were to "follow their faith;" they were to "consider the end of their conversation."

The Christian Hebrews were to "remember" their pastors who had guided and taught them; *i.e.*, they were not to forget them, they were often to think of them, to recall to mind the wholesome instructions they had given them, and the holy example they had set before them. It is not one of the creditable points in the character of human nature that we are so apt to consign to oblivion those to whom we have been deeply indebted. This tendency operates in reference to deceased pastors as well as other benefactors. He who consults his own spiritual improvement will guard against it. We are so constituted that religious truth makes a deeper impression on us, and a holy example exercises a more powerful influence on us, when the one is stated and the other exhibited by an individual to whom we are closely connected, and whom we personally esteem and love; and if we do not give way to an ungrateful forgetfulness, the circumstance of that individual being no more on earth, instead of diminishing, will increase that impression and influence. In this way departed friends, and especially departed pastors, will promote the spiritual improvement of those with whom they were connected long after their death.

While the Apostle exhorts them generally to remember with affectionate gratitude their departed pastors, he particularly urges them to "follow their faith." It is not very easy to fix the precise import of these words. "Faith," as I have often had occasion to state, usually signifies one of two things: either that act or state of mind which we term believing, or that which is the object of the mind in that state or act, *i.e.*, the thing believed. It also sometimes signifies the virtue of fidelity, or faithfulness.

Understanding the word in the first sense, the meaning is, 'Your departed teachers were eminent believers. They were strong in faith, and thus gave glory to God. They remained unshaken in their belief of the doctrines of Christ, and did not yield to the impulses of the evil heart of unbelief. Follow them. Be ye also strong in faith. Let nothing shake your conviction, that in having received the Gospel, you have not followed a cunningly devised fable; but that it is a faithful saying, and worthy of all acceptation, the very truth most sure.'

Understanding the word in the second sense, the meaning is, 'There are many diverse and strange doctrines now taught you; beware of giving heed to them. Do not change your creed; hold by the belief of your deceased pastors; follow their faith. They were, many of them, inspired men, who spake to you as they were moved by the Holy Ghost. The doctrine they taught you was the true doctrine of Christ, and they gave you the fullest evidence of this. Do not be carried away by the pretences of these innovators. Recollect your original instructors; and hold fast the form of sound words which ye have learned of them, in faith and love which is in Christ Jesus.'

Understanding the word "faith" in the last sense, as equivalent to 'fidelity,' the meaning is, 'Your departed teachers continued stedfast in the faith, and profession, and practice of Christianity till the close of their life. They were faithful to their great Master—faithful even to death. Imitate their fidelity. Be followers of them, as they were of Christ.'

In whichever of these senses you understand the words, they convey an important and appropriate meaning. I confess that I find it difficult to determine which is the preferable mode of interpretation. I hesitate between the second and the third. When I consider the injunction as connected with that contained in the 9th verse, I am disposed to prefer the second : 'Hold fast the faith of your primitive and inspired instructors, now with God, and do not adopt the diverse and strange doctrines which are pressed upon you by new and self-appointed teachers.' When I look at it in its connection with the clause to which it is immediately attached—"considering the end of their conversation"—I am disposed to prefer the third : 'Reflecting on the manner in which they finished their course. Be imitators of their fidelity.'

The third duty which the Apostle enjoins on the Christian Hebrews in reference to their departed pastors, is the consideration of "the end of their conversation." "Conversation" here is just equivalent to—'manner of life:' their sentiments, affections, and habits as Christians. "The *end* of their conversation" is the result, the termination—or, to use rather a familiar, but still a very expressive word, the *upshot*, of their Christian course. These good men continued faithful to the death, and died in the faith of Christ, and the hope of eternal life in Him. Some of them, like Stephen and James the brother of John, suffered martyrdom, but they were "more than conquerors through Him that loved them." The dying scenes of such men were well fitted to confirm the faith of their surviving brethren. When the Christians returned from witnessing Stephen's martyrdom, must they not have said within themselves, 'Jesus Christ is well worth dying for !' and, instead of fearing, must they not rather have coveted a similar end to their conversation ? When ministers on their deathbed are enabled to exhibit an example of the power of the faith of the Gospel to sustain and console the mind, amid exanimating sickness and agonizing pain, and in the prospect of the awful solemnities of judgment, and the untried realities of an eternal and unchangeable state, it is very much fitted to operate as a motive on their people to imitate at once their faith and their fidelity.

I am rather disposed to think that the phrase, "end of their conversation," looks beyond death into the unseen world. The Apostle's exhortation seems to be, 'Consider not only how their course closed in this world, but consider in what it has terminated in a future world.' He seems to turn their mind to the same glorious scene which was presented to the mental view of John the divine. He as it were bids them contemplate their departed pastors " standing before the throne, and before the Lamb, clothed with white robes, and palms in their hands, and crying with a loud voice, Salvation to our God, that sitteth on the throne, and to the Lamb;" and says to them, ' These are those who had the rule over you, and who spoke to you the word of God. They have overcome by the blood of the Lamb, and by the word of their testimony; and they loved not their lives to the death. " They have come out of great tribulation, and have washed their robes and made them white in the blood of the Lamb. Therefore are they before the throne of God, and serve Him day and night in His temple. And He that sitteth on the throne shall dwell among them. They shall hunger no more, neither thirst any more; neither shall the sun light on them, nor any heat; for the Lamb, who is in the midst of the throne, shall feed them, and lead them to fountains of living water; and God shall wipe away all tears from their eyes." This is the end of their conversation. Faithful unto death, they have obtained a crown of life.' The consideration of the state of glory and blessedness into which their departed faithful pastors had entered, was certainly very well fitted to induce the Hebrew Christians to hold fast their faith, and to emulate their faithfulness.

To this exhortation to remember their departed pastors, and especially so to consider the termination of their Christian course as to imitate their faith and fidelity, the Apostle subjoins the emphatic words, "Jesus Christ the same yesterday, and to-day, and for ever." One is almost tempted to suspect that these words have fallen out of their proper place. They would come in well between the 5th and 6th verses. But this conjecture is unsupported by external evidence, and therefore cannot be entertained.

These words are obviously elliptical. The ellipsis may be supplied in two ways: Jesus Christ is the same yesterday, to-day, and for ever;' or, 'Let Jesus Christ be the same yesterday, to-day, and for ever.' Understanding the words as an assertion, the meaning is not, I apprehend, 'Jesus Christ is the unchangeable Jehovah,' though that is a truth, and an infinitely important one; but, 'Jesus Christ never changes;' *i.e.*, either, 'His mind, as that mind has been made known to you by your inspired teachers, who are now with Him, can never change, so that any new doctrine brought to you under His name must be false. Men's opinions are constantly changing, but Jesus Christ is "the same yesterday, to-day, and for ever," —His doctrines are invariable.' Or, 'He ever lives; and His affection and care of His people are unchanged and unchangeable. Your most valuable pastors must die, but He ever lives; and He ever lives to protect and bless those who put their confidence in Him.'

I am disposed to understand the words rather as an exhortation than as a statement. The same reasons which led me to consider the fourth verse as an exhortation, influence me in taking a similar view of the verse now before us. It stands in the midst of exhortations, a number of which are expressed in the same elliptical manner. 'Let Jesus Christ be the same yesterday, to-day, and for ever;' *i.e.*, let Him be the same to you. He is the same in Himself; His person is as certainly divine, His doctrine is as true, His promises are as trustworthy, His laws as wise and good, as ever they were. You have embraced Him as your Saviour, and your Teacher, and your Lord. Why should you abandon Him? He really is what your pastors, now with the Lord, represented Him to be, and what you, believing their representations, have acknowledged Him to be. By your steady adherence to Him in all His characters, make it plain that to you, in your estimation, He is "the same yesterday, to-day, and for ever."

The exhortation which follows naturally rises out of this. Ver. 9. "Be not carried about with divers and strange doctrines: for it is a good thing that the heart be established with grace; not with meats, which have not profited them that have been occupied therein."

"Divers doctrines" are doctrines different from the doctrines of pure Christianity; "strange doctrines" are doctrines foreign to, alien from, these doctrines. "To be carried about," or carried hither and thither, by these doctrines, is to have the mind brought into an unsettled state, which naturally produces a corresponding unsteadiness of conduct. The doctrines spoken of by the Apostle, as is plain from what follows, referred to the Jewish doctrines respecting clean or unclean meats, according as they were or were not to be offered on the altar; and probably he has in view the attempt, which was very early made, to connect Judaism with Christianity.

"For it is a good thing that the heart be established with grace; not with meats, which have not profited them that have been occupied therein." "To have the heart established," is a Jewish phrase, directly referring to the effect of food in producing refreshment, and used as equivalent to—'to obtain real satisfaction.' The Apostle's sentiment is this: '*Grace*'—i.e., the free favour of God to sinners, as revealed in the Gospel—'is far more fitted to give solid, permanent satisfaction to the mind and heart, than a superstitious regard to distinction of meats.' The man who understands and believes the truth with regard to the grace of God bringing salvation, walks at liberty, keeping God's commandments, is taught to "deny ungodliness and worldly lusts, and to live soberly, righteously, and godly in this present world;" but the man who is fettered with notions that this species of food is lawful and that unlawful,—that the first may be safely eaten, but that the other must be avoided, under the penalty of incurring God's displeasure,—has his mind occupied with trifles, which lead away from the great fundamental duties of piety and virtue, and, having no solid ground of hope towards God, can have no settled or rational tranquillity of mind.

The Apostle adds, what indeed to us must be very obvious, that "they who have occupied themselves with these things had not been profited." Every deviation from the purity of primitive truth, and from the simplicity of primitive usage, must be hurtful to those who indulge in it. The advice contained in these words, though having a peculiar reference to the circumstances of the Hebrew Christians, is full of important instruction to us. For more than a hundred years the Church in this country has not been so much harassed as of late with "divers and strange doctrines."[1] Had the description been meant for

[1] This was originally written in 1830, when what were called the Row heresies were exciting very general attention.—ED.

those dogmas which have been, and are still, so sedulously inculcated, it could not have been more appropriate. The doctrines of the sinfulness of our Lord's human nature, of universal pardon, and of the identity of the faith of the Gospel with an assurance of personal salvation, are certainly " divers and strange doctrines;" and the duty of Christians in general in reference to them, is very distinctly stated in the passage before us. They are not to be " carried about" by them; they are not to be tossed to and fro with these words of doctrine. They will " not profit those who occupy themselves therewith."

It is a fact as honourable to Christianity as disgraceful to human nature, that the difficulty with which that religion has hitherto made its way in our world has been owing, not to its faults, but to its excellences; and that those qualities which chiefly recommend it to the admiration of the higher and uncorrupted orders of intelligent beings, as " the manifold wisdom of God," are the very qualities which have excited the contempt and loathing, the neglect and opposition of mankind, and led the great majority of those in every age to whom its claims have been addressed, to consider it as absolute foolishness. Purity, simplicity, and spirituality are the leading features of Christianity; and it is because it is pure, and simple, and spiritual that it is so much admired in heaven, and so much despised on earth—that holy angels " desire to look into" it, and that depraved men " make light of it."

The fondness of man for what is *material* in religion, and his disrelish of what is *spiritual*, is strikingly illustrated in the extreme difficulty which was experienced by the primitive teachers of Christianity in weaning the Jews, even such of them as by profession had embraced the Gospel, from their excessive attachment to a system which had so much in it to strike the senses as Judaism. The manner in which these inspired men laboured to attain this end, discovers " the wisdom from above" by which they were guided. They showed the Jews, whether converted or unconverted, that everything that was excellent under the former economy had a counterpart under the new order of things still more excellent; that the spiritual reality was far better than the material shadow; and that what was glorious had now no glory, " by reason of the glory that excelleth." They showed them, that if we Christians have no visible, material manifestation of the divine glory on earth, towards which we bodily draw near when we worship, we have the spiritual Divinity in heaven, to whom in spirit we approach, in exercises which employ our highest faculties, and interest our best affections; that, if we have no splendid temple like that of Jerusalem, within whose sacred precincts acceptable homage can be presented to Jehovah, we have access to the omnipresent God at all times, and in all circumstances; that, if we have no order of priests like that of Aaron to transact our business with God, we have, in the person of the incarnate Son of God, "a great High Priest," who has by the sacrifice of Himself expiated our sins, and who "ever lives to make intercession for us."

In the passage which comes now before us for explication, we find the Apostle applying this mode of reasoning to the subject of *sacred meats*, on which the Jews seem to have valued themselves. Of many of the offerings which were laid on the altar of Jehovah part only was consumed, and the rest reserved as food, either for the priests, or for the offerer and his guests. This food was considered as peculiarly sacred, and the eating of it viewed as an important religious privilege. In the verse which immediately precedes the passage for exposition, the Apostle, in reference to these sacred meats, had said in effect, 'The grace of God—the free favour of God to sinners, manifested in the Gospel—understood and believed, will do the heart more good than the use of any kind of food, however sacred.' And in the paragraph, on the illustration of which I am about to enter, he shows that Christians had a species of spiritual sacred food, far more holy than any which the Jewish people, or even the Aaronical priesthood, were permitted to taste.

Vers. 10-12. "We have an altar, whereof they have no right to eat which serve the tabernacle. For the bodies of those beasts, whose blood is brought into the sanctuary by the high priest for sin, are burnt without the camp. Wherefore Jesus also, that He might sanctify the people with His own blood, suffered without the gate." I shall endeavour first to explain the meaning of these words, and then illustrate the general sentiment which they express.

Before doing this, however, I shall quote Tholuck's beautiful sketch of the Apostle's train of thought :—"The asyndeton gives greater emphasis to the thought. The reference to what precedes is this: 'If ye would indeed hold by βρώματα, or meats, ye have surely far more excellent βρώματα, or meats, in Christianity than in Judaism.' The thought contained in the image that Christians have a higher altar, leads first of all to the idea, that Jesus, as the great sacrifice of atonement, is the true βρῶμα, or meat, of the faithful. The sacrifice of Christ naturally suggests the idea of His sufferings. Then comes the thought, we should be the companions of His sufferings, and even for His sake go out of the city, the emblem of this earthly existence, and endure a death like His, of pain and shame. And then comes the additional thought, that as Christ is the true sacrifice, all our sacrifices are of a figurative and spiritual kind,—no longer sin-offerings and expiatory sacrifices, but simply sacrifices of praise; and these are not to consist merely in words, but also in good works. Such is the brilliant chain of thought from ver. 10 to ver. 16."

It is quite plain that the language in the 10th verse is elliptical. Nor is it difficult to supply the ellipsis: "We"—*i.e.*, we Christians as opposed to Jews—"we have an altar, of which we have a right to eat, but of which they who serve the tabernacle have no right to eat." By "the altar" we are either to understand the sacrifice laid on the altar, or, what comes to the same thing, the phrase, "to eat of," or from, "the altar," is to be understood as meaning, to eat of the sacred food which had been offered on the altar. "Those who serve the tabernacle," or rather, 'those who minister in the tabernacle,' are, I apprehend, the Levitical priesthood. There were, as we have already remarked, certain sacrifices of which the offerer and his friends were allowed to eat a part; and of by far the greater number of sacrifices a considerable portion was assigned to the priests.[1] But there was a class of offerings of which the priest was not allowed to appropriate the smallest part to himself: the animal was considered as entirely devoted to God, and was wholly burnt with fire, either on the altar, or in a clean place without the camp, while Israel was in the wilderness, and without the city, after the erection of the temple at Jerusalem.[2]

Now it appears to me that the Apostle says, 'We Christians are allowed to feast—spiritually, of course—on a sacrifice belong-

---

[1] Lev. vi. 26; Num. xviii. 9, 10; Lev. vii. 34; Num. vi. 19; Lev. vii. 15, xix. 6.

[2] Lev. xvi. 14–16, 27; iv. 3–12.

ing to that class of which not only no ordinary Israelite, but no priest, was under the law allowed to taste.' The sacrifice referred to is plainly the sacrifice which our Lord, as our great High Priest, offered up once for all, even the sacrifice of Himself. Of the class of sacrifices to which the Apostle refers, and which was not a large class, the sacrifice for the sins of the people on the great day of atonement was the most remarkable; and I think there can be no doubt that this sacrifice was directly in his view when he made the statement which we are considering. That sacrifice was not to be used as food: the blood was to be brought into the holy place, which is here equivalent to the holy of holies; and after certain portions had been burnt on the altar, all the rest was to be taken without the camp, or without the city, and there burnt to ashes. Instead of being allowed to be eaten, it was considered as entirely a devoted thing; and he that touched it was not permitted to mingle with the congregation of Israel till he had submitted to certain lustratory rites. Now the sacrifice of our Lord Jesus belongs to this class. When He suffered, it was that by the shedding of His blood " He might sanctify the people ;" *i.e.*, expiate the sins of the spiritual Israel of God, and fit them for acceptable spiritual intercourse with God. His sacrifice was a propitiatory sacrifice for the sins of all His people, answering to the sacrifice for the sins of all Israel on the great day of atonement. And that our Lord's sacrifice was of this character, was marked by His suffering death without the gates of Jerusalem, as the bodies of the victims offered for the sins of the Israelitish people were consumed without the camp, or without the city. Maimonides says, What originally was not lawful to be done in the camp, it was afterwards unlawful to do in the city.

The sacrifice of Christ plainly, then, belongs to that class of sacrifices of which not only the Israelites generally, but the priests, ay, even the high priest, were forbidden to participate. We Christians are permitted spiritually to feast on this sacrifice—to " eat the flesh and to drink the blood of the Son of man." We are allowed to feed on the sacrifice offered up for our sins, and not for our sins only, but for the sins of the whole people of God. And we thus have a far higher privilege in reference to sacred food, not merely than the Israelites, but even than the priests themselves enjoyed. Such seems to me the general meaning of the passage. The meaning of the Apostle does not seem to be, as some have supposed, 'We Christians have an altar'—meaning the Lord's table—' to which no Jew, continuing to practise the rites of Judaism, can be admitted;' nor, 'We have a sacrifice on which we spiritually feed, but of which no Jew, continuing to practise the rites of Judaism, can participate;' but, 'We Christians are allowed to feed on the propitiatory sacrifice for our own sins, the sins of the people of God, which even the priests under the Old Testament economy were not permitted to do.'

Thus it appears that these words contain a statement, and a proof of that statement. The statement is, 'We Christians, with regard to sacred food, have higher privileges, not only than the Jews, but even than the Jewish priests. We are allowed to feast on a sacrifice of the highest and holiest kind, which they were not.' The proof is, 'The highest and holiest kind of sacrifice was that which was offered on the great day of atonement for the sins of the people of God. Of that sacrifice even the priests were not permitted to eat. The blood was brought into the holy place, and what was not burnt on the altar was consumed without the camp, or without the city. The sacrifice of Jesus Christ was a sacrifice of this highest and holiest kind. It was a sacrifice for sin—it was a sacrifice for the sins of the whole spiritual people of God; and to mark it as the antitype of the sacrifice for sin on the great day of atonement, He suffered without the gates of Jerusalem. On this sacrifice we Christians are permitted to feed. We eat the flesh and we drink the blood of the Son of man, offered in sacrifice for our sins.' The conclusion is direct and inevitable: 'We Christians have higher privileges in reference to sacred food, not merely than the Jews, but than the Jewish priests. We have an altar of which they have no right to eat who serve the tabernacle.'

Having thus endeavoured to ascertain the meaning of the Apostle's words, let us proceed to illustrate the sentiment which they contain. Fully to perceive the meaning and design of this statement, thus most satisfactorily proved, it will be necessary to inquire into the nature and value of the privilege of the Jews and the Jewish priests in feeding on sacrifices; then to inquire into the nature and value of the privilege of Christians in feeding spiritually on the sacrifice of Christ; and then, by a comparison of these, to evince the superiority of the latter to the former.

With regard to the privilege of the Jews and the Jewish priests, it is quite plain, whatever superstitious notions might be entertained by them, that the flesh which had been offered in sacrifice was not better as food than any other flesh of the same quality, and that the mere eating it could be of no spiritual advantage to the individual; just as, whatever superstitious notions may be entertained respecting the bread and wine in the Lord's Supper, they have no qualities as bodily nourishment different from common bread and wine, and the mere eating the one and drinking the other can communicate no spiritual benefit. Sacrifice was emblematical, and feasting on sacrifice was emblematical also. Eating the flesh of the sacrifice was, I apprehend, emblematical of two things, or perhaps, to speak more accurately, of two aspects of the same thing. Eating of the sacrifice was a natural emblem of deriving from the sacrifice the advantages it was intended to secure—expiation of ceremonial guilt, removal of ceremonial pollution, and access to the external ordinances of the tabernacle and temple worship. As the altar is in Scripture represented as God's table— Mal. i. 7; Ps. l. 12, 13; Ezek. xxxix. 20, xli. 22—eating of the sacrifice is emblematical of being in a state of reconciliation with God: sitting at His table, and eating of the sacrifice which had been presented to Him, interested in the blessings promised, and secured from the evils threatened, in the Old Covenant. This, whatever extravagant notions the Jews might entertain on the subject, seems to have been the true nature and value of the privilege of feeding on sacrifices.

Now let us inquire into the nature and value of the privilege enjoyed by Christians. They "eat the flesh and drink the blood of the Son of man," who gave Himself a sacrifice and an offering in the room of His people. I need scarcely say the language is figurative; that eating and drinking are not to be understood literally, but spiritually. But what is meant by spiritually feeding on the sacrifice of Christ—spiritually eating His flesh and drinking His blood? It is, in plain words, our deriving from the sacrifice of Christ the blessings which it is intended and calculated to obtain. This we do by the belief of the truth respecting this sacrifice. Believing that truth, we have the forgiveness of our sins, the sanctification of our natures, and spiritual favourable intercourse with God as our reconciled Father. We have in Him the redemption that is through His blood, even the forgiveness of sins; we are washed and sanctified; we have access with boldness to the throne of grace. We have not merely the emblems of these in the Lord's Supper, but in the faith of the truth of the Gospel respecting the sacrifice of Christ we have these invaluable blessings themselves; and seated spiritually at the table of a reconciled Divinity, we feast along with Him. That which satisfied His justice, magnified His law, glorified all His perfections, and gave Him perfect satisfaction, is that which quiets our conscience, transforms our nature, rejoices our heart. We find enjoyment in that in which He finds enjoyment: "our fellowship is with the Father." We hear Him saying, as it were, in reference to the sacrifice of His Son, 'I am fully satisfied;' and our souls echo back, 'So are we.' He says, "This is My Son, in whom I am well pleased;" and we reply, 'This is our Saviour, and He is all our salvation and all our desire.'

It will not require many words to show the superiority, the infinite superiority, of the privilege of the Christian as to *sacred food*, above that of the Jewish people, and even of the Jewish priests. They had merely, in eating the sacrifices, the *emblem* of blessings; we, in spiritually feeding on the sacrifice of Christ, have the blessings themselves. They had but the emblems of expiation, and forgiveness, and purification, and fellowship with God; we have expiation, and forgiveness, and purification, and fellowship with God. But this is by no means all. The blessings of which, in eating the sacrifices, they enjoyed the emblems, were of a kind far inferior to the blessings of which we, in eating spiritually the sacrifice of Christ, actually participate. What is expiation and forgiveness of ceremonial guilt to the expiation and forgiveness of moral guilt? What is external purification to inward sanctification? What is external communion to spiritual fellowship? Nor is even this all. The circumstance that it was but a part of the sacrifice that was set before them that they were allowed to eat of, probably intimated —and the circumstance that there were certain sacrifices, and those of the most solemn and sacred nature, of which they were not permitted to participate at all, certainly intimated—

that complete atonement had not been made for them, and that God and the worshipper were not yet altogether at peace; whereas we, in the faith of the truth, are permitted to feast on the whole sacrifice of Jesus Christ. We not only eat His flesh, but we do what none of the priests durst do with regard to any of the sacrifices, we drink His blood. We enjoy the full measure of benefit which His sacrifice was designed to secure. We are allowed to feed freely on the highest and holiest of all sacrifices. Our reconciliation with God is complete, our fellowship with Him intimate and delightful.

The bearing of this statement on the Apostle's object is direct and obvious. It is a striking illustration of the general principle of the Epistle. 'In Christ you have all that you had under Moses, and much more. Let your unbelieving brethren boast of their privileges with regard to *sacred food*: you enjoy far higher privileges than they, or even than their venerated priests. Even *they* durst not eat of the sacrifice of atonement for all the people of Israel. But *you* are permitted daily, hourly, without ceasing, to feast on the sacrifice of the incarnate Son of God, who suffered, the Just One in the room of the unjust, who gave Himself an offering of a sweet smelling savour in the room of all the sanctified ones.'

From this statement the Apostle draws an important practical inference in the 13th verse. "Let us go forth therefore unto Him without the camp, bearing His reproach."[1]

The meaning and force of this exhortation are not difficult to perceive. If Jesus, the incarnate Son of God, in order to expiate our sins, submitted to become a sin-offering—voluntarily subjected Himself to so much suffering and shame, and if we, from our interest in this sacrifice, enjoy such invaluable privileges; let us cheerfully submit to whatever suffering and shame we may be exposed to in cleaving to Him and His cause. There He is, hanging on a cross as one accursed—cast out of the holy city as unworthy even to die within its walls. But who is this? "A man approved of God"—"the Holy One and the Just"—"the Brightness of the Father's glory"—"God mani-

[1] No Seceder should be ignorant that this was the text from which William Wilson of Perth, one of the illustrious four who were the fathers of the Scottish Secession, preached on the day that by civil authority he was prevented from officiating in the parish church.

fest in flesh;" and "He is wounded for our iniquities, and bruised for our transgressions, and the chastisement of our peace is on Him, and our healing is in His wounds." Shall we then seek to enjoy worldly honour and pleasure by remaining among His murderers? Shall we not leave the city, and take our place by the cross of our Saviour, and willingly bear whatever reproach and suffering may be cast on us for our attachment to Him? Is it not quite reasonable and right that we should even be willing to be crucified for Him who was crucified for us?

It is impossible to conceive the duty of the Christian Hebrews, readily to sacrifice worldly advantages, and submit cheerfully to suffering and reproach for the cause of Christ, more cogently recommended than in these words. And it does seem probable that the Apostle meant to suggest, by this way of stating the truth, that an entire separation from their unbelieving countrymen, and an entire abandonment of the overdated Mosaic institution, were called for on their part, in order to an unreserved devotement of themselves to Jesus Christ; and that this, whatever it might cost them, should be immediately made by them.[1] The Apostle adds, in the 14th verse, a powerful additional reason for their thus willingly submitting to such reproaches and sufferings as an honest attachment to Jesus Christ might bring upon them. Ver. 14. "For here have we no continuing city, but we seek one to come."

Some have supposed that the Apostle refers here to the approaching destruction of Jerusalem, and the final overthrow of the temple worship and the economy to which it belonged. We rather think his idea is, 'The sacrifices we may be called on to make, the sufferings we may be called on to endure, the reproaches which may be cast on us for our attachment to Christ, ought not to make any very deep impression on us. We are but pilgrims and strangers here; we have no fixed residence, no continuing city. This is not our home. But we have a home, at which in due time we shall arrive. To get safely

---

[1] Chrysostom is a good interpreter in many cases, but he does not sustain his character when from this passage he, in his 32d Hom. on this Epistle, teaches that Christians, after the example of Christ, should be buried *extra urbem*. It would have been well, however, if the practice, for which so whimsical a reason is assigned by the Byzantine bishop, had been universally followed.

there, is the great matter. This is what we are seeking; and if we succeed in this—of which, if we be real Christians, there is no doubt—that home will far more than make amends for all the toils and sufferings we have met with on our road to it. These reproaches and sufferings for Christ's sake will soon pass away; and in the heavenly Jerusalem above, from which we shall never be called on to go out, we shall meet with an abundant compensation for all the sufferings, the privations, and reproaches we may be called to sustain in the cause of our Lord while here below.'

While there is a peculiar propriety in these words, viewed as addressed to the Hebrew Christians, in their substance they are applicable to Christians in every country and in every age. All who by faith have feasted on the sacrifice of Christ, are bound by gratitude and duty cheerfully to submit to all the reproach and suffering which may be involved in an honest and open profession of attachment to Him, and dutiful observance of all His ordinances. It is their duty to renounce the world, and all that is in it, even their lawful enjoyments, when these come in competition with their adherence to Christ. They are not, as it has been very justly remarked, to steal out of the camp or city, but they are boldly to go forth, making a public profession of their dependence on Christ's atonement, and their subjection to His authority. And they are to do this under a deep conviction that all that is earthly is transitory, and that what is spiritual is alone permanent. All the worldly advantages which may be purchased by unfaithfulness to our Lord will soon be as if they had never been; nothing will remain but the shame and punishment. All the worldly disadvantages which may be incurred by faithfulness to our Lord will also soon be as if they had never been, and nothing will remain but "the recompense of reward," the "exceeding and eternal weight of glory." May we all who name the name of Christ be enabled to be "faithful to the death, that we may obtain the crown of life."

## CONCLUSION.

PRIVILEGE and duty are very closely connected under the Christian economy. All the Christian's duties, when rightly understood, will be found to be privileges, and all his privileges will be found sources of obligation and motives to duty. We have, in the paragraph of which our subject of exposition forms a part, a very interesting view of the leading privileges and duties of Christians in their intimate mutual connection. The description is given in language borrowed from the Jewish economy. Christians, as they need a high priest, have such an high priest as they need in Jesus Christ, the incarnate Son of God. On that all-perfect sacrifice for sin which He has offered up in His own spotless obedience unto the death, they as a holy priesthood are allowed spiritually to feed; enjoying thus a higher privilege than belonged to the Jewish people, or even to the Jewish priesthood, under the former dispensation. They have no sacrifice of atonement to offer for themselves: that is not necessary; for "by His own sacrifice He has for ever perfected"—*i.e.*, completely expiated the sins of all—"them who are sanctified," of the whole body of the separated ones. They do not need to present a sacrifice of expiation: that has been done in their room. What remains for them is to feast on that sacrifice; or, in other words, to enjoy the glorious results of this all-perfect sacrifice, in reconciliation with God, peace of conscience, and the joyful hope of the glory of God.

But while they have no sacrifice of atonement to offer, they still, as a spiritual priesthood, are required to offer spiritual sacrifices to God; and the fact that the perfection of the Saviour's atoning sacrifice supersedes entirely the necessity of their attempting to do anything for the expiation of their own sins, is the most powerful of all motives to their diligent discharge of their duties as spiritual priests, in presenting themselves to God a "living sacrifice, holy and acceptable, which is their reasonable service."

What are some of those sacrifices which gratitude to Christ, for giving Himself for our sins a sacrifice and offering, should induce Christians to present, may be learned from the 15th and 16th verses. Vers. 15, 16. " By Him therefore let us offer the sacrifice of praise to God continually, that is, the fruit of our lips, giving thanks to His name. But," or *and*, " to do good and to communicate forget not: for with such sacrifices God is well pleased."

The Jews were required to offer not only sacrifices of expiation, but sacrifices of thanksgiving. "The thank-offering consisted in the presentation of an ox, sheep, or goat, which was brought by the offerer to the altar, and slain by him at the south side of it. The priest received the blood and sprinkled it round the altar. The fat was burnt on the altar. The breast and the shoulder—the former of which was to be heaved, and the latter waved by the offerer—belonged to the priest. The rest was applied to the purpose of a sacrificial feast for the offerer and his friends. These offerings were sometimes presented in token of gratitude for some particular blessing received from God, and sometimes as an expression of a habitual sentiment of thankfulness for God's continual kindness. The first of these kinds of thank-offerings was united with meat-offerings, consisting of unleavened cakes and a leavened loaf, which went to the priests."[1]

Under the Christian dispensation there were no such material thank-offerings, but there was something far better. We Christians are bound by obligations peculiarly strong and tender to present a thank-offering to God; but the thank-offering we are to present is not anything material: it is "the fruit of the lips, giving thanks to God's name." What we present is not the offspring of an animal; but, as the Prophet Hosea expresses it, "the calves of our lips;" not the fruit of the earth, but "the fruit of our lips." The words, "giving thanks to His name," are to be joined in construction with the word "lips:" 'our lips giving thanks to His name.' "The fruit of our lips giving thanks to God's name"—*i.e.*, giving thanks to God as revealed to us—is just a circumlocution for our grateful acknowledgments. "Let us offer the sacrifice of praise, the fruit of our lips giving thanks to His name," is just equivalent to—'Let us gratefully acknowledge the divine kindness.'

What is the particular divine benefit for which the Apostle here calls on Christians to give thanks, it is not difficult to perceive. It is indicated by the word *therefore*, which plainly looks back to the preceding statement. A sacrifice of expiation has been presented for us, in the offering of the body of Christ once for all. That sacrifice has been accepted of God; and this is intimated to us by our being permitted spiritually to feast on this sacrifice. "We have been redeemed to God by the blood of His Son;" "Christ has died for us, the Just One in the room of the

[1] *Winer's Bib. Dict.*, as quoted by Dr Pye Smith.

unjust," and "His blood cleanses us from all sin;" and "in Him we have redemption through His blood, the forgiveness of sin, according to the riches of divine grace." It is *therefore* that we ought to "offer the sacrifice of praise" to Him who appointed, to Him who accepted, the great atoning sacrifice— to Him who gave His Son for us—to Him who gives His Son to us.

This spiritual sacrifice of thanksgiving we are to present to God *continually*. The sacrifices under the law could only be presented at particular times, and in particular places; but our spiritual services may be presented at any time, in any place. And as they may, so they ought, to be presented continually. Not that we are to be uninterruptedly engaged in praise, but that we are frequently to be so employed; and that we are constantly to cherish a grateful sense of the divine kindness in the appointment and acceptance of the great sacrifice of atonement, and in permitting us habitually spiritually to feast on it, so as always to be ready to avail ourselves of every proper opportunity of expressing these sentiments in praise and thanksgiving.

This spiritual sacrifice of thanksgiving to God we are continually to present *by Christ Jesus*. By *Him*. All the sacrifices of the people of Israel under the law were offered by, through the medium of, the priests. All our religious services must be presented through the mediation of our Lord Jesus Christ—in a dependence on what He did on earth, and is doing in heaven. It is only when viewed in connection with His atonement and intercession that any of our religious services can be acceptable to God.

But praise is not the only species of thank-offering which Christians are required to present to God. "Thanksgiving is good," as Mr Henry quaintly but justly remarks, "but thanks-living is better." The Apostle accordingly adds, ver. 16, "To do good and to communicate forget not."

The connective particle rendered "but," is merely *connective*. It is equivalent to 'moreover.' I can scarcely doubt that the Apostle here refers to the custom of the Jews, who were accustomed to send portions of the sacrificial feast, on the eucharistic sacrifices, to the poor: Lev. vii. 14; Deut. xii. 12, xiv. 29, xvi. 11. It is the duty of Christians to express their gratitude to God for His goodness to them, through Christ Jesus, by doing good; *i.e.*, by performing acts of beneficence—in feeding the hungry, clothing the naked, relieving the distressed; and in this way communicating to their poor and afflicted brethren of the blessings Providence has conferred on them,—" doing good to all men, especially to those who are of the household of faith." While the terms are of that general kind as to express beneficence and the communication of benefits generally, it seems probable that the Apostle had a direct reference to doing good by communicating to others those blessings for which they were especially bound to give thanks. It is the duty of Christians to do good to their fellow-men by communicating to them, so far as this is competent to them, those heavenly and spiritual blessings for which they are bound continually to give thanks to God by Christ Jesus.

The motive by which the Apostle enforces the duty of offering these spiritual sacrifices of praise and beneficence, and the communication of benefits, is a very powerful one : " With these sacrifices God is well pleased." These were sacrifices with which God at all times was well pleased—better pleased than with external, positive religious duties. "I will have mercy," said He, "and not sacrifice." With regard to praise, we find the psalmist saying, " Whoso offereth praise glorifieth Me : and to him that ordereth his conversation aright will I show the salvation of God." "I will praise the name of God with a song, and will magnify Him with thanksgiving."[1] And with regard to well-doing and communicating we find the prophet saying, " Is it such a fast that I have chosen ? a day for a man to afflict his soul ? is it to bow down his head as a bulrush, and to spread sackcloth and ashes under him ? wilt thou call this a fast, and an acceptable day to the Lord ? Is not this the fast that I have chosen ? to loose the bands of wickedness, to undo the heavy burdens, and to let the oppressed go free, and that ye break every yoke ? Is it not to deal thy bread to the hungry, and that thou bring the poor that are cast out to thy house ? when thou seest the naked, that thou cover him ; and that thou hide not thyself from thine own flesh ? Then shall thy light break forth as the morning, and thine health shall spring forth speedily ; and thy righteousness shall go before thee : the glory of the Lord shall be thy rere-ward."[2] But it is probable that the

[1] Ps. l. 23, lxix. 30.    [2] Isa. lviii. 5-8.

Apostle's design was to convey the idea, that these were now the only kind of thank-offerings which were acceptable to God. The ceremonial thank-offerings had ceased to be pleasing to Him; for the economy to which they belonged had come to an end. These spiritual eucharistic sacrifices are the only ones which, under the new and spiritual dispensation, are agreeable to Him.

When the Apostle says that praise, and kindness, and liberality, are sacrifices which are acceptable to God, I trust I need scarcely say he does not intend to represent them as available to remove the divine displeasure, or to propitiate the divine favour. They are not expiatory sacrifices at all. Expiatory virtue is to be found only in the great atoning sacrifice of our Lord. He merely means,—God approves of them; they are well pleasing to Him. This surely is a very strong incitement to offer such sacrifices, " an exceeding great reward" for offering them. Beyond this the highest aspirations of a Christian cannot go. It is all he can wish; it is above all that he can think. To have the approbation of good men is delightful; to have the approbation of our own conscience is more delightful still; but to have the approbation of God, this is surely the highest recompense a creature can reach. This approbation is very strongly expressed in the word of God already. "God is not unrighteous, to forget your work and labour of love which ye have showed toward His name, in that ye have ministered to the saints, and do minister." "My God shall supply all your need according to His riches in glory by Christ Jesus."[1] It will be still more illustriously displayed when the Son appears in the glory of the Father, and in the presence of an assembled universe proclaims to those who, as a token of gratitude to God for the blessings of the Christian salvation, have " done good and communicated :" " For I was an hungered, and ye gave Me meat : I was thirsty, and ye gave Me drink : I was a stranger, and ye took Me in : naked, and ye clothed Me : I was sick, and ye visited Me : I was in prison, and ye came unto Me. Then shall the righteous answer Him, saying, Lord, when saw we Thee an hungered, and fed Thee? or thirsty, and gave Thee drink? When saw we Thee a stranger, and took Thee in? or naked, and clothed Thee? Or when saw we Thee sick, or in prison, and came unto Thee? And the King shall answer and

---

[1] Phil. iv. 19.

say unto them, Verily I say unto you, Inasmuch as ye have done it unto one of the least of these My brethren, ye have done it unto Me."[1]

The next duty which the Apostle enjoins on the Hebrew Christians, is obedience to their spiritual rulers. He had formerly pointed out to them their duty in reference to their deceased pastors, ver. 7; now he points out their duty to their living pastors, and enforces its performance by very powerful motives. Ver. 17. " Obey them that have the rule over you, and submit yourselves: for they watch for your souls, as they that must give account; that they may do it with joy, and not with grief: for that is unprofitable for you."

I have already had an opportunity of explaining to you the nature and extent of Church rule.[2] The Hebrew Christians were to be obedient to their spiritual rulers. They were to consider the Christian ministry as an ordinance of Christ; and they were to yield obedience to those who filled it, in so far as they taught them the doctrines and commandments of Jesus Christ. They were not to obey them with a slavish, implicit respect to their authority, but they were to obey them from an enlightened regard to Christ's authority; and they were to submit themselves, not only in receiving with humility their instructions, but also their faithful reproofs and admonitions.

The motives to the conscientious performance of these duties are contained in the concluding part of the verse:—" They watch for your souls, as those who must give an account." Christian pastors, if they are at all what they ought to be, " watch for the souls" of those who have called them to take the oversight of them in the Lord. The spiritual improvement, the everlasting salvation of their people, is their great object; and to gain this great object, they *watch*. They know, that to gain it, constant attention is necessary; and they endeavour to yield it. They occupy a place of trust: they have not only been called by their people, but they have been commissioned by their Lord. They have been entrusted with the care of a portion of that " Church which He purchased with His own blood;" and they know that " they must give account." They must do so at the close of life, when the command comes forth, " Give an account of thy stewardship; thou must be no longer

---

[1] Matt. xxv. 35–40.     [2] *Vide* pp. 234, 235.

steward;" and at the great day of judgment, when both ministers and people " must give an account to God." But this is not all: they must give account even here. Ministers ought to keep up a constant intercourse with their great Master. They ought to bear their people on their hearts before the Lord. If their work prospers,—if the souls of their people seem to prosper and be in health,—then they ought with joy and thankfulness to give an account of this to Him; and if, on the other hand, the souls of their people seem languid and diseased,—if ignorance and carelessness prevail,—if " questions gendering strife rather than godly edifying" occupy their attention,—if there " be among them roots of bitterness," or " enemies of the cross of Christ,"—then too ought the Christian minister to pour out his sorrows before the Lord, giving his account " with grief." It is to this giving account that, I apprehend, the Apostle refers in the passage before us.

The consideration of these facts should induce the Christian people to " obey" their pastor, and " submit themselves." He may urge on you unpalatable truth—he may utter sharp reproofs; but recollect he has no choice; remember he is " a man under authority." Put the question, Has he said anything that Christ has not said? If he has, disregard him; if he has not, blame him not,—he has but discharged his duty to his Master and to you; and recollect, you cannot in this case disregard the servant without doing dishonour to the Master. If he had been appointed to amuse you, to " speak smooth things" to you, you might reasonably find fault with him for his uncompromising statements and his keen rebukes. But he " watches for your souls." Your spiritual improvement, your everlasting salvation, is his object; and therefore he must not, to spare your feelings, endanger your souls. It were cruel kindness in the physician, to save a little present pain, to allow a fatal disease to fix its roots in the constitution, which must by and by produce far more suffering than what is now avoided, and not only suffering, but death.

The last clause of the verse is connected with the first clause: " Obey them that have the rule over you, and submit yourselves, that when they give in their account, they may give it in with joy, and not with grief; for that is unprofitable to you." If a minister is but *faithful*, so far as he himself is concerned, he may, he must, give in his account with joy. Whether the Gospel, as administered by him, be "the savour of life unto life" or "of death unto death," if he is but faithful, he will be "a sweet savour of Christ unto God," in them that perish as well as in them that believe; his unsuccessful as well as his successful labours will meet the approbation of the great Master, and obtain an abundant "recompense of reward." But so far as his people are concerned, the account given in by him will be joyful or sorrowful just in proportion to his success; and for him to give in a joyful account, is profitable for them; for him to give in a sorrowful account, is unprofitable. It affords the purest satisfaction to a Christian minister to find that his labours among his people are "not in vain in the Lord;" that the thoughtless are becoming serious; that those alarmed about their spiritual interests are seeking and finding rest in the faith of the truth, and the well-grounded hope of eternal life; and that those who have believed through grace are growing up in all things to Him who is the Head, becoming more intelligent and active, more harmless and useful, more weaned from earth, more fit for heaven. Every Christian minister, if he deserve the name at all, can in some measure say, with the Apostle John, "I have no greater joy than to hear that my children walk in truth;"[1] or with the Apostle Paul, "For what is our hope, or joy, or crown of rejoicing? are not even ye in the presence of our Lord Jesus Christ at His coming? For ye are our glory and joy."[2] In these circumstances he gives his account to his Master with joy, and thus is profitable to his people. His holy joy enables him to prosecute with growing alacrity the duties of his office; and the great Head of the Church, by a still further communication of divine influence, shows His satisfaction with His obedient children. On the other hand, if the members of a Christian church do not obey their pastor in the Lord and submit themselves, and if their souls obviously are not prospering under his ministry, it must be with a sad heart that he gives in his account to his Lord.

It is very strikingly said by Dr Owen, With what sighing, and groaning, and mourning, the accounts of faithful ministers to Christ are often accompanied, He alone knows, and the last day will manifest. For the accounts of ministers to be given

[1] 3 John 4.     [2] 1 Thess. ii. 19, 20.

in in this way, is not profitable for their people.[1] The heart of the minister is discouraged; the great Master is displeased; the tokens of His favour are withdrawn; spiritual barrenness prevails; and the clouds seem, as it were, commanded to rain no rain on the unfruitful vineyard.

The Apostle now solicits from the Hebrew Christians an interest in their prayers, ver. 18. "Pray for us." The Apostle was fully persuaded of two things: that all the blessings he stood in need of could be obtained from God, from God alone; and that prayer was the appointed means of obtaining these blessings. Hence we find him very frequently requesting the prayers of the churches: 2 Cor. i. 11; Eph. vi. 19; Col. iv. 3; 2 Thess. iii. 1. By soliciting the prayers of the Hebrew Christians, he also intimates the high opinion he entertained of them as righteous men, whose prayers would "avail much." He adds, "For we trust that we have a good conscience, willing in all things to live honestly."

There never was a man more exposed to obloquy than the Apostle Paul; and it seems likely that unfavourable reports had been circulated among the Hebrew Christians respecting him. It is in reference to these that he says, "We trust we have a good conscience, in all things willing to live honestly." 'Though my name may be cast out as evil, and I may suffer as if I were an evil-doer, yet I am conscious of my own integrity and faithfulness in the ministry committed to me. I am desirous of conducting myself *honourably* in all circumstances. I do not walk in craftiness, nor do I handle the word of God deceitfully; but my rejoicing is this, the testimony of my conscience, that in simplicity and godly sincerity, not with fleshly wisdom, but by the grace of God, I have had my conversation in the world.'[2]

---

[1] ἀλυσιτελές, one of the ἅπαξ λεγόμενα, so far as regards the New Testament. By a common figure, it is used to mean more than it expresses. It is = 'hurtful.' We have a curious illustration of the meaning of the word in the address which the comic poet, in Athenæus l. iv., puts in the mouth of a drunkard, to an abstinent philosopher or water-drinker,—a teetotaller of those days:—

> Ἀλυσιτελὴς εἶ τῇ πόλει, πίνων ὕδωρ,
> Τὸν γὰρ γεωργὸν καὶ τὸν ἔμπορον κακοῖς·
> Ἐγὼ δὲ τὰς προσόδους μεθύων καλὰς ποιῶ.

[2] This passage is quoted with great effect by Richard Alleine in his valedictory discourse to his people, on leaving them in consequence of the Act of Conformity, 1662.

He presses his request on them from a reference to his present circumstances. The Apostle had been among the Christian Hebrews formerly; he wished to be restored to them. He considers their prayers as means well fitted for gaining his desire, knowing that, in the government of His Church, Jesus Christ has a great regard to the prayers of His people. Whether the Apostle obtained his wish or not, we do not know, nor is it at all material. Whatever appears to us duty in any particular case, we may, we ought to desire and to pray for, though the event we wish for may never take place. The secret purposes of God are not the rule of our prayers. If Apostles needed the prayers of the churches, how much more ordinary ministers! " Brethren, pray for us."

One of the best methods of enforcing our recommendations of duties to others, is to exemplify them ourselves. This is the plan which the Apostle adopted in reference to the duty of mutual intercession. He had just been requesting an interest in the prayers of the Hebrew Christians, and he immediately shows them that they had an interest in his. He had just been bidding them pray for him, and he straightway commences praying for them. He had just said, " Brethren, pray for us," and he now says, vers. 20, 21, "Now the God of peace, that brought again from the dead our Lord Jesus, that great Shepherd of the sheep, through the blood of the everlasting covenant, make you perfect in every good work to do His will, working in you that which is well-pleasing in His sight, through Jesus Christ; to whom be glory for ever and ever. Amen."

This sublime and comprehensive prayer—which, properly speaking, forms the appropriate conclusion of the Epistle, for what follows is plainly a kind of postscript—deserves, and will reward, our most considerate attention. Our attention must be directed in succession—(1) to the descriptive appellation under which the Apostle addresses the object of prayer—"The God of peace, who brought again from the dead our Lord Jesus, that great Shepherd of the sheep, by the blood of the everlasting covenant;" (2) to the prayer itself—that God, as the God of peace, would " make them perfect in every good work to do His will, working in them that which was well-pleasing in His sight, by Jesus Christ;" and (3) the doxology or ascription of praise with which the prayer closes—"To Him be glory for ever and ever. Amen."

Let us then, first, consider the import of the descriptive appellation under which the Apostle addresses the great object of prayer. Before we enter on an inquiry into the meaning of this appellation, it will be proper to endeavour to settle a question respecting the construction of this clause of the verse, the determination of which materially affects the sense. The words, "through the blood of the everlasting covenant," may either be connected with the phrase, "brought again from the dead," or with the dignified title given to Jesus Christ, "the great Shepherd of the sheep;"—they may either be viewed as descriptive of the manner in which His resurrection was accomplished, or of the manner in which He became "the great Shepherd of the sheep." A good sense may be brought out of the words according to either of these two modes of connecting them. The usage of the original language admits of either. Looking merely at the Greek words, I should be disposed to say the latter method of connecting them is the more natural of the two, and that the Apostle's idea is, that Christ became the great Shepherd of the sheep by means of His voluntary oblation of Himself; *i.e.*, obtained for Himself that supreme authority over the Church which is implied in His being "the great Shepherd of the sheep." Yet when I consider that—though it is most true that Christ purchased the Church with His own blood, and was exalted on account of His expiatory sufferings as "Head over all things to His Church"—"in the days of His flesh" He takes to Himself the appellation, "the good Shepherd," and that it was as "the good Shepherd," in the discharge of the duties rising out of this character, that He "laid down His life for the sheep," it appears to me more probable that the first method of connecting the words is that which gives us the Apostle's idea: that His resurrection from the dead was "through the blood of the everlasting covenant." What is the meaning of that assertion, will appear, we trust, by and by.

Having settled this question of construction, let us proceed to the exposition of the descriptive appellation here given to the object of prayer. In order distinctly to bring out the thoughts involved in such a complicated form of expression as that now before us, it is often found advisable to reverse, or at any rate considerably to change, the order in which they stand. The following are the thoughts in what I apprehend is their natural order—the order in which they presented themselves to the Apostle's mind:—Jesus Christ our Lord is the great Shepherd of the sheep. As the great Shepherd of the sheep He submitted to death. As the great Shepherd of the sheep He has been brought again from the dead by God. When God brought Him again from the dead, He did so through the blood of the everlasting covenant. In bringing Jesus our Lord from the dead by the blood of the everlasting covenant, God acted as the God of peace; and it is to God, as having manifested Himself to be the God of peace by bringing our Lord Jesus from the dead through the blood of the everlasting covenant, that the Apostle addresses his prayers in behalf of the Hebrew Christians. Let us shortly illustrate these most important truths.

(1.) Jesus our Lord is "the great Shepherd of the sheep." What class of persons is described under the figurative denomination, "the sheep?" What is to be understood by Jesus our Lord being their Shepherd? and what by His being the great Shepherd? To the first of these questions a most satisfactory answer will be found in the words of our Lord in the tenth chapter of the Gospel by John. The description extends from the 11th verse down to the 30th. The sum of His statement is, that the sheep are those whom the Father has given Him, both Jews and Gentiles, for whom He laid down His life, who hear His voice and follow Him, to whom He gives eternal life, and who "will never perish, because none can pluck them out of His, and out of His Father's hand." They are plainly that innumerable multitude out of every kindred, and people, and tongue, and nation, which He redeems to God by His blood,—the same class of persons who in the preceding part of the Epistle are represented as "the heirs of salvation;" "the many children to be brought to glory" through "the captain of their salvation being made perfect through suffering;" the "holy brethren" of the Messiah; the "partakers of the heavenly calling;" those that through believing do enter into the promised rest; "partakers of Christ;" "the heirs of the promise;" "they that are called;" "they that come to God by Christ;" "the sanctified" ones by the offering of Christ's body once for all; those who have "received the kingdom that cannot be moved." "The sheep" is just another name for genuine Christians, viewed as separated from the rest of the world, and placed under the peculiar care of Christ as their Shepherd.

This naturally leads us to inquire what is meant by His being termed the Shepherd of the sheep. Many very learned interpreters have considered that the figurative expression "shepherd" is intended chiefly, if not solely, to convey the idea of *teacher, instructor*. I apprehend, however, that this is a mistake, and that this idea, if included, is but a subordinate one; that the word "shepherd," when used figuratively, both in the Old and New Testament, denotes one who presides over a collection of people, who governs, guides, and protects them—a leader, a guard, a defender, a chief, a king. David's being raised to the supreme government of the Israelitish people is represented as his being made their shepherd: Ps. lxxviii. 70-72. In the First Epistle of Peter, chap. ii. 25, *shepherd*, and *bishop*, or overseer, are used as equivalent expressions. The idea intended to be conveyed is obviously this: He is placed over them for the purpose of doing everything that is necessary for promoting their happiness. It is just a figurative expression equivalent in meaning to the literal expression "Saviour."

But our Lord is not only termed "the Shepherd," but "that great Shepherd of the sheep." He may receive this appellation to distinguish Him from all others who are called shepherds, as He is termed "the King of kings, and the Lord of lords;" or to mark Him as the superior of all those who in His Church receive the name of shepherds or pastors—in which case the phrase is equivalent to that used by Peter—the chief Shepherd; or to mark His transcendent personal dignity, as in the use of the same epithet in the expression, "A great High Priest, Jesus the Son of God." I have sometimes thought that, both in this expression, and in our Lord's own expression, "the good," or that good "Shepherd," there is an allusion to the numerous predictions of the Messiah under the character of a Shepherd in the Old Testament prophecies. The following are specimens of the predictions I refer to: "O Zion, that bringest good tidings, get thee up into the high mountain; O Jerusalem, that bringest good tidings, lift up thy voice with strength: lift it up, be not afraid; say unto the cities of Judah, Behold your God! Behold, the Lord God will come with strong hand, and His arm shall rule for Him: behold, His reward is with Him, and His work before Him. He shall feed His flock like a shepherd; He shall gather the lambs with His arm, and carry them in His bosom, and shall gently lead those that are with young." "And I will set up one Shepherd over them, and He shall feed them, even My servant David; He shall feed them, and He shall be their Shepherd. And I the Lord will be their God, and My servant David a prince among them: I the Lord have spoken it."[1] The full import of the expression seems to be—'Jesus our Lord, the Divine Saviour of the spiritual people of God, promised to the fathers.'

(2.) This "great Shepherd of the sheep" submitted to death. This is not indeed stated in so many words, but it is obviously implied, both in the phrase, "brought again from the dead," and in that of "the blood of the everlasting covenant." He submitted to death; and He submitted to death as a victim. His blood was the blood of a victim, or expiatory sacrifice, shed to ratify a covenant of peace. "The good Shepherd gave His life for the sheep." "All we like sheep had gone astray; we had turned every one to his own way; and the Lord laid on Him the iniquity of all. Exaction was made, and He became answerable. And He was wounded for our transgressions, He was bruised for our iniquities: and the chastisement of our peace was upon Him; and by His stripes we are healed. He gave His soul a sacrifice for sin." But as "the great Shepherd" laid down His life in order to save His sheep, in obedience to the will of His Father, so He laid it down "that He might take it again." It was not possible that *He* should continue bound with the fetters of death.

(3.) God "brought Him again from the dead." These words represent the resurrection of our Lord as an act of divine power. No power inferior to divine could have accomplished it. The question of the Apostle to king Agrippa, "Why should it be thought a thing incredible that God should raise the dead?" implies that it might well be accounted an incredible thing that any one else should. The resurrection of Jesus Christ is sometimes spoken of as His own work. "Destroy this temple," He says, "and in three days I will raise it up again. This He said of the temple of His body." And, "As the Father raiseth up the

---

[1] Isa. xl. 9–11; Ezek. xxxiv. 23, 24.

dead, and quickeneth them, even so the Son quickeneth whom He will." This will not, however, in any degree appear to be inconsistent with the declaration in the passage before us, by any one who understands the principles of the economy of redemption. The Father in that economy is the representative of divinity—the sustainer of its majesty, the vindicator of its rights. The Son acts in a subordinate character. Whatever He says, He says in the name of the Father; whatever He does, He does by the power of the Father. "The Father who dwelleth in Me, He doth the works." When He was raised from the dead, He was raised by the power of the Father; *i.e.*, by the power of God. But the words before us do not so much represent the resurrection as an act of mere power, as an act of rectoral justice.

(4.) God brought "the great Shepherd of the sheep"—who had given His life for the sheep—"from the dead, by the blood of the everlasting covenant." The covenant here referred to is obviously that divine constitution or arrangement by which spiritual and eternal blessings are secured for the guilty and depraved children of men, through the mediation of the incarnate Son of God. This covenant is termed "the everlasting covenant" to distinguish it from other covenants or arrangements made by God, and especially from that covenant or arrangement which was made with the Israelites at Sinai, and which, as it referred directly to temporal blessings, was intended only for temporary duration. This new covenant is never to give place to any other.

"The blood" of this covenant is the blood by the shedding of which this covenant was ratified. When illustrating the ninth chapter of the Epistle, I had occasion at considerable length to show you that it is the doctrine of the Apostle, that in all covenants or arrangements made by God for conferring blessings on sinful men, there has always been an assertion of His rights as the just and holy Moral Governor of the world; and that the form this assertion of His rights has uniformly taken, has been that of the death of a propitiatory victim; and that the dignity of the victim necessarily bore a proportion to the value of the benefits secured by the covenant. The blood of animal propitiatory victims confirmed the first covenant. The blood of the incarnate Only-begotten of God confirmed the new and better covenant; *i.e.*, the obedience to the death of the incarnate Son of God as the substitute of sinners, makes it consistent with, illustrative of, the divine holiness, and justice, and faithfulness, as well as goodness, to bestow pardon on the guilty, and salvation on the lost children of men, believing in Jesus.

The resurrection of our Lord is represented as the result of this shedding of His blood, by which the everlasting covenant was confirmed. He was " brought again from the dead by the blood of the everlasting covenant." His obedience to the death was the procuring cause of His own resurrection, as well as of the salvation of His people, which is the result of that resurrection. The Father loved the Son, had complacency in Him, because, in compliance with His will, He laid down His life for the sheep; and this was the manner in which He manifested His complacency. Because He humbled Himself, therefore He highly exalted Him.

(5.) In bringing our Lord Jesus from the dead, God acted in the character of "the God of peace." This is an appellation of the Divinity peculiar to the Apostle Paul, and frequently occurring in his writings: Rom. xv. 33, xvi. 20; 1 Cor. xiv. 33; 2 Thess. iii. 16. The word "peace" is often used as equivalent to 'prosperity,' happiness in general; and "the God of peace" may be considered as equivalent to—' the God who is the author of happiness.' The proper signification of the word, however, is ' reconciliation ;' and I think there can be but very little doubt that it has its proper primary signification here. "The God of peace," or reconciliation, is the pacified, the reconciled Divinity. It is just equivalent to the more fully expressed character of God—" God in Christ, reconciling the world to Himself, not imputing to men their trespasses; seeing He has made Him to be sin for us, who knew no sin, that we might be made the righteousness of God in Him." God was displeased with man on account of sin; *i.e.*, in plain words, not merely was man's sin the object of His moral disapprobation, but, in the ordinary course of things, man's final happiness was inconsistent with the honour of His character as the righteous Governor of the world, and (what is but another way of expressing the same truth) with the principles of His moral administration, and the happiness of His intelligent subjects generally. This incompatibility could be removed only by some display of the divine displeasure against sin, and of the righteousness and reasonableness of the law man had violated, fully equivalent to that which would have been given by the condemning sanction of the law being allowed to take its course in reference to the offenders. This has been given in the substituted obedience and sufferings of the incarnate Son. These have "magnified the law, and made it honourable." God is now "just, and the justifier of the ungodly"—"the just God and the Saviour." "His righteousness is declared through His Son being set forth a propitiation in His blood." And the first display, and the satisfactory proof, that God is now "the God of peace," is His raising His Son, our Surety, from the dead, and giving Him "all power in heaven and earth," "that He may give eternal life to as many as the Father has given Him."

It is finely said by Dr Owen: "The well-spring of the whole dispensation of grace lies in the bringing again our Lord Jesus Christ from the dead, through the blood of the everlasting covenant. Had not the will of God been fully executed, atonement made for sin, the Church sanctified, the law accomplished, and the threatenings satisfied, Christ could not have been brought from the dead. The death of Christ, if He had not risen, could not have completed our redemption; we should have been yet in our sins. For evidence would have been given that atonement was not made. The bare resurrection of Christ, or the bringing Him from the dead, would not have saved us; for so any other man may be raised by the power of God. But the bringing of Christ again from the dead by the blood of the everlasting covenant, is that which gives assurance of the complete redemption and salvation of the Church."

Now, it is to God as having manifested Himself to be "the God of peace"—the pacified Divinity—by "bringing again from the dead our Lord Jesus," when, as "the great Shepherd," He had given His life for the sheep, that the Apostle addresses his prayers in behalf of the Hebrew Christians. Indeed, this is the only character in which the Divinity can be rationally addressed by sinful men, or in behalf of sinful men. Without a reference to that atonement which was completed in the death of the Son of God, and the completeness of which is demonstrated by His resurrection, no spiritual and saving blessing can be reasonably expected by sinners from Him who is "glorious in holiness," and " can by no means clear the guilty." But from the pacified Divinity every heavenly and spiritual blessing may be expected; and, contemplating God in this character, we may go near Him, even to His seat, asking blessings both for ourselves and others—" drawing near with boldness to the throne of grace," in the faith of Him "who was given for our offences, and raised again for our justification," "that we may obtain mercy, and find grace to help in the time of need." Such is the appellation under which the Apostle addresses his intercessions for the Hebrew Christians to the object of prayer—the pacified Divinity, manifesting His reconciled character in the resurrection of Jesus, " the great Shepherd," on the ground of His having fully satisfied the demands of His law and justice, in giving His life for the sheep, in giving Himself a sacrifice and an offering that He might bring them to God.

We proceed now to inquire into the import of the prayer which the Apostle here presents. He prays that "the God of peace" would make the Hebrew Christians " perfect in every good work to do His will, working in you that which is well-pleasing in His sight."

The prayer consists of two parts; the one referring to the end, and the other to the means of gaining that end. The Apostle prays that the Christian Hebrews might be "made perfect in every good work to do His will;" and He prays that, in order to do this, He would " work in them that which is well-pleasing in His sight, through Jesus Christ."

The first petition is, that God would "make them perfect in every good work to do His will." These English words do not convey any very clear and distinct signification. The word translated " make perfect," properly signifies 'to set to rights what is out of order,' thus preparing it for its proper use. Its meaning will be best illustrated by referring to some of the passages where it occurs. Rom. ix. 22, the " vessels of wrath" are represented as "*fitted*"—the same word as that used here—"for destruction." "The worlds" are said to have been "*framed*" —*i.e.*, ' arranged, put in order from the chaotic state,' and thus fitted for their several purposes—" by the word of God:" Heb. xi. 3. " A body" is said to be " prepared " for our Lord : Heb. x. 5. And it is said, Eph. iv. 13, that Christ " gave some teachers, for the perfecting of the saints, for the work of the ministry"—*i.e.*, to fit or prepare holy men for the work of the ministry,—"that the body of Christ—*i.e.*, the Church—" may be edified." We apprehend the word has the same meaning here as in the passages to which I have just referred. The Apostle prays that " the God of peace" would fit or prepare the Hebrew Christians " to do His will in every good work." We are all by nature utterly unfit to obey the divine will; we do not know it, we do not love it. God alone can render us fit for doing His will; and this is true, not only with regard to unregenerate, but with regard to regenerate men. " Without Him we can do nothing." " Our sufficiency is of God."

The Apostle's prayer is a very extensive one. He wishes not only that they might be prepared to do the will of God, but to do the whole will of God—"to do His will in every good work;" *i.e.*, in the performance of every duty, moral and religious. The will of God is our sanctification—our sanctification wholly, in the whole man—"soul, body, and spirit;" and it is the Apostle's prayer that the Hebrew Christians might be enabled by God to be perfect and entire, wanting nothing.

The second petition refers to the means by which this end is to be gained. The Hebrew Christians are to be prepared for doing the will of God " in every good work," by God's " working in them that which is well-pleasing in His sight, by Jesus Christ."[1] In order to external good works, there must be internal good principles. In order to conformity to the law of God in the life, there must be conformity to the will of God in the heart. That in us which is " well-pleasing in God's sight," is just a mode of thinking and of feeling which is conformable to His will. The way in which God does this, is not by miraculously implanting such a mode of thinking and feeling within us. That God could do this, if it so pleased Him, we have no reason to doubt; but He acts according to the laws of our intelligent and moral nature. In His word He has given us a plain, well-accredited revelation of His *mind*. By the influence of His Spirit, which our depravity renders absolutely necessary, He leads us to understand and believe this revelation. The revealed mind of God, understood and believed by us, becomes our mind; and our mind being brought into accordance with God's mind, our will, according to the constitution of our

---

[1] εὐάρεστον ἐνώπιον αὐτοῦ = טוֹב לְפָנָיו.

nature, is brought into accordance with God's will. It is thus that God, by His word and Spirit, "works in us that which is well-pleasing in His sight."

It is plain from these remarks, that God's working in us does not make us passive. It is plain that, in order to our having in us "that which is well-pleasing in His sight," we must carefully study the Scriptures, and accompany our study of the Scriptures with earnest prayer to God for that divine influence without which they cannot be understood and believed. While we use the means—and we act like madmen if we do not use the means—and look for the end, we are never to forget that His *working in us* is necessary to enable us "both to will and to do;" and when the use of the means is effectual, we are to ascribe to Him all the glory, saying, 'It was not I, but the grace of God that is in me. It is not so much I that live as Christ that lives in me.'

The expression, "by Jesus Christ," admits of a twofold connection, and, of course, of a twofold explication. It may either be connected with the phrase, "that which is well-pleasing in His sight," or with the phrase, "working in us." In the first case the meaning is, that whatever good is wrought in the mind of man is acceptable to God, through Jesus Christ. We owe to Him, not only the pardon of our sins and the sanctification of our nature, but we owe also the acceptance of our imperfectly sanctified hearts and lives to His mediation. In the second case the meaning is, that, while the Holy Spirit is the direct agent, all God's sanctifying operations on the mind of man, are carried on with a reference to the mediation of our Lord Jesus Christ. There is no communication of divine influence from "the God of peace," but in and by Jesus Christ, and by virtue of His mediation.

The third thing in the Apostle's prayer which requires consideration is, the doxology or ascription of praise with which it closes: "To whom be glory for ever and ever." It is impossible, from the construction, to determine with absolute certainty whether this ascription of praise refer to "the God of peace" or to Jesus Christ. We know that both are worthy of eternal honour and praise, and that both shall receive them. We find that glory is ascribed to each separately, and to both together, in other passages of Scripture. To the Father separately: Phil.

iv. 20, "Now unto God and our Father be glory for ever and ever. Amen." To the Son separately: Rev. i. 5, 6, "Unto Him that loved us, and washed us from our sins in His own blood, and hath made us kings and priests unto God and His Father; to Him be glory and dominion for ever and ever. Amen." To both together: Rev. v. 13, "And every creature which is in heaven, and on the earth, and under the earth, and such as are in the sea, and all that are in them, heard I saying, Blessing, and honour, and glory, and power, be unto Him that sitteth upon the throne, and unto the Lamb, for ever and ever." It appears to me, however, that though Christ be the nearest relative, yet, as "the God of peace" is the person addressed and principally spoken of in the prayer, the ascription of praise is to be considered as addressed to Him. "The God of peace" well deserves to be praised and glorified for ever, for all He has done for, and for all He has done in, His redeemed people. The "bringing again from the dead our Lord Jesus, that great Shepherd of the sheep," and His "preparing His people in every good work to do His will," by "working in them that which is well-pleasing in His sight," are themes worthy of the songs of eternity. In these dispensations He displays a power and a wisdom, a holiness and a grace, which richly deserve everlasting praise. And as they deserve it, so they shall receive it. The Apostle's pious wish, in which every Christian will cordially acquiesce, will be fully realized. A song ever new shall be unceasingly raised by the nations of the saved to "the God of peace," who reconciled them to Himself by the blood of His Son, and declared the reconciliation by His glorious resurrection; and who, by the instrumentality of His word and the power of His Spirit, "prepared them for doing His will in every good work, by working in them that which is well-pleasing in His sight." "Amen," adds the Apostle. So it ought to be, so let it be, so shall it be. "And let all the people say, *Amen*, and *Amen*."

This is, properly speaking, the conclusion of the Epistle; and a more appropriate one could not have been conceived. What follows in the four following verses is of the nature of a postscript. This is a usual practice with the Apostle. Similar postscripts are attached to the Epistles to the Romans and Philippians, and to both the Epistles to Timothy.

The 22d verse contains an affectionate request that they would take kindly what on his part was meant kindly. "I beseech you, brethren, suffer the word of exhortation; for I have written a letter to you in few words." The Hebrew Christians were, like all other Christians, Paul's spiritual brethren; but I think it very likely he here referred to the natural relation in which they stood to him as Hebrews. It was as Hebrews—as persons possessed with Jewish prejudices—that they especially needed, and were in danger of not "suffering, the word of exhortation." It is equivalent to—'Remember, I am your brother, and both feel the affection, and am warranted to use the freedom, of a brother.'

"The word of exhortation" is just equivalent to—'this hortatory discourse.' Some have supposed that the Apostle refers only to those parts of the Epistle that consist of direct exhortation, such as the beginning of the 2d chapter, the 6th, the latter part of the 10th, the 12th, and the 13th chapters. We rather apprehend that he means 'this hortatory discourse' as a general description of the whole Epistle. And a juster one could not be conceived; for what is the Epistle, from beginning to end, but a most impressive and well-supported exhortation to persevere in the faith and profession of the Gospel, notwithstanding all the temptations to abandon them to which they were exposed?

To "suffer," or bear, this hortatory discourse, is a phrase which obviously implies, that in it there were many things opposed to their prejudices, and which, therefore, they might be dissatisfied and displeased with. I do not know that the meaning of the exhortation can be better given than in the words of Dr Owen: "Let no prejudices, no inveterate opinions, no apprehension of severity in its admonitions and threatenings, provoke you against it, render you impatient under it, and so cause you to lose the benefit of it. Christians should beware of turning away from statements and exhortations merely because they are not very agreeable to them. That may be the very reason why they are peculiarly required by them."

The reason of this injunction is given in the close of the verse: "For I have written a letter to you in few words."[1] It may appear strange that the Apostle uses such language with regard to this Epistle, as it is the largest of his Epistles, with the

---

[1] διὰ βραχέων (ῥημάτων); *i.e.*, δι' ὀλίγων,—1 Pet. v. 12.

exception of that written to the Romans, and as he seems to have considered his Epistle to the Galatians a long one : " Ye see how long a letter I have written to you with mine own hand." The remark in the Epistle to the Galatians refers either to the size and form of the Greek characters, which the Apostle does not seem to have been accustomed to write, or to the letter being long for an autograph, he being in the habit of employing an amanuensis. Length and shortness are comparative terms. A very short letter on an unimportant subject may be too long, and a very long letter on an important subject may be too short. The Apostle's meaning is, 'I have written to you concisely.' And who that has read the Epistle is not convinced of this?[1] I have delivered nearly one hundred lectures of an hour's length on this Epistle; and yet I am persuaded I have but very imperfectly brought out those "treasures of wisdom and knowledge" which are contained in these brief terms.

The force of the conciseness of the Apostle's style, as a reason why his brethren should "bear the word of exhortation," is not difficult to perceive. It is equivalent to—'If there be anything apparently harsh and unpalatable in the exhortation, impute it to the circumstance that I have had so much to communicate within a moderate compass, that there was no room to smooth down all asperities.'

The 23d verse gives some interesting information respecting a distinguished Christian evangelist, and the Apostle's intention of speedily visiting the Hebrew Christians : " Know ye that our brother Timothy is set at liberty ; with whom, if he come shortly, I will see you." Timothy, of whose history we have a number of notices in the Acts of the Apostles, seems to have accompanied the Apostle in very many of his journeyings, and to have served with him as a son with a father in the work of the Gospel. Having been with him in Judea, his worth and excellences were well known to the churches there. He does not seem to have gone to Rome with the Apostle, but he probably followed him there; and it would appear from this passage that he had been cast into prison as an associate of Paul, or for preaching the Gospel himself. From this imprisonment he had

---

[1] " It is reasonable to suppose that the writer means to say that he had written briefly, considering the importance and difficulty of the subjects of which he had treated. And who will deny this ?"—STUART.

been delivered; and it seems to have been his intention to avail himself of his deliverance to visit the brethren in Judea. The Apostle intimates his intention to accompany Timothy in this journey, if he should undertake it soon; at the same time, hinting that, if Timothy could not come speedily, it was doubtful whether his work would permit him to do so or not. We do not know whether these expectations were ever fulfilled.

The words in the 24th verse seem plainly addressed to those individuals to whom the letter was sent, and by whom it was to be communicated to the Church. He charges them to "salute" —*i.e.*, to express his kind and respectful affection, first to the office-bearers, and then to the members of the churches of Judea. The members are called *saints—separated ones*, set apart by God for Himself—separated from "the world lying under the wicked one"—devoted to the love, and fear, and service of God and His Son. Such are the only proper members of the visible Church; such are the only true members of the Church invisible. "They of Italy salute you;"[1] that is, 'The Christians in Italy send you the assurance of their cordial regard.' How does Christianity melt down prejudices! Romans and Jews, Italians and Hebrews, were accustomed to regard each other with contempt and hatred. But in Christ Jesus there is neither Roman nor Jew, neither Italian nor Hebrew: all are one. Christians of different countries should take all proper opportunities of testifying their mutual regard to each other. It is calculated to strengthen and console, and to knit them closer and closer in love. Proper expressions of love increase love on both sides.

The Epistle is concluded with the usual sign in the Apostle's Epistles, written probably by his own hand. "Grace be with you all. Amen." "Grace" here is the grace of God—the divine sovereign kindness. What a comprehensive, kind wish is this: 'May you be the objects of the continued love of the greatest, the wisest, and the best Being in the universe; and

---

[1] Οἱ ἀπὸ τῆς Ἰταλίας may signify, 'those who have come from Italy'—those Italians who have been obliged to leave their country and come to some other country. In this way some interpreters render it, especially those who deny the Pauline origin of the Epistle. It may signify Italians generally, including Romans; but supposing the Epistle to have been written from Rome, it probably signifies the Christians from other parts of Italy, at the time residing in Rome. Tholuck's note deserves to be read.

may He constantly bestow on you proofs of His peculiar love and care!' "His favour is life, His loving-kindness is better than life." Nothing better, for time or for eternity, can be desired for ourselves or for others than the grace of God. Infinite power to guard, infinite wisdom to guide, infinite excellence and love to excite and gratify all the affections of the heart for ever and ever.

And now I close these illustrations of the Epistle to the Hebrews. Happier hours than those which I have spent in composing these expository discourses, I can scarcely expect to spend on this side the grave. I trust the study of the Epistle has not been without some improvement, as well as much enjoyment, to myself. I shall rejoice if at last it shall be found that others also have been made better and happier by it. All is now over with the author and his readers, as to his illustrating the Epistle, and their listening to these illustrations; but there remains the improvement to be made, and the account to be given in. God requireth the things which are past, and so should we. Let me request those who have accompanied me thus far, seriously to review the whole Epistle, and ask themselves, Do we understand it better, and do we feel more strongly the sanctifying and consoling influence of the doctrines which it unfolds? Can we say with greater conviction of the truth than formerly, We need a High Priest—we have a High Priest— we are well pleased with our High Priest; we have acknowledged Jesus as our High Priest; we will hold fast our acknowledgment; He died for us—we will live for Him; and if He calls us, we will die for Him; we will trace His steps on the earth, we will wait His coming in the clouds? If this be the case even in one individual, I shall not have laboured in vain: if it has been the case with a number of individuals, I shall have received a full reward.

Πρὸς Ἑβραίους ἐγράφη ἀπὸ τῆς Ἰταλίας διὰ Τιμοθέου.

The 23d verse of the 13th chapter sufficiently proves that this hypograph is not genuine. Like many of the other hypographs of the Apostolical Epistles, it is the mere conjecture of an ignorant and inconsiderate transcriber. "These inscriptions are," as Hallett well says, "not of the least authority. It is a pity they should be printed in the Bible." In some MSS., after ἐγράφη, Ἑβραιστὶ is added. Instead of ἀπὸ τῆς Ἰταλίας, one codex has ἀπὸ Ῥώμης, and another, ἀπ' Ἀθηνῶν.

www.ingramcontent.com/pod-product-compliance
Lightning Source LLC
Chambersburg PA
CBHW071428300426
44114CB00013B/1351